ESSENTIAL
Korean
Vocabulary

Learn the Key Words and Phrases
Needed to Speak Korean Fluently

T0151481

KYUBYONG PARK

TUTTLE Publishing

Tokyo | Rutland, Vermont | Singapore

"Books to Span the East and West"

Tuttle Publishing was founded in 1832 in the small New England town of Rutland, Vermont [USA]. Our core values remain as strong today as they were then—to publish best-in-class books which bring people together one page at a time. In 1948, we established a publishing office in Japan—and Tuttle is now a leader in publishing English-language books about the arts, languages and cultures of Asia. The world has become a much smaller place today and Asia's economic and cultural influence has grown. Yet the need for meaningful dialogue and information about this diverse region has never been greater. Over the past seven decades, Tuttle has published thousands of books on subjects ranging from martial arts and paper crafts to language learning and literature—and our talented authors, illustrators, designers and photographers have won many prestigious awards. We welcome you to explore the wealth of information available on Asia at **www.tuttlepublishing.com**.

Published by Tuttle Publishing, an imprint of Periplus Editions (HK) Ltd.

www.tuttlepublishing.com

Copyright © 2014 Kyubyong Park

ISBN 978-0-8048-4325-6

Distributed by

North America, **Latin America & Europe**	**Japan**	**Asia Pacific**
Tuttle Publishing	Tuttle Publishing	Berkeley Books Pte. Ltd.
364 Innovation Drive	Yaekari Building, 3rd Floor,	3 Kallang Sector #04-01
North Clarendon,	5-4-12 Osaki	Singapore 349278
VT 05759-9436 U.S.A.	Shinagawa-ku, Tokyo 141 0032	Tel: (65) 6741-2178
Tel: 1 (802) 773-8930	Tel: (81) 3 5437-0171	Fax: (65) 6741-2179
Fax: 1 (802) 773-6993	Fax: (81) 3 5437-0755	inquiries@periplus.com.sg
info@tuttlepublishing.com	sales@tuttle.co.jp	www.tuttlepublishing.com
www.tuttlepublishing.com	www.tuttle.co.jp	

First edition
25 24 23 22 21   10 9 8 7 6 5   2108VP
Printed in Malaysia

Contents

Preface

For most of us who are old enough to have lost our magical ability to acquire language without conscious effort, learning a new language is not easy. You need to memorize a lot of new words and expressions. Some people prefer learning new vocabulary purely through their daily activities to memorizing words in vocabulary books. However, if you can anticipate what language elements you are likely to come across while talking to someone or reading something, you can be better prepared. By studying the entries in this book, you will get a feel for what words or expressions native speakers use in certain situations.

This book holds more than 8,000 essential Korean words/expressions marked by three different symbols ⦂ / ⦂ / ° according to their weight. There are two things I want you to keep in mind. First, use the weight symbols wisely. Do not be overwhelmed by the amount of words in this book. It can be a strategy to go for more important words first. Second, do not simply flip through the meanings of the headwords. I strongly encourage you to pay attention to the words in bold in each example phrase/sentence, which shows which word or words the headword is frequently used with. This is called collocation, a concept you will find very important as you progress in your studies.

This is not a grammar book. I expect you to know some basic Korean grammar, and I assume that you also know how to read and write Hangul, the Korean script. Some Korean books for foreigners use romanization to write Korean words, rather than Hangul. I understand that Hangul may look strange to English speakers' eyes at first sight. This is to be expected when encountering a new and foreign writing system. The good news is that Hangul is very easy to learn. And more importantly, all Koreans use it. In my opinion, these are reasons enough to learn Hangul.

This book was originally published by Nexus under the title *Survival Korean Vocabulary* in 2007. In repurposing it for Tuttle, I changed more than the title. I've added more than two thousand words and rewritten almost all the examples, and I reorganized the themes and the word categorizations.

In writing this book, I owe the following sources a great debt.

The basic model on which this book is based is Barron's *Mastering Vocabulary Series*.

I am thankful to all dictionary editors and developers. I know how agonizing the job of compiling a dictionary is. I referred to the following dictionaries throughout the time I worked on this book.

Doosan Dong-A editorial staff. *Doosan Dong-A's Prime Korean-English Dictionary*. 3rd edition. Doosan Dong-A, 2010.
Neungyule editorial staff. *Neungyule Korean-English Dictionary*. Neungyule Education Inc., 2006.

It was not easy to establish themes and categorize more than 8,000 words. The following books were a big help to me in this task.

Darakwon Voca Club. Deongeori VOCA. Vols. 1-4. Darakwon, 2010-11.
Kim, Eung-mo. *Hangugeo Sinchegwallyeon Jadongsa Nanmalbat*. Pagijong, 1996.
Kim, Eung-mo. *Eoneopyohyeon Jadongsa Naeyongyeongu*. Pagijong, 2000.
Kim, Eung-mo. *Ilsangeoneo Jadongsa Nanmalbat*. Pagijong, 2000.
Sin, Hyeon-suk; Kim, Mi-hyeong; Im, So-young; Im Hye-won. *Uimiro Bullyuhan Hyeondae Hangugeo Hakseup Sajeon*. Hangukmunhwasa, 2000.

Kyubyong Park

At a Glance

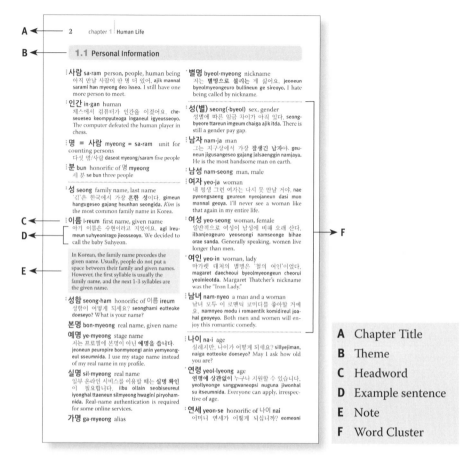

1.1 Personal Information

사람 sa·ram person, people, human being
아직 만날 사람이 한 명 더 있어. ajik mannal sarami han myeong deo isseo. I still have one more person to meet.

인간 in·gan human
체스에서 컴퓨터가 인간을 이겼어요. cheseuseo keompyuteoga inganeul igyeosseoyo. The computer defeated the human player in chess.

명 = 사람 myeong = sa·ram unit for counting persons
다섯 명/사람 daseot myeong/saram five people

분 bun honorific of 명 myeong
세 분 se bun three people

성 seong family name, last name
'김'은 한국에서 가장 흔한 성이다. gimeun hangugeseo gajang heunhan seongida. *Kim* is the most common family name in Korea.

이름 i·reum first name, given name
아기 이름은 수현이라고 지었어요. agi ireumeun suhyeonirago jieosseoyo. We decided to call the baby Suhyeon.

In Korean, the family name precedes the given name. Usually, people do not put a space between their family and given names. However, the first syllable is usually the family name, and the next 1-3 syllables are the given name.

성함 seong·ham honorific of 이름 ireum
성함이 어떻게 되세요? seonghami eotteoke doeseyo? What is your name?

본명 bon·myeong real name, given name

예명 ye·myeong stage name
저는 프로필에 본명이 아닌 예명을 씁니다. jeoneun peuropire bonmyeongi anin yemyeongeul sseumnida. I use my stage name instead of my real name in my profile.

실명 sil·myeong real name
일부 온라인 서비스를 이용할 때는 실명 확인이 필요합니다. ilbu ollain seobiseureul iyonghal ttaeneun silmyeong hwagini piryohamnida. Real-name authentication is required for some online services.

가명 ga·myeong alias

별명 byeol·myeong nickname
지는 별명으로 불리는 게 싫어요. jeoneun byeolmyeongeuro bullineun ge sireoyo. I hate being called by nickname.

성(별) seong(-byeol) sex, gender
성별에 따른 임금 차이가 아직 있다. seongbyeore ttareun imgeum chaiga ajik itda. There is still a gender pay gap.

남자 nam·ja man
그는 지구상에서 가장 잘생긴 남자야. geuneun jigusangeseo gajang jalsaenggin namjaya. He is the most handsome man on earth.

남성 nam·seong man, male

여자 yeo·ja woman
내 평생 그런 여자는 다시 못 만날 거야. nae pyeongsaeng geureon nyeojaneun dasi mon mannal geoya. I'll never see a woman like that again in my entire life.

여성 yeo·seong woman, female
일반적으로 여성이 남성에 비해 오래 산다. ilbanjeogeuro yeoseongi namseonge bihae orae sanda. Generally speaking, women live longer than men.

여인 yeo·in woman, lady
마가렛 대처의 별명은 '철의 여인'이었다. magaret daecheoui byeolmyeongeun cheorui yeoinieotda. Margaret Thatcher's nickname was the "Iron Lady."

남녀 nam·nyeo a man and a woman
남녀 모두 이 로맨틱 코미디를 좋아할 거예요. namnyeo modu i romaentik komidireul joahal geoyeyo. Both men and women will enjoy this romantic comedy.

나이 na·i age
실례지만, 나이가 어떻게 되세요? sillyejiman, naiga eotteoke doeseyo? May I ask how old you are?

연령 yeol·lyeong age
연령에 상관없이 누구나 지원할 수 있습니다. yeollyeonge sanggwaneopsi nuguna jiwonhal su itseumnida. Everyone can apply, irrespective of age.

연세 yeon·se honorific of 나이 nai
어머니 연세가 어떻게 되십니까? eomeoni

A Chapter Title
B Theme
C Headword
D Example sentence
E Note
F Word Cluster

Symbols and Abbreviations

⦂ ⦂ ⦁	Importance of the headword
ɪᴅɪᴏᴍ	Idiom
A = B	A and B are almost always interchangeable. e.g. 아줌마 **a·jum·ma** = 아주머니 **a·ju·meo·ni**
A ≒ B	A and B are similar in meaning, but it is not always possible to substitute one for another, e.g. 독신 **dok·sin** ≒ 미혼 **mi·hon**
A | B	B is derived from A, which is substituted by ~ in B, e.g. 경험 | ~하다 **gyeong·heom | ~·ha·da** (→ 경험 | 경험하다 **gyeong·heom | gyeong·heom·ha·da**)
A ← B	A, which is considered correct, is often misspelled as B, e.g. 쌍둥이 **ssang·dung·i** ← 쌍둥이 **ssang·dong·i** (→ 쌍둥이 O, 쌍둥이 X)
sth	something
sb	somebody

가명 겪다 경험 고인 고향 국적 기저귀 기혼 기흔

자 꼬마 나이 남녀 남성 남자 년생

노인 늙다 독신 돌 돌아가시다 되다 띠 만 매장

명 묘 묘비 묘지 무덤 별명 본명 분 사람 살

살다 삶 상 생년월일 생신 생일 서명 성

성숙하다 성인 성장 성함 세 소녀 소년 수명

숙녀 숨지다 시신 신분증 싱글 아가씨 아기

chapter **1** | Human Life

아이 아저씨 아줌마 애도 어른

어리다 어린아이 여성 여자 연령 연세

예명 유부녀 유서 유언 이름 인생 일생 장례 장례식

젊다 젊음 주민등록증 주소 죽다 죽음 중반

직업 처녀 철 청년 청소년 청춘 체험 총각 출생

칠순 탄생 태어나다 팔순 화장 환갑 후반

1.1 Personal Information

사람 sa·ram person, people, human being
아직 만날 사람이 한 명 더 있어. **ajik mannal sarami han myeong deo isseo.** I still have one more person to meet.

인간 in·gan human
체스에서 컴퓨터가 인간을 이겼어요. **cheseueseo keompyuteoga inganeul igyeosseoyo.** The computer defeated the human player in chess.

명 = 사람 myeong = sa·ram unit for counting persons
다섯 명/사람 **daseot myeong/saram** five people

분 bun honorific of 명 **myeong**
세 분 **se bun** three people

성 seong family name, last name
'김'은 한국에서 가장 **흔한 성**이다. **gimeun hangugeseo gajang heunhan seongida.** *Kim* is the most common family name in Korea.

이름 i·reum first name, given name
아기 이름은 수현이라고 지었어요. **agi ireumeun suhyeonirago jieosseoyo.** We decided to call the baby Suhyeon.

> In Korean, the family name precedes the given name. Usually, people do not put a space between their family and given names. However, the first syllable is usually the family name, and the next 1-3 syllables are the given name.

성함 seong·ham honorific of 이름 **ireum**
성함이 어떻게 되세요? **seonghami eotteoke doeseyo?** What is your name?

본명 bon·myeong real name, given name

예명 ye·myeong stage name
저는 프로필에 본명이 아닌 **예명을 씁니다.** **jeoneun peuropire bonmyeongi anin yemyeongeul sseumnida.** I use my stage name instead of my real name in my profile.

실명 sil·myeong real name
일부 온라인 서비스를 이용할 때는 **실명 확인**이 필요합니다. **ilbu ollain seobiseureul iyonghal ttaeneun silmyeong hwagini piryohamnida.** Real-name authentication is required for some online services.

가명 ga·myeong alias

별명 byeol·myeong nickname
저는 **별명으로 불리는** 게 싫어요. **jeoneun byeolmyeongeuro bullineun ge sireoyo.** I hate being called by nickname.

성(별) seong(·byeol) sex, gender
성별에 따른 임금 차이가 아직 있다. **seongbyeore ttareun imgeum chaiga ajik itda.** There is still a gender pay gap.

남자 nam·ja man
그는 지구상에서 가장 **잘생긴 남자**야. **geuneun jigusangeseo gajang jalsaenggin namjaya.** He is the most handsome man on earth.

남성 nam·seong man, male

여자 yeo·ja woman
내 평생 그런 여자는 다시 못 만날 거야. **nae pyeongsaeng geureon nyeojaneun dasi mon mannal geoya.** I'll never see a woman like that again in my entire life.

여성 yeo·seong woman, female
일반적으로 여성이 남성에 비해 오래 산다. **ilbanjeogeuro yeoseongi namseonge bihae orae sanda.** Generally speaking, women live longer than men.

여인 yeo·in woman, lady
마가렛 대처의 별명은 '철의 여인'이었다. **magaret daecheoui byeolmyeongeun cheorui yeoinieotda.** Margaret Thatcher's nickname was the "Iron Lady."

남녀 nam·nyeo a man and a woman
남녀 모두 이 로맨틱 코미디를 좋아할 거예요. **namnyeo modu i romaentik komidireul joahal geoyeyo.** Both men and women will enjoy this romantic comedy.

나이 na·i age
실례지만, 나이가 어떻게 되세요? **sillyejiman, naiga eotteoke doeseyo?** May I ask how old you are?

연령 yeol·lyeong age
연령에 상관없이 누구나 지원할 수 있습니다. **yeollyeonge sanggwaneopsi nuguna jiwonhal su itseumnida.** Everyone can apply, irrespective of age.

연세 yeon·se honorific of 나이 **nai**
어머니 연세가 어떻게 되십니까? **eomeoni**

yeonsega eotteoke doesimnikka? How old is your mother?

살 sal age, years
몇 살이세요? **myeot sariseyo?** How old are you?

세 se age, years
만 5세 미만의 아이는 입장이 무료입니다. **man ose mimanui aineun ipjangi muryoimnida.** Admission is free for children under five.

만 man in Western age
만으로 서른여섯 살입니다. **maneuro seoreunnyeoseot sarimnida.** I'm now 36 years old.

The traditional way of counting someone's age in Korea is different than in Western countries. In Korea, people begin counting a child's age while the child is still in the womb, so a newborn baby is one year old in Korean thinking. Then, the baby turns two on the following New Year's day. People use the expression 만으로 **maneuro** to show the Western age.

년생 nyeon·saeng word used to say what year you were born in
A: 몇 년생이세요? B: 78년생이에요. A: **myeon nyeonsaengiseyo?** B: **chilsippallyeonsaengieyo.** A: What year were you born in? B: I was born in 1978.

대 dae (certain times of) one's age

초반 cho·ban early phase
그 사람은 30대 초반이에요. **geu sarameun samsipdae chobanieyo.** He is in his early 30s.

중반 jung·ban middle phase

후반 hu·ban latter phase
범인은 20대 중반에서 후반의 남성으로 보입니다. **beomineun isipdae jungbaneseo hubanui namseongeuro boimnida.** The suspect looks like a male in his mid to late 20s.

독신 ≒ 미혼 dok·sin ≒ mi·hon unmarried person
저는 평생을 독신으로/미혼으로 살 생각입니다. **jeoneun pyeongsaengeul doksineuro/mihoneuro sal saenggagimnida.** I decided to remain single for the rest of my life.

싱글 = 솔로 sing·geul = sol·lo single person
저는 서른 살이고 싱글입니다/솔로입니다. **jeoneun seoreun sarigo singgeurimnida/solloimnida.** I'm 30 years old and single.

배우자 bae·u·ja spouse
배우자의 이름과 주민등록번호를 써 주세요. **baeujaui ireumgwa jumindeungnokbeonhoreul sseo juseyo.** Fill in your spouse's name and social security number.

총각 chong·gak unmarried man
한국에서는 **농촌 총각**들이 결혼하기 어렵다. **hangugeseoneun nongchon chonggakdeuri gyeolhonhagi eoryeopda.** It's difficult for Korean men in the countryside to marry.

처녀 cheo·nyeo unmarried woman

기혼 gi·hon married (person)
기혼이세요, 미혼이세요? **gihoniseyo, mihoniseyo?** Are you married or single?

기혼자 gi·hon·ja married person

유부남 yu·bu·nam married man

유부녀 yu·bu·nyeo married woman

신분증 sin·bun·jeung identification, ID card
신분증을 보여 주세요. **sinbunjeungeul boyeo juseyo.** Please show me your identification.

주민등록증 ju·min·deung·nok·jeung identification, ID card, social security card
주민등록증을 분실했어요. **jumindeungnokjeungeul bunsilhaesseoyo.** I lost my ID card.

주소 ju·so address
주소를 아래 줄에 써 주세요. **jusoreul arae jure sseo juseyo.** Please write your address on the line below.

생년월일 saeng·nyeo·nwo·ril date of birth
생년월일이 어떻게 되세요? **saengnyeonworiri eotteoke doeseyo?** What's your date of birth?

국적 guk·jeok nationality

고향 go·hyang birthplace, hometown
고향이 어디세요? **gohyangi eodiseyo?** What's your hometown?

직업 ji·geop occupation
직업이 무엇입니까? **jigeobi mueosimnikka?** What is your occupation?

서명 = 사인 | ~하다 seo·myeong = sa·in | ~·ha·da signature | to sign
여기에 서명해/사인해 주세요. **yeogie seomyeonghae/sainhae juseyo.** Sign here, please.

1.2 Life, Stages of Life, Death

일생 il·saeng lifetime
일생에 다시 없을 기회를 놓치지 마세요. il-saenge dasi eopseul gihoereul lochiji maseyo. Don't miss this opportunity of a lifetime.

(한)평생 (han·)pyeong·saeng (in one's) whole life
평생 혼자 살고 싶지는 않아요. pyeongsaeng honja salgo sipjineun anayo. I don't want to live the single life forever.

인생 in·saeng human life, lifetime
오늘은 내 인생 최악의 날이었어. oneureun nae insaeng choeagui narieosseo. It was the worst day of my life.

삶 sam life
침대에서 나오기도 싫고 **삶의 의욕**을 다 잃어 버린 느낌이야. chimdaeeseo naogido silko sal-mui uiyogeul da ireobeorin neukkimiya. I can't get out of bed. I think I've lost my will to live.

수명 su·myeong life expectancy
통계적으로 볼 때 여자가 남자보다 **수명이** 길 다. tonggyejeogeuro bol ttae yeojaga namjabo-da sumyeongi gilda. Statistically women live longer than men.

살다 sal·da to live
저는 늘 대도시에서 살고 싶었어요. jeoneun neul daedosieseo salgo sipeosseoyo. I've al-ways wanted to live in a big city.

경험 | ~하다 gyeong·heom | ~·ha·da ex-perience | to experience
이 분야에서 경험보다 중요한 것은 없습니다. i bunyaeseo gyeongheomboda jungyohan geo-seun eopseumnida. Nothing is more impor-tant in this field than experience.

체험 | ~하다 che·heom | ~·ha·da experi-ence | to experience

겪다 gyeok·da to experience, undergo, suffer
저는 제가 직접 **겪은 일**에 대해서 씁니다. jeoneun jega jikjeop gyeokkeun ire daehaeseo sseumnida. I write about the things I've ex-perienced first hand.

아기 a·gi baby
제가 없는 동안 **아기** 좀 **봐** 주시겠어요? jega eomneun dongan agi jom bwa jusigesseoyo? Could you look after my baby while I'm away?

태어나다 tae·eo·na·da to be born
저는 부산에서 태어났어요. jeoneun busa-neseo taeeonasseoyo. I was born in Busan.

귀(가) 빠지다 gwi(·ga) ppa·ji·da to be born
오늘은 바로 제 **귀가 빠진** 날이에요. oneureun baro je gwiga ppajin narieyo. Today is my birthday.

> Since ears are the first part of a newborn seen by its parents, 귀 빠진 날 **gwi ppajin nal**, *the day one's ears popped out*, refers to one's birthday.

출생 | ~하다 chul·saeng | ~·ha·da birth | to be born
한국에서는 출생 후 한 달 이내에 **출생 신고** 를 해야 합니다. hangugeseoneun chulsaeng hu han dal inaee chulsaeng singoreul haeya hamnida. In Korea, you must register a new birth within a month.

탄생 | ~하다 tan·saeng | ~·ha·da birth | to be born
공주님의 탄생을 축하합니다! gongjunimui tansaengeul chukhahamnida! Congrats on your new baby girl!

생일 saeng·il birthday
늦었지만 **생일** 축하해! neujeotjiman saengil chukhahae! Happy belated birthday!

생신 saeng·sin honorific of 생일 **saengil**

띠 tti Chinese zodiac sign
저는 말띠예요. jeoneun malttiyeyo. I was born in the Year of the Horse.

돌 ← 돐 dol one's first birthday
내일이 제 아들 돌이에요. naeiri je adeul do-rieyo. Tomorrow is my son's first birthday.

쌍둥이 ← 쌍동이 ssang·dung·i ← ssang·dong·i twins
그들은 쌍둥이지만 외모가 전혀 다르다. geu-deureun ssangdungijiman oemoga jeonhyeo dareuda. They are twins, but they look to-tally different.

기저귀 gi·jeo·gwi diaper
여보, 아기 **기저귀** 좀 **갈아** 줘. yeobo, agi gi-jeogwi jom gara jwo. Honey, please change the baby's diaper.

유모차 yu·mo·cha stroller

아기가 유모차에서 자고 있다. **agiga yumo·chaeseo jago itda.** A baby is sleeping in the stroller.

아이 = 애 a·i = ae child, toddler
아이들이/애들이 바깥에서 눈사람을 만들고 있다. **aideuri/aedeuri bakkateseo nunsarameul mandeulgo itda.** The children are making a snowman outside.

어린아이 = 어린애 ≒ 어린이 eo·ri·na·i = eo·ri·nae ≒ eo·ri·ni child
어린아이들은/어린애들은 외국어를 빨리 배운다. **eorinaideureun/eorinaedeureun oegugeoreul ppalli baeunda.** Children learn a second language quickly.

어린이도 돈을 내야 하나요? **eorinido doneul laeya hanayo?** Do children have to pay?

꼬마 kko·ma kid

어리다 eo·ri·da young, little
나는 어려서부터 책 읽는 것을 좋아했다. **naneun eoryeoseobuteo chaek ingneun geoseul joahaetda.** I have liked reading since I was little.

소년 so·nyeon boy
그는 소년 시절을 해외에서 보냈다. **geuneun sonyeon sijeoreul haeoeeseo bonaetda.** He has spent his childhood living overseas.

소녀 so·nyeo (little) girl
아내는 어쩔 때는 아직도 소녀처럼 보여요. **anaeneun eojjeol ttaeneun ajikdo sonyeocheoreom boyeoyo.** My wife sometimes looks like a little girl.

청소년 cheong·so·nyeon youth, juvenile
요즘 청소년들은 빨리 유행을 받아들이는 경향이 있어요. **yojeum cheongsonyeondeureun ppalli yuhaengeul badadeurineun gyeonghyangi isseoyo.** The youth nowadays tend to adopt new fashions quickly.

자라(나)다 ja·ra(·na)·da to grow (up)
저는 부산에서 태어났지만 서울에서 자랐어요. **jeoneun busaneseo taeeonatjiman seoureseo jarasseoyo.** I was born in Busan, but grew up in Seoul.

성장 | ~하다 seong·jang | ~·ha·da growth, development | to grow up
저는 시골에서 성장했어요. **jeoneun sigoreseo seongjanghaesseoyo.** I grew up in the country side.

되다 doe·da to become
부모님은 제가 의사가 되길 바라셨어요. **bumonimeun jega uisaga doegil barasyeosseoyo.** My parents wanted me to become a doctor.

사춘기 sa·chun·gi adolescence, puberty
사춘기에는 많은 신체적, 정신적 변화가 일어난다. **sachungieneun maneun sinchejeok, jeongsinjeok byeonhwaga ireonanda.** Many physical and mental changes occur during adolescence.

철 cheol discretion, sense
너 왜 이리 철이 없어? 철 좀 들어! **neo wae iri cheori eopseo? cheol jom deureo!** Why are you so immature? Act your age!

성숙하다 seong·su·ka·da mature
그 아이는 나이에 비해 성숙했어. **geu aineun naie bihae seongsukaesseo.** He is mature for his age.

성인 seong·in adult, grown-up
성인 표 두 장이랑 아이 표 한 장이요. **seongin pyo du jangirang ai pyo han jangiyo.** Two adult tickets and one child ticket, please.

어른 eo·reun adult, grown-up; elders
아들아이는 어른이 되면 과학자가 되고 싶어해요. **adeuraineun eoreuni doemyeon gwahakjaga doego sipeo haeyo.** My son wants to be a scientist when he grows up.

어른들을 공경해야 한다. **eoreundeureul gonggyeonghaeya handa.** You should respect senior citizens.

청년 = 젊은이 cheong·nyeon = jeol·meu·ni young man, young people
그는 훌륭한 청년으로/젊은이로 자라났다. **geuneun hullyunghan cheongnyeoneuro/jeolmeuniro jaranatda.** He has grown into a fine young man.

신사 sin·sa gentleman
신사 숙녀 여러분! **sinsa sungnyeo yeoreobun!** Ladies and gentlemen!

숙녀 sung·nyeo lady
그 말괄량이 아가씨가 아름다운 숙녀가 되었군요. **geu malgwallyangi agassiga areumdaun sungnyeoga doeeotgunnyo.** The tomboy has grown up into a beautiful lady.

아가씨 a·ga·ssi young lady, miss

청춘 cheong·chun youth
마음은 아직 청춘이에요. **maeumeun ajik cheongchunieyo.** I am still young at heart.

젊다 jeom·da young
여기에 **젊은 연인**들이 많이 옵니다. **yeogie jeolmeun nyeonindeuri mani omnida.** A lot of young couples come here.

젊음 jeol·meum youth

아줌마 = 아주머니 a·jum·ma = a·ju·meo·ni middle-aged woman; ma'am
아줌마/아주머니, 여기가 어디예요? **ajumma/ajumeoni, yeogiga eodiyeyo?** Ma'am, where am I?

아저씨 a·jeo·ssi middle-aged man; mister
그는 열다섯 살이지만, 아저씨처럼 보인다. **geuneun nyeoldaseot sarijiman, ajeossicheoreom boinda.** Though he is fifteen, he looks like a middle-aged man.

노인 no·in senior citizen
한국의 지하철에는 노인들을 위한 자리가 따로 있다. **hangugui jihacheoreneun noindeureul wihan jariga ttaro itda.** The subways in Korea have special seats for senior citizens.

늙다 neuk·da old; to get old
그 사람은 나이보다 **늙어 보인다**. **geu sarameun naiboda neulgeo boinda.** He looks old for his age.
어떤 유명인들은 늙지 않는 것 같다. **eotteon nyumyeongindeureun neukji anneun geot gatda.** Some celebrities don't seem to age.

환갑 = 회갑 hwan·gap = hoe·gap the age of sixty
아버지는 내년이 환갑이세요/회갑이세요. **abeojineun naenyeoni hwangabiseyo/hoegabiseyo.** My father will turn sixty next year.

Traditionally, Koreans have believed in a 60-year life cycle, giving the 60th year its own importance and significance. Thus, a person's 60th birthday is a very important time of celebration.

칠순 chil·sun the age of seventy
이번 주 일요일에 할머니 **칠순 잔치**를 합니다. **ibeon ju iryoire halmeoni chilsun janchireul hamnida.** We're having my grandmother's 70th birthday party this Sunday.

팔순 pal·sun the age of eighty
아버지는 **팔순이 넘으셨지만** 아직 정정하세요. **abeojineun palsuni neomeusyeotjiman ajik jeongjeonghaseyo.** My father is still very vigorous, even though he's over 80.

죽다 juk·da to die

담배를 계속 피우면 젊은 나이에 죽을지도 몰라. **dambaereul gyesok piumyeon jeolmeun naie jugeuljido molla.** Keep smoking and you'll probably die young.

죽음 ju·geum death

숨지다 sum·ji·da to die
결국 그는 **숨진 채** 발견되었다. **gyeolguk geuneun sumjin chae balgyeondoeeotda.** In the end, he was found dead.

사망 | ~하다 sa·mang | ~·ha·da death, passing | to die
그는 교통사고로 사망했다. **geuneun gyotongsagoro samanghaetda.** He died young in a car accident.

돌아가시다 do·ra·ga·si·da to die, pass away
부모님은 두 분 다 돌아가셨어요. **bumonimeun du bun da doragasyeosseoyo.** Both of my parents have passed away.

In Korean, there are many expressions for *to die*. 죽다 is the generic word and is used for people, plants and animals. 사망하다 is a formal, legal term. 숨지다 is mostly used to describe death from an accident. Finally, 돌아가시다 is a euphemism for death. The last three terms are used for people only.

고인 go·in the dead, the deceased

유서 yu·seo will, last will and testament
고인은 **유서를 남기지** 않았습니다. **goineun nyuseoreul lamgiji anatseumnida.** The deceased didn't leave a will.

유언 yu·eon will, testament
그녀는 자신의 재산을 딸에게 모두 남긴다는 **유언을 남겼다**. **geunyeoneun jasinui jaesaneul ttarege modu namgindaneun nyueoneul lamgyeotda.** She made out a will leaving everything to her daughter.

(초)상 (cho·)sang sb's death; funeral
저 집에 **초상이 난** 모양이야. **jeo jibe chosangi nan moyangiya.** It looks like someone died in that family.

장례 jang·nye funeral

장례식 jang·nye·sik funeral ceremony
여러 장관들이 **장례식에 참석했다**. **yeoreo janggwandeuri jangnyesige chamseokaetda.** Several ministers were present at the funeral.

애도 | ~하다 ae·do | ~·ha·da condolences, mourning | to lament, mourn
진심으로 **애도의 말씀**을 드립니다. jinsimeuro aedoui malsseumeul deurimnida. Please accept my condolences.

시신 si·sin dead body

묘지 myo·ji burial ground, cemetery

묻다 mut·da to bury
그들은 고인을 **국립묘지에 묻었다**. geudeureun goineul gungnimmyojie mudeotda. They buried the dead in the National Cemetery.

매장 | ~하다 mae·jang | ~·ha·da burial | to bury, inter

묻히다 mu·chi·da to be buried
많은 병사들이 묘비도 없이 **공동묘지에 묻혔다**. maneun byeongsadeuri myobido eopsi gongdongmyojie muchyeotda. Many soldiers were buried without tombstones in the cemetery.

무덤 mu·deom grave, tomb
무덤을 **훼손하는** 것은 법적으로 금지되어 있다. mudeomeul hwesonhaneun geoseun beopjeogeuro geumjidoeeo itda. It's against the law to violate a grave.

묘 = 산소 myo = san·so grave, tomb
이번 주말에 가족들과 아버지 산소에/묘에 갈 생각입니다. ibeon jumare gajokdeulgwa abeoji sansoe/myoe gal saenggagimnida. I'm planning to visit my father's grave with my family this weekend.

묘비 myo·bi tombstone

화장 | ~하다 hwa·jang | ~·ha·da cremation | to cremate
그녀는 자신이 죽으면 화장을 해 달라고 부탁했다. geunyeoneun jasini jugeumyeon hwajangeul hae dallago butakaetda. She requested that she be cremated.

가슴 가운뎃손가락 거칠다 고르다 고소하다 고요하다

관절 관찰 관찰력 근육 기미 날카롭다 내다보다

노랫소리 뇌 눈가 다리 다크서클 돌아보다

두리번거리다 뒤꿈치 들려오다 따뜻하다 딱딱하다

딸꾹질 땀 뜨겁다 맛없다 매운맛 맹장 머리

목 목구멍 무디다 무릎 미각 미지근하다 발 밟다

배설물 변 보다 볼 부드럽다 부위 뼈 사랑니 살피다

chapter **2** | **The Human Body**

새콤하다 소란 소름 손바닥 숨시야 신장 심장 싸다 쓰다

쓴맛 악취 양발 양팔 어금니 어깨 어둡다 얼굴

엄지 여드름 엿듣다 엿보다 오른발 오른손 오른팔 온몸

웃음소리 응시 이 입술 잇몸 자궁 장기 젖 주름 주목

지켜보다 척수 쳐다보다 촉각 축축하다 트림 팔꿈치 팔

목 폐 푹신하다 향 어리 허벅지 호흡 혹 훑어보다

2.1 External Body Parts

몸 mom body
몸을 살짝 앞으로 기울여 보세요. **momeul saljjak apeuro giullyeo boseyo.** Lean forward slightly.

온몸 = 전신 on·mom = jeon·sin whole body
머리부터 발끝까지 **온몸이/전신이** 가려워요. **meoributeo balkkeutkkaji onmomi/jeonsini garyeowoyo.** My whole body itches from head to toe.

신체 sin·che body
이 바이러스는 **신체 접촉**을 통해 감염된다. **i baireoseuneun sinche jeopchogeul tonghae gamyeomdoenda.** This virus is transmitted through physical contact.

인체 in·che human body

부위 bu·wi part, region, spot
상처 주변 **부위**가 점점 더 붓고 있어요. **sangcheo jubyeon buwiga jeomjeom deo butgo isseoyo.** The area around the wound is swelling.

머리 meo·ri head
머리를 부딪힌 후로 머리가 빠져요. **meorireul budichin huro meoriga ppajyeoyo.** My hair has been falling out since I got hit on the head.

고개 go·gae head
그는 낙담해서 **고개**를 저었다. **geuneun nakdamhaeseo gogaereul jeoeotda.** He shook his head in despair.

머리(카락) = 머리칼 meo·ri(·ka·rak) = meo·ri·kal hair
음식에 **머리카락/머리칼**이 있어! **eumsige meorikaragi/meorikari isseo!** There's a hair in my food!

얼굴 eol·gul face
저는 술만 마시면 **얼굴**이 빨개져요. **jeoneun sulman masimyeon eolguri ppalgaejyeoyo.** My face turns red whenever I drink alcohol.

낯 nat face
저는 **낯**을 많이 **가려서** 새로운 사람들에게 마음을 여는 데 많은 시간이 걸려요. **jeoneun nacheul mani garyeoseo saeroun saramdeurege maeumeul lyeoneun de maneun sigani geollyeoyo.** I'm very shy of strangers, and need a lot of time to open up to new people.

이마 i·ma forehead
네 **이마**에 열이 있잖아. **ne imae yeori itjana.** Your forehead feels hot.

볼 = 뺨 bol = ppyam cheek
저는 원래 오른쪽 **볼**에/**뺨**에 점이 있었어요. **jeoneun wollae oreunjjok bore/ppyame jeomi isseosseoyo.** I had a birthmark on my right cheek.

턱 teok chin
우리 가족들은 전부 **턱**이 **뾰족해요**. **uri gajokdeureun jeonbu teogi ppyojokaeyo.** Everyone in my family has a pointed chin.

눈 nun eye
눈을 감고 소원을 빌어 봐. **nuneul gamgo sowoneul bireo bwa.** Close your eyes and make a wish.

눈가 nun·ga eye rim
그녀는 **눈가**에 주름이 있다. **geunyeoneun nungae jureumi itda.** She has wrinkles around her eyes.

눈동자 nun·dong·ja pupil
어두운 곳에 가면 **눈동자**가 **커진다**. **eoduun gose gamyeon nundongjaga keojinda.** One's pupils dilate in the dark.

눈썹 nun·sseop eyebrow
운이 좋게도 저는 **눈썹**이 아주 **진해서** 그릴 필요가 없어요. **uni jokedo jeoneun nunsseobi aju jinhaeseo geuril piryoga eopseoyo.** I'm lucky to have such thick eyebrows—I don't have to use an eyebrow pencil.

속눈썹 song·nun·sseop eyelashes
이 마스카라는 **속눈썹**이 긴 분에게 딱입니다. **i maseukaraneun songnunsseobi gin bunege ttagimnida.** This mascara is perfect for long eyelashes.

코 ko nose
제 남동생은 눈썹이 짙고 **코**가 **오똑해요**. **je namdongsaengeun nunsseobi jitgo koga ottukaeyo.** My younger brother has thick eyebrows and a sharp nose.

귀 gwi ear
귀가 울려요. **gwiga ullyeoyo.** My ears are ringing.

입 ip mouth

입을 크게 **벌리세요**. ibeul keuge beolliseyo. Open your mouth wide.

입술 ip·sul lips
입술이 계속 **트고** 갈라져요. ipsuri gyesok teugo gallajyeoyo. I keep getting chapped lips.

잇몸 in·mom gums
잇몸이 많이 **부으셨군요**. inmomi mani bueusyeotgunnyo. Your gums are so swollen.

혀 hyeo tongue
혀를 내밀어 보세요. hyeoreul laemireo boseyo. Stick out your tongue.

이(빨) i(·ppal) tooth
식사 후에 이를 꼭 **닦으세요**. siksa hue ireul kkok dakkeuseyo. Don't forget to brush your teeth after eating.

치아 chi·a tooth
사탕은 치아에 좋지 않습니다. satangeun chi-ae jochi anseumnida. Candy is not good for your teeth.

사랑니 sa·rang·ni wisdom tooth
아무래도 **사랑니를 뽑으셔야** 할 것 같습니다. amuraedo sarangnireul ppobeusyeoya hal geot gatseumnida. I think you should have your wisdom teeth extracted.

어금니 eo·geum·ni molar
아래쪽 어금니에 충치가 있어요. araejjok eo-geumnie chungchiga isseoyo. I have a cavity in one of my lower molars.

목 mok neck; throat
목이 아파요. mogi apayo. I have a sore throat. OR I hurt my neck.

목구멍 mok·gu·meong throat

팔 pal arm
팔을 위로 죽 **뻗어** 보세요. pareul wiro juk ppeodeo boseyo. Put your arms straight up.

오른팔 o·reun·pal right arm

왼팔 oen·pal left arm

양팔 yang·pal both arms

팔꿈치 pal·kkum·chi elbow
3개월 전에 골프를 치다가 **팔꿈치를 다쳤어요**. samgaewol jeone golpeureul chidaga pal-kkumchireul dachyeosseoyo. I hurt my elbow while playing golf three months ago.

팔목 = 손목 pal·mok = son·mok wrist
컴퓨터 작업을 오래 하고 나면 항상 **팔목이/**

손목이 아파요. keompyuteo jageobeul orae hago namyeon hangsang palmogi/sonmogi apayo. My wrists always get sore after working at the computer for such a long time.

손 son hand
손이 참 따뜻하시네요. soni cham ttatteuta-sineyo. You have warm hands.

오른손 o·reun·son right hand

왼손 oen·son left hand
저는 왼손으로 글씨를 써요. jeoneun oensoneuro geulssireul sseoyo. I write with my left hand.

양손 yang·son both hands

손등 son·deung back of one's hand
그는 손등으로 얼굴의 땀을 닦았다. geuneun sondeungeuro eolgurui ttameul dakkatda. He wiped the sweat off his face with the back of his hand.

손바닥 son·ba·dak palm
손바닥이 위를 향하게 역기를 잡으세요. son-badagi wireul hyanghage yeokgireul jabeuseyo. Grip the weights with your palms facing upwards.

주먹 ju·meok fist
주먹 꼭 쥐어 보세요. jumeok kkok jwieo boseyo. Make a tight fist.

손가락 son·ga·rak finger
아기들이 **손가락을 깨무는** 것은 나쁜가요? agideuri songarageul kkaemuneun geoseun nappeungayo? Is it bad for babies to bite their fingers?

엄지(손가락) eom·ji(·son·ga·rak) the thumb

집게손가락 = 검지 jip·ge·son·ga·rak = geom·ji index finger

가운뎃손가락 = 중지 ga·un·det·son·ga·rak = jung·ji the middle finger

약지 yak·ji ring finger

새끼손가락 sae·kki·son·ga·rak the little finger

손톱 son·top nail
너 **손톱** 좀 **깎아야겠다**. neo sontop jom kka-kkayagetda. You need to cut your nails.

어깨 eo·kkae shoulder
양팔을 어깨 위로 올리세요. yangpareul eo-kkae wiro olliseyo. Raise your arms above your shoulders.

겨드랑이 gyeo·deu·rang·i armpit
저는 겨드랑이에서 땀이 과도하게 났어요.
jeoneun gyeodeurangieseo ttami gwadohage
nasseosseoyo. I used to sweat excessively under my arms.

가슴 ga·seum chest; breast; heart
요즘 들어 **가슴이** 자주 **답답해요. yojeum deureo gaseumi jaju dapdapaeyo.** Recently, I often feel pressure in my chest.

작은 가슴이 제 콤플렉스예요. jageun gaseumi je kompeullekseuyeyo. I have a complex because of my small breasts.

어젯밤에 별 이유 없이 **가슴이** 마구 **뛰기** 시작했어요. eojetbame byeol iyu eopsi gaseumi magu ttwigi sijakaesseoyo. Last night my heart started pounding hard for no reason.

배 bae stomach, belly
밥을 많이 먹어서 **배가** 너무 **불러. babeul mani meogeoseo baega neomu bulleo.** I ate too much and now my stomach feels too full.

배꼽 bae·kkop navel, belly button

등 deung back
A: 다리가 너무 아파. B: 그럼 내 **등에 업혀.**
A: dariga neomu apa. B: geureom nae deunge eopyeo. A: My legs are killing me. B: Ride on my back, then.

허리 heo·ri waist
움직일 때마다 **허리가** 너무 **아파요. umjigil ttaemada heoriga neomu apayo.** Whenever I move, my back really hurts.

옆구리 yeop·gu·ri side, flank
흉곽 바로 아래 왼쪽 옆구리에 통증이 있어요. hyunggwak baro arae oenjjok yeopgurie tongjeungi isseoyo. I feel pain on the left side just below my rib cage.

엉덩이 eong·deong·i buttocks, butt
하루 종일 앉아 있었더니 **엉덩이가 아파요.** haru jongil anja isseotdeoni eongdeongiga apayo. My butt hurts from sitting down all day.

다리 da·ri leg
축구를 하다가 **다리를 다쳤어요. chukgureul hadaga darireul dachyeosseoyo.** I hurt my leg while playing soccer.

가랑이 ga·rang·i crotch

허벅지 heo·beok·ji thigh

무릎 mu·reup knee
그는 **무릎을 꿇고** 용서를 빌었다. geuneun

mureupeul kkulko yongseoreul bireotda. He got down on his knees and asked for forgiveness.

종아리 jong·a·ri calf
그는 야구공에 종아리를 맞았다. geuneun yagugonge jongarireul majatda. He got hit on the calf by a baseball.

발 bal foot
발을 탁자 위에 올려놓지 마라. bareul takja wie ollyeonochi mara. Don't put your feet on the table!

오른발 o·reun·bal right foot

왼발 oen·bal left foot

양발 yang·bal both feet

발등 bal·deung top of the foot

발바닥 bal·ba·dak sole

뒤꿈치 = 발꿈치 dwi·kkum·chi = bal·kkum·chi heel
신이 너무 작아서 **뒤꿈치가/발꿈치가 까졌어요.** sini neomu jagasseo dwikkumchiga/balkkumchiga kkajyeosseoyo. My shoes are so tight that my heels were blistered.

발목 bal·mok ankle
등산하다가 **발목을 삐었어요.** deungsanhadaga balmogeul ppieosseoyo. I sprained my ankle while mountain climbing.

발가락 bal·ga·rak toe

엄지발가락 eom·ji·bal·ga·rak big toe

새끼발가락 sae·kki·bal·ga·rak little toe
새끼발가락 구부릴 수 있어? saekkibalgarak guburil su isseo? Can you bend your little toe?

발톱 bal·top toenail, claw
문에 찍혀서 **발톱이 빠졌어요.** mune jjikyeoseo baltobi ppajyeosseoyo. I jammed my toe on the door and lost my toenail.

피부 pi·bu skin
흰옷이 너의 **까만 피부랑** 잘 어울리는구나. huinosi neoui kkaman piburang jal eoullineunguna. White clothes go well with your dark skin tones.

털 teol hair, fur
저는 팔에 털이 굉장히 많아요. jeoneun pare teori goengjanghi manayo. I have extremely hairy arms.

수염 su·yeom facial hair

그는 짧은 회색 **수염을** 기르고 있었다. geuneun jjalbeun hoesaek suyeomeul gireugo isseotda. He had a short gray beard.

기미 gi·mi freckle

주근깨 ju·geun·kkae freckle

그는 갈색 머리에 주근깨가 있었다. geuneun galsaek meorie jugeunkkaega isseotda. He had brown hair and freckles.

여드름 yeo·deu·reum pimple

여드름을 짜다가 세균에 감염될 수도 있다. yeodeureumeul jjadaga segyune gamyeomdoel sudo itda. If you squeeze your pimples, you might spread germs.

주름(살) ju·reum(·sal) wrinkle, crease

시어머니는 얼굴에 주름살 하나 없으세요. sieomeonineun eolgure jureumsal hana eopseuseyo. My mother-in-law doesn't have any wrinkles on her face.

다크서클 da·keu·seo·keul dark circles

점 jeom mole

나는 작년에 얼굴에 있는 **점들을 뺐다**. naneun jangnyeone eolgure inneun jeomdeureul ppaetda. I had some moles removed from my face.

혹 hok bump, lump

어쩌다 이마에 **혹이 생긴 거야?** eojjeoda imae hogi saenggin geoya? How did you get a bump on your forehead?

2.2 Internal Organs, Bodily Functions

장기 jang·gi organ

뼈 ppyeo bone

다행히 뼈에는 이상이 없네요. dahaenghi ppyeoeneun isangi eomneyo. Luckily, the bone is all right.

살 sal flesh

운동을 시작한 후로 **살이 쪘어요**. undongeul sijakan huro sari jjyeosseoyo. I have gained weight since I started exercising.

근육 geu·nyuk muscle

근육은 내부 장기들을 보호한다. geunyugeun naebu janggideureul bohohanda. Muscles protect the internal organs.

인대 in·dae ligament

축구를 하다 **인대가** 늘어났어요. chukgureul hada indaega neureonasseoyo. I pulled a ligament while playing soccer.

관절 gwan·jeol joint

비만은 관절에 무리를 줄 수 있다. bimaneun gwanjeore murireul jul su itda. Obesity can strain the joints.

뇌 noe brain

공룡들은 보통 뇌가 작았다. gongnyongdeureun botong noega jagatda. Dinosaurs usually had small brains.

척수 cheok·su spinal cord

심장 sim·jang heart

스트레스는 **심장** 질환의 주요 원인 중 하나 다. seuteureseuneun simjang jilhwanui juyo wonin jung hanada. Stress is one of the major causes of heart disease.

혈관 hyeol·gwan blood vessel

동맥 dong·maek artery

정맥 jeong·maek vein

혈관은 동맥과 정맥으로 되어 있다. hyeolgwaneun dongmaekgwa jeongmaegeuro doeeo itda. Blood vessels are composed of veins and arteries.

모세혈관 mo·se·hyeol·gwan capillary

폐 = 허파 pye = heo·pa lung

위 wi stomach

저는 수년간 위에 문제가 있어 왔어요. jeoneun sunyeongan wie munjega isseo wasseoyo. I've had trouble with my stomach for years.

간 gan liver

술을 많이 드셔서 **간이 상했습니다**. sureul mani deusyeoseo gani sanghaetseumnida. You have ruined your liver from drinking too much alcohol.

쓸개 sseul·gae gall bladder

췌장 chwe·jang pancreas

맹장 maeng·jang appendix

지난 달에 **맹장 제거** 수술을 받았어요. jinan dare maengjang jegeo susureul badasseoyo. I had an appendectomy last month.

신장 = 콩팥 sin·jang = kong·pat kidney

음경 eum·gyeong penis

정자 jeong·ja semen

자궁 ja·gung womb

세포 se·po cell

염색체 yeom·saek·che chromosome

호흡 | ~하다 ho·heup | ~·ha·da breathing | to breathe
천천히 그리고 깊게 호흡하세요. cheoncheonhi geurigo gipge hoheupaseyo. Breathe slowly and deeply.

숨 sum breath
잠깐만 숨을 참으세요. jamkkanman sumeul chameuseyo. Hold your breath for a moment.

쉬다 swi·da to breathe
숨을 쉬기 너무 괴로워요. sumeul swigi neomu goerowoyo. I have much difficulty in breathing.

소화 | ~하다 so·hwa | ~·ha·da digestion | to digest
어젯밤 먹은 게 소화가 잘 안 돼요. eojetbam meogeun ge sohwaga jal an dwaeyo. I'm having trouble digesting what I ate last night.

배설 | ~하다 bae·seol | ~·ha·da excretion | to excrete

배설물 bae·seol·mul excretion

(대)변 = 똥 (dae·)byeon = ttong stool

소변 = 오줌 so·byeon = o·jum urine, pee

마렵다 ma·ryeop·da to feel an urge to urinate
오줌이 마려워요. ojumi maryeowoyo. I have to pee.

누다 nu·da to take (a pee or a dump)
몇 주간 똥을 못 누었어요. myeot jugan ttongeul mon nueosseoyo. I haven't taken a shit in weeks.

싸다 ssa·da to take (a pee or a dump)
나는 열두 살이 될 때까지 이불에 오줌을 쌌다. naneun nyeoldu sari doel ttaekkaji ibure ojumeul ssatda. I wet my bed until I was 12.

땀 ttam sweat
날이 너무 더워서 가만 있어도 땀이 나네요.

nari neomu deowoseo gaman isseodo ttami naneyo. It's so hot that I am sweating even when I'm sitting still.

피 ≒ 혈액 pi ≒ hyeo·raek blood

생리 saeng·ni period, menses
생리가 불규칙해. 산부인과에 가 봐야 할까 봐. saengniga bulgyuchikae. sanbuingwae ga bwaya halkka bwa. I have irregular periods. I think I should go see a gynecologist.

흘리다 heul·li·da to shed, sweat, bleed, drool
그 남자는 부상으로 피를 많이 흘렸다. geu namjaneun busangeuro pireul mani heullyeotda. The injured man lost a lot of blood.

눈곱 ← 눈꼽 nun·gop ← nun·kkop sleep
요즘 들어 눈곱이 많이 끼어요. yojeum deureo nungobi mani kkieoyo. These days I keep getting sleep in my eyes.

젖 jeot milk
저는 젖이 안 나와서 아들한테 분유를 먹일 수밖에 없었어요. jeoneun jeoji an nawaseo adeulhante bunyureul meogil subakke eopseosseoyo. I didn't produce much breast milk so I had to give my son formula.

딸꾹질 | ~하다 ttal·kkuk·jil | ~·ha·da hiccup | to hiccup
딸꾹질이 안 멈춰요. ttalkkukjiri an meomchwoyo. I can't stop my hiccups.

하품 | ~하다 ha·pum | ~·ha·da yawn | to yawn
이 일이 너무 지겨워서 하품이 계속 나. i iri neomu jigyeowoseo hapumi gyesok na. This is so boring that I keep yawning.

방귀 bang·gwi gas, fart
누가 방귀 꼈니? nuga banggwi kkwieonni? Who farted?

트림 | ~하다 teu·rim | ~·ha·da burp | to burp
수유 중과 수유 후에 아기에게 트림을 시키세요. suyu junggwa suyu hue agiege teurimeul sikiseyo. Burp your baby both during and at the end of a feeding.

소름 so·reum goosebumps
경기를 보다 몸에 소름이 돋았다. gyeonggireul boda mome soreumi dodatda. I had goosebumps from just watching the game.

2.3 The Senses

감각 gam·gak sense
행복한 사람들은 대체로 **유머 감각**이 뛰어나
다. haengbokan saramdeureun daechero yumeo
gamgagi ttwieonada. Most people who are
happy have a great sense of humor.

시각 si·gak sight, vision
저는 열네 살 때 오토바이 사고로 **시각을 잃었
습니다.** jeoneun nyeolle sal ttae otobai sagoro
sigageul ireotseumnida. I lost my vision at the
age of 14 in a motorbike accident.

시선 si·seon one's eyes
왜 내 **시선을** 피하는 거야? wae nae siseoneul
pihaneun geoya? Why do you avoid eye contact with me?

시야 si·ya view, sight
비가 오는 날에는 앞유리에 김이 서려 운전
중 **시야를 방해할** 수 있습니다. biga oneun
nareneun amnyurie gimi seoryeo unjeon jung
siyareul banghaehal su itseumnida. On a rainy
day, fog on the windshield can block your
view while driving.

보다 bo·da to see, watch, look
거울 좀 그만 봐. geoul jom geuman bwa. Stop
looking in the mirror.

보이다 bo·i·da to be seen, look (like)
오늘 왜 그렇게 **우울해 보여**? oneul wae geureoke uulhae boyeo? Why do you look so sad?

바라보다 ba·ra·bo·da to look (at)
왜 먼 산 바라보고 있어? Wae meon san barabogo isseo? Why are you looking out at that
faraway hill afar?

쳐다보다 chyeo·da·bo·da to gaze, stare
다른 사람을 **빤히 쳐다보는** 것은 실례예요.
dareun sarameul ppanhi chyeodaboneun geoseun sillyeyeyo. It is not polite to stare at
others.

지켜보다 ji·kyeo·bo·da to watch, observe
코치는 아이들이 축구를 하는 것을 지켜보고
있다. kochineun aideuri chukgureul haneun
geoseul jikyeobogo itda. The coach is watching the children play soccer.

응시 | ~하다 eung·si | ~·ha·da stare, gaze
| to stare, gaze
그는 멍하니 **허공을 응시하고** 있었다. geu-
neun meonghani heogongeul eungsihago isseotda. He was blankly gazing into space.

주시 | ~하다 ju·si | ~·ha·da gaze, obser-
vation | to keep an eye on
당국은 현 **사태를 주시하고** 있습니다. danggugeun hyeon sataereul jusihago itseumnida.
The authorities are keeping an eye on the
present situation.

주목 | ~하다 ju·mok | ~·ha·da attention |
to pay attention
저는 부모님으로부터 아무 **주목을 받지** 못했
어요. jeoneun bumonimeurobuteo amu jumo-
geul batji motaesseoyo. I didn't get any attention from my parents.

노려보다 no·ryeo·bo·da to stare at, glare at
그들은 서로를 한참 동안 노려봤다. geudeu-
reun seororeul hancham dongan noryeobwatda.
They stared at each other for a while.

살펴보다 sal·pyeo·bo·da to examine,
search, check
내가 차 안을 살펴볼게. naega cha aneul sal-
pyeobolge. I'll go check in the car.

살피다 sal·pi·da to check, look (around)
길을 건너기 전에 **주위를** 잘 살펴라. gireul
geonneogi jeone juwireul jal salpyeora. Look
before you cross the street.

관찰 | ~하다 gwan·chal | ~·ha·da observ-
ation | to observe
이 박사는 현미경으로 미생물을 관찰하고 있
다. i baksaneun hyeonmigyeongeuro misaeng-
mureul gwanchalhago itda. Dr. Lee is observing
microorganisms through a microscope.

관찰력 gwan·chal·lyeok power of obser-
vation

훑어보다 hul·teo·bo·da to look over, skim
through
보고서를 훑어보고 오자가 있는지 확인해라.
bogoseoreul hulteobogo ojaga inneunji hwaginhaera. Skim through the report and check
for any spelling mistakes.

올려다보다 ol·lyeo·da·bo·da to look up
(at)

내려다보다 nae·ryeo·da·bo·da to look
down

내다보다 nae·da·bo·da to look out (of)
수업 시간에는 **창밖을 내다보지** 마라. sueop
siganeneun changbakkeul laedaboji mara.
Don't look out the window during class.

들여다보다 deu·ryeo·da·bo·da to look in (to)
냉장고 안을 **들여다봐도** 먹을 것이 없었다. naengjanggo aneul deullyeodabwado meogeul geosi eopseotda. I looked into the refrigerator but there was nothing to eat.

엿보다 ≒ 훔쳐보다 yeot·bo·da ≒ hum·chyeo·bo·da to peep
어떤 상황인지 사무실 안을 **살짝 엿보고/훔쳐보고** 와라. eotteon sanghwanginji samusil aneul saljjak yeotbogo/humchyeobogo wara. Peep into the office to see what's going on.
그는 열쇠 구멍을 통해 엿보다가/훔쳐보다가 잡혔다. geuneun nyeolsoe gumeongeul tonghae yeobodaga/humchyeobodaga japyeotda. He was caught peeping through the keyhole.

둘러보다 dul·leo·bo·da to look around
A: 도와 드릴까요? B: 아뇨, **그냥 둘러보는** 거예요. A: dowa deurilkkayo? B: anyo, geunyang dulleoboneun geoyeyo. A: May I help you? B: No, thanks. I'm just looking around.

두리번거리다 du·ri·beon·geo·ri·da to look around
나는 혹시 카메라가 숨겨져 있지 않을까 싶어 계속 **주위를 두리번거렸다.** naneun hoksi kameraga sumgyeojyeo itji aneulkka sipeo gyesok juwireul duribeongeoryeotda. I kept looking around to see if there was a hidden camera.

돌아보다 do·ra·bo·da to look back
그는 뒤도 돌아보지 않고 가 버렸다. geuneun dwido doraboji anko ga beoryeotda. He walked away without looking back.

청각 cheong·gak sense of hearing

소리 so·ri sound, noise
다락에서 이상한 **소리가** 나요. darageseo isanghan soriga nayo. There is a strange noise coming from the attic.

웃음소리 u·seum·so·ri laughter

울음소리 u·reum·so·ri cry, twitter

노랫소리 no·raet·so·ri singing voice

듣다 deut·da to hear, listen
내 말 좀 **들어 봐.** nae mal jom deureo bwa. Please, listen to me.

밝다 bak·da keen, acute, sharp
어머니는 **귀가** 아주 **밝으세요.** eomeonineun gwiga aju balgeuseyo. My mother has very sharp ears.

어둡다 eo·dup·da bad, weak
저는 **귀가 어두운데** 다른 사람의 얘기를 아주 잘 들어 준다는 말을 많이 들어왔어요. jeoneun gwiga eoduunde dareun saramui yaegireul aju jal deureo jundaneun mareul mani deureowasseoyo. I have a hearing difficulty, and yet I've been told I'm a very good listener.

들리다 deul·li·da to be heard, sound
이상하게 **들릴지도** 모르지만, 내가 한 말은 사실입니다. isanghage deulliljido moreujiman, naega han mareun sasirimnida. Strange as it may sound, what I said is true.

들려오다 deul·lyeo·o·da to be heard, sound
귀에 익은 **목소리가 들려왔다.** gwie igeun moksoriga deullyeowatda. I heard a familiar voice.

엿듣다 yeot·deut·da to eavesdrop, overhear
누군가 우리 **통화** 내용을 **엿듣고** 있는 것 같아요. nugunga uri tonghwa naeyongeul lyeotdeutgo inneun geot gatayo. I think someone is listening to our phone conversations.

귀가 간지럽다 gwi·ga gan·ji·reop·da one's ears are burning
누가 내 말 하고 다니나 봐. **귀가 간지러워.** nuga nae mal hago danina bwa. gwiga ganjireowo. I think someone's talking about me. My ears are burning.

조용하다 | 조용히 jo·yong·ha·da | jo·yong·hi silent, quiet | silently, quietly
저는 아주 **조용한 동네**에 살았었어요. jeoneun aju joyonghan dongnee sarasseosseoyo. I used to live in a very quiet neighborhood.

고요하다 go·yo·ha·da quiet, tranquil, calm
숲은 **사방이 고요했다.** supeun sabangi goyohaetda. The forest was completely silent.

소란 | ~스럽다 so·ran | ~·seu·reop·da disturbance, fuss | noisy, loud
왜 이렇게 소란스러워? wae ireoke soranseureowo? What's all this commotion?

시끄럽다 si·kkeu·reop·da noisy, loud
주변이 너무 **시끄러워요.** jubyeoni neomu sikkeureowoyo. It's too noisy around here.

미각 mi·gak (sense of) taste

맛 mat taste, flavor
커피 맛이 어때? keopi masi eottae? How does the coffee taste?

단맛 dan·mat sweet taste
이 사과는 **단맛이 난다.** i sagwaneun danmasi nanda. This apple has a sweet taste.

쓴맛 sseun·mat bitter taste
사탕을 먹어 봐. 쓴맛이 좀 덜할 거야. satang-eul meogeo bwa. sseunmasi jom deolhal geoya. Eat some candy. It will help you get rid of the bitter taste.

매운맛 mae·un·mat spicy taste

짠맛 jjan·mat salty taste

입맛 = 밥맛 = 식욕 im·mat = bam·mat = si·gyok appetite
오늘은 **입맛이/밥맛이/식욕이 없다.** oneu-reun immasi/bammasi/sigyogi eopda. I have no appetite today.

맛있다 ma·sit·da delicious
이 집에서 뭐가 제일 맛있어요? i jibeseo mwo-ga jeil masisseoyo? What's your best dish?

맛없다 ma·deop·da to taste bad
악! 정말 맛없다! ak! jeongmal madeopda! Ugh! It tastes terrible!

싱겁다 sing·geop·da bland
국이 좀 싱거워요. gugi jom singgeowoyo. The soup is a little bland.

짜다 jja·da salty
생선이 너무 짠데. saengseoni neomu jjande. The fish is too salty.

달다 dal·da sweet, sugary
차가 너무 달아요. chaga neomu darayo. The tea is too sugary.

달콤하다 dal·kom·ha·da sweet
갑자기 달콤한 게 먹고 싶어요. gapjagi dalkomhan ge meokgo sipeoyo. Suddenly, I feel like eating something sweet.

맵다 maep·da hot, spicy
한국의 어떤 양념들은 정말 매워요. hangugui eotteon nyangnyeomdeureun jeongmal mae-woyo. Some Korean seasonings are very spicy.

매콤하다 mae·kom·ha·da hot, spicy
오늘 저녁에는 뭔가 매콤한 걸 먹고 싶어요. oneul jeonyeogeneun mwonga maekomhan geol meokgo sipeoyo. I feel like having something spicy for dinner tonight.

시다 si·da sour
레몬이 신 것은 산 때문이다. remoni sin geo-seun san ttaemunida. A lemon is sour because of its citric acid.

새콤하다 sae·kom·ha·da sour
새콤한 맛을 좋아하신다면 레몬즙을 한 스푼 넣으셔도 됩니다. saekomhan maseul joahasin-damyeon lemonjeubeul han seupun neoeu-syeodo doemnida. If you like it sour, you may add a spoon of lemon juice.

상큼하다 sang·keum·ha·da fresh, refreshing
상큼한 주스가 마시고 싶다. sangkeumhan ju-seuga masigo sipda. I feel like drinking some fresh juice.

떫다 tteol·da bitter, sour, astringent
왜 감은 떫은 건가요? wae gameun tteolbeun geongayo? Why are persimmons astringent?

쓰다 sseu·da bitter
몸에 좋은 약은 입에 쓰다. mome joeun nya-geun ibe sseuda. Good medicine tastes bitter.

고소하다 go·so·ha·da (to taste) like sesame
과자가 참 고소하네요. gwajaga cham goso-haneyo. The cookies are really nutty.

느끼하다 neu·kki·ha·da greasy
이 피자는 너무 느끼해. i pijaneun neomu neu-kkihae. The pizza is too greasy.

비리다 bi·ri·da fishy
나는 **비린** 생선들을 좋아하지 않는다. naneun birin saengseondeureul joahaji anneunda. I don't like fish with strong fishy smell.

담백하다 dam·bae·ka·da light, clean
음식을 담백하게 드세요. eumsigeul dambae-kage deuseyo. Eat lightly.

....

후각 hu·gak sense of smell

냄새 naem·sae smell, odor
저는 **담배 냄새가** 정말 싫어요. jeoneun dam-bae naemsaega jeongmal sireoyo. I really hate the smell of cigarette smoke.

악취 ak·chwi bad smell
하수구에서 **악취가** 나요. hasugueseo akchwi-ga nayo. There is a bad smell coming from the drain.

향긋하다 hyang·geu·ta·da fragrant, aromatic
라벤더는 요리에 **향긋한 향**을 더해 줍니다. rabendeoneun nyorie hyanggeutan hyangeul deohae jumnida. Lavender adds a fragrant flavor to cuisine.

향(기) hyang(·gi) scent, fragrance
이 꽃은 향기가 좋아요. i kkocheun hyanggiga joayo. This flower has a nice fragrance.

맡다 mat·da to smell
지금은 감기에 걸려서 **냄새를 못 맡아요.** ji-geumeun gamgie geollyeoseo naemsaereul mon matayo. I can't smell a thing because of my cold.

촉각 chok·gak sense of touch

느끼다 neu·kki·da to feel

느낌 neu·kkim feeling, sense
그 사람이 떠날 것 같은 느낌이 들어. geu sarami tteonal geot gateun neukkimi deureo. I have a feeling that he will leave.

가렵다 ga·ryeop·da itchy
등이 가려워요. deungi garyeowoyo. My back itches.

간지럽다 gan·ji·reop·da itchy, tickle
간지러워, 그만해. ganjireowo, geumanhae. Stop tickling me.

따갑다 tta·gap·da stinging
손이 따가워요. soni ttagawoyo. I feel stinging sensation in my hand.

시리다 si·ri·da cold
찬물을 마시면 **이가 시려요.** chanmureul masimyeon iga siryeoyo. My teeth ache whenever I drink cold water.

감촉 = 촉감 gam·chok = chok·gam touch, feel
이 천은 **감촉이/촉감이 부드러워요.** i cheoneun gamchogi/chokgami budeureowoyo. This fabric feels soft.

딱딱하다 ttak·tta·ka·da hard, stiff
빵이 말라서 딱딱해졌다. ppangi mallaseo ttakttakaejyeotda. The bread has dried out and became hard.

단단하다 dan·dan·ha·da hard, solid
이런 종류의 나무는 단단합니다. ireon jong-nyuui namuneun dandanhamnida. This kind of wood is solid.

물렁(물렁)하다 mul·leong(·mul·leong)·ha·da soft, tender
할머니는 치아가 안 좋으셔서 **물렁한 과일을** 즐겨 드세요. halmeonineun chiaga an joeusyeo-seo mulleonghan gwaireul jeulgyeo deuseyo. My grandmother has bad teeth, so she likes to eat soft fruit.

푹신(푹신)하다 puk·sin(·puk·sin)·ha·da very soft
이 소파는 푹신푹신하고 편하다. i sopaneun puksinpuksinhago pyeonhada. This sofa is very soft and comfortable.

차다 ≒ 차갑다 cha·da ≒ cha·gap·da cold, chilly
바람이 차니 따뜻하게 입어라. barami chani ttatteutage ibeora. Dress warmly because the wind is chilly.
방바닥이 **얼음같이 차가워요.** bangbadagi eo-reumgachi chagawoyo. The floor is as cold as ice.

시원하다 si·won·ha·da cool
물이 시원하네요. muri siwonhaneyo. The water feels cool.

미지근하다 mi·ji·geun·ha·da lukewarm
마지막으로 미지근한 물에 헹궈 내세요. ma-jimageuro mijigeunhan mure henggwo naeseyo. Lastly, rinse it in lukewarm water.

따스하다 tta·seu·ha·da warm
이제 따스한 봄 기운이 느껴진다. ije ttaseu-han bom giuni neukkyeojinda. Now I can feel the warmth of spring.

따뜻하다 tta·tteu·ta·da warm
따뜻한 물 한 잔만 주시겠어요? ttatteutan mul han janman jusigesseoyo? Can I have a glass of warm water?

뜨겁다 tteu·geop·da hot, burning
조심하세요. 뜨거워요. josimhaseyo. tteugeo-woyo. Be careful, it's very hot.

표면 pyo·myeon surface

거칠다 geo·chil·da rough, coarse
달의 표면은 고르지 않고 거친 것으로 알려져 있다. darui pyomyeoneun goreuji anko geochin geoseuro allyeojyeo itda. The surface of the moon is known to be rough and uneven.

매끄럽다 = 매끈하다 mae·kkeu·reop·da = mae·kkeun·ha·da smooth, soft
비타민 시는 피부를 매끄럽게/매끈하게 한다. bitamin sineun pibureul maekkeureopge/maekkeunhage handa. Vitamin C can help the skin look smooth.

끈적(끈적)하다 = 끈적거리다 kkeun·jeok(·kkeun·jeok)·ha·da = kkeun·jeok·geo·ri·da sticky
반죽이 너무 끈적하면/끈적거리면 밀가루를 약간 더 넣으세요. banjugi neomu kkeunjeoka-

myeon/kkeunjeokgeorimyeon milgarureul lyak-gan deo neoeuseyo. Add a small amount of flour if the dough is too sticky.

부드럽다 bu·deu·reop·da soft
나는 부드러운 침대를 안 좋아한다. naneun budeureoun chimdaereul an joahanda. I don't like soft beds.

울퉁불퉁하다 ul·tung·bul·tung·ha·da un-even, bumpy
꽉 잡아! 길이 울퉁불퉁해지는 것 같아. kkwak jaba! giri ultungbultunghaejineun geot gata. Hold on! The road is going to get a little bumpy.

고르다 go·reu·da even

날카롭다 nal·ka·rop·da sharp
새의 부리가 날카롭다. saeui buriga nalkaropda. The bird's beak is sharp.

뾰족하다 ppyo·jo·ka·da sharp, pointed

무디다 mu·di·da blunt, dull
이 칼은 샐러드용으로 특수 제작되어 날 끝이 무딥니다. i kareun saelleodeuyongeuro teuksu jejakdoeeo nal kkeuchi mudimnida. This knife has a blunt blade especially designed for salad.

미끄럽다 mi·kkeu·reop·da slippery, slick
조심해! 바닥이 미끄러워. josimhae! badagi mikkeureowo. Be careful! The floor is slip-pery.

축축하다 chuk·chu·ka·da damp, wet
그녀의 얼굴과 온몸이 땀으로 축축하게 젖었다. geunyeoui eolgulgwa onmomi ttameuro chukchukage jeojeotda. Her face and whole body were wet with sweat.

감다 개다 개다 거울 걸레 골다 구멍 기르다

깎다 깔다 깨끗이 깨끗하다 깨우다 꾸미다

꾸미다 꿈 낮잠 내놓다 늦잠 다듬다 다리다 닦다

닦다 달다 담그다 담요 더럽다 드라이어 로션

갈리다 말리다 맡기다 먼지 면도기 목욕 목욕탕

미용실 바느질 바싹 베다 불리다 비누 비우다 빗

빗다 빗자루 빨다 사우나 살림 새우다 샤워 샴푸

세수 세제 세탁 세탁소 손질 수면 쉬다 스킨

chapter **3** | **Daily Activities**

심부름 쓰레받기 쓸다 씻기다 씻다 악몽 양치 얼룩

엉망 염색 이발소 이불 일회용품 잠 잠꼬대 잠들다

잠자다 재활용 정리 족집게 졸다 졸리다

지우다 집안일 찜질방 청소 청소기 취하다

치실 치약 치우다 침대 칫솔 태우다

파마 푹 행주 헹구다 화장 화장품 유지

3.1 Sleeping, Relaxing

일상 | ~적 il·sang l~·jeok everyday life | daily, everyday
인터넷은 이제 우리 **일상**의 일부예요. inteoneseun ije uri ilsangui ilbuyeyo. Now the Internet is part of our daily life.

잠 jam sleep
커피를 마시면 밤에 **잠**이 안 **와요**. keopireul masimyeon bame jami an wayo. I can't sleep at night if I drink coffee.

수면 su·myeon sleep
저는 만성적인 **수면** 장애가 있어요. jeoneun manseongjeogin sumyeon jangaega isseoyo. I have a chronic sleep disorder.

낮잠 nat·jam nap, doze
낮잠을 너무 많이 **잤더니** 잠이 안 온다. natjameul leomu mani jatdeoni jami an onda. I took a long nap and now I can't sleep.

늦잠 neut·jam oversleeping
오늘 **늦잠**을 **자서** 학교에 지각했어요. oneul leutjameul jasseo hakgyoe jigakaesseoyo. I overslept this morning and was late for school.

자다 ja·da to sleep
밤에 잠은 잘 **잤어**? bame jameun jal jasseo? Did you sleep well?

주무시다 ju·mu·si·da honorific of 자다 jada
안녕히 **주무셨**어요? annyeonghi jumusyeosseoyo? Did you have a good sleep?

잠들다 jam·deul·da to go to sleep, fall asleep
쉿! 아기가 방금 **잠들었어**. swit! agiga banggeum jamdeureosseo. Hush! The baby's just fallen asleep.

잠자다 jam·ja·da to sleep
잠자기 전에 이를 닦아라. jamjagi jeone ireul dakkara. Brush your teeth before going to bed.

잠자리 jam·ja·ri bed, sleeping place
어젯밤 일찍 **잠자리**에 들었다. eojetbam iljjik jamjarie deureotda. I went to bed early last night.

> **잠자리**, which means *bed*, is pronounced /잠짜리/. Its homograph 잠자리 which is pronounced as it's written means *dragonfly*.

눕다 nup·da to lie

저는 보통 자리에 눕자마자 자요. jeoneun botong jarie nupjamaja jayo. I usually fall asleep as soon as I lie down.

졸다 jol·da to doze off
수업 시간 내내 **졸았어요**. sueop sigan naenae jorasseoyo. I dozed off and slept during the entire class.

졸음 jo·reum sleepiness

눈을 붙이다 nu·neul bu·chi·da to get a little sleep
잠깐 **눈** 좀 **붙이지** 그러세요? jamkkan nun jom buchiji geureoseyo? Why don't you get some shuteye?

졸리다 ← 졸립다 jol·li·da ← jol·lip·da to feel sleepy
하루 종일 **졸려요**. haru jongil jollyeoyo. I feel sleepy all day long.

꿈 kkum dream
좋은 **꿈** 꿰! joeun kkum kkwo! Sweet dreams!

악몽 ang·mong nightmare, bad dream

꾸다 kku·da to dream (a dream)
악몽을 **꿨어요**. angmongeul kkwosseoyo. I had a bad dream.

잠꼬대 | ~하다 jam·kko·dae l ~·ha·da sleep talking | to talk in one's sleep
내 동생은 **잠꼬대**가 심하다. nae dongsaengeun jamkkodaega simhada. My little brother often talks in his sleep.

골다 gol·da to snore
남편은 잘 때 **코**를 심하게 **골아요**. nampyeoneun jal ttae koreul simhage gorayo. My husband snores loudly in his sleep.

새우다 sae·u·da to stay up (all night)
책을 읽다 **밤을 새웠어요**. chaegeul ikda bameul saewosseoyo. I stayed up all night reading a book.

밤새우다 bam·sae·u·da to stay up all night

침대 chim·dae bed
일어나자마자 **침대** 정리부터 해라. ireonajamaja chimdae jeongnibuteo haera. As soon as you wake up, you need to tidy your bed.

이불 i·bul covers
나는 잘 때 **이불**을 **걷어차는** 습관이 있다. naneun jal ttae ibureul geodeochaneun seupgwani

itda. I have a habit of kicking the covers off in my sleep.

담요 ← 담뇨 dam·nyo blanket
밤에는 추우니까 **담요 한 장**을 더 달라고 해라. **bameneun chuunikka damnyo han jangeul deo dallago haera.** Ask for another blanket because it's going to be cold tonight.

덮다 deop·da to cover
그녀는 환자에게 **담요를 덮어** 주었다. **geunyeoneun hwanjaege damnyoreul deopeo jueotda.** She covered the patient with a blanket.

요 yo Korean-style mattress
요가 너무 얇다. **yoga neomu yalda.** The mattress is too thin.

깔다 kkal·da to spread, lay
이불 깔아라. **ibul kkarara.** Spread out the sheets.

펴다 pyeo·da to spread

개다 gae·da to fold up

베개 be·gae pillow
이 **베개**는 너무 높아요. 다른 베개를 좀 갖다 주실래요? **i begaeneun neomu nopayo. dareun begaereul jom gatda jusillaeyo?** This pillow is too thick. Would you please bring me another one?

베다 be·da to use (a pillow)
너무 부드러운 **베개를 베고** 자면 목에 좋지 않다. **neomu budeureoun begaereul bego jamyeon moge jochi anta.** A pillow that is too soft is bad for your neck.

깨다 kkae·da to wake (up)
새벽에 **잠이 깨서** 다시 못 잤어요. **saebyeoge jami kkaeseo dasi mot jasseoyo.** I woke up at dawn and couldn't go back to sleep.

일어나다 i·reo·na·da to get up, wake up
벌써 일어난 거야? **beolsseo ireonan geoya?** Are you up already?

깨우다 kkae·u·da to wake, awake
한 시간 뒤에 깨워 줄래? **han sigan dwie kkaewo jullae?** Can you wake me up after an hour?

휴식 hyu·sik rest, break
저에겐 휴식이 필요해요. **jeoegen hyusigi piryohaeyo.** I need a break.

푹 puk deeply, very much

쉬다 swi·da to rest, relax
푹 쉬면 괜찮을 거야. **puk swimyeon gwaenchaneul geoya.** You will feel better after you have a good rest.

취하다 chwi·ha·da to take, have, get
충분한 **수면과 휴식을 취하셔야** 합니다. **chungbunhan sumyeongwa hyusigeul chwihasyeoya hamnida.** You need to get plenty of sleep and rest.

머리(를) 식히다 meo·ri(·reul) si·ki·da to have a brief rest
잠깐 **머리를 식히러** 산책 나갔어요. **jamkkan meorireul sikireo sanchaek nagasseoyo.** He went for a walk to cool off.

3.2 Personal Grooming

씻다 ssit·da to wash
집에 오자마자 **손을 씻어라.** **jibe ojamaja soneul ssiseora.** Wash your hands as soon as you get home.

씻기다 ssit·gi·da to wash
저는 밤마다 **아기를 씻깁니다.** **jeoneun bammada agireul ssitgimnida.** I bathe my baby every night.

닦다 dak·da to clean, wipe; to brush (one's teeth)
그 선수는 수건으로 얼굴의 **땀을 닦았다.** **geu seonsuneun sugeoneuro eolgurui ttameul dakkatda.** The athlete wiped the sweat off his face with a towel.

이를 닦으면 잇몸에서 피가 나요. **ireul dakkeumyeon inmomeseo piga nayo.** My gums bleed when I brush my teeth.

세수 | ~하다 se·su | ~·ha·da face washing | to wash one's face
나 아직 세수도 안 했어. **na ajik sesudo an haesseo.** I haven't even washed my face yet.

양치(질) | ~하다 yang·chi(·jil) | ~·ha·da teeth brushing | to brush one's teeth
저는 양치를 하루에 세 번 합니다. **jeoneun nyangchireul harue se beon hamnida.** I brush my teeth three times a day.

면도 | ~하다 myeon·do | ~·ha·da shave, shaving | to shave

아침에 면도하다가 베었어요. achime myeon-dohadaga beeosseoyo. I cut myself while shaving this morning.

샤워 | ~하다 sya·wo | ~·ha·da shower | to take a shower
저는 샤워를 늘 아침에 해요. jeoneun sya-woreul leul achime haeyo. I always take a shower in the morning.

목욕 | ~하다 mo·gyok | ~·ha·da bath | to take a bath
저는 일주일에 한 번 목욕을 합니다. jeoneun iljuire han beon mogyogeul hamnida. I take a bath once a week.

비누 bi·nu soap
저는 어릴 때부터 샴푸 대신 비누로 머리를 감았어요. jeoneun eoril ttaebuteo syampu daesin binuro meorireul gamasseoyo. I've washed my hair with soap instead of shampoo since I was young.

수건 = 타월 su·geon = ta·wol towel
머리 말릴 수건/타월 있어? meori mallil su-geon/tawol isseo? Do you have a towel to dry your hair with?

치약 chi·yak toothpaste

칫솔 chit·sol toothbrush

치실 chi·sil floss

면도기 myeon·do·gi razor

(공중)목욕탕 (gong·jung·)mo·gyok·tang (public) bath house

사우나 sa·u·na sauna

스파 seu·pa spa

찜질방 jjim·jil·bang Korean dry sauna

감다 gam·da to wash (one's hair)
저는 밤에 머리를 감아요. jeoneun bame meo-rireul gamayo. I wash my hair every night.

말리다 mal·li·da to dry
드라이어로 머리를 잘 말려라. deuraieoro meorireul jal mallyeora. Blow-dry your hair well.

빗다 bit·da to comb
나 머리 빗게 거울 좀 줘. na meori bitge geoul jom jwo. I need a mirror so I can see to comb my hair.

샴푸 syam·pu shampoo

(헤어)드라이어 = 드라이기 (he·eo·) deu·ra·i·eo = deu·ra·i·gi hairdryer

빗 bit comb

기르다 gi·reu·da to grow, wear
수염을 기르는 중이에요. suyeomeul gireu-neun jungieyo. I'm letting my mustache grow.

다듬다 da·deum·da to trim, polish
끄트머리를 다듬어 주세요. kkeuteumeorireul dadeumeo juseyo. Just trim the ends of my hair, please.

손질 | ~하다 son·jil | ~·ha·da trimming | to trim, fix
손톱 손질을 받고 싶어요. sontop sonjireul batgo sipeoyo. I want to get a manicure.

깎다 ≒ 자르다 kkak·da ≒ ja·reu·da to cut; to have one's hair cut
왜 그렇게 머리를 짧게 깎았어/잘랐어? wae geureoke meorireul jjalge kkakkasseo/jalla-sseo? Why did you have your hair cut so short?

머리를 깎다/자르다 **meorireul kkakda/ jareuda** can mean *to cut someone else's hair* or *to get one's hair cut.*

손톱깎이 son·top·kka·kki nail clippers

족집게 jok·jip·ge tweezers

미용실 = 미장원 mi·yong·sil = mi·jang·won beauty parlor
요즘은 남자들도 많이들 미용실에/미장원에 갑니다. yojeumeun namjadeuldo manideul mi-yongsire/mijangwone gamnida. These days many men go to beauty parlors.

미용사 mi·yong·sa hairdresser

이발소 i·bal·so barbershop
저 건물에 이발소 표시가 있다. jeo geonmure ibalso pyosiga itda. There's a barber pole on that building.

이발사 i·bal·sa barber

파마 | ~하다 pa·ma | ~·ha·da perm | to get a perm
파마 어디서 했어? pama eodiseo haesseo? Where did you get your hair permed?

염색 | ~하다 yeom·saek | ~·ha·da dyeing | to dye, color

머리를 **검게 염색해** 주세요. meorireul geomge yeomsaekae juseyo. Can you dye my hair black?

삭발 | ~하다 sak·bal | ~·ha·da shaved head | to shave one's head
그들은 여성 운전 금지에 대한 항의의 표시로 삭발을 했다. geudeureun nyeoseong unjeon geumjie daehan hanguiui pyosiro sakbareul haetda. They shaved their heads as a sign of protest against the ban on female drivers.

화장 | ~하다 hwa·jang | ~·ha·da makeup | to wear makeup
저는 평소에는 화장을 안 해요. jeoneun pyeongsoeneun hwajangeul an haeyo. Usually I don't wear makeup.

꾸미다 kku·mi·da to adorn
당신은 꾸미지 않아도 예뻐. dangsineun kkumiji anado yeppeo. You are still beautiful without makeup.

화장품 hwa·jang·pum cosmetics
화장품을 아낄 수 있는 여러 방법이 있어요. hwajangpumeul akkil su inneun nyeoreo bang-beobi isseoyo. There are lots of ways to save on cosmetics.

거울 geo·ul mirror
누나는 하루 종일 **거울을** 들여다봐요. nuna-neun haru jongil geoureul deuryeodabwayo. My older sister looks into the mirror all day long.

향수 hyang·su perfume, cologne
한 여성 판매 직원이 제 팔목에 **향수를 뿌렸어요.** han nyeoseong panmae jigwoni je pal-moge hyangsureul ppuryeosseoyo. A saleslady sprayed perfume on my wrist.

팩 paek face pack

스킨 seu·kin toner

로션 ro·syeon lotion
피부가 건조해지지 않도록 **로션을** 자주 **바르세요.** pibuga geonjohaejiji antorok rosyeoneul jaju bareuseyo. Apply lotion frequently to prevent dry skin.

크림 keu·rim cream

매니큐어 mae·ni·kyu·eo nail polish

3.3 Chores, Housework

집안일 ji·ban·nil household chores
집안일에는 끝이 없다. jibanireuneun kkeuchi eopda. There is no end to household chores.

살림 | ~하다 sal·lim | ~·ha·da housekeeping | to housekeep
저희 아빠는 집에서 살림을 하세요. jeohui appaneun jibeseo sallimeul haseyo. My dad stays home and manages the household.

빨래 | ~하다 ppal·lae | ~·ha·da laundry | to do the laundry
빨래는 햇볕에서 더 빨리 마른다. ppallaeneun haetbyeoteseo deo ppalli mareunda. The laundry will dry faster in the sun.

손빨래 | ~하다 son·ppal·lae | ~·ha·da hand-wash | to hand wash
이 스웨터는 손빨래해야 합니다. i seuwe-teoneun sonppallaehaeya hamnida. This sweater must be hand washed.

세탁 | ~하다 se·tak | ~·ha·da doing the laundry | to do the laundry
와이셔츠 한 장 세탁하는 데 얼마예요? wai-syeocheu han jang setakaneun de eolmayeyo? How much does it cost to dry-clean a dress shirt?

빨다 ppal·da to wash, clean
옷을 빨아 봤지만, 얼룩이 지워지지 않았다. oseul ppara bwatjiman, eollugi jiwojiji anatda. I tried washing it, but the stain won't come out.

담그다 dam·geu·da to soak, put sth in water
그 드레스는 물에 담그지 마. geu deureseu-neun mure damgeuji ma. Don't soak the dress in water.

불리다 bul·li·da to soak, steep
반 시간 정도 옷을 물에 불려라. ban sigan jeongdo oseul mure bullyeora. Soak the clothes in water for half an hour.

헹구다 heng·gu·da to rinse
따뜻한 물로 헹궈라. ttatteutan mullo heng-gwora. Rinse off with warm water.

짜다 jja·da to wring out, squeeze
옷을 짜면 안 되는 거 꼭 기억하세요. oseul jjamyeon an doeneun geo kkok gieokaseyo. Remember not to wring out the clothes.

널다 neol·da to hang up
빨래를 잘 짠 다음 널어라. ppallaereul jal jjan daeum neoreora. Wring out the laundry well and hang it out to dry.

바싹 ba·ssak completely

마르다 ma·reu·da to run dry
빨래가 **바싹** 말랐어. ppallaega bassak mallaseo. The laundry has dried completely.

말리다 mal·li·da to dry
빨래를 그늘에서 말려라. ppallaereul geuneureseo mallyeora. Dry the laundry in the shade.

젖다 jeot·da to get wet
비에 **옷이** 다 **젖었다.** bie osi da jeojeotda. My clothes got wet in the rain.

걷다 geot·da to gather (up), bring in
비 온다! **빨래 걷어라.** bi onda! ppallae geodeora. It's raining! Bring the laundry inside.

개다 gae·da to fold
빨래를 빨리, 그리고 잘 **개는** 요령을 알려 드릴게요. ppallaereul ppalli, geurigo jal gaeneun nyoryeongeul allyeo deurilgeyo. I'll show you the quickest and most efficient way to fold laundry.

때 ttae dirt
흰옷은 **때가** 잘 **탄다.** huinoseun ttaega jal tanda. White clothes get dirty easily.

얼룩 eol·luk stain

자국 ja·guk mark, stain

흔적 heun·jeok trace, mark

묻다 mut·da to be stained with
너 셔츠에 **흙 묻었어.** neo syeocheue heuk mudeosseo. You got dirt on your shirt.

없애다 eop·sae·da to remove, get rid of
얼룩을 **없애 주세요.** eollugeul eopsae juseyo. Can you remove the stains?

지우다 ji·u·da to remove

제거 | **~하다** je·geo | ~·ha·da removal, elimination | to remove, get rid of
부드러운 천으로 표면의 **때를 제거해라.** budeureoun cheoneuro pyomyeonui ttaereul jegeohaera. Remove any dirt from the surface with a soft cloth.

세탁기 se·tak·gi washing machine

세제 se·je detergent, cleanser

세제를 너무 많이 **넣지** 마. sejereul leomu mani neochi ma. Don't add too much detergent.

세탁소 se·tak·so laundry

맡기다 mat·gi·da to put, leave
세탁기가 고장 나서 옷을 **세탁소에 맡겨야** 했다. setakgiga gojang naseo oseul setaksoe matgyeoya haetda. My washing machine broke, so I had to take my clothes to the laundry.

찾다 chat·da to pick up
언제 찾으러 올까요? eonje chajeureo olkkayo? When can I pick it up?

심부름 | **~하다** sim·bu·reum | ~·ha·da errand | to run an errand
심부름 좀 해 줄래? simbureum jom hae jullae? Can you run an errand for me?

다리미 da·ri·mi iron
다리미 만지지 마. darimi manjiji ma. Don't touch the iron.

다림질 | **~하다** da·rim·jil | ~·ha·da ironing | to iron
이 옷은 뒤집어서 다림질하세요. i oseun dwijibeoseo darimjilhaseyo. Iron these clothes on the reverse side.

다리다 da·ri·da to iron
이 **바지** 좀 **다려** 주세요. i baji jom daryeo juseyo. Please have these pants ironed.

청소 | **~하다** cheong·so | ~·ha·da cleaning | to clean
오늘은 화장실 청소를 할 거야. oneureun hwajangsil cheongsoreul hal geoya. Today I'm going to clean my bathroom.

치우다 chi·u·da to clean, tidy, clear
테이블 치우는 거 좀 도와줘. teibeul chiuneun geo jom dowajwo. Help me clear the table.

정리 ≒ **정돈** | **~하다** jeong·ni ≒ jeong·don | ~·ha·da arrangement | to arrange, organize
옷장 정리하는 것 좀 도와줄래? otjang jeongnihaneun geot jom dowajullae? Could you give me a hand with arranging the closet?
네 물건들 정리/정돈 좀 해. ne mulgeondeul jeongni/jeongdon jom hae. Put your things in order.

깨끗하다 | **깨끗이** kkae·kkeu·ta·da | kka·

kkeu·si clean | cleanly, neatly
제 방은 깨끗함과는 거리가 멀어요. **je bang-eun kkaekkeutamgwaneun georiga meoreoyo.** My room is far from being neat and clean.

더럽다 deo·reop·da dirty, filthy
옷이 왜 그렇게 더러워? **osi wae geureoke deoreowo?** Why are your clothes so dirty?

지저분하다 ji·jeo·bun·ha·da dirty, messy
사무실이 지저분하면 직원들이 일에 집중하기가 힘들어요. **samusiri jijeobunhamyeon jigwondeuri ire jipjunghagiga himdeureoyo.** When the office is messy, it is hard for the employees to focus on their jobs.

엉망 eong·mang wreck, mess, ruin
제 방 정말 엉망이죠? **je bang jeongmal eongmangijyo?** My room is really messy, isn't it?

· ·

먼지 meon·ji dust

털다 teol·da to dust, brush
방 구석구석의 **먼지를 털어** 내는 것은 쉬운 일이 아니었다. **bang guseokguseogui meonjireul teoreo naeneun geoseun swiun iri anieotda.** It was no easy task to dust the whole room.

빗자루 bit·ja·ru broom

쓸다 sseul·da to sweep
바닥 쓸었니? **badak sseureonni?** Have you swept the floor?

쓰레받기 sseu·re·bat·gi dust pan

담다 dam·da to put sth in
나는 유리 조각을 빗자루로 쓸어 **쓰레받기에 담았다. naneun nyuri jogageul bitjaruro sseureo sseurebatgie damatda.** I swept the glass shards into a dust pan.

걸레 geol·le rag, mop

닦다 dak·da to mop, clean, wipe, brush
걸레로 **바닥 좀 닦아라. geollero badak jom dakkara.** Clean the floor with a mop.

청소기 cheong·so·gi vacuum cleaner
청소기 어디에 뒀어? **cheongsogi eodie dwosseo?** Where did you put the vacuum cleaner?

돌리다 dol·li·da to work, operate
여보, 침실에 **청소기 좀 돌려** 줄래? **yeobo, chimsire cheongsogi jom dollyeo jullae?** Honey, will you vacuum the bedroom, please?

· ·

쓰레기 sseu·re·gi garbage, waste

쓰레기 양을 줄이려고 노력해야 한다. **sseuregi yangeul juriryeogo noryeokaeya handa.** We must try to reduce the amount of garbage.

휴지 hyu·ji waste paper

쓰레기통 = 휴지통 sseu·re·gi·tong = hyu·ji·tong wastebasket, trash can
쓰레기는 쓰레기통에/휴지통에 버려라. **sseuregineun sseuregitonge/hyujitonge beoryeora.** Throw the garbage into the trash can.

버리다 beo·ri·da to throw away

비우다 bi·u·da to empty out
휴지통 좀 **비워** 줄래요? **hyujitong jom biwo jullaeyo?** Could you empty the trash can?

태우다 tae·u·da to burn
허가 없이 쓰레기를 태울 수 없습니다. **heoga eopsi sseuregireul taeul su eopseumnida.** You can't burn garbage without permission.

일회용 il·hoe·yong disposable

일회용품 il·hoe·yong·pum disposable product
우리 모두 **일회용품의 사용**을 줄여야 한다. **uri modu ilhoeyongpumui sayongeul juryeoya handa.** We should reduce the use of disposable products.

재활용 | ~하다 jae·hwa·ryong | ~·ha·da recycling | to recycle, reuse
재활용 쓰레기는 분리해서 배출하세요. **jaehwaryong sseuregineun bullihaeseo baechulhaseyo.** Separate recyclable waste products before you take them out.

재활용품 jae·hwa·ryong·pum recyclable materials

내놓다 nae·no·ta to put sth out
쓰레기 **밖에 내놓았어**? **sseuregi bakke naenoasseo?** Did you take out the garbage?

배출 | ~하다 bae·chul | ~·ha·da discharge | to put sth out, send out

· ·

바느질 | ~하다 ba·neu·jil | ~·ha·da sewing | to sew

실 sil thread

바늘 ba·neul needle

달다 dal·da to hoist, attach, wear
내 옷에 **단추 좀 달아** 줄래? **nae ose danchu jom dara jullae?** Can you sew a button on for me?

구멍 gu·meong hole, pit
양말에 **구멍이** 났어요. yangmare gumeongi nasseoyo. The socks have holes in them.

···

설거지 | ~하다 ← 설겆이 seol·geo·ji | ~·ha·da dish-washing | to wash the dishes
아버지는 엄마가 설거지하는 걸 가끔 도와주세요. abeojineun eommaga seolgeojihaneun geol gakkeum dowajuseyo. Dad sometimes helps mom wash the dishes.

고무장갑 go·mu·jang·gap rubber gloves
설거지할 때는 **고무장갑을 껴라**. seolgeojihal ttaeneun gomujanggabeul kkyeora. Put on rubber gloves when you do the dishes.

행주 haeng·ju dishcloth
행주로 상 좀 닦아 줄래? haengjuro sang jom dakka jullae? Can you wipe the table with the dish cloth?

수세미 su·se·mi scouring pad

가리다 가만있다 가져가다 가져오다 감다
건너다 건드리다 건지다 걸어오다 구르다
굽히다 긁다 깜박이다 꺼내다 꼬집다 끄르다 끌다
놓다 내려가다 내밀다 넘어오다 넘어지다
ᄂ다 놓아두다 놓이다 눕다 늘어서다 다가오다
ᄂ녀가다 달다 달려가다 달리다 담다 던지다
덮이다 데려오다 도달하다 돌아오다 닫다
따르다 떠나다 떨다 떼다 뚫다 뛰다
뛰어내리다 뛰어다니다 뛰어들다 뛰어오르다

chapter **4** | Movement

만지다 매다 멈추다 묶다 밀다 받다 뱉다
붙다 비비다 비키다 빠져나가다 빠져나오다
빠지다 빨다 뻗다 새기다 서다 섞다 숨기다
ᄎ치다 쑤시다 쓰러지다 씌우다 안다 업다 오가다
ᄆ리다 올라가다 올리다 움직임 일어나다
잡다 접근 접촉 젓다 정지 제자리 쥐다 지나치
다 지다 집다 짜다 쪼개다 찢다 출입 통하
다 풀리다 할퀴다 핥다 흘러나오다 흘러내리다

4.1 Hand Movement

손짓 | ~하다 son·jit l ~·ha·da (hand) gesture | to gesture, sign
그녀는 손짓을 하며 시계를 가리켰다. **geunyeoneun sonjiseul hamyeo sigyereul garikyeotda.** She gesticulated at the clock.

가리키다 ← 가르키다 ga·ri·ki·da ← ga·reu·ki·da to point, indicate
그 여자 아이는 말없이 한 건물을 가리켰다. **geu yeoja aineun mareopsi han geonmureul garikyeotda.** The girl quietly pointed at a building.

대다 dae·da to put, touch
상처 부위에 아이스 팩을 대고 있어. **sangcheo buwie aiseu paegeul daego isseo.** Put an ice pack over the injury.

닿다 da·ta to touch, reach
이 약은 아이들 손에 닿지 않는 곳에 두세요. **i yageun aideul sone dachi anneun gose duseyo.** Make sure you keep this medicine out of reach of children.

만지다 man·ji·da to touch
만지지 마시오! **manjiji masio!** Don't touch it!

접촉 | ~하다 jeop·chok l ~·ha·da contact, touch | to touch, make contact
환자와의 신체 접촉을 피하시오. **hwanjawaui sinche jeopchogeul pihasio.** Avoid physical contact with patients.

짚다 jip·da to put one's hand on
의사는 내게 몇 주간 목발을 짚고 다녀야 한다고 말했다. **uisaneun naege myeot jugan mokbareul jipgo danyeoya handago malhaetda.** The doctor said I should walk on crutches for a few weeks.

건드리다 geon·deu·ri·da to touch, jog
엉뚱한 버튼을 건드린 것 같아요. **eongttunghan beoteuneul geondeurin geot gatayo.** I think I touched the wrong button.

더듬(거리)다 deo·deum(·geo·ri)·da to grope, fumble
나는 스위치를 찾아 어둠 속을 더듬었다. **naneun seuwichireul chaja eodum sogeul deodeumeotda.** I groped around in the dark for the switch.

쓰다듬다 sseu·da·deum·da to stroke, pet
강아지 한번 쓰다듬어 봐도 돼요? **gangaji hanbeon sseudadeumeo bwado dwaeyo?** Can I pet your puppy?

짜다 jja·da to wring out, squeeze
저는 치약을 중간에서부터 짭니다. **jeoneun chiyageul junggaseobuteo jjamnida.** I squeeze the toothpaste tube from the middle.

비틀다 bi·teul·da to twist
왜 불쌍한 인형 팔을 비틀고 있니? **wae bulssanghan inhyeong pareul biteulgo inni?** Why are you twisting the arm of that poor doll?

꼬집다 kko·jip·da to pinch
나는 꿈을 꾸고 있는 게 아닌가 싶어 내 볼을 꼬집었다. **naneun kkumeul kkugo inneun ge aninga sipeo nae boreul kkojibeotda.** I pinched my cheek to make sure that I wasn't dreaming.

주무르다 ju·mu·reu·da to massage
어깨 좀 주물러 줄래? **eokkae jom jumulleo jullae?** Can you massage my shoulders for me?

접다 jeop·da to fold
종이를 반으로 접으세요. **jongireul baneuro jeobeuseyo.** Fold the paper in half.

펴다 pyeo·da to unfold, open
교과서 10쪽을 펴세요. **gyogwaseo sipjjogeul pyeoseyo.** Open your textbook to page ten.

쥐다 jwi·da to hold, clasp, clench
주먹을 쥐었다 폈다 해 볼래? **jumeogeul jwieotda pyeotda hae bollae?** Open and close your hand.

(붙)잡다 (but·)jap·da to hold, catch
제 손 꽉 잡으세요. **je son kkwak jabeuseyo.** Hold my hand tight.

악수 | ~하다 ak·su l ~·ha·da handshake | to shake hands
한국 사람들은 인사할 때 항상 악수를 하지는 않습니다. **hanguk saramdeureun insahal ttae hangsang aksureul hajineun anseumnida.** Koreans don't always shake hands when they greet one another.

붙들다 but·deul·da to hold, catch
그들은 나를 붙들고 계속 얘기를 해 댔다. **geudeureun nareul butdeulgo gyesok yaegireul hae daetda.** They held me and kept talking to me.

뭉치다 mung·chi·da to form a lump
아이들이 눈을 뭉치고 있다. **aideuri nuneul mungchigo itda.** The children are making snowballs.

붙이다 bu·chi·da to stick, attach

이력서에 **사진 붙이는** 걸 깜빡했어. iryeok-seoe sajin buchineun geol kkamppakaesseo. I forgot to attach my photo to my resume.

붙다 but·da to stick (to), adhere (to)
너 옷에 **껌 붙었어.** neo ose kkeom buteosseo. You have gum stuck to your clothes.

뜯다 tteut·da to take sth off, tear sth off
얼른 **봉투를 뜯어** 봐. eolleun bongtureul tteudeo bwa. Open the envelope quickly.

떼다 tte·da to take sth off, detach
내 어깨에서 **손 떼라.** nae eokkaeeseo son ttera. Take your hands off my shoulder.

떨어지다 tteo·reo·ji·da to come off, fall off
꽃잎들이 눈처럼 떨어졌다. kkonnipdeuri nuncheoreom tteoreojyeotda. The petals have fallen to the ground like snow.

놓다 no·ta to release, let go
이 손 놓으세요. i son noeuseyo. Let go of my hand.

놓아주다 = 놔주다 no·a·ju·da = nwa·ju·da to release, let go
아버지는 언제나 잡은 고기들을 모두 놓아주고는/놔주고는 했어요. abeojineun eonjena jabeun gogideureul modu noajugoneun/nwajugoneun haesseoyo. Dad always used to release the fish back into the water.

찢다 jjit·da to tear, rip
이 책을 찢은 사람이 누구야? i chaegeul jjijeun sarami nuguya? Who tore this book?

째다 jjae·da to cut
의사는 **상처를 째고** 고름을 짜냈다. uisaneun sangcheoreul jjaego goreumeul jjanaetda. The doctor cut open the wound and squeezed out the pus.

쪼개다 jjo·gae·da to split
녀석은 그 사과를 **반으로 쪼개** 나에게 주었다. nyeoseogeun geu sagwareul baneuro jjogae naege jueotda. He cut the apple in half and shared it with me.

따다 tta·da to pick, pluck
아이들을 데리고 우리 농장에 **포도를 따러** 오세요. aideureul derigo uri nongjange podoreul ttareo oseyo. Take your kids to pick grapes at our farm.

꺾다 kkeok·da to break, snap
나뭇가지를 꺾으면 안 된다. namutgajireul kkeokkeumyeon an doenda. You should not break the branch.

부러뜨리다 = 부러트리다 bu·reo·tteu·ri·da = bu·reo·teu·ri·da to break off, fracture

놓치다 no·chi·da to miss
포수가 공을 놓쳤다. posuga gongeul lochyeotda. The catcher missed the ball.

흘리다 heul·li·da to drop
영수증을 어디에 흘린 것 같아요. yeongsujeungeul eodie heullin geot gatayo. I think I might have dropped the receipt somewhere.

떨어뜨리다 = 떨어트리다 tteo·reo·tteu·ri·da = tteo·reo·teu·ri·da to drop
방금 손수건을 떨어뜨리셨어요/떨어트리셨어요. banggeum sonsugeoneul tteoreotteurisyeosseoyo/tteoreoteurisyeosseoyo. You just dropped your handkerchief.

빠뜨리다 = 빠트리다 ppa·tteu·ri·da = ppa·teu·ri·da to drop
핸드폰을 물에 빠뜨린/빠트린 다음에 어떻게 해야 하죠? haendeuponeul mure ppatteurin/ppateurin daeume eotteoke haeya hajyo? What should I do after I dropped my phone in water?

던지다 deon·ji·da to throw
그는 할 수 있는 한 멀리 공을 던졌다. geuneun hal su inneun han meolli gongeul deonjyeotda. He threw the ball as far as he could.

집다 jip·da to pick up
나는 허리를 숙여 책을 집었다. naneun heorireul sugyeo chaegeul jibeotda. I bent over to pick up the book.

줍다 jup·da to pick up
휴지를 주워서 휴지통에 버려라. hyujireul juwoseo hyujitonge beoryeora. Pick up the garbage and throw it into the garbage bin.

누르다 nu·reu·da to press
6층 좀 눌러 주시겠어요? yukcheung jom nulleo jusigesseoyo? Can you please press the button for the 6th floor for me?

바르다 ba·reu·da to apply, put on
이 보습제를 매일 발라라. i boseupjereul maeil ballara. Apply this moisturizer every day.

흔들다 heun·deul·da to shake, swing
마시기 전에 잘 흔드세요. masigi jeone jal heundeuseyo. Shake well before drinking.

흔들리다 heun·deul·li·da to shake, swing, rock, roll

갑자기 배가 심하게 흔들렸다. **gapjagi baega simhage heundeullyeotda.** Suddenly our boat began rocking violently.

젓다 jeot·da to stir; to row
팬에 들러붙지 않도록 계속 저으세요. **paene deulleobutji antorok gyesok jeoeuseyo.** Stir constantly so that it doesn't stick to the pan.

섞다 seok·da to mix, blend
사발에 모든 재료를 넣고 섞어 주세요. **sabare modeun jaeryoreul leoko seokkeo juseyo.** Put all of the ingredients into a bowl and mix well.

뒤집다 dwi·jip·da to turn sth inside out, turn sth over
저는 보통 셔츠를 뒤집어서 널어요. **jeoneun botong syeocheureul dwijibeoseo neoreoyo.** I usually turn my shirts inside out before I hang them up.

엎다 eop·da to turn over
실수로 재떨이를 엎었어요. **silsuro jaetteori·reul eopeosseoyo.** I accidentally knocked over the ashtray.

깨(뜨리)다 kkae(·tteu·ri)·da to break, smash
엄마가 제일 아끼는 꽃병을 깨뜨렸어. 난 이제 죽었어. **eommaga jeil akkineun kkotbyeongeul kkaetteuryeosseo. nan ije jugeoseo.** I broke mom's favorite vase. She's going to kill me.

부수다 ← 부시다 bu·su·da ← bu·si·da to break, smash
도둑이 **창문을 부수고** 달아났다. **dodugi changmuneul busugo daranatda.** The robber broke the window and ran away.

파(내)다 pa(·nae)·da to dig, excavate
그는 부하들에게 깊은 **구덩이를 파도록** 시켰다. **geuneun buhadeurege gipeun gudeongireul padorok sikyeotda.** He ordered his men to dig a deep hole.

뚫다 ttul·ta to dig, pierce
너 귀 뚫은 거야? **neo gwi ttureun geoya?** Have you had your ears pierced?

캐(내)다 kae(·nae)·da to dig, lift
사람들이 **금을 캐고** 있었다. **saramdeuri geumeul kaego isseotda.** The people were mining for gold.

새기다 sae·gi·da to carve, engrave
우리는 액자 뒷면에 우리의 **이름을 새겨** 넣었다. **urineun aekja dwinmyeone uriui ireumeul saegyeo neoeotda.** We engraved our names on the back of the frame.

긁다 geuk·da to scratch, scrape
등 좀 긁어 줘. **deung jom geulgeo jwo.** Scratch my back.

할퀴다 hal·kwi·da to scratch
고양이가 발톱으로 **얼굴을 할퀴었어요. go·yangiga baltobeuro eolgureul halkwieosseoyo.** My cat clawed me in the face.

비비다 ← 부비다 bi·bi·da ← bu·bi·da to rub
눈을 비비지 마세요. **nuneul bibiji maseyo.** Don't rub your eyes.

문지르다 mun·ji·reu·da to rub
벌에 쏘였을 때 문지르면 상태를 악화시킬 뿐이다. **beore ssoyeosseul ttae munjireumyeon sangtaereul akhwasikil ppunida.** Rubbing the spot where the bee stung you will only make it worse.

치다 chi·da to hit, strike
그 녀석이 먼저 저를 쳤어요! **geu nyeoseogi meonjeo jeoreul chyeosseoyo!** He hit me first!

때리다 ttae·ri·da to beat, hit
어젯밤 형이 저를 때렸어요. **eojetbam hyeongi jeoreul ttaeryeosseoyo.** Last night my brother hit me.

패다 pae·da to beat
그 선수는 기자를 두들겨 패고 카메라를 박살냈다. **geu seonsuneun gijareul dudeulgyeo paego kamerareul baksal laetda.** The player beat the reporter up and smashed her camera.

두드리다 du·deu·ri·da to rap, beat, knock
누군가 창문을 두드리는 소리가 들렸다. **nugunga changmuneul dudeurineun soriga deullyeotda.** I heard a knock on the window.

손뼉 son·ppyeok palm and fingers
그가 **손뼉을 치자** 불이 켜졌다. **geuga sonppyeogeul chija buri kyeojyeotda.** When he clapped his hands, the lights turned on.

두다 du·da to put, set
책상 위에 두세요. **chaeksang wie duseyo.** Put it on the desk.

놓다 no·ta to lay, put
이 상자 어디에 놓을까요? **i sangja eodie noeulkkayo?** Where do I put this box?

놓이다 no·i·da to be laid, be put

놓아두다 = 놔두다 no·a·du·da = nwa·du·da to leave
그대로 놓아두세요/놔두세요. geudaero noaduseyo/nwaduseyo. Please leave them as they are.

내놓다 nae·no·ta to put out, take out
쓰레기를 **바깥에 내놓아라.** sseuregireul bakkate naenoara. Take the garbage out.

들여놓다 deu·ryeo·no·ta to bring in; to purchase
가구는 집 **안으로 들여놓아라.** gaguneun jip aneuro deuryeonoara. Bring the furniture into the house.

내려놓다 nae·ryeo·no·ta to put down
가방은 거기에 내려놓으세요. gabangeun geogie naeryeonoeuseyo. Put the bag down there.

올려놓다 ol·lyeo·no·ta to put sth on
파일은 책상 위에 올려놓았어요. paireun chaeksang wie ollyeonoasseoyo. I put the files on your desk.

얹다 eon·da to put on, lay
버터를 얹어 드릴까요? beoteoreul eonjeo deurilkkayo? Do you want butter on that?

쌓다 ssa·ta to pile, stack
그는 책들을 아무렇게나 쌓아 두었다. geuneun chaekdeureul amureokena ssaa dueotda. He piled the books in a heap.

쌓이다 ssa·i·da to pile up, be stacked
요에 먼지가 쌓여 있었다. yoe meonjiga ssayeo isseotda. The mattress was covered with dust.

들다 deul·da to raise, hold
반대하시는 분은 손을 들어 주세요. bandaehasineun buneun soneul deureo juseyo. Raise your hand if you have any objections.

걸다 geol·da to hang
이 사탕 바구니를 문에 걸어라. i satang bagunireul mune georeora. Hang this candy basket on the door.

달다 dal·da to hoist, attach, wear
창문에 커튼을 달아 주세요. changmune keoteuneul dara juseyo. Hang the curtain on the window.

매달다 mae·dal·da to hang, suspend
누가 고양이 목에 방울을 매달 것인가? nuga goyangi moge bangureul maedal geosinga? Who shall hang the bell around the cat's neck?

넣다 neo·ta to put (sth in)
주머니에 손을 넣지 마라. jumeonie soneul leochi mara. Don't put your hand in your pocket.

집어넣다 ji·beo·neo·ta to put (sth in)
침대 시트를 **안으로 집어넣어** 드릴까요? chimdae siteureul aneuro jibeoneoeo deurilkkayo? Do you want me to tuck the sheets in for you?

담다 dam·da to put, hold
이 물건들을 가방에 담아라. i mulgeondeureul gabange damara. Put these items in the bag.

꽂다 kkot·da to put, stick
이 책을 맨 위 책꽂이에 꽂아 두어라. i chaegeul maen wi chaekkkojie kkoja dueora. Put this book on the top shelf.

끼우다 kki·u·da to put, insert
그녀는 책에 **책갈피를 끼워** 두었다. geunyeoneun chaege chaekgalpireul kkiwo dueotda. She put a bookmark in her book.

찌르다 jji·reu·da to pierce, stab
범인은 행인을 찌르고 달아났다. beomineun haengineul jjireugo daranatda. The suspect stabbed a passerby and ran off.

쑤시다 ssu·si·da to pick, poke
다른 사람들 앞에서 **이 쑤시지** 마라. dareun saramdeul apeseo i ssusiji mara. Don't pick your teeth in public.

후비다 hu·bi·da to pick
코를 후비면 안 됩니다. koreul hubimyeon an doemnida. You should not pick your nose.

박다 bak·da to drive, hammer
벽에 **못을 박는** 방법 말고 딴 방법 없을까? byeoge moseul bangneun bangbeop malgo ttan bangbeop eopseulkka? Is there any other option beside hammering the nail into the wall?

박히다 ba·ki·da to be stuck, be embedded in
발에 **유리 조각이 박혔어요.** bare yuri jogagi bakyeosseoyo. I have a piece of glass stuck in my foot.

꺼내다 kkeo·nae·da to pull, take out
고기가 완전히 익으면 오븐에서 꺼내세요. gogiga wanjeonhi igeumyeon obeuneseo kkeonaeseyo. When the meat is cooked thoroughly, remove it from the oven.

끄집어내다 kkeu·ji·beo·nae·da to pull, take out

그는 가방에서 낡은 책 한 권을 끄집어냈다. geuneun gabangeseo nalgeun chaek han gwoneul kkeujibeonaetda. He took an old book from his bag.

빼다 ppae·da to take out, remove
야, 주머니에서 손 빼라. **ya, jumeonieseo son ppaera.** Hey, take your hands out of your pockets.

뽑다 ppop·da to pull out, take out
어머니는 꽃밭의 잡초를 뽑고 계세요. **eomeonineun kkotbatui japchoreul ppopgo gyeseyo.** My mother is weeding her flower bed.

건지다 geon·ji·da to scoop, fish out
연못에서 공을 건지는 데 쓸 긴 막대를 찾고 있어요. **yeonmoseseo gongeul geonjineun de sseul gin makdaereul chatgo isseoyo.** I'm looking for a long stick to get the ball out of the pond.

푸다 pu·da to scoop
밥 좀 퍼. **bap jom peo.** Scoop rice.

열다 yeol·da to open
열어 봐. 깜짝 선물이야. **yeoreo bwa. kkamjjak seonmuriya.** Open it up. It's a surprise gift.

열리다 yeol·li·da to open, unscrew
바지 지퍼 열렸어. **baji jipeo yeollyeosseo.** Your fly is open.

닫다 dat·da to close
문을 닫고 들어와라. **muneul datgo deureowara.** Close the door behind you.

닫히다 da·chi·da to close, shut
문이 안 닫혀요. **muni an dachyeoyo.** The door won't shut.

덮다 deop·da to cover, close
이불 덮어라. **ibul deopeora.** Cover yourself with the blanket.

씌우다 ssui·u·da to cover
용기에 덮개를 씌워 놓으세요. **yonggie deopgaereul ssuiwo noeuseyo.** Keep the cover on the container.

덮이다 deo·pi·da to be covered

잠그다 ← 잠구다 jam·geu·da ← jam·gu·da to lock
누가 서랍 잠갔어요? **nuga seorap jamgasseoyo?** Who locked the drawer?

잠기다 jam·gi·da to be locked, be fastened
문이 잠겼는지 확인해라. **muni jamgyeonneunji hwaginhaera.** Check if the door is locked.

감추다 gam·chu·da to hide, disguise
뒤에 감추고 있는 게 뭐야? **dwie gamchugo inneun ge mwoya?** What are you hiding behind your back?

숨기다 sum·gi·da to hide, conceal
결국 아내는 벽장 안에 숨긴 돈을 찾아냈어요. **gyeolguk anaeneun byeokjang ane sumgin doneul chajanaesseoyo.** Finally, my wife found the money hidden in the closet.

가리다 ga·ri·da to screen, hide
안 보여. 앞을 가리지 마. **an boyeo. apeul gariji ma.** I can't see. Don't block my view.

막다 mak·da to stop, prevent
나는 손바닥으로 귀를 막았다. **naneun sonbadageuro gwireul magatda.** I covered my ears with my hands.

묶다 muk·da to tie, bind
개를 묶어 놓아라. **gaereul mukkeo noara.** Tie up the dog.

매다 mae·da to tie, fasten
안전벨트 매. **anjeonbelteu mae.** Fasten your seat belt.

감다 gam·da to wind (up), coil
의사 선생님은 상처를 세척하고 붕대를 감아 주었다. **uisa seonsaengnimeun sangcheoreul secheokago bungdaereul gama jueotda.** The doctor cleansed the wound and applied a dressing.

말다 mal·da to roll
종이 가장자리를 접고 그다음 말아 주세요. **jongi gajangjarireul jeopgo geudaeum mara juseyo.** Fold over the edge of the paper, then roll it up.

싸다 ssa·da to wrap
남은 음식 좀 싸 주시겠어요? **nameun eumsik jom ssa jusigesseoyo?** Can you wrap these leftovers up for me?

감싸다 gam·ssa·da to cover, wrap
화상 부위를 붕대로 감싸세요. **hwasang buwireul bungdaero gamssaseyo.** Cover the burn with a dressing.

풀다 pul·da to untie, unfasten
안전벨트 풀어도 돼요? **anjeonbelteu pureodo dwaeyo?** May I unfasten my seat belt?

풀리다 pul·li·da to come untied
실이 엉켜서 안 풀려요. **siri eongkyeoseo an pullyeoyo.** The threads are intertwined and can't be undone.

끄르다 kkeu·reu·da to undo, untie
선물 끌러 봐. seonmul kkeulleo bwa. Unwrap the present.

....

밀다 mil·da to push
차 미는 거 도와 드릴까요? cha mineun geo dowa deurilkkayo? Shall I help you push the car?

당기다 dang·gi·da to pull, draw
문을 밀지 말고 당기세요. muneul milji malgo danggiseyo. Don't push the door, just pull it.

끌다 kkeul·da to pull, draw
그녀는 여행 **가방을 끌고** 있었다. geunyeoneun nyeohaeng gabangeul kkeulgo isseotda. She was pulling a suitcase.

잡아당기다 = 끌어당기다 ja·ba·dang· gi·da = kkeu·reo·dang·gi·da to pull, draw

돌리다 dol·li·da to turn, spin
나는 방에서 나오려고 문의 **손잡이를 돌렸다.** naneun bangeseo naoryeogo munui sonjabireul dollyeotda. I turned the handle of the door to get out of the room.

틀다 teul·da to turn
속도를 줄이고 핸들을 **오른쪽으로 트세요.** sokdoreul jurigo haendeureul oreunjjogeuro teuseyo. Slow down and turn the steering wheel to the right.

주다 ju·da to give
나는 그녀에게 생일 선물로 시계를 주었다. naneun geunyeoege saengil seonmullo sigyereul jueotda. I gave her a watch for her birthday.

드리다 deu·ri·da humble word of 주다 juda
제가 드린 책 읽어 보셨어요? jega deurin

chaek ilgeo bosyeosseoyo? Have you read the book I gave you?

돌려주다 dol·lyeo·ju·da to give back
그는 내 책을 돌려주지 않았다. geuneun nae chaegeul dollyeojuji anatda. He didn't give my book back to me.

건네주다 geon·ne·ju·da to pass
소금 좀 건네줄래? sogeum jom geonnejullae? Can you pass me the salt?

받다 bat·da to get, take
생일 선물로 뭐 받고 싶어? saengil seonmullo mwo batgo sipeo? What do you want for your birthday?

주고받다 ju·go·bat·da to exchange
우리는 아직도 **이메일을 주고받는다.** urineun ajikdo imeireul jugobanneunda. We still exchange emails with each other.

....

안다 an·da to hug, hold
내가 짐을 들 테니 당신이 **아이** 좀 **안아요.** naega jimeul deul teni dangsini ai jom anayo. You can hold the baby, and I'll carry the luggage.

안기다 an·gi·da to be embraced
아기가 엄마 **품에 안겨** 자고 있다. agiga eomma pume angyeo jago itda. A baby is sleeping in her mom's arms.

껴안다 kkyeo·an·da to hug, cuddle

끌어안다 kkeu·reo·an·da to hug, cuddle

포옹 | ~하다 po·ong | ~·ha·da embrace, hug | to embrace, hug
선수들은 경기가 끝난 뒤 포옹을 주고받았다. seonsudeureun gyeonggiga kkeunnan dwi poongeul jugobadatda. The players embraced each other after the match.

4.2 Body Movement

몸짓 mom·jit gesture, motion
우리는 손짓과 몸짓으로 의사소통을 했어요. urineun sonjitgwa momjiseuro uisasotongeul haesseoyo. We communicated through signs and gestures.

동작 dong·jak movement, motion, gesture
그 사람은 **동작이 느린** 편이에요. geu sarameun dongjagi neurin pyeonieyo. His movements are rather slow.

자세 ja·se posture
나쁜 자세는 허리 통증을 유발할 수 있다. nappeun jaseneun heori tongjeungeul lyubalhal su itda. Bad posture can cause back pains.

끄덕이다 kkeu·deo·gi·da to nod
제 말이 들리면 **고개를 끄덕이세요.** je mari deullimyeon gogaereul kkeudeogiseyo. Nod if you can hear me.

젓다 jeot·da to shake

그는 단호하게 **머리를 저었다**. geuneun dan-hohage meorireul jeoeotda. He shook his head decisively.

갸웃거리다 = 갸웃하다 gya·ut·geo·ri·da = gya·u·ta·da to tilt

감다 gam·da to close (one's eyes)
눈을 감고 소원을 빌어 봐. nuneul gamgo sowoneul bireo bwa. Close your eyes and make a wish.

뜨다 tteu·da to open (one's eyes)
이제 **눈을 떠도** 됩니다. ije nuneul tteodo doemnida. You can open your eyes now.

깜박이다 = 깜박거리다 kkam·ba·gi·da = kkam·bak·geo·ri·da to blink
평균적으로 사람들은 1분에 15–20회 **눈을 깜박인다/깜박거린다**. pyeonggyunjeogeuro saramdeureun ilbune siboeseo isiphoe nuneul kkambaginda/kkambakgeorinda. On average a person blinks 15-20 times in a minute.

윙크 | ~하다 wing·keu | ~·ha·da wink | to wink
저 여자가 방금 나한테 **윙크한** 것 같아. jeo yeojaga banggeum nahante wingkeuhan geot gata. I think that girl just winked at me.

물다 mul·da to bite; to hold sth in one's mouth
모기가 **물었나** 봐. mogiga mureonna bwa. I think a mosquito bit me.

그는 늘 입에 **담배를 물고** 작업을 한다. geuneun neul ibe dambaereul mulgo jageobeul handa. He always works with a cigarette in his mouth.

깨물다 kkae·mul·da to bite, gnaw
저는 **손톱을 깨무는** 나쁜 버릇이 있어요. jeoneun sontobeul kkaemuneun nappeun beoreusi isseoyo. I have a bad habit of biting my nails.

뱉다 baet·da to spit
왜 길에 **침을 뱉어**? wae gire chimeul baeteo? Why did you spit on the street?

빨다 ppal·da to suck
아기가 엄마의 **젖을 빨고** 있다. agiga eommaui jeojeul ppalgo itda. A baby is nursing at his mother's breast.

다물다 da·mul·da to shut (one's mouth)
입 **다물어**! ip damureo! Shut up!

불다 bul·da to blow, breathe

뜨거우니 불어서 식혀라. tteugeouni bureoseo sikyeora. It's hot. Blow on it to cool it down.

핥다 hal·da to lick
우리 고양이는 매일 아침 내 **얼굴을 핥으면서** 잠을 깨워요. uri goyangineun maeil achim nae eolgureul halteumyeonseo jameul kkaewoyo. My cat wakes me up by licking my face every morning.

업다 eop·da to carry sb on one's back
당신이 **아기를 업어**. dangsini agireul eobeo. Carry the baby on your back.

지다 ji·da to carry sth on one's back
그 배낭은 제가 지고 갈게요. geu baenangeun jega jigo galgeyo. Let me carry the pack.

기대다 gi·dae·da to lean on
창문에 기대지 마. 위험해. changmune gidaeji ma. wiheomhae. Don't lean on the window. It's dangerous.

돌다 dol·da to turn
코너에서 **오른쪽으로** 도세요. koneoeseo oreunjjogeuro doseyo. Turn right at the corner.

돌아서다 do·ra·seo·da to turn around
그는 돌아서서 가 버렸다. geuneun doraseoseo ga beoryeotda. He turned and went away.

구르다 gu·reu·da to roll over
지난 달에 **계단에서** 굴러서 팔이 부러졌어요. jinan dare gyedaneseo gulleoseo pari bureojyeosseoyo. I fell down the stairs last month and broke my arms.

뒹굴다 dwing·gul·da to roll over
개가 **진흙에서** 뒹굴고 있다. gaega jinheulgeseo dwinggulgo itda. The dog is rolling in the mud.

움츠리다 um·cheu·ri·da to shrink, withdraw
그들은 추워서 **어깨를 움츠렸다**. Geudeureun chuwoseo eokkaereul umcheuryeotda. They hunched their shoulders from the cold.

웅크리다 ung·keu·ri·da to crouch, huddle
사람들이 놀라 탁자 밑으로 **몸을 웅크렸다**. saramdeuri nolla takja miteuro momeul ungkeuryeotda. People cowered under the tables.

굽히다 gu·pi·da to bend, stoop
그 남자는 몸을 굽혀 내 스카프를 주워 주었다. geu namjaneun momeul gupyeo nae seukapeureul juwo jueotda. He bent down and picked up my scarf.

구부리다 gu·bu·ri·da to bend, stoop
무릎을 **구부리지** 않고 발가락에 손이 닿습니까? mureupeul guburiji anko balgarage soni dasseumnikka? Can you touch your toes without bending your knees?

숙이다 su·gi·da to bend, bow (one's head)
어른에게 인사할 때는 **고개를 숙여야지**. eoreunege insahal ttaeneun gogaereul sugyeoyaji. Bow your head when greeting your elders.

벌리다 beol·li·da to open, spread
지하철에서 **다리를 벌리면** 안 됩니다. jihacheoreseo darireul beollimyeon an doemnida. Don't spread your legs in the subway.

뻗다 ppeot·da to reach, stretch
양팔을 쭉 **뻗으세요**. yangpareul jjuk ppeodeuseyo. Stretch out your arms.

내밀다 nae·mil·da to stick out, stretch out
입을 크게 벌리고 **혀를 내밀어** 보세요. ibeul keuge beolligo hyeoreul laemireo boseyo. Open your mouth and stick out your tongue.

오므리다 o·meu·ri·da to narrow, close
다리를 좀 **오므려** 주세요. darireul jom omeuryeo juseyo. Please close your legs.

떨다 tteol·da to shake, quiver
다리 **떨지** 마. dari tteolji ma. Stop shaking your legs.

숨다 sum·da to hide
책상 밑에 **숨어** 봤자 소용없어. chaeksang mite sumeo bwatja soyongeopseo. It is no use hiding under the desk.

서다 seo·da to stand
여기에 **한 줄로 서** 주세요. yeogie han jullo seo juseyo. Please stand in one line over here.

일어서다 i·reo·seo·da to stand up
일어서서 말씀해 주세요. ireoseoseo malsseumhae juseyo. Please stand up when you speak.

일어나다 i·reo·na·da to stand up, get up
오래 앉았다 **일어날** 때 현기증이 나요. orae anjatda ireonal ttae hyeongijeungi nayo. When I stand up after sitting for a long time, I get dizzy.

늘어서다 neu·reo·seo·da to line up
많은 사람들이 표를 사려고 **늘어서서 있었다**. maneun saramdeuri pyoreul saryeogo neureoseo iseotda. Many people lined up to buy tickets.

앉다 an·da to sit
그들은 앞자리에 나란히 **앉았다**. geudeureun apjarie naranhi anjatda. They sat side by side in the first row.

주저앉다 ju·jeo·an·da to drop down, flop down
나는 그 소식을 듣고 **바닥에 주저앉았다**. naneun geu sosigeul deutgo badage jujeoanjatda. I fell to the floor in shock at the news.

쪼그리다 jjo·geu·ri·da to crouch, squat
오래 **쪼그리고** 앉아 있었더니 다리에 쥐가 나요. orae jjogeurigo anja isseotdeoni darie jwiga nayo. I've been squatting so long that I have got a cramp in my leg.

꿇다 kkul·ta to kneel
그녀는 **무릎을 꿇고** 용서를 빌었다. geunyeoneun mureupeul kkulko yongseoreul bireotda. She went down on her knees and asked for forgiveness.

눕다 nup·da to lie
그 사람은 **침대에 누워** 책을 읽고 있었어요. geu sarameun chimdaee nuwo chaegeul ikgo isseosseoyo. He was lying on the bed reading a book.

엎드리다 eop·deu·ri·da to lie face down
저는 **엎드려서 자요**. jeoneun eopdeuryeoseo jayo. I sleep on my stomach.

넘어지다 neo·meo·ji·da to fall, trip
오늘 아침에 계단에서 **넘어졌어**. oneul achime gyedaneseo neomeojyeosseo. I fell down the stairs this morning.

엎어지다 eo·peo·ji·da to fall down
오늘 아침 돌에 걸려 **엎어져** 팔목을 삐었다. oneul achim dore geollyeo eopeojyeo palmogeul ppieotda. This morning I tripped over a stone and twisted my wrist.

쓰러지다 sseu·reo·ji·da to fall down, collapse
그 사람 오늘 아침에 심장마비로 **쓰러졌대**. geu saram oneul achime simjangmabiro sseureojyeotdae. I heard he had collapsed with a heart attack this morning.

미끄러지다 mi·kkeu·reo·ji·da to slip
얼음에서 **미끄러져서** 팔이 부러졌어요. eoreumeseo mikkeureojyeoseo pari bureojyeosseoyo. I slipped on the ice and broke my arm.

걷다 geot·da to walk

저는 우리 집 앞 공원을 걷는 걸 좋아해요. jeoneun uri jip ap gongwoneul geonneun geol joahaeyo. I like to walk in the park in front of my house.

(발)걸음 (bal·)geo·reum step, pace
걸음이 굉장히 **빠르시네요**. georeumi goeng-janghi ppareusineyo. You walk so fast.

절다 jeol·da to limp
제 남동생은 왼쪽 **다리를** 약간 **절어요**. je namdongsaengeun oenjjok darireul lyakgan jeo-reoyo. My younger brother walks with a slight limp in his left leg.

기다 gi·da to crawl, creep
우리 아기는 아직 기지도 못해. uri agineun ajik gijido motae. My baby can't even crawl yet.

뛰다 ttwi·da to run; to jump
복도에서 뛰지 마라. bokdoeseo ttwiji mara. Don't run in the hall.
침대에서 뛰지 마라. chimdaeeseo ttwiji mara. Don't jump on the bed.

달리다 dal·li·da to run
저는 100미터를 15초에 달릴 수 있습니다. jeoneun baengmiteoreul sibochoe dallil su it-seumnida. I can run 100 meters in 15 sec-onds.

차다 cha·da to kick
너 일부러 내 **다리 찬 거지**? neo ilbureo nae dari chan geoji? You kicked my leg on pur-pose, didn't you?

딛다 = 디디다 dit·da = di·di·da to step, tread
지하철 안은 **발 디딜** 틈도 없었다. jihacheol aneun bal didil teumdo eopseotda. There was no room to set down your foot on the subway.

밟다 bap·da to step on
발을 **밟아서** 죄송합니다. bareul balbaseo joe-songhamnida. Please excuse me for stepping on your foot.

4.3 Horizontal Movement, Vertical Movement

움직이다 um·ji·gi·da to move
팔을 움직일 수 있습니까? pareul umjigil su itseumnikka? Can you move your arms?
움직이지 마세요. umjigiji maseyo. Stay still.

움직임 um·ji·gim movement, motion

이동 | ~하다 i·dong | ~·ha·da movement, migration | to move, travel, migrate
홍수 지역 주민들은 안전한 장소로 이동했다. hongsu jiyeok jumindeureun anjeonhan jangso-ro idonghaetda. The residents of the flooded district moved to a safe place.

서다 seo·da to stop
야, 거기 서! 서라니까! ya, geogi seo! seora-nikka! Hey, stop right there! Stop!

정지 | ~하다 jeong·ji | ~·ha·da stop, halt | to stop, halt
정지한 물체의 운동에너지는 0이다. jeongji-han mulcheui undongeneojineun nyeongida. The kinetic energy of a stationary object is zero.

멈추다 meom·chu·da to stop, halt
갑자기 팩스가 **작동을 멈췄어요**. gapjagi paekseuga jakdongeul meomchwosseoyo. Sud-denly the fax machine stopped working.

눈물이 멈추지 않아요. nunmuri meomchuji anayo. Tears keep falling.

멎다 meot·da to stop
드디어 **기침이 멎었어**. deudieo gichimi meo-jeosseo. Finally the coughing stopped.

제자리 je·ja·ri the original place
제자리 달리기는 아주 좋은 준비 운동입니다. jejari dalligineun aju joeun junbi undongimnida. Running in place is a great warm-up exercise.

가만(히) ga·man(·hi) motionlessly, still, just as it is
지금 그대로 **가만 뒤라**. jigeum geudaero ga-man dwora. Leave it as it is now.

가만있다 ga·ma·nit·da to stay motionless
아이가 1분도 가만있지를 못해요. aiga ilbun-do gamanitjireul motaeyo. My child can't sit still for a minute.

가다 ga·da to go
나 방금 너희 집에 갔었는데 너 없더라. na banggeum neohui jibe gasseonneunde neo eop-deora. I just went to your house and you were not there.

나아가다 na·a·ga·da to proceed, progress

배가 천천히 나아갔다. **baega cheoncheonhi naagatda.** The boat proceeded slowly.

걸어가다 geo·reo·ga·da to go on foot
걸어갈래요? 아니면 차로 갈래요? **georeogallaeyo? animyeon charo gallaeyo?** Would you like to go on foot or by car?

달려가다 = 뛰어가다 dal·lyeo·ga·da = ttwi·eo·ga·da to go running
어디를 그렇게 급하게 달려가니/뛰어가니? **eodireul geureoke geupage dallyeogani/ttwieogani?** Where are you running off to so fast?

출발 | ~하다 chul·bal | ~·ha·da departure | to depart, leave
부산으로 가는 기차가 오후 한 시에 출발한다. **busaneuro ganeun gichaga ohu han sie chulbalhanda.** The train to Busan departs at 1 p.m.

떠나다 tteo·na·da to leave, depart
다음 주에 한국을 떠나 고국으로 돌아가요. **daeum jue hangugeul tteona gogugeuro doragayo.** I'll leave Korea and return home next week.

뜨다 tteu·da to leave, move on
강의 중에는 자리를 뜨지 말아 주십시오. **gangui jungeneun jarireul tteuji mara jusipsio.** Please do not leave the room in the middle of the lecture.

나서다 na·seo·da to leave, start
나는 집을 나서자마자 뛰기 시작했다. **naneun jibeul laseojamaja ttwigi sijakaetda.** I began to run as soon as I left home.

(되)돌아가다 (doe·)do·ra·ga·da to return (to)
저에게는 돌아갈 고향이 없어요. **jeoegeneun doragal gohyangi eopseoyo.** I have no hometown to return to.

다녀가다 da·nyeo·ga·da to come by
오늘 어머님이 다녀가셨어요. **oneul eomeonimi danyeogasyeosseoyo.** My mother-in-law stopped by today.

오다 o·da to come
언제 오세요? **eonje oseyo?** When are you coming?

걸어오다 geo·reo·o·da to come on foot
우리가 얼마나 걸어온 거죠? **uriga eolmana georeoon geojyo?** How far have we come on foot?

달려오다 = 뛰어오다 dal·lyeo·o·da = ttwi·eo·o·da to come running
비명 소리를 듣고 이웃들이 달려왔다/뛰어왔다. **bimyeong sorireul deutgo iutdeuri dallyeowatda/ttwieowatda.** The neighbors came running when they heard the screams.

도착 | ~하다 do·chak | ~·ha·da arrival | to arrive
열차가 아직 도착하지 않았다. **yeolchaga ajik dochakaji anatda.** The train has not arrived yet.

이르다 = 다다르다 i·reu·da = da·da·reu·da to arrive, reach
우리는 정오에 산 정상에 이르렀다/다다랐다. **urineun jeongoe san jeongsange ireureotda/dadaratda.** We reached the summit of the mountain at midday.

도달하다 do·dal·ha·da to arrive, reach
집에 도달해서야 열쇠를 놓고 온 것을 알았어요. **jibe dodalhaeseoya yeolsoereul loko on geoseul arasseoyo.** I didn't realize that I had forgotten my key until I reached home.

(되)돌아오다 (doe·)do·ra·o·da to return (to), come back
다섯 시 전에 집에 돌아와야 해. **daseot si jeone jibe dorawaya hae.** You should get back home before 5 p.m.

다녀오다 da·nyeo·o·da to go and get back
일본을 하루 만에 다녀올 수 있나요? **ilboneul haru mane danyeool su innayo?** Is it possible to go to Japan and come back within a day?

오가다 o·ga·da to come and go
이제는 아무도 이 거리를 오가지 않습니다. **ijeneun amudo i georireul ogaji anseumnida.** Now nobody comes and goes on this street.

옮기다 om·gi·da to move, take
이 상자 옮기는 것 좀 도와줄래? **i sangja omgineun geot jom dowajullae?** Can you help me move this box?

데려가다 de·ryeo·ga·da to take
아빠가 우리를 영화관에 데려가 주셨다. **appaga urireul lyeonghwagwane deryeoga jusyeotda.** My dad took us to the movies.

가져가다 ga·jyeo·ga·da to take, carry
학교에 우산 가져가라. **hakgyoe usan gajyeogara.** Take your umbrella to school with you.

데려오다 de·ryeo·o·da to bring, fetch
그녀는 파티에 자기 남자 친구를 데려왔다.

geunyeoneun patie jagi namja chingureul deryeowatda. She brought her boyfriend to the party.

가져오다 ga·jyeo·o·da to bring
내가 부탁한 책 가져왔니? **naega butakan chaek gajyeowanni?** Did you bring the book I asked for?

모이다 mo·i·da to gather, flock
아이들이 놀이터에 모였다. **aideuri noriteoe moyeotda.** The children gathered on the playground.

흩어지다 heu·teo·ji·da to scatter, disperse
흩어져서 계속 찾아보자. **heuteojyeoseo gyesok chajaboja.** Let's scatter and keep searching.

지나가다 ji·na·ga·da to pass by, go by
이 버스가 서울역을 지나가나요? **i beoseuga seoullyeogeul jinaganayo?** Does this bus pass by Seoul Station?

지나치다 ji·na·chi·da to pass by, go by
책에 열중해서 정류장을 지나칠 뻔했어요. **chaege yeoljunghaeseo jeongnyujangeul jinachil ppeonhaesseoyo.** I was so engrossed in the book that I almost missed my stop.

통과 | ~하다 tong·gwa | ~·ha·da passage | to pass
하루에 만 대가 넘는 차량이 그 터널을 통과한다. **harue man daega neomneun charyangi geu teoneoreul tonggwahanda.** Over ten thousand vehicles pass through that tunnel each day.

통하다 tong·ha·da to go through
옆문을 통해 건물을 빠져나왔어요. **yeommuneul tonghae geonmureul ppajyeonawasseoyo.** I left the building through a side door.

스치다 seu·chi·da to graze, brush
그녀가 내 옆을 스쳐 가자 심장이 두근거렸다. **geunyeoga nae yeopeul seuchyeo gaja simjangi dugeungeoryeotda.** My heart was beating hard after she brushed past me.

뒷걸음(질)치다 = 뒷걸음질하다
dwit·geo·reum(·jil)·chi·da = dwit·geo·reum·jil·ha·da to step back
저는 무서워서 뒷걸음질쳤어요/뒷걸음질했어요. **jeoneun museowoseo dwitgeoreumjilchyeosseoyo/dwitgeoreumjilhaesseoyo.** I stepped back in fear.

물러서다 mul·leo·seo·da to step back
그는 물러서서 액자를 제대로 걸었는지 살펴보았다. **geuneun mulleoseoseo aekjareul jedaero georeonneunji salpyeoboatda.** He stepped back to see if he had hung the picture correctly.

비키다 bi·ki·da to step aside
좀 비켜 주실래요? **jom bikyeo jusillaeyo?** May I get through?

따르다 tta·reu·da to follow, go after
오늘은 엄마를 따라 백화점에 갔어요. **oneureun eommareul ttara baekwajeome gasseoyo.** Today I followed my mother to the department store.

따라가다 tta·ra·ga·da to follow, go after
내가 따라가도 돼? **naega ttaragado dwae?** Can I tag along?

따라오다 tta·ra·o·da to follow, come with
저를 따라오세요. **jeoreul ttaraoseyo.** Follow me.

따라다니다 tta·ra·da·ni·da to follow, chase, tag along
왜 자꾸 내 뒤를 따라다니는 거야? **wae jakku nae dwireul ttaradanineun geoya?** Why do you keep following me around?

접근 | ~하다 jeop·geun | ~·ha·da approach | to approach, come close
접근 금지 **jeopgeun geumji** Off Limits

다가가다 da·ga·ga·da to approach
나는 그 여자 아이에게 다가가서 이름을 물었다. **naneun geu yeoja aiege dagagaseo ireumeul mureotda.** I approached her and asked her name.

다가오다 da·ga·o·da to approach, to come up
곰이 다가오자 그는 죽은 체했다. **gomi dagaoja geuneun jugeun chehaetda.** When the bear approached, he played dead.

다가서다 da·ga·seo·da to approach
내 뒤에 바짝 다가서라. **nae dwie bajjak dagaseora.** Come stand close behind me.

들어가다 deu·reo·ga·da to enter, go into
들어가지 마시오! **deureogaji masio!** Do not enter!

들어오다 deu·reo·o·da to enter, come in
신선한 공기가 들어오게 창문을 열어라. **sinseonhan gonggiga deureooge changmuneul lyeoreora.** Open the window so we can get some fresh air.

출입 | ~하다 chu·rip | ~·ha·da access | to enter

관계자 외 출입 금지 gwangyeja oe churip geumji Authorized Personnel Only

이 건물은 외부인이 출입할 수 없습니다. i geonmureun oebuini churipal su eopseumnida. This building is off-limits to visitors.

뛰어들다 ttwi·eo·deul·da to run, dash

물속으로 뛰어들고 싶어요. mulsogeuro ttwi-eodeulgo sipeoyo. I want to dive into the water.

나가다 na·ga·da to go out

할머니는 집을 나간 이후로 소식이 없어요. halmeonineun jibeul lagan ihuro sosigi eopseoyo. There hasn't been any news of my grandmother since she left home.

뛰어나가다 = 달려나가다 ttwi·eo·na·ga·da = dal·lyeo·na·ga·da to run out

빠져나가다 ppa·jyeo·na·ga·da to get out, escape

그는 뒷문으로 살짝 빠져나갔다. geuneun dwinmuneuro saljjak ppajyeonagatda. He quietly slipped out the back door.

나오다 na·o·da to come out

총을 버리고 집 밖으로 나와라! chongeul beorigo jip bakkeuro nawara! Throw out your gun and come out of the house!

뛰어나오다 = 달려나오다 ttwi·eo·na·o·da = dal·lyeo·na·o·da to run out

빠져나오다 ppa·jyeo·na·o·da to get out, escape

흘러나오다 heul·leo·na·o·da to flow out

상처에서 피가 흘러나왔다. sangcheoeseo piga heulleonawatda. Blood came flowing out of the wound.

새다 sae·da to leak, escape

저런! 천장에서 물이 새잖아. jeoreon! cheonjangeseo muri saejana. Oh my God! The ceiling is leaking.

뛰어다니다 ttwi·eo·da·ni·da to run around

실내에서 뛰어다니지 마세요. sillaeeseo ttwieodaniji maseyo. Do not run around indoors.

돌아다니다 do·ra·da·ni·da to go around

우리는 밤에 서울을 돌아다녔다. urineun bame seoureul doradanyeotda. We toured Seoul at night.

넘다 neom·da to cross, pass, go over

선을 넘지 마세요. seoneul leomji maseyo. Don't cross the line.

넘어가다 neo·meo·ga·da to cross

이 언덕을 넘어가면 작은 마을이 나온다. i eondeogeul leomeogamyeon jageun maeuri naonda. You can see a small village after you cross over the hill.

넘어오다 neo·meo·o·da to cross

뛰어넘다 ttwi·eo·neom·da to jump over

건너다 geon·neo·da to cross

길을 건널 때 조심해라. gireul geonneol ttae josimhaera. Be careful while crossing the street.

오르다 o·reu·da to climb, go up

남편은 주말마다 산에 오릅니다. nampyeoneun jumalmada sane oreumnida. My husband goes hiking on weekends.

뛰어오르다 ttwi·eo·o·reu·da to jump, run up

달리는 차에 뛰어오르는 것은 매우 위험합니다. dallineun chae ttwieooreuneun geoseun maeu wiheomhamnida. It is very dangerous to jump on a running car.

올라가다 ol·la·ga·da to go up, rise, climb

올라가는 에스컬레이터를 타세요. ollaganeun eseukeolleiteoreul taseyo. Take the escalator upstairs.

올라오다 ol·la·o·da to come up

14층으로 올라오세요. sipsacheungeuro ollaoseyo. Come up to the 14th floor.

올리다 ol·li·da to raise, lift

팔을 어깨 위로 올려 보세요. pareul eokkae wiro ollyeo boseyo. Raise your arms over your shoulders.

내리다 nae·ri·da to lower; get off

트럭에서 짐 내리는 것 좀 도와줄래? teureogeseo jim naerineun geot jom dowajullae? Would you help me unload the truck?

다음 역에서 내리세요. daeum nyeogeseo naeriseyo. Get off at the next stop.

뛰어내리다 ttwi·eo·nae·ri·da to jump

절벽에서 뛰어내리는 게 별로 재미있을 것 같지 않아요. jeolbyeogeseo ttwieonaerineun ge byeollo jaemiisseul geot gatji anayo. It doesn't look so fun to jump off a cliff.

흘러내리다 heul·leo·nae·ri·da   to roll down, run down

눈물이 뺨을 타고 흘러내렸다. nunmuri ppyameul tago heulleonaeryeotda. Tears rolled down my cheeks.

내려가다 nae·ryeo·ga·da to go down

한 층 더 내려가세요. han cheung deo naeryeogaseyo. Go down one more floor.

내려오다 nae·ryeo·o·da to come back down

산은 올라가는 것보다 내려오는 것이 더 위험해요. saneun ollaganeun geotboda naeryeooneun geosi deo wiheomhaeyo. It's more dangerous to descend a mountain than to ascend it.

오르내리다 o·reu·nae·ri·da to go up and down

할아버지는 계단을 오르내리기 힘들어하세요. harabeojineun gyedaneul oreunaerigi himdeureohaseyo. My grandfather has difficulty going up and down the stairs.

떨어지다 tteo·reo·ji·da to fall, drop

사다리에서 떨어졌는데 이상하게도 멀쩡해요. sadarieseo tteoreojyeonneunde isanghagedo meoljjeonghaeyo. I fell off the ladder, but strangely I'm fine.

추락 | ~하다 chu·rak | ~·ha·da fall, drop | to fall, drop

그는 비행기 **추락** 사고로 사망했다. geuneun bihaenggi churak sagoro samanghaetda. He died in a plane crash.

빠지다 ppa·ji·da to fall in

반지가 **물에 빠졌어요**. banjiga mure ppajyeosseoyo. I dropped my ring into the water.

chapter 5 | Health and Medicine

5.1 General State of Health

건강 | ~하다 geon·gang | ~·ha·da health | healthy
저는 아주 건강해요. jeoneun aju geongang-haeyo. I'm as healthy as a horse.

튼튼하다 teun·teun·ha·da healthy, strong
다행히 저희 아이는 아주 튼튼해요. dahaeng-hi jeohui aineun aju teunteunhaeyo. Luckily, my child is very healthy.

가뿐하다 ga·ppun·ha·da refreshed
푹 자고 났더니 몸이 가뿐했다. puk jago nat-deoni momi gappunhaetda. I felt refreshed after getting a good night's sleep.

(허)약하다 (heo·)ya·ka·da weak, frail
저는 몸이 약해서 감기에 자주 걸려요. jeo-neun momi yakaeseo gamgie jaju geollyeoyo. I'm so frail that I often catch colds.

피로 = 피곤 | ~하다 pi·ro = pi·gon | ~·ha·da tiredness, fatigue | tired, fatigued
저녁을 먹고 나자 갑자기 피로가/피곤이 몰려 왔다. jeonyeogeul meokgo naja gapjagi piroga/pigoni mollyeowatda. After finishing dinner, I suddenly felt tired.

오늘 하루 종일 운전을 했더니 몹시 피곤하다/피로하다. oneul haru jongil unjeoneul haet-deoni mopsi pigonhada/pirohada. I'm very tired as I have driven all day.

지치다 ji·chi·da to be exhausted, be tired
지쳐서 말할 힘도 없어. jichyeoseo malhal him-do eopseo. I'm too tired to talk.

힘들다 him·deul·da hard, tough
힘든 하루였어요. himdeun haruyeosseoyo. It was a tough day.

과로 | ~하다 gwa·ro | ~·ha·da overwork | to overwork
그는 과로로 젊은 나이에 죽었다. geuneun gwaroro jeolmeun naie jugeotda. He died young from overworking.

아프다 a·peu·da sick, painful
그 사람은 아파서 못 왔어. geu sarameun apa-seo mot wasseo. He couldn't come because he was ill.

고통스럽다 go·tong·seu·reop·da painful, agonizing
몇 시간씩 앉아 있는 것은 고통스러운 일이에요. myeot siganssik anja inneun geoseun go-tongseureoun irieyo. It's painful to keep sit-ting for hours.

쑤시다 ssu·si·da to ache, be sore
온몸이 쑤셔요. onmomi ssusyeoyo. I feel sore all over.

쓰(라)리다 sseu(·ra)·ri·da sore
팔꿈치 까진 데가 쓰라려요. palkkumchi kkajin dega sseuraryeoyo. I skinned my elbow and it hurts.

저리다 jeo·ri·da numb, asleep
자고 일어나니 손이 저렸다. jago ireonani soni jeoryeotda. My hands were numb when I woke up.

병 byeong disease, illness
어떤 사람들은 음식으로 많은 병을 치료할 수 있다고 믿는다. eotteon saramdeureun eumsi-geuro maneun byeongeul chiryohal su itdago minneunda. Some people believe that many diseases can be cured with food.

질병 jil·byeong disease, illness
이들 박테리아는 식중독이나 장티푸스와 같은 질병을 일으킬 수 있다. ideul bakterianeun sikjungdogina jangtipuseuwa gateun jilbyeong-eul ireukil su itda. These bacteria can cause illnesses such as food poisoning or typhoid.

전염병 jeo·nyeom·byeong infectious disease

병균 byeong·gyun germ

면역 myeo·nyeok immunity
만성적인 스트레스는 면역 체계를 약화시킬 수 있습니다. manseongjeogin seuteureseu-neun myeonyeok chegyereul yakwasikil su it-seumnida. Chronic stress can weaken your immune system.

걸리다 geol·li·da to catch, get sick
감기에 걸린 것 같아요. gamgie geollin geot gatayo. I think I have a cold.

나다 na·da to have, get, catch
나는 네가 병이 날 줄 알았어. naneun nega byeongi nal jul arasseo. I thought you might be sick.

갑자기 열이 나요. gapjagi yeori nayo. Sud-denly I have a fever.

들다 deul·da to have, get, catch
어쩌다 눈에 멍이 든 거니? eojjeoda nune meongi deun geoni? How did you get a black eye?

감염 | ~되다 ga·myeom | ~·doe·da infection | to be infected
폐렴은 다양한 병균에 의해 폐가 감염되어 발생하는 병이다. **pyeryeomeun dayanghan byeonggyune uihae pyega gamyeomdoeeo balsaenghaneun byeongida.** Pneumonia is a lung inflammation which can be caused by a variety of viruses and bacteria.

전염 | ~되다 jeo·nyeom | ~·doe·da contagion | to be communicated
이 병은 공기를 매개로 전염된다. **i byeongeun gonggireul maegaero jeonyeomdoenda.** This disease is transmitted through the air.

옮다 om·da to catch, be communicated
수영장에서 **눈병이 옮았습니다.** **suyeongjangeseo nunbyeongi olmatseumnida.** I got eye infection from the swimming pool.

옮기다 om·gi·da to infect, transmit
내 생각에는 네가 나한테 **감기를 옮긴** 것 같아. **nae saenggageneun nega nahante gamgireul omgin geot gata.** I think you gave me your cold.

확산 | ~되다 hwak·san | ~·doe·da spread, diffusion | to spread, diffuse
해외로부터 전염병이 유입되어 확산되는 것을 방지하기 위한 노력이 있었다. **haeoerobuteo jeonyeombyeongi yuipdoeeo hwaksandoeneun geoseul bangjihagi wihan noryeogi isseotda.** There was an attempt to prevent the spread of contagious diseases from overseas.

퍼지다 peo·ji·da to spread
신종플루가 전국적으로 퍼졌다. **sinjongpeulluga jeongukjeogeuro peojyeotda.** The Swine Flu has spread throughout the country.

증세 = 증상 jeung·se = jeung·sang symptom
증세가/증상이 어때요? **jeungsega/jeungsangi eottaeyo?** What are your symptoms?

기운 gi·un symptom, sign
A: 왜 그렇게 기운이 없어? B: 감기 기운이 있어. **A: wae geureoke giuni eopseo? B: gamgi giuni isseo.** A: Why are you so down? B: I think I have a cold.

후유증 hu·yu·jeung aftereffect
피해자들 대부분이 사고 후유증을 경험했다. **pihaejadeul daebubuni sago huyujeungeul gyeongheomhaetda.** Most of the victims experienced post-traumatic stress after the accident.

고통 ≒ 아픔 go·tong ≒ a·peum pain, agony
이 약을 먹으면 고통이/아픔이 덜해질 겁니다. **i yageul meogeumyeon gotongi/apeumi deolhaejil geomnida.** This medicine will ease the pain.

통증 tong·jeung pain, ache
가슴에 **통증이 있으면** 즉시 의사를 부르세요. **gaseume tongjeungi isseumyeon jeuksi uisareul bureuseyo.** If you feel pain in your chest, call the doctor at once.

시달리다 si·dal·li·da to suffer, be harassed
많은 개, 고양이들이 차 **멀미에 시달린다는** 걸 아세요? **maneun gae, goyangideuri cha meolmie sidallindaneun geol aseyo?** Do you know that many dogs and cats suffer from car sickness?

앓다 al·ta to suffer (from), be sick
그 사람은 **심장병을 앓고** 있다. **geu sarameun simjangbyeongeul alko itda.** He suffers from a heart disease.

의사 ui·sa doctor
의사 선생님이 심각한 게 아니라고 그러셨어요. **uisa seonsaengnimi simgakan ge anirago geureosyeosseoyo.** The doctor told me that it's nothing serious.

간호사 gan·ho·sa nurse
한국에는 남자 간호사가 아주 적다. **hangugeneun namja ganhosaga aju jeokda.** There are very few male nurses in Korea.

환자 hwan·ja patient, invalid
1025호실 환자 언제 퇴원해요? **cheonisibohosil hwanja eonje toewonhaeyo?** When is the patient in Room 1025 going to be discharged?

병원 byeong·won hospital, clinic
딸아이가 지금 아파서 병원에 있어요. **ttaraiga jigeum apaseo byeongwone isseoyo.** My daughter is sick so she's in the hospital now.

종합병원 jong·hap·byeong·won general hospital

개인병원 gae·in·byeong·won clinic

보건소 bo·geon·so community health center
독감 예방 접종은 각 보건소를 통해 무료로 맞을 수 있습니다. **dokgam yebang jeopjong-eun gak bogeonsoreul tonghae muryoro majeul su itseumnida.** Vaccinations for the flu are available for free at every community health center.

동물병원 dong·mul·byeong·won pet clinic

병실 byeong·sil hospital room
어머니는 수술 후 병실로 옮겨졌어요. **eo-meonineun susul hu byeongsillo omgyeojyeo-sseoyo.** My mother was moved to a hospital room after the surgery.

진료실 = 진찰실 jil·lyo·sil = jin·chal·sil doctor's office
여기 내과 진료실이/진찰실이 어디예요? **yeogi naegwa jillyosiri/jinchalsiri eodiyeyo?** Can you tell me where the internal medicine ward is?

입원실 i·bwon·sil patient's room

수술실 su·sul·sil operating room

응급실 eung·geup·sil emergency room

호(실) ho(·sil) room number
병실이 몇 호실이죠? **byeongsiri myeo tosiri-jyo?** What's your hospital room number?

입원 | ~하다 i·bwon | ~·ha·da hospitalization | to be hospitalized
얼마나 오래 입원해 계셨어요? **eolmana orae ibwonhae gyesyeosseoyo?** How long were you hospitalized?

간호 | ~하다 gan·ho | ~·ha·da nursing, care | to nurse, care for
병원에 입원해 있는 동안 아내가 저를 간호했어요. **byeongwone ibwonhae inneun dongan anaega jeoreul ganhohaesseoyo.** My wife cared for me while I was in the hospital.

보살피다 bo·sal·pi·da to take care of, look after
그녀는 병든 남편을 헌신적으로 보살폈다. **geunyeoneun byeongdeun nampyeoneul heon-sinjeogeuro bosalpyeotda.** She looked after her ailing husband with great devotion.

돌보다 dol·bo·da to take care of, look after
치매 환자를 돌보는 일은 쉬운 일이 아니다. **chimae hwanjareul dolboneun ireun swiun iri anida.** It's not easy to look after a patient with Alzheimer's.

병문안 = 문병 byeong·mu·nan = mun·byeong visit to a sick person
주말에 다른 사람들과 함께 병원으로 박 대리 **병문안을/문병을** 갈 생각입니다. **jumare da-reun saramdeulgwa hamkke byeongwoneuro bak daeri byeongmunaneul/munbyeongeul gal saenggagimnida.** I'll go see Mr. Park in the hospital with the others.

의식 ui·sik consciousness
어제 아들이 학교에서 **의식을** 잃고 쓰러졌어요. **eoje adeuri hakgyoeseo uisigeul ilko sseu-reojyeosseoyo.** Yesterday my son lost his consciousness and collapsed at school.
할머니는 아직도 **의식이** 없으세요. **halmeoni-neun ajikdo uisigi eopseuseyo.** My grand-mother is still unconscious.

깨어나다 kkae·eo·na·da to come around, become conscious again
깨어나 보니 병원 침대에 누워 있었다. **kkaeeona boni byeongwon chimdaee nuwo isseotda.** When I came around, I was lying in a hospital bed.

낫다 nat·da to be cured, recover from
암은 쉽게 낫는 병이 아니다. **ameun swipge nanneun byeongi anida.** Cancer is not something that can be easily cured.

회복 | ~하다 hoe·bok | ~·ha·da recovery | to recover from
수술 후에 그 환자는 아주 빨리 회복했다. **su-sul hue geu hwanjaneun aju ppalli hoebokaet-da.** After the operation, the patient recov-ered very quickly.

극복하다 ≒ 이겨내다 geuk·bo·ka·da ≒ i·gyeo·nae·da to overcome
그녀는 암을 극복했다/이겨냈다. **geunyeo-neun ameul geukbokaetda/igyeonaetda.** She fought against cancer and won.

퇴원 | ~하다 toe·won | ~·ha·da leaving the hospital | to be discharged
하루 빨리 퇴원하시기를 바랍니다. **haru ppalli toewonhasigireul baramnida.** I hope you get out of the hospital soon.

진료 ≒ 진찰 | ~하다 jil·lyo ≒ jin·chal | ~·ha·da (medical) treatment | to give medical treatment
진료/진찰 시간은 오전 10시에서 오후 5시입니다. jillyo/jinchal siganeun ojeon nyeolsieseo ohu daseotsiimnida. Office hours are from 10 a.m. to 5 p.m.

치료 | ~하다 chi·ryo | ~·ha·da treatment, cure | to treat
어머니는 약물 치료를 받고 계세요. eomeonineun nyangmul chiryoreul batgo gyeseyo. My mother is undergoing medical treatment.

검사 | ~하다 geom·sa | ~·ha·da examination, test | to examine, check
방금 검사 결과가 나왔습니다. banggeum geomsa gyeolgwaga nawatseumnida. We just got your test results.

진단 | ~하다 jin·dan | ~·ha·da diagnosis | to diagnose
나는 폐렴 진단을 받았다. naneun pyeryeom jindaneul badatda. I was diagnosed with pneumonia.

처방 | ~하다 cheo·bang | ~·ha·da prescription | to prescribe
항생제 처방을 받으면 지정된 복용량을 정확히 지키세요. hangsaengje cheobangeul badeumyeon jijeongdoen bogyongnyangeul jeonghwaki jikiseyo. If you receive prescribed antibiotics, follow the dosage instructions exactly.

건강검진 geon·gang·geom·jin checkup, physical examination
마지막으로 건강검진을 받으신 게 언제죠? majimageuro geonganggeomjineul badeusin ge eonjejyo? When was the last time you had a checkup?

청진기 cheong·jin·gi stethoscope
의사가 청진기를 이용해 진찰했다. uisaga cheongjingireul iyonghae jinchalhaetda. The doctor used the stethoscope in his examination.

체온 che·on body temperature
체온을 재겠습니다. cheoneul jaegetseumnida. Let me check your temperature.

맥박 maek·bak pulse

혈압 hyeo·rap blood pressure

맥박과 혈압은 정상입니다. maekbakgwa hyeorabeun jeongsangimnida. Your pulse and blood pressure are normal.

엑스레이 ek·seu·re·i X-ray
뼈가 골절되었는지 엑스레이를 찍어 봅시다. ppyeoga goljeoldoeeonneunji ekseureireul jjigeo bopsida. Let's get it X-rayed to check if the bone is broken.

내시경 nae·si·gyeong endoscope

엠알아이 e·ma·ra·i MRI

수술 | ~하다 su·sul | ~·ha·da operation, surgery | to operate
수술 전에는 아무것도 드시면 안 됩니다. susul jeoneneun amugeotdo deusimyeon an doemnida. You're not allowed to eat anything before the operation.

마취 | ~하다 ma·chwi | ~·ha·da anesthesia | to anesthetize
국소 마취는 몇 시간이면 풀립니다. gukso machwineun myeot siganimyeon pullimnida. The local anesthetic will wear off in a few hours.

주사 ju·sa injection, shot
독감 예방 주사는 맞았어요? dokgam yebang jusaneun majasseoyo? Did you get a flu shot?

마사지 | ~하다 ma·sa·ji | ~·ha·da massage | to massage
마사지가 통증을 줄이는 데 도움이 될 거예요. masajiga tongjeungeul jurineun de doumi doel geoyeyo. Massages will help reduce the pain.

응급처치 eung·geup·cheo·chi first aid
소방관이 현장에서 부상자에게 응급처치를 했다. sobanggwani hyeonjangeseo busangjaege eunggeupcheochireul haetda. The firefighters gave the wounded first aid at the scene.

인공호흡 in·gong·ho·heup mouth-to-mouth

심폐소생술 sim·pye·so·saeng·sul CPR

소독 | ~하다 so·dok | ~·ha·da disinfection | to disinfect
일단 상처 부위를 알코올로 소독하겠습니다. ildan sangcheo buwireul alkoollo sodokagetseumnida. First, I'll disinfect the wound with alcohol.

5.3 Medicine

약 yak medicine, drug
약 기운이 나타나는 것 같아. yak giuni nata-naneun geot gata. I feel the medicine is starting to take effect.

감기약 gam·gi·yak cold medicine

기침약 gi·chim·nyak cough medicine

두통약 du·tong·nyak headache medicine

멀미약 meol·mi·yak motion sickness medicine

설사약 seol·sa·yak diarrhea medicine

소독약 so·dong·nyak disinfectant

안약 a·nyak eye drops

소화제 so·hwa·je digestive

진통제 jin·tong·je painkiller

항생제 hang·saeng·je antibiotic

해열제 hae·yeol·je fever reducer

진통제 jin·tong·je painkiller

수면제 su·myeon·je sleeping pill

한약 ha·nyak Chinese medicine
한약을 복용하는 동안에는 술을 드시면 안 됩니다. hanyageul bogyonghaneun donganeneun sureul deusimyeon an doemnida. You aren't allowed to drink alcohol while taking this Chinese medicine.

알약 al·lyak tablet, pill

알 al unit for counting sth round
이 알약을 한 번에 한 알씩 하루에 세 번 드세요. i allyageul han beone han alssik harue se beon deuseyo. Take one pill three times a day.

가루약 ga·ru·yak powdered medicine

구급약 gu·geum·nyak first-aid medicine

연고 yeon·go ointment
상처 부위에 매일 이 **연고를** 바르세요. sangcheo buwie maeil i yeongoreul bareuseyo.

Apply this ointment to the wound every day.

반창고 ban·chang·go bandage, sticking plaster
상처 부위에 **반창고를** 붙여라. sangcheo buwie banchanggoreul buchyeora. Put a bandage on the wound.

밴드 baen·deu Band-Aid

파스 pa·seu skin patch; pain relief cream

붕대 bung·dae bandage
붕대는 최대한 자주 **갈아** 주세요. bungdaeneun choedaehan jaju gara juseyo. Change the bandage as often as possible.

약국 yak·guk pharmacy, drugstore
2층에 약국이 있습니다. icheunge yakgugi itseumnida. There is a pharmacy on the second floor.

약사 yak·sa pharmacist
비타민 제품을 고를 때 약사에게 조언을 구하세요. bitamin jepumeul goreul ttae yaksaege joeoneul guhaseyo. Ask your pharmacist for advice when selecting vitamins.

처방전 cheo·bang·jeon prescription
이 약은 처방전이 있어야 합니다. i yageun cheobangjeoni isseoya hamnida. You need a prescription for this medicine.

먹다 meok·da to take (medicine)
식사하고 30분 후에 **약 먹는** 것 잊지 마세요. siksahago samsipbun hue yak meongneun geot itji maseyo. Be sure to take this medicine 30 minutes after every meal.

복용 | ~하다 bo·gyong | ~·ha·da internal use | to take a dose

부작용 bu·ja·gyong side effect
부작용이 있으면 즉시 **복용을** 중단하세요. bujagyongi isseumyeon jeuksi bogyongeul jungdanhaseyo. Stop taking the medicine immediately if there's any sign of side effects.

5.4 Departments of a Hospital

내과 nae·gwa internal medicine department

소화불량 so·hwa·bul·lyang indigestion

체하다 che·ha·da to have an upset stomach
체했을 때 페퍼민트 차를 마시면 울렁거림이 덜해질 수 있다. **chehaesseul ttae pepeominteu chareul masimyeon ulleonggeorimi deolhaejil su itda.** If you have an upset stomach, peppermint tea will help ease your nausea.

배탈 bae·tal stomachache

설사 | ~하다 seol·sa | ~·ha·da diarrhea | to suffer from diarrhea
배탈이 나서 밤새 설사를 했어요. **baetari naseo bamsae seolsareul haesseoyo.** My stomach was upset and I had diarrhea all night.

변비 byeon·bi constipation
요즘에 변비가 심해졌어요. **yojeume byeonbiga simhaejyeosseoyo.** These days my constipation has been getting worse.

식중독 sik·jung·dok food poisoning

(구)토(하다) (gu·)to(·ha·da) vomit | to vomit
파르보 바이러스는 설사와 구토를 유발한다. **pareubo baireoseuneun seolsawa gutoreul lyubalhanda.** The parvovirus causes diarrhea and vomiting.

비만 bi·man obesity
과식은 비만의 주 원인이다. **gwasigeun bimanui ju woninida.** Overeating is the main cause of obesity.

간염 ga·nyeom hepatitis

위염 wi·yeom gastritis

고혈압 go·hyeo·rap high blood pressure

뇌졸중 noe·jol·jung stroke

빈혈 bin·hyeol anemia

감기 gam·gi cold, flu
엄마한테서 감기가 옮았어요. **eommahanteseo gamgiga olmasseoyo.** I caught a cold from my mother.

몸살 mom·sal illness from fatigue, body ache
몸살 기운이 좀 있어요. **momsal giuni jom isseoyo.** I feel sore all over today.

독감 dok·gam flu, influenza
지금 전국에 독감이 유행이에요. **jigeum jeonguge dokgami yuhaengieyo.** Influenza is raging throughout the country now.

열 yeol fever
열이 있으면 자리에 누워 쉬어라. **yeori isseumyeon jarie nuwo swieora.** Go to bed if you have a fever.

기침 | ~하다 gi·chim | ~·ha·da cough | to cough
기침을 시작하면 멈추지를 않아요. **gichimeul sijakamyeon meomchujireul anayo.** When I start coughing, I can't stop.

콧물 kon·mul mucus
어젯밤부터 콧물이 계속 나요. **eojetbambuteo konmuri gyesok nayo.** I have had runny nose since last night.

재채기 jae·chae·gi sneeze
재채기가 계속 나와요. **jaechaegiga gyesok nawayo.** I keep on sneezing.

가래 ga·rae phlegm
목에 가래가 계속 끼어요. **moge garaega gyesok kkieoyo.** I have some phlegm in my throat.

두통 du·tong headache
두통이 심해요. **dutongi simhaeyo.** I have a bad headache.

폐렴 pye·ryeom pneumonia

암 am cancer
아버지는 작년에 말기 암 진단을 받았다. **abeojineun jangnyeone malgi am jindaneul badatda.** My father was diagnosed with terminal cancer last year.

종양 jong·yang tumor
위에서 종양이 발견되었습니다. **wieseo jongyangi balgyeondoeeotseumnida.** A tumor was discovered in your stomach.

··

이비인후과 i·bi·in·hu·gwa ear-nose-and-throat department

비염 bi·yeom rhinitis

축농증 chung·nong·jeung sinus infection

··

외과 oe·gwa surgery department
외과 치료를 받으세요. **oegwa chiryoreul ba-**

deuseyo. Get some surgical treatment.

성형외과 seong·hyeong·oe·gwa plastic surgery

정형외과 jeong·hyeong·oe·gwa orthopedic surgery

다치다 da·chi·da to hurt, be wounded
어쩌다 **다치셨어요**? eojjeoda dachisyeosseoyo? How did you get hurt?

부러지다 bu·reo·ji·da to break, fracture
다리가 **부러진** 것 같아요. dariga bureojin geot gatayo. I think my leg is broken.

골절 | ~되다 gol·jeol | ~·doe·da fracture | to be fractured

마비 | ~되다 ma·bi | ~·doe·da paralysis | to be paralyzed
저는 오토바이 사고로 **하반신이 마비되었습니다**. jeoneun otobai sagoro habansini mabi-doeeotseumnida. I was paralyzed from the waist down in a motorcycle accident.

삐다 ppi·da to sprain, twist
어제 **허리를 삐었어요**. eoje heorireul ppieosseoyo. Yesterday I strained my back.

깁스 gip·seu plaster cast
팔에 **깁스를** 하셔야 합니다. pare gipseureul hasyeoya hamnida. You need a cast on your arm.

깁스 derives from the German word *Gips*.

목발 mok·bal crutches
당분간 **목발을** 짚고 다니세요. dangbungan mokbareul jipgo daniseyo. You need to use crutches for the time being.

출혈 chul·hyeol bleeding
그는 수술 중 **과다 출혈**로 사망했다. geuneun susul jung gwada chulhyeollo samanghaetda. He died from excessive bleeding during the operation.

코피 ko·pi nosebleed
요즘 들어 자주 **코피가 나요**. yojeum deureo jaju kopiga nayo. Lately I often have nosebleeds.

상처 sang·cheo injury, wound, scar
다행히 **상처가** 깊진 않습니다. dahaenghi sangcheoga gipjin anseumnida. Fortunately the wound is not deep.

부상 bu·sang injury, wound
사람들은 **부상을 입은** 선수를 병원으로 데려갔다. saramdeureun busangeul ibeun seonsureul byeongwoneuro deryeogatda. They took

the injured player to the hospital.

흉터 hyung·teo scar
저는 왼쪽 뺨에 **흉터가** 있어요. jeoneun oen-jjok ppyame hyungteoga isseoyo. I have a scar on my left cheek.

멍 meong bruise
어쩌다 **멍이** 들었어요? eojjeoda meongi deureosseoyo? How did you get the bruise?

치과 chi·gwa dental clinic, the dentist's
나는 **치과에** 가는 것이 가장 싫다. naneun chigwae ganeun geosi gajang silta. The last place I want to go is a dental clinic.

충치 chung·chi decayed tooth, cavity

때우다 ttae·u·da to fill, patch up
어제 **충치를** 금으로 **때웠어요**. eoje chung-chireul geumeuro ttaewosseoyo. Yesterday I had some cavities repaired with gold fillings.

뽑다 ≒ 빼다 ppop·da ≒ ppae·da to pull out
다음 주에 치과에 가서 **사랑니를 뽑을/뺄** 거예요. daeum jue chigwae gaseo sarangnireul ppobeul/ppael geoyeyo. I'm going to go to the dentist's to have a wisdom tooth pulled.

교정 | ~하다 gyo·jeong | ~·ha·da correction | to correct
얼마간은 **치아 교정**을 받는 걸 고민했었어요. eolmaganeun chia gyojeongeul banneun geol gominhaesseosseoyo. I had thought about having my teeth straightened for some time.

스케일링 seu·ke·il·ling scaling
6개월에 한 번 **스케일링을** 받으세요. yukgae-wore han beon seukeillingeul badeuseyo. You need to get your teeth cleaned every 6 months.

임플란트 im·peul·lan·teu dental implant

안과 an·gwa ophthalmic department, eye clinic
눈에 뭐가 들어가서 **안과에** 가야겠어. nune mwoga deureogaseo angwae gayagesseo. I need to go to an eye clinic because I've got something in my eye.

시력 si·ryeok eyesight, vision
최근에 **시력이** 많이 **떨어졌어요**. choegeune siryeogi mani tteoreojyeosseoyo. Recently my eyes have gotten a lot worse.

눈병 nun·byeong eye disease
눈병을 예방하려면 손을 자주자주 씻으세요.

nunbyeongeul yebangharyeomyeon soneul jaju-jaju ssiseuseyo. To prevent eye disease, you should wash your hands often.

근시 geun·si nearsightedness

난시 nan·si astigmatism

색맹 saeng·maeng color blindness

피부과 pi·bu·gwa department of dermatology

피부병 pi·bu·byeong skin disease

알레르기 al·le·reu·gi allergy
저는 꽃가루 알레르기가 있어요. jeoneun kkotgaru allereugiga isseoyo. I have a pollen allergy.

알레르기 derives from the German word *Allergie.*

두드러기 du·deu·reo·gi hives

무좀 mu·jom athlete's foot
무좀은 곰팡이균에 의해 발생되는 피부병입니다. mujomeun gompangigyune uihae balsaengdoeneun pibubyeongimnida. Athlete's foot is a skin disease caused by a fungus.

물집 mul·jip blister
왼발바닥에 물집이 잡혔어요. oenbalbadage muljibi japyeosseoyo. I've got blisters on the sole of my left foot.

습진 seup·jin eczema

염증 yeom·jeung infection

고름 go·reum pus

곪다 gom·da fester
상처가 곪아서 통증이 심해요. sangcheoga golmaseo tongjeungi simhaeyo. The wound festered and caused me intense agony.

신경정신과 sin·gyeong·jeong·sin·gwa department of neuropsychiatry

현기증 hyeon·gi·jeung dizziness, vertigo

어지럽다 eo·ji·reop·da dizzy
자리에서 일어날 때 자주 어지러워요. jarieseo ireonal ttae jaju eojireowoyo. I often feel dizzy when I stand up.

멀미 meol·mi motion sickness

우울증 u·ul·jeung depression

지금 심한 우울증에 시달리고 있어요. jigeum simhan uuljeunge sidalligo isseoyo. I'm suffering from severe depression.

스트레스 seu·teu·re·seu stress
일하면서 스트레스를 많이 받으세요? ilhamyeonseo seuteureseureul mani badeuseyo? Are you under a lot of stress from work?

건망증 geon·mang·jeung forgetfulness
저는 건망증이 꽤 심한 편이에요. jeoneun geonmangjeungi kkwae simhan pyeonieyo. I tend to forget things quite easily.

불면증 bul·myeon·jeung insomnia
요즘 밤마다 불면증에 시달려요. yojeum bammada bulmyeonjeunge sidallyeoyo. These days I've been suffering from insomnia.

수면제 su·myeon·je sleeping pill
수면제가 정말로 우리 몸에 그렇게 해롭나요? sumyeonjega jeongmallo uri mome geureoke haeromnayo? Are sleeping pills really that bad for your health?

중독 jung·dok poisoning
한 가족이 일산화탄소 중독으로 병원에 입원했다. han gajogi ilsanhwatanso jungdogeuro byeongwone ibwonhaetda. A family was taken to the hospital after being poisoned by carbon monoxide.

치매 chi·mae Alzheimer's

노망 no·mang senility

비뇨기과 bi·nyo·gi·gwa department of urology

산부인과 san·bu·in·gwa obstetrics and gynecology

소아과 so·a·gwa pediatric hospital

한의원 ha·nui·won Korean medical clinic

한의사 ha·nui·sa doctor for Korean medicine

침 chim acupuncture
어제 한의원에 가서 침을 맞고 왔어. eoje hanuiwone gaseo chimeul matgo wasseo. I had acupuncture done at a Chinese medical clinic yesterday.

뜸 tteum moxibustion
어제 허리에 뜸을 떴어요. eoje heorie tteumeul tteosseoyo. I had moxibustion done on my back yesterday.

가엾다 간절하다 감성 감정 감탄 걱정 겁 고독 고민 골치 공
포 관심 괴로움 괴롭다 궁금하다 귀찮다 그리워하다
그립다 기막히다 기분 기뻐하다 기쁘다 기절 긴장 긴장감
끔찍하다 난처하다 놀랍다 뉘우치다 답답하다 당혹스럽다
당황하다 동정심 두근거리다 따분하다 떨다 떨리다 마음
무서움 무서워하다 무안하다 민망하다 바라다 반성 부끄러움
부끄럽다 부러워하다 부럽다 분하다 뿌듯하다 서럽다 서운하다

chapter 6 | Feelings

성의 소원 슬프다 신 신경 신경질 신기하다 신나다 실망
싫다 심리 심정 아쉽다 안쓰럽다 애 애정 어리둥절하다
어색하다 어이없다 억울하다 열 열등감 외로움 욕심
우울하다 울음 웃기다 웃음 유쾌하다 자신 재미없다
존중 즐거워하다 증오 지겹다 쩔쩔매다 창피하다 탐 탐내다
편하다 행복 허무하다 후련하다 흐느끼다 흐뭇하다 흥미롭다 흥분

6.1 Pleasure, Affection, Wishes, Awe, Sympathy

감정 gam·jeong feelings, emotion
아버지는 **감정 표현**을 잘 안 하세요. abeo-jineun gamjeong pyohyeoneul jal an haseyo. My father hardly shows any emotion.

감(수)성 gam(·su)·seong sensibility
십대들은 사춘기에 **감수성이 예민하다**. sip-daedeureun sachungie gamsuseongi yeminha-da. Teenagers can be very sensitive during puberty.

마음 = 맘 ma·eum = mam mind, heart
마음/맘 편히 가져라. maeum/mam pyeonhi gajyeora. Try to relax.

기분 gi·bun feelings, mood
지금은 **웃**을 **기분**이 아니에요. jigeumeun useul gibuni anieyo. I'm not in the mood for laughter.

심정 sim·jeong feelings, heart
지금 울고 싶은 심정이야. jigeum ulgo sipeun simjeongiya. I feel like crying.

심리 sim·ni psychology, mentality
나는 여자들의 **심리를 이해할** 수가 없다. na-neun nyeojadeurui simnireul ihaehal suga eop-da. I can't understand a woman's mentality.

자부심 = 긍지 ja·bu·sim = geung·ji pride, self-esteem
네가 하는 일에 **자부심을/긍지를 가져라**. nega haneun ire jabusimeul/geungjireul gajyeo-ra. Take pride in your work.

자신(감) ja·sin(·gam) self-confidence
저는 춤에는 **자신이 없어요**. jeoneun chume-neun jasini eopseoyo. I have no confidence at all when it comes to dancing.

자존심 ja·jon·sim self-esteem, pride
자존심이 강한 사람은 대개 일을 열심히 한다. jajonsimi ganghan sarameun daegae ireul lyeolsimhi handa. People who think highly of themselves usually work hard.

열등감 = 콤플렉스 yeol·deung·gam = kom·peul·lek·seu (inferiority) complex
저는 평생 제 큰형에 대한 **열등감에/콤플렉스에 시달려** 왔어요. jeoneun pyeongsaeng je keunhyeonge daehan nyeoldeunggame/kompeullekseue sidallyeo wasseoyo. I've suffered from an inferiority complex towards my big brother throughout my life.

기쁘다 gi·ppeu·da glad, happy
와 주셔서 기쁩니다. wa jusyeoseo gippeumni-da. I'm glad you could come.

기쁨 gi·ppeum pleasure, happiness

기뻐하다 gi·ppeo·ha·da to rejoice, be happy
선생님이 널 보면 기뻐하실 거야. seonsaeng-nimi neol bomyeon gippeohasil geoya. Your teacher would be happy if she saw you.

웃다 ut·da to laugh, smile
웃어야 할지 울어야 할지 모르겠네요. useoya halji ureoya halji moreugenneyo. I'm not sure whether to laugh or cry.

웃음 u·seum laugh, laughter
반 학생들 모두 선생님의 농담에 **웃음을 터뜨렸다**. ban haksaengdeul modu seonsaengnimui nongdame useumeul teotteuryeotda. The whole class burst into laughter at the teacher's joke.

배꼽(이) 빠지다 bae·kkop(·i) ppa·ji·da to laugh one's head off
어제 TV 보다가 **배꼽 빠지게 웃었어**. eoje tibeui bodaga baekkop ppajige useosseo. I laughed my head off while watching TV yesterday.

행복 | ~하다 haeng·bok | ~·ha·da happiness | happy
당신이 있어서 행복해요. dangsini isseoseo haengbokaeyo. You make me happy.

즐겁다 jeul·geop·da pleasant, happy
즐거운 시간 보내세요. jeulgeoun sigan bonae-seyo. Have a good time.

즐거움 jeul·geo·um joy, pleasure

즐거워하다 jeul·geo·wo·ha·da to feel happy, enjoy

재미 jae·mi fun, interest

재미있다 = 재밌다 jae·mi·it·da = jae·mit·da fun, funny
오늘 밤 재미있었어/재밌었어? oneul bam jaemiisseosseo/jaemisseosseo? Did you have fun tonight?

흥미롭다 heung·mi·rop·da interesting

웃기다 ut·gi·da fun, humorous
그 영화는 웃기면서 동시에 슬프다. geu yeonghwaneun utgimyeonseo dongsie seul-peuda. The movie is funny and sad at the same time.

우습다 u·seup·da fun, humorous

신 sin joy, delight

신나다 sin·na·da to be excited, be happy
오늘 밤은 **신나게** 놀자. oneul bameun sinnage nolja. Let's have fun tonight.

맛(이) 나다 mat(·i) na·da to be funny, be interesting
요즘은 일할 **맛이** 안 **나**. yojeumeun ilhal masi an na. I don't feel like working these days.

상쾌하다 sang·kwae·ha·da fresh, refreshing
찬물로 샤워를 하고 나니 상쾌해. chanmullo syaworeul hago nani sangkwaehae. I feel refreshed after taking a cold shower.

유쾌하다 yu·kwae·ha·da cheerful, pleasant
그 사람하고 얘기를 하고 있으면 참 유쾌해요. geu saramhago yaegireul hago isseumyeon cham nyukwaehaeyo. It feels pleasant to talk with him.

편(안)하다 | 편히 pyeon(·an)·ha·da | pyeon·hi comfortable, relaxed | comfortably
저는 혼자 있을 때가 제일 편해요. jeoneun honja isseul ttaega jeil pyeonhaeyo. I feel most comfortable when I am alone.

반갑다 ban·gap·da glad, pleasant
그것 참 반가운 일이군요. geugeot cham bangaun irigunnyo. That's a very good thing.

반가움 ban·ga·um delight, joy

만족 | ~하다 | ~스럽다 man·jok | ~·ha·da | ~·seu·reop·da satisfaction | to be satisfied | satisfactory
저는 늘 그 사람이 하는 일에 만족합니다. jeoneun neul geu sarami haneun ire manjokamnida. I am always satisfied with his work.

뿌듯하다 ppu·deu·ta·da satisfied, proud
제가 누군가에게 도움이 될 수 있어 뿌듯합니다. jega nugungaege doumi doel su isseo ppudeutamnida. I'm happy I can be of service to someone.

흐뭇하다 heu·mu·ta·da pleased, satisfied
자네 부모님이 자네를 보셨다면 흐뭇해하셨을 거야. jane bumonimi janereul bosyeotdamyeon heumutaehasyeosseul geoya. Your parents would be happy if they saw you.

자랑 | ~하다 | ~스럽다 ja·rang | ~·ha·da | ~·seu·reop·da boast | to boast, show off | proud
나는 한국인인 것이 자랑스럽다. naneun

hanguginin geosi jarangseureopda. I am very proud of being Korean.

·····

사랑 | ~하다 | ~스럽다 sa·rang | ~·ha·da | ~·seu·reop·da love | to love | lovely
자기는 날 얼마나 사랑해? jagineun nal eolmana saranghae? How much do you love me?

애정 ae·jeong love, affection
포옹은 애정의 표현이다. poongeun aejeongui pyohyeonida. Hugging is a sign of affection.

정 jeong affection
엄마는 **정이 많으세요**. eommaneun jeongi maneuseyo. My mom has a warm heart.

정성 jeong·seong true heart
정성이 담긴 선물로 당신의 사랑을 표현하세요. jeongseongi damgin seonmullo dangsinui sarangeul pyohyeonhaseyo. Express your love with a heartfelt gift.

성의 seong·ui sincerity
그녀의 대답에는 **성의가 없었다**. geunyeoui daedabeneun seonguiga eopseotda. Her reply lacked enthusiasm.

진심 jin·sim sincerity, true heart
진심으로 사과드려요. jinsimeuro sagwadeuryeoyo. I sincerely apologize.

신경 sin·gyeong care, concern
신경 쓰지 마. singyeong sseuji ma. Never mind.

관심 gwan·sim interest, concern
저는 미술에 별로 **관심이 없어요**. jeoneun misure byeollo gwansimi eopseoyo. I'm not very interested in art.

반하다 ban·ha·da to fall in love
저는 제 아내에게 **첫눈에 반했어요**. jeoneun je anaeege cheonnune banhaesseoyo. I fell in love with my wife at first sight.

끌리다 kkeul·li·da to be drawn, be attracted
저는 나쁜 남자들한테 끌려요. jeoneun nappeun namjadeulhante kkeullyeoyo. I'm attracted to bad boys.

좋아하다 jo·a·ha·da to like, enjoy
운동을 하는 것, 보는 것 둘 다 좋아합니다. undongeul haneun geot, boneun geot dul da joahamnida. I like both playing and watching sports.

마음이 있다 ma·eu·mi it·da to be interested in sth/sb
너 그 사람한테 **마음이 있어**? neo geu saram-

hante maeumi isseo? Are you interested in her?

아끼다 a·kki·da to cherish, treasure
이건 제가 제일 아끼는 그림이에요. igeon jega jeil akkineun geurimieyo. This is the picture I cherish the most.

소중하다 so·jung·ha·da precious, valuable, dear
생명보다 소중한 것은 없습니다. saengmyeongboda sojunghan geoseun eopseumnida. Nothing is more precious than life.

둘도 없다 dul·do eop·da (there's) no one like sb
제 아내 같은 여자는 세상에 둘도 없을 거예요. je anae gateun nyeojaneun sesange duldo eopseul geoyeyo. There's probably no woman in the world like my wife.

존경 | ~하다 jon·gyeong | ~·ha·da respect, admiration | to respect, esteem
요즘 아이들은 더 이상 선생님을 존경하지 않는다. yojeum aideureun deo isang seonsaengnimeul jongyeonghaji anneunda. These days students do not respect their teachers any more.

존중 | ~하다 jon·jung | ~·ha·da respect | to respect, honor
네 의사를 존중한다. ne uisareul jonjunghanda. I respect your decision.

그립다 geu·rip·da to miss, long for
학창 시절이 그립네요. hakchang sijeori geurimneyo. I miss my school days.

그리움 geu·ri·um longing

그리워하다 geu·ri·wo·ha·da to miss, long for

....

바라다 ba·ra·da to wish, hope, want

바람 ba·ram wish, desire
그의 마지막 바람은 평안하게 죽는 것이다. geuui majimak barameun pyeonganhage jungneun geosida. His last wish is to die in peace.

People often make a mistake of saying 바램 **baraem** or 바래요 **baraeyo** when they should have said 바람 **baram** or 바라요 **barayo.**

원하다 won·ha·da to wish, hope, want
원하신다면 늦게까지 계셔도 됩니다. wonhasindamyeon neutgekkaji gyesyeodo doemnida. You may stay late if you wish.

희망 | ~하다 hui·mang | ~·ha·da hope, wish | to hope, wish
그녀의 부정적인 대답이 내 모든 희망을 날려 버렸다. geunyeoui bujeongjeogin daedabi nae modeun huimangeul lallyeo beoryeotda. Her negative reply blew all my hopes away.

소망 | ~하다 so·mang | ~·ha·da hope, wish | to hope, wish
새해 소망이 뭐예요? saehae somangi mwoyeyo? What is your New Year's wish?

소원 | ~하다 so·won | ~·ha·da hope, wish | to hope, wish
제 소원은 통일입니다. je sowoneun tongirimnida. My sole wish is the reunification of our country.

간절하다 gan·jeol·ha·da ardent, desperate
차가운 맥주 생각이 간절합니다. chagaun maekju saenggagi ganjeolhamnida. I crave cold beer.

빌다 bil·da to wish, pray
행운을 빌어. haenguneul bireo. Good luck to you.

꿈꾸다 kkum·kku·da to dream of
많은 사람들이 성공을 꿈꾼다. maneun saramdeuri seonggongeul kkumkkunda. Many people dream of success.

기대 | ~하다 gi·dae | ~·ha·da expectation | to expect
우리는 그렇게 많은 사람들을 기대하지는 않았어요. urineun geureoke maneun saramdeureul gidaehajineun anasseoyo. We weren't expecting so many people.

호기심 ho·gi·sim curiosity
민수는 호기심이 무척 강한 아이다. Minsuneun hogisimi mucheok ganghan aida. Minsu is such a curious child.

궁금하다 gung·geum·ha·da curious
걔는 세상 모든 것이 다 궁금한가 봐. gyaeneun sesang modeun geosi da gunggeumhanga bwa. It seems like he's curious about everything in the world.

궁금증 gung·geum·jeung curiosity
나는 궁금증을 풀기 위해 직접 실험을 하기로 결심했다. naneun gunggeumjeungeul pulgi wihae jikjeop silheomeul hagiro gyeolsimhaetda. I decided to do the experiment myself to satisfy my curiosity.

....

감탄 | ~하다 gam·tan | ~·ha·da wonder | to wonder, be impressed
우리는 산꼭대기에서 보이는 경치를 감탄하며 바라보았다. urineun sankkokdaegieseo boineun gyeongchireul gamtanhamyeo baraboatda. We admired the view from the top of the mountain.

감동 늑 감격 | ~하다 | ~적 gam·dong 늑 gam·gyeok | ~·ha·da | ~·jeok deep emotion | to be touched, be moved | touching, moving
그 영화 정말 감동적이었어요. geu yeonghwa jeongmal gamdongjeogieosseoyo. The movie was so touching.
그는 상을 받고 **감격의/감동의 눈물을** 흘렸다. geuneun sangeul batgo gamgyeogui/gamdongui nunmureul heullyeotda. He was moved to tears when accepting the award.

감명 gam·myeong impression
선생님의 말씀에 깊은 **감명을** 받았습니다. seonsaengnimui malsseume gipeun gammyeongeul badatseumnida. I was deeply impressed with your words.

동정 | ~하다 dong·jeong | ~·ha·da sympathy, pity | to sympathize, pity

동정심 dong·jeong·sim sympathy, pity

내게서 동정심을 기대하지 마라. naegeseo dongjeongsimeul gidaehaji mara. Don't expect any pity from me.

불쌍하다 bul·ssang·ha·da pitiful, pathetic
동물원의 동물들이 불쌍해요. dongmurwonui dongmuldeuri bulssanghaeyo. I feel pity for the animals in the zoo.

가엾다 = 가엽다 ga·yeop·da pitiful, pathetic
가엾기도/가엽기도 해라. gayeopgido haera. What a pity!

딱하다 tta·ka·da pitiful, pathetic
그 사람들 처지가 참 **딱하네요.** geu saramdeul cheojiga cham ttakaneyo. They're in a pitiful situation.

안쓰럽다 ← 안스럽다 an·sseu·reop·da ← an·seu·reop·da pitiful, pathetic
그는 불쌍한 아이가 안쓰러워 약간의 돈을 주었다. geuneun bulssanghan aiga ansseureowo yakganui doneul jueotda. He gave that poor child some money since he felt sorry for her.

안되다 an·doe·da sorry
그것 참 안됐군요. geugeot cham andwaetgunnyo. That's too bad.

> 안되다 is always used in the past tense.

6.2 Anger, Hate, Displeasure, Sorrow, Loneliness

분노 | ~하다 bun·no | ~·ha·da anger, wrath | to get angry
그녀의 얼굴은 분노로 새빨개졌다. geunyeoui eolgureun bunnoro saeppalgaejyeotda. Her face turned red with anger.

피가 거꾸로 솟다 pi·ga geo·kku·ro sot·da one's blood boils
그 얘기를 들으니 **피가 거꾸로 솟았다.** geu yaegireul deureuni piga geokkuro sosatda. That story makes my blood boil.

화 hwa anger
그때는 **화를** 풀고 싶지 않았어요. geuttaeneun hwareul pulgo sipji anasseoyo. I didn't want to let go of my anger at that time.

화나다 hwa·na·da to be angry
나한테 화났어? nahante hwanasseo? Are you mad at me?

화내다 hwa·nae·da to get angry

나는 이제껏 아내가 화내는 걸 본 적이 없다. naneun ijekkeot anaega hwanaeneun geol bon jeogi eopda. I've never seen my wife angry.

약 yak anger, annoyance
약 올라 죽겠어요. yak olla jukgesseoyo. I'm so pissed off.

열 yeol anger
김 과장님은 가끔 사람을 정말 **열 받게** 해요. gim gwajangnimeun gakkeum sarameul jeongmal lyeol batge haeyo. Mr. Kim sometimes pisses me off.

분하다 bun·ha·da angry, resentful
분해서 잠이 안 와요. bunhaeseo jami an wayo. I'm so angry I can't sleep.

원통하다 won·tong·ha·da angry, resentful
대학에 안 간 것이 원통해요. daehage an gan geosi wontonghaeyo. I regret I didn't go to college.

억울하다 eo·gul·ha·da unfair, angry
저는 억울하게 직장에서 잘렸어요. jeoneun eogulhage jikjangeseo jallyeosseoyo. I was unfairly fired from my job.

미치다 mi·chi·da to go crazy
요즘 들어 미친 사람처럼 혼잣말을 자주 해요. yojeum deureo michin saramcheoreom honjanmareul jaju haeyo. These days, I often talk to myself like a madman.

(얄)밉다 (yal·)mip·da detestable
저 남자 미워 죽겠어. jeo namja miwo jukgesseo. That guy is so hateful.

미움 mi·um hate, hatred

미워하다 mi·wo·ha·da to hate

가슴에 못(을) 박다 ga·seu·me mot(·eul) bak·da to break sb's heart
그 말이 네 엄마 가슴에 못을 박는 말인 거 아니? geu mari ne eomma gaseume moseul bangneun marin geo ani? Do you know what you said broke your mother's heart?

싫다 sil·ta hateful
나는 예의 없는 사람이 제일 싫어. naneun yeui eomneun sarami jeil sireo. I hate impolite people the most.

싫어하다 si·reo·ha·da to hate, dislike
저는 아무것도 하지 않고 앉아 있는 것을 싫어해요. jeoneun amugeotdo haji anko anja inneun geoseul sireohaeyo. I hate sitting around and doing nothing.

증오 | ~하다 jeung·o | ~·ha·da hate, hatred | to loath, hate
사랑의 반대말은 증오가 아니라 무관심이다. sarangui bandaemareun jeungoga anira mugwansimida. The opposite of love is not hate, but indifference.

괴씸하다 gwae·ssim·ha·da disgusted

눈 밖에 나다 nun ba·kke na·da to get on sb's wrong side, be out of favor
지각을 자주 해서 선생님 눈 밖에 났어요. jigageul jaju haeseo seonsaengnim nun bakke nasseoyo. I got on the wrong side of my teacher because I was often late.

무관심 | ~하다 mu·gwan·sim | ~·ha·da indifference | indifferent, unconcerned
많은 사람들이 정치에 무관심하다. maneun saramdeuri jeongchie mugwansimhada. Many people are uninterested in politics.

마음이 없다 ma·eu·mi eop·da to not be interested in sth/sb
그 여자는 나한테 마음이 없는 것 같아. geu yeojaneun nahante maeumi eomneun geot gata. She doesn't seem interested in me.

담(을) 쌓다 dam(·eul) ssa·ta to have no interest
아들 녀석은 공부랑은 담을 쌓았어요. adeul lyeoseogeun gongburangeun dameul ssaasseoyo. My boy has no interest at all in studying.

무시 | ~하다 mu·si | ~·ha·da disregard | to ignore, disregard
그는 나에게 사람들의 비난을 무시하라고 충고했다. geuneun naege saramdeurui binaneul musiharago chunggohaetda. He advised me to ignore people's criticism.

불쾌하다 bul·kwae·ha·da unpleasant, displeased
불쾌하시게 했다면 사과드립니다. bulkwaehasige haetdamyeon sagwadeurimnida. I apologize if I have offended you.

불쾌감 bul·kwae·gam displeasure

불편하다 bul·pyeon·ha·da uncomfortable, awkward
그 여자랑 있으면 마음이 불편해. geu yeojarang isseumyeon maeumi bulpyeonhae. I feel uncomfortable with her.

거북하다 geo·bu·ka·da uncomfortable, awkward
그 말씀은 듣기 거북합니다. geu malsseumeun deutgi geobukamnida. I feel uncomfortable hearing that.

짜증 | ~스럽다 jja·jeung | ~·seu·reop·da irritation, annoyance | irritated
내 여자 친구는 가끔 나를 짜증스럽게 해. nae yeoja chinguneun gakkeum nareul jjajeungseureopge hae. My girlfriend sometimes annoys me.

신경질 sin·gyeong·jil irritation, annoyance
그의 끝없는 불평에 신경질이 났다. geuui kkeudeomneun bulpyeonge singyeongjiri natda. He got on my nerves with his endless ranting.

성질 seong·jil temper
그 사람 성질 건드리지 마라. geu saram seongjil geondeuriji mara. Don't provoke him.

성질나다 seong·jil·la·da to be angry

성질내다 = 성질부리다 seong·jil·lae·da = seong·jil·bu·ri·da to lose one's temper

˙귀찮다 gwi·chan·ta troublesome, tiresome
지금은 모든 게 다 귀찮아. jigeumeun modeun ge da gwichana. I'm sick and tired of everything.

성가시다 seong·ga·si·da annoying, bothersome
성가시게 해서 죄송합니다. seonggasige haeseo joesonghamnida. I'm sorry to trouble you.

⫶괴롭다 goe·rop·da painful, distressed
치과에 가는 건 괴로운 일이다. chigwae ganeun geon goeroun irida. It's a painful experience to go to the dentist.

˙괴로움 goe·ro·um pain, suffering

˙괴로워하다 goe·ro·wo·ha·da to be tormented

⫶답답하다 dap·da·pa·da feel heavy; stifling
걱정이 있어서 가슴이 답답해요. geokjeongi isseoseo gaseumi dapdapaeyo. I felt heavy with worry.

˙속상하다 sok·sang·ha·da upset, annoyed
파티에 갈 수가 없어서 속상해. patie gal suga eopseoseo soksanghae. I'm upset because I can't go to the party.

⫶불만 | ~스럽다 bul·man | ~·seu·reop·da dissatisfaction, complaint | dissatisfied
회사의 정책에 불만이 있습니까? hoesaui jeongchaege bulmani itseumnikka? Do you have any complaints about company policies?

못마땅하다 mon·ma·ttang·ha·da dissatisfied, unhappy
뭐가 그렇게 못마땅한 거야? mwoga geureoke monmattanghan geoya? What made you so upset?

˙실망 | ~하다 | ~스럽다 sil·mang | ~·ha·da | ~·seu·reop·da disappointment | to get disappointed | disappointing
실망하기에는 이르다. silmanghagieneun ireuda. It's too early to be disappointed.

ᴵᴰᴹ기(가) 꺾이다 = 기(가) 죽다 gi(·ga) kkeo·kki·da = gi(·ga) juk·da to be discouraged
부모님의 반대에도 불구하고 그는 기가 꺾이지/죽지 않았다. bumonimui bandaeedo bulguhago geuneun giga kkeokkiji/jukji anatda. Despite opposition from his parents, he did not lose heart.

실망감 sil·mang·gam sense of disappointment

ᴵᴰᴹ등(을) 돌리다 deung(·eul) dol·li·da to turn one's back on sb
모든 사람이 그에게서 등을 돌렸어요. modeun sarami geuegeseo deungeul dollyeosseoyo. Everyone turned their backs on him.

˙절망 | ~하다 | ~스럽다 | ~적 jeol·mang | ~·ha·da | ~·seu·reop·da | ~·jeok despair | to lose hope | hopeless, despairing | hopeless
상황은 절망적이다. sanghwangeun jeolmangjeogida. The situation is hopeless.

절망감 jeol·mang·gam sense of despair

⫶슬프다 seul·peu·da sad, sorrowful
이거 슬픈 영화인가요? igeo seulpeun nyeonghwaingayo? Is this a sad movie?

⫶슬픔 seul·peum sorrow, sadness
그는 깊은 슬픔에 잠겨 있다. geuneun gipeun seulpeume jamgyeo itda. He's lost in deep sorrow.

⫶슬퍼하다 seul·peo·ha·da to grieve, be sad

⫶눈물 nun·mul tear
여러분은 자신이 한 일에 대한 후회의 눈물을 얼마나 자주 흘리십니까? yeoreobuneun jasini han ire daehan huhoeui nunmureul eolmana jaju heullisimnikka? How often do you shed tears of regret for what you have done?

⫶울다 ul·da to cry, weep
남자도 울고 싶을 때가 있어요. namjado ulgo sipeul ttaega isseoyo. Men sometimes want to cry, too.

˙울음 u·reum crying, weeping
아기가 울음을 그치지 않아요. agiga ureumeul geuchiji anayo. The baby won't stop crying.

ᴵᴰᴹ목(을) 놓아 울다 mok(·eul) no·a ul·da to weep bitterly
엄마는 외할머니의 장례식에서 목을 놓아 우셨어요. eommaneun oehalmeoniui jangnyesigeseo mogeul loa usyeosseoyo. Mom wept bitterly at her mother's funeral.

흐느끼다 heu·neu·kki·da to weep, sob
그녀의 양 어깨가 흐느낌으로 떨렸다. geunyeoui yang eokkaega heuneukkimeuro tteollyeotda. Her shoulders were racked with sobs.

훌쩍이다 = 훌쩍거리다 hul·jjeo·gi·da = hul·jjeok·geo·ri·da to weep, sob

서럽다 seo·reop·da sad, sorrowful
그는 서럽게 울었다. geuneun seoreopge ureotda. He gave a deep sob.

서러움 = 설움 seo·reo·um = seo·rum sorrow, sadness

서러워하다 seo·reo·wo·ha·da to grieve, be sad

우울하다 ≒ 울적하다 u·ul·ha·da ≒ ul·jeo·ka·da gloomy, depressed
오늘 왜 그리 우울해/울적해 보여? oneul wae geuri uulhae/uljeokae boyeo? Why are you looking so down today?
비가 오는 날은 마음이 울적해. biga oneun nareun maeumi uljeokae. I feel blue on rainy days.

불행 | ~하다 bul·haeng | ~·ha·da misfortune, unhappiness | unhappy
그의 성격은 불행했던 어린 시절과 관련돼 있다. geuui seonggyeogeun bulhaenghaetdeon eorin sijeolgwa gwallyeondwae itda. The way his personality turned out has to do with his unhappy childhood.

외롭다 oe·rop·da lonely, solitary
나 너무 외로워. na neomu oerowo. I feel so lonely.

외로움 oe·ro·um loneliness

고독 | ~하다 go·dok | ~·ha·da loneliness | lonely, solitary
어떤 의미에서 모든 인간은 고독하다. eotteon uimieseo modeun inganeun godokada. Every human being is lonely in a sense.

쓸쓸하다 sseul·sseul·ha·da lonely, solitary
모두가 떠나고 나니 기분이 너무 쓸쓸했다. moduga tteonago nani gibuni neomu sseul-sseulhaetda. I felt so lonely after everybody left.

허전하다 heo·jeon·ha·da empty, desolate
아들을 군대에 보내고 나니 마음이 허전했어요. adeureul gundaee bonaego nani maeumi heojeonhaesseoyo. I felt empty after sending my son off to the army.

허무하다 heo·mu·ha·da vain, futile
가끔 모든 것이 허무하게 느껴진다. gakkeum modeun geosi heomuhage neukkyeojinda. Sometimes I feel everything is in vain.

6.3 Greed, Regret, Anxiety, Boredom

욕심 yok·sim greed
욕심에는 끝이 없다. yoksimeneun kkeuchi eopda. Greed has no limits.

욕망 yong·mang desire
그는 권력에 대한 욕망에 사로잡혀 있다. geuneun gwollyeoge daehan nyongmange saro-japyeo itda. He is driven by his desire for power.

탐 tam greed

탐나다 tam·na·da desirable

탐내다 tam·nae·da to covet
남의 것을 탐내지 마라. namui geoseul tam-naeji mara. Do not covet what is not yours.

침(을) 흘리다 chim(·eul) heul·li·da to be desirous of
남의 물건에 침을 흘리지 마라. namui mulgeone chimeul heulliji mara. Do not covet what belongs to others.

배(를) 채우다 bae(·reul) chae·u·da to look after only one's own interest

개는 자기 배 채우는 것밖에 몰라요. gyaeneun jagi bae chaeuneun geotbakke mollayo. He only knows how to look after his own interest.

눈(이) 멀다 nun(·i) meol·da to be blinded by
그 사람은 돈에 눈이 먼 사람이야. geu sara-meun done nuni meon saramiya. He's blinded by money.

부럽다 bu·reop·da envious
난 네가 부러워. nan nega bureowo. I envy you.

부러워하다 bu·reo·wo·ha·da to envy

질투 | ~하다 jil·tu | ~·ha·da jealousy | to be jealous of
제 가장 친한 친구가 다른 애들이랑 어울리는 것을 보니 질투가 났어요. je gajang chinhan chinguga dareun aedeurirang eoullineun geo-seul boni jiltuga nasseoyo. I was full of jealousy when I saw my best friend hanging out with her other friends.

배(가) 아프다 bae(·ga) a·peu·da to be green with envy

솔직히 성공한 친구를 보면 **배가 아파요**. soljiki seonggonghan chingureul bomyeon bae-ga apayo. Frankly, I'm jealous of my friend's success.

> This idiom also appears in a famous Korean proverb, 사촌이 땅을 사면 배가 아프다 **sachoni ttangeul samyeon baega apeuda**, which literally means "If your cousin buys land, you get a stomachache." This means that people become easily jealous of their neighbor's success.

질투심 jil·tu·sim sense of jealousy
솔직히 가끔 언니에게 **질투심을 느낍니다**. soljiki gakkeum eonniege jiltusimeul leukkimnida. To be honest, sometimes I feel jealous of my older sister.

(시)샘 (si·)saem jealousy, envy
그녀는 친한 친구가 새 자전거를 자랑하자 **샘이 났다**. geunyeoneun chinhan chinguga sae jajeongeoreul jaranghaja saemi natda. She became green with envy when her best friend boasted about her new bike.

아쉽다 a·swip·da sorry, sad
아쉽지만 이만 집에 가 봐야 해. aswipjiman iman jibe ga bwaya hae. It's too bad that I have to go home.

서운하다 = 섭섭하다 seo·un·ha·da = seop·seo·pa·da sorry, disappointed
이렇게 가시니 서운하네요/섭섭하네요. ireoke gasini seounhaneyo/seopseopaneyo. I'm so sorry that you are leaving like this.

아깝다 a·kkap·da regrettable, sad
이 모자는 버리기 아까워요. i mojaneun beorigi akkawoyo. This hat is still too good to throw away.

안타깝다 an·ta·kkap·da regrettable, sad
참 안타까운 일이네요. cham antakkaun irineyo. I'm sorry to hear that.

후회 | ~하다 | ~스럽다 hu·hoe | ~·ha·da | ~·seu·reop·da regret | to regret | regretful
그 사람을 보낸 게 후회스러워요. geu saram_eul bonaen ge huhoeseureowoyo. I regret having let him go.

ᴵᴰᴹ**가슴(을) 치다 = 땅(을) 치다** ga·seum(·eul) chi·da = ttang(·eul) chi·da to bitterly regret
나는 거기 가지 않은 것을 **가슴을/땅을 치고** 후회했다. naneun geogi gaji aneun geoseul ga-seumeul/ttangeul chigo huhoehaetda. I bitter-

ly regretted not having gone there.

한 | ~스럽다 han | ~·seu·reop·da resentment | regretful
부모님이 살아 계실 때 잘하지 못한 게 한이에요. bumonimi sara gyesil ttae jalhaji motan ge hanieyo. I regret not being good to my parents while they were alive.

반성 | ~하다 ban·seong | ~·ha·da self-reflection | to regret, reflect on
저는 제가 한 일들을 깊이 반성하고 있습니다. jeoneun jega han ildeureul gipi banseongha-go itseumnida. I deeply regret what I have done.

뉘우치다 nwi·u·chi·da to reflect, regret
그녀의 얼굴에는 **뉘우치는 기색**이 없었다. geunyeoui eolgureneun nwiuchineun gisaegi eopseotda. Her face showed no sign of regret.

걱정 | ~하다 | ~스럽다 geok·jeong | ~·ha·da | ~·seu·reop·da worry, anxiety | to worry | worried, anxious
아들 녀석이 나중에 커서 뭐가 될지 걱정스러워. adeul lyeoseogi najunge keoseo mwoga doelji geokjeongseureowo. I worry so much about my son's future.

근심 | ~하다 | ~스럽다 geun·sim | ~·ha·da | ~·seu·reop·da worry, anxiety | to worry | worried, anxious
자신이 어찌할 수 없는 일들에 대해 근심하지 마세요. jasini eojjihal su eomneun ildeure dae-hae geunsimhaji maseyo. Don't worry about things you can't control.

고민 | ~하다 | ~스럽다 go·min | ~·ha·da | ~·seu·reop·da worry | to worry | worried, anxious
체중이 빠져서 고민이다. chejungi ppajyeoseo gominida. I'm worried because I'm losing weight.

한숨 han·sum deep breath, sigh
그녀는 깊은 한숨을 내쉬고는 아무 말 없이 떠났다. geunyeoneun gipeun hansumeul laeswigoneun amu mal eopsi tteonatda. She sighed deeply and left without a word.

ᴵᴰᴹ**마음에 걸리다** ma·eu·me geol·li·da trouble one's mind
어제가 결혼 기념일이었는데 깜빡한 게 **마음에 걸려요**. eojega gyeolhon ginyeo-mireonneunde kkamppakan ge maeume geol-lyeoyo. I forgot yesterday was our wedding anniversary. It's eating at me.

애 ae anxiety, impatience
시간이 얼마 남지 않아서 **애가 탔다. sigani eolma namji anaseo aega tatda.** I was really upset that time was running out.

애(가) 타다 ae(·ga) ta·da to be worried sick
시간이 다 돼 가는데 걔가 안 와서 **애가 타요. sigani da dwae ganeunde gyaega an waseo aega tayo.** I'm worried sick because it's almost time but he's not here.

애(를) 태우다 = 가슴(을) 태우다 = 속(을) 태우다 ae(·reul) tae·u·da = ga·seum(·eul) tae·u·da = sok(·eul) tae·u·da to worry
그런 일로 **애를/가슴을/속을 태울** 것 없다. **geureon illo aereul/gaseumeul/sogeul taeul geot eopda.** Don't fuss over it.

속(을) 뒤집다 sok(·eul) dwi·jip·da to provoke, annoy
남편이란 사람이 말만 하면 제 **속을 뒤집어 놔요. nampyeoniran sarami malman hamyeon je sogeul dwijibeo nwayo.** My husband always says things that get me riled up.

속(을) 썩이다 sok(·eul) sseo·gi·da to worry
부모님 **속** 좀 그만 **썩여라. bumonim sok jom geuman sseogyeora.** Stop worrying your parents.

골치 gol·chi head
골치 아파. **golchi apa.** It's troublesome.

불안 | ~하다 bu·ran | ~·ha·da anxiety, uneasiness | anxious, uneasy
내일 있을 면접 때문에 불안해서 잠이 안 와. **naeil isseul myeonjeop ttaemune buranhaeseo jami an wa.** I can't sleep because I'm anxious about tomorrow's interview.

초조하다 cho·jo·ha·da restless, nervous, anxious
모두가 시험 결과를 초조하게 기다리고 있다. **moduga siheom gyeolgwareul chojohage gidari-go itda.** Everybody is edgy about my test results.

염려 | ~하다 yeom·nyeo | ~·ha·da worry, anxiety | to worry
염려하지 마세요. **yeomnyeohaji maseyo.** Don't worry.

우려 | ~하다 u·ryeo | ~·ha·da concern, worry, fear | to be concerned, worry
정부는 이 사안에 대해 **우려를 표명했다. jeongbuneun i saane daehae uryeoreul pyo-myeonghaetda.** The government expressed concern about this issue.

막막하다 mang·ma·ka·da uncertain, at a loss
뭘 해서 먹고 살지 막막해요. **mwol haeseo meokgo salji mangmakaeyo.** I'm at a loss as to what to do for a living.

안심하다 an·sim·ha·da to feel relieved, relax
이제 안심해도 돼. **ije ansimhaedo dwae.** You can relax now.

진정하다 jin·jeong·ha·da to calm down, relax
진정하고 내 말 좀 들어 봐. **jinjeonghago nae mal jom deureo bwa.** Calm down and listen to me.

지루하다 ← 지리하다 ji·ru·ha·da ← ji·ri·ha·da boring; bored
A: 그 영화 어땠어? B: 정말 지루했어. **A: geu yeonghwa eottaesseo? B: jeongmal jiruhaesseo.** A: How was the movie? B: It was so boring!
지루해 죽겠어! jiruhae jukgesseo! I'm bored to death.

지겹다 ji·gyeop·da boring; bored, sick and tired
지겨운 하루였어요. **jigyeoun haruyeosseoyo.** It's been such a long day!
내가 하는 일이 너무 **지겨워요. naega haneun iri neomu jigyeowoyo.** I'm sick and tired of my job.

싫증 sil·jeung dislike
우리 아이는 뭐든 빨리 **싫증을 내요. uri aineun mwodeun ppalli silcheungeul laeyo.** My child easily loses interest in things.

질리다 jil·li·da to be sick and tired of
이 노래는 아무리 들어도 질리지 않을 것 같아요. **i noraeneun amuri deureodo jilliji aneul geot gatayo.** I don't think I'll ever get tired of this song no matter how much I listen to it.

심심하다 sim·sim·ha·da bored
하루 종일 집에만 있으니 **심심해 죽겠어. haru jongil jibeman isseuni simsimhae jukgesseo.** I'm bored to death from being stuck in the house all day long.

따분하다 tta·bun·ha·da boring, dull; bored
그 사람 참 따분해. **geu saram cham ttabunhae.** He is so boring.

재미없다 jae·mi·eop·da boring, dull
살면서 그렇게 재미없는 영화는 처음이야. **salmyeonseo geureoke jaemieomneun nyeong-**

hwaneun cheoeumiya. I've never seen such a boring movie in my life.

방바닥(을) 긁다 bang·ba·dak(·eul) geuk·da to hang around at home
주말 내내 **방바닥만** 긁었어요. jumal laenae bangbadangman geulgeosseoyo. I just hung around at home all weekend.

This idiom describes the situation someone lies down all day long watching TV or taking a nap because he or she has nothing to do.

6.4 Tension, Fear, Surprise, Embarrassment

긴장 | ~하다 gin·jang | ~·ha·da tension | to get nervous
A: 지금 너무 긴장돼. B: 정말? 긴장하지 마. A: jigeum neomu ginjangdwae. B: jeongmal? ginjanghaji ma. A: I'm so nervous. B: Really? Don't be.

긴장감 gin·jang·gam sense of tension

손에 땀을 쥐다 so·ne tta·meul jwi·da to be very excited
시합은 처음부터 마지막까지 **손에 땀을 쥐게** 했다. sihabeun cheoeumbuteo majimakkkaji sone ttameul jwige haetda. It was a thrilling game from start to finish.

떨다 tteol·da to shake, tremble
떨지 말고 침착해. tteolji malgo chimchakae. Stop trembling and stay calm.

떨리다 tteol·li·da to shake, tremble

흥분 | ~하다 heung·bun | ~·ha·da excitement | to be excited, get upset
흥분하지 마. heungbunhaji ma. Calm down.

두근거리다 = 두근대다 du·geun·geo·ri·da = du·geun·dae·da to pound, palpitate
내가 꿈꾸던 날이 다가오자 **심장이 두근거리기/두근대기** 시작했다. naega kkumkkudeon nari dagaoja simjangi dugeungeorigi/dugeundaegi sijakaetda. My heart started to pound as the long-awaited day approached.

가슴(이) 뛰다 ga·seum(·i) ttwi·da one's heart pounds
난 걔만 보면 **가슴이** 마구 **뛰어**. nan gyaeman bomyeon gaseumi magu ttwieo. I feel my heart beating faster whenever I see him.

설레다 ← 설레이다 seol·le·da ← seol·le·i·da to get excited
오늘 밤이 우리의 첫 데이트라서 되게 설레요. oneul bami uriui cheot deiteuraseo doege seolleyo. I'm so excited because tonight is our first date.

홀가분하다 hol·ga·bun·ha·da lighthearted
시험이 끝나서 홀가분해요. siheomi kkeunnaseo holgabunhaeyo. I feel relieved that the test is over.

후련하다 hu·ryeon·ha·da relieved
너에게 사실을 털어놓으니 **마음이 후련하다**. neoege sasireul teoreonoeuni maeumi huryeonhada. I feel relieved that I told you the truth.

어깨가 가볍다 eo·kkae·ga ga·byeop·da to feel relieved
그 일을 끝내고 나니 **어깨가 가볍겠네**. geu ireul kkeunnaego nani eokkaega gabyeopgenne. You must feel relieved now that the work is finished.

시원하다 si·won·ha·da refreshed, relieved
일을 그만뒀더니 **속이 시원해요**. ireul geumandwotdeoni sogi siwonhaeyo. Now that I've quit my job, I feel free.

무섭다 ≒ 두렵다 mu·seop·da ≒ du·ryeop·da afraid, scared
'무서운 영화' 봤어요? 하나도 안 무서웠어요. museoun nyeonghwa bwasseoyo? hanado an museowosseoyo. Have you seen *Scary Movie*? I was not scared at all.

무서움 ≒ 두려움 mu·seo·um ≒ du·ryeo·um fear, dread

무서워하다 ≒ 두려워하다 mu·seo·wo·ha·da ≒ du·ryeo·wo·ha·da to be afraid
실수하는 걸 무서워하지/두려워하지 마세요. silsuhaneun geol museowohaji/duryeowohaji maseyo. Don't be afraid of making a mistake.

공포 | ~스럽다 gong·po | ~·seu·reop·da fear, terror | frightening
나는 공포로 그 자리에 얼어붙고 말았다. naneun gongporo geu jarie eoreobutgo maratda. I was glued to the spot in terror.

겁 geop fear, fright

겁나다 geom·na·da frightened
저는 운전이 겁나요. jeoneun unjeoni geom-nayo. I am frightened of driving.

겁내다 geom·nae·da to fear

끔찍하다 kkeum·jji·ka·da terrible, awful
사고 현장은 끔찍했다. sago hyeonjangeun kkeumjjikaetda. The scene of the accident was terrible.

깜짝 kkam·jjak with surprise

놀라다 nol·la·da to be surprised
내 예전 여자 친구가 결혼했다는 소식에 **깜짝 놀랐어.** nae yejeon nyeoja chinguga gyeolhon-haetdaneun sosige kkamjjak nollasseo. I was very surprised at the news that my ex-girl-friend had gotten married.

놀랍다 nol·lap·da surprising, amazing

놀라움 nol·la·um surprise

간(이) 떨어지다 gan(·i) tteo·reo·ji·da to be frightened, be startled
깜짝 놀랐잖아! 간 떨어질 뻔했어. kkamjjak nollatjana! gan tteoreojil ppeonhaesseo. Geez! You scared me to death.

신기하다 sin·gi·ha·da amazing, wonderful
사람들이 자기 부모를 닮는 걸 보면 참 신기해요. saramdeuri jagi bumoreul damneun geol bomyeon cham singihaeyo. It's amazing how people resemble their parents.

충격 | ~적 chung·gyeok | ~·jeok shock, impact | shocking
나는 내 친구의 죽음에 큰 **충격을 받았다.** naneun nae chinguui jugeume keun chunggyeo-geul badatda. I was shocked by the death of my friend.

기절 | ~하다 gi·jeol | ~·ha·da faint | to faint, pass out
이 그림을 보고 기절할 뻔했어요. i geurimeul bogo gijeolhal ppeonhaesseoyo. I almost fainted seeing this picture.

하늘이 노랗다 ≒ 하늘이 무너지다 ha·neu·ri no·ra·ta ≒ ha·neu·ri mu·neo·ji·da to feel like the world is caving in
그 시험을 다시 봐야 한다는 생각을 하니 **하늘이 노래졌다.** geu siheomeul dasi bwaya han-daneun saenggageul hani haneuri noraejyeot-da. My head started to spin at the very thought that I had to take the exam again.

엄마가 돌아가셨을 때는 **하늘이 무너지는 것** 같았다. eommaga doragasyeosseul ttaeneun haneuri muneojineun geot gatatda. I felt like the world was caving in when my mom passed away.

당황하다 | 당황스럽다 dang·hwang·ha·da | dang·hwang·seu·reop·da to be embarrassed | embarrassed
왜 그렇게 당황하세요? wae geureoke dang-hwanghaseyo? Why are you so embarrassed?

쩔쩔매다 jjeol·jjeol·mae·da to be at a loss, be flustered
걔는 여자들 앞에서는 무슨 말을 할지 몰라 쩔쩔맨다. gyaeneun nyeojadeul apeseoneun museun mareul halji molla jjeoljjeolmaenda. He is at a loss for words in front of women.

당혹스럽다 dang·hok·seu·reop·da embarrassed
당혹스러워 얼굴이 화끈거렸다. danghokseu-reowo eolguri hwakkeungeoryeotda. My face blushed with embarrassment.

꿀 먹은 벙어리 kkul meo·geun beong·eo·ri cat got sb's tongue
왜 갑자기 **꿀 먹은 벙어리**가 됐어? wae gapja-gi kkul meogeun beongeoriga dwaesseo? Cat suddenly got your tongue?

꿀 먹은 벙어리 literally means *a mute who has eaten honey*. Long ago, a student once got caught by his teacher for eating honey without permission. The student couldn't say a word because he had the honey in his mouth. Ever since, a 꿀 먹은 벙어리 has been used to refer to a person who hides the truth for some reason.

기막히다 gi·ma·ki·da dumbfounded
기막혀서 말이 안 나오는구나. gimakyeoseo mari an naoneunguna. I am at a loss for words.

어이없다 ← 어의없다 eo·i·eop·da ← eo·ui·eop·da dumbfounded
그건 정말 어이없는 규정이다. geugeon jeong-mal eoieomneun gyujeongida. It is such a silly rule.

곤란하다 gol·lan·ha·da embarrassing, awkward
그 질문은 대답하기 곤란합니다. geu jilmu-neun daedapagi gollanhamnida. That's an em-barrassing question to answer.

난처하다 = 난감하다 nan·cheo·ha·da = nan·gam·ha·da embarrassing, awkward

제 **입장이 난처합니다/난감합니다**. je ipjangi nancheohamnida/nangamhamnida. I'm in an awkward position.

어리둥절하다 eo·ri·dung·jeol·ha·da embarrassed, confused
그녀는 **어리둥절한 표정**을 지었다. geunyeoneun eoridungjeolhan pyojeongeul jieotda. She had a puzzled look on her face.

부끄럽다 bu·kkeu·reop·da shy; ashamed
제 자신이 **부끄러워요**. je jasini bukkeureowoyo. I'm so ashamed of myself.

부끄러움 bu·kkeu·reo·um shyness; sense of shame
그는 **부끄러움이 많아서** 국왕에게 직접 말을 걸지 못했다. geuneun bukkeureoumi manaseo gugwangege jikjeop mareul geolji motaetda. He was too shy to address the king directly.

수줍다 su·jup·da shy, bashful

수줍음 su·ju·beum shyness
저는 **수줍음이 많아요**. jeoneun sujubeumi manayo. I am so shy.

창피하다 chang·pi·ha·da ashamed, embarrassed

네가 **창피할 이유는 없어**. nega changpihal iyuneun eopseo. There's no reason for you to be ashamed.

무안하다 mu·an·ha·da embarrassed
나는 **무안해서** 그녀의 눈을 똑바로 쳐다볼 수가 없었다. naneun muanhaeseo geunyeoui nuneul ttokbaro chyeodabol suga eopseotda. I was too embarrassed to look her in the eye.

민망하다 min·mang·ha·da embarrassed
결혼 전에 아내에게 썼던 연애 편지를 생각하면 **민망해요**. gyeolhon jeone anaeege sseotdeon nyeonae pyeonjireul saenggakamyeon minmanghaeyo. I cringe when I think of the love letters I wrote to my wife before we got married.

쑥스럽다 ssuk·seu·reop·da shy, bashful
이런 말 하기 **쑥스럽지만**, 저는 변비가 있어요. ireon mal hagi ssukseureopjiman, jeoneun byeonbiga isseoyo. I'm embarrassed to say this but I have constipation.

어색하다 eo·sae·ka·da awkward
낯선 사람과 같이 있으면 **어색해요**. natseon saramgwa gachi isseumyeon eosaekaeyo. I feel awkward to be with strangers.

산주 검토 간주 간주 검토 견해 결론 결심 결정 경계 경계심 고려 고르다 고안하다
고정관념 관점 교훈 구별 궁리 그럴듯하다 기념 기억나다 기억력 기울이다 까먹다 깜빡
깨닫다 납득 눈뜨다 다짐하다 대조 독창성 독창적 돌이키다 드러내다 떠오르다 마음먹
망각 매달리다 모르다 몰두 몰라보다 믿음 발상 밝혀내다 밝히다 분간하다 분류
비교 상상 상상력 생각 생각나다 선택 시험 신뢰 신용 아이디어 알다
알아내다 알아듣다 알아보다 알아차리다 양해 연상 열중하다 예감 예측 오해 유추 의사
의심 이성 인식 입장 입증 전념하다 전망 주의 지능 지지 짐작 집중 착각 참고
참조 창안하다 창의성 찾아내다 추측 탐구 파악 판단 판단력 평가 표시 표현 해석
헤아리다 헷갈리다 혼동 회상 회의 검토 견해 결론 결심 결정 경계 경계심 고려
고르다 고안하다 고정관념 관점 교훈 구별 궁리 그럴듯하다 기념 기억나다 기억력 기울이다
까먹다 깜빡 깨닫다 납득 눈뜨다 다짐하다 대조 독창성 독창적 돌이키다 드러내다
떠오르다 마음먹다 망각 매달리다 모르다 몰두 몰라보다 믿음 발상 밝혀내다
밝히다 분간하다 분류 비교 상상 상상력 생각 생각나다 선택 시험 신뢰 신용

chapter 7 | Thoughts

아이디어 알다 알아내다 알아듣다 알아보다 알아차리다 양해 연상 열중하다 예감 예측
오해 유추 의사 의심 이성 인식 입장 입증 전념하다 전망 주의 지능 지지 짐작
집중 착각 참고 참조 창안하다 창의성 찾아내다 추측 탐구 파악 판단 판단력 평가
표시 표현 해석 헤아리다 헷갈리다 혼동 회상 회의 견해 결론 결심 결정 경계 경계심
고려 고르다 고안하다 고정관념 관점 교훈 구별 궁리 그럴듯하다 기념 기억나다 기억력
기울이다 까먹다 깜빡 깨닫다 납득 눈뜨다 다짐하다 대조 독창성 독창적 돌이키다
드러내다 떠오르다 마음먹다 망각 매달리다 모르다 몰두 몰라보다 믿음 발상
밝혀내다 밝히다 분간하다 분류 비교 상상 상상력 생각 생각나다 선택 시험
신뢰 신용 아이디어 알다 알아내다 알아듣다 알아보다 알아차리다 양해 연상 열중하다
감 예측 오해 유추 의사 의심 이성 인식 입장 입증 전념하다 전망 주의 지능 지지
짐작 집중 착각 참고 참조 창안하다 창의성 찾아내다 추측 탐구 파악 판단 판단력
평가 표시 표현 해석 헤아리다 헷갈리다 혼동 회상 회의

7.1 Thinking, Believing, Doubting, Ideas

생각 | ~하다 saeng·gak | ~·ha·da thought, thinking | to think
저의 문제는 종종 생각하지 않고 말한다는 거예요. jeoui munjeneun jongjong saenggakaji anko malhandaneun geoyeyo. The problem with me is that I often act without thinking.

사고 | ~하다 sa·go | ~·ha·da thinking, thought | to think
논리적 사고는 문제를 해결하고 합리적 결정을 내리게 한다. nollijeok sagoneun munjereul haegyeolhago hamnijeok gyeoljeongeul laerige handa. Logical thinking helps you solve problems and make good decisions.

사고력 sa·go·ryeok thinking ability
외국어 학습은 사고력을 향상시킬 수 있다. oegugeo hakseubeun sagoryeogeul hyangsangsikil su itda. Learning a foreign language can improve one's thinking ability.

(심사)숙고 | ~하다 (sim·sa·)suk·go | ~·ha·da deliberation | to think over, deliberate
심사숙고 끝에 귀하를 선발하지 않기로 결정했음을 알려드리게 되어 유감입니다. simsasukgo kkeute gwihareul seonbalhaji ankiro gyeoljeonghaesseumeul allyeodeurige doeeo yugamimnida. After careful consideration, we regret to inform you that you have not been selected for this position.

궁리 | ~하다 gung·ni | ~·ha·da deliberation | to think over, deliberate
아무리 궁리해도 좋은 방법을 모르겠다. amuri gungnihaedo joeun bangbeobeul moreugetda. I can think of no good way to get this done.

고려 | ~하다 go·ryeo | ~·ha·da consideration | to consider
외국으로 가는 것을 진지하게 고려하고 있습니다. oegugeuro ganeun geoseul jinjihage goryeohago itseumnida. I'm seriously considering going abroad.

여기다 yeo·gi·da to regard, consider
그는 자신을 슈퍼맨으로 여기고 있다. geuneun jasineul syupeomaeneuro yeogigo itda. He considers himself superman.

간주 | ~하다 gan·ju | ~·ha·da consideration | to regard, consider
시험 중에 말을 하면 부정행위로 간주하겠습니다. siheom junge mareul hamyeon bujeonghaengwiro ganjuhagetseumnida. Talking during the test will be considered cheating.

생각나다 saeng·gang·na·da to come to mind
그 사람 얼굴은 아는데 이름이 생각나지 않아요. geu saram eolgureun aneunde ireumi saenggangnaji anayo. I know his face, but I can't remember his name.

떠오르다 tteo·o·reu·da to occur
좋은 생각이 떠올랐어요. joeun saenggagi tteoollasseoyo. A good idea occurred to me.

눈에 밟히다 nu·ne bal·pi·da can't get sth/sb out of one's mind
두고 온 아이들이 자꾸 눈에 밟혀요. dugo on aideuri jakku nune balpyeoyo. I can't get the kids I left behind out of my mind.

....

믿다 mit·da to believe
그 사람한테 여러 번 말했는데 아직도 내 말을 안 믿어. geu saramhante yeoreo beon malhaenneunde ajikdo nae mareul an mideo. I've told him again and again, but he still doesn't believe me.

믿음 mi·deum trust, faith

신념 sin·nyeom belief, principle
그는 자신의 신념을 결코 굽히지 않았다. geuneun jasinui sinnyeomeul gyeolko gupiji anatda. He never gave up his principles.

신뢰 | ~하다 sil·loe | ~·ha·da trust, faith | to trust, have faith
이번 사건으로 경찰에 대한 신뢰가 크게 떨어졌다. ibeon sageoneuro gyeongchare daehan silloega keuge tteoreojyeotda. The case has seriously damaged the credibility of the police.

신용 | ~하다 si·nyong | ~·ha·da credit, credibility | to trust, believe
이것은 우리의 신용에 있어 아주 중요한 문제다. igeoseun uriui sinyonge isseo aju jungyohan munjeda. This is very important to our credibility.

지지 | ~하다 ji·ji | ~·ha·da support, backing | to support, back up
그 계획은 사람들의 지지를 얻지 못했다. geu gyehoegeun saramdeurui jijireul eotji motaetda. The plan failed to receive support from the people.

확신 | ~하다 hwak·sin | ~·ha·da conviction, confidence | to be sure, be certain
저는 우리 팀이 이길 것을 확신합니다. jeoneun uri timi igil geoseul hwaksinhamnida. I'm sure that our team will win.

의심 | ~하다 | ~스럽다 ui·sim | ~·ha·da | ~·seu·reop·da doubt | to doubt | doubtful
지금 나를 의심하는 거야? jigeum nareul uisimhaneun geoya? You don't believe me?
그 사람 말이 사실인지 의심스러워. geu saram mari sasirinji uisimseureowo. I have doubts about whether he is telling the truth.

의문 ui·mun doubt, question

회의 hoe·ui doubt, skepticism

의견 ui·gyeon opinion
그 사람한테 네 의견을 말하지 그래? geu saramhante ne uigyeoneul malhaji geurae? Why don't you tell him your opinion?

견해 gyeon·hae view, opinion
당신의 정치적 견해를 밝혀 주십시오. dangsinui jeongchijeok gyeonhaereul balkyeo jusipsio. State your political views, please.

의사 ui·sa mind, idea
아마 제가 제 의사를 제대로 전달하지 못한 것 같습니다. ama jega je uisareul jedaero jeondalhaji motan geot gatseumnida. Maybe I have failed to express myself clearly.

아이디어 a·i·di·eo idea
이 부분에 참신한 아이디어가 꼭 필요합니다. i bubune chamsinhan aidieoga kkok piryohamnida. I definitely need some fresh ideas for this.

발상 bal·sang idea, thinking
그것 참 독창적인 발상이군요. geugeot cham dokchangjeogin balsangigunnyo. That's a very original idea.

편견 = 선입견 pyeon·gyeon = seo·nip·gyeon prejudice, bias
그녀는 장애인에 대한 편견을/선입견을 극복하기 위해 노력해 왔다. geunyeoneun jangaeine daehan pyeongyeoneul/seonipgyeoneul geukbokagi wihae noryeokae watda. She has tried to overcome others' prejudice against people with disabilities.

고정관념 go·jeong·gwan·nyeom stereotype

고정관념을 깨라. gojeonggwannyeomeul kkaera. Think outside of the box.

입장 ip·jang position, stance
입장을 바꿔 놓고 생각해 봐. ipjangeul bakkwo noko saenggakae bwa. Put yourself in my shoes.

관점 gwan·jeom point of view, viewpoint
이 문제는 보는 관점에 따라 다양한 의견이 존재한다. i munjeneun boneun gwanjeome ttara dayanghan uigyeoni jonjaehanda. Opinions on this issue vary according to your viewpoint.

밝히다 bal·ki·da to reveal, disclose
그는 그 도전을 받아들이겠다는 의사를 밝혔다. geuneun geu dojeoneul badadeurigetdaneun uisareul balkyeotda. He made public his intention to accept the challenge.

드러내다 ≒ 나타내다 deu·reo·nae·da ≒ na·ta·nae·da to show, reveal, express
그는 자신의 감정을 잘 드러내지/나타내지 않는다. geuneun jasinui gamjeongeul jal deureonaeji/natanaeji anneunda. He doesn't express his feelings well.

드러나다 ≒ 나타나다 deu·reo·na·da ≒ na·ta·na·da to come out, be exposed
진실은 드러나게 되어 있다. jinsireun deureonage doeeo itda. The truth will come out.

표현 | ~하다 pyo·hyeon | ~·ha·da expression | to express, show
애매한 표현을 피해라. aemaehan pyohyeoneul pihaera. Avoid ambiguous expressions.

표시 | ~하다 pyo·si | ~·ha·da expression | to express
그들은 내 결정에 강한 불만을 표시했다. geudeureun nae gyeoljeonge ganghan bulmaneul pyosihaetda. They expressed strong dissatisfaction with my decision.

주관적 ju·gwan·jeok subjective
이 기사는 너무 주관적이에요. i gisaneun neomu jugwanjeogieyo. This article is too subjective.

객관적 gaek·gwan·jeok objective
우리는 그 훈련의 효과에 대한 객관적 증거를 수집 중에 있습니다. urineun geu hullyeonui hyogwae daehan gaekgwanjeok jeunggeoreul sujip junge itseumnida. We're collecting objective evidence of the training's effectiveness.

7.2 Remembering, Resolving, Deciding, Being Careful

기억 | ~하다 gi·eok | ~·ha·da memory | to remember
저는 여전히 그 사고를 또렷이 기억합니다. **jeoneun nyeojeonhi geu sagoreul ttoryeosi gieokamnida.** I still have clear memories of the accident.

기억나다 gi·eong·na·da to come to mind
너무 오래돼서 기억이 나지 않네요. **neomu oraedwaeseo gieogi naji anneyo.** It's been so long I can't remember.

기억력 gi·eong·nyeok memory, ability to remember
그녀는 **놀라운 기억력**을 갖고 있다. **geunyeoneun nollaun gieongnyeogeul gatgo itda.** She has a remarkable memory.

추억 chu·eok memory, recollection
이 노래를 들을 때면 첫사랑과의 **추억에 잠기게** 됩니다. **i noraereul deureul ttaemyeon cheotsaranggwaui chueoge jamgige doemnida.** When I listen to this song, I'm lost in memories of my first love.

기념 | ~하다 gi·nyeom | ~·ha·da commemoration | to commemorate, celebrate
그 행사는 그의 사망 40주년을 기념해서 열렸다. **geu haengsaneun geuui samang sasipjunyeoneul ginyeomhaeseo yeollyeotda.** The event was held to commemorate the 40th anniversary of his death.

떠올리다 tteo·ol·li·da to recall
그 사건은 과거 고통스러웠던 **기억을 떠올리게** 했다. **geu sageoneun gwageo gotongseureowotdeon gieogeul tteoollige haetda.** The incident reminded me of my past sufferings.

연상 | ~하다 yeon·sang | ~·ha·da association | to recall
왠지 이 그림은 아프리카를 연상하게 한다. **waenji i geurimeun apeurikareul lyeonsanghage handa.** For some reason this picture reminds me of Africa.

여행 하면 뭐가 연상되세요? **yeohaeng hamyeon mwoga yeonsangdoeseyo?** What do you associate with traveling?

회상 | ~하다 hoe·sang | ~·ha·da reminiscence, recollection | to recall, recollect
그 당시를 회상하면 그 모든 게 꿈만 같아요. **geu dangsireul hoesanghamyeon geu modeun ge kkumman gatayo.** When I look back upon those days, it all seems like a dream.

(되)돌아보다 (doe·)do·ra·bo·da to look back, think back
어릴 때를 돌아보면 나는 참 개구쟁이 소년이었다. **eoril ttaereul dorabomyeon naneun cham gaegujaengi sonyeonieotda.** When I look back on my childhood, I see that I was a mischievous boy.

돌이키다 do·ri·ki·da to look back on, reflect on
돌이켜 보니, 그 사람들과 어울리는 게 아니었다. **dorikyeo boni, geu saramdeulgwa eoullineun ge anieotda.** In retrospect, I shouldn't have hung out with them.

깜빡 | ~하다 kkam·ppak | ~·ha·da completely, with a flash | to forget
내일이 결혼 기념일이라는 걸 깜빡했어요. **naeiri gyeolhon ginyeomirraneun geol kkamppakaesseoyo.** I almost forgot that tomorrow is my wedding anniversary.

잊(어버리)다 it(·eo·beo·ri)·da to forget
아차, 깜빡 잊어버렸어. **acha, kkamppak ijeobeoryeosseo.** Oh, I completely forgot.

까먹다 kka·meok·da (informal) to forget
까먹기 전에 말해야지. 너한테 전화 왔어. **kkameokgi jeone malhaeyaji. neohante jeonhwa wasseosseo.** Before I forget, there was a call for you.

망각 | ~하다 mang·gak | ~·ha·da oblivion | to forget
망각은 축복이다. **manggageun chukbogida.** Oblivion is bliss.

결심 | ~하다 gyeol·sim | ~·ha·da resolution | to resolve, make up one's mind
패스트푸드를 안 먹기로 결심했어. **paeseu teupudeureul an meokgiro gyeolsimhaesseo.** I made up my mind not to eat junk food.

마음먹다 ma·eum·meok·da to resolve, make up one's mind
대학원에 지원하기로 마음먹었어요. **daehagwone jiwonhagiro maeummeogeosseoyo.** I've decided to apply for graduate school.

다짐하다 da·jim·ha·da to promise, resolve
그는 범인을 반드시 잡겠다고 다짐했다. **geuneun beomineul bandeusi japgetdago dajimhaetda.** He was determined to catch the culprit at any cost.

각오 | ~하다 ga·go | ~·ha·da determination, resolution | to be determined, resolve
각오 단단히 해라. **gago dandanhi haera.** Brace yourself.

결정 | (결)정하다 gyeol·jeong | (gyeol·)jeong·ha·da decision | to decide
대다수가 그 **결정**을 받아들이지 않았다. **daedasuga geu gyeoljeongeul badadeuriji anatda.** The majority didn't accept the decision.
주말을 어떻게 보낼 건지 아직 정하지 않았어요? **jumareul eotteoke bonael geonji ajik jeonghaji anasseoyo?** Have you decided how you'll spend the weekend yet?

결론 gyeol·lon conclusion
성급하게 **결론** 내리지 마라. **seonggeupage gyeollon naeriji mara.** Don't jump to conclusions.

조심하다 | 조심스럽다 jo·sim·ha·da | jo·sim·seu·reop·da to watch out, be careful | careful
조심해! 위험해. **josimhae! wiheomhae.** Be careful! It's very dangerous.

접시에 조심스럽게 내려놓으세요. **jeopsie josimseureopge naeryeonoeuseyo.** Lay it down on the plate carefully.

주의 ≒ 유의 | ~하다 ju·ui ≒ yu·ui | ~·ha·da care, caution | to beware, pay attention
주의/유의 사항을 읽어 봤어? **juui/yuui sahangeul ilgeo bwasseo?** Have you read the directions?
깨지기 쉬워요. 떨어뜨리지 않게 주의하세요/유의하세요. **kkaejigi swiwoyo. tteoreotteuriji anke juuihaseyo/yuuihaseyo.** It's fragile. Be careful not to drop it.

경계 | ~하다 gyeong·gye | ~·ha·da guard, alert | to be on the alert
경찰은 사람들에게 수상한 상자를 경계하라고 경고했다. **gyeongchareun saramdeurege susanghan sangjareul gyeonggyeharago gyeonggohaetda.** Police warned people to be on the alert for suspicious packages.

경계심 = 경각심 gyeong·gye·sim = gyeong·gak·sim wariness

7.3 Knowing, Understanding, Reasoning

알다 al·da to know
그들 중 답을 아는 사람은 아무도 없었다. **geudeul jung dabeul aneun sarameun amudo eopseotda.** None of them knew the answer.

인식 ≒ 인지 | ~하다 in·sik ≒ in·ji | ~·ha·da recognition, perception | to recognize, perceive
흡연이 얼마나 위험한지 인식하지/인지하지 못하는 사람도 있다. **heubyeoni eolmana wiheomhanji insikaji/injihaji motaneun saramdo itda.** Some people do not realize how dangerous smoking is.
모두들 이 규정을 인지하고 있습니까? **modudeul i gyujeongeul injihago itseumnikka?** Is everyone aware of the policy?

알아보다 a·ra·bo·da to recognize, identify
이 중에서 네 신발을 알아보겠니? **i jungeseo ne sinbareul arabogenni?** Do you recognize your shoes from among these?

깨닫다 kkae·dat·da to realize, become aware
그는 자신이 틀렸다는 사실을 깨닫지 못했다. geuneun jasini teullyeotdaneun sasireul kkaedatji motaetda. He didn't realize he was wrong.

깨달음 kkae·da·reum enlightenment

교훈 gyo·hun lesson, moral
이번 경험이 너에게 좋은 교훈이 될 거야. **ibeon gyeongheomi neoege joeun gyohuni doel geoya.** This experience will be a good lesson for you.

눈뜨다 nun·tteu·da to become aware, realize
아이들은 어른들이 생각하는 것보다 훨씬 일찍 성에 눈뜬다. **aideureun eoreundeuri saenggakaneun geotboda hwolssin iljjik seonge nuntteunda.** Children become sexually aware much earlier than many people think.

알아차리다 a·ra·cha·ri·da to become aware, realize
나는 누군가 나를 따라오고 있음을 알아차렸다. **naneun nugunga nareul ttaraogo isseumeul aracharyeotda.** I noticed someone was following me.

알아내다 a·ra·nae·da to find, discover, detect
그 사건에 대해 뭔가 알아낸 게 있나요? **geu sageone daehae mwonga aranaen ge innayo?** Did you find out anything about the case?

찾아내다 cha·ja·nae·da to find, discover

모르다 mo·reu·da not to know
그 사람이 나를 모르는 게 분명했다. **geu sarami nareul moreuneun ge bunmyeonghaetda.** It was clear that he did not know me.

몰라보다 mol·la·bo·da to fail to recognize
할머니는 치매에 걸리셔서 엄마도 몰라보신다. **halmeonineun chimaee geollisyeoseo eommado mollabosinda.** My grandmother has Alzheimer's so she can't even recognize my mom.

·······

이해 | ~하다 i·hae | ~·ha·da understanding | to understand
네가 집중하지 않기 때문에 설명을 이해하지 못하는 거야. **nega jipjunghaji anki ttaemune seolmyeongeul ihaehaji motaneun geoya.** You don't understand the explanation because you aren't paying attention.

이해력 i·hae·ryeok power of understanding

지능 ji·neung intelligence, intellect

이성 i·seong reason, rationality

논리 nol·li logic, reasoning

앞뒤가 맞다 ap·dwi·ga mat·da to be consistent
네 말은 **앞뒤가 안 맞아**. **ne mareun apdwiga an maja.** Your story doesn't make sense.

헤아리다 he·a·ri·da to guess, understand

알아듣다 a·ra·deut·da to understand, follow
알아듣기 쉽게 말해 줘. **aradeutgi swipge malhae jwo.** Please tell me in a simple way.

파악 | ~하다 pa·ak | ~·ha·da grasp, understanding | to understand, grasp
그녀는 얘기의 **요점을 파악하지** 못했다. **geunyeoneun yaegiui yojeomeul paakaji motaetda.** She failed to grasp the point of the story.

납득 | ~하다 nap·deuk | ~·ha·da understanding | to accept, understand
네가 나라면 납득할 수 있겠니? **nega naramyeon napdeukal su itgenni?** If you were in my place, would you accept this?

양해 | ~하다 yang·hae | ~·ha·da understanding | to understand
양해해 주셔서 감사합니다. **yanghaehae jusyeoseo gamsahamnida.** Thank you for your understanding.

오해 | ~하다 o·hae | ~·ha·da misunderstanding | to misunderstand
내 말 오해하지 마. **nae mal ohaehaji ma.** Don't get me wrong.

착각 | ~하다 chak·gak | ~·ha·da illusion, delusion | to mistake
죄송해요, 제 친구로 착각했어요. **joesonghaeyo, je chinguro chakgakaesseoyo.** I'm sorry, I mistook you for my friend.

혼동 | ~하다 hon·dong | ~·ha·da confusion | to confuse, mistake
사람들은 자주 저를 제 형하고 혼동해요. **saramdeureun jaju jeoreul je hyeonghago hondonghaeyo.** People often confuse me for my older brother.

헷갈리다 het·gal·li·da to be confusing; to be confused
여기 교통 표지판이 너무 헷갈려요. **yeogi gyotong pyojipani neomu hetgallyeoyo.** The traffic signs here are very confusing.

·······

추측 | ~하다 chu·cheuk | ~·ha·da guess, supposition | to guess, suppose
그것은 추측에 불과하다. **geugeoseun chucheuge bulgwahada.** It is no more than a guess.

짐작 | ~하다 jim·jak | ~·ha·da guess, conjecture | to guess, assume
리모컨이 어디 있을지 전혀 짐작이 안 가. **rimokeoni eodi isseulji jeonhyeo jimjagi an ga.** I have no idea where the remote might be.

그럴듯하다 geu·reol·deu·ta·da plausible
또 **그럴듯한 핑계**를 생각해 냈구나. **tto geureoldeutan pinggyereul saenggakae naetguna.** You came up with a plausible excuse again.

예감 ye·gam hunch, premonition
내 **불길한 예감**이 맞았어. **nae bulgilhan yegami majasseo.** My ominous feeling proved right.

전망 jeon·mang view, prospect, outlook
취업 전망이 여전히 어두워. **chwieop jeonmangi yeojeonhi eoduwo.** The outlook on employment remains gloomy.

가정 | ~하다 ga·jeong | ~·ha·da supposi-

tion, speculation, hypothesis | to suppose, assume
이건 어디까지나 가정이야. **igeon eodikkajina gajeongiya.** This is a mere hypothesis.

유추 | ~하다 yu·chu | ~·ha·da inference | to infer
이 자료로 유추할 수 있는 것은 무엇입니까? **i jaryoro yuchuhal su inneun geoseun mueosimnikka?** What can be inferred from this data?

예측 | ~하다 ye·cheuk | ~·ha·da predic-

tion, forecast | to predict, foresee
사실 내일 날씨는 아무도 예측할 수 없다. **sasil laeil lalssineun amudo yecheukal su eopda.** Actually, no one can predict tomorrow's weather.

예상 | ~하다 ye·sang | ~·ha·da expectation, prediction | to expect, predict
내가 예상했던 것보다 조금 쉬웠어. **naega yesanghaetdeon geotboda jogeum swiwosseo.** It was a little easier than I had expected.

7.4 Researching

연구 | ~하다 yeon·gu | ~·ha·da study, research | to study, research
저희는 이 약의 효과에 대한 연구를 하고 있습니다. **jeohuineun i yagui hyogwae daehan nyeongureul hago itseumnida.** We are doing research on the effects of this medicine.

탐구 | ~하다 tam·gu | ~·ha·da study, research | to study, research
이 장에서는 종교와 문명의 관계를 탐구한다. **i jangeseoneun jonggyowa munmyeongui gwangyereul tamguhanda.** This chapter explores the relationship between religion and civilization.

증명 | ~하다 jeung·myeong | ~·ha·da proof | to prove, verify
자신이 한 말을 증명할 수 있나요? **jasini han mareul jeungmyeonghal su innayo?** Can you prove what you said?

검증 | ~하다 geom·jeung | ~·ha·da verification | to verify
그 이론은 아직 검증이 되지 않았다. **geu ironeun ajik geomjeungi doeji anatda.** The theory has not been verified yet.

입증 | ~하다 ip·jeung | ~·ha·da proof | to prove, verify
제가 어제 그곳에 있었다는 것을 입증할 수 있는 사진이 있습니다. **jega eoje geugose isseotdaneun geoseul ipjeunghal su inneun sajini itseumnida.** I have pictures to prove I was there yesterday.

밝혀내다 bal·kyeo·nae·da to unearth, disclose
경찰은 피해자의 **사인을 밝혀내기** 위해 부검을 실시했다. **gyeongchareun pihaejaui saineul balkyeonaegi wihae bugeomeul silsihaetda.** Investigators performed an autopsy to deter-

mine the cause of the victim's death.

규명 | ~하다 gyu·myeong | ~·ha·da identification | to identify, determine
베토벤의 정확한 **사인을 규명하기** 위해 많은 사람들이 노력하고 있다. **betobenui jeonghwakan saineul gyumyeonghagi wihae maneun saramdeuri noryeokago itda.** Many are trying to determine the exact cause of Beethoven's death.

조사 | ~하다 jo·sa | ~·ha·da investigation | to investigate
저는 사건의 원인을 조사하고 있습니다. **jeoneun sageonui wonineul josahago itseumnida.** I am looking into the causes of the accident.

알아보다 a·ra·bo·da to check, investigate
제가 알아볼게요. **jega arabolgeyo.** Let me look into it.

참고 | ~하다 cham·go | ~·ha·da reference | to refer, consult
많은 도서관에서 **참고 도서**는 대출이 안 됩니다. **maneun doseogwaneseo chamgo doseoneun daechuri an doemnida.** In many libraries, reference books are not allowed to be checked out.

참조 | ~하다 cham·jo | ~·ha·da reference, consultation | to refer, consult
자세한 사항은 **홈페이지를 참조하세요**. **jasehan sahangeun hompeijireul chamjohaseyo.** Refer to our homepage for details.

창안하다 chang·an·ha·da to invent, originate
그는 열일곱 살 때 이 **이론을 창안했다**. **geuneun nyeorilgop sal ttae i ironeul changanhaetda.** He came up with this theory at the age of 17.

고안하다 go·an·ha·da to invent, originate
그가 이 보안 시스템을 고안했습니다. geuga i boan siseutemeul goanhaetseumnida. He designed this security system.

창의적 chang·ui·jeok creative, original
저는 늘 제 자신이 대단히 창의적인 사람이라고 생각해 왔습니다. jeoneun neul je jasini daedanhi changuijeogin saramirago saenggakae watseumnida. I have always considered myself a highly creative person.

창의성 = 창의력 chang·ui·seong = chang·ui·ryeok ingenuity, creativity
아내는 창의성이/창의력이 풍부합니다. anaeneun changuiseongi/changuiryeogi pungbuhamnida. My wife is a woman of creativity.

독창적 dok·chang·jeok original
그녀의 음악은 매우 독창적이다. geunyeoui eumageun maeu dokchangjeogida. Her music is truly original.

독창성 dok·chang·seong creativity, originality
그의 사진에는 독창성이 전혀 없다. geuui sajineun dokchangseongi jeonhyeo eopda. His photos are completely lacking in originality.

상상 | ~하다 sang·sang | ~·ha·da imagination | to imagine
너를 여기서 만날 거라고는 상상도 못했어. neoreul lyeogiseo mannal georagoneun sangsangdo motaesseo. I never expected to see you here.

상상력 sang·sang·nyeok imaginative power
그의 놀라운 이야기들이 내 상상력을 자극했다. geuui nollaun iyagideuri nae sangsangnyeogeul jageukaetda. His astonishing stories stimulated my imagination.

집중 | ~하다 jip·jung | ~·ha·da concentration | to focus, concentrate
밥 먹을 때는 먹는 데만 집중해라. bap meogeul ttaeneun meongneun deman jipjunghaera. Focus on your food while you are eating.

집중력 jip·jung·nyeok power of concentration
그는 놀라운 집중력을 보였다. geuneun nollaun jipjungnyeogeul boyeotda. He showed remarkable powers of concentration.

열중하다 yeol·jung·ha·da to be absorbed in
그는 글쓰기에 열중해서 그녀가 오는 것도 알아채지 못했다. geuneun geulsseugie yeoljung-haeseo geunyeoga oneun geotdo arachaeji motaetda. He was so absorbed in his writing that he didn't see her coming.

몰두 | ~하다 mol·du | ~·ha·da absorption, preoccupation | to be absorbed in
지난 1년간, 저는 새 소프트웨어를 개발하는 일에 몰두해 왔어요. jinan illyeongan, jeoneun sae sopeuteuweeoreul gaebalhaneun ire molduhae wasseoyo. For the past year, I've been entirely occupied with developing a new software.

전념하다 jeon·nyeom·ha·da to devote oneself, concentrate
그녀는 음악에만 전념하기로 결심했다. geunyeoneun eumageman jeonnyeomhagiro gyeolsimhaetda. She decided to devote herself to music.

주의 ju·ui attention

기울이다 gi·u·ri·da to pay (attention)
선생님 말씀에 좀 더 주의를 기울여라. seonsaengnim malsseume jom deo juuireul giuryeora. Pay more attention to what your teacher says.

매달리다 mae·dal·li·da to stick to
일에 매달려 있다 보니 하루가 금세 가 버렸다. ire maedallyeo itda boni haruga geumse ga beoryeotda. The day flew by quickly while I focused on my work.

선택 | ~하다 seon·taek | ~·ha·da choice, selection | to choose, pick
이 중에서 하나를 선택해. i jungeseo hanareul seontaekae. Choose one of these.

고르다 go·reu·da to choose, select
먹고 싶은 거 다 골라. meokgo sipeun geo da golla. Just pick out whatever you want to eat.

판단 | ~하다 pan·dan | ~·ha·da judgment | to judge
너의 판단에 맡길게. neoui pandane matgilge. It depends on your judgment.

판단력 pan·dan·nyeok judgment
탐욕이 그의 판단력을 마비시켰다. tamyogi geuui pandannyeogeul mabisikyeotda. His covetousness blinded his judgment.

구별 | ~하다 gu·byeol | ~·ha·da distinction | to distinguish
거짓과 참을 구별하는 것은 쉽지 않았다. geojitgwa chameul gubyeolhaneun geoseun swipji anatda. It was not easy to distinguish the truth from the lies.

분간하다 bun·gan·ha·da to distinguish, tell
그들의 어머니 말고는 아무도 그들 쌍둥이를 분간하지 못했다. geudeurui eomeoni malgoneun amudo geudeul ssangdungireul bunganhaji motaetda. Nobody apart from their mother could tell the twins apart.

구분 | ~하다 gu·bun | ~·ha·da division, classification; distinction | to divide, classify; to distinguish, tell
참가자들은 두 그룹으로 구분할 수 있습니다. chamgajadeureun du geurubeuro gubunhal su itseumnida. The participants are classified into two groups.
나는 목소리로는 그들을 구분해 낼 수 없었다. naneun moksorironeun geudeureul gubunhae nael su eopseotda. I couldn't tell their voices apart.

가르다 ga·reu·da to divide, split
팀은 어떻게 가를까? timeun eotteoke gareulkka? How should we divide up the team?

나누다 na·nu·da to divide, classify, sort
물건들을 크기별로 나누어 줄래? mulgeondeureul keugibyeollo nanueo jullae? Can you sort things by their size?

분류 | ~하다 bul·lyu | ~·ha·da classification, categorization | to classify, categorize
우리는 책을 주제에 따라 분류했다. urineun chaegeul jujee ttara bullyuhaetda. We classified the books by subject.

분석 | ~하다 bun·seok | ~·ha·da analysis | to analyze
우리는 패배의 원인을 분석해야 한다. urineun paebaeui wonineul bunseokaeya handa. We should analyze why we were defeated.

비교 | ~하다 bi·gyo | ~·ha·da comparison | to compare
그 애를 자기 형이랑 비교하지 마세요. geu aereul jagi hyeongirang bigyohaji maseyo. You should not compare him with his older brother.

대조 | ~하다 dae·jo | ~·ha·da contrast | to compare, contrast, check
번역을 원문과 대조해 보세요. beonyeogeul wonmungwa daejohae boseyo. Compare the translation with its original.

평가 | ~하다 pyeong·ga | ~·ha·da evaluation | to evaluate, estimate

자신의 기준으로 다른 사람을 평가하는 것은 옳지 않다. jasinui gijuneuro dareun sarameul pyeonggahaneun geoseun olchi anta. It is not right to judge others by your own standard.

종합 | ~하다 jong·hap | ~·ha·da composite, general | to synthesize, put together
우리의 의견을 종합해 보면 해결책을 찾아낼 수 있을 거야. uriui uigyeoneul jonghapae bomyeon haegyeolchaegeul chajanael su isseul geoya. If we put our thoughts together, we can find a solution.

요약 | ~하다 yo·yak | ~·ha·da summary | to summarize
다음 중 위 지문을 가장 잘 요약한 것은? daeum jung wi jimuneul gajang jal lyoyakan geoseun? Which of the following best summarizes the above passage?

검토 | ~하다 geom·to | ~·ha·da examination, check, review | to examine, review
그 문제는 검토 중입니다. geu munjeneun geomto jungimnida. The matter is under examination.

해석 | ~하다 hae·seok | ~·ha·da interpretation | to interpret
나는 그녀의 침묵을 긍정의 의미로 해석했다. naneun geunyeoui chimmugeul geungjeongui uimiro haeseokaetda. I interpreted her silence as a yes.

점검 | ~하다 jeom·geom | ~·ha·da check, inspection | to check, inspect
1년에 한 번 가스 안전 점검을 받아야 합니다. illyeone han beon gaseu anjeon jeomgeomeul badaya hamnida. You should have a gas safety check every year.

확인 | ~하다 hwa·gin | ~·ha·da confirmation | to confirm
떠나기 전에 예약을 확인해야 한다. tteonagi jeone yeyageul hwaginhaeya handa. You should confirm the reservation before leaving.

시험 = 테스트 | ~하다 si·heom = te·seu·teu | ~·ha·da test | to test
다음 문항들은 당신의 공간 지각 능력을 시험할/테스트할 것입니다. daeum munhangdeureun dangsinui gonggan jigak neungnyeogeul siheomhal/teseuteuhal geosimnida. The following questions are designed to test your spatial perception.

가능하다 개선 거들다 결과 계획 고생 구비하다

고만두다 그만하다 기다리다 꾸준하다 끈기

끊임없다 끝내다 끝없다 노력 늦추다 다시

다하다 다행히 단념 달성 대가 도로 도움 따르다

또 마련하다 마치다 모방 목적 목표 미루다

바꾸다 반복 방식 법 보람 보상 보완 보충

불가능 성과 수 수정 스스로 시도 시행 식 실시

chapter **8** | Actions

실행 실현 쓰다 애쓰다 어쩌다가 연기 연속

열심히 영향 예비 완료 완성 우연히 운 유지

의욕 의존 의지하다 이룩하다 이용 이용자 인내 일부러

작용 잘 재수 저절로 저지르다 적용 적응 전환

조절 조정 종료 준비 줄 중단 지속 지원 최선

포기 한번 해내다 행동 행운 행위 활용 힘쓰다

8.1 Endeavors, Outcomes

행동 | ~하다 haeng·dong | ~·ha·da act, behavior | to act, behave
나는 네 그런 행동을 이해할 수가 없어. na·neun ne geureon haengdongeul ihaehal suga eopseo. I don't understand why you behave that way.

행위 haeng·wi act, action, deed
자살은 스스로 자신의 목숨을 의도적으로 끊는 행위이다. jasareun seuseuro jasinui moksumeul uidojeogeuro kkeunneun haengwiida. Suicide is the act of taking one's own life.

짓 jit (offensive) act
그건 미친 짓이야. geugeon michin jisiya. That's an act of madness.

하다 ha·da to do
내가 할게. naega halge. I'll do it.

저지르다 jeo·ji·reu·da to commit, do (a bad act)
그 아이가 무슨 짓을 저지를지는 아무도 모른다. geu aiga museun jiseul jeojireuljineun amudo moreunda. Nobody knows what the child will do next.

노력 | ~하다 no·ryeok | ~·ha·da effort, endeavor | to try, endeavor
지금은 가능한 한 많은 의견을 들으려고 노력 중이에요. jigeumeun ganeunghan han maneun uigyeoneul deureuryeogo noryeok jungieyo. I'm trying to listen to as many opinions as possible.

애쓰다 ae·sseu·da to try, endeavor
애쓴 보람이 없구나. aesseun borami eopguna. All my efforts were in vain.

기(를) 쓰다 gi(·reul) sseu·da to make every effort
몸이 안 좋았지만 산 정상까지 기를 쓰고 올라갔어요. momi an joatjiman san jeongsangkkaji gireul sseugo ollagasseoyo. I felt ill, but I climbed with all my might to the top of the mountain.

힘쓰다 him·sseu·da to strive, make an effort
우리는 천연자원을 보존하기 위해 힘쓰고 있습니다. urineun cheonyeonjawoneul bojonhagi wihae himsseugo itseumnida. We're striving to protect our natural resources.

최선 choe·seon best

다하다 da·ha·da to carry out, fulfill
최선을 다해 돕겠습니다. choeseoneul dahae dopgetseumnida. I'll do my best to help you.

열심히 yeol·sim·hi hard, diligently
너 정말 공부 열심히 했구나. neo jeongmal gongbu yeolsimhi haetguna. You must have studied very hard.

의지 ui·ji will, volition
어머니는 의지가 강한 분이세요. eomeonineun uijiga ganghan buniseyo. My mother has a strong will.

의욕 ui·yok will, desire
그분은 언제나 열정과 의욕이 넘쳐 보여요. geubuneun eonjena yeoljeonggwa uiyogi neomchyeo boyeoyo. He always seems to be full of passion and desire.

열정 yeol·jeong passion, ardor
그녀는 책을 쓰는 데 열정을 쏟았다. geunyeoneun chaegeul sseuneun de yeoljeongeul ssodatda. She put her heart and soul into writing her book.

끈기 kkeun·gi patience, tenacity
그 일은 상당한 끈기와 의지를 요한다. geu ireun sangdanghan kkeungiwa uijireul lyohanda. It requires a lot of tenacity and determination.

인내 | ~하다 in·nae | ~·ha·da patience, endurance | to endure, bear
인내하는 사람이 마지막에 남는다. innaehaneun sarami majimage namneunda. It is people with perseverance who survive.

인내심 = 참을성 in·nae·sim = cha·meul·seong patience, perseverance
그 사람은 인내심이/참을성이 아주 강하다. geu sarameun innaesimi/chameulseongi aju ganghada. He is very patient.

견디다 gyeon·di·da to endure, bear, stand
이렇게 추운 날씨는 못 견디겠어요. ireoke chuun nalssineun mot gyeondigesseoyo. I can't stand this cold weather.

참다 cham·da to bear, endure
조금만 더 참아. jogeumman deo chama. Hang on just a little longer.

적응 | ~하다 jeo·geung | ~·ha·da adaptation | to adapt
새 학교에 적응하는 일은 쉽지 않았다. sae

hakgyoe jeogeunghaneun ireun swipji anatda. It was not easy to adapt to life at the new school.

기다리다 gi·da·ri·da to wait, hold on
잠시 기다려 주세요. **jamsi gidaryeo juseyo.** Please hang on a minute.

목(이) 빠지게 기다리다 = 눈(이) 빠지도록 기다리다 mok(·i) ppa·ji·ge gi·da·ri·da = nu(·ni) ppa·ji·do·rok gi·da·ri·da to wait for sb eagerly
왜 이렇게 늦었어? 목이/눈이 빠지도록 기다렸잖아. **wae ireoke neujeosseo? mogi/nuni ppajidorok gidaryeotjana.** Why are you so late? I waited and waited for you.

고생 | ~하다 go·saeng | ~·ha·da suffering | to have a hard time
그 집 찾느라고 정말 고생 많이 했어. **geu jip channeurago jeongmal gosaeng mani haesseo.** I had a really hard time finding the house.

애(를) 먹다 ae(·reul) meok·da to have trouble
여기 찾느라고 애를 먹었어요. **yeogi channeurago aereul meogeosseoyo.** I had a hard time finding this place.

운 un luck, fortune
운이 좋으시네요! 그게 저희한테 있는 마지막 물건이거든요. **uni joeusineyo! Geuge jeohuihante inneun majimak mulgeonigedeunnyo.** You're in luck! It's the last one we have in stock.

행운 haeng·un good luck
너 같은 친구를 둔 건 나한테 정말 행운이야. **neo gateun chingureul dun geon nahante jeongmal haenguniya.** I'm lucky to have a friend like you.

재수 jae·su luck, fortune
재수 없는 소리 하지 마. **jaesu eomneun sori haji ma.** Don't say such awful things.

우연히 u·yeon·hi by accident, by chance
길에서 우연히 그녀를 보았다. **gireseo uyeonhi geunyeoreul boatda.** By chance, I saw her on the street.

어쩌다(가) eo·jjeo·da(·ga) accidentally, by chance; sometimes, occasionally
어쩌다가 여기까지 오게 됐어요. **eojjeodaga yeogikkaji oge dwaesseoyo.** I happened to come here.

다행히 da·haeng·hi luckily

다행히도 열쇠를 다시 찾았어요. **dahaenghido yeolsoereul dasi chajasseoyo.** Luckily I found the key again.

의존 | ~하다 ui·jon | ~·ha·da dependence, reliance | to depend on
한국 경제는 전통적으로 수출에 의존합니다. **hanguk gyeongjeneun jeontongjeogeuro suchure uijonhamnida.** The Korean economy traditionally depends on exports.

의지하다 ui·ji·ha·da to depend on
남편은 제가 의지할 수 있는 유일한 사람이에요. **nampyeoneun jega uijihal su inneun nyuilhan saramieyo.** My husband is the only person I can depend on.

돕다 ≒ 도와주다 dop·da ≒ do·wa·ju·da to help
도와줘서 고마워. **dowajwoseo gomawo.** Thank you for your help.

도움 do·um help, aid
도움이 되어 기쁩니다. **doumi doeeo gippeumnida.** I'm happy I could help.

거들다 geo·deul·da to help
식탁 정리하는 거 좀 거들어 줄래? **siktak jeongnihaneun geo jom geodeureo jullae?** Will you help me clear the table?

발 벗고 나서다 bal beot·go na·seo·da to roll up one's sleeves
걔는 친구 일이라면 발 벗고 나선다. **gyaeneun chingu iriramyeon bal beotgo naseonda.** He is always ready to lend a helping hand to his friend.

기여 = 공헌 | ~하다 gi·yeo = gong·heon | ~·ha·da contribution | to contribute
그 선수는 승리에 크게 기여했다/공헌했다. **geu seonsuneun seungnie keuge giyeohaetda/gongheonhaetda.** That athlete made a great contribution to the victory.

지원 | ~하다 ji·won | ~·ha·da support, aid | to support, back up
정부로부터 재정 지원을 받습니까? **jeongburobuteo jaejeong jiwoneul batseumnikka?** Do you have financial support from the government?

의도 | ~하다 | ~적 ui·do | ~·ha·da | ~·jeok intention | to intend | intentional
화나게 할 의도는 없었어요. **hwanage hal uidoneun eopseosseoyo.** I did not intend to make you upset.

일부러 il·bu·reo on purpose, deliberately
너 일부러 그런 거지? **neo ilbureo geureon geoji?** You did that on purpose, didn't you?

스스로 seu·seu·ro by oneself, for oneself
숙제는 **스스로 해라**. **sukjeneun seuseuro haera.** Do your homework yourself.

저절로 jeo·jeol·lo by itself, naturally
문이 저절로 열렸다. **muni jeojeollo yeol-lyeotda.** The door opened by itself.

직접 jik·jeop personally, directly
알고 싶으면 직접 그곳에 가 봐. **algo sipeu-myeon jikjeop geugose ga bwa.** If you want to know, go there and see for yourself.

....

목적 mok·jeok purpose, goal, aim
여기 온 목적이 뭡니까? **yeogi on mokjeogi mwomnikka?** What's the purpose of coming here?

수단 su·dan means, way, measure
목적은 수단을 정당화하지 않는다. **mokjeo-geun sudaneul jeongdanghwahaji anneunda.** The ends do not justify the means.

방법 bang·beop way, means
부자가 되는 빠른 방법이 없을까? **bujaga doe-neun ppareun bangbeobi eopseulkka?** Isn't there a quicker way to become rich?

법 beop way, method
새 친구를 사귀는 좋은 법은 말을 건네는 것이다. **sae chingureul sagwineun joeun beobeun mareul geonneneun geosida.** A good way to make a new friend is to start a conversation with him or her.

줄 jul way
영어 할 **줄 아세요**? **yeongeo hal jul aseyo?** Can you speak English?

수 su means, way
너는 할 **수 있어**. **neoneun hal su isseo.** You can do it.

방식 bang·sik way, means, style
저는 제 방식대로 할게요. **jeoneun je bangsik-daero halgeyo.** I'll do it my own way.

식 sik way
나한테 그런 식으로 말하지 마세요. **nahante geureon sigeuro malhaji maseyo.** Don't talk to me that way.

기회 gi·hoe opportunity, chance
한 번 더 **기회를 주세요**. **han beon deo gihoe-reul juseyo.** Give me another chance, please.

흉내 hyung·nae imitation, takeoff
내 친구 민준이는 다른 사람 **흉내를** 잘 **낸다**. **nae chingu minjunineun dareun saram hyung-naereul jal laenda.** My friend Minjun is good at imitating others.

모방 | ~하다 mo·bang | ~·ha·da imitation, copy | to imitate, copy
그 사람 말투는 모방이 불가능하다. **geu sa-ram maltuneun mobangi bulganeunghada.** No one can copy his way of speaking.

따르다 tta·reu·da to follow
아이들은 부모를 **따라** 하면서 배운다. **ai-deureun bumoreul ttara hamyeonseo baeunda.** Children learn by imitating their parents.

....

반복 = 되풀이 | ~하다 ban·bok = doe·pu·ri | ~·ha·da repetition | to repeat
그들은 같은 **실수를 반복하지/되풀이하지** 않기 위해 매우 신중했다. **geudeureun gateun silsureul banbokaji/doepurihaji anki wihae maeu sinjunghaetda.** They were very careful not to repeat the same mistakes.

또 tto once more, again
또 먹어? **tto meogeo?** Are you eating again?

다시 da·si again, once more
다시 한 번 말씀해 주실래요? **dasi han beon malsseumhae jusillaeyo?** Could you say that again, please?

도로 do·ro again, back
왜 도로 오는 거야? **wae doro oneun geoya?** Why are you coming back?

잘 jal well
잘 알고 있어요. **jal algo isseoyo.** I am well aware of it.

제대로 je·dae·ro properly, right
제대로 좀 해! **jedaero jom hae!** Do it right!

....

이용 | ~하다 i·yong | ~·ha·da use | to use, utilize
주차할 데가 없으니까 **대중교통을 이용하는** 게 나을 거야. **juchahal dega eopseunikka dae-junggyotongeul iyonghaneun ge naeul geoya.** It will be better to use public transportation because there's no parking available.

사용 | ~하다 sa·yong | ~·ha·da use | to use
여기 있는 물건들은 사용하시면 안 됩니다. **yeogi inneun mulgeondeureun sayonghasi-myeon an doemnida.** You are not allowed to use these here.

┊ **쓰다** sseu·da to use
어떤 카메라를 쓰세요? eotteon kamerareul sseuseyo? What kind of camera do you use?

° **이용자 ≒ 사용자** i·yong·ja ≒ sa·yong·ja user

┊ **적용 | ~하다** jeo·gyong | ~·ha·da application | to apply
변경 사항들을 적용하려면 컴퓨터를 껐다 켜시오. byeongyeong sahangdeureul jeogyongharyeomyeon keompyuteoreul kkeotda kyeosio. Restart your computer to apply these changes.

┊ **활용 | ~하다** hwa·ryong | ~·ha·da application, practical use | to use, apply
이번 기회를 최대한 활용해야 해. ibeon gihoereul choedaehan hwaryonghaeya hae. I should make the most of this opportunity.

┊ **결과** gyeol·gwa result
결과에 너무 신경 쓰지 마라. gyeolgwae neomu singyeong sseuji mara. You should not care so much about the results.

성과 seong·gwa result, outcome
이 논문은 2년간의 연구의 성과입니다. i nonmuneun inyeonganui yeonguui seonggwaimnida. This thesis is the fruit of over two years of research.

┊ **뚜껑(을) 열다** ttu·kkeong(·eul) yeol·da to see what has happened
뚜껑을 열고 보니 결과는 예상과 달랐다. ttukkeongeul lyeolgo boni gyeolgwaneun yesanggwa dallatda. The result turned out to be different from what I expected.

┊ **보람** bo·ram fruit, outcome
노력한 보람이 있어서 기뻐요. noryeokan borami isseoseo gippeoyo. I'm happy my efforts have paid off.

° **대가** dae·ga reward
대가를 바라고 한 일이 아닙니다. daegareul barago han iri animnida. I didn't do this for a reward.

° **보상** bo·sang reward

° **영향** yeong·hyang influence, effect
흡연이 건강에 해로운 영향을 끼치는 것은 놀라운 일이 아니다. heubyeoni geongange haeroun nyeonghyangeul kkichineun geoseun nollaun iri anida. Not surprisingly smoking has a harmful effect on your health.

┊ **효과 | ~적** hyo·gwa | ~·jeok effect, effec-tiveness | effective
그 약 효과가 있어? geu yak yogwaga isseo? Does that medicine work?
이 차는 두통에 정말 효과적이에요. i chaneun dutonge jeongmal hyogwajeogieyo. This tea is really good for headaches.

° **반응 | ~하다** ba·neung | ~·ha·da response, reaction | to respond, react
영화에서 그녀의 연기는 비평가들의 호의적인 반응을 이끌어냈다. yeonghwaeseo geunyeoui yeongineun bipyeonggadeurui houijeogin baneungeul ikkeureonaetda. Her acting in the film has drawn a favorable response from the critics.

° **작용 | ~하다** ja·gyong | ~·ha·da action, effect | to act, work
인생에서 때로는 운이 크게 작용한다. insaengeseo ttaeroneun uni keuge jagyonghanda. Luck often plays a big role in life.

° **이루다** i·ru·da to achieve, fulfill
그는 자신이 원하는 바를 이루기 위해 늘 최선을 다한다. geuneun jasini wonhaneun bareul irugi wihae neul choeseoneul dahanda. He always does his best to achieve what he wants.

° **이룩하다** i·ru·ka·da to achieve, accomplish
중국은 최근 수년간 급격한 경제 성장을 이룩했다. junggugeun choegeun sunyeongan geupgyeokan gyeongje seongjangeul irukaetda. China has made dramatic economic progress in recent years.

° **해내다** hae·nae·da to achieve, manage, complete
그는 맡은 일은 반드시 해낸다. geuneun mateun ireun bandeusi haenaenda. He always completes his given tasks.

달성 | ~하다 dal·seong | ~·ha·da achievement, accomplishment | to achieve, accomplish
우리는 목표를 달성했지만 아직 끝나지 않았습니다. urineun mokpyoreul dalseonghaetjiman ajik kkeunnaji anatseumnida. We've achieved our goal, but it's not over.

° **실현 | ~하다** sil·hyeon | ~·ha·da realization | to realize
마침내 제 사무실을 갖는 오랜 꿈을 실현했습니다. machimnae je samusireul ganneun oraen kkumeul silhyeonhaetseumnida. I have finally realized my longtime dream of having my own office.

: **성공 | ~하다** seong·gong | ~·ha·da success | to succeed
실패는 성공의 어머니다. **silpaeneun seonggongui eomeonida.** Failure is a stepping stone to success.

: **잘되다** jal·doe·da to go well, succeed
수술은 다행히 잘되었습니다. **susureun dahaenghi jaldoeeotseumnida.** Fortunately, the operation was a success.

: **실패 | ~하다** sil·pae | ~·ha·da failure | to fail
캠페인은 실패로 끝났다. **kaempeineun silpaero kkeunnatda.** The campaign ended in failure.

: **안되다** an·doe·da to go badly
일이 안될 때 그는 늘 다른 사람들 탓을 한다. **iri andoel ttae geuneun neul dareun saramdeul taseul handa.** When things go badly, he always blames others.

: **가능성** ga·neung·seong possibility
승리할 가능성은 없다. **seungnihal ganeungseongeun eopda.** There's no possibility of winning.

: **가능하다** ga·neung·ha·da possible
믿는 사람에게는 모든 것이 가능하다. **minneun saramegeneun modeun geosi ganeunghada.** All things are possible for those who believe.

: **불가능 | ~하다** bul·ga·neung | ~·ha·da impossibility | impossible
보고서를 일주일 내에 끝내는 것은 불가능해요. **bogoseoreul iljuil laee kkeunnaeneun geoseun bulganeunghaeyo.** It is impossible to finish the report in one week.

8.2 Course of Practice

: **목표** mok·pyo goal, aim, target
우리 목표는 우승입니다. **uri mokpyoneun useungimnida.** Our goal is to win this tournament.

: **계획 | ~하다** gye·hoek | ~·ha·da plan | to plan
언제 출발할 계획이니? **eonje chulbalhal gyehoegini?** When do you plan to leave?

: **세우다** se·u·da to plan, form
장기적인 경력 계획을 세워라. **janggijeogin gyeongnyeok gyehoegeul sewora.** Make a long-term plan for your career.

구상 | ~하다 gu·sang | ~·ha·da plan, design | to plan
그 프로젝트는 아직 구상 단계에 있다. **geu peurojekteuneun ajik gusang dangyee itda.** The project is still in the conceptual stage.

: **준비 | ~하다** jun·bi | ~·ha·da preparation | to prepare
지원하기 전에 제가 특별히 준비해야 할 것이 있습니까? **jiwonhagi jeone jega teukbyeolhi junbihaeya hal geosi itseumnikka?** Is there anything special I should prepare before applying?

갖추다 gat·chu·da to prepare; to be furnished, be equipped
그녀는 교사로서 충분한 자격을 갖추고 있다. **geunyeoneun gyosaroseo chungbunhan jagyeogeul gatchugo itda.** She is well qualified as a teacher.
이 호텔은 방마다 에어컨을 갖추고 있다. **i hotereun bangmada eeokeoneul gatchugo itda.** Each room in this hotel is equipped with an air conditioner.

구비하다 gu·bi·ha·da to be furnished, be equipped
주방에는 조리 도구가 구비되어 있습니다. **jubangeneun jori doguga gubidoeeo itseumnida.** Kitchens are equipped with cooking utensils.

대비 | ~하다 dae·bi | ~·ha·da preparation | to prepare
비 올 때를 대비해서 우산을 가져가라. **bi ol ttaereul daebihaeseo usaneul gajyeogara.** You should take an umbrella in case of rain.

: **마련하다** ma·ryeon·ha·da to prepare, arrange
그는 내가 거리를 전전할 때 내게 잘 곳과 먹을 것을 마련해 주었다. **geuneun naega georireul jeonjeonhal ttae naege jal gotgwa meogeul geoseul maryeonhae jueotda.** He gave me a place to sleep and food to eat when I was living on the streets.

예비 ye·bi reserve, spare
예비 열쇠가 있어? **yebi yeolsoega isseo?** Do you have a spare key?

실행 | ~하다 sil·haeng | ~·ha·da practice, action | to carry out
그것은 **실행 가능한** 계획이 아니다. geugeo-seun silhaeng ganeunghan gyehoegi anida. That's not a viable proposition.

시행 | ~하다 si·haeng | ~·ha·da enforcement, implementation | to carry out
새 법은 다음 달부터 시행된다. sae beobeun daeum dalbuteo sihaengdoenda. The law comes into effect next month.

실시 | ~하다 sil·si | ~·ha·da implementation | to implement, carry out
내일부터 겨울 **세일**을 실시합니다. naeilbuteo gyeoul seireul silsihamnida. We're having a winter sale starting tomorrow.

시도 | ~하다 si·do | ~·ha·da try, attempt | to try, attempt
그 계획은 시도해 볼 만하다. geu gyehoegeun sidohae bol manhada. The plan is worth a try.

한번 han·beon on trial
제가 한번 해 볼게요. jega hanbeon hae bol-geyo. Let me give it a try.

- -

미루다 mi·ru·da to delay, postpone
오늘 할 일을 내일로 미루지 마라. oneul hal ireul laeillo miruji mara. Don't put off till tomorrow what you can do today.

연기 | ~하다 yeon·gi | ~·ha·da delay | to delay, postpone
회의가 내일로 연기되었다. hoeuiga naeillo yeongidoeeotda. The meeting was postponed until tomorrow.

늦추다 neut·chu·da to delay, postpone
나는 한 시간 가까이 출발을 늦추었다. naneun han sigan gakkai chulbareul leutchueotda. I delayed my departure by nearly an hour.

- -

계속 | ~하다 gye·sok | ~·ha·da continuously | to continue, keep (on)
이번 달 말까지는 계속 바쁠 것 같아. ibeon dal malkkajineun gyesok bappeul geot gata. I think I'll be busy until the end of the month.
베토벤은 귀가 먼 후에도 작곡을 계속했다. betobeneun gwiga meon huedo jakgogeul gyesokaetda. Beethoven continued composing even after he went deaf.

유지 | ~하다 yu·ji | ~·ha·da maintenance | to keep, maintain
현재 **상태**를 유지하는 것이 쉽지 않다. hyeon-jae sangtaereul lyujihaneun geosi swipji anta.

It's not easy to maintain present conditions.

지속 | ~하다 | ~적 ji·sok | ~·ha·da | ~·jeok continuance | to keep, maintain | continuous
증상이 2주 이상 지속되면 의사와 상의하세요. jeungsangi iju isang jisokdoemyeon uisawa sanguihaseyo. Consult your doctor if the symptoms persist for more than two weeks.

연속 | ~하다 | ~적 yeon·sok | ~·ha·da | ~·jeok continuity, continuance | to continue | consecutive
가위바위보를 연속해서 열 번 이겼어요. gawibawiboreul lyeonsokaeseo yeol beon igyeo-sseoyo. I won rock-paper-scissors ten times in a row.

끊임없다 | 끊임없이 kkeu·ni·meop·da | kkeu·ni·meop·si constant | constantly, without stop
비가 하루 종일 끊임없이 내렸다. biga haru jongil kkeunimeopsi naeryeotda. The rain continued unceasingly throughout the day.

꾸준하다 | 꾸준히 kku·jun·ha·da | kku·jun·hi steady, constant | steadily, constantly
박사 학위를 받은 여성의 수가 꾸준히 증가해 왔다. baksa hagwireul badeun nyeoseongui suga kkujunhi jeunggahae watda. There has been a steady increase in the number of women receiving PhDs.

끝없다 | 끝없이 kkeu·deop·da | kkeu·deop·si endless | without end
그 사람들의 끝없는 불평이 지겨워. geu saramdeurui kkeudeomneun bulpyeongi jigyeowo. I'm tired of their endless complaining.

- -

변경 | ~하다 byeon·gyeong | ~·ha·da modification, change | to modify, change
일정은 사전 통보 없이 변경될 수 있습니다. iljeongeun sajeon tongbo eopsi byeongyeong-doel su itseumnida. The schedule can be changed without prior notice.

바꾸다 ba·kku·da to change, switch
생각을 바꿨어. saenggageul bakkwosseo. I changed my mind.

전환 | ~하다 jeon·hwan | ~·ha·da change, switch | to change, switch
우리 **발상**을 전환해 봅시다. uri balsangeul jeonhwanhae bopsida. Let's change the way we think.

수정 | ~하다 su·jeong | ~·ha·da modification, change | to modify, change

계획의 많은 부분이 수정되었다. **gyehoegui maneun bubuni sujeongdoeeotda.** Much of the plan has been changed.

개선 ｜ ~하다 gae·seon ｜ ~·ha·da improvement ｜ to improve
근본적인 해결책은 너의 **체질을 개선하는 거야.** **geunbonjeogin haegyeolchaegeun neoui chejireul gaeseonhaneun geoya.** The fundamental solution is to improve your physical condition.

보완 ｜ ~하다 bo·wan ｜ ~·ha·da supplementation ｜ to supplement, complement
우리는 **약점을 보완하기** 위해 최선을 다했다. **urineun nyakjeomeul bowanhagi wihae choeseoneul dahaetda.** We did our best to make up for the weakness.

보충 ｜ ~하다 bo·chung ｜ ~·ha·da supplement ｜ to supplement, make up for
이번 주 토요일에 **보충 수업이** 있어요. **ibeon ju toyoire bochung sueobi isseoyo.** We have a make-up class this Saturday.

조절 ｜ ~하다 jo·jeol ｜ ~·ha·da control, adjustment ｜ to control, adjust
발이 바닥에 완전히 닿도록 의자 **높이를 조절하세요.** **bari badage wanjeonhi datorok uija nopireul jojeolhaseyo.** Adjust the height of your chair so your feet can rest completely on the floor.

조정 ｜ ~하다 jo·jeong ｜ ~·ha·da adjustment ｜ to adjust
모임을 다음 주 화요일로 조정해 주실 수 있나요? **moimeul daeum ju hwayoillo jojeonghae jusil su innayo?** Could you reschedule the meeting for next Tuesday?

중단 ｜ ~하다 jung·dan ｜ ~·ha·da halt, interruption ｜ to stop, halt
비가 와서 게임이 중단되었다. **biga waseo geimi jungdandoeeotda.** The game was stopped due to the rain.

중지 ｜ ~하다 jung·ji ｜ ~·ha·da halt ｜ to stop, cease
사격 중지! **sagyeok jungji!** Hold your fire!

포기 ｜ ~하다 po·gi ｜ ~·ha·da abandonment ｜ to give up, abandon
이번에는 절대 포기 안 할 거야. **ibeoneneun jeoldae pogi an hal geoya.** I'll absolutely not give up this time.

단념 ｜ ~하다 dan·nyeom ｜ ~·ha·da abandonment ｜ to give up, abandon

그녀는 해외 유학 **계획을 단념했다.** **geunyeoneun haeoe yuhak gyehoegeul dannyeomhaetda.** She gave up the idea of studying abroad.

그만하다 geu·man·ha·da to stop, quit
농담은 그만해. **nongdameun geumanhae.** Stop joking around.

그만두다 geu·man·du·da to stop, quit, drop
작년에 **학교를 그만뒀어요.** **jangnyeone hakgyoreul geumandwosseoyo.** I left school last year.

손(을) 떼다 = 발(을) 빼다 son(·eul) tte·da = bal(·eul) ppae·da to quit, drop out
나는 이번 일에서 **손을 떼겠어/발을 빼겠어.** **naneun ibeon ireseo soneul ttegesseo/bareul ppaegesseo.** I quit.

종료 ｜ ~하다 jong·nyo ｜ ~·ha·da end, close ｜ to put an end to
꽉 찬 화면 방식을 종료하려면 ESC를 누르세요. **kkwak chan hwamyeon bangsigeul jongnyoharyeomyeon ieseusireul lureuseyo.** Press ESC to exit full screen mode.

완료 ｜ ~하다 wal·lyo ｜ ~·ha·da completion ｜ to complete, finish
공사가 언제 완료될지는 아무도 모른다. **gongsaga eonje wallyodoeljineun amudo moreunda.** Nobody knows when the construction will be completed.

완성 ｜ ~하다 wan·seong ｜ ~·ha·da completion ｜ to complete, finish
이 소설을 올해 말까지 완성하고 싶어요. **i soseoreul olhae malkkaji wanseonghago sipeoyo.** I'd like to finish this novel by the end of the year.

마무리 ｜ ~하다 ma·mu·ri ｜ ~·ha·da the finishing touches ｜ to finish, complete
프로젝트는 **마무리 단계에** 있다. **peurojekteuneun mamuri dangyee itda.** The project is in its final stage.

끝내다 = 끝맺다 kkeun·nae·da = kkeun·maet·da to finish, put an end to
이번 주 안으로 일을 다 끝내세요/끝맺으세요. **ibeon ju aneuro ireul da kkeunnaeseyo/kkeunmaejeuseyo.** Finish all the work within this week.

마치다 ma·chi·da to end, to finish
이 일을 마치는 데 3일 정도 걸릴 겁니다. **i ireul machineun de samil jeongdo geollil geomnida.** It will take around three days to finish this work.

가난 가치관 감정적 개성 건방지다 겸손 경우 고리타분하다

고지식하다 고집 곧다 곱슬 귀머거리 깔끔하다 꼴 꼼꼼하다

죄죄하다 낙천적 눈빛 능동적 능력 다정하다 당당하다 동안

하다 따뜻하다 매너 맹인 명랑하다 모습 몸무게 못나다

되다 무능하다 무례 무책임하다 미소 바보 배려 버릇

벙어리 부정적 불친절하다 비겁하다 비관적 비굴하다 비열하다

빼다 사정 살 상황 생기다 생김새 성격 성실하다

소질 소탈하다 솔직하다 수동적 신세 안색 야위다

chapter **9** | Describing People

약하다 얌전하다 억지 언어장애인 예민하다 예절 오똑하다

오만하다 외모 울상 위대하다 유명하다 인격

살다 잘하다 재주 점잖다 정중하다 지경 지혜

지혜롭다 찌푸리다 차림 착하다 창백하다 책임감

천재 첫인상 체격 체형 초라하다 태도 터놓다 파마

풍만하다 함부로 활기 훌륭하다

9.1 Situations

상황 sang·hwang situation
지난 몇 년간 **상황이** 나아지고 있다. jinan myeon nyeongan sanghwangi naajigo itda. The situation has been improving for the past few years.

사정 sa·jeong circumstances, situation, story
사정이 있어서 못 갔어요. sajeongi isseoseo mot gasseoyo. I couldn't go there for a certain reason.

형편 hyeong·pyeon circumstances
저는 과외를 받을 **형편이** 못 됩니다. jeoneun gwaoereul badeul hyeongpyeoni mot doemnida. I can't afford to get private lessons.

여건 yeo·geon conditions
그들의 생활 **여건은** 열악했다. geudeurui saenghwal lyeogeoneun nyeorakaetda. Their living conditions were poor.

조건 jo·geon condition
부가 행복의 필수 조건은 아니다. buga haengbogui pilsu jogeoneun anida. Wealth is not an essential condition for happiness.

경우 gyeong·u case, circumstances
어떤 경우에도 이 규칙들을 준수해야 합니다. eotteon gyeonguedo i gyuchikdeureul junsuhaeya hamnida. You must follow these rules under all circumstances.

처지 cheo·ji position, circumstances
나 지금 여행갈 처지가 못 돼. na jigeum nyeohaenggal cheojiga mot dwae. I'm not in a position to go on a trip.

신세 sin·se position, circumstances
내 신세가 참 불쌍해요. nae sinsega cham bulsanghaeyo. I'm so pathetic.

지경 ji·gyeong circumstances, situation, story
그 은행은 파산 지경에 이르렀다. geu eunhaengeun pasan jigyeonge ireureotda. The bank is on the verge of bankruptcy.

배보다 배꼽이 크다 bae·bo·da bae·kko·bi keu·da the tail is wagging the dog
배보다 배꼽이 더 커요. baeboda baekkobi deo keoyo. It's a case of the tail wagging the dog.

바쁘다 ba·ppeu·da busy
이번 주 내내 바빴어요. ibeon ju naenae bappasseoyo. I've been busy all this week.

눈코 뜰 새(가) 없다 nun·ko tteul sae(·ga) eop·da to be as busy as a bee
지난주에 이사를 해서 **눈코 뜰 새 없이** 바빴어요. jinanjue isareul haeseo nunko tteul sae eopsi bappasseoyo. Last week I moved out, so I was as busy as a bee.

급하다 | 급히 geu·pa·da | geu·pi urgent, pressing | hurriedly
천천히 하세요. 급할 것 없어요. cheoncheonhi haseyo. geupal geot eopseoyo. Take your time. There's no rush.

분주하다 bun·ju·ha·da busy
엄마는 지금 저녁 준비로 분주하세요. eommaneun jigeum jeonyeok junbiro bunjuhaseyo. My mom is busy preparing dinner now.

서두르다 = 서둘다 seo·du·reu·da = seo·dul·da to rush, hurry
왜 그렇게 서둘러? wae geureoke seodulleo? Why are you in such a hurry?

어서 eo·seo quickly
어서 오세요. eoseo oseyo. Welcome.

촉박하다 chok·ba·ka·da tight
시간이 촉박해요. sigani chokbakaeyo. I'm very short on time.

발등에 불이 떨어지다 bal·deung·e bu·ri tteo·reo·ji·da last minute
발등에 불이 떨어질 때까지 뭐 했니? baldeunge buri tteoreojil ttaekkaji mwo haenni? What were you doing until the last minute?

내 코가 석 자 nae ko·ga seok ja to have one's own problems
나도 다른 사람을 돕고 싶지만 지금은 **내 코가 석 자야**. nado dareun sarameul dopgo sipjiman jigeumeun nae koga seok jaya. I wish I could help others, but I have to take care of my own problems now.

> This idiom can be literally translated "My nose is running 3 feet." The incredibly long, runny nose represents one's own problem that should be given priority over others.

한가하다 han·ga·ha·da free
요즘 한가해요. yojeum hangahaeyo. I'm free these days.

잘살다 jal·sal·da to be rich
저희는 예전보다 잘살아요. jeohuineun

yejeonboda jalsarayo. We are better off than we used to be.

* **넉넉하다** neong·neo·ka·da well-to-do, well off
저희 집은 그리 넉넉한 편이 아니에요. jeohui jibeun geuri neongneokan pyeoni anieyo. My family is not very well-to-do.

‖ **가난 | ~하다** ga·nan | ~·ha·da poverty | poor
저는 가난한 집에서 태어났어요. jeoneun gananhan jibeseo taeeonasseoyo. I was born poor.

9.2 Appearances

* **외모** oe·mo appearance, look
사람을 외모로 판단하지 마라. sarameul oemoro pandanhaji mara. Don't judge a man by his appearance.

‖ **모습** mo·seup figure, form
코끼리가 거울에 비친 자신의 모습을 바라보고 있다. kokkiriga geoure bichin jasinui moseubeul barabogo itda. An elephant is looking at its reflection in the mirror.

생김새 saeng·gim·sae appearance, looks

* **꼴** kkol (offensive) look, state
네 꼴 보기 싫어! ne kkol bogi sireo! I don't want to see you!

‖ **생기다** saeng·gi·da to look like
A: 나 여자 친구 생겼어. B: 정말? 어떻게 생겼어? A: na yeoja chingu saenggyeosseo. B: jeongmal? eotteoke saenggyeosseo? A: I have finally found a girlfriend. B: Really? What does she look like?

‖ **미인 = 미녀** mi·in = mi·nyeo beauty, beautiful woman

미남 mi·nam handsome man

동안 dong·an baby face

‖ **곱다** gop·da beautiful, lovely
고운 피부를 갖는 것은 사람들이 생각하는 것보다 쉽습니다. goun pibureul ganneun geoseun saramdeuri saenggakaneun geotboda swipseumnida. Getting a smooth complexion is easier than you may think.

* **우아하다** u·a·ha·da elegant
하이힐을 신고 우아하게 걷고 싶어요. haihireul singo uahage geotgo sipeoyo. I'd like to walk gracefully in high heels.

오뚝하다 o·ttu·ka·da sharp
코가 참 오뚝하시네요. koga cham ottukasineyo. You have a very sharp nose.

‖ **매력 | ~적** mae·ryeok | ~·jeok charm, attraction | attractive
그녀는 밝고 똑똑하고 매력적이다. geunyeoneun balgo ttokttokago maeryeokjeogida. She is bright, smart, and attractive.

‖ **아름답다** a·reum·dap·da beautiful, pretty
오늘 당신 정말 아름답군. oneul dangsin jeongmal areumdapgun. You look stunning today.

‖ **예쁘다** ye·ppeu·da pretty
제 아내는 인형처럼 예뻐요. je anaeneun inhyeongcheoreom yeppeoyo. My wife is as pretty as a doll.

‖ **잘생기다** jal·saeng·gi·da good-looking, handsome
남자 친구는 잘생기지는 않았지만, 매력이 있어요. namja chinguneun jalsaenggijineun anatjiman, maeryeogi isseoyo. My boyfriend is not handsome, but he is charming.

Note that 잘생겼다 **jalsaenggyeotda** is used to describe a man who IS handsome.

‖ **멋** meot charm, flavor, stylishness

* **멋지다 = 멋있다** meot·ji·da = meo·sit·da wonderful, nice
그 드레스 입으니까 멋지다/멋있다. geu deureseu ibeunikka meotjida/meositda. You look nice in that dress.

* **섹시하다** sek·si·ha·da sexy, hot
그녀는 난간에 기대어 **섹시한 포즈**를 취했다. geunyeoneun nangane gidaeeo seksihan pojeureul chwihaetda. She struck a sexy pose leaning against the rail.

‖ **귀엽다** gwi·yeop·da cute
너는 웃을 때가 귀여워. neoneun useul ttaega gwiyeowo. You're cute when you laugh.

* **못생기다 = 못나다** mot·saeng·gi·da = mon·na·da ugly, unattractive

저는 왜 이렇게 못생겼을까요/못났을까요? jeoneun wae ireoke motsaenggyeosseulkkayo/ monnasseulkkayo? Why am I so ugly?

Note that the past tense 못생겼다 **motsaeng-gyeotda** and 못났다 **monnatda** are used to describe a person who IS ugly.

인상 in·sang looks, features; impression
인상 쓰지 마. insang sseuji ma. Don't frown.
아내를 처음 보았을 때 사실 거만하다는 인상을 받았어요. anaereul cheoeum boasseul ttae sasil geomanhadaneun insangeul badasseoyo. When I first saw my wife, I had the impression that she was arrogant.

첫인상 cheo·din·sang first impression
한국의 첫인상이 어땠어요? hangugui cheo-dinsangi eottaesseoyo? What was your first impression of Korea?

이미지 i·mi·ji image, impression
좋은 이미지를 유지하는 것이 연예인들에게는 중요하다. joeun imijireul lyujihaneun geosi yeo-nyeindeuregeneun jungyohada. Maintaining a good image is important for entertainers.

눈빛 nun·bit eyes, light in one's eyes
그녀는 나를 **차가운 눈빛**으로 노려보았다. geunyeoneun nareul chagaun nunbicheuro no-ryeoboatda. She stared at me glassily.

표정 pyo·jeong expression, look
그녀의 **시무룩한 표정**을 보고 나는 그녀가 기분이 상했음을 알았다. geunyeoui simurukan pyojeongeul bogo naneun geunyeoga gibuni sanghaesseumeul aratda. When I looked at her sullen face, I realized that I had hurt her.

짓다 jit·da to make, show, express
그렇게 우스꽝스러운 **표정 짓지** 마. geureoke useukkwangseureoun pyojeong jitji ma. Stop making such funny expressions.

미소 mi·so smile
수지는 늘 환한 **미소를 띠고** 있다. sujineun neul hwanhan misoreul ttigo itda. Suji always wears a bright smile.

울상 ul·sang long face
왜 울상을 짓고 있어? wae ulsangeul jitgo isseo? Why the long face?

안색 an·saek complexion

창백하다 chang·bae·ka·da pale
너 **안색이 창백해** 보여. neo ansaegi changbae-kae boyeo. You look pale.

찌푸리다 = **찡그리다** jji·pu·ri·da = jjing·geu·ri·da to frown
모두들 그의 옷차림을 보고 **얼굴을 찌푸렸다/찡그렸다**. modudeul geuui otcharimeul bogo eolgureul jjipuryeotda/jjinggeuryeotda. Everyone frowned at what he was wearing.

시무룩하다 si·mu·ru·ka·da sulky, sullen
왜 오늘따라 그렇게 시무룩해 보여? wae oneulttara geureoke simurukae boyeo? Why do you look so gloomy today?

(옷)차림 (ot·)cha·rim dress, attire, getup

옷이 날개 o·si nal·gae clothes make the man
역시 옷이 날개야. 사람이 달라 보이네. yeoksi osi nalgaeya. sarami dalla boine. Clothes make the man. You look like a different person.

단정하다 dan·jeong·ha·da neat, tidy
대부분의 여자들이 용모가 단정한 남자를 원한다. daebubunui yeojadeuri yongmoga dan-jeonghan namjareul wonhanda. Most women want a well-groomed man.

깔끔하다 ≒ **말끔하다** kkal·kkeum·ha·da ≒ mal·kkeum·ha·da neat, tidy
그녀는 언제나 옷차림이 깔끔하다/말끔하다. geunyeoneun eonjena otcharimi kkalkkeumha-da/malkkeumhada. She always dresses neatly.

세련되다 se·ryeon·doe·da refined, sophisticated
그 정장을 입으니 세련돼 보이네요. geu jeongjangeul ibeuni seryeondwae boineyo. You look sharp in that suit.

Note that the past tense 세련됐다 **seryeond-waetda** is always used to describe someone who IS sophisticated.

야하다 ya·ha·da erotic, sexual

초라하다 cho·ra·ha·da shabby, poor
그 남자는 옷차림이 초라하고 머리가 단정하지 않았다. geu namjaneun otcharimi chorahago meoriga danjeonghaji anatda. He dressed shabbily, and his hair was badly brushed.

꾀죄죄하다 kkoe·joe·joe·ha·da dirty, grubby, unkempt
그는 초라하고 꾀죄죄해 보였다. geuneun chorahago kkoejoejoehae boyeotda. He looked shabby and unkempt.

수수하다 su·su·ha·da pleasantly plain
저는 수수하고 편한 차림을 좋아합니다.

jeoneun susuhago pyeonhan charimeul joahamnida. I like to dress simply and casually.

촌스럽다 chon·seu·reop·da countrified
제 생각에 제 문제는 옷을 좀 촌스럽게 입는 것인 것 같아요. je saenggage je munjeneun oseul jom chonseureopge imneun geosin geot gatayo. I think my problem is that I dress like a country bumpkin.

체격 che·gyeok build, frame

덩치 = 몸집 deong·chi = mom·jip build, frame
그는 의외로 덩치가/몸집이 작았다. geuneun uioero deongchiga/momjibi jagatda. He had a smaller build than I thought.

체형 che·hyeong body type
저희 가족은 모두 키가 크고 마른 **체형**을 갖고 있어요. jeohui gajogeun modu kiga keugo mareun chehyeongeul gatgo isseoyo. All of my family members are tall and have a thin frame.

몸매 mom·mae figure, form
좋은 몸매를 갖고 싶으시면 규칙적으로 운동하세요. joeun mommaereul gatgo sipeusimyeon gyuchikjeogeuro undonghaseyo. If you want to have a nice figure, you need to exercise regularly.

건장하다 geon·jang·ha·da big and strong
그 남자는 **체격**이 **건장했다**. geu namjaneun chegyeogi geonjanghaetda. He had a big, strong build.

왜소하다 wae·so·ha·da small, undersized
저는 눈에 띄지 않는 왜소한 소년이었습니다. jeoneun nune ttuiji anneun waesohan sonyeonieotseumnida. I was an undersized boy who didn't get noticed very much.

뚱뚱하다 ttung·ttung·ha·da fat, overweight
이 옷 입으니까 나 뚱뚱해 보이지 않아? i on nibeunikka na ttungttunghae boiji ana? Do I look fat in these clothes?

마르다 ma·reu·da thin, slim
남편은 상당히 마른 편이에요. nampyeoneun sangdanghi mareun pyeonieyo. My husband is quite thin.

> Note that the past tense 말랐다 **mallatda** is always used to describe someone who IS thin.

야위다 ya·wi·da to become thin, grow gaunt
얼굴이 야위셨군요. eolguri yawisyeotgunnyo. Your face is gaunt.

뼈와 가죽뿐이다 ppyeo·wa ga·juk·ppu·ni·da to be all skin and bones
한 달간 다이어트를 했더니 남은 게 **뼈와 가죽뿐이야**. han dalgan daieoteureul haetdeoni nameun ge ppyeowa gajukppuniya. I'm all skin and bones after a month on a diet.

풍만하다 pung·man·ha·da voluptuous
그녀는 가슴이 풍만했다. geunyeoneun gaseumi pungmanhaetda. She had full breasts.

통통하다 tong·tong·ha·da plump

날씬하다 ≒ 늘씬하다 nal·ssin·ha·da ≒ neul·ssin·ha·da slim, slender
어떻게 그렇게 **날씬한/늘씬한 몸매**를 유지하십니까? eotteoke geureoke nalssinhan/neulssinhan mommaereul lyujihasimnikka? How do you manage to stay so slim?

몸무게 = 체중 mom·mu·ge = che·jung (body) weight
나 몸무게가/체중이 좀 늘었어. na mommugega/chejungi jom neureosseo. I gained some weight.

살 sal flesh, fat

빼다 ppae·da to lose
앞으로 5킬로는 더 빼야 해요. apeuro okilloneun deo ppaeya haeyo. I need to lose another five kilograms.

빠지다 ppa·ji·da to fall out
살이 진짜 많이 **빠졌군요**. sari jinjja mani ppajyeotgunnyo. You've really lost a lot of weight.

찌다 jji·da to gain (weight)
너는 살이 좀 **쪄야겠다**. neoneun sari jom jjyeoyagetda. I think you'd better gain some weight.

키 ≒ 신장 ki ≒ sin·jang height
키가/신장이 얼마예요? kiga/sinjangi eolmayeyo? How tall are you?

크다 keu·da tall
A: **키가 크시네요.** B: 아니에요. 딱 한국 남자 평균 신장이에요. A: kiga keusineyo. B: anieyo. ttak hanguk namja pyeonggyun sinjangieyo. A: You're tall. B: Not really. I'm just about average height for a Korean man.

작다 jak·da short
그 여자는 **키가 작고** 약간 통통한 편이다. geu yeojaneun kiga jakgo yakgan tongtonghan pyeonida. She is short and a little plump.

힘 him strength, energy, power
그는 **힘이** 엄청 세다. geuneun himi eomcheong seda. He is very strong.

기운 gi·un energy, power

세다 se·da strong, powerful

약하다 ya·ka·da weak

(헤어)스타일 (he·eo·)seu·ta·il hairstyle
헤어스타일을 바꿔 볼까 생각 중이다. heeoseutaireul bakkwo bolkka saenggak jungida. I'm thinking of changing my hairstyle.

생머리 saeng·meo·ri straight hair

곱슬(머리) gop·seul(·meo·ri) curly hair

단발(머리) dan·bal(·meo·ri) bob

파마(머리) pa·ma(·meo·ri) perm, permanent

곱슬곱슬하다 gop·seul·gop·seul·ha·da curly, wavy
저는 태어날 때부터 **머리카락이 곱슬곱슬했어요.** jeoneun taeeonal ttaebuteo meorikaragi gopseulgopseulhaesseoyo. I've got naturally curly hair.

대머리 dae·meo·ri bald head
제가 처음 남편을 만났을 때, 남편은 대머리가 아니었어요. jega cheoeum nampyeoneul mannasseul ttae, nampyeoneun daemeoriga anieosseoyo. When I first met my husband, he wasn't bald.

금발 geum·bal blonde hair

흰머리 huin·meo·ri gray hair
저는 스무 살 때 **흰머리가 나기** 시작했어요. jeoneun seumu sal ttae huinmeoriga nagi sijakaesseoyo. I started getting gray hair when I turned 20.

세다 se·da to turn gray
머리가 얼마나 빨리 **세는지는** 유전자에 달려 있다. meoriga eolmana ppalli seneunjineun nyujeonjae dallyeo itda. How early our hair becomes gray is determined by our genes.

목소리 mok·so·ri voice
제발 **목소리** 좀 낮추세요. jebal moksori jom natchuseyo. Please keep your voice down.

부드럽다 bu·deu·reop·da soft, mild
그 남자는 **목소리가** 아주 **부드러웠다.** geu namjaneun moksoriga aju budeureowotda. He had such a gentle voice.

허스키하다 heo·seu·ki·ha·da husky, hoarse
그녀는 **허스키한 목소리로** 음울한 노래를 불렀다. geunyeoneun heoseukihan moksoriro eumulhan noraereul bulleotda. She sang a melancholy song in a husky voice.

장애인 jang·ae·in the disabled
이 엘리베이터는 **장애인 전용**입니다. i ellibeiteoneun jangaein jeonyongimnida. This elevator is reserved for the disabled.

시각장애인 si·gak·jang·ae·in visually impaired person

맹인 maeng·in blind person
그녀는 태어날 때부터 **맹인**이었다. geunyeoneun taeeonal ttaebuteo maenginieotda. She has been blind since birth.

장님 jang·nim blind person

장님, 벙어리, and 귀머거리 are offensive words for the handicapped.

멀다 meol·da to go (blind or deaf)
저는 어릴 때 성홍열을 앓고 **눈이 멀었어요.** jeoneun eoril ttae seonghongnyeoreul alko nuni meoreosseoyo. I went blind from having scarlet fever as a kid.

제 형은 두 살 때 **귀가 멀었어요.** je hyeongeun du sal ttae gwiga meoreosseoyo. My older brother became deaf when he was two years old.

청각장애인 cheong·gak·jang·ae·in hearing-impaired person

귀머거리 gwi·meo·geo·ri deaf person

먹다 meok·da to go (deaf)
귀 안 **먹었으니까** 소리 지르지 마. gwi an meogeosseunikka sori jireuji ma. Stop yelling! I'm not deaf.

언어장애인 eo·neo·jang·ae·in speech-impaired person

벙어리 beong·eo·ri mute

9.3 Personality, Ability, Habits, Manners

성격 seong·gyeok personality, character
많은 부부가 **성격** 차이로 이혼한다. maneun bubuga seonggyeok chairo ihonhanda. Many couples get divorced because their personalities are too different.

인격 in·gyeok character, personality
스포츠는 **인격** 형성에 도움이 된다. seupocheuneun ingyeok hyeongseonge doumi doenda. Sports help build character.

인간성 in·gan·seong humanity, human nature
내 친구 영찬이는 **인간성이** 참 **좋다**. nae chingu yeongchanineun inganseongi cham jota. My friend Youngchan is a man of good character.

가치관 ga·chi·gwan values
우리는 **가치관의** 차이 때문에 헤어졌어요. urineun gachigwanui chai ttaemune heeojyeosseoyo. We broke up because of our difference in values.

마음씨 ma·eum·ssi nature, disposition
따님이 **마음씨가** 참 **곱군요**. ttanimi maeumssiga cham gopgunnyo. Your daughter has a heart of gold.

교양 gyo·yang refinement
그는 **교양** 있는 사람이다. geuneun gyoyang inneun saramida. He is a man of culture.

지혜 ji·hye wisdom
경험은 지혜의 아버지다. gyeongheomeun jihyeui abeojida. Experience is the father of wisdom.

개성 gae·seong individuality
당신은 **개성이** 강한 편인가요? dangsineun gaeseongi ganghan pyeoningayo? Do you have a strong personality?

장점 jang·jeom advantage, merit

단점 dan·jeom flaw, shortcoming
솔직함은 그의 장점인 동시에 단점이다. soljikameun geuui jangjeomin dongsie danjeomida. Frankness is both his strength and weakness.

능력 neung·nyeok ability
그건 제 능력 밖의 일이에요. geugeon je neungnyeok bakkui irieyo. That's beyond what I can do.

재능 jae·neung talent, gift, aptitude
그는 수학에 **천부적인 재능을** 보였다. geuneun suhage cheonbujeogin jaeneungeul boyeotda. He showed a natural aptitude for mathematics.

소질 so·jil talent, gift, aptitude
저는 그림에 **소질이** 없어요. jeoneun geurime sojiri eopseoyo. I have no talent for painting.

재주 jae·ju talent, skill, knack
그는 사람을 다루는 **재주가** 있다. geuneun sarameul daruneun jaejuga itda. He is good at managing people.

적성 jeok·seong aptitude
이 일은 제 **적성에** 잘 **맞아요**. i ireun je jeokseonge jal majayo. This job suits me well.

흥미 heung·mi interest
저는 스포츠에는 **흥미가** 없어요. jeoneun seupocheuneneun heungmiga eopseoyo. I'm not interested in sports.

실력 sil·lyeok ability, skill
그 사람들한테 네 실력을 보여줘. geu saramdeulhante ne sillyeogeul boyeojwo. Show your ability to them.

솜씨 som·ssi skill, ability
요리 솜씨가 정말 좋으시군요. yori somssiga jeongmal joeusigunnyo. Your cooking is great.

자격 ja·gyeok qualification
지원 자격이 어떻게 돼요? jiwon jagyeogi eotteoke dwaeyo? What are the requirements for this job?

습관 seup·gwan habit
저는 손톱을 물어 뜯는 **나쁜 습관이** 있어요. jeoneun sontobeul mureo tteunneun nappeun seupgwani isseoyo. I have a bad habit of biting my nails.

버릇 beo·reut habit; manners
아직도 그 **버릇** 못 **고쳤니**? ajikdo geu beoreut mot gochyeonni? Haven't you stopped that bad habit yet?
요즘 젊은 사람들은 **버릇이** 없어요. yojeum jeolmeun saramdeureun beoreusi eopseoyo. Young people these days have no manners.

태도 tae·do attitude
우리 아이는 태도에 문제가 있어요. uri aineun taedoe munjega isseoyo. My child has an attitude problem.

매너 mae·neo manners
매너가 참 좋으시군요. maeneoga cham joeusi-gunnyo. You have such good manners.

예절 ≒ 예의 ye·jeol ≒ ye·ui manners, etiquette
앉을 자리를 안내 받기 전까지 기다리는 게 예의입니다. anjeul jarireul annae batgi jeon-kkaji gidarineun ge yeuiimnida. It's common courtesy to wait until you're shown a seat.
그 사람은 참 예의가/예절이 바르다. geu sarameun cham yeuiga/yejeori bareuda. He is very courteous.

9.4 Positive Qualities

착하다 cha·ka·da good-natured
남편은 조용하고 착한 사람이에요. nampyeo-neun joyonghago chakan saramieyo. My husband is quiet and good-natured.

도덕적 ≒ 윤리적 do·deok·jeok ≒ yul·li·jeok ethical, moral
도덕적인/윤리적인 생활을 하기 위해 꼭 신앙심이 깊어야만 하는 것은 아니다. dodeokjeo-gin/yullijeogin saenghwareul hagi wihae kkok sinangsimi gipeoyaman haneun geoseun anida. One doesn't have to be religious to lead a moral life.
어떤 의미에서 지구온난화는 윤리적인 문제다. eotteon uimieseo jiguonnanhwaneun nyulli-jeogin munjeda. In a sense, global warming is an ethical issue.

양심적 yang·sim·jeok conscientious
사람들은 정치인들이 양심적으로 행동하기를 기대한다. saramdeureun jeongchiindeuri yangsimjeogeuro haengdonghagireul gidaehan-da. People expect politicians to be conscientious.

가슴에 손(을) 얹다 ga·seu·me son(·eul) eon·da to try to be conscientious
가슴에 손을 얹고 생각해 봐. gaseume soneul leongo saenggakae bwa. I want you to sincerely ask yourself.

인간적 in·gan·jeok humane, human
전쟁 포로들은 인간적인 대우를 받게 되어 있다. jeonjaeng porodeureun inganjeogin daeu-reul batge doeeo itda. Prisoners of war are to be treated in a humane fashion.

관대하다 ≒ 너그럽다 gwan·dae·ha·da ≒ neo·geu·reop·da generous, tolerant
아내는 애들한테 너무 관대해요/너그러워요. anaeneun aedeulhante neomu gwandaehaeyo/neogeureowoyo. My wife is way too lenient with our children.

가슴(이) 넓다 = 마음(이) 넓다 = 속(이) 넓다 ga·seum(·i) neol·da = ma·eum(·i) neol·da = sok(·i) neol·da to be generous
그 사람은 굉장히 가슴이/마음이/속이 넓은 사람이에요. geu sarameun goengjanghi gaseu-mi/maeumi/sogi neolbeun saramieyo. He is a very generous man.

원만하다 won·man·ha·da amicable, easy-going
저는 대인 관계가 원만하지 못한 편입니다. jeoneun daein gwangyega wonmanhaji motan pyeonimnida. I have problems dealing with people.

발(이) 넓다 bal(·i) neol·da to have a wide acquaintance
저는 이 분야에 발이 넓은 편입니다. jeoneun i bunyae bari neolbeun pyeonimnida. I have many acquaintances in this field.

털털하다 teol·teol·ha·da easygoing, unaffected
저는 제 자신이 솔직하고 털털한 사람이라고 생각합니다. jeoneun je jasini soljikago teol-teolhan saramirago saenggakamnida. I think I'm a straightforward and easygoing person.

소탈하다 so·tal·ha·da easygoing, unaffected
나는 그녀의 소탈한 태도에 끌렸다. naneun geunyeoui sotalhan taedoe kkeullyeotda. I was drawn to her unaffected manner.

친절 | ~하다 chin·jeol | ~·ha·da kindness | kind
감사합니다. 정말 친절하시네요. gamsaham-nida. jeongmal chinjeolhasineyo. Thank you. You're very kind.

배려 | ~하다 bae·ryeo | ~·ha·da care, consideration | to consider, care
배려해 주셔서 감사합니다. baeryeohae jusyeoseo gamsahamnida. Thank you for your consideration.

다정하다 ≒ 상냥하다 da·jeong·ha·da ≒ sang·nyang·ha·da kind, friendly
그들 부부는 우리를 **다정한/상냥한** 미소로 반겨 주었다. geudeul bubuneun urireul dajeonghan/sangnyanghan misoro bangyeo jueotda. The couple welcomed us with the sweetest smile.

따뜻하다 tta·tteu·ta·da warm, warm-hearted
그는 마음이 **따뜻하고** 배려가 깊다. geuneun maeumi ttatteutago baeryeoga gipda. He is warm-hearted and considerate.

자상하다 ja·sang·ha·da thoughtful, considerate
저는 **자상한** 아버지가 되고 싶어요. jeoneun jasanghan abeojiga doego sipeoyo. I want to be a loving father.

인자하다 in·ja·ha·da benevolent, kind

정직하다 jeong·ji·ka·da honest, truthful
어제 뭘 했는지 **정직하게** 말해라. eoje mwol haenneunji jeongjikage malhaera. Be honest about what you did yesterday.

곧다 got·da upright, righteous
그는 **정직하고 곧은** 사람이다. geuneun jeongjikago godeun saramida. He is an honest and upright man.

바르다 ba·reu·da upright
다른 사람이 있거나 없거나 **바르게** 행동해라. dareun sarami itgeona eopgeona bareuge haengdonghaera. Behave properly in private as well as in public.

솔직하다 | 솔직히 sol·ji·ka·da | sol·ji·ki honest, open | honestly
저는 **솔직한** 사람입니다. jeoneun soljikan saramimnida. I'm an honest man.

진솔하다 jin·sol·ha·da honest, open
우리 문제에 대해 **진솔한 대화**를 나눠 보자. uri munjee daehae jinsolhan daehwareul lanwo boja. Let's have an honest talk about our problems.

터놓다 teo·no·ta to open one's heart
터놓고 말할게요. teonoko malhalgeyo. I'll be honest with you.

순수 | ~하다 sun·su | ~·ha·da purity | pure, innocent
순수한 것과 순진한 건 달라요. sunsuhan geotgwa sunjinhan geon dallayo. There is a difference between being pure and being naive.

순진하다 sun·jin·ha·da innocent, naive
그 큰돈을 그 자식한테 주다니 너 참 **순진하구나**. geu keundoneul geu jasikante judani neo cham sunjinhaguna. You are really naive to give so much money to that bastard.

소박하다 so·ba·ka·da simple
저는 **소박하게** 살고 싶어요. jeoneun sobakage salgo sipeoyo. I want to live simply.

검소하다 geom·so·ha·da thrifty, frugal
그들은 부자지만 **검소한 생활**을 한다. geudeureun bujajiman geomsohan saenghwareul handa. Though wealthy, they live a frugal life.

성실하다 seong·sil·ha·da faithful, sincere
철수 씨는 매사에 **성실해요**. cheolsu ssineun maesae seongsilhaeyo. Cheolsu always does his best.

착실하다 chak·sil·ha·da faithful, sincere
감옥에 몇 년간 형을 살고 나온 후 그는 **착실하게 살겠다고** 마음먹었다. gamoge myeon nyeongan hyeongeul salgo naon hu geuneun chaksilhage salgetdago maeummeogeotda. After his years in prison, he has resolved to become a good person.

진실하다 jin·sil·ha·da truthful, sincere
왜 너는 그 사람이 **진실하지** 않다고 말하는 거니? wae neoneun geu sarami jinsilhaji antago malhaneun geoni? Why do you say he's insincere?

부지런하다 bu·ji·reon·ha·da diligent
대체로 한국 사람들은 부지런하다. daechero hanguk saramdeureun bujireonhada. Most Koreans are diligent.

진지하다 jin·ji·ha·da serious, earnest
캐나다 이민을 **진지하게** 생각 중이야. kaenada imineul jinjihage saenggak jungiya. I'm seriously considering emigrating to Canada.

믿음직하다 = 믿음직스럽다 mi·deum·ji·ka·da = mi·deum·jik·seu·reop·da reliable, trustworthy
믿음직한/믿음직스러운 직원은 늘 제때에 일을 끝내는 사람이다. mideumjikan/mideumjikseureoun jigwoneun neul jettae ireul kkeunnaeneun saramida. A reliable employee is one who always completes his work in a timely manner.

책임감 chae·gim·gam sense of responsibility
책임감이 강한 사람은 회사에서 환영받는다.

chaegimgami ganghan sarameun hoesaeseo hwannyeongbanneunda. People with a strong sense of responsibility are welcomed by the company.

어깨가 무겁다 eo·kkae·ga mu·geop·da to shoulder a heavy responsibility
아기가 생기고 나니 **어깨가 무거워요**. agiga saenggigo nani eokkaega mugeowoyo. I feel burdened with responsibility now that I have a baby.

신중하다 | 신중히 sin·jung·ha·da | sin·jung·hi cautious, prudent | cautiously
좀 더 신중했어야 했는데. jom deo sinjung-haesseoya haenneunde. I should have been more prudent.

입이 무겁다 i·bi mu·geop·da can keep a secret
걱정 마. 나는 **입이 무거워**. geokjeong ma. na-neun ibi mugeowo. Don't worry. I can keep a secret.

꼼꼼하다 | 꼼꼼히 kkom·kkom·ha·da | kkom·kkom·hi meticulous, precise | meticulously
설명서를 **꼼꼼하게** 읽고 참고를 위해 보관하십시오. seolmyeongseoreul kkomkkomhage ilgo chamgoreul wihae bogwanhasipsio. Please read the instructions carefully and keep them for reference.

철저하다 | 철저히 cheol·jeo·ha·da | cheol·jeo·hi thorough | thoroughly
그녀는 맡은 일에 아주 철저하다. geunyeo-neun mateun ire aju cheoljeohada. She is very thorough about her responsibilities.

겸손 | ~하다 gyeom·son | ~·ha·da modesty | modest, humble
그의 친절하고 **겸손한 태도**는 모두에게 감명을 주었다. geuui chinjeolhago gyeomsonhan tae-doneun moduege gammyeongeul jueotda. His kind and modest attitude touched everybody.

공손하다 gong·son·ha·da polite, courteous
그녀는 늘 모두에게 공손하다. geunyeoneun neul moduege gongsonhada. She's always polite to everyone.

정중하다 jeong·jung·ha·da polite, courteous
정중한 사과가 길거나 장황할 필요는 없다. jeongjunghan sagwaga gilgeona janghwanghal piryoneun eopda. A polite apology doesn't have to be long and dramatic.

침착하다 chim·cha·ka·da calm, poised
일본인들은 지진에도 불구하고 침착했다. il-bonindeureun jijinedo bulguhago chimchakaet-da. The Japanese remained calm despite the earthquake.

차분하다 cha·bun·ha·da calm, cool
그는 차분하지만 단호한 목소리로 내게 말했다. geuneun chabunhajiman danhohan mok-soriro naege malhaetda. He spoke to me in a calm but firm voice.

태연하다 tae·yeon·ha·da calm, cool, nonchalant
그녀 앞에서 그의 가슴은 마구 뛰었지만, 그는 애써 태연한 척했다. geunyeo apeseo geuui gaseumeun magu ttwieotjiman, geuneun ae-sseo taeyeonhan cheokaetda. His heart was pounding as he stood in front of her, but he pretended to be calm.

눈도 깜짝 안 하다 nun·do kkam·jjak an ha·da to not blink an eye
어떻게 **눈도 깜짝 안 하고** 거짓말을 할 수가 있어? eotteoke nundo kkamjjak an hago geojin-mareul hal suga isseo? How could you lie so blatantly without batting an eyelid?

평온 | ~하다 pyeong·on | ~·ha·da tranquility, serenity | calm, peaceful
저는 아름답고 평온한 한 마을에서 태어났어요. jeoneun areumdapgo pyeongonhan han maeureseo taeeonasseoyo. I was born in a beautiful, tranquil village.

얌전하다 yam·jeon·ha·da gentle, mild
아이들이 참 얌전하네요. aideuri cham nyam-jeonhaneyo. Your kids are very well-behaved.

순하다 sun·ha·da gentle, mild
이 아기는 참 순하네. i agineun cham sunhane. This baby is so docile.

조용하다 jo·yong·ha·da silent, quiet
그는 밥 먹을 때만 조용하다. geuneun bam meogeul ttaemun joyonghada. He is quiet only while he is eating.

과묵하다 gwa·mu·ka·da reticent
그는 과묵한 사람이다. geuneun gwamukan sa-ramida. He is a man of few words.

점잖다 jeom·jan·ta gentle, decent
아버지는 아주 점잖은 분이셨어요. abeoji-neun aju jeomjaneun bunisyeosseoyo. My father was a gentleman.

무게를 잡다 mu·ge·reul jap·da to be serious
갑자기 왜 **무게를 잡고** 그래? **gapjagi wae mugereul japgo geurae?** Why are you suddenly so serious?

지혜롭다 ji·hye·rop·da wise
네가 이것을 **지혜롭게** 극복할 거라 믿어. **nega igeoseul jihyeropge geukbokal geora mideo.** I believe you'll overcome this with wisdom.

현명하다 hyeon·myeong·ha·da wise
그날 집에 있기로 한 것은 **현명한 선택**이었다. **geunal jibe itgiro han geoseun hyeonmyeonghan seontaegieotda.** It was wise that I chose to stay home on that day.

속(이) 깊다 sok(·i) gip·da to be mature and considerate
걔는 나이에 비해 **속이** 참 **깊은** 것 같아요. **gyaeneun naie bihae sogi cham gipeun geot gatayo.** He seems to be mature for his age.

유능하다 yu·neung·ha·da competent
회사의 미래는 **유능한 인재**에 달려 있습니다. **hoesaui miraeneun nyuneunghan injaee dallyeo itseumnida.** The future success of a company depends on having competent workers.

똑똑하다 ttok·tto·ka·da smart, clever
아드님이 참 똑똑하군요. **adeunimi cham ttokttokagunnyo.** Your son is really smart.

영리하다 yeong·ni·ha·da smart, clever

천재 cheon·jae genius
의심의 여지 없이 리오넬 메시는 축구 천재이다. **uisimui yeoji eopsi rionel mesineun chukgu cheonjaeida.** Undoubtedly Lionel Messi is a football genius.

융통성 yung·tong·seong flexibility
그는 그 문제를 **융통성** 있게 처리했다. **geuneun geu munjereul lyungtongseong itge cheorihaetda.** He dealt with the matter flexibly.

적극적 jeok·geuk·jeok active, aggressive
그 사람은 매사에 늘 적극적이다. **geu saraemeun maesae neul jeokgeukjeogida.** He is always aggressive in everything he does.

능동적 neung·dong·jeok active
리더가 되려면 **능동적인 성격**을 갖춰야 한다. **rideoga doeryeomyeon neungdongjeogin seonggyeogeul gatchwoya handa.** To become a leader, you have to develop an active personality.

긍정적 geung·jeong·jeok positive, affirmative
긍정적으로 생각하렴. **geungjeongjeogeuro saenggakaryeom.** Look on the bright side.

낙천적 nak·cheon·jeok optimistic
저는 미래에 대해 낙천적이에요. **jeoneun miraee daehae nakcheonjeogieyo.** I am optimistic about the future.

이성적 i·seong·jeok rational, reasonable
차분히 이성적으로 생각해 보세요. **chabunhi iseongjeogeuro saenggakae boseyo.** Stay calm. Think rationally.

논리적 nol·li·jeok logical
그것이 이 문제에 대한 유일한 **논리적 설명**이다. **geugeosi i munjee daehan nyuilhan nollijeok seolmyeongida.** It's the only logical explanation for this matter.

합리적 ham·ni·jeok rational, reasonable
그녀가 **합리적 선택**을 하리라 믿습니다. **geunyeoga hamnijeok seontaegeul harira mitseumnida.** I believe she will make a rational decision.

엉뚱하다 eong·ttung·ha·da unpredictable, strange
내 조카는 엉뚱한 구석이 많다. **nae jokaneun eongttunghan guseogi manta.** My nephew can be unpredictable.

비범하다 bi·beom·ha·da extraordinary
그녀는 글쓰기에 **비범한 재능**을 갖고 있다. **geunyeoneun geulsseugie bibeomhan jaeneungeul gatgo itda.** She has an extraordinary talent for writing.

평범하다 pyeong·beom·ha·da ordinary
더 이상은 평범하게 살고 싶지 않아요. **deo isangeun pyeongbeomhage salgo sipji anayo.** I don't want to live an ordinary life anymore.

용기 yong·gi courage
소영 씨에게 데이트 신청할 **용기가** 안 **나요.** **soyeong ssiege deiteu sincheonghal lyonggiga an nayo.** I have no courage to ask Soyoung out.

용감하다 yong·gam·ha·da brave, courageous
그런 말을 하다니 참 용감하구나. **geureon mareul hadani cham nyonggamhaguna.** You are so brave to say those things.

간(이) 크다 gan(·i) keu·da to be brave, be courageous

누나는 **간이 커서** 밤에도 혼자 잘 다녀요. nu-naneun gani keoseo bamedo honja jal danyeo-yo. My sister is confident enough to often go out alone at night.

Traditionally, 간 **gan**, the liver, was thought to regulate energy in the body. Accordingly, it is closely associated with courage in many Korean proverbs/idioms.

당당하다 dang·dang·ha·da confident, dignified
그 사람은 언제나 당당해 보인다. **geu sara-meun eonjena dangdanghae boinda.** He always looks confident.

어깨를 펴다 eo·kkae·reul pyeo·da to have confidence
넌 잘못한 게 없어. **어깨 펴고** 다녀. neon jal-motan ge eopseo. eokkae pyeogo danyeo. You did nothing wrong. Be confident.

활달하다 hwal·dal·ha·da outgoing, lively
그녀는 다른 십대 소녀들처럼 활달한 소녀였다. geunyeoneun dareun sipdae sonyeodeulcheo-reom hwaldalhan sonyeoyeotda. She was out-going, just like any other teenage girl.

씩씩하다 ssik·ssi·ka·da energetic, spirited
그는 천성적으로 씩씩한 소년이었다. geu-neun cheonseongjeogeuro ssikssikan sonyeo-nieotda. He was by nature a spirited boy.

명랑하다 ≒ 쾌활하다 myeong·nang·ha·da ≒ kwae·hwal·ha·da cheerful

활기 hwal·gi energy, vigor
정민이는 늘 **활기가 넘쳐**. jeongminineun neul hwalgiga neomchyeo. Jeonmin is always full of energy.

기가 살다 gi·ga sal·da to become confident
동생은 엄마 앞에서는 **기가 살아서** 자기 마음대로 해요. dongsaengeun eomma apeseoneun giga saraseo jagi maeumdaero haeyo. My younger brother is more confident when he is with mom and does whatever he wants.

느긋하다 neu·geu·ta·da relaxed, carefree
왜 나는 그냥 쉬면서 **느긋하게** 즐기면 안 되는 거야? wae naneun geunyang swimyeonseo neugeutage jeulgimyeon an doeneun geoya? Why can't I just relax and enjoy myself?

재미있다 jae·mi·it·da fun, entertaining
그는 아주 재미있는 사람이어서 좋은 아빠가

될 거야. geuneun aju jaemiinneun saramieoseo joeun appaga doel geoya. He'll be a fantastic dad because he is so funny.

유쾌하다 yu·kwae·ha·da happy, cheerful
아버지는 유쾌한 분이셔서 세상에 걱정이 없으세요. abeojineun nyukwaehan bunisyeoseo sesange geokjeongi eopseuseyo. My dad is a very cheerful man and nothing is too much trouble for him.

유머러스하다 yu·meo·reo·seu·ha·da humorous
저는 유머러스한 남자가 좋아요. jeoneun nyumeoreoseuhan namjaga joayo. I like men with a good sense of humor.

발휘 | ~하다 bal·hwi | ~·ha·da display, exhibition | to demonstrate, display
제가 스스로의 **능력을 발휘하지** 못했을 때 저 자신에게 화가 납니다. jega seuseuroui neung-nyeogeul balhwihaji motaesseul ttae jeo jasinege hwaga namnida. I get mad at myself when I don't perform to the best of my ability.

잘나다 jal·la·da good, distinguished
그 여자는 자기가 잘난 줄 알아. geu yeoja-neun jagiga jallan jul ara. She thinks she's an important person.

Note that the past tense 잘났다 **jallatda** is always used to describe someone who IS good. However, this is often meant sarcastically.

잘하다 jal·ha·da to do sth well
요리를 잘하는 여자가 제 이상형이에요. yori-reul jalhaneun nyeojaga je isanghyeongieyo. My ideal woman is one who cooks well.

위대하다 wi·dae·ha·da great
세종대왕은 한글을 만든 위대한 왕이었다. sejongdaewangeun hangeureul mandeun wi-daehan wangieotda. Sejong was a great king who invented the Korean alphabet.

영웅 yeong·ung hero, heroine
이순신 장군은 우리나라의 **국가적 영웅**이다. isunsin jangguneun urinaraui gukgajeok nyeon-gungida. Admiral Yi Sunshin is a national hero of Korea.

훌륭하다 hul·lyung·ha·da excellent, great, honorable
그녀는 **훌륭한** 교사다. geunyeoneun hul-lyunghan gyosada. She is a superb teacher.

탁월하다 ta·gwol·ha·da excellent, superior

그는 **탁월한 지도자**예요. geuneun tagwolhan jidojayeyo. He is an excellent leader.

* **뛰어나다** ttwi·eo·na·da outstanding, good
그녀는 우리 시대의 가장 **뛰어난 가수** 중 하나다. geunyeoneun uri sidaeui gajang ttwieonan gasu jung hanada. She is one of the most outstanding singers of our time.

* **우수하다** u·su·ha·da excellent, superb

* **둘째 가라면 서럽다** dul·jjae ga·ra·myeon seo·reop·da second to none
저는 운동에 있어서는 **둘째 가라면 서러운 사람**이에요. jeoneun undonge isseoseoneun duljjae garamyeon seoreoun saramieyo. I'm second to none at sports.

* **타고나다** ta·go·na·da to be gifted

그 사람은 **타고난 배우**야. geu sarameun tagonan baeuya. He is a gifted actor.

* **그릇이 크다** geu·reu·si keu·da to have great potential
이 아이는 제가 아는 누구보다 **그릇이** 큽니다. 커서 훌륭한 사람이 될 거예요. i aineun jega aneun nuguboda geureusi keumnida. keoseo hullyunghan sarami doel geoyeyo. This boy has greater potential than anyone I've ever seen. He will grow up to be a great man.

* **유명하다** yu·myeong·ha·da famous
저는 그 사람이 그렇게 **유명한** 축구 선수인지 몰랐어요. jeoneun geu sarami geureoke yumyeonghan chukgu seonsuinji mollasseoyo. I didn't know he was such a famous soccer player.

9.5 Negative Qualities

* **못되다** mot·doe·da bad, mean
너 정말 **못됐어**! neo jeongmal motdwaesseo! You are so mean!

> Note that the past tense 못됐다 **motdwaet-da** is always used to describe someone who IS mean.

* **나쁘다** na·ppeu·da bad, mean
그들은 소문만큼 **나쁜** 사람들은 아니다. geudeureun somunmankeum nappeun saramdeureun anida. They are not as bad as people say they are.

* **비열하다** bi·yeol·ha·da nasty, base
저는 여러분이 그의 **비열한 거짓말**을 꿰뚫어볼 수 있으리라 믿습니다. jeoneun nyeoreobuni geuui biyeolhan geojinmareul kkwettureobol su isseurira mitseumnida. I believe you'll see through his scummy lies.

* **비도덕적 ≒ 비윤리적** bi·do·deok·jeok ≒ bi·yul·li·jeok immoral, unethical
나는 의사가 자기 가족 중 누군가를 수술하는 것이 **비도덕적**이라고/**비윤리적**이라고 생각한다. naneun uisaga jagi gajok jung nugungareul susulhaneun geosi bidodeokjeogirago/biyullijeogirago saenggakanda. I think it is unethical for doctors to operate upon their family members.

* **비양심적** bi·yang·sim·jeok unscrupulous
몇몇 **비양심적**인 공무원들이 자신들의 지위를 이용해 뇌물을 받았음이 드러났다.

myeonmyeot biyangsimjeogin gongmuwondeuri jasindeurui jiwireul iyonghae noemureul badasseumi deureonatda. It turned out that a few unscrupulous officials had abused their positions and accepted bribes.

* **비인간적** bi·in·gan·jeok inhumane
사형 제도가 **비인간적**이라고 생각하는 사람들이 있다. sahyeong jedoga biinganjeogirago saenggakaneun saramdeuri itda. Some people believe the death penalty is inhumane.

* **비굴하다** bi·gul·ha·da servile, abject
비굴해지고 싶지 않아요. bigulhaejigo sipji anayo. I don't want to be servile.

* **비겁하다** bi·geo·pa·da cowardly
나는 **비겁하게** 말 한마디 하지 않았다. naneun bigeopage mal hanmadi haji anatda. I was too cowardly to say a word.

* **겁** geop fear, fright
겁이 나서 죽을 뻔했어요. geobi naseo jugeul ppeonhaesseoyo. I almost died from fear.

* **간이 작다** ga·ni jak·da to be cowardly
나는 **간이 작아서** 그런 일은 못 해. naneun gani jagaseo geureon ireun mo tae. I am not brave enough to do such a thing.

* **간이 콩알만 해지다** ga·ni kong·al·man hae·ji·da to be scared out of one's wits
지갑이 없어진 줄 알고 **간이 콩알만 해졌어요**. jigabi eopseojin jul algo gani kongalman haejyeosseoyo. I was scared out of my wits,

thinking I had lost my purse.

옹졸하다 ong·jol·ha·da narrow-minded, petty
그때를 돌아보면 나는 참 옹졸했다. geuttae-reul dorabomyeon naneun cham ongjolhaetda. When I look back on that time, I see that I was so narrow-minded.

못나다 mon·na·da stupid, foolish
오늘 **못난 소리**만 계속해서 미안해. oneul monnan soriman gyesokaeseo mianhae. I'm sorry I keep saying stupid things today.

> Note that the past tense 못났다 monnatda is always used to describe someone who IS stupid.

그릇이 작다 geu·reu·si jak·da to be a man of small capacity
그는 그 일을 맡기에는 **그릇이** 너무 **작아**. geuneun geu ireul matgieneun geureusi neomu jaga. He doesn't have what it takes to undertake the job.

속(이) 좁다 sok(·i) jop·da to be narrow-minded
그 사람 그렇게 **속이 좁은** 줄 몰랐어요. geu saram geureoke sogi jobeun jul mollasseoyo. I didn't know he was so narrow-minded.

편협하다 pyeon·hyeo·pa·da narrow-minded, prejudiced
그 정치인은 여성에 대한 **편협한 시각**을 드러냈다. geu jeongchiineun nyeoseonge daehan pyeonhyeopan sigageul deureonaetda. The politician was narrow-minded when it came to women.

까다롭다 kka·da·rop·da particular, fussy
왜 그렇게 **까다롭게** 구니? wae geureoke kkadaropge guni? Why are you being so difficult?

예민하다 ye·min·ha·da edgy, sensitive
어젯밤에 한숨도 못 자서 지금 **신경이** 좀 **예민해요**. eojetbame hansumdo mot jaseo jigeum singyeongi jom yeminhaeyo. I'm very sensitive today because I didn't sleep at all last night.

불친절하다 bul·chin·jeol·ha·da unkind, unfriendly

퉁명스럽다 tung·myeong·seu·reop·da abrupt, brusque
호텔 직원들은 다소 퉁명스럽고 불친절했다. hotel jigwondeureun daso tungmyeongseureopgo bulchinjeolhaetda. The staff at the hotel was somewhat brusque and unfriendly.

무뚝뚝하다 mu·ttuk·ttu·ka·da abrupt, brusque
그는 무뚝뚝한 것 같지만 알고 보면 재밌는 사람이다. geuneun muttukttukan geot gatjiman algo bomyeon jaeminneun saramida. Although he seems brusque, he's actually fun.

매정하다 mae·jeong·ha·da cold-hearted
그렇게 말씀하시다니 매정하시네요. geureoke malsseumhasidani maejeonghasineyo. It was heartless of you to say that.

냉정하다 naeng·jeong·ha·da cold-hearted, cold
예진이에게 도와 달라고 했는데 냉정하게 거절하더라. yejiniege dowa dallago haenneunde naengjeonghage geojeolhadeora. I asked Yejin for help, but she turned me down coldly.

쌀쌀맞다 ssal·ssal·mat·da cold, cool
왜 저를 **쌀쌀맞게** 대하셨어요? wae jeoreul ssalssalmatge daehaseosseoyo? Why did you give me the cold shoulder?

차갑다 cha·gap·da cold, cool
그녀는 **인상이 차갑지**만 그렇다고 나쁜 사람은 아니다. geunyeoneun insangi chagapjiman geureotago nappeun sarameun anida. She seems cold, but that doesn't mean she's a bad person.

독하다 do·ka·da spiteful; dogged, firm
그들은 독한 말을 서로 주고받았다. geudeureun dokan mareul seoro jugobadatda. They spat venomous words at each other.
아내는 독하게 다이어트 중이에요. anaeneun dokage daieoteu jungieyo. My wife is on a harsh diet.

피도 눈물도 없다 pi·do nun·mul·do eop·da to be cold-blooded
그 사람은 **피도 눈물도 없는** 인간이야. geu sarameun pido nunmuldo eomneun inganiya. He is cold-blooded.

엄(격)하다 eom(·gyeok)·ha·da strict, rigorous
저희 선생님은 아주 엄한 분이세요. jeohui seonsaengnimeun aju eomhan buniseyo. My teacher is very strict.

음흉하다 eum·hyung·ha·da wicked, evil
그는 음흉한 눈초리로 나를 쳐다보았다. geuneun eumhyunghan nunchoriro nareul chyeodaboatda. He gave me an evil glance.

약삭빠르다 ≒ **약다** yak·sak·ppa·reu·da ≒ yak·da clever, cunning

그녀는 음흉하고 약삭빠르다/약았다. **geu-nyeoneun eumhyunghago yaksakppareuda/ya-gatda.** She is sly and clever.

계산적 gye·san·jeok calculating
영화에서 그는 냉정하고 계산적인 인물을 연기했다. **yeonghwaeseo geuneun naeng-jeonghago gyesanjeogin inmureul yeongihaet-da.** In the film he portrayed a cold and calculating character.

척 = 체 | ~하다 cheok = che | ~·ha·da
pretense | to pretend
나는 그를 못 본 척했다/체했다. **naneun geureul mot bon cheokaetda/chehaetda.** I pretended not to see him.

잘난 척/체 좀 그만해. **jallan cheok/che jom geumanhae.** Stop putting on airs.

사치스럽다 sa·chi·seu·reop·da luxurious
복권에 당첨된 뒤 그는 **사치스러운 생활**을 했다. **bokgwone dangcheomdoen dwi geuneun sa-chiseureoun saenghwareul haetda.** After winning the lottery, he lived a life of luxury.

불성실하다 bul·seong·sil·ha·da faithless
그들은 그의 **불성실한** 근무 **태도**를 더 이상 참지 못하고 해고했다. **geudeureun geuui bul-seongsilhan geunmu taedoreul deo isang cham-ji motago haegohaetda.** They could no longer put up with his half-hearted attitude at work and fired him.

입만 살다 im·man sal·da all talk (and no action)
그 사람은 입만 살았어. **geu sarameun imman sarasseo.** He's all talk and no action.

무책임하다 mu·chae·gim·ha·da irresponsible
일이 끝나지 않았는데 가다니 자네 참 무책임하군. **iri kkeunnaji ananneunde gadani jane cham muchaegimhagun.** You're so irresponsible for leaving before the work is done.

게으르다 ge·eu·reu·da lazy, idle
게으른 건 여전하구나. **geeureun geon nyeo-jeonhaguna.** You are as lazy as ever.

나태하다 na·tae·ha·da lazy, idle, indolent
학창 시절에 나태했던 게 후회스러워요. **hakchang sijeore nataehaetdeon ge huhoeseu-reowoyo.** I regret having been idle during my school days.

손가락 하나 까딱하지 않다 son·ga·rak ha·na kka·tta·ka·ji an·ta to do nothing and idle away
남편은 주말에는 집에서 **손가락 하나 까딱 안해요.** nampyeoneun jumareneun jibeseo songa-rak hana kkattak an haeyo. My husband does not lift a finger when he's at home on weekends.

경솔하다 gyeong·sol·ha·da rash, hasty
그런 식으로 일을 그만둔 것은 **경솔한 짓**이었어요. **geureon sigeuro ireul geumandun geo-seun gyeongsolhan jisieosseoyo.** It was rash of you to quit your job like that.

입이 가볍다 i·bi ga·byeop·da to have a big mouth
그렇게 **입이 가벼운** 사람한테 비밀 얘기를 하는 게 아니었는데. **geureoke ibi gabyeoun saramhante bimil lyaegireul haneun ge ani-eonneunde.** I shoudn't have told my secret to such a big mouth.

안일하다 a·nil·ha·da lackadaisical
내 안일한 정신 상태 때문에 우리 계획이 틀어졌다. **nae anilhan jeongsin sangtae ttaemune uri gyehoegi teureojyeotda.** My lackadaisical state of mind attitude spoiled our plans.

간이 붓다 ga·ni but·da to be out of one's mind
선생님께 그런 말을 하다니 너 **간이 부었구나.** seonsaengnimkke geureon mareul hadani neo gani bueotguna. You must be out of your mind to say such a thing to your teacher.

마구 ≒ 막 ma·gu ≒ mak recklessly
그 사람의 문제는 돈을 **마구/막 쓴다는** 점이다. **geu saramui munjeneun doneul magu/mak sseundaneun jeomida.** His problem is that he spends money like water.

함부로 ham·bu·ro carelessly, rashly
함부로 말하지 마! hamburo malhaji ma! Don't talk carelessly.

둔하다 dun·ha·da slow, stupid, dense
나는 둔해서 상황이 어떻게 돌아가는지 몰랐다. **naneun dunhaeseo sanghwangi eotteoke doraganeunji mollatda.** I was too dense to understand what was going on.

급하다 geu·pa·da impatient, rash
저는 **성격이** 아주 **급해서** 줄을 서서 기다리는 걸 싫어해요. **jeoneun seonggyeogi aju geupae-seo jureul seoseo gidarineun geol sireohaeyo.** I'm very impatient and hate waiting in line.

덜렁대다 = 덜렁거리다 deol·leong·dae·da = deol·leong·geo·ri·da careless
덜렁대지/덜렁거리지 좀 마. **deolleongdaeji**

deolleonggeoriji jom ma. Stop being so careless.

수다스럽다 su·da·seu·reop·da talkative
저는 수다스러운 남자를 안 좋아해요. **jeoneun sudaseureoun namjareul an joahaeyo.** I don't like talkative men.

·········

오만하다 ≒ 거만하다 o·man·ha·da ≒ geo·man·ha·da arrogant, proud
나는 그의 오만함을/거만함을 참을 수가 없었다. **naneun geuui omanhameul/geomanhameul chameul suga eopseotda.** I couldn't bear his arrogance.
그 여자는 사람들에게 **거만한 태도로** 지시를 하고는 했다. **geu yeojaneun saramdeurege geomanhan taedoro jisireul hagoneun haetda.** She used to command people to do things in an arrogant manner.

어깨에 힘(을) 주다 = 목에 힘(을) 주다 eo·kkae·e him(·eul) ju·da = mo·ge him(·eul) ju·da to be arrogant, be in high spirits
그 사람은 딸이 검사라고 **어깨에/목에 힘을** 주고 다녀. **geu sarameun ttari geomsarago eokkaee/moge himeul jugo danyeo.** He goes around boasting that his daughter is a prosecutor.

건방지다 geon·bang·ji·da arrogant, impudent
내가 뭘 해야 할지 건방지게 나한테 가르치려 드는 거냐? **naega mwol haeya halji geonbangjige nahante gareuchiryeo deuneun geonya?** How dare you tell me what should and shouldn't I do?

버릇없다 beo·reu·deop·da ill-mannered, ill-behaved
요즘에는 버릇없는 애들이 많아요. **yojeumeneun beoreudeomneun aedeuri manayo.** Children these days have no manners at all.

무례 | ~하다 mu·rye | ~·ha·da rudeness, disrespect | impolite, rude
제 말이 무례했다면 사과드립니다. **je mari muryehaetdamyeon sagwadeurimnida.** I apologize if that sounded rude.

뻔뻔하다 = 뻔뻔스럽다 ppeon·ppeon·ha·da = ppeon·ppeon·seu·reop·da shameless, brazen
여기 다시 나타나다니 참 **뻔뻔하구나/뻔뻔스럽구나! yeogi dasi natanadani cham ppeonppeonhaguna/ppeonppeonseureopguna!** You have a lot of nerve to show up here again!

얼굴이 두껍다 eol·gu·ri du·kkeop·da to be shameless
나한테 돈을 꾸러 오다니 참 **얼굴도 두껍다. nahante doneul kkureo odani cham eolguldo dukkeopda.** You're so shameless. How dare you come to borrow money from me?

·········

멍청하다 meong·cheong·ha·da stupid, foolish
그 말을 믿을 만큼 제가 멍청하지는 않습니다. **geu mareul mideul mankeum jega meongcheonghajineun anseumnida.** I'm not so stupid as to believe that.

머리가 모자라다 meo·ri·ga mo·ja·ra·da to be short on brains
그는 좋은 사람이지만 **머리가 좀 모자라요. geuneun joeun saramijiman meoriga jom mojarayo.** He is a nice person but short on brains.

머리가 비다 meo·ri·ga bi·da to be empty-headed
그 여자는 예쁘게는 생겼는데 **머리가 비었다. geu yeojaneun yeppeugeneun saenggyeonneunde meoriga bieotda.** She's got the looks, but she's empty-headed.

어리석다 ≒ 미련하다 eo·ri·seok·da ≒ mi·ryeon·ha·da foolish, absurd
네가 그의 제안을 받아들인 건 **어리석은/미련한 짓이었어. nega geuui jeaneul badadeurin geon eoriseogeun/miryeonhan jisieosseo.** It was foolish of you to accept his offer.

바보 ba·bo fool, idiot
바보 같은 짓 하지 마. babo gateun jit haji ma. Don't be a fool.

귀가 얇다 gwi·ga yal·da to be easily influenced by what others say
당신은 **귀가** 너무 **얇아요. dangsineun gwiga neomu yalbayo.** You are too easily influenced by what people say.

고집 | ~스럽다 go·jip | ~·seu·reop·da stubbornness | stubborn
고집 부리지 마라. gojip buriji mara. Stop being stubborn.

억지 | ~스럽다 eok·ji | ~·seu·reop·da stubbornness | stubborn
그 여자는 왕왕 말도 안 되는 **억지를 쓴다. geu yeojaneun wangwang maldo an doeneun eokjireul sseunda.** She often makes ridiculous demands.

떼 tte tantrum

고지식하다 go·ji·si·ka·da inflexible
그 여자는 좀 고지식한 편이에요. **geu yeoja-neun jom gojisikan pyeonieyo.** She tends to go by the book.

앞뒤가 막히다 ap·dwi·ga ma·ki·da to be narrow-minded, be stubborn
우리 아버지는 **앞뒤가 꽉 막힌** 분이에요. **uri abeojineun apdwiga kkwak makin bunieyo.** My father is so narrow-minded and inflexible.

....

소극적 so·geuk·jeok passive
그 기업은 시장의 변화에 소극적으로 대처하다 도산하고 말았다. **geu gieobeun sijangui byeonhwae sogeukjeogeuro daecheohada dosanhago maratda.** The company dealt with the market changes passively and this led to its bankruptcy.

수동적 su·dong·jeok passive
수동적으로 일하지 마라. **sudongjeogeuro il-haji mara.** Don't be a passive worker!

부정적 bu·jeong·jeok negative
긍정적으로 생각하는 것보다 부정적으로 생각하는 것이 훨씬 더 쉽다. **geungjeongjeogeuro saenggakaneun geotboda bujeongjeogeuro saenggakaneun geosi hwolssin deo swipda.** It is much easier to think negatively than positively.

비관적 bi·gwan·jeok pessimistic
저는 삶을 비관적으로 바라보는 사람들의 입장을 이해합니다. **jeoneun salmeul bigwanjeogeuro baraboneun saramdeurui ipjangeul ihaehamnida.** I can understand those who have a pessimistic view on life.

냉소적 naeng·so·jeok cynical, sarcastic
그는 사랑과 관계에 대해 냉소적이다. **geuneun saranggwa gwangyee daehae naengsojeogida.** He is cynical about love and relationships.

감정적 gam·jeong·jeok emotional
나는 감정적인 사람보다는 이성적인 사람이 좋아. **naneun gamjeongjeogin sarambodaneun iseongjeogin sarami joa.** I like a reasonable person more than an emotional person.

재미없다 jae·mi·eop·da boring, dull
은하는 착하지만 재미없는 사람이다. **eunhaneun chakajiman jaemieomneun saramida.** Eunha is kind but boring.

따분하다 tta·bun·ha·da boring, dull
고리타분하다 = 고루하다 go·ri·ta·bun·ha·da = go·ru·ha·da stuffy, old-fashioned
왜 대부분의 어른들이 그렇게 고리타분한지/고루한지 이해가 안 돼. **wae daebubunui eoreundeuri geureoke goritabunhanji/goruhanji ihaega an dwae.** I don't understand why most grown-ups are so obstinate.

....

무능하다 mu·neung·ha·da incompetent, incapable
그 자신을 빼고 모두들 그가 무능하다고 생각했다. **geu jasineul ppaego modudeul geuga muneunghadago saenggakaetda.** Everyone but himself thought he was incompetent.

못하다 mo·ta·da to be poor at
저는 노래를 못해요. **jeoneun noraereul motaeyo.** I am poor at singing.

서투르다 = 서툴다 seo·tu·reu·da = seo·tul·da poor at, unskilled
제가 젓가락질이 좀 서툴러요. **jega jeotgarakjiri jom seotulleoyo.** I'm poor at using chopsticks.

간섭 감사 거절 거짓말 거참 걸다 경고 고집

고함 고함치다 구박 군 권유 글쎄 금하다 꺼대다

까어들다 논의 논쟁 놀리다 대들다 더듬다 덕분

들어주다 떠들다 말 말없이 말투 맹세 무슨

바람에 발언 발표 보고 복 부정 비난 비명

거리다 사양 삼가다 설득 설명 세상에 소개 소리

다 속삭이다 수고 쉬 승낙 시인 시키다 신청

chapter **10** Speaking

안녕 암시 애원 야 야유 약속 어떠하다

떡하다 어찌 언급 얼버무리다 예 예언 왜 욕 우기다

원 위로 유머 음 응 의문 이르다 이야기

성 제시 제안 죄송하다 주장 지껄이다 지적

질문 찬성추천 충고 탓 통보 투정 트집 폭로

항의 험담 혼나다 혼잣말 환영 횡설수설

10.1 Talking

말 | ~하다 mal | ~·ha·da word, speech | to say, speak
이거 내가 말했다고 아무한테도 말하지 마. **igeo naega malhaetdago amuhantedo malhaji ma.** Don't tell anyone I told you this.

말씀 | ~하다 mal·sseum | ~·ha·da honorific of 말 mal | honorific of 말하다
진작 말씀하시지 그러셨어요. **jinjak malsseumhasiji geureosyeosseoyo.** You should have said it earlier.

발언 | ~하다 ba·reon | ~·ha·da comment, remark | to make a comment
그의 **경솔한 발언**이 모두를 화나게 했다. **geuui gyeongsolhan bareoni modureul hwanage haetda.** His careless remarks made everybody angry.

높임말 = 경어 = 존댓말 no·pim·mal = gyeong·eo = jon·daen·mal honorific
아이들은 어른들에게 **높임말을/경어를/존댓말을 써야** 합니다. **aideureun eoreundeurege nopimmareul/gyeongeoreul/jondaenmareul sseoya hamnida.** Children should use honorifics when speaking to their elders.

반말 | ~하다 ban·mal | ~·ha·da familiar forms of words | to talk down to
반말하지 마세요. **banmalhaji maseyo.** Don't talk down to me.

말(을) 놓다 mal(·eul) no·ta to talk using familiar forms
우리 나이가 같은데 **말 놓을까요**? **uri naiga gateunde mal loeulkkayo?** Since we're the same age, why don't we speak more casually?

언급 | ~하다 eon·geup | ~·ha·da mention | to mention
그 문제는 다시 언급하지 않기로 하자. **geu munjeneun dasi eongeupaji ankiro haja.** Let's not mention it again.

한마디 han·ma·di a word
그녀는 말 **한마디 없이** 밥만 먹었다. **geunyeoneun mal hanmadi eopsi bamman meogeotda.** She ate without saying a word.

소위 = 이른바 so·wi = i·reun·ba so-called
소위/이른바 유기농 식품에 대한 관심이 점점 커지고 있다. **sowi/ireunba yuginong sikpume daehan gwansimi jeomjeom keojigo itda.** There

has been an increasing interest in so-called organic products.

말하자면 = 이를테면 mal·ha·ja·myeon = i·reul·te·myeon so to speak, as it were
최 박사님은 말하자면/이를테면 걸어다니는 사전이에요. **choe baksanimeun malhajamyeon/ireultemyeon georeodanineun sajeonieyo.** Dr. Choi is, so to speak, a walking dictionary.

말투 mal·tu way of speaking
나는 그 사람 말투가 마음에 안 들어. **naneun geu saram maltuga maeume an deureo.** I don't like his way of speaking.

유창하다 yu·chang·ha·da fluent
그 사람은 영어가 유창해요. **geu sarameun nyeongeoga yuchanghaeyo.** He speaks English fluently.

어눌하다 eo·nul·ha·da inarticulate

말없이 ma·reop·si silently, without a word
그녀는 말없이 듣고만 있었다. **geunyeoneun mareopsi deutgoman isseotda.** She was listening without saying a word.

침묵 | ~하다 chim·muk | ~·ha·da silence | to be silent
침묵은 금이다. **chimmugeun geumida.** Silence is golden.

닥치다 ≒ 다물다 dak·chi·da ≒ da·mul·da (offensive) to shut up
입 닥쳐/다물어! **ip dakchyeo/damureo!** Shut up!

발표 | ~하다 bal·pyo | ~·ha·da announcement, presentation | to make public, present
우승자는 다음 달에 발표됩니다. **useungjaneun daeum dare balpyodoemnida.** The winner will be announced next month.

강연 | ~하다 gang·yeon | ~·ha·da lecture, speech | to deliver a lecture or speech
강연 잘 들었습니다. **gangyeon jal deureotseumnida.** I enjoyed your speech.

연설 | ~하다 yeon·seol | ~·ha·da speech, address | to give a speech, address
대통령의 연설은 유머가 가득했다. **daetongnyeongui yeonseoreun nyumeoga gadeukaetda.** The President's speech was full of humor.

선언 | ~하다 seo·neon | ~·ha·da announcement, declaration | to announce, declare
이로써 올림픽의 **개막을 선언합니다.** irosseo ollimpigui gaemageul seoneonhamnida. I hereby declare the opening of the Olympic Games.

대화 | ~하다 dae·hwa | ~·ha·da talk, conversation | to talk, converse
오랜 **대화** 끝에 그들은 헤어지기로 결정했다. oraen daehwa kkeute geudeureun heeojigiro gyeoljeonghaetda. After a long talk, they decided to break up.

회화 hoe·hwa talk, conversation
이번 방학 기간에 **영어 회화**를 정복하고 싶어요. ibeon banghak gigane yeongeo hoehwareul jeongbokago sipeoyo. I'd like to master English conversation for this vacation.

화제 hwa·je topic of conversation
야구가 우리 대화의 **주된 화제**였다. yaguga uri daehwaui judoen hwajeyeotda. Baseball was the major topic of our conversation.

도마 위에 오르다 do·ma wi·e o·reu·da to be in the hot seat
그 배우가 홈페이지에 남긴 글이 **도마 위에** 올라 있어요. geu baeuga hompeijie namgin geuri doma wie olla isseoyo. The actor's post on his website became the subject of controversy.

This expression is used when you are receiving criticism like a fish being sliced up on the cutting board.

이야기 = 얘기 | ~하다 i·ya·gi = yae·gi | ~·ha·da story, talk | to talk, tell
아무한테도 **이야기하지/얘기하지** 마. amuhantedo iyagihaji/yaegihaji ma. Don't tell anyone.

옛날이야기 = 옛날얘기 yen·nal·li·ya·gi = yen·nal·lyae·gi old story

들려주다 deul·lyeo·ju·da to tell, let sb hear
내가 어렸을 때 할머니는 자주 **옛날이야기를 들려주셨다.** naega eoryeosseul ttae halmeonineun jaju yennariyagireul deullyeojusyeotda. When I was little, my grandmother often used to tell me stories about the past.

걸다 geol·da to speak, talk
아까 길에서 외국인이 **말을 걸어** 와서 당황했어요. akka gireseo oegugini mareul georeo waseo danghwanghaesseoyo. I was embarrassed when a foreigner struck up a conversation with me on the street a while ago.

꺼내다 kkeo·nae·da to bring up, raise
그 주제를 **꺼내는** 목적이 뭡니까? geu jujereul kkeonaeneun mokjeogi mwomnikka? What's the purpose of bringing up that topic?

수다 su·da chatter

떨다 tteol·da to have (a chat)
그들은 전화로 몇 시간이고 **수다를 떨었다.** geudeureun jeonhwaro myeot siganigo sudareul tteoreotda. They chatted on the phone for hours.

잡담 | ~하다 jap·dam | ~·ha·da chat, chatter | to chat, chatter
사람들은 너무 많은 시간을 잡담으로 허비하는 경향이 있다. saramdeureun neomu maneun siganeul japdameuro heobihaneun gyeonghyangi itda. People tend to waste too much time chatting.

지껄이다 ji·kkeo·ri·da (offensive) to chat
그 녀석 또 **헛소리를 지껄이고** 있어. geu nyeoseok tto heotsorireul jikkeorigo isseo. He's talking a load of crap again!

진담 jin·dam serious talk
그 말 **진담**이야? geu mal jindamiya? Are you serious?

농담 | ~하다 nong·dam | ~·ha·da joke | to joke, kid
농담이야. nongdamiya. Just kidding.

유머 yu·meo humor, wit
정수는 **유머 감각**이 뛰어나서 사람들에게 인기가 많아요. jeongsuneun nyumeo gamgagi ttwieonaseo saramdeurege ingiga manayo. Jeongsu has a great sense of humor and that's why he is so popular with people.

비밀 bi·mil secret
비밀 지킬 수 있어? bimil jikil su isseo? Can you keep a secret?

고백 | ~하다 go·baek | ~·ha·da confession | to confess
고백할 게 있는데요, 사랑합니다. gobaekal ge inneundeyo, saranghamnida. I have a confession to make—I love you.

털어놓다 teo·reo·no·ta to confess, disclose
솔직히 **털어놓는** 게 어때? soljiki teoreonon-

neun ge eottae? Why can't you be honest with me?

입 밖에 내다 ip ba·kke nae·da to disclose, reveal

이 일을 **입 밖에 내면** 큰일 난다. i ireul ip bakke naemyeon keunil landa. If you don't keep your mouth shut about this, we'll be in big trouble.

떠들다 tteo·deul·da to chat, make noise

수업 시간에 떠들지 마라. sueop sigane tteodeulji mara. Don't talk during class.

소곤거리다 = 소곤대다 so·gon·geo·ri·da = so·gon·dae·da to whisper

너희 둘 뭘 그렇게 소곤거리고/소곤대고 있어? neohui dul mwol geureoke sogongeorigo/sogondaego isseo? What are you two whispering about?

속삭이다 sok·sa·gi·da to whisper

그들은 속삭이듯 말했다. geudeureun soksagideut malhaetda. They talked in a whisper.

중얼거리다 = 중얼대다 jung·eol·geo·ri·da = jung·eol·dae·da to mutter, murmur

그는 알아들을 수 없는 말을 중얼거렸다/중얼댔다. geuneun aradeureul su eomneun mareul jungeolgeoryeotda/jungeoldaetda. He muttered something unintelligible.

혼잣말 | ~하다 hon·jan·mal | ~·ha·da talking to oneself | to talk to oneself

저는 가끔 혼잣말을 하는 습관이 있어요. jeoneun gakkeum honjanmareul haneun seupgwani isseoyo. I have a habit of talking to myself.

더듬다 deo·deum·da to stutter, stammer

저는 어릴 때 말을 심하게 더듬었어요. jeoneun eoril ttae mareul simhage deodeumeosseoyo. When I was little, I stammered badly.

얼버무리다 eol·beo·mu·ri·da to hedge

얼버무리지 말고 분명히 대답해라. eolbeomuriji malgo bunmyeonghi daedapaera. Stop mumbling. Answer clearly.

헛소리 | ~하다 heot·so·ri | ~·ha·da nonsense | to talk nonsense

헛소리 그만해! heotsori geumanhae! Cut the crap!

횡설수설 | ~하다 hoeng·seol·su·seol | ~·ha·da nonsense | to talk nonsense

횡설수설하지 말고 핵심을 말해. hoengseolsuseolhaji malgo haeksimeul malhae. Stop meandering and get to the point.

말(을) 돌리다 mal(·eul) dol·li·da to beat around the bush

말 돌리지 말고 핵심을 말해 봐. mal dolliji malgo haeksimeul malhae bwa. Stop beating around the bush and get to the point.

거짓말 | ~하다 geo·jin·mal | ~·ha·da lie | to lie

내가 자기한테 거짓말한 걸 알면 나를 더 미워할 텐데. naega jagihante geojinmalhan geol almyeon nareul deo miwohal tende. If she finds out that I lied to her, she is going to hate me even more.

변명 | ~하다 byeon·myeong | ~·ha·da excuse, justification | to give an excuse

늦은 데 대한 변명이 필요한데. neujeun de daehan byeonmyeongi piryohande. I need an excuse for being late.

핑계 ping·gye excuse, pretext

그녀는 아프다는 핑계를 대고 결근했다. geunyeoneun apeudaneun pinggyereul daego gyeolgeunhaetda. She was absent from work on the pretext of being sick.

소설(을) 쓰다 so·seol(·eul) sseu·da to make up story

소설 좀 그만 써. soseol jom geuman sseo. Stop making up stories.

얼굴에 씌어 있다 eol·gu·re ssui·eo it·da to be written all over one's face

거짓말하지 마. 얼굴에 다 씌어 있어. geojinmalhaji ma. eolgure da ssuieo iseo. Don't lie. It's written all over your face.

장담 | ~하다 jang·dam | ~·ha·da assurance, guarantee | to assure

100퍼센트 장담합니다. baekpeosenteu jangdamhamnida. I'm 100 percent sure.

큰소리 keun·so·ri big talk

큰소리치다 keun·so·ri·chi·da to talk big

그는 큰소리쳤지만 아무것도 안 했다. geuneun keunsorichyeotjiman amugeotdo an haetda. He talked big but did nothing.

과장 | ~하다 gwa·jang | ~·ha·da exaggeration | to exaggerate

그가 천재라는 말은 결코 과장이 아니다. geuga cheonjaeraneun mareun gyeolko gwajangi anida. It is no exaggeration to say that he is a genius.

허풍 heo·pung brag, bluff

걔는 허풍이 심해. gyaeneun heopungi simhae. He's full of hot air.

소문 so·mun rumor, gossip
네가 회사를 그만두었다는 소문을 들었어. nega hoesareul geumandueotdaneun somuneul deureosseo. Rumor has it that you left the company.

소리치다 so·ri·chi·da to shout, yell
나는 누군가 도와달라고 소리치는 것을 들었다. naneun nugunga dowadallago sorichineun geoseul deureotda. I heard someone shouting for help.

외치다 oe·chi·da to shout, yell
시위자들은 정부 정책에 반대하는 구호를 외쳤다. siwijadeureun jeongbu jeongchaege bandaehaneun guhoreul oechyeotda. The protesters shouted slogans against government policy.

고함 go·ham shout, yell

고함치다 go·ham·chi·da to shout, yell
왜 나한테 고함치고 그래? wae nahante gohamchigo geurae? Why are you yelling at me?

비명 bi·myeong scream, shriek
아파서 비명을 지를 뻔했어요. apaseo bimyeongeul jireul ppeonhaesseoyo. I almost shouted out in pain.

지르다 ji·reu·da to shout, yell
공공장소에서 소리 지르지 마. gonggongjang-soeseo sori jireuji ma. Don't yell in public.

부르다 bu·reu·da to call
나 불렀어? na bulleosseo? Did you call me?

10.2 Titles, Greetings, Showing Gratitude, Apologizing

씨 ssi Mr., Ms.

군 gun Mr.

양 yang Miss

군 and 양 are used for people who are much younger than you.

인사 | ~하다 in·sa | ~·ha·da greeting | to greet
이제 작별 인사를 해야 할 것 같아. ije jakbyeol insareul haeya hal geot gata. I'm afraid I must say goodbye.

(큰·)절 | ~하다 (keun·)jeol | ~·ha·da deep bow | to bow deeply
추석 때 아이들은 할아버지, 할머니께 큰절을 한다. chuseok ttae aideureun harabeoji, halmeonikke keunjeoreul handa. Children bow deeply to their grandparents on Chuseok.

안녕 | ~하다 | ~히 an·nyeong | ~·ha·da | ~·hi hi, hello (familiar form) | to be fine | peacefully
소영 씨, 안녕하세요? soyeong ssi, annyeong-haseyo? Soyoung, hello?
안녕히 계세요. annyeonghi gyeseyo. Goodbye.
안녕히 가세요. annyeonghi gaseyo. Goodbye.

반갑다 ban·gap·da glad, happy
만나서 반갑습니다. mannaseo bangapseum-nida. Nice to meet you.

뵙다 = 뵈다 boep·da = boe·da to see, meet
처음 뵙겠습니다. cheoeum boepgetseumnida. Nice to meet you.

소개 | ~하다 so·gae | ~·ha·da introduction | to introduce
제 소개를 하겠습니다. je sogaereul hagetseumnida. Let me introduce myself.

별일 byeol·lil big deal, particular thing
별일 없으시죠? byeollil eopseusijyo? Is everything all right?

덕분 = 덕택 deok·bun = deok·taek thanks to, due to
덕분에/덕택에 잘 지냅니다. deokbune/deok-taege jal jinaemnida. I'm doing well.

안부 an·bu regards
부모님께 안부 전해 주세요. bumonimkke anbu jeonhae juseyo. Please say hello to your parents for me.

환영 | ~하다 hwa·nyeong | ~·ha·da welcome | to welcome
환영합니다! hwanyeonghamnida! Welcome!

축하 | ~하다 chu·kha | ~·ha·da congratulation | to congratulate
생일 축하해! saengil chukhahae! Happy Birthday!

복 bok luck
새해 복 많이 받으세요. saehae bok mani badeuseyo. Happy New Year!

감사 | ~하다 gam·sa l ~·ha·da thanks | to thank
도와주셔서 감사합니다. **dowajusyeoseo gam-sahamnida.** Thank you for helping me.

고맙다 go·map·da thankful
정말 고맙다. **jeongmal gomapda.** Thank you so much.

> 감사하다 and 고맙다 are the two main expressions showing thankfulness. They are mostly interchangeable, but when you use 반말 **banmal** (casual speech) only 고맙다 is used.

뭘 = 천만에 mwol = cheon·ma·ne don't mention it
A: 고마워요. B: 뭘요/천만에요. **A: goma-woyo. B: mwollyo/cheonmaneyo.** A: Thank you. B: Don't mention it.

수고 | ~하다 su·go l ~·ha·da trouble, effort | to take the trouble
수고 많으셨어요. **sugo maneusyeosseoyo.** Thank you for the hard work.

사과 | ~하다 sa·gwa l ~·ha·da apology | to apologize
나는 내가 한 일에 대해 사과하고 싶지 않아. **naneun naega han ire daehae sagwahago sipji ana.** I don't want to apologize for what I've done.

미안하다 mi·an·ha·da sorry
늦어서 미안해. **neujeoseo mianhae.** I'm sorry I'm late.

죄송하다 joe·song·ha·da sorry
방해해서 죄송합니다. **banghaehaeseo joe-songhamnida.** I'm sorry to disturb you.

> 죄송하다 sounds more polite and formal than 미안하다.

실례 | ~하다 sil·lye l ~·ha·da discourtesy | to excuse
잠시 실례하겠습니다. **jamsi sillyehagetseum-nida.** Excuse me for a moment.

괜찮다 gwaen·chan·ta fine, okay
괜찮아요. **gwaenchanayo.** I'm okay.

10.3 Questioning, Answering

묻다 mut·da to ask
더 이상 묻지 마. **deo isang mutji ma.** No more questions.

여쭈다 = 여쭙다 yeo·jju·da = yeo·jjup·da humble word of 묻다 **mutda**
하나만 여쭤 봐도 될까요? **hanaman nyeojjwo bwado doelkkayo?** Can I ask you a question?

물어보다 mu·reo·bo·da to ask
뭐 좀 물어볼 게 있는데. **mwo jom mureobol ge inneunde.** I have a question for you.

문의 | ~하다 mu·nui l ~·ha·da inquiry | to inquire
문의할 사항이 있으시면 제 비서에게 연락 주세요. **munuihal sahangi isseusimyeon je bi-seoege yeollak juseyo.** For more information, please contact my assistant.

질문 | ~하다 jil·mun l ~·ha·da question | to ask a question
제 질문이 바로 그겁니다. **je jilmuni baro geugeomnida.** That's what I'm asking you.

물음 mu·reum question
그녀는 내 물음에 답하지 않았다. **geunyeo-** neun nae mureume dapaji anatda. She didn't answer my question.

의문 ui·mun doubt, question
의문 나는 점이 있으시면 질문하세요. **uimun naneun jeomi isseusimyeon jilmunhaseyo.** If you have any questions, just ask.

누구 nu·gu who, whom
실례지만 전화 거신 분은 누구세요? **sillyeji-man jeonhwa geosin buneun nuguseyo?** May I ask who's calling, please?

누가 nu·ga who (shortened form of 누구가 **nuguga**)
이 소설 누가 썼지? **i soseol luga sseotji?** Who wrote this novel?

언제 eon·je when
언제 시간 되세요? **eonje sigan doeseyo?** When are you free?

어디 eo·di where
어디 가세요? **eodi gaseyo?** Where are you going?

무엇 = 뭐 mu·eot = mwo what

궁금한 게 있으면 무엇이든/뭐든 물어보세요. **gunggeumhan ge isseumyeon mueosideun/mwodeun mureoboseyo.** Feel free to ask me if you have any questions.

무슨 mu·seun what, what kind of
그게 무슨 뜻이야? **geuge museun tteusiya?** What do you mean?

어느 eo·neu which, what
어느 것이 더 좋으세요? **eoneu geosi deo joeuseyo?** Which one do you prefer?

어떤 eo·tteon which, what, how
어떤 색깔을 찾고 계세요? **eotteon saekkkareul chatgo gyeseyo?** What color are you looking for?

웬 wen what
웬 소란이야? **wen soraniya?** What's this commotion about?

어떻게 eo·tteo·ke how, what
어떻게 해야 할지 모르겠어요. **eotteoke haeya halji moreugesseoyo.** I don't know what to do.

어찌 eo·jji how, why
어찌 된 일이야? **eojji doen iriya?** What happened?

얼마나 eol·ma·na how
한국에 온 지 얼마나 됐어요? **hanguge on ji eolmana dwaesseoyo?** How long have you been in Korea?

왜 wae why
왜 그렇게 생각해? **wae geureoke saenggakae?** Why do you think so?

어째서 eo·jjae·seo how come
어째서 오늘 학교에 안 간 거니? **eojjaeseo oneul hakgyoe an gan geoni?** How come you didn't go to school today?

웬일 wen·nil what matter, what reason
웬일로 이렇게 일찍 일어났어? **wenillo ireoke iljjik ireonasseo?** Why did you get up so early?

(도)대체 (do·)dae·che on earth, in the world
도대체 무슨 말이야? **dodaeche museun mariya?** What on earth are you talking about?

하필 ha·pil why of all things
왜 하필 일요일에 비가 오는 거야? **wae hapil iryoire biga oneun geoya?** Why does it always rain on Sunday of all days?

어떠하다 = 어떻다 eo·tteo·ha·da = eo·tteo·ta how

요즘 몸은 좀 어때요? **yojeum momeun jom eottaeyo?** How do you feel these days?

어떡하다 eo·tteo·ka·da what to do
시험에서 떨어지면 나 어떡하지? **siheomeseo tteoreojimyeon na eotteokaji?** What should I do if I fail the exam?

그렇지 geu·reo·chi right?
농담이지, 그렇지? **nongdamiji, geureochi?** You are kidding, right?

(대)답 | ~하다 (dae·)dap | ~·ha·da answer, reply | to answer, reply
그건 그 사람이 대답할 수 없는 질문이야. **geugeon geu sarami daedapal su eomneun jilmuniya.** It's a question he couldn't answer.

답변 | ~하다 dap·byeon | ~·ha·da answer, reply | to answer, reply
신속한 답변을 주시면 고맙겠습니다. **sinsokan dapbyeoneul jusimyeon gomapgetseumnida.** We'd appreciate your quick reply.

응답 | ~하다 eung·dap | ~·ha·da answer, reply | to answer, reply
대부분의 사람들이 새 법률에 반대한다고 응답했다. **daebubunui saramdeuri sae beomnyure bandaehandago eungdapaetda.** Most people answered by saying that they were opposed to the new law.

(말)대꾸 | ~하다 (mal·)dae·kku | ~·ha·da back talk | to talk back
어른한테 말대꾸하지 마라. **eoreunhante maldaekkuhaji mara.** Don't talk back to your elders.

인정 | ~하다 in·jeong | ~·ha·da acknowledgment, approval | to admit, concede
그녀는 절대로 자신의 실수를 인정하지/시인하지 않는다. **geunyeoneun jeoldaero jasinui silsureul injeonghaji/siinhaji anneunda.** She never admits a mistake.

시인 | ~하다 si·in | ~·ha·da acknowledgment, approval | to admit, concede

긍정 | ~하다 geung·jeong | ~·ha·da affirmation | to affirm, acknowledge
그는 그 진술을 부정도 긍정도 하지 않았다. **geuneun geu jinsureul bujeongdo geungjeongdo haji anatda.** He neither denied nor affirmed the statement.

부정 ≒ 부인 | ~하다 bu·jeong ≒ bu·in | ~·ha·da denial | to deny
그것은 부정할/부인할 수 없는 사실이다. **geugeoseun bujeonghal/buinhal su eomneun sasirida.** It cannot be denied.

그래 geu·rae yes, OK
나도 그래. **nado geurae.** Yes, me too.

그럼 geu·reom sure, exactly
A: 올 거야? B: 그럼! **A: ol geoya? B: geureom!** A: Will you come? B: Sure.

응 = 어 eung = eo yes (familiar form)
A: 너도 갈래? B: 응/어, 그래. **A: neodo gallae? B: eung/eo, geurae.** A: You want to join us? B: Sure.

물론 mul·lon of course
A: 나랑 결혼해 줄래? B: 그럼, 물론이지. **A: narang gyeolhonhae jullae? B: geureom, mulloniji.** A: Will you marry me? B: Yes, of course.

당연하다 | 당연히 dang·yeon·ha·da | dang·yeon·hi natural, reasonable, of course | of course, absolutely
A: 축구 좋아하세요? B: 당연하죠! **A: chukgu joahaseyo? B: dangyeonhajyo!** A: Do you like soccer? B: Absolutely!

음 eum um, well
음, 네 말이 맞을지도 모르겠네. **eum, ne mari majeuljido moreugenne.** Well, you may be right.

글쎄 geul·sse well
글쎄, 그 옷이 나한테 맞을지 모르겠어. **geulsse, geu osi nahante majeulji moreugesseo.** Well, I wonder if the clothes suit me.

네 = 예 ne = ye yes (honorific of 응 eung)
A: 어제 학교 갔었니? B: 네/예. **A: eoje hakgyo gasseonni? B: ne/ye.** A: Did you go to school yesterday? B: Yes.

뭐 mwo what
뭐? 안 들려. **mwo? an deullyeo.** What? I can't hear you.

아니(야) a·ni(·ya) no (familiar form)
A: 자? B: 아니, 깨어 있어. **A: ja? B: ani, kkaeeo isseo.** A: Are you sleeping? B: No, I'm awake.

아니요 = 아뇨 ← 아니오 a·ni·yo = a·nyo ← a·ni·o no (honorific of 아니 ani)
A: 이 애가 당신 아들인가요? B: 아니요/아뇨, 내 딸이에요. **A: i aega dangsin adeuringayo? B: aniyo/anyo, nae ttarieyo.** A: Is this your son? B: No, it's my daughter.

10.4 Requesting, Accepting, Refusing, Ordering, Forbidding

부탁 | ~하다 bu·tak | ~·ha·da request | to ask, request
부탁 하나 해도 될까요? **butak hana haedo doelkkayo?** Can I ask you a favor?

애원 | ~하다 ae·won | ~·ha·da plea | to plead
나는 그에게 가지 말라고 애원했다. **naneun geuege gaji mallago aewonhaetda.** I pleaded with him not to go.

제발 je·bal please
제발 좀 서둘러. **jebal jom seodulleo.** Please, hurry.

호소 | ~하다 ho·so | ~·ha·da appeal, plea | to appeal, plead
정부는 국민들에게 절전을 호소하고 있다. **jeongbuneun gungmindeurege jeoljeoneul hosohago itda.** The government is appealing to people to save electricity.

사정하다 sa·jeong·ha·da to beg, plead
나는 이모에게 돈을 빌려 달라고 사정했다. **naneun imoege doneul billyeo dallago sajeong-** haetda. I pleaded with my aunt to lend me some money.

청하다 cheong·ha·da to ask, request
필요하다면 친구들이나 가족들에게 **도움을 청하세요.** **piryohadamyeon chingudeurina gajokdeurege doumeul cheonghaseyo.** Ask friends and family members for help if you need it.

손(을) 벌리다 son(·eul) beol·li·da to ask for money
아무리 힘들어도 동생한테 **손을 벌릴** 수는 없어요. **amuri himdeureodo dongsaenghante soneul beollil suneun eopseoyo.** No matter how hard it gets, I can't ask my younger brother for money.

조르다 jo·reu·da to pester, nag
딸아이가 일주일째 인형을 사 달라고 조르고 있어요. **ttaraiga iljuiljjae inhyeongeul sa dallago joreugo isseoyo.** My daughter has been nagging me to buy her a doll for a week.

요구 ≒ 요청 | ~하다 yo·gu ≒ yo·cheong | ~·ha·da demand, ask | to demand

죄송하지만 당신의 **요구를/요청**을 들어줄 수 가 없습니다. **joesonghajiman dangsinui yogureul/yocheongeul deureojul suga eopseumnida.** I'm sorry but I can't meet your demands.

신청 | ~하다 sin·cheong | ~·ha·da request | to request, ask
지금 저한테 **데이트 신청하는** 건가요? **jigeum jeohante deiteu sincheonghaneun geongayo?** Are you asking me out?

들어주다 deu·reo·ju·da to grant
어려운 **부탁인데** 들어줄래? **eoryeoun butaginde deureojullae?** Can I ask you a big favor?

수락 | ~하다 su·rak | ~·ha·da acceptance, consent | to accept, agree
귀하의 **제안을** 기꺼이 **수락하겠습니다. gwihaui jeaneul gikkeoi surakagetseumnida.** I am more than happy to accept your offer.

허락 ≒ 허가 | ~하다 heo·rak ≒ heo·ga | ~·ha·da permission, consent | to permit, allow
나는 아들 녀석에게 영화 보러 가도 좋다고 **허락했다. naneun adeul lyeoseogege yeonghwa boreo gado jotago heorakaetda.** I allowed my son to go to the movies.
이곳에 출입하려면 **사전 허가가/허락이** 필요합니다. **igose churiparyeomyeon sajeon heogaga/heoragi piryohamnida.** You need to get prior approval to enter this place.

승인 | ~하다 seung·in | ~·ha·da approval | to approve
죄송하지만 손님 카드가 승인이 안 되네요. **joesonghajiman sonnim kadeuga seungini an doeneyo.** I'm afraid your credit card application has not been approved.

허용 | ~하다 heo·yong | ~·ha·da permission | to permit
이곳은 외부인의 **출입이 허용되지** 않습니다. **igoseun oebuinui churibi heoyongdoeji anseumnida.** Unauthorized people are not allowed to enter this place.

승낙 | ~하다 seung·nak | ~·ha·da consent, permission | to permit, approve
부모님께 **결혼 승낙**은 받았어? **bumonimkke gyeolhon seungnageun badasseo?** Did you get your parents' permission to get married?

동의 | ~하다 dong·ui | ~·ha·da agreement, consent | to agree, consent
수학여행에 대한 부모님의 **서면 동의**가 필요

합니다. **suhangnyeohaenge daehan bumonimui seomyeon donguiga piryohamnida.** Written parental consent is required for school trips.

찬성 | ~하다 chan·seong | ~·ha·da agreement, consent | to be for, agree
찬성이야, **반대**야? **chanseongiya, bandaeya?** Are you for or against it?

거절 | ~하다 geo·jeol | ~·ha·da refusal | to refuse, reject
그들은 우리의 **요청**을 **거절했다. geudeureun uriui yocheongeul geojeolhaetda.** They rejected our request.

거부 | ~하다 geo·bu | ~·ha·da refusal | to refuse, reject
택시 기사가 **승차를 거부하는** 것은 법으로 금지돼 있다. **taeksi gisaga seungchareul geobuhaneun geoseun beobeuro geumjidwae itda.** It is prohibited by law for taxi drivers to refuse to take passengers.

사양 | ~하다 sa·yang | ~·ha·da declining | to decline
고맙지만, **사양**할게요. **gomapjiman, sayanghalgeyo.** No, thank you.

명령 | ~하다 myeong·nyeong | ~·ha·da order, command | to order, command
저한테 **명령**하지 마세요. **jeohante myeongnyeonghaji maseyo.** Don't order me around.

지시 | ~하다 ji·si | ~·ha·da directions, instructions | to direct, instruct, order
팀장은 나에게 다음 주 월요일까지 보고서를 제출하라고 **지시했다. timjangeun naege daeum ju woryoilkkaji bogoseoreul jechulharago jisihaetda.** My boss instructed me to hand in the report by next Monday.

시키다 si·ki·da to order, make sb do
내가 **시키는** 대로 했어? **naega sikineun daero haesseo?** Did you do what I told you to do?

만들다 man·deul·da to make
그녀의 행동은 모두를 분노하게 **만들었다. geunyeoui haengdongeun modureul bunnohage mandeureotda.** Her behavior made everyone angry.

강요 | ~하다 gang·yo | ~·ha·da coercion | to force, compel
엄마는 가끔 내가 먹고 싶지 않은 걸 먹으라고 **강요**한다. **eommaneun gakkeum naega meokgo sipji aneun geol meogeurago gangyohanda.** My mother sometimes forces me to eat what I don't want to eat.

등(을) 떠밀다 deung(·eul) tteo·mil·da to force sb to do sth
주위에서 **등을 떠밀어서** 오게 됐어요. juwieseo deungeul tteomireoseo oge dwaeseoyo. People pushed me into coming here.

엎드려 절 받기 eop·deu·ryeo jeol bat·gi to twist sb's arm
엎드려 절 받고 싶지는 않지만, 내 생일에 뭐 없어? eopdeuryeo jeol batgo sipjineun anchiman, nae saengire mwo eopseo? I don't want to twist your arm for a present, but didn't you get something for my birthday?

금지 | ~하다 geum·ji | ~·ha·da prohibition | to prohibit, ban

박물관에서는 사진 촬영이 금지되어 있다. bangmulgwaneseoneun sajin chwaryeongi geumjidoeeo itda. You are not allowed to take pictures in the museum.

금하다 geum·ha·da to prohibit, ban, forbid
영화관 내 음식물 반입을 금합니다. yeonghwagwan nae eumsingmul banibeul geumhamnida. You are not allowed to bring food into the theater.

삼가다 ← 삼가하다 sam·ga·da ← sam·ga·ha·da to abstain, refrain
실내에서는 **흡연을 삼가시오**. sillaeeseoneun heubyeoneul samgasio. Please refrain from smoking indoors.

10.5 Scolding, Blaming, Abusing, Swearing, Complaining, Protesting

꾸중 = 꾸지람 | ~하다 kku·jung = kku·ji·ram | ~·ha·da scolding | to scold
오늘 엄마한테 **꾸중을/꾸지람을** 들어서 기분이 별로예요. oneul eommahante kkujungeul/kkujirameul deureoseo gibuni byeolloyeyo. I'm in a bad mood today because I got scolded by my mother.

꾸짖다 ≒ 나무라다 kku·jit·da ≒ na·mu·ra·da to scold
선생님이 반 친구들 앞에서 나를 **꾸짖으셨다/나무라셨다**. seonsaengnimi ban chingudeul apeseo nareul kkujijeusyeotda/namurasyeotda. The teacher gave me a scolding in front of my classmates.

야단 ya·dan scolding
선생님에게 말대꾸를 하다 **야단을 맞았다**. seonsaengnimege maldaekkureul hada yadaneul majatda. I got a scolding from my teacher for talking back to him.

혼내다 hon·nae·da to scold

손(을) 보다 son(·eul) bo·da to teach sb a lesson
그 녀석 **손** 좀 **봐** 줘야겠어. geu nyeoseok son jom bwa jwoyagesseo. I should teach him a lesson.

혼나다 hon·na·da to be scolded

뜨거운 맛을 보다 tteu·geo·un ma·seul bo·da to get into trouble
주식을 하다 이번에 아주 **뜨거운 맛을 봤어요**. jusigeul hada ibeone aju tteugeoun maseul

bwasseoyo. I got my fingers badly burnt in the stock market.

잔소리 | ~하다 jan·so·ri | ~·ha·da nitpicking | to nitpick, nag
아내는 **잔소리가 심한** 편이에요. anaeneun jansoriga simhan pyeonieyo. My wife nags me a lot.

바가지(를) 긁다 ba·ga·ji(·reul) geuk·da to nag, henpeck one's husband
술을 마시고 집에 들어가면 아내가 **바가지를 긁어요**. sureul masigo jibe deureogamyeon anaega bagajireul geulgeoyo. My wife nags me whenever I return home drunk.

귀(가) 따갑다 ≒ 귀에 못이 박히다 gwi(·ga) tta·gap·da ≒ gwi·e mo·si ba·ki·da to have heard sth a thousand times
그 얘기라면 **귀가 따갑도록** 들었어요. geu yaegiramyeon gwiga ttagapdorok deureosseoyo. I've heard that story a thousand times.
엄마는 저에게 공부하라는 얘기를 **귀에 못이 박힐** 정도로 하세요. eommaneun jeoege gongbuharaneun yaegireul gwie mosi bakil jeongdoro haseyo. I am sick and tired of my mom continually telling me to study.

핀잔 pin·jan scolding
근무 중에 잡담을 하다 팀장에게 **핀잔을 들었어요**. geunmu junge japdameul hada timjangege pinjaneul deureosseoyo. I got told off by the team manager for chatting at work.

구박 | ~하다 gu·bak | ~·ha·da abuse | to abuse
제발 나 구박 좀 그만해. **jebal la gubak jom geumanhae.** Please stop being so hard on me.

원망 | ~하다 | ~스럽다 won·mang | ~·ha·da | ~·seu·reop·da resentment | to blame | resentful
나중에 내 원망은 하지 마. **najunge nae wonmangeun haji ma.** Don't blame me later.

탓 | ~하다 tat | ~·ha·da fault, blame | to blame
너는 왜 늘 다른 사람 탓을 하니? **neoneun wae neul dareun saram taseul hani?** Why do you always blame others?

IDM 누워서 침 뱉기 nu·wo·seo chim baet·gi cutting off your nose to spite your face
친구 욕해 봤자 **누워서 침 뱉기**예요. **chingu yokae bwatja nuwoseo chim baetgiyeyo.** Talking ill of your friends is like cutting off your nose to spite your face.

비난 | ~하다 bi·nan | ~·ha·da criticism, reproach | to criticize
나는 **비난을 받아도** 싸. **naneun binaneul bada-do ssa.** I deserve to be blamed.

비판 | ~하다 | ~적 bi·pan | ~·ha·da | ~·jeok criticism | to criticize | critical
그의 행동은 다른 교사들에게 **강한 비판**을 받아 왔다. **geuui haengdongeun dareun gyosa-deurege ganghan bipaneul bada watda.** His behavior has been strongly criticized by other teachers.
남편은 제가 하는 모든 일에 비판적이에요. **nampyeoneun jega haneun modeun ire bipanjeogieyo.** My husband is critical of everything I do.

험담 | ~하다 heom·dam | ~·ha·da slander | to speak ill of
그녀는 자주 다른 직원들 험담을 한다. **geu-nyeoneun jaju dareun jigwondeul heomdameul handa.** She often bad-mouths other employees.

트집 teu·jip fault, blemish
괜한 **트집** 좀 **잡지** 마라. **gwaenhan teujip jom japji mara.** Stop being so picky.

헐뜯다 heol·tteut·da to speak ill of
두 후보는 토론에서 상대를 헐뜯었다. **du huboneun toroneseo sangdaereul heoltteu-deotda.** The two candidates slandered each other during the debate.

고자질 | ~하다 go·ja·jil | ~·ha·da snitching | to snitch on, tell on
네가 선생님한테 나를 고자질했니? **nega seonsaengnimhante nareul gojajilhaenni?** Did you report me to the teacher?

이르다 i·reu·da to tell (on), snitch on
엄마한테 이르면 죽을 줄 알아. **eommahante ireumyeon jugeul jul ara.** I'll kill you if you tell mom.

욕 | ~하다 yok | ~·ha·da swear word, abuse | to curse, cuss
아이들 앞에서 욕하지 마세요. **aideul apeseo yokaji maseyo.** Don't swear in front of the children.

IDM 입이 거칠다 i·bi geo·chil·da to have a foul mouth
입이 거친 사람이랑 가까이하지 마. **ibi geochin saramirang gakkaihaji ma.** Don't hang out with people who have foul mouths.

악담 | ~하다 ak·dam | ~·ha·da curse | to curse, abuse
그 사람 없는 데서 다른 사람 악담하지 마라. **geu saram eomneun deseo dareun saram ak-damhaji mara.** Don't speak ill of others behind their backs.

야유 | ~하다 ya·yu | ~·ha·da jeer | to jeer
관객들은 가수에게 **야유를 보냈다. gwan-gaekdeureun gasuege yayureul bonaetda.** The audience booed the singer.

저주 | ~하다 jeo·ju | ~·ha·da curse | to curse
세상을 저주한다고 무슨 소용이 있어? **sesangeul jeojuhandago museun soyongi isseo?** What good is it to curse the world?

비웃다 bi·ut·da to laugh at, sneer
김 과장님이 내 보고서를 보고 비웃었어요. **gim gwajangnimi nae bogoseoreul bogo biuseo-sseoyo.** Mr. Kim sneered at my report.

조롱 | ~하다 jo·rong | ~·ha·da ridicule | to ridicule, scoff
걔의 **조롱하는 말투**를 더 이상은 못 참겠어. **gyaeui joronghaneun maltureul deo isangeun mot chamgesseo.** I can't stand his derisive way of talking anymore.

빈정거리다 bin·jeong·geo·ri·da to be sarcastic
그의 목소리에 **빈정거림이 묻어** 있었다. **geuui moksorie binjeonggeorimi mudeo isseotda.** There was a touch of sarcasm in his voice.

말에 뼈가 있다 ma·re ppyeo·ga it·da there is sth meaningful in what sb says
그 사람 **말에**는 **뼈가 있어요**. geu saram mareneun ppyeoga isseoyo. Everything he says is charged with meaning.

비꼬다 bi·kko·da to be sarcastic
그렇게 **비꼬지** 마. geureoke bikkoji ma. Don't be so sarcastic.

놀리다 nol·li·da to tease, make fun of
지금 나 **놀리는** 거야? jigeum na nollineun geoya? Are you making fun of me?

불평 | ~하다 bul·pyeong | ~·ha·da word of complaint | to complain
제발 **불평** 좀 그만해. jebal bulpyeong jom geumanhae. Please stop complaining.

투덜거리다=투덜대다 tu·deol·geo·ri·da = tu·deol·dae·da to grumble, complain
투덜거린다고/**투덜댄**다고 변하는 건 없어. tudeolgeorindago/tudeoldaendago byeonhaneun geon eopseo. Complaining won't change anything.

투정 | ~하다 tu·jeong | ~·ha·da word of complaint | to complain
아이가 **반찬 투정**이 심해요. aiga banchan tujeongi simhaeyo. My child is very picky about food.

푸념 | ~하다 pu·nyeom | ~·ha·da complaint | to whine, complain
그는 자신의 처지에 대해 자주 **푸념을 늘어놓는다**. geuneun jasinui cheojie daehae jaju punyeomeul leureononneunda. He often whines on and on about his situation.

하소연 | ~하다 ha·so·yeon | ~·ha·da appeal, complaint | to whine, appeal
나한테 **하소연**해 봤자 소용 없어. nahante hasoyeonhae bwatja soyong eopseo. It's no use whining to me.

항의 | ~하다 hang·ui | ~·ha·da complaint, protest | to complain, protest
그들은 그 결정에 **항의**하여 사직했다. geudeureun geu gyeoljeonge hanguihayeo sajikaetda. They resigned in protest of the decision.

반대 | ~하다 ban·dae | ~·ha·da objection, opposition | to object, oppose
저는 그 계획에 **반대**합니다. jeoneun geu gyehoege bandaehamnida. I'm against the plan.

대들다 dae·deul·da to challenge, defy
그녀는 조용히 말했지만 아무도 감히 그녀에게 **대들지** 못했다. geunyeoneun joyonghi malhaetjiman amudo gamhi geunyeoege daedeulji motaetda. She spoke quietly but no one dared to defy her.

따지다 tta·ji·da to quibble
별것 아닌 일로 **따지지** 마라. byeolgeot anin illo ttajiji mara. Stop quibbling over silly stuff.

10.6 Promising, Insisting, Suggesting, Encouraging, Praising

약속 | ~하다 yak·sok | ~·ha·da promise | to promise
조용히 있겠다고 **약속**할게요. joyonghi itgetdago yaksokalgeyo. I promise you that I'll be very quiet.

맹세 | ~하다 maeng·se | ~·ha·da vow, pledge | to swear, vow
다시는 술 안 마실 것을 **맹세**할게. dasineun sul an masil geoseul maengsehalge. I swear I won't drink again.

바람(을) 맞다 ba·ram(·eul) mat·da to get stood up
친구한테 **바람을 맞**아서 기분이 별로예요. chinguhante barameul majaseo gibuni byeolloyeyo. I'm in a bad mood because my friend stood me up.

주장 | ~하다 ju·jang | ~·ha·da assertion, opinion | to insist, maintain
그는 나를 본 적이 없다고 **주장**했다. geuneun nareul bon jeogi eopdago jujanghaetda. He claimed that he had never seen me.

고집 | ~하다 go·jip | ~·ha·da stubbornness | to insist, stick to
고집 부리지 마. gojip buriji ma. Stop being stubborn.

우기다 u·gi·da to insist, persist
그는 자신이 몇 분 만에 그것을 고칠 수 있다고 **우겼다**. geuneun jasini myeot bun mane geugeoseul gochil su itdago ugyeotda. He insisted he could fix it in a few minutes.

강조 | ~하다 gang·jo | ~·ha·da emphasis | to emphasize, highlight

인질들의 안전이 최우선이라는 점을 다시 한 번 강조하고 싶습니다. **injildeurui anjeoni choeuseoniraneun jeomeul dasi hanbeon gangjohago sipseumnida.** I want to stress again that the safety of the hostages comes first.

....

제안 | ~하다 je·an | ~·ha·da suggestion, offer | to suggest, propose
귀하의 **제안**은 검토 중에 있습니다. **gwihaui jeaneun geomto junge itseumnida.** Your proposal is under consideration.

건의 | ~하다 geo·nui | ~·ha·da proposal, suggestion | to propose, suggest
건의 사항 있나요? **geonui sahang innayo?** Do you have any suggestions?

제의 | ~하다 je·ui | ~·ha·da suggestion, offer | to suggest, propose
그 회사로부터 **입사 제의**를 받았어요. **geu hoesarobuteo ipsa jeuireul badasseoyo.** I got a job offer from that company.

추천 | ~하다 chu·cheon | ~·ha·da recommendation | to recommend
어떤 식당을 **추천**하고 싶으세요? **eotteon sikdangeul chucheonhago sipeuseyo?** Which restaurant would you recommend?

....

권유 | 권(유)하다 gwo·nyu | gwon(·yu)·ha·da advice, suggestion | to suggest, advise
의사 선생님이 제게 수영을 **권유**했어요. **uisa seonsaengnimi jege suyeongeul gwonyuhaesseoyo.** The doctor recommended that I swim.

권장 | ~하다 gwon·jang | ~·ha·da encouragement | to encourage, recommend
우리는 이 프로그램에 여러분의 적극적인 참여를 **권장**합니다. **urineun i peurogeuraeme yeoreobunui jeokgeukjeogin chamyeoreul gwonjanghamnida.** We encourage your active participation in this program.

설득 | ~하다 seol·deuk | ~·ha·da persuasion | to persuade, convince
아무도 남편이 마음을 바꾸도록 **설득**할 수 없어요. **amudo nampyeoni maeumeul bakkudorok seoldeukal su eopseoyo.** Nobody can convince my husband to change his mind.

충고 | ~하다 chung·go | ~·ha·da advice | to advise
충고 한마디 할게. **chunggo hanmadi halge.** Let me give you a piece of advice.

조언 | ~하다 jo·eon | ~·ha·da advice, tip | to advise
그는 내게 병원에 가 보라고 **조언**했다. **geuneun naege byeongwone ga borago joeonhaetda.** He advised me to go to the doctor.

참견 | ~하다 cham·gyeon | ~·ha·da interference | to interfere
이건 네가 **참견**할 문제가 아니다. **igeon nega chamgyeonhal munjega anida.** This is none of your business.

간섭 | ~하다 gan·seop | ~·ha·da interference | to interfere
어머니는 제 생활에 지나치게 **간섭**하세요. **eomeonineun je saenghware jinachige ganseopaseyo.** My mother meddles in my life too much.

끼어들다 kki·eo·deul·da interfere

....

칭찬 | ~하다 ching·chan | ~·ha·da compliment, praise | to compliment, praise
제가 **칭찬**을 받을 자격이 있는지 모르겠습니다. **jega chingchaneul badeul jagyeogi inneunji moreugetseumnida.** I'm not sure I deserve the praise.

입에 침이 마르다 i·be chi·mi ma·reu·da to brag, praise
그는 친구들에게 **입에 침이 마르도록** 며느리 칭찬을 했다. **geuneun chingudeurege ibe chimi mareudorok myeoneuri chingchaneul haetda.** He praised his daughter-in-law nonstop to his friends.

격려 | ~하다 gyeong·nyeo | ~·ha·da encouragement | to encourage
선수들에게 **격려의 박수**를 부탁드립니다. **seonsudeurege gyeongnyeoui baksureul butakdeurimnida.** Please give a round of applause to the players.

비행기(를) 태우다 bi·haeng·gi(·reul) tae·u·da to praise sb to the skies
왜 갑자기 사람 **비행기를 태우는** 거야? **wae gapjagi saram bihaenggireul taeuneun geoya?** Hey, why are you heaping all of this praise on me?

위로 | ~하다 wi·ro | ~·ha·da consolation | to console, comfort
위로해 주셔서 고맙습니다. **wirohae jusyeoseo gomapseumnida.** Thank you for your sympathy.

달래다 dal·lae·da to soothe, comfort

그녀는 우는 **아기를 달래려고** 했지만 소용 없었다. **geunyeoneun uneun agireul dallaeryeogo haetjiman soyong eopseotda.** She tried to calm the baby but to no avail.

타이르다 ta·i·reu·da to reason, explain

그는 인내심을 가지고 조용히 딸을 타일렀다. **geuneun innaesimeul gajigo joyonghi ttareul tailleotda.** He tried to reason with his daughter quietly and patiently.

10.7 Discussing, Arguing, Explaining, Informing

의논 | ~하다 ui·non | ~·ha·da discussion, consultation | to discuss, consult
너랑 의논할 게 있어. **neorang uinonhal ge isseo.** I have something to discuss with you.

논의 | ~하다 no·nui | ~·ha·da discussion, debate | to discuss
우리는 오늘 환경을 보전하기 위해 무엇을 해야 할지 논의하기 위해 이 자리에 모였습니다. **urineun oneul hwangyeongeul bojeonhagi wihae mueoseul haeya halji nonuihagi wihae i jarie moyeotseumnida.** We are here today to discuss what we should do to protect our environment.

상의 | ~하다 sang·ui | ~·ha·da consultation | to discuss
어떻게 나랑 한마디 **상의도 없이** 직장을 관둘 수 있어? **eotteoke narang hanmadi sanguido eopsi jikjangeul gwandul su isseo?** Why did you quit your job without saying a word to me?

머리(를) 모으다 meo·ri(·reul) mo·eu·da to put heads together
우리가 **머리를 모으면** 무슨 방법이 있을 거야. **uriga meorireul moeumyeon museun bangbeobi isseul geoya.** We will figure out a way if we all put our heads together.

상담 | ~하다 sang·dam | ~·ha·da advice, consultation | to consult
스스로 하기 전에 먼저 **전문가와 상담하세요.** **seuseuro hagi jeone meonjeo jeonmungawa sangdamhaseyo.** You should consult an expert before trying to do it yourself.

면담 | ~하다 myeon·dam | ~·ha·da face-to-face talk | to have a face-to-face talk
오늘 오후에 지도 교수님하고 면담이 있어요. **oneul ohue jido gyosunimhago myeondami isseoyo.** I have a meeting with my supervisor this afternoon.

토론 | ~하다 to·ron | ~·ha·da debate, discussion | to debate, discuss

활발한 토론을 기대합니다. **hwalbalhan toroneul gidaehamnida.** I look forward to a lively debate.

논쟁 | ~하다 non·jaeng | ~·ha·da dispute, argument | to argue
과학자들은 인류의 역사에 대해 **논쟁을 벌여** 왔다. **gwahakjadeureun illyuui yeoksae daehae nonjaengeul beoryeo watda.** Scientists have argued about the history of mankind.

언쟁 ≒ 말싸움 = 말다툼 | ~하다 eon·jaeng ≒ mal·ssa·um = mal·da·tum | ~·ha·da quarrel, argument | to argue
어제 제일 친한 친구와 아무것도 아닌 일로 **언쟁을/말싸움을/말다툼을 벌였어요.** eoje jeil chinhan chinguwa amugeotdo anin illo eonjaengeul/malssaumeul/maldatumeul beoryeosseoyo. Yesterday I had an argument with my best friend over a trivial matter.

너와 이 문제로 언쟁하고/말싸움하고/말다툼하고 싶지 않아. **neowa i munjero eonjaenghago/malssaumhago/maldatumhago sipji ana.** I don't want to quarrel with you over this.

설명 | ~하다 seol·myeong | ~·ha·da explanation | to explain
내가 왜 늦게 도착했는지 설명할게요. **naega wae neutge dochakaenneunji seolmyeonghalgeyo.** Let me explain why I arrived late.

해설 | ~하다 hae·seol | ~·ha·da explanation, exposition | to explain
이 책은 상대성이론에 대해 쉽게 해설하고 있다. **i chaegeun sangdaeseongirone daehae swipge haeseolhago itda.** This book explains the theory of relativity in plain terms.

진술 | ~하다 jin·sul | ~·ha·da statement | to state
당신에게 무슨 일이 있었는지 정확히 진술해 주세요. **dangsinege museun iri isseonneunji jeonghwaki jinsulhae juseyo.** State exactly what happened to you.

구술 | ~하다 gu·sul | ~·ha·da oral statement | to tell, talk
다음번에 **구술 시험**을 보겠습니다. daeumbeone gusul siheomeul bogetseumnida. We will have an oral exam next time.

뒷받침하다 dwit·bat·chim·ha·da to support, back up

대다 dae·da to make, give
당신의 주장을 뒷받침할 **증거를 댈** 수 있어요? dangsinui jujangeul dwitbatchimhal jeunggeoreul dael su isseoyo? Can you give proof of your claim?

제시 | ~하다 je·si | ~·ha·da presentation | to produce, present
증거로 **제시된** 모든 문서는 원본이어야 합니다. jeunggeoro jesidoen modeun munseoneun wonbonieoya hamnida. All documents presented as proof must be the originals.

제공 | ~하다 je·gong | ~·ha·da supply | to provide
그 목격자는 경찰에 믿을 만한 **정보를 제공했다.** geu mokgyeokjaneun gyeongchare mideul manhan jeongboreul jegonghaetda. The witness provided the police with reliable information.

이유 ≒ 까닭 i·yu ≒ kka·dak reason
네가 화낼 **이유가/까닭이** 없는 것 같은데. nega hwanael iyuga/kkadalgi eomneun geot gateunde. I don't think you have a reason to get angry.

동기 dong·gi motive
살인 **동기가** 불확실합니다. sarin donggiga bulhwaksilhamnida. The motive for the murder is uncertain.

근거 geun·geo grounds, basis, foundation
네가 하고 있는 말은 **근거가 없어.** nega hago inneun mareun geungeoga eopseo. What you are saying is groundless.

예 ye example
좀 더 구체적인 **예를 들어** 주실 수 있나요? jom deo guchejeogin yereul deureo jusil su innayo? Could you please give me a more specific example?

때문 ttae·mun because (of), since
뭐 **때문에** 늦었어? mwo ttaemune neujeosseo? Why were you late?

바람에 ba·ra·me because (of), since
늦잠 자는 **바람에** 늦었어요. neutjam janeun

barame neujeosseoyo. I was late because I overslept.

인하다 in·ha·da to be caused by
폭우로 **인해** 경기가 취소되었다. poguro inhae gyeonggiga chwisodoeeotda. Due to heavy rain, the game was canceled.

괜히 = 공연히 gwaen·hi = gong·yeon·hi in vain, for no reason
괜히/공연히 말했나 봐. gwaenhi/gongyeonhi malhaenna bwa. I shouldn't have said that.

의하다 ui·ha·da to be due to
일기예보**에 의하면** 이번 주도 더울 거래. ilgiyeboe uihamyeon ibeon judo deoul georae. According to the weather forecast, it will be hot this week, too.

알리다 al·li·da to inform, notify
언제 내려야 할지 좀 **알려** 주세요. eonje naeryeoya halji jom allyeo juseyo. Please let me know when I should get off.

통보 ≒ 통지 | ~하다 tong·bo ≒ tong·ji | ~·ha·da notice, notification | to notify
면접 결과는 이메일로 **통보해/통지해** 드리겠습니다. myeonjeop gyeolgwaneun imeillo tongbohae/tongjihae deurigetseumnida. We'll notify you the result of your interview by e-mail.

보고 | ~하다 bo·go | ~·ha·da report | to report
보고할 특별한 사항은 없습니다. bogohal teukbyeolhan sahangeun eopseumnida. There's nothing special to report.

폭로 | ~하다 pong·no | ~·ha·da disclosure | to disclose, reveal
그녀는 제 비밀을 세상에 **폭로하겠다고** 협박했어요. geunyeoneun je bimireul sesange pongnohagetdago hyeopbakaesseoyo. She threatened to reveal my secrets to the world.

지적 | ~하다 ji·jeok | ~·ha·da pointing out | to point out
아빠는 내가 전혀 생각하지 못했던 것들에 대해 늘 **지적하세요.** appaneun naega jeonhyeo saenggakaji motaetdeon geotdeure daehae neul jijeokaseyo. My dad always points out things I've never paid attention to before.

암시 | ~하다 am·si | ~·ha·da suggestion, hint | to imply
그 소설은 **문학적 암시로** 가득하다. geu soseoreun munhakjeok amsiro gadeukada. The novel is full of literary allusions.

밝히다 bal·ki·da to make public

그녀는 대선 출마 **의사를 밝혔다**. geunyeo-neun daeseon chulma uisareul balkyeotda. She made public her intentions to run for presidency.

공개 | ~하다 gong·gae | ~·ha·da opening to the public | to make public
범인의 사진이 **언론에 공개되었다**. beominui sajini eollone gonggaedoeeotda. The picture of the culprit was released to the press.

경고 | ~하다 gyeong·go | ~·ha·da warning | to warn
그들은 전기가 끊길 거라고 우리에게 **경고했다**. geudeureun jeongiga kkeunkil georago uriege gyeonggohaetda. They notified us in advance that the electricity would be turned off.

주의 ju·ui warning
경비원이 내게 사진을 찍지 말라고 **주의를 주었다**. gyeongbiwoni naege sajineul jjikji mallago juuireul jueotda. The guard asked me not to take any pictures.

예고 | ~하다 ye·go | ~·ha·da notice | to give notice, warn
시어머니가 아무 **예고 없이** 나타나셔서 당황했어요. sieomeoniga amu yego eopsi natanasyeoseo danghwanghaesseoyo. I was embarrassed that my mother-in-law showed up at my house without any notice.

예언 | ~하다 ye·eon | ~·ha·da prophecy | to foretell
그 예언은 오래 뒤에 현실이 되었다. geu yeeoneun orae dwie hyeonsiri doeeotda. The prediction came true a long time later.

유언 | ~하다 yu·eon | ~·ha·da will | to have a will
아버지는 자신의 재산을 사회에 환원하겠다는 유언을 남기셨어요. abeojineun jasinui jaesaneul sahoee hwanwonhagetdaneun nyueoneul lamgisyeosseoyo. My father made a will donating his assets to society.

10.8 Interjections

거참 geo·cham oh, oh dear
거참, 이상하네. geocham, isanghane. How strange it is!

맙소사 map·so·sa oh no
맙소사! 엉망진창이네. mapsosa! eongmangjinchangine. Oh no! What a mess!

아(아) a(·a) ah, oh

원 won gosh

세상에 se·sang·e boy!
원 세상에! 언제 그렇게 됐니? won sesange! eonje geureoke dwaenni? Oh no! When did it happen?

아이고 ≒ 아유 ← 아이구 a·i·go ≒ a·yu ← a·i·gu oh, oops, my goodness
아이고/아유, 깜짝이야. aigo/ayu, kkamjjagiya. Oh! You surprised me.

아하 a·ha aha

앗 ≒ 악 at ≒ ak ah, oh, ugh!
앗/악, 지갑을 놓고 왔어! at/ak, jigabeul loko wasseo! Dear me! I've left my wallet.

어머 eo·meo oh
어머, 가엾어라. eomeo, gayeopseora. Oh, poor thing!

어머 is mostly used by women rather than men.

오 o oh
오, 잘됐네. o, jaldwaenne. Oh, good.

저런 jeo·reon oh dear

야 ya hey!

야 is used when an adult calls a child, or between close friends.

저 jeo well, um
저, 혹시 저를 아세요? jeo, hoksi jeoreul aseyo? Um, do I know you?

만세 man·se hurrah

야호 ya·ho hurrah
야호, 우리가 해냈어! yaho, uriga haenaesseo! Hurrah! We did it!

쉬 = 쉿 swi = swit shh
쉬/쉿! 아무한테도 말하지 마. swi/swit! amuhantedo malhaji ma. Shhhh! Don't tell anybody.

아야 a·ya ouch!
아야, 내 발 밟았어! aya, nae bal balbasseo! Ouch! You stepped on my toe!

타카나 감탄사 고유어 관형사 괄호 글자 낭독 느낌표 단일어

호 대명사 독어 동사 동의어 된소리 따옴표 뜻 띄어쓰기

시아어 로마자 마침표 말레이어 명사 모음v목적어 문법 문자

장 문장부호 문장성분 물음표 밑줄 반대말 받침 발음

베트남어 보어 복합어 부사 사투리 서술어 소문자 속어

사 스페인어 시제 쓰기 쓰다 아람문자 아랍어 어간 어미

어원 어휘 언어 영어 오자 외국어 외래어 용어

chapter **11** | Language

우리말 의미 이탈리아어 인도네시아어 인칭 일어

기 읽다 자 작은따옴표 절 접두사 접미사 조사 주어

줄 중괄호 중국어 중성 찍다 치다 큰따옴표

키릴문자 태 터키어 통하다 파생어 포르투갈어 표준어 품사

프랑스어 한국어 한글 한자 형용사 화법

히라가나 힌디어

11.1 Languages

언어 eo·neo language
국제연합의 **공식 언어**는 아랍어, 중국어, 영
어, 불어, 러시아어, 스페인어이다. gukjeyeon-
habui gongsik eoneoneun arabeo, junggugeo,
yeongeo, bureo, reosiaeo, seupeineoida. The
official languages of the United Nations are
Arabic, Chinese, English, French, Russian,
and Spanish.

표준어 pyo·ju·neo standard language

사투리 = 방언 sa·tu·ri = bang·eon dia-
lect, accent

한국어 = 한국말 han·gu·geo = han·
gung·mal Korean
한국어/한국말 잘하시네요. hangugeo/
hangungmal jalhasineyo. You speak Korean
very well.

우리말 u·ri·mal our language

외국어 oe·gu·geo foreign language
하실 줄 아는 외국어 있으세요? hasil jul aneun
oegugeo isseuseyo? Can you speak any foreign languages?

영어 yeong·eo English

일(본)어 il(·bon)·eo Japanese

중국어 jung·gu·geo Chinese

스페인어 = 서반아어 seu·pe·i·neo =
seo·ba·na·eo Spanish

힌디어 hin·di·eo Hindi

아랍어 a·ra·beo Arabic

포르투갈어 po·reu·tu·ga·reo Portuguese

러시아어 reo·si·a·eo Russian

독(일)어 dok(·il)·eo German

말레이어 mal·le·i·eo Malay

인도네시아어 in·do·ne·si·a·eo Indonesian

베트남어 be·teu·na·meo Vietnamese

프랑스어 = 불어 peu·rang·seu·eo =
bu·reo French

터키어 teo·ki·eo Turkish

이탈리아어 = 이태리어 i·tal·li·a·eo =
i·tae·ri·eo Italian

타갈로그어 ta·gal·lo·geu·eo Tagalog

11.2 Writing, Punctuation

문자 mun·ja   script, character, letter,
alphabet
한글은 **표음 문자**다. hangeureun pyoeum mun-
jada. Hangul is a phonetic alphabet.

한글 han·geul Hangul, Korean alphabet
한글은 매우 과학적이다. hangeureun maeu
gwahakjeogida. Hangul is very scientific.

로마자 ro·ma·ja Roman alphabet

대문자 dae·mun·ja capital

소문자 so·mun·ja lower case letter

한자 han·ja Chinese character
한자는 배우기 너무 어려워요. hanjaneun baeugi neomu eoryeowoyo. Chinese characters
are so difficult to learn.

가나 ga·na kana

히라가나 hi·ra·ga·na hiragana

가타카나 ga·ta·ka·na katakana

아랍문자 a·ram·mun·ja Arabic script

키릴문자 ki·ril·mun·ja Cyrillic alphabet

문장부호 mun·jang·bu·ho   punctuation
mark

마침표 ma·chim·pyo period

물음표 mu·reum·pyo question mark

느낌표 neu·kkim·pyo exclamation mark

쉼표 swim·pyo comma

따옴표 tta·om·pyo quotation mark

큰따옴표 keun·tta·om·pyo double quotation
mark

작은따옴표 ja·geun·tta·om·pyo single quotation mark

찍다 jjik·da to put, dot

왜 문장 끝에 **마침표를 찍지** 않았니? wae munjang kkeute machimpyoreul jjikji ananni? Why didn't you put a period at the end of the sentence?

기호 gi·ho sign, symbol, mark

괄호 gwal·ho parenthesis

소괄호 = 원괄호 so·gwal·ho = won·gwal·ho parenthesis, round bracket

중괄호 = 활괄호 jung·gwal·ho = hwal·gwal·ho brace, curly bracket ({})

대괄호 = 각괄호 dae·gwal·ho = gak·gwal·ho square bracket ([])

줄 jul line

밑줄 mit·jul underline

치다 chi·da to put sth in parenthesis, underline, circle
밑줄 친 부분을 영어로 번역하시오. mitjul chin bubuneul lyeongeoro beonyeokasio. Translate the underlined parts into English.

긋다 geut·da to draw, rule
틀린 부분에 줄을 죽 그어라. teullin bubune jureul juk geueora. Cross out the incorrect parts.

11.3 Words, Text

단어 da·neo word, vocabulary
저는 심지어 **기본적인 단어**들도 몰라요. jeoneun simjieo gibonjeogin daneodeuldo mollayo. I don't even know the basic words.

낱말 nan·mal word

어휘 eo·hwi vocabulary

용어 yong·eo term, terminology
저는 **컴퓨터 용어**들을 잘 몰라요. jeoneun keompyuteo yongeodeureul jal mollayo. I'm not familiar with computer terminology.

어원 eo·won etymology

고유어 go·yu·eo native tongue

외래어 oe·rae·eo loanword

한자어 han·ja·eo Sino-Korean word

동의어 = 유의어 dong·ui·eo = yu·ui·eo synonym

반대말 = 반의어 ban·dae·mal = ba·nui·eo antonym

속어 so·geo slang

신(조)어 sin(·jo)·eo coinage

속담 sok·dam saying, proverb

정의 | ~하다 jeong·ui | ~·ha·da definition | to define
성공의 정의가 무엇인가? seonggongui jeong·uiga mueosinga? What is the definition of success?

의미 | ~하다 ui·mi | ~·ha·da meaning | to mean
민주주의는 대중에 의한 통치를 의미한다. minjujuuineun daejunge uihan tongchireul uimihanda. Democracy means rule by the people.

뜻 | ~하다 tteut | ~·ha·da meaning, sense | to mean
이 문장이 무슨 뜻인지 모르겠어요. i munjangi museun tteusinji moreugesseoyo. I don't get what this sentence means.

통하다 tong·ha·da to make sense
이 문장은 뜻이 안 통한다. i munjangeun tteusi an tonghanda. This sentence doesn't make sense.

읽기 = 독해 il·gi = do·kae reading

읽다 ik·da to read
한글 읽을 수 있으세요? hangeul ilgeul su isseuseyo? Can you read Hangul?

낭독 | ~하다 nang·dok | ~·ha·da reading | to read aloud

쓰기 sseu·gi writing

쓰다 sseu·da to write
대부분의 한국 아이들은 학교에 들어가기 전에 읽고 쓸 수 있습니다. daebubunui hanguk aideureun hakgyoe deureogagi jeone ikgo sseul su itseumnida. Most Korean children can read and write before they enter school.

맞춤법 mat·chum·beop orthography

철자 cheol·ja spelling

띄어쓰기 ttui·eo·sseu·gi word spacing

오자 o·ja misspelling

11.4 Linguistic Terms

자음 ja·eum consonant

모음 mo·eum vowel

초성 cho·seong initial consonant

중성 jung·seong middle vowel

: 받침 = 종성 bat·chim = jong·seong final consonant, coda

> In Korean, the final consonant of a syllable is placed below the vowel. That's where the term 받침, which literally means *support*, came from.

: 글자 geul·ja letter
독일어 명사의 첫 글자는 늘 대문자로 쓴다는 거 기억하세요. **dogireo myeongsaui cheot geuljaneun neul daemunjaro sseundaneun geo gieokaseyo.** Remember that the first letter of a German noun is always capitalized.

· 자 ja letter
200자 원고지 **ibaekja wongoji** 200 squares of writing paper

: 발음 | ~하다 ba·reum | ~·ha·da pronunciation | to pronounce
이 단어는 두 가지 발음이 있어요. **i daneoneun du gaji bareumi isseoyo.** There are two pronunciations of this word.

예사소리 = 평음 ye·sa·so·ri = pyeong·eum plain consonant

된소리 = 경음 doen·so·ri = gyeong·eum fortis

거센소리 = 격음 geo·sen·so·ri = gyeo·geum aspirated consonant

> The terms 예사소리, 된소리, and 거센소리 are used to explain the contrast among the Korean consonants ㄱ/ㄷ/ㅂ/ㅅ/ㅈ, ㄲ/ㄸ/ㅃ/ㅆ/ㅉ, and ㅋ/ㅌ/ㅍ/ㅊ.

단일어 da·ni·reo simplex

복합어 bo·kha·beo compound

파생어 pa·saeng·eo derivative

접두사 jeop·du·sa prefix

접미사 jeom·mi·sa suffix

어간 eo·gan stem

어미 eo·mi ending

품사 pum·sa part of speech

명사 myeong·sa noun

대명사 dae·myeong·sa pronoun

수사 su·sa numeral

동사 dong·sa verb

형용사 hyeong·yong·sa adjective

관형사 gwan·hyeong·sa determiner

부사 bu·sa adverb

조사 jo·sa particle, postposition

> In Korean, particles are attached to nouns, pronouns, numerals, adverbs, or endings to denote the grammatical function of the preceding word.

감탄사 gam·tan·sa interjection

· 문법 mun·beop grammar

시제 si·je tense

격 gyeok case

태 tae voice

법 beop mood

인칭 in·ching person

화법 hwa·beop speech

구 gu phrase

절 jeol clause

문장 mun·jang sentence
다음 문장에서 잘못된 부분을 고치세요. **da-eum munjangeseo jalmotdoen bubuneul go-chiseyo.** Correct any mistakes in the following sentence.

문장성분 mun·jang·seong·bun sentence component

주어 ju·eo subject

서술어 seo·su·reo predicate

목적어 mok·jeo·geo object

보어 bo·eo complement

가격 가발 가격 가발 가방 가죽 가지다 가짜 값 걸치다 걸옷
결제 교복 교환 구두 구입 군복 귀걸이 깎다 꽉 끈 끼다 끼다
나일론 내다 내리다 내복 단추 두르다 렌즈 맞다 매다 면
모자 모직 무늬 물건 반바지 반지 반품 배송 백화점 벌
벗다 브래지어 브랜드 비닐봉지 비단 비싸다 사다 샌들 센터
소유 속옷 수영복 슈퍼 시장 신 신다 싸다 쓰다 안경
액세서리 양산 어울리다 얼마 영수증 오르다 옷 외투 우산
운동복 유행 인상 인하 입다 입히다 잠바 잠옷 점원 조끼
주머니 줄 지퍼 진짜 책가방 카드 카운터 켤레 티셔츠 파자마
판매 팔다 팔리다 패션 편의점 한복 할부 핸드백 허리띠

chapter **12** | Clothing and Shopping

현금 환불 가방 가죽 가지다 가짜 값 걸치다 걸옷 결제
교복 교환 구두 구입 군복 귀걸이 깎다 꽉 끈 끼다 끼다 나일
론 내다 내리다 내복 단추 두르다 렌즈 맞다 매다 면
모자 모직 무늬 물건 반바지 반지 반품 배송 백화점 벌 벗다
브래지어 브랜드 비닐봉지 비단 비싸다 사다 샌들 센터 소유
속옷 수영복 슈퍼 시장 신 신다 싸다 쓰다 안경
액세서리 양산 어울리다 얼마 영수증 오르다 옷 외투 우산
운동복 유행 인상 인하 입다 입히다 잠바 잠옷 점원 조끼
주머니 줄 지퍼 진짜 책가방 카드

12.1 Clothing

옷 ot clothes, clothing
세일 기간 동안에 옷을 싸게 살 수 있어. **seil gigan dongane oseul ssage sal su isseo.** You can buy clothes for cheap during sales.

벌 beol set, pair (for clothes)
바지 한 벌 **baji han beol** a pair of trousers

입다 ip·da to wear (clothes)
가끔 저는 무엇을 입어야 할지 마음을 못 정해요. **gakkeum jeoneun mueoseul ibeoya halji maeumeul mot jeonghaeyo.** Sometimes I can't make up my mind what to wear.

걸치다 geol·chi·da to wear, slip on
아직 추워. 코트 걸쳐라! **ajik chuwo. koteu geolchyeora!** It's still cold. Put your coat on!

갈아입다 ga·ra·ip·da to change
옷 갈아입을 거야. 데이트가 있거든. **ot garaibeul geoya. deiteuga itgeodeun.** I'm going to go change. I've got a date.

입히다 i·pi·da to dress, put on
아이에게 가벼운 옷을 입히세요. **aiege gabyeoun oseul ipiseyo.** Dress your child in light clothing.

벗다 beot·da to take off
실내에서는 모자를 벗는 게 어때? **sillaeeseoneun mojareul beonneun ge eottae?** Why don't you take off your hat indoors?

벗기다 beot·gi·da to take off, undress
항상 같은 순서로 아이의 옷을 벗기세요. **hangsang gateun sunseoro aiui oseul beotgiseyo.** Always undress your child in the same sequence.

어울리다 eo·ul·li·da to match, suit
넥타이랑 셔츠가 잘 어울리네. **nektairang syeocheuga jal eoulline.** The tie and the shirt match.

꽉 kkwak tight

끼다 kki·da to pinch, be tight
이 옷은 너무 꽉 껴서 숨을 못 쉬겠어요. **i oseun neomu kkwak kkyeoseo sumeul mot swigesseoyo.** These clothes are so tight that I can't breathe.

딱 ttak perfectly

맞다 mat·da to fit
이 옷은 저한테 딱 맞아요. **i oseun jeohante ttak majayo.** This dress fits me perfectly.

패션 pae·syeon fashion, style

최신 choe·sin the newest
이 스타일이 최신 유행하고 있어요. **i seutairi choesin nyuhaenghago isseoyo.** This style is very fashionable.

유행 | ~하다 yu·haeng | ~·ha·da fashion, trend | to be in fashion
올 여름은 70년대 패션이 다시 유행하고 있다. **ol lyeoreumeun chilsimnyeondae paesyeoni dasi yuhaenghago itda.** The 70s look is back in style this summer.

의류 ui·ryu clothing, clothes

양복 yang·bok suit
이 넥타이는 네 양복이랑 잘 어울릴 거야. **i nektaineun ne yangbogirang jal eoullil geoya.** I guess this tie will go with your suit.

정장 jeong·jang suit, formal dress

한복 han·bok *hanbok*

The *hanbok* is a Korean traditional clothing which is often characterized by its vibrant colors and wide seams. Nowadays, people only wear it on special occasions such as Chuseok and New Year's Day.

운동복 un·dong·bok sportswear

수영복 su·yeong·bok swimwear

교복 gyo·bok school uniform

군복 gun·bok military uniform

잠옷 ja·mot sleepwear

파자마 pa·ja·ma pajamas

옷감 ot·gam cloth, material, fabric

섬유 seo·myu fiber, textile

면 = 솜 myeon = som cotton

비단 bi·dan silk

모직 mo·jik woolen fabric

가죽 ga·juk leather

나일론 na·il·lon nylon

천 cheon cloth, fabric

겉옷 geo·dot   outer clothing

셔츠 = 남방 syeo·cheu = nam·bang   shirt

: **티셔츠** ti·syeo·cheu   T-shirt
어제 산 이 티셔츠를 교환하고 싶은데요. **eoje san i tisyeocheureul gyohwanhago sipeundeyo.** I would like to exchange this T-shirt which I bought yesterday.

' **와이셔츠** wa·i·syeo·cheu   dress shirt

> There are two theories for the origin of 와이 셔츠. One is that it comes from *white shirt*, and the other is that the name comes from its Y-shape.

: **스웨터** seu·we·teo   sweater
나는 보통 겨울용 스웨터를 여름에 산다. **naneun botong gyeoullyong seuweteoreul lyeoreume sanda.** I usually buy winter sweaters in summer.

조끼 jo·kki   vest

: **블라우스** beul·la·u·seu   blouse
이 까만 블라우스는 상당히 고급스럽다. **i kkaman beullauseuneun sangdanghi gogeupseureopda.** This black blouse is very elegant.

' **잠바 = 점퍼** jam·ba = jeom·peo   jacket

외투 = 코트 oe·tu = ko·teu   coat

──────────

: **바지** ba·ji   pants, trousers
바지에 얼룩이 묻었어요. **bajie eollugi mudeosseoyo.** I got a stain on my pants.

반바지 ban·ba·ji   shorts

: **청바지** cheong·ba·ji   (blue) jeans
청바지는 간편하다. **cheongbajineun ganpyeonhada.** Jeans are comfortable.

: **치마 = 스커트** chi·ma = seu·keo·teu   skirt
요즘 긴 치마가/스커트가 유행이다. **yojeum gin chimaga/seukeoteuga yuhaengida.** Long skirts are in fashion these days.

미니스커트 mi·ni·seu·keo·teu   miniskirt

: **원피스** won·pi·seu   (one-piece) dress

속옷 = 내의 so·got = nae·ui   underwear

내복 nae·bok   long underwear

러닝 reo·ning   undershirt

: **팬티** paen·ti   underpants, briefs

브래지어 = 브라 beu·rae·ji·eo = beu·ra   bra

──────────

' **소매** so·mae   sleeve
소매가 너무 길어요. **somaega neomu gireoyo.** The sleeves are too long.

' **걷다** geot·da   to roll up
더우면 소매를 걷어. **deoumyeon somaereul geodeo.** Roll up your sleeves if you feel hot.

: **(호)주머니** (ho·)ju·meo·ni   pocket

: **단추 = 버튼** dan·chu = beo·teun   button

지퍼 ji·peo   zipper

: **무늬** mu·nui   pattern, design

12.2 Accessories

: **액세서리 = 장신구 ← 악세사리**
aek·se·seo·ri = jang·sin·gu ← ak·se·sa·ri accessories

: **모자** mo·ja   hat, cap

가발 ga·bal   wig

: **우산** u·san   umbrella

양산 yang·san   parasol

: **쓰다** sseu·da   to wear (hat, glasses, umbrella, etc.)
사진 속에서 야구 **모자를 쓰고** 있는 사람이 누구야? **sajin sogeseo yagu mojareul sseugo inneun sarami nuguya?** Who's this man with the baseball cap in the picture?

──────────

목도리 ≒ 스카프 mok·do·ri ≒ seu·ka·peu   scarf, muffler

' **두르다** du·reu·da   to wrap sth around
외출할 때 **목도리를** 둘러라. **oechulhal ttae mokdorireul dulleora.** Put on your scarf before going outside.

──────────

: **목걸이** mok·geo·ri   necklace
저희 시어머니는 **진주 목걸이**를 많이 갖고 계세요. **jeohui sieomeonineun jinju mokgeorireul**

mani gatgo gyeseyo. My mother-in-law has many pearl necklaces.

귀걸이 = 귀고리 gwi·geo·ri = gwi·go·ri earring
여자 친구에게 선물할 귀걸이를/귀고리를 찾고 있어요. yeoja chinguege seonmulhal gwi-georireul/gwigorireul chatgo isseoyo. I'm looking for earrings as a gift for my girlfriend.

(넥)타이 (nek·)ta·i necktie, tie

허리띠 = 혁대 = 벨트 heo·ri·tti = hyeok·dae = bel·teu belt
허리띠가/혁대가/벨트가 제 허리에 너무 짧아요. heorittiga/hyeokdaega/belteuga je heorie neomu jjalbayo. The belt won't go around my waist.

매다 mae·da to wear (necklace, earrings, tie, belt, etc.)
그 남자는 늘 같은 넥타이만 맨다. geu namjaneun neul gateun nektaiman maenda. He always wears the same tie.

시계 si·gye clock, watch

차다 cha·da to wear (watch)
왜 시계를 오른팔에 차고 다니니? wae sigyereul oreunpare chago danini? Why do you wear your watch on your right wrist?

가방 ga·bang bag, sack

책가방 chaek·ga·bang school bag

핸드백 haen·deu·baek handbag

메다 me·da to carry, shoulder
그 여자는 어깨에 핸드백을 메고 있었다. geu yeojaneun eokkaee haendeubaegeul mego isseotda. She was carrying a purse on her shoulder.

안경 an·gyeong glasses
그는 책을 읽을 때는 안경을 쓴다. geuneun chaegeul ilgeul ttaeneun angyeongeul sseunda. He wears glasses when he reads books.

렌즈 ren·jeu contact lens

반지 ban·ji ring
그는 손가락에 결혼 반지를 끼고 있었다. geuneun songarage gyeolhon banjireul kkigo isseotda. He was wearing a wedding ring on his finger.

장갑 jang·gap gloves

끼다 kki·da to wear (glasses, lens, ring, or gloves)

코트 입고 장갑 끼는 거 잊지 마. koteu ipgo janggap kkineun geo itji ma. Don't forget to wear a coat and gloves.

스타킹 seu·ta·king stockings

양말 yang·mal socks
그러니까 자꾸 양말에 구멍이 나지. geureonikka jakku yangmare gumeongi naji. That's why your socks keep getting holes.

짝 jjak pair
양말이 짝이 안 맞네. yangmari jjagi an manne. These socks don't match.

신(발) sin(·bal) shoes, footwear
신발 사이즈가 어떻게 되세요? sinbal saijeuga eotteoke doeseyo? What's your shoe size?

켤레 kyeol·le set, pair (for shoes or socks)
구두 한 켤레 gudu han kyeolle a pair of shoes

구두 gu·du shoes, dress shoes
구두 닦으세요. gudu dakkeuseyo. Shine your shoes.

끈 kkeun string
네 신발 끈 풀렸어. ne sinbal kkeun pullyeosseo. Your laces are undone.

줄 jul string, cord

슬리퍼 seul·li·peo slippers

샌들 saen·deul sandals

장화 jang·hwa boots

운동화 un·dong·hwa sneakers, running shoes
운동화를 신고 직장에 간다고? undonghwareul singo jikjange gandago? Do you wear sneakers to the office?

신다 sin·da to wear (shoes, socks, etc.)
양말을 신고 난 후에 신발을 신어라. yangmareul singo nan hue sinbareul sineora. Put on your shoes after you have put on your socks.

지갑 ji·gap wallet, purse
그는 자기 아내와 아이들 사진을 지갑에 넣어 가지고 다닌다. geuneun jagi anaewa aideul sajineul jigabe neoeo gajigo daninda. He carries a picture of his wife and children in his wallet.

손수건 son·su·geon handkerchief

12.3 Shopping

‡ **쇼핑 sho·ping** shopping
저는 토요일에 늘 **쇼핑을 해요**. jeoneun to-yoire neul syopingeul haeyo. On Saturdays, I always go shopping.

‡ **가게 ≒ 상점 ga·ge ≒ sang·jeom** shop, store
한국에서는 많은 가게들이/상점들이 늦게까지 문을 연다. hangugeseoneun maneun gagedeuri/sangjeomdeuri neutgekkaji muneul lyeonda. In Korea, many stores are open until late.

‡ **슈퍼(마켓) syu·peo(·ma·ket)** supermarket
새 **슈퍼마켓이 들어섰다**. sae syupeomakesi deureoseotda. A new supermarket has been opened.

* **편의점 pyeo·nui·jeom** convenience store

‡ **백화점 bae·khwa·jeom** department store
쇼핑하러 **백화점 가자**. syopinghareo baekhwajeom gaja. Let's go shopping at the department store.

‡ **센터 sen·teo** center
지금 쇼핑 **센터**에 와 있어. jigeum syoping senteoe wa isseo. I'm at a mall now.

* **매장 mae·jang** shop, store, department
남성복 **매장**은 5층에 있습니다. namseongbok maejangeun ocheunge itseumnida. The men's department is on the fifth floor.

‡ **시장 si·jang** market
한국에 가면 **재래 시장**에 가 보고 싶어요. hanguge gamyeon jaerae sijange ga bogo sipeoyo. I want to visit a traditional market when I go to Korea.

‡ **자동판매기 = 자판기 ja·dong·pan·mae·gi = ja·pan·gi** vending machine
자동판매기에/**자판기**에 넣을 잔돈 있어? jadongpanmaegie/japangie neoeul jandon isseo? Do you have change for the vending machine?

‡ **가지다 = 갖다 ga·ji·da = gat·da** to have, own
차를 **가지고**/**갖고** 계신가요? chareul gajigo/gatgo gyesingayo? Do you have a car?

* **소유 | ~하다 so·yu | ~·ha·da** possession, ownership | to own, possess
이 건물은 누구 **소유**예요? i geonmureun nugu soyuyeyo? Who owns this building?

‡ **얻다 eot·da** to get, acquire
종이랑 볼펜을 좀 **얻을** 수 있을까요? jongirang bolpeneul jom eodeul su isseulkkayo? Can I get some paper and a ballpoint pen?

‡ **구하다 gu·ha·da** to look for, seek
점원 **구함** jeomwon guham Salesperson Wanted

‡ **물건 mul·geon** thing, stuff
사용한 후에 내 **물건들을** 돌려줘. sayonghan hue nae mulgeondeureul dollyeojwo. Give my stuff back after you use it.

‡ **개 gae** piece, unit
초콜릿 두 **개** chokollit du gae two pieces of chocolate

‡ **진짜 jin·jja** real thing
얼핏 봐도 그건 **진짜**가 아니야. eolpit bwado geugeon jinjjaga aniya. One glance is enough to know it is not real.

‡ **가짜 ga·jja** fake, imitation
나는 이 가방이 진짜인지 **가짜**인지 구분이 안 돼요. naneun i gabangi jinjjainji gajjainji gubuni an dwaeyo. I can't tell whether this purse is genuine or not.

‡ **고객 ≒ 손님 go·gaek ≒ son·nim** customer, patron
단골 **고객**님들께는/**손님**들께는 특별 할인을 해 드립니다. dangol gogaengnimdeulkkeneun/sonnimdeulkkeneun teukbyeol harineul hae deurimnida. We give a special discount to our regular customers.

‡ **점원 jeo·mwon** clerk, shop assistance
점원 한 명이 곧 도와드릴 거예요. jeomwon han myeongi got dowadeuril geoyeyo. One of the salesclerks will take care of you at once.

‡ **사다 sa·da** to buy
뭐 **샀니**? mwo sanni? What did you buy?

* **구입 ≒ 구매 | ~하다 gu·ip ≒ gu·mae | ~·ha·da** purchase | to purchase, buy
구입하신/**구매**하신 물건은 무료로 배달해 드립니다. guipasin/gumaehasin mulgeoneun muryoro baedalhae deurimnida. Products bought here will be delivered free of charge.
대량으로 **구매**하시면 할인해 드립니다. daeryangeuro gumaehasimyeon harinhae deurimnida. If you buy in bulk, we'll give you a discount.

팔다 pal·da to sell
여기서 파는 물건들은 품질이 좋다. yeogiseo paneun mulgeondeureun pumjiri jota. The materials that they sell here have good quality.

판매 | ~하다 pan·mae | ~·ha·da sale | to sell

팔리다 pal·li·da to be sold
이 모델은 나오자마자 모두 팔렸어요. i modereun naojamaja modu pallyeosseoyo. This model sold out as soon as it was released.

날개(가) 돋친 듯 팔리다 nal·gae(·ga) dot·chin deut pal·li·da to sell like hot cakes
이 책은 요즘 날개 돋친 듯 팔리고 있어요. i chaegeun nyojeum nalgae dotchin deut palligo isseoyo. This book is selling like hot cakes these days.

할인 | ~하다 ha·rin | ~·ha·da discount | to discount
저희 매장의 모든 품목이 이번 주에 최고 30 퍼센트까지 **할인 판매**를 합니다. jeohui maejangui modeun pummogi ibeon jue choego sampippeosenteukkaji harin panmaereul hamnida. All products in our shop are on sale for up to 30% off this week.

깎다 kkak·da to discount
너무 비싸요. 조금만 **깎아 주세요.** neomu bissayo. jogeumman kkakka juseyo. It's too expensive. Could you lower the price a little?

교환 | ~하다 gyo·hwan | ~·ha·da exchange | to exchange

반품 | ~하다 ban·pum | ~·ha·da return | to return
구매하신 상품은 교환이나 반품이 안 됩니다. gumaehasin sangpumeun gyohwanina banpumi an doemnida. We do not accept exchanges or returns for purchased items.

환불 | ~하다 hwan·bul | ~·ha·da refund | to refund
환불하고 싶은데요. hwanbulhago sipeundeyo. I'd like to get a refund.

값 gap price, value
값이 또 올랐어. gapsi tto ollasseo. The price has risen again.

가격 ga·gyeok price
맘에 들어? 가격은 어때? mame deureo? gagyeogeun eottae? Do you like it? What's the price?

얼마 eol·ma how much

이거 얼마예요? igeo eolmayeyo? How much is this?

비싸다 bi·ssa·da expensive, costly
이게 더 낫네. 하지만 더 비싸. ige deo nanne. hajiman deo bissa. This is better but it's more expensive.

싸다 ≒ 저렴하다 ssa·da ≒ jeo·ryeom·ha·da cheap, inexpensive
특히 해외 구매는 온라인 쇼핑이 대체로 더 쌉니다/저렴합니다. teuki haeoe gumaeneun ollain syopingi daechero deo ssamnida/jeoryeomhamnida. Online shopping is usually cheaper, especially if you buy from overseas.

싸구려 ssa·gu·ryeo cheapie
싸구려라 질이 별로군. ssaguryeora jiri byeollogun. The quality is not good because it's cheap.

오르다 o·reu·da to increase, rise
이번 주 들어 **가격이** 많이 **올랐어요.** ibeon ju deureo gagyeogi mani ollasseoyo. The price has increased drastically this week.

올리다 ol·li·da to raise, increase

인상 | ~하다 in·sang | ~·ha·da raise, rise | to raise, increase
인상된 가격이 언제부터 적용돼요? insangdoen gagyeogi eonjebuteo jeogyongdwaeyo? When will the price increase go into effect?

인하 | ~하다 in·ha | ~·ha·da reduction, markdown | to lower

내리다 nae·ri·da to fall, go down; to lower, let down
A: 가격이 내렸어요? B: 네. 올해부터 가격을 1000원 내렸어요. A: gagyeogi naeryeosseoyo? B: ne. olhaebuteo gagyeogeul cheonwon naeryeosseoyo. A: Has the price gone down? B: Yes. We dropped the price by a thousand won.

가격표 ga·gyeok·pyo price tag

상표 sang·pyo trademark

브랜드 beu·raen·deu brand

계산 | ~하다 gye·san | ~·ha·da payment | to pay
따로따로 계산할게요. ttarottaro gyesanhalgeyo. Split the bill, please.

결제 | ~하다 gyeol·je | ~·ha·da payment | to pay

카드로 결제해도 되나요? kadeuro gyeoljehae-do doenayo? Can I pay by credit card?

˚지불 | ~하다 ji·bul | ~·ha·da payment | to pay
요금은 어떻게 지불하시겠습니까? yogeu-meun eotteoke jibulhasigetseumnikka? How would you like to pay?

⠸내다 nae·da to pay
제가 낼게요. jega naelgeyo. I'll pay.

˚현금 hyeon·geum cash
제가 지금 **현금**이 **부족해요**. jega jigeum hyeon-geumi bujokaeyo. I'm short on cash now.

⠸(신용)카드 (si·nyong·)ka·deu card, credit card

일시불 il·si·bul lump sum payment

할부 hal·bu installment plan
일시불로 할까요, 아니면 할부로 할까요? il-sibullo halkkayo, animyeon halburo halkkayo? Would you like to pay in a lump sum or on an installment plan?

⠸수표 su·pyo check
죄송하지만 저희는 수표를 받지 않는데요. joesonghajiman jeohuineun supyoreul batji an-neundeyo. I'm sorry, but we don't accept checks.

⠸카운터 = 계산대 ka·un·teo = gye·san·dae counter
계산은 카운터에서/계산대에서 하시면 됩니다. gyesaneun kaunteoeseo/gyesandaeeseo hasimyeon doemnida. You can pay at the counter.

계산서 gye·san·seo check, bill

계산서 부탁합니다. gyesanseo butakamnida. Check, please.

영수증 yeong·su·jeung receipt
영수증 필요하신가요? yeongsujeung piryo-hasingayo? Do you need a receipt?

⠸포장 | ~하다 po·jang | ~·ha·da packing, packaging | to wrap, pack
포장해 드릴까요? pojanghae deurilkkayo? Shall I wrap it up for you?

⠸봉지 bong·ji bag, sack

⠸비닐봉지 bi·nil·bong·ji plastic bag

˚바구니 ba·gu·ni basket
A: 비닐봉지 필요하세요? B: 아니요, 바구니 가져왔어요. A: binilbongji piryohaseyo? B: aniyo, baguni gajyeowasseoyo. A: Do you need a plastic bag? B: No, I brought a basket.

⠸배달 | ~하다 bae·dal | ~·ha·da delivery | to deliver
배달해 주시나요? baedalhae jusinayo? Do you deliver?

배송 | ~하다 bae·song | ~·ha·da ship-ping, delivery | to ship, deliver
전국 어디나 48시간 이내에 배송해 드립니다. jeonguk eodina sasippalsigan inaee baesong-hae deurimnida. We deliver to anywhere in the country within 48 hours.

택배 taek·bae delivery service, courier service
택배 기사가 곧 도착할 거예요. taekbae gisaga got dochakal geoyeyo. The courier should be here any minute.

가리다 가스레인지 간식 겨자 고추 국물 굴 굶다

름 기름 김 깍두기 껌 꿀 끓이다 냄비 녹이다

차 다지다 당근 도마 된장찌개 두부 딸기

콩 떡 떡국 라면 레몬 마늘 마시다 메뉴판

밤 배고프다 버섯 병 보다 비빔밥

삶다 삼계탕 상 생선 샴페인 섞이다 소시지

쇠고기 수박 숟가락 술 술병 술집

chapter **13** | Food and Eating

스테이크 시키다 식다 식사 식성 식탁 식품

신하다 쌀 썰다 안주 양념 양배추 양주 양파

영양 오이 와인 요리 요리사 우동 원샷 익히다

떨이 재료 전자레인지 주스 죽 중국집 짬뽕 찌다

기름 참외 찻잔 채식주의자 취하다 커피 케이크

첩 콜라 타다 탄수화물 탕수육 통 튀기다 피망 햄

13.1 Food, Beverages

음식 eum·sik food
매운 음식도 괜찮아? maeun eumsikdo gwaen-chana? Are you OK with spicy food?

식품 sik·pum food, groceries
요즘 **건강 식품**이 인기를 얻고 있다. yojeum geongang sikpumi ingireul eotgo itda. Health foods have been gaining in popularity these days.

식료품 sing·nyo·pum groceries
처음 이곳에 이사 왔을 때 걸어서 닿는 거리에 **식료품 가게**가 있다는 게 참 좋았어요. cheoeum igose isa wasseul ttae georeoseo danneun georie singnyopum gagega itdaneun ge cham joasseoyo. When I first moved here, I was so excited to have a grocery store within walking distance.

식량 sing·nyang food, rations

영양 yeong·yang nutrition
삼계탕은 **영양**이 풍부합니다. samgyetangeun nyeongyangi pungbuhamnida. *Samgyetang* is nutritious.

영양소 yeong·yang·so nutrient
이 음식에는 **영양소**가 골고루 **들어 있다**. i eumsigeneun nyeongyangsoga golgoru deureo itda. This food is nutritionally balanced.

탄수화물 tan·su·hwa·mul carbohydrate
단백질 dan·baek·jil protein
지방 ji·bang fat
이 초콜릿은 **지방**이 적어. i chokolliseun jibangi jeogeo. This chocolate is low in fat.

비타민 bi·ta·min vitamin
무기질 mu·gi·jil mineral

한식 han·sik Korean food
쌀 ssal rice
죽은 쌀에 물을 많이 넣고 끓인 거야. jugeun ssare mureul mani neoko kkeurin geoya. *Juk* is rice cooked with lots of water.

밥 bap steamed rice
밥 좀 더 주시겠어요? bap jom deo jusigesseoyo? Can I have some more rice?

공기 gong·gi bowl
밥 한 공기 더 주세요. bap pan gonggi deo juseyo. A bowl of rice, please.

반찬 ban·chan side dish
밥은 숟가락으로, 반찬은 젓가락으로 드세요. babeun sutgarageuro, banchaneun jeotgarageuro deuseyo. Eat rice with a spoon and eat side dishes with chopsticks.

김치 gim·chi kimchi

Kimchi is the most popular Korean side dish. It is made with radishes, cabbage, cucumbers, etc., which are fermented in salt and red pepper.

김 gim dried seaweed
깍두기 kkak·du·gi *kkakdugi*

Kkakdugi is a kind of kimchi that is made with sliced radishes.

김밥 gim·bap kimbap
많은 아이들이 소풍에 도시락으로 **김밥**을 싸 온다. maneun aideuri sopunge dosirageuro gimbabeul ssa onda. Many children bring kimbap on picnic lunches.

Kimbap is made by rolling rice in a piece of dried laver, with spinach, eggs, carrots, and different kinds of vegetables of your choosing. It is a very popular dish for picnics and can also be eaten as a snack.

비빔밥 bi·bim·bap *bibimbap*

Bibimbap is a rice dish, mixed with different kinds of fresh vegetables, seasoned with red pepper paste.

볶음밥 bo·kkeum·bap fried rice
죽 juk rice porridge
저는 배가 아프면 보통 죽을 먹어요. jeoneun baega apeumyeon botong jugeul meogeoyo. I usually eat rice porridge when I have a stomachache.

냉면 naeng·myeon *naengmyeon*

Naengmyeon is a Korean traditional cold noodle that is served in a stock seasoned with vinegar and mustard. Koreans enjoy it particularly in the summer.

국수 guk·su noodles

칼국수 kal·guk·su *kalguksu*

Kalguksu is a noodle dish. The noodles are made with flour dough, which is first flattened by a roller and then cut into thin, long strips. They are then boiled in chicken stock.

국 guk Korean soup

국물 gung·mul soup broth
국물이 옷에 튀었어. gungmuri ose twieosseo. The soup splattered on my clothes.

건더기 geon·deo·gi the solid ingredients in a soup

떡국 tteok·guk *tteokguk*, rice cake soup

Tteokguk is a clear soup made with sliced rice cake. It is a tradition in Korea to eat this soup on the morning of Chinese New Year's Day.

미역국 mi·yeok·guk *miyeokguk* (seaweed soup)

Miyeokguk is a clear soup made with boiled seaweed. In Korea, people eat it on their birthdays.

찌개 ← 찌게 jji·gae ← jji·ge stew

김치찌개 gim·chi·jji·gae kimchi stew

된장찌개 doen·jang·jji·gae bean paste stew

갈비탕 gal·bi·tang beef-rib soup

삼계탕 sam·gye·tang *samgyetang*
한국 사람들은 쉽게 지치는 여름날 삼계탕을 즐겨 찾는다. hanguk saramdeureun swipge jichineun nyeoreumnal samgyetangeul jeulgyeo channeunda. Koreans enjoy *samgyetang* in summer because they get exhausted easily.

Samgyetang is a soup made with boiled chicken, ginseng, sweet rice, and jujube. This is a very popular dish, especially during the summer as it energizes the body during Korea's extremely hot weather.

설렁탕 ← 설농탕 seol·leong·tang ← seol·long·tang *seolleongtang*
사람들은 보통 설렁탕을 깍두기와 함께 먹는다. saramdeureun botong seolleongtangeul kkakdugiwa hamkke meongneunda. People usually eat *seolleongtang* with *kkakdugi*.

Seolleongtang is a dish that combines rice with a soup made with beef stock.

떡볶이 tteok·bo·kki *tteokbokki*

Tteokbokki is one of the most popular Korean snack foods made from rice cake, fish cake, and red chili sauce.

튀김 twi·gim fried food

볶음 bo·kkeum stir-fry

불고기 bul·go·gi *bulgogi*

Bulgogi is a Korean barbecue in which marinated pork or beef is grilled before serving.

갈비 gal·bi ribs

떡 tteok *tteok*, rice cake

Tteok is rice cake made with cooked sticky rice. It is a popular snack in Korea and is especially known as traditional holiday food.

송편 song·pyeon *songpyeon* (a type of rice cake)
송편은 한국인들이 추석에 먹는 특별한 음식이에요. songpyeoneun hangugindeuri chuseoge meongneun teukbyeolhan eumsigieyo. *Songpyeon* is a special food that Koreans eat on Chuseok.

Songpyeon is a kind of traditional rice cake made with rice dough and red beans. People make this for Korean Thanksgiving.

중식 jung·sik Chinese food

자장면 = 짜장면 ja·jang·myeon = jja·jang·myeon *jajangmyeon*
자장면/짜장면 시켜 먹자. jajangmyeon/jjajangmyeon sikyeo meokja. Let's order *jajangmyeon* for lunch.

Jajangmyeon is a noodle dish that mixes ground pork, onion, zucchini with Chinese sauce. Along with 짬뽕 jjamppong, this is one of the most popular Chinese dishes in Korea.

짬뽕 jjam·ppong *jjamppong*

Jjamppong is a noodle dish combined with stir-fried seafood and vegetables, then boiled in stock.

탕수육 tang·su·yuk sweet and sour pork

만두 man·du dumpling

일식 il·sik Japanese food

라면 ra·myeon ramen
라면은 불면 맛없어. ramyeoneun bulmyeon madeopseo. Soggy ramen is unappetizing.

오뎅 = 어묵 o·deng = eo·muk oden

우동 = 가락국수 u·dong = ga·rak·guk·su udon

초밥 = 스시 cho·bap = seu·si sushi

단무지 dan·mu·ji pickled radish

양식 yang·sik Western food

스테이크 seu·te·i·keu steak

스파게티 seu·pa·ge·ti spaghetti

피자 pi·ja pizza

수프 ← 스프 su·peu soup

카레 ka·re curry

빵 ppang bread
요즘에는 많은 사람들이 아침에 밥 대신 빵을 먹는다. yojeumeneun maneun saramdeuri achime bap daesin ppangeul meongneunda. These days, many people eat bread instead of rice for breakfast.

빵 derives from the Portuguese word *pão*.

식빵 sik·ppang plain bread

케이크 ← 케익 ke·i·keu ← ke·ik cake

햄버거 haem·beo·geo hamburger

샌드위치 saen·deu·wi·chi sandwich

소시지 ← 소세지 so·si·ji ← so·se·ji sausage

햄 haem ham

치즈 chi·jeu cheese

고기 go·gi meat, fish

돼지고기 dwae·ji·go·gi pork

쇠고기 = 소고기 soe·go·gi = so·go·gi beef

닭고기 dak·go·gi chicken, poultry

생선 saeng·seon fish
저는 생선이랑 채소만 먹어요. jeoneun saeng-seonirang chaesoman meogeoyo. I eat only fish and vegetables.

생선 is used only in the context of food. When you refer to a fish living in the water, you should say 물고기 **mulgogi** instead.

새우 sae·u shrimp

게 ge crab

멸치 myeol·chi anchovy

오징어 o·jing·eo squid

굴 gul oyster

미역 mi·yeok seaweed

채소 = 야채 chae·so = ya·chae vegetable

토마토 to·ma·to tomato

상추 ← 상치 sang·chu ← sang·chi lettuce
저는 언제나 고기를 상추에 싸 먹어요. jeoneun eonjena gogireul sangchue ssa meogeoyo. I always eat meat wrapped in lettuce.

배추 bae·chu Chinese cabbage

양배추 yang·bae·chu cabbage

피망 pi·mang bell pepper, paprika

감자 gam·ja potato

고구마 go·gu·ma sweet potato

옥수수 ok·su·su corn

무 ← 무우 mu ← mu·u radish

시금치 si·geum·chi spinach

고추 go·chu chili pepper

버섯 beo·seot mushroom

호박 ho·bak pumpkin, squash

당근 dang·geun carrot

오이 o·i cucumber

파 pa green onion, scallion

양파 yang·pa onion

나물 na·mul herbs

콩나물 kong·na·mul bean sprouts

두부 du·bu tofu

과일 **gwa·il** fruit

씨 **ssi** seed

껍질 **kkeop·jil** skin, peel

수박 **su·bak** watermelon

통 **tong** head
수박 한 통 **subak han tong** a watermelon

감 **gam** persimmon

참외 **cha·moe** Korean melon

딸기 **ttal·gi** strawberry

귤 **gyul** mandarin orange, tangerine

복숭아 **bok·sung·a** peach

오렌지 **o·ren·ji** orange

레몬 **re·mon** lemon

사과 **sa·gwa** apple

배 **bae** pear

포도 **po·do** grape

바나나 **ba·na·na** banana

송이 **song·i** bunch (of bananas or grapes)
포도 한 송이 **podo han songi** a bunch of grapes

밤 **bam** chestnut

과자 **gwa·ja** cookie
과자 내 거 좀 남겨 둬. **gwaja nae geo jom namgyeo dwo.** Leave some cookies for me.

껌 **kkeom** chewing gum

사탕 **sa·tang** candy

초콜릿 ← 초콜렛 **cho·kol·lit** ← **cho·kol·let** chocolate
살을 빼고 싶으면 초콜릿을 그만 먹어. **sareul ppaego sipeumyeon chokolliseul geuman meogeo.** If you want to lose weight, you have to cut out chocolate from your diet.

아이스크림 **a·i·seu·keu·rim** ice cream
여기 아이스크림은 굉장히 맛있어요. **yeogi aisseukeurimeun goengjanghi masisseoyo.** They have delicious ice cream here.

땅콩 **ttang·kong** peanut

양념 | ~하다 **yang·nyeom | ~·ha·da** seasoning | to season
국을 뭘로 양념했어요? **gugeul mwollo yangnyeomhaesseoyo?** What did you season the soup with?

조미료 **jo·mi·ryo** seasoning

소금 **so·geum** salt
국에 소금이 너무 많이 들어갔다. **guge sogeumi neomu mani deureogatda.** The soup is too salty.

깨소금 **kkae·so·geum** powdered sesame mixed with salt

설탕 **seol·tang** sugar

꿀 **kkul** honey

기름 **gi·reum** oil

참기름 **cham·gi·reum** sesame oil
참기름 냄새가 고소하다. **chamgireum naemsaega gosohada.** Sesame oil is aromatic.

식용유 **si·gyong·yu** cooking oil
야채 볶을 때 식용유를 쓸까요, 버터를 쓸까요? **yachae bokkeul ttae sigyongnyureul sseulkkayo, beoteoreul sseulkkayo?** Should I use oil or butter for frying the vegetables?

소스 **so·seu** sauce

마요네즈 **ma·yo·ne·jeu** mayonnaise

버터 **beo·teo** butter

케첩 **ke·cheop** ketchup

식초 **sik·cho** vinegar

후추 **hu·chu** pepper

밀가루 **mil·ga·ru** wheat flour

마늘 **ma·neul** garlic

겨자 **gyeo·ja** mustard

간장 **gan·jang** soy sauce

고추장 **go·chu·jang** *gochujang*, red pepper paste

된장 **doen·jang** (fermented) soybean paste

고춧가루 **go·chut·ga·ru** chili powder

물 **mul** water
너무 짜면 물 마셔. **neomu jjamyeon mul masyeo.** Drink some water if it's too salty.

모금 **mo·geum** sip
물 한 모금만 주세요. **mul han mogeumman juseyo.** Please let me have a sip of water.

음료(수) **eum·nyo(·su)** drink, beverage

이 식당은 음료수를 공짜로 제공한다. i sik-dangeun eumnyosureul gongjjaro jegonghanda. This restaurant serves free soft drinks.

주스 ju·seu juice
100퍼센트 천연 **과일 주스** baekpeosenteu cheonyeon gwail juseu 100 percent pure fruit juice

사이다 sa·i·da lemon-lime soda, Sprite™

콜라 kol·la cola, Coke™
사람들은 보통 피자를 콜라와 함께 먹는다. saramdeureun botong pijareul kollawa hamkke meongneunda. People usually have pizza with coke.

커피 keo·pi coffee
매일 아침 **커피** 향이 나를 깨운다. maeil achim keopi hyangi nareul kkaeunda. The smell of coffee wakes me up every morning.

차 cha tea
A: 커피 마실래? **차 마실래**? B: 아무거나. A: keopi masillae? cha masillae? B: amugeona. A: Do you want coffee or tea? B: It's all the same to me.

녹차 nok·cha green tea

홍차 hong·cha black tea

인삼차 in·sam·cha ginseng tea

우유 u·yu milk

요구르트 ← **야구르트** yo·gu·reu·teu ← ya·gu·reu·teu yogurt

술 sul alcoholic drink
어제 **술**을 너무 많이 **마셨더니** 머리가 아파요. eoje sureul leomu mani masyeotdeoni meo-riga apayo. I have a hangover because I had too much to drink last night.

맥주 maek·ju beer
저는 **맥주 마실래요**. jeoneun maekju masil-laeyo. I'll have a beer.

소주 so·ju soju
저는 소주 몇 잔이 고작이에요. jeoneun soju myeot jani gojagieyo. I can only drink a few shots of soju.

> Soju is the most popular Korean alcoholic beverage. It has a transparent color, and is known for its stinging taste.

막걸리 mak·geol·li *makgeolli*

> *Makgeolli* is a Korean traditional liquor which has a somewhat opaque and white color.

양주 yang·ju hard liquor

샴페인 syam·pe·in champagne

와인 = 포도주 wa·in = po·do·ju wine
이 **와인**은/포도주는 디저트로 제격이야. i waineun/podojuneun dijeoteuro jegyeogiya. This wine is ideal for dessert.

13.2 Eating, Drinking, Smoking

먹다 meok·da to eat
A: 밥 한 공기 더 드실래요? B: 더 이상 못 먹겠어. A: bap pan gonggi deo deusillaeyo? B: deo isang mot meokgesseo. A: Do you want another bowl of rice? B: I can't eat anymore.

마시다 ma·si·da to drink
마실 것 좀 드릴까요? masil geot jom deuril-kkayo? Can I get you something to drink?

입에 대다 i·be dae·da to eat, drink
그는 음식을 **입에도 대지** 않았다. geuneun eumsigeul ibedo daeji anatda. He didn't even touch the food.

드시다 = 잡수시다 deu·si·da = jap·su·si·da honorific of 먹다 meokda

식사 | ~하다 sik·sa | ~·ha·da meal | to have a meal
점심 식사하셨어요? jeomsim siksahasyeo-sseoyo? Have you had lunch?

끼니 kki·ni meal
또 햄버거로 **끼니를 때운** 거야? tto haembeo-georo kkinireul ttaeun geoya? Did you make do with a hamburger again?

끼 kki meal
저는 하루에 한 **끼**만 먹습니다. jeoneun harue han kkiman meokseumnida. I only eat one meal a day.

아침 a·chim breakfast

점심 jeom·sim lunch

저녁 jeo·nyeok dinner

간식 gan·sik snack
점심을 적게 먹어서 세 시에 **간식을 먹었어요**. jeomsimeul jeokge meogeoseo se sie gansigeul meogeosseoyo. Since I had so little for lunch, I had a snack at three.

군것질 | ~하다 gun·geot·jil | ~·ha·da eating between meals | to eat between meals
딸아이가 군것질을 너무 좋아해서 걱정이에요. ttaraiga gungeotjireul leomu joahaeseo geokjeongieyo. I'm worried my daughter likes snacks too much.

푸다 pu·da to scoop
밥 좀 퍼. bap jom peo. Scoop rice.

덜다 deol·da to take food from one's plate
먹을 만큼 덜어서 먹어라. meogeul mankeum deoreoseo meogeora. Get your own serving and dig in.

배고프다 bae·go·peu·da hungry
배고파 죽겠어. baegopa jukgesseo. I'm starving.

고프다 go·peu·da hungry
저는 아직 **배 안 고파요**. jeoneun ajik bae an gopayo. I am not hungry yet.

꼬르륵 kko·reu·reuk rumbling
배에서 자꾸 **꼬르륵 소리가 나요**. baeeseo jakku kkoreureuk soriga nayo. My stomach keeps growling.

출출하다 chul·chul·ha·da a little hungry
출출한데 먹을 것 좀 있어? chulchulhande meogeul geot jom isseo? I'm a little hungry. Do you have something to eat?

시장하다 si·jang·ha·da hungry
되게 시장하셨나 봐요. doege sijanghasyeonna bwayo. You must have been very hungry.

배부르다 bae·bu·reu·da full, stuffed
배불러서 더는 못 먹겠어. baebulleoseo deoneun mot meokgesseo. I am full and can't eat anymore.

부르다 bu·reu·da full
이제 **배가 불러요**. ije baega bulleoyo. Now I'm stuffed.

과식 | ~하다 gwa·sik | ~·ha·da overeating | to overeat
과식은 몸에 해로워요. gwasigeun mome haerowoyo. Overeating is bad for your health.

입이 짧다 i·bi jjal·da to be a picky eater, have a small appetite
제가 **입이 짧은** 편이어서 많이 안 먹어요. jega ibi jjalbeun pyeonieoseo mani an meogeoyo. I have a small appetite and don't eat much.

목마르다 mong·ma·reu·da thirsty
목말라 죽겠어. mongmalla jukgesseo. I'm dying of thirst.

마르다 ma·reu·da thirsty
목이 마른데 마실 것 좀 있어? mogi mareunde masil geot jom isseo? I'm thirsty. Is there anything to drink?

갈증 gal·jeung thirst
갈증이 나기 전에 물을 마셔라. galjeungi nagi jeone mureul masyeora. Drink water before you feel thirsty.

식성 sik·seong appetite
아내는 **식성이 까다로워요**. anaeneun sikseongi kkadarowoyo. My wife is a picky eater.

가리다 ga·ri·da to be choosy, be picky
저는 음식을 가리지 않는 편이에요. jeoneun eumsigeul gariji anneun pyeonieyo. I'm not particular about food.

채식 chae·sik vegetarian diet
언제부터 채식을 하셨어요? eonjebuteo chaesigeul hasyeosseoyo? When did you become a vegetarian?

채식주의자 chae·sik·ju·ui·ja vegetarian

다이어트 | ~하다 da·i·eo·teu | ~·ha·da diet | to diet
나 지금 다이어트 중이야. na jigeum daieoteu jungiya. I'm dieting.

굶다 gum·da to starve, skip a meal
하루 종일 굶었어요. haru jongil gulmeosseoyo. I haven't eaten all day.

손가락(을) 빨다 son·ga·rak(·eul) ppal·da to starve
직장을 구해야 하는데. **손가락 빨** 수는 없잖아. jikjangeul guhaeya haneunde. songarak ppal suneun eopjana. I need to get a job because I can't just starve.

거르다 geo·reu·da to skip (a meal)
입맛이 없어서 **점심을 걸렀어요**. immasi eopseosseo jeomsimeul geolleoseoyo. I skipped lunch because I had no appetite.

하늘이 노랗다 ha·neu·ri no·ra·ta to almost faint from hunger
저는 한 끼만 굶어도 **하늘이 노랗게** 보여요.

jeoneun han kkiman gulmeodo haneuri norake boyeoyo. I will feel faint even if I skip just one meal.

집다 jip·da to pick up
젓가락으로 집어 봐. jeotgarageuro jibeo bwa. Try to pick it up with chopsticks.

찍다 jjik·da to spear
포크로 찍어 먹어. pokeuro jjigeo meogeo. Spear it with a fork.

씹다 ssip·da to chew, bite
나는 음식을 잘 씹지 않는다. naneun eumsigeul jal ssipji anneunda. I don't usually chew my food well.

꿀꺽 kkul·kkeok gulp
그는 목에서 침을 꿀꺽 삼켰다. geuneun mogeseo chimeul kkulkkeok samkyeotda. He gulped.

삼키다 sam·ki·da to swallow
삼킬 때 목이 아파요. samkil ttae mogi apayo. My throat hurts when I swallow.

따르다 tta·reu·da to pour

쏟다 ssot·da to spill, pour
죄송해요. 커피를 쏟았어요. joesonghaeyo. keopireul ssodaseoyo. I'm sorry. I spilled the coffee.

넘치다 neom·chi·da to overflow, brim over
그만 따라. 잔이 넘치잖아. geuman ttara. jani neomchijana. Stop pouring. The glass is overflowing.

타다 ta·da to mix; to make (coffee)
커피에 프림 타? keopie peurim ta? Do you want me to add sugar to your coffee?
커피 타 줄까? keopi ta julkka? Do you want me to make coffee?

따다 tta·da to open, unlock; to get, pick
병 좀 따 봐. byeong jom tta bwa. Open the bottle.

숟가락 sut·ga·rak spoon
저기, 잠시만요! 숟가락이 더러워요. jeogi, jamsimannyo! sutgaragi deoreowoyo. Waiter, please! This spoon is dirty.

젓가락 jeot·ga·rak chopstick
저는 아직 젓가락 사용이 불편해요. jeoneun ajik jeotgarak sayongi bulpyeonhaeyo. I'm still uncomfortable using chopsticks.

수저 su·jeo spoon and chopsticks

포크 po·keu fork

탁자 = 테이블 tak·ja = te·i·beul table
내 친구는 옛날식 탁자를/테이블을 사고 싶어 한다. nae chinguneun yennalsik takjareul/teibeureul sago sipeo handa. My friend wants to buy an antique table.

식탁 sik·tak dining table
식사 후에 식탁을 치워 주세요. siksa hue siktageul chiwo juseyo. After eating, please clear the dining table.

(밥)상 (bap·)sang dining table
상 차리는 것 좀 도와줄래? sang charineun geot jom dowajullae? Can you help me set the table?

그릇 geu·reut bowl

접시 jeop·si dish, plate

주전자 ju·jeon·ja kettle

컵 keop cup
물 한 컵 mul han keop a cup of water

잔 jan cup, glass
잔이 깨져 있어요. jani kkaejyeo isseoyo. The glass is broken.
커피 한 잔 keopi han jan a cup of coffee

찻잔 chat·jan teacup

술 sul alcohol
술을 마신 후에 운전을 하면 절대로 안 됩니다. sureul masin hue unjeoneul hamyeon jeoldaero an doemnida. You should never drive after drinking.

음주 eum·ju drinking
지나친 음주는 건강에 해롭습니다. jinachin eumjuneun geongange haeropseumnida. Excessive drinking is bad for your health.

안주 an·ju food served with alcoholic drinks
안주는 뭘로 시킬까? anjuneun mwollo sikilkka? What appetizer should we order?

병 byeong bottle, jar
맥주 한 병 maekju han byeong a bottle of beer

마개 ma·gae stopper
마개가 너무 꽉 잠겨서 열리지가 않아요. magaega neomu kkwak jamgyeoseo yeollijiga anayo. The stopper is so tight I can't get it open.

술잔 sul·jan glass of alcohol
다들 **술잔**을 높이 **드세요**. 건배합시다. dadeul suljaneul lopi deuseyo. geonbaehapsida. Everyone raise your glasses. Let's make a toast.

술병 sul·byeong (liquor) bottle
술병이 비었잖아. 다른 거 하나 더 따야겠어. sulbyeongi bieotjana. dareun geo hana deo tta-yagesseo. This bottle is empty. I'll have to open another.

술자리 sul·ja·ri drinking party
어제 친구들과 **술자리**를 가졌다. eoje chingu-deulgwa suljarireul gajyeotda. I had a drink with my friends yesterday.

한잔 | ~하다 han·jan | ~·ha·da a drink | to have a drink
오늘은 제가 **한잔** 살게요. oneureun jega han-jan salgeyo. Let me buy you a drink today.

건배 | ~하다 geon·bae | ~·ha·da toast, cheers | to toast
건배! geonbae! Cheers!

원샷 | ~하다 won·syat | ~·ha·da bottoms up | to drink up
자, 원샷! ja, wonsyat! Bottoms up!

주량 ju·ryang drinking capacity
주량이 얼마나 되세요? juryangi eolmana doe-seyo? How much can you drink?

과음 | ~하다 gwa·eum | ~·ha·da heavy drinking | to drink to excess
어젯밤에 **과음**했더니 속이 안 좋아요. eojet-bame gwaeumhaetdeoni sogi an joayo. I have a stomachache from drinking too much last night.

IDM **코가 삐뚤어지게 (술을) 마시다** ko·ga ppi·ttu·reo·ji·ge (su·reul) ma·si·da to drink like a fish
오늘 밤은 **코가 삐뚤어지게** 마셔 보자. oneul bameun koga ppittureojige masyeo boja. Let's drink like a fish tonight.

취하다 chwi·ha·da to get drunk
내가 보기에는 너 **취했어**. naega bogieneun neo chwihaesseo. I think you're drunk.

(술)주정 (sul·)ju·jeong bad drinking habit
그 사람은 술만 취하면 **주정**을 부린다. geu sarameun sulman chwihamyeon jujeongeul bu-rinda. He acts recklessly whenever he's drunk.

IDM **필름이 끊기다** pil·leu·mi kkeun·ki·da to pass out drunk

어젯밤에는 **필름이 끊겨서** 집에 어떻게 왔는지 기억이 안 나요. eojetbameneun pilleumi kkeunkyeoseo jibe eotteoke wanneunji gieogi an nayo. I passed out last night, and I don't remember how I got back home.

> 필름 in this idiom represents memories or consciousness.

멀쩡하다 meol·jjeong·ha·da sober
저 지금 **멀쩡해요**. jeo jigeum meoljjeong-haeyo. I'm sober.

토하다 to·ha·da to vomit, throw up
토할 것 같아요. tohal geot gatayo. I feel like throwing up.

담배 dam·bae cigarette

피우다 pi·u·da to smoke
담배 피워도 될까요? dambae piwodo doel-kkayo? May I smoke?

흡연 | ~하다 heu·byeon | ~·ha·da smok-ing | to smoke
흡연 금지 heubyeon geumji No Smoking

금연 | ~하다 geu·myeon | ~·ha·da non-smoking | to quit smoking
내 새해 결심은 **금연**이다. nae saehae gyeol-simeun geumyeonida. My New Year's resolu-tion is to quit smoking.

끊다 kkeun·ta to cut, stop, quit
담배를 **끊고** 싶지만 그게 잘 안 돼요. dambae-reul kkeunko sipjiman geuge jal an dwaeyo. I want to quit smoking but I can't.

(담배)꽁초 (dam·bae·)kkong·cho ciga-rette butt
담배꽁초를 버리지 마시오. dambae-kkongchoreul beoriji masio. Do not discard cigarette butts.

라이터 ra·i·teo (cigarette) lighter
라이터 있으세요? raiteo isseuseyo? Do you have a lighter?

성냥 seong·nyang match
A: **성냥** 있으세요? B: 미안합니다, 담배를 안 피워서요. A: seongnyang isseuseyo? B: mian-hamnida, dambaereul an piwosseoyo. A: Do you have a match? B: I'm sorry, but I don't smoke.

재떨이 ← 재털이 jae·tteo·ri ← jae·teo·ri ashtray
재떨이 좀 비워 주시겠어요? jaetteori jom biwo jusigesseoyo? Could you empty the ash-tray?

13.3 Places to Eat/Drink

식당 = 음식점 sik·dang = eum·sik·jeom
restaurant
이 식당이/음식점이 네가 전에 추천했던 곳이
야? i sikdangi/eumsikjeomi nega jeone
chucheonhaetdeon gosiya? Is this the restaurant you recommended?

레스토랑 re·seu·to·rang Western-style
restaurant
그 레스토랑은 예약을 해야 해. geu reseu-
torangeun yeyageul haeya hae. Reservations
are required at that restaurant.

뷔페 ← 부페 bwi·pe ← bu·pe buffet restaurant

한식집 han·sik·jip Korean restaurant

중국집 jung·guk·jip Chinese restaurant
중국집에서 저녁 먹을까? junggukjibeseo jeo-
nyeok meogeulkka? How about having dinner at a Chinese restaurant?

일식집 il·sik·jip Japanese restaurant

빵집 = 제과점 ppang·jip = je·gwa·jeom
bakery, bakeshop
많은 아빠들이 집에 돌아가는 길에 **빵집에/제
과점에** 들른다. maneun appadeuri jibe dora-
ganeun gire ppangjibe/jegwajeome deulleunda.
Many dads stop by a bakery on their way
back home.

카페 = 커피숍 ka·pe = keo·pi·syop café
저는 자주 그 카페에서/커피숍에서 시간을 보
냅니다. jeoneun jaju geu kapeeseo/keopisyo-
beseo siganeul bonaemnida. I often hang out
at the café.

찻집 = 다방 chat·jip = da·bang coffee
shop, teahouse
근처 찻집에/다방에 갑시다. geuncheo
chatjibe/dabange gapsida. Let's go to a nearby teahouse.

술집 sul·jip bar, pub
새로 생긴 술집에 가 보자. saero saenggin
suljibe ga boja. Let's check out the new bar.

바 ba bar

호프집 ho·peu·jip pub

포장마차 po·jang·ma·cha *pojangmacha*,
food stall
우리 포장마차 가서 한잔하자. uri pojangma-
cha gaseo hanjanhaja. Let's have a drink at a
food stall.

Pojangmacha is a place that sells street food
and alcoholic beverages. It is usually set up
as a stall on the street and sells a variety of
snacks.

요리사 yo·ri·sa cook

주방장 ju·bang·jang chef

종업원 jong·eo·bwon employee, worker
그녀는 **종업원 관리**를 잘한다. geunyeoneun
jongeobwon gwallireul jalhanda. She does a
good job managing her employees.

메뉴 me·nyu menu
오늘의 메뉴는 뭔가요? oneurui menyuneun
mwongayo? What is on the menu today?

메뉴판 me·nyu·pan menu (board)
메뉴판 좀 갖다 주세요. menyupan jom gatda
juseyo. Please give me the menu.

주문 | ~하다 ju·mun | ~·ha·da order | to
order
주문하신 음식 나왔습니다. jumunhasin eumsik nawatseumnida. Here's your order.

시키다 si·ki·da to order
한참 전에 음식을 시켰는데 아직 안 나왔어
요. hancham jeone eumsigeul sikyeonneunde
ajik an nawasseoyo. I ordered a while ago, but
I didn't get my food yet.

인분 in·bun serving(s)
그는 언제나 2인분을 시킨다. geuneun eonjena
iinbuneul sikinda. He always orders two portions of food.

공짜 ← 꽁짜 gong·jja ← kkong·jja free of
charge
세상에 공짜는 없어. sesange gongjjaneun eopseo. Nothing's free in life.

무료 mu·ryo free of charge
음료수는 무료입니다. eumnyosuneun muryoimnida. Beverages are free.

서비스 seo·bi·seu service; free of charge
이곳의 서비스는 믿을 만합니다. igosui seobi-
seuneun mideul manhamnida. The service
here is reliable.
이건 서비스입니다. igeon seobiseuimnida.
This is on the house.

13.4 Cooking

요리 | ~하다 yo·ri | ~·ha·da cooking | to cook
오늘은 요리할 기분이 아니에요. oneureun nyorihal gibuni anieyo. I'm not in the mood to cook.

다듬다 da·deum·da to trim, prepare
콩나물 좀 다듬어라. kongnamul jom dadeumeora. Prepare the bean sprouts.

손질 | ~하다 son·jil | ~·ha·da trimming | to trim, prepare
재료 손질하는 것 좀 도와줄래? jaeryo sonjilhaneun geot jom dowajullae? Can you help me prepare the ingredients?

썰다 sseol·da to cut, chop, slice
고기를 어떻게 썰어 드릴까요? gogireul eotteoke sseoreo deurilkkayo? How shall I cut the meat for you?

자르다 ja·reu·da to cut
무를 얇게 잘라 주세요. mureul lyalge jalla juseyo. Cut the daikon into thin slices.

갈다 gal·da to grind, rub
우선 말린 감자를 갈아 주세요. useon mallin gamjareul gara juseyo. First, grind the dried potatoes.

섞다 seok·da to mix, blend
잘 섞어서 밥 위에 부으세요. jal seokkeoseo bap wie bueuseyo. Mix well and pour over rice.

섞이다 seo·kki·da to be mixed
달걀이 다른 재료들과 잘 섞일 때까지 계속 저으세요. dalgyari dareun jaeryodeulgwa jal seokkil ttaekkaji gyesok jeoeuseyo. Keep stirring till the eggs are well blended with other ingredients.

무치다 mu·chi·da to mix sth with seasoning
나물 좀 무쳐라. namul jom muchyeora. Mix the vegetables with seasoning.

젓다 jeot·da to stir
요리하는 동안 가끔 저어 주세요. yorihaneun dongan gakkeum jeoeo juseyo. Stir occasionally while cooking.

반죽 | ~하다 ban·juk | ~·ha·da dough, paste | to knead, dough
밀가루를 우유에 잘 섞은 뒤 반죽하세요. milgarureul uyue jal seokkeun dwi banjukaseyo. Mix the flour with the milk to form a paste.

붓다 but·da to pour
물을 좀 더 부어 봐. mureul jom deo bueo bwa. Pour some more water.

까다 kka·da to peel, hull, shell
할 일 없으면 마늘 좀 까라. hal il eopseumyeon maneul jom kkara. Peel some garlic if you have nothing to do.

벗기다 beot·gi·da to take off, peel, skin
생선 비늘을 벗겨야 해요? saengseon bineureul beotgyeoya haeyo? Do you want me to scale the fish?

다지다 da·ji·da to mince, chop up
양파랑 마늘을 잘게 다져라. yangparang maneureul jalge dajyeora. Chop the onions and garlic into small pieces.

데우다 de·u·da to heat, warm
우유 좀 데워 줄까? uyu jom dewo julkka? Do you want me to warm the milk up for you?

데치다 de·chi·da to blanch, parboil
채소를 볶기 전에 살짝 데쳐 주세요. chaesoreul bokgi jeone saljjak dechyeo juseyo. Blanch the vegetables prior to stir-frying.

끓이다 kkeu·ri·da to boil
잠시만 기다리세요. 주전자에 물을 끓이고 있어요. jamsiman gidariseyo. jujeonjae mureul kkeurigo isseoyo. Hold on a moment. I'm boiling water in the kettle.

끓다 kkeul·ta to boil
시금치를 끓는 물에 넣어라. sigeumchireul kkeulleun mure neoeora. Put the spinach in the boiling water.

삶다 sam·da to boil
삶은 달걀 있어요? salmeun dalgyal isseoyo? Do you have hard-boiled eggs?

익히다 i·ki·da to cook, boil
고기를 바싹 익혀 주세요. gogireul bassak ikyeo juseyo. I'd like my meat well done.

익다 ik·da to ripen, be done
돼지고기 다 익은 거 맞아? dwaejigogi da igeun geo maja? Are you sure the pork is done?

타다 ta·da to burn, be burned
스테이크 안 타게 잘 보고 있어라. seuteikeu an tage jal bogo isseora. Keep your eye on the steak so that it won't burn.

튀기다 twi·gi·da to fry
생선을 약 5분간 튀겨라. **saengseoneul lyak obungan twigyeora.** Fry the fish for about 5 minutes.

튀다 twi·da to spatter, splash
기름이 사방에 튀어 있었다. **gireumi sabange twieo isseotda.** Oil was spattered everywhere.

볶다 bok·da to stir-fry
양파를 약한 불에서 볶아 주세요. **yangpareul lyakan bureseo bokka juseyo.** Stir-fry the onions in oil over low heat.

굽다 gup·da to roast, grill
방금 구운 빵이야. **banggeum guun ppangiya.** The bread is freshly baked.

찌다 jji·da to steam
찐 감자 좋아해? **jjin gamja joahae?** Do you like steamed potatoes?

김 gim steam
밥솥에서 김이 **빠져** 나갈 때까지 기다리세요. **bapsoteseo gimi ppajyeo nagal ttaekkaji gidariseyo.** Wait until the steam escapes from the cooker.

식히다 si·ki·da to cool, chill
음식을 내놓기 전에 최소 한 시간은 식히세요. **eumsigeul laenoki jeone choeso han siganeun sikiseyo.** Chill for at least 1 hour prior to serving.

식다 sik·da to cool down, get cold
국이 식을 때까지 기다려라. **gugi sigeul ttaekkaji gidaryeora.** Wait for the soup to cool down.

간 gan saltiness

보다 bo·da to taste, try
간 좀 봐. 간이 맞아? **gan jom bwa. gani maja?** Taste this. Is it well seasoned?

재료 jae·ryo material, ingredient

신선하다 sin·seon·ha·da fresh, new

저희 식당은 **신선한 재료**만을 사용합니다. **jeohui sikdangeun sinseonhan jaeryomaneul sayonghamnida.** My restaurant uses only fresh ingredients.

싱싱하다 sing·sing·ha·da fresh
채소가 아주 **싱싱해** 보이네요. **chaesoga aju singsinghae boineyo.** The vegetables look fresh.

썩다 sseok·da to rot, decay
이런! 사과가 썩었어. **ireon! sagwaga sseogeosseo.** Oops! The apple is rotten!

상하다 sang·ha·da to go bad
장마철에는 **음식이** 쉽게 **상하죠.** **jangmacheoreuneun eumsigi swipge sanghajyo.** Food goes bad easily during the rainy season.

얼리다 eol·li·da to freeze
고기를 얼려서 보관하세요. **gogireul eollyeoseo bogwanhaseyo.** Preserve the meat by freezing it.

녹이다 no·gi·da to melt
버터를 녹여서 서늘한 곳에 치워 두세요. **beoteoreul logyeoseo seoneulhan gose chiwo duseyo.** Melt the butter and set it aside to cool.

오븐 o·beun oven

가스레인지 ga·seu·re·in·ji gas stove

전자레인지 jeon·ja·re·in·ji microwave

밥솥 bap·sot rice cooker

도마 do·ma cutting board

칼 kal knife

식칼 sik·kal kitchen knife

프라이팬 peu·ra·i·paen frying pan

냄비 ← **남비** naem·bi ← nam·bi pot

뚜껑 ttu·kkeong cover, cap, top
냄비 뚜껑 어디 갔어? **naembi ttukkeong eodi gasseo?** Where's the pan lid?

가구 가구 가스 거실 건넌방 건전지 계단 공부방

공원 구역 굴뚝 기숙사 난로 냉방 냉장고

다리 다세대주택 단독주택 대도시 대문 댁 댐

시 동네 라디오 리모컨 마당 마을 밀리다

방 방문 방바닥 벤치 변기 보증금 부동산 부엌

부채 불 블라인드 빌딩 생활 서랍 서재 석유

풍기 세면대 소파 수도 수돗물 숯 시골 시설

chapter **14** Living
Arrangements

안방 양로원 연기 열 열쇠 옆방 옆집 오디오

온돌 옷방 욕실 욕조 원룸 월세 위층 유리창

이웃 이웃집 임대 장롱 장식 전국 전세 주거

주택 지방 지역 지하 집 집세 채 책꽂이

장 천장 치다 치르다 침대 침실 텔레비전

하숙집 현관 화장대 화장실 휘발유

14.1 Places

전국 | ~적 jeon·guk | ~·jeok   the whole country | countrywide
독감이 **전국적으로** 유행하고 있다. dokgami jeongukjeogeuro yuhaenghago itda. The flu has spread throughout the country.

수도 su·do capital
서울은 한국의 **수도**다. seoureun hangugui sudoda. Seoul is the capital of Korea.

수도권 su·do·gwon capital area
수도권의 교통 체증이 심각하다. sudogwonui gyotong chejeungi simgakada. The traffic jams in the capital area are serious.

지방 ji·bang area, region; the provinces
이 **지방**은 사과로 유명합니다. i jibangeun sagwaro yumyeonghamnida. This region is famous for its apples.

지방 학생들은 대개 학교 주변에서 자취를 합니다. jibang haksaengdeureun daegae hakgyo jubyeoneseo jachwireul hamnida. Most students from the provinces live apart from their family in places near their schools instead.

도시 do·si city, town
바쁜 **도시 생활**로부터 벗어나고 싶어요. bappeun dosi saenghwallobuteo beoseonago sipeoyo. I want to escape from the busy city life.

대도시 dae·do·si metropolis, big city
많은 사람들이 일자리를 찾아 대도시로 온다. maneun saramdeuri iljarireul chaja daedosiro onda. Many people come to big cities to find work.

도심 = 시내 do·sim = si·nae downtown
저는 도심에서/시내에서 운전하는 걸 좋아하지 않습니다. jeoneun dosimeseo/sinaeeseo unjeonhaneun geol joahaji anseumnida. I don't like driving downtown.

시외 si·oe countryside

시골 si·gol rural area
저는 시골에서 자랐어요. jeoneun sigoreseo jarasseoyo. I grew up in the countryside.

구역 gu·yeok area, quarter, zone
금연 **구역** geumnyeon guyeok smoke-free area

지역 ji·yeok area, region
저는 이 **지역**을 아주 잘 알아요. jeoneun i jiyeogeul aju jal arayo. I know this area very well.

가구 ga·gu household, family

마을 ma·eul village, town
이 마을에는 고작 다섯 가구가 산다. i maeureneun gojak daseot gaguga sanda. There are only five families living in this village.

동네 dong·ne neighborhood, town
이 **동네**에 공원이 있어요? i dongnee gongwoni isseoyo? Is there a park in this neighborhood?

주민 ju·min resident
이 **동네 주민**이세요? i dongne juminiseyo? Are you a local resident?

....

시설 si·seol facilities
저희 대학은 올해 초 장애인을 위한 시설을 확장했습니다. jeohui daehageun olhae cho jangaeineul wihan siseoreul hwakjanghaetseumnida. Our university expanded facilities for the disabled early this year.

공원 gong·won park
공원에 산책 갈까? gongwone sanchaek galkka? How about going for a walk in the park?

벤치 ben·chi bench

회관 hoe·gwan meeting hall
사람들이 **마을 회관**에 모여 있다. saramdeuri maeul hoegwane moyeo itda. People are gathered in the town hall.

경로당 gyeong·no·dang senior citizen center

고아원 go·a·won orphanage

양로원 yang·no·won nursing home

광장 gwang·jang square, plaza
수천 명의 성난 시민들이 **광장**으로 모여들었다. sucheon myeongui seongnan simindeuri gwangjangeuro moyeodeureotda. Thousands of angry citizens have gathered in the plaza.

댐 daem dam

다리 da·ri bridge
다리 밑으로 개울이 흘러요. dari miteuro gaeuri heulleoyo. A stream flows under the bridge.

....

집 jip house, home
A: 수지 집에 있어요? B: 아뇨, 지금 없어요.

A: suji jibe isseoyo? B: anyo, jigeum eopseoyo.
A: Is Suji in? B: No, she is not home now.

채 chae unit for counting houses
나는 집이 두 채 있다. **naneun jibi du chae itda.**
I have two houses.

댁 daek honorific of 집 **jip**

생활 | ~하다 saeng·hwal | ~·ha·da life |
to live
이곳의 **생활 환경**은 정말 열악해. **igosui saenghwal hwangyeongeun jeongmal lyeorakae.** The living conditions here are really poor.

생활비 saeng·hwal·bi living expenses
시골보다 도시가 **생활비**가 훨씬 많이 **들어요**. **sigolboda dosiga saenghwalbiga hwolssin mani deureoyo.** The cost of living is much higher in the city than in the countryside.

거주 | ~하다 geo·ju | ~·ha·da residence |
to live, reside
이곳 기후는 사람이 거주하기에 적합하지 않다. **igot gihuneun sarami geojuhagie jeokapaji anta.** The weather here is unfit for human habitation.

주거 ju·geo dwelling, residence

이웃 i·ut neighbor
우리 이웃은 아주 좋은 사람들이다. **uri iuseun aju joeun saramdeurida.** Our neighbors are very nice.

이웃집 i·ut·jip neighbor's house

옆집 yeop·jip next door
엄마는 옆집에 사세요. **eommaneun nyeopjibe saseyo.** My mom lives next door.

부동산 = 복덕방 bu·dong·san = bok· deok·bang real estate office
이 거리에 부동산이/복덕방이 많이 밀집해 있다. **i georie budongsani/bokdeokbangi mani**

miljipae itda. Many real estate offices are concentrated on this street.

(집)주인 (jip·)ju·in house owner, landlord
집주인하고 얘기하고 싶어요. **jipjuinhago yaegihago sipeoyo.** I'd like to speak with the landlord.

세입자 se·ip·ja tenant

임대 | ~하다 im·dae | ~·ha·da lease | to rent, lease
임대 기간이 다음 달에 끝나요. **imdae gigani daeum dare kkeunnayo.** The lease expires next month.

전세 jeon·se *jeonse*, (key-money) lease

Jeonse is a way to lease a house unique to South Korea. Instead of paying monthly, the tenant gives the landlord a large amount of key money, and he gets it back when the lease ends.

월세 wol·se monthly rent
이 집은 월세가 50만 원이다. **i jibeun wolsega osimman wonida.** The rent for this house is five hundred thousand won a month.

보증금 bo·jeung·geum deposit

집세 jip·se house rent

치르다 chi·reu·da to pay
집세를 치렀나요? **jipsereul chireonnayo?** Did you pay the rent?

밀리다 mil·li·da to be overdue
집세가 두 달이나 밀려 있다. **jipsega du darina millyeo itda.** I am two months behind in rent.

이사 | ~하다 i·sa | ~·ha·da move | to move
어디로 이사하세요? **eodiro isahaseyo?** Where are you moving to?

14.2 Houses, Furnishings, Miscellaneous Items

주택 ju·taek house
이 동네에는 고급 **주택**들이 많아요. **i dongneeneun gogeup jutaekdeuri manayo.** There are lots of luxurious houses in this neighborhood.

단독주택 dan·dok·ju·taek single-unit house

다세대주택 = 연립주택 = 빌라 da·se·

dae·ju·taek = yeol·lip·ju·taek = bil·la town house

아파트 a·pa·teu apartment, condominium
우리는 같은 아파트에 삽니다. **urineun gateun apateue samnida.** We live in the same apartment.

오피스텔 o·pi·seu·tel studio, efficiency apartment

저는 오피스텔에 살고 있어요. **jeoneun opi-seutere salgo isseoyo.** I live in an efficiency apartment.

원룸 won·num studio
가구가 완비된 원룸을 찾고 있습니다. **gaguga wanbidoen wonnumeul chatgo itseumnida.** I'm looking for a furnished studio apartment.

건물 geon·mul building
이 건물을 짓는 데 삼 년이 걸렸다. **i geon-mureul jinneun de sam nyeoni geollyeotda.** The construction of this building took three years.

빌딩 bil·ding (modern) building

기숙사 gi·suk·sa residence hall

하숙집 ha·suk·jip boarding house
그는 사무실 근처의 하숙집에서 산다. **geu-neun samusil geuncheoui hasukjibeseo sanda.** He lives in a boarding house near the office.

셋방 set·bang rented room
저는 학교 근처 셋방에 살아요. **jeoneun hak-gyo geuncheo setbange sarayo.** I live in a rent-ed room near the school.

현관(문) hyeon·gwan(·mun) (front) door, (front) entrance
신발은 현관에서 벗으세요. **sinbareun hyeon-gwaneseo beoseuseyo.** Take off your shoes at the front door.

문 mun door, gate
문 닫고 들어오세요. **mun datgo deureooseyo.** Close the door behind you.

정문 jeong·mun front gate

대문 dae·mun main entrance
대문 잠그는 것 잊지 마. **daemun jamgeuneun geot itji ma.** Don't forget to lock the gates.

창(문) chang(·mun) window
그녀는 창문을 한 달에 한 번 청소한다. **geu-nyeoneun changmuneul han dare han beon cheongsohanda.** She cleans the windows once a month.

유리창 yu·ri·chang (glass) window
유리창이 너무 지저분해요. **yurichangi neomu jijeobunhaeyo.** The window is so dirty.

열쇠 yeol·soe key
열쇠 여분이 있나요? **yeolsoe yeobuni innayo?** Do you have a spare key?

벽 byeok wall

거실의 벽은 지금 막 칠했습니다. **geosirui byeogeun jigeum mak chilhaetseumnida.** The walls of the living room have just been painted.

담(장) dam(·jang) wall, fence
공이 담 너머로 넘어갔다. **gongi dam neo-meoro neomeogatda.** The ball went over the fence.

층 cheung floor, story
영업부는 5층에 있습니다. **yeongeopbuneun ocheunge itseumnida.** The sales department is on the fifth floor.

위층 wi·cheung upstairs

아래층 a·rae·cheung downstairs

복도 bok·do hallway
복도에 물건을 놓아 두면 안 됩니다. **bokdoe mulgeoneul loa dumyeon an doemnida.** You shouldn't leave stuff in the hallway.

계단 gye·dan stairs, staircase
이 계단은 지하실로 이어진다. **i gyedaneun ji-hasillo ieojinda.** These stairs lead down to the basement.

엘리베이터 = 승강기 el·li·be·i·teo = seung·gang·gi elevator
엘리베이터가/승강기가 멈췄어. 관리인을 불러야 해. **ellibeiteoga/seungganggiga meom-chwosseo. gwalliineul bulleoya hae.** The eleva-tor is stuck; you will have to call the building manager.

에스컬레이터 e·seu·keol·le·i·teo escala-tor

실내 sil·lae indoor
따뜻한 실내에 있어라. **ttatteutan sillaee isseo-ra.** Stay indoors where it's warm.

방 bang room
내 방에서는 거리가 내다보인다. **nae bange-seoneun georiga naedaboinda.** My room over-looks the street.

방바닥 bang·ba·dak floor of the room

방문 bang·mun door of a room

안방 an·bang main room
안방의 가구를 바꿔야겠어요. **anbangui gagu-reul bakkwoyagesseoyo.** We should change the furniture in the master bedroom.

침실 chim·sil bedroom

우리는 침실이 두 개 있는 아파트를 구하고 있어요. urineun chimsiri du gae inneun apateureul guhago isseoyo. We're looking for an apartment with two bedrooms.

건넌방 ← 건너방 geon·neon·bang ← geon·neo·bang the room across from the main room
건넌방에 가서 놀아라. geonneonbange gaseo norara. Go play in another room.

옆방 yeop·bang next room
부모님이 옆방에 계신다. bumonimi yeopbange gyesinda. My parents are in the next room.

옷방 ot·bang dressing room

거실 geo·sil living room
아버지는 거실에서 낮잠을 자고 계세요. abeojineun geosireseo natjameul jago gyeseyo. My dad is napping in the living room.

마루 ma·ru floor
나는 마루를 쓸 테니까 너는 닦아. naneun marureul sseul tenikka neoneun dakka. I'll sweep the floor and you mop, OK?

천장 ← 천정 cheon·jang ← cheon·jeong ceiling
그 건물은 천장이 높다. geu geonmureun cheonjangi nopda. The building has high ceiling.

부엌 = 주방 ← 부억 bu·eok = ju·bang kitchen
아내는 부엌에서/주방에서 음식을 준비하고 있습니다. anaeneun bueokseo/jubangeseo eumsigeul junbihago itseumnida. My wife is preparing meals in the kitchen.

화장실 hwa·jang·sil restroom, toilet
화장실이 어디 있어요? hwajangsiri eodi isseoyo? Where is the restroom?

욕실 yok·sil bathroom
욕실이 너무 작은 게 아쉽네요. yoksiri neomu jageun ge aswimneyo. Too bad the bathroom is too small.

변기 byeon·gi toilet
변기가 막혔으니 사용하지 마라. byeongiga makyeosseuni sayonghaji mara. Don't use the toilet because it's clogged.

세면대 se·myeon·dae basin

욕조 yok·jo bathtub

수도꼭지 su·do·kkok·ji faucet
수도꼭지에서 물이 떨어져요. sudokkokjieseo

muri tteoreojyeoyo. The faucet is dripping.

서재 seo·jae study

공부방 gong·bu·bang study

지하실 ji·ha·sil basement

옥상 ok·sang rooftop

지붕 ji·bung roof
지붕은 비, 열, 햇빛, 바람을 막는다. jibungeun bi, yeol, haetbit, barameul mangneunda. A roof protects against rain, heat, sunlight, and wind.

굴뚝 gul·ttuk chimney

다락(방) da·rak(·bang) attic

베란다 be·ran·da veranda

지하 ji·ha basement
여성들이 지하 주차장에 주차하는 것은 위험하다. yeoseongdeuri jiha juchajange juchahaneun geoseun wiheomhada. It is dangerous for women to use the underground parking lots.

실외 ≒ 야외 si·roe ≒ ya·oe the outside, the outdoors
실외/야외 수영장은 겨울에 문을 닫습니다. siroe/yaoe suyeongjangeun gyeoure muneul datseumnida. The outdoor swimming pool is closed during winter.

마당 ≒ 뜰 ≒ 정원 ma·dang ≒ tteul ≒ jeong·won yard, garden

창고 chang·go warehouse, storage
A: 소파 어디 있어? B: 창고에. A: sopa eodi isseo? B: changgoe. A: Where is the sofa? B: In the warehouse.

가구 ga·gu furniture
그 가구는 아주 현대적인 것 같아. geu gaguneun aju hyeondaejeogin geot gata. The furniture looks very modern to me.

침대 chim·dae bed
A: 내 열쇠 어디 갔지? B: 침대 위는 봤어? A: nae yeolsoe eodi gatji? B: chimdae wineun bwasseo? A: Where is my key? B: Did you check the bed?

옷장 ot·jang wardrobe

장롱 jang·nong wardrobe

화장대 hwa·jang·dae vanity

책꽂이 chaek·kko·ji bookshelf

책을 다시 **책꽂이에 꽂아라**. chaegeul dasi chaekkkojie kkojara. Put the book back on the shelf.

책장 chaek·jang bookcase

서랍 seo·rap drawer
팬티는 맨 아래 서랍에 있다. paentineun maen arae seorabe itda. The underpants are in the bottom drawer.

소파 ← 쇼파 so·pa ← syo·pa sofa
나는 **소파에 앉아** 책을 읽으며 저녁을 보내는 걸 좋아한다. naneun sopae anja chaegeul ilgeumyeo jeonyeogeul bonaeneun geol johanda. I like to spend my evenings on the sofa reading books.

냉장고 naeng·jang·go refrigerator, fridge
아내는 **최신형 냉장고**를 사고 싶어해요. anaeneun choesinhyeong naengjanggoreul sago sipeohaeyo. My wife would like to buy the latest refrigerator.

텔레비전 ← 테레비 tel·le·bi·jeon ← te·re·bi television (set)
텔레비전 소리 좀 줄여라. tellebijeon sori jom juryeora. Turn down the TV.

리모컨 ri·mo·keon remote control

라디오 ra·di·o radio

오디오 o·di·o stereo system

냉방 naeng·bang air conditioning

에어컨 e·eo·keon air conditioner
왜 **에어컨을 껐어요?** 더워 죽겠어요. wae eeokeoneul kkeosseoyo? deowo jukgesseoyo. Why did you turn off the air conditioner? I'm dying from the heat.

선풍기 seon·pung·gi electric fan
선풍기 앞에서 머리를 말려라. seonpunggi apeseo meorireul mallyeora. Dry your hair in front of the fan.

부채 bu·chae fan
나는 **선풍기보다 부채**가 더 좋아. naneun seonpunggiboda buchaega deo joa. I prefer hand-held fans to electric fans.

장식 | ~하다 jang·sik | ~·ha·da decoration | to decorate
식탁 위에 꽃이 장식되어 있었다. siktak wie kkochi jangsikdoeeo isseotda. The table was decorated with flowers.

커튼 ← 커텐 keo·teun ← keo·ten curtain
방에 빛이 좀 들어오게 **커튼을 열어** 주시겠어요? bange bichi jom deureooge keoteuneul lyeoreo jusigesseoyo? Could you please open the curtains to let more light into the room?

블라인드 beul·la·in·deu the blinds
블라인드 좀 내려도 될까요? beullaindeu jom naeryeodo doelkkayo? Do you mind if I lower the blinds?

치다 chi·da to draw, close
어두워졌으니 **커튼을 쳐라**. eoduwojyeosseuni keoteuneul chyeora. It's dark outside. Close the curtains.

14.3 Fuel, Energy

에너지 e·neo·ji energy
에너지를 절약합시다. eneojireul jeoryakapsida. Let's save energy.

연료 yeol·lyo fuel
이 나무는 연료로 사용됩니다. i namuneun nyeollyoro sayongdoemnida. This wood is used as fuel.

기름 gi·reum gasoline, gas, oil
제 차는 **기름**을 많이 **먹어요**. je chaneun gireumeul mani meogeoyo. My car uses so much gas.

석유 seo·gyu oil, petroleum

휘발유 hwi·bal·lyu gasoline, gas

가스 ga·seu gas
가스 밸브 잠갔는지 확인해라. gaseu baelbeu jamganneunji hwaginhaera. Make sure you turned off the gas valve.

주유소 ju·yu·so gas station
저는 지금 주유소에서 아르바이트를 하고 있어요. jeoneun jigeum juyusoeseo areubaiteureul hago isseoyo. I currently work part-time at a gas station.

전기 jeon·gi electricity
간밤의 심한 비바람으로 **전기가 끊겼어요**.

ganbamui simhan bibarameuro jeongiga kkeun-kyeosseoyo. The electricity was cut off due to the storm last night.

건전지 = 배터리 geon·jeon·ji = bae·teo·ri battery

충전 | ~하다 chung·jeon | ~·ha·da charge | to (re)charge
이 배터리는 충전용인가요? i baeteorineun chungjeonnyongingayo? Is this a rechargeable battery?

불 bul fire; light
어렸을 때 목이 **불**에 데었어요. eoryeosseul ttae mogi bure deeosseoyo. My neck got scalded when I was little.
불이 너무 **어두워요**. buri neomu eoduwoyo. The light is too dim.

연탄 yeon·tan briquette
북한에서는 부유한 사람들만이 겨울에 **연탄**을 사용할 수 있다. bukhaneseoneun buyuhan saramdeulmani gyeoure yeontaneul sayonghal su itda. In North Korea, only rich people can use coal briquettes for fuel in the winter.

숯 sut charcoal

열 yeol heat
컴퓨터는 동작하면서 부산물로 **열**을 발생시킨다. keompyuteoneun dongjakamyeonseo busanmullo yeoreul balsaengsikinda. All computers generate heat as a by-product of use.

난방 nan·bang heating
이 건물은 **난방 시설**이 열악하다. i geonmureun nanbang siseori yeorakada. This building has a poor heating system.

난로 nal·lo heater, stove
난로에 불 좀 피울까? nannoe bul jom piulkka? Do you want me to start a fire in the fireplace?

보일러 bo·il·leo boiler, furnace
갑자기 뜨거운 물이 안 나와. 보일러에 문제가 있나 봐. gapjagi tteugeoun muri an nawa. boilleoe munjega inna bwa. Suddenly my hot water stopped working. There must be something wrong with the boiler.

온돌 on·dol *ondol*

Ondol is a traditional Korean heating system. Nowadays, there are pipes underneath the floor, through which heated water flows and warms the room.

수돗물 su·don·mul tap water, running water
추후 공지가 있을 때까지 **수돗물**을 마시지 않기를 부탁드립니다. chuhu gongjiga isseul ttaekkaji sudonmureul masiji ankireul butakdeurimnida. We recommend not drinking the tap water until further notice.

화재 hwa·jae fire
지진 후에 큰 **화재**가 발생했다. jijin hue keun hwajaega balsaenghaetda. A big fire broke out after the earthquake.

타다 ta·da to burn, blaze
뭔가 **타는** 냄새 안 나? mwonga taneun naemsae an na? Don't you smell something burning?

연기 yeon·gi smoke
저 건물은 연기로 가득 찼다. jeo geonmureun nyeongiro gadeuk chatda. That building is filled with smoke.

소화기 so·hwa·gi fire extinguisher
소화기는 1년 두 번 이상 점검을 해야 한다. sohwagineun illyeon du beon isang jeomgeomeul haeya handa. Fire extinguishers should be checked at least twice a year.

같이 결혼 결혼기념일 결혼식 고모 고모부

관하다 교제 남 남매 녀 다툼 대접 대하다 동갑

동생 둘째 따로 딸아이 마누라 마주치다

파중 막내 막내아들 말리다 며느리 모시다 모친

미팅 배웅 별거 본가 부모 부부 부인 부친

사귀다 사귀다 사위 사이 사이좋다 삼촌

서로 성 시댁 시집 시집 시집가다 아들

chapter 15 | Family and Social Relations

아들아이 아버지 아빠 아이 애인 약혼식

어머니 언니 여동생 여보 오빠 외아들

용서 우정 위자료 위하다 이별 이성 인연 임부 입덧

자식 작은아버지 장가가다 장남 장녀 장인 조카 진통

질녀 집안 차녀 찾아가다 처가 청첩장 청혼 조대

축의금 출산 친정 친하다 큰아버지 키스 태아 피임

할아버지 형 형제 혼인 혼자 화해

15.1 Family

가정 ga·jeong home, family
요즘은 거의 모든 가정에 인터넷이 연결되어 있어요. **yojeumeun geoui modeun gajeonge inteonesi yeongyeoldoeeo isseoyo.** Almost every home is hooked up to the Internet nowadays.

가족 ga·jok family
어머니가 **가족을 부양하고** 계세요. **eomeoniga gajogeul buyanghago gyeseyo.** My mother supports our family.

식구 sik·gu family member
식구들 모두가 감기에 걸렸다. **sikgudeul moduga gamgie geollyeotda.** The whole family has caught a cold.

집안 ji·ban home, family
명절을 맞아 온 집안 식구가 모였다. **myeongjeoreul maja on jiban sikguga moyeotda.** The whole family has gathered together to celebrate a holiday.

가장 ga·jang head of a family
이 모금 행사는 십대 **소년 소녀 가장**을 돕기 위한 것입니다. **i mogeum haengsaneun sipdae sonyeon sonyeo gajangeul dopgi wihan geosimnida.** The purpose of this fundraiser is to help teenagers who are the breadwinners of their families.

(가정)주부 (ga·jeong·)ju·bu homemaker
엄마는 **평범한** 가정주부세요. **eommaneun pyeongbeomhan gajeongjubuseyo.** My mom is an ordinary housewife.

부모 bu·mo parents
이번 여름에 부모님이랑 여행 갈 계획이에요. **ibeon nyeoreume bumonimirang yeohaeng gal gyehoegieyo.** I'm planning a trip with my parents this summer.

아버지 a·beo·ji father
아버지는 연세가 어떻게 되십니까? **abeojineun nyeonsega eotteoke doesimnikka?** How old is your father?

부친 bu·chin father

아빠 a·ppa dad

어머니 eo·meo·ni mother
어머니는 내가 태어날 때까지 일을 계속했다. **eomeonineun naega taeeonal ttaekkaji ireul gyesokaetda.** My mother continued to work until I was born.

모친 mo·chin mother

엄마 eom·ma mom

할아버지 ha·ra·beo·ji grandfather
할아버지는 늘 일찍 주무세요. **harabeojineun neul iljjik jumuseyo.** My grandfather always goes to bed early.

할머니 hal·meo·ni grandmother
할머니는 제주도에 사세요. **halmeonineun jejudoe saseyo.** My grandmother lives on Jeju Island.

자녀 ja·nyeo children, sons and daughters
자녀가 몇이세요? **janyeoga myeochiseyo?** How many children do you have?

자녀 is usually used to refer to someone else's children.

자식 ja·sik children, sons and daughters
남편과 저는 자식을 원해요. **nampyeongwa jeoneun jasigeul wonhaeyo.** My husband and I want a child.

아이 = 애 a·i = ae child, sons and daughters
저희는 아이가/애가 없어요. **jeohuineun aiga/aega eopseoyo.** We have no children.

남 nam son

녀 nyeo daughter
저는 2남 1녀 중 막내예요. **jeoneun inam illyeo jung mangnaeyeyo.** I'm the youngest of two sons and one daughter.

첫째 = 맏이 cheot·jjae = ma·ji the eldest
저는 사 남매 중 첫째예요/맏이예요. **jeoneun sa nammae jung cheotjjaeyeyo/majiyeyo.** I'm the eldest of four children.

둘째 dul·jjae second child

막내 mang·nae the youngest

아들 a·deul son
저는 아들 하나와 딸 하나예요. **jeoneun adeul hanawa ttal hanayeyo.** I have a son and a daughter.

아들아이 = 아들애 a·deu·ra·i = a·deu·rae (one's) son
아들아이가/아들애가 내년에 초등학교에 들

어가요. adeuraiga/adeuraega naenyeone cho-deunghakgyoe deureogayo. My son enters elementary school next year.

아드님 a·deu·nim (sb else's) son
아드님이 정말 자랑스러우시겠어요. adeunimi jeongmal jarangseureousigesseoyo. You must be very proud of your son.

장남 = 큰아들 jang·nam = keu·na·deul eldest son
한국에서는 주로 장남이/큰아들이 부모님과 함께 살았다. hangugeseoneun juro jangnami/keunadeuri bumonimgwa hamkke saratda. In Korea, the eldest son usually used to live with his parents.

차남 = 작은아들 cha·nam = ja·geu·na·deul second son

막내아들 mang·nae·a·deul youngest son

외(동)아들 oe(·dong)·a·deul only son
그들은 작년에 사고로 **외아들**을 **잃었다**. geudeureun jangnyeone sagoro oeadeureul ireotda. They lost their only son in an accident last year.

딸 ttal daughter

딸아이 = 딸애 tta·ra·i = tta·rae (one's) daughter
저는 **딸아이**를/딸애를 늦게 **얻었어요**. jeoneun ttaraireul/ttaraereul leutge eodeosseoyo. I had a daughter late in my life.

따님 tta·nim (sb else's) daughter

장녀 = 큰딸 jang·nyeo = keun·ttal eldest daughter

차녀 = 작은딸 cha·nyeo = ja·geun·ttal second daughter

막내딸 mang·nae·ttal youngest daughter

외동딸 oe·dong·ttal only daughter

손주 son·ju grandchild
아버지는 손주를 원하세요. abeojineun sonjureul wonhaseyo. My father wants grandchildren.

손자 son·ja grandson
그는 손자에게 울음을 그치면 케이크를 주겠다고 약속했다. geuneun sonjaege ureumeul geuchimyeon keikeureul jugetdago yaksokaetda. He promised his grandson a cake if he stopped crying.

손녀 son·nyeo granddaughter
그녀는 손녀에게 많은 돈을 남겨주었다. geunyeoneun sonnyeoege maneun doneul lamgyeojueotda. She left a lot of money to her granddaughter.

형제 hyeong·je brother, sibling
형제가 몇이나 되세요? hyeongjega myeochina doeseyo? How many siblings do you have?

남매 nam·mae brother and sister
그는 다섯 남매를 두었다. geuneun daseot nammaereul dueotda. He has five sons and daughters.

자매 ja·mae sisters
저는 세 자매 중 막내예요. jeoneun se jamae jung mangnaeyeyo. I'm the youngest of three sisters.

형 hyeong boy's elder brother
형은 호주에서 살고 있습니다. hyeongeun ho-jueseo salgo itseumnida. My older brother lives in Australia.

In Korea, people don't call their older siblings by their names. Instead, they use 형, 오빠, 누나, or 언니 according to the gender of the speakers and their older siblings.

오빠 o·ppa girl's elder brother
그녀는 자기 오빠를 아주 많이 존경한다. geunyeoneun jagi opparaeul aju mani jongyeonghanda. She looks up to her brother very much.

누나 nu·na boy's elder sister
우리 엄마는 혼자서 나와 누나 둘을 길렀다. uri eommaneun honjaseo nawa nuna dureul gilleotda. My mom raised me and my two sisters by herself.

언니 eon·ni girl's elder sister
어제는 언니 집에서 잤어요. eojeneun eonni jibeseo jasseoyo. I slept at my older sister's house last night.

동생 dong·saeng younger sibling
저는 동생과 사이가 안 좋아요. jeoneun dongsaenggwa saiga an joayo. I am not on good terms with my younger brother/sister.

여동생 yeo·dong·saeng younger sister

남동생 nam·dong·saeng younger brother

부부 bu·bu (married) couple, husband and wife

요즘에는 아이를 원하지 않는 부부가 많아요. **yojeumeneun aireul wonhaji anneun bubuga manayo.** These days, many couples don't want to have kids.

: 남편 nam·pyeon husband
남편은 패션에 무관심해요. **nampyeoneun paesyeone mugwansimhaeyo.** My husband isn't interested in fashion.

: 아내 = 와이프 a·nae = wa·i·peu wife
이제 나도 아내가 필요하다. **ije nado anaega piryohada.** Now I need a wife.

: 부인 bu·in honorific of 아내 **anae**
부인은 어디 계세요? **buineun eodi gyeseyo?** Where is your wife?

˙ 마누라 ma·nu·ra wife
어젯밤에 마누라랑 싸웠어요. **eojetbame manurarang ssawosseoyo.** I argued with my wife last night.

마누라 is a casual term for *wife*. It can be very inappropriate to use it to refer to someone else's wife.

: 여보 yeo·bo darling, honey, sweetheart
다녀왔어요, 여보. **danyeowasseoyo, yeobo.** I'm home, honey!

사돈 sa·don in-laws
우리는 사돈 간입니다. **urineun sadon ganimnida.** We're in-laws.

: 사위 sa·wi son-in-law
사위는 변호사예요. **sawineun byeonhosayeyo.** My son-in-law is a lawyer.

: 며느리 myeo·neu·ri daughter-in-law
아내는 며느리와 잘 지냅니다. **anaeneun myeoneuriwa jal jinaemnida.** My wife gets along with our daughter-in-law.

: 시부모 si·bu·mo husband's parents
저희는 시부모님과 함께 삽니다. **jeohuineun sibumonimgwa hamkke samnida.** We live with our parents-in-law.

: 시아버지 si·a·beo·ji husband's father
시아버지는 최근에 돌아가셨어요. **siabeojineun choegeune doragasyeosseoyo.** My father-in-law passed away recently.

A woman calls her husband's father 아버님 **abeonim.**

: 시어머니 si·eo·meo·ni husband's mother
시어머니는 좋은 분이시지만 저는 아직 어머

님이 어려워요. **sieomeonineun joeun bunisijiman jeoneun ajik geomeonimi eoryeowoyo.** My mother-in-law is kind but I still feel uncomfortable with her.

A woman calls her husband's mother 어머님 **eomeonim.**

˙ 장인 jang·in wife's father
장인 어른은 작년에 은퇴하셨습니다. **jangin eoreuneun jangnyeone euntoehasyeotseumnida.** My father-in-law retired last year.

A man calls his wife's father 장인 어른 **jangin eoreun** or 아버님 **abeonim.**

˙ 장모 jang·mo wife's mother
우리는 일요일에 장인, 장모님을 찾아뵐 예정이다. **urineun iryoire jangin, jangmonimeul chajaboel yejeongida.** We're visiting my wife's parents on Sunday.

A man calls his wife's mother 장모님 **jangmonim** or 어머님 **eomeonim.**

: 시집 si·jip husband's parents' home
이번 설에 시집에 가 봐야 해요. **ibeon seore sijibe ga bwaya haeyo.** I should go to my in-laws' house for the Lunar New Year.

˙ 시댁 si·daek honorific of 시집 **sijip**

˙ 친정 chin·jeong married woman's parents' home
아내는 친정에 가 있어요. **anaeneun chinjeonge ga isseoyo.** My wife stays at her parents' home.

본가 bon·ga parents' home
본가는 서울에 있습니다. **bonganeun seoure itseumnida.** My parents live in Seoul.

처가 cheo·ga wife's home
처가 쪽 친척들과 친하세요? **cheoga jjok chincheokdeulgwa chinhaseyo?** Are you close to your wife's relatives?

친가 chin·ga father's side

외가 oe·ga mother's side; mother's parents' home

˙ 친척 chin·cheok relative
오직 **가까운 친척**들만이 결혼식에 참석했다. **ojik gakkaun chincheokdeulmani gyeolhonsige chamseokaetda.** Only the nearest relatives were present at the wedding.

삼촌 ← 삼춘 sam·chon ← sam·chun uncle
나는 어릴 때 삼촌과 함께 살았다. naneun eoril ttae samchongwa hamkke saratda. I lived with my uncle when I was little.

큰아버지 keu·na·beo·ji older brother of one's father

큰어머니 keu·neo·meo·ni wife of 큰아버지 keunabeoji

작은아버지 ja·geun·a·beo·ji younger brother of one's father

작은어머니 = 숙모 ja·geun·eo·meo·ni = sung·mo wife of 작은아버지 jageunabeoji

고모 go·mo sister of one's father

우리 고모와 아버지는 많이 닮았습니다. uri gomowa abeojineun mani dalmatseumnida. My aunt and my father look so much alike.

고모부 go·mo·bu husband of 고모 gomo

이모 i·mo sister of one's mother
이모가 졸업 선물로 시계를 주셨다. imoga joreop seonmullo sigyereul jusyeotda. My aunt gave me a watch as a graduation present.

이모부 i·mo·bu husband of 이모 imo

사촌 ← 사춘 sa·chon ← sa·chun cousin

조카 jo·ka nephew, niece

질녀 jil·lyeo niece

15.2 Relationships, Making Friends, Dating

인간관계 in·gan·gwan·gye relationship, human relations
인간관계에서 의사소통만큼 중요한 것도 없다. ingangwangyeeseo uisasotongmankeum jungyohan geotdo eopda. Communication is the most important thing in relationships.

만나다 man·na·da to meet, see
어제 철민이를 **우연히 만났어.** eoje cheolminireul uyeonhi mannasseo. I ran into Cheolmin yesterday.

만남 man·nam meeting

마주치다 ma·ju·chi·da to run into
어제 길에서 예전 남자 친구와 마주쳤다. eoje gireseo yejeon namja chinguwa majuchyeotda. Yesterday I ran into my ex-boyfriend on the street.

헤어지다 he·eo·ji·da to break up
저는 작년에 아내와 헤어졌어요. jeoneun jangnyeone anaewa heeojyeosseoyo. My wife and I divorced last year.

이별 | ~하다 i·byeol | ~·ha·da farewell, parting | to part
사랑하는 사람과 이별하는 일은 힘든 법이다. saranghaneun saramgwa ibyeolhaneun ireun himdeun beobida. It's hard to say goodbye to someone you love.

작별 | ~하다 jak·byeol | ~·ha·da farewell, parting | to part
그는 **작별 인사도** 없이 파티를 빠져나갔다. geuneun jakbyeol insado eopsi patireul ppa-

jyeonagatda. He slipped out of the party without saying goodbye.

초대 ≒ 초청 | ~하다 cho·dae ≒ cho·cheong | ~·ha·da invitation | to invite
귀하를 저희의 결혼식에 초대합니다/초청합니다. gwihareul jeohuiui gyeolhonsige chodaehamnida/chocheonghamnida. We have invited you to our wedding.

오늘 이렇게 한국어에 관한 **초청 강연**을 할 수 있게 되어 영광스럽게 생각합니다. oneul ireoke hangugeoe gwanhan chocheong gangyeoneul hal su itge doeeo yeonggwangseureopge saenggakamnida. It is a great honor today to give a guest lecture on the Korean language.

모시다 mo·si·da to invite

초대장 ≒ 초청장 cho·dae·jang ≒ cho·cheong·jang letter of invitation

선물 | ~하다 seon·mul | ~·ha·da present, gift | to give a present
미안해. **선물**을 준비 못 했어. mianhae. seonmureul junbi mot haesseo. I'm sorry, but I didn't get you anything.

참석 | ~하다 cham·seok | ~·ha·da attendance, presence | to attend, be present
시간을 내어 참석해 주셔서 감사드립니다. siganeul laeeo chamseokae jusyeoseo gamsadeurimnida. I appreciate your taking the time to come here.

방문 | ~하다 bang·mun | ~·ha·da visit | to visit

방문해 주셔서 감사합니다. **bangmunhae jusyeoseo gamsahamnida.** Thank you for coming to see us.

찾아가다 cha·ja·ga·da to go, visit, call

들르다 deul·leu·da to drop by
아빠가 전화해서 **사무실에 좀 들르라고** 하셨어. **appaga jeonhwahaeseo samusire jom deulleurago hasyeosseo.** Daddy called and asked me to drop by his office.

찾아오다 cha·ja·o·da to come, visit
말도 없이 찾아와서 죄송해요. **maldo eopsi chajawaseo joesonghaeyo.** Sorry to have come without notice.

마중 ma·jung going out to welcome sb
제가 기차역으로 **마중 나갈게요.** **jega gichayeogeuro majung nagalgeyo.** I'll pick you up at the railway station.

데리다 de·ri·da to pick sb up
언제 **데리러 갈까? eonje derireo galkka?** When should I pick you up?

맞(이하)다 mat(·i·ha)·da to welcome, receive
가게 주인은 손님들을 현관에서 맞았다. **gage juineun sonnimdeureul hyeongwaneseo majatda.** The shop owner welcomed the customers at the door.

대접 | ~하다 dae·jeop | ~·ha·da reception, treatment | to treat
그녀는 우리에게 근사한 **저녁을 대접했다.** **geunyeoneun uriege geunsahan jeonyeogeul daejeopaetda.** She treated us to a great dinner.

배웅 | ~하다 bae·ung | ~·ha·da seeing sb off | to see sb off, see sb out
배웅해 줘서 고맙습니다. **baeunghae jwoseo gomapseumnida.** Thanks for seeing me off.

남 nam others, strangers
남들 말에 신경 쓸 것 없어. **namdeul mare singyeong sseul geot eopseo.** Don't pay attention to what others say.

상대방 = 상대편 sang·dae·bang = sang·dae·pyeon the other
상대방이/상대편이 어떻게 느낄지 생각해 봐. **sangdaebangi/sangdaepyeoni eotteoke neukkilji saenggakae bwa.** Think of how the other party would feel.

혼자 hon·ja a single person; alone
너 혼자만 알고 있어. **neo honjaman algo isseo.** Keep this to yourself.

나는 도시에서 혼자 살고 부모님은 시골에 사셔. **naneun dosieseo honja salgo bumonimeun sigore sasyeo.** I live alone in the city and my parents live in the country.

홀로 hol·lo alone

각자 gak·ja each one, separately
각자 계산하자. **gakja gyesanhaja.** Let's split the bill.

따로(따로) tta·ro(·tta·ro) separately
저는 부모님이랑 따로 살아요. **jeoneun bumonimirang ttaro sarayo.** I live separately from my parents.

같이 = 함께 ga·chi = ham·kke together
우리랑 같이/함께 갈래? **urirang gachi/hamkke gallae?** Do you want to join us?

서로 seo·ro each other, one another
우리는 서로 연락하지 않는다. **urineun seoro yeollakaji anneunda.** We don't keep in touch with each other.

같이하다 = 함께하다 ga·chi·ha·da = ham·kke·ha·da to share, join
오늘 점심 같이할까요/함께할까요? **oneul jeomsim gachihalkkayo/hamkkehalkkayo?** Shall we have lunch together?

대하다 dae·ha·da to treat; concerning
그녀는 나를 가족처럼 대했다. **geunyeoneun nareul gajokcheoreom daehaetda.** She treated me like one of her own family.
너에 대해 모두 알고 있다고 생각했어. **neoe daehae modu algo itdago saenggakaesseo.** I thought I knew everything about you.

관하다 gwan·ha·da concerning, regarding
그에 관해서는 한마디도 하고 싶지 않아요. **geue gwanhaeseoneun hanmadido hago sipji anayo.** I don't want to say a word regarding him.

위하다 wi·ha·da for
우리는 먹기 위해 사는 걸까? 아니면 살기 위해 먹는 걸까? **urineun meokgi wihae saneun geolkka? animyeon salgi wihae meongneun geolkka?** Do we live to eat, or eat to live?

친구 chin·gu friend
소라는 제 가장 **친한 친구**예요. **soraneun je gajang chinhan chinguyeyo.** Sora is my best friend.

사귀다 sa·gwi·da to get along, get close to
저는 성격이 내성적이라서 **친구를 빨리 사귀**

지 못해요. jeoneun seonggyeogi naeseongjeogiraseo chingureul ppalli sagwiji motaeyo. I'm slow to make friends because I'm introverted.

동갑 dong·gap the same age
우리는 동갑이었고 곧 친한 친구가 되었다. urineun donggabieotgo got chinhan chinguga doeeotda. We were the same age and soon became close friends.

또래 tto·rae peer, same age group
아들아이는 또래 애들만큼 말을 잘하지 못해요. adeuraineun ttorae aedeulmankeum mareul jalhaji motaeyo. My son just doesn't talk as well as other kids of his age.

우정 u·jeong friendship
우정은 남녀 모두에게 중요하다. ujeongeun namnyeo moduege jungyohada. Friendships are important for both men and women.

사이 sa·i relationship
그날 이후로 그녀와 나는 사이가 멀어졌다. geunal ihuro geunyeowa naneun saiga meoreojyeotda. After that day, she and I drifted apart.

간 gan between, among
종교 차이가 두 사람 간에 갈등을 불러왔다. jonggyo chaiga du saram gane galdeungeul bulleowatda. Religious differences caused conflict between the two.

사이좋다 sa·i·jo·ta on good terms
저는 제가 아는 모든 사람과 사이좋게 잘 지내요. jeoneun jega aneun modeun saramgwa saijoke jal jinaeyo. I get along with everybody I know.

IDM 마음이 통하다 ma·eu·mi tong·ha·da to be on the same wavelength
아내와 저는 처음부터 마음이 잘 통했어요. anaewa jeoneun cheoeumbuteo maeumi jal tonghaesseoyo. My wife and I really hit it off from the moment we met.

IDM 손발(이) 맞다 son·bal(·i) mat·da to be like-minded
우리는 손발이 잘 맞아요. urineun sonbari jal majayo. We make a good team.

친하다 chin·ha·da close
우리가 더 친해졌으면 좋겠어요. uriga deo chinhaejyeosseumyeon jokesseoyo. I hope we become closer.

인기 in·gi popularity
민수는 정말 재미있어서 사람들에게 인기가 많다. minsuneun jeongmal jaemiisseoseo saram-

deurege ingiga manta. Everybody likes Minsu because he is so funny.

싸우다 ssa·u·da to fight, argue
싸우지 좀 마! ssauji jom ma! Stop fighting!

싸움 ssa·um fight

다투다 da·tu·da to quarrel, argue
요즘 여자 친구랑 자주 다퉈요. yojeum nyeoja chingurang jaju datwoyo. These days I often quarrel with my girlfriend.

다툼 da·tum quarrel, argument

IDM 발(을) 끊다 bal(·eul) kkeun·ta to stop visiting
어쩌면 그렇게 발을 딱 끊을 수가 있어요? eojjeomyeon geureoke bareul ttak kkeuneul suga isseoyo? How could you stop coming here?

IDM 거리가 생기다 geo·ri·ga saeng·gi·da to feel some distance from sb
개와 다툰 이후로 거리가 생겼어요. gyaewa datun ihuro georiga saenggyeosseoyo. After the argument, I felt some distance from him.

IDM 거리를 두다 geo·ri·reul du·da to keep one's distance
그 애랑 잠시 거리를 두고 싶어. geu aerang jamsi georireul dugo sipeo. I'd like to keep my distance from him for a while.

말리다 mal·li·da to stop, keep
싸움을 말리다 맞았어요. ssaumeul mallida majasseoyo. I got hit while trying to stop the fight.

화해 | ~하다 hwa·hae | ~·ha·da reconciliation | to reconcile
그만 싸우고 화해해. geuman ssaugo hwahaehae. Stop fighting and make up.

IDM 발이 손이 되도록 빌다 ba·ri so·ni doe·do·rok bil·da to beg and plead
나는 발이 손이 되도록 빌었지만 소용없었다. naneun bari soni doedorok bireotjiman soyong-eopseotda. I begged and pleaded to no avail.

용서 | ~하다 yong·seo | ~·ha·da forgiveness | to forgive
그건 실수였어요. 제발 용서해 주세요. geugeon silsuyeosseoyo. jebal lyongseohae juseyo. It was a mistake. Please forgive me.

이성 i·seong the opposite sex
고등학생은 이성을 만날 기회가 많지 않다. godeunghaksaengeun iseongeul mannal gihoega manchi anta. High school students don't

have many opportunities to meet members of the opposite sex.

눈(이) 높다 nun(·i) nop·da to be picky
그 사람은 여자 보는 **눈이** 너무 **높아**. geu sarameun nyeoja boneun nuni neomu nopa. He is picky about women.

사귀다 sa·gwi·da to date, go out
사귀는 사람이 있어요. sagwineun sarami isseoyo. I'm seeing someone.

교제 | ~하다 gyo·je | ~·ha·da dating, romantic relationship | to date, go out
두 사람 **교제한** 지 얼마나 된 거야? du saram gyojehan ji eolmana doen geoya? How long have you two been together?

미팅 mi·ting group blind date
저는 **미팅을** 한 번도 안 해 봤어요. jeoneun mitingeul han beondo an hae bwasseoyo. I have never gone on a group blind date.

소개팅 so·gae·ting blind date
소개팅 시켜 줄까? sogaeting sikyeo julkka? Do you want me to set you up on a blind date?

애인 ae·in lover, boyfriend, girlfriend
예쁜 **애인이** 생겼으면 좋겠어요. yeppeun aeini saenggyeosseumyeon jokeseoyo. I wish I had a cute girlfriend.

연인 yeo·nin one's love, couple
우리는 **연인보다** 좋은 친구로 지내기로 했어요. urineun nyeoninboda joeun chinguro jinaegiro haesseoyo. We decided that we make better friends than lovers.

커플 keo·peul couple
우리는 사귄 지 오래된 **커플입니다**. urineun sagwin ji oraedoen keopeurimnida. We've been seeing each other for a long time.

자기 ja·gi darling, honey, sweetheart
나는 **자기밖에** 없어. naneun jagibakke eopseo. You are everything to me, darling.

데이트 | ~하다 de·i·teu | ~·ha·da date | to date, have a date
지금 **데이트** 신청하는 건가요? jigeum deiteu sincheonghaneun geongayo? Are you asking me out now?

연애 | ~하다 yeo·nae | ~·ha·da date, love | to have a relationship

우리는 7년 **연애** 끝에 헤어졌다. urineun chillyeon nyeonae kkeute heeojyeotda. We broke up after seven years of dating.

인연 i·nyeon tie, connection
저 두 사람은 **하늘이 맺어준 인연**이야. jeo du sarameun haneuri maejeojun inyeoniya. Those two are a match made in heaven.

운명 un·myeong fate
그녀는 **운명을** 받아들이기를 거부했다. geunyeoneun unmyeongeul badadeurigireul geobuhaetda. She refused to accept her fate.

성 | ~적 seong | ~·jeok sex | sexual
그녀는 **성적 매력이** 넘친다. geunyeoneun seongjeok maeryeogi neomchinda. She exudes sex appeal.

키스 = 입맞춤 | 키스하다 = 입맞추다 ki·seu = im·mat·chum | ki·seu·ha·da = im·mat·chu·da kiss | to kiss
첫 **키스는/입맞춤은** 어땠나요? cheot kiseuneun/immanchumeun eottaennayo? How was your first kiss?

뽀뽀 | ~하다 ppo·ppo | ~·ha·da kiss, peck | to kiss
아빠한테 **뽀뽀**. appahante ppoppo. Give Daddy a kiss.

> **뽀뽀** is usually used in the context of non-sexual relationships such as parents and children.

성관계 = 섹스 | ~하다 seong·gwan·gye = sek·seu | ~·ha·da sex, intercourse | to have sex
저는 혼전 **성관계를/섹스를** 반대합니다. jeoneun honjeon seonggwangyereul/sekseureul bandaehamnida. I disapprove of premarital sex.

콘돔 kon·dom condom

피임 | ~하다 pi·im | ~·ha·da contraception | to practice contraception
콘돔은 가장 효과적인 **피임 방법**입니다. kondomeun gajang hyogwajeogin piim bangbeobimnida. Condoms are the most effective method of contraception.

15.3 Marriage, Childbirth, Divorce

약혼 | ~하다 ya·khon | ~·ha·da engagement | to be engaged
저는 약혼을 했지만 약혼녀를 정말로 얼마나 사랑하는지 모르겠어요. jeoneun nyakhoneul haetjiman nyakhonnyeoreul jeongmallo eolmana saranghaneunji moreugesseoyo. I'm engaged, but I don't know how much I really love my fiancée.

약혼식 ya·khon·sik engagement ceremony

약혼자 ya·khon·ja fiancé

약혼녀 ya·khon·nyeo fiancée

청혼 | ~하다 cheong·hon | ~·ha·da proposal | to propose
나는 그녀에게 청혼했지만 거절 당했다. naneun geunyeoege cheonghonhaetjiman geojeol danghaetda. I asked her to marry me and she said no.

결혼 | ~하다 gyeol·hon | ~·ha·da marriage | to marry, get married
저는 3년 전에 결혼했어요. jeoneun samnyeon jeone gyeolhonhaesseoyo. I got married three years ago.

국수(를) 먹게 해 주다 guk·su(·reul) meok·ge hae ju·da to tie the knot
언제 국수 먹게 해 줄 거예요? eonje guksu meokge hae jul geoyeyo? When are you tying the knot?

> This idiom is rooted in the Korean tradition of giving long noodles to wedding guests.

혼인 | ~하다 ho·nin | ~·ha·da marriage | to marry, get married
혼인 신고는 했어? honin singoneun haesseo? Have you registered your marriage?

장가 jang·ga marriage

장가가다 jang·ga·ga·da to get married, take a wife
저는 장가를 일찍 갔어요. jeoneun janggareul iljjik gasseoyo. I got married early.

시집 si·jip marriage

시집가다 si·jip·ga·da to get married, take a husband
딸아이가 통 시집갈 생각을 안 해요. ttaraiga tong sijipgal saenggageul an haeyo. My daughter is not at all interested in getting married.

청첩장 cheong·cheop·jang wedding invitation
언제 **청첩장을** 돌려야 할지 모르겠어요. eonje cheongcheopjangeul dollyeoya halji moreugesseoyo. I'm wondering when I should send out wedding invitations.

결혼식 gyeol·hon·sik wedding ceremony
내 결혼식에 올 거지? nae gyeolhonsige ol geoji? Will you come to my wedding?

예식장 ye·sik·jang wedding hall
시월에는 **예식장을** 구하기가 쉽지 않아요. siworeneun yesikjangeul guhagiga swipji anayo. It's not easy to find a wedding hall in October.

신랑 sil·lang groom

신부 sin·bu bride
결혼식이 끝나자 신랑과 신부가 키스했다. gyeolhonsigi kkeunnaja sillanggwa sinbuga kiseuhaetda. The bride and groom kissed when the wedding ceremony ended.

주례 ju·rye officiant
제 대학교수님이 **주례를** 서 주셨어요. je daehakgyosunimi juryereul seo jusyeosseoyo. My professor officiated at my wedding.

웨딩드레스 we·ding·deu·re·seu wedding dress

부케 bu·ke bouquet

축가 chuk·ga nuptial song

축의금 chu·gui·geum congratulatory money
결혼식 축의금은 얼마 냈어? gyeolhonsik chuguigeumeun eolma naesseo? How much congratulatory money did you give at his wedding?

피로연 pi·ro·yeon banquet reception

신혼여행 sin·hon·nyeo·haeng honeymoon
신혼여행은 발리로 가고 싶어요. sinhonnyeohaengeun balliro gago sipeoyo. I want to go to Bali for my honeymoon.

신혼부부 sin·hon·bu·bu newlyweds
그 사람들은 아직도 신혼부부 같아요. geu saramdeureun ajikdo sinhonbubu gatayo. They still look like newlyweds.

결혼기념일 gyeol·hon·gi·nyeo·mil wedding anniversary
오늘은 저희의 다섯 번째 결혼기념일입니다. oneureun jeohuiui daseot beonjjae gyeolhonginyeomirimnida. Today is our 5th wedding anniversary.

임신 | ~하다 im·sin | ~·ha·da pregnancy | to conceive, get pregnant
아내는 임신 6개월이에요. anaeneun imsin nyukgaeworieyo. My wife is six months pregnant.

가지다 = 갖다 ga·ji·da = gat·da to have
아내가 **아기를 가졌어요.** anaega agireul gajyeosseoyo. My wife is pregnant.

임(산)부 im(·san)·bu pregnant woman
이 자리는 임산부를 위한 자리입니다. i jarineun imsanbureul wihan jariimnida. This seat is reserved for pregnant women.

입덧 ip·deot morning sickness
아내는 **입덧이 심해서** 아무것도 못 먹어요. anaeneun ipdeosi simhaeseo amugeotdo mon meogeoyo. My wife can't eat anything because of her morning sickness.

산모 san·mo mother

태아 tae·a embryo, fetus
산모와 태아 모두 건강합니다. sanmowa taea modu geonganghamnida. Both the mother and the fetus are healthy.

출산 | ~하다 chul·san | ~·ha·da childbirth, delivery | to give birth to, bear
출산 예정일이 언제예요? chulsan yejeongiri eonjeyeyo? When is your baby due?

분만 | ~하다 bun·man | ~·ha·da childbirth, delivery | to give birth
저는 세 아이를 모두 **자연 분만**으로 낳았어요. jeoneun se aireul modu jayeon bunmaneuro naasseoyo. I had three children by natural childbirth.

낳다 na·ta to give birth to, bear
아내가 어젯밤 **딸을 낳았어.** anaega eojetbam ttareul laasseo. My wife gave birth to a daughter last night.

진통 jin·tong contraction, labor pains
그녀는 5분마다 **진통을 느꼈다.** geunyeoneun obunmada jintongeul leukkyeotda. She had contractions every 5 minutes.

유산 | ~하다 yu·san | ~·ha·da miscarriage | to miscarry
그녀는 임신 10주 만에 유산했다. geunyeoneun imsin sipju mane yusanhaetda. She had a miscarriage after 10 weeks of pregnancy.

바람(을) 피우다 ba·ram(·eul) pi·u·da to have an affair
남편이 **바람을 피워서** 이혼했어요. nampyeoni barameul piwoseo ihonhaesseoyo. I got a divorce because my husband cheated on me.

이혼 | ~하다 i·hon | ~·ha·da divorce | to divorce
요새 우리나라에서는 부부 세 쌍 중 한 쌍이 이혼한다. yosae urinaraeseoneun bubu se ssang jung han ssangi ihonhanda. One in every three marriages ends in divorce in our country nowadays.

별거 | ~하다 byeol·geo | ~·ha·da separation | to separate
저희 부부가 별거한 지 거의 1년이 다 되었어요. jeohui bubuga byeolgeohan ji geoui illyeoni da doeeosseoyo. We've been separated for almost a year.

위자료 wi·ja·ryo alimony
그는 아내에게 **막대한 위자료**를 지불해야 했다. geuneun anaeege makdaehan wijaryoreul jibulhaeya haetda. He had to pay a huge alimony to his wife.

재혼 | ~하다 jae·hon | ~·ha·da second marriage | to remarry
저는 5년 전에 재혼했어요. jeoneun onyeon jeone jaehonhaesseoyo. I got remarried five years ago.

가르치다 가설 건축학 경영학 경제학 고교 공책

와 과학 과학 교감 교문 교사 교실 교장 국립

국어 근본적 기구 기준 다니다 담임 답

입 동창 등록 등록금 떨어지다 맞다 문구 물리

리학 미술 박스 반장 발명 보고서 복사기 분필

사립 상식 색연필 선배 성적 세미나 수준 수학자

시험지 진입생 신청 신청서 실습 심리학 심리학자 양호실

chapter **16** | Education, School, and Study

어학연수 언어학 여고생 연구자 연필 예습 외우다

음악 의학 이수 입학 입학식 자원봉사 장학금 재학생

점심시간 정치학 조교 조퇴 종 중간고사 중학교

중학생 지구과학 지도 지리 지우개 지침 진리

상 철학 초등학생 총장 풀 프린터 필통

학년 학번 학습 학원 학장 학점 한문 합격자

16.1 Students, Faculty

교육 gyo·yuk education
그녀는 매우 **좋은 교육**을 받았다. geunyeoneun maeu joeun gyoyugeul badatda. She's received a very good education.

학생 hak·saeng student
학생 할인이 됩니까? haksaeng harini doemnikka? Do you have discounts for students?

남학생 nam·hak·saeng male student

여학생 yeo·hak·saeng female student
우리 반은 남학생보다 여학생이 많아. uri baneun namhaksaengboda yeohaksaengi mana. My class has more female students than male students.

초등학생 cho·deung·hak·saeng elementary school student
한국의 초등학생 수는 점점 더 감소하는 추세에 있다. hangugui chodeunghaksaeng suneun jeomjeom deo gamsohaneun chusee itda. The number of South Korea's elementary school students has been on a steady decline.

중학생 jung·hak·saeng junior high school student
많은 중학생들이 담배를 피우나요? maneun junghaksaengdeuri dambaereul piunayo? Do many junior high school students smoke?

고등학생 go·deung·hak·saeng high school student
나는 내년에 고등학생이 된다. naneun naenyeone godeunghaksaengi doenda. I'll be in high school next year.

여고생 yeo·go·saeng female high school student

대학생 dae·hak·saeng university student
내 여자 친구는 나보다 네 살 어린 대학생이야. nae yeoja chinguneun naboda ne sal eorin daehaksaengiya. My girlfriend is an undergraduate who is four years younger than me.

여대생 yeo·dae·saeng female university student
그녀는 여대생들을 대상으로 여성의 사회 진출에 대한 연설을 했다. geunyeoneun nyeodaesaengdeureul daesangeuro yeoseongui sahoe jinchure daehan nyeonseoreul haetda. She delivered a speech on the advancement of women in society to an audience of college girls.

신입생 si·nip·saeng first-year student, freshman
오늘 밤에 **신입생 환영회**가 있습니다. oneul bame sinipsaeng hwanyeonghoega itseumnida. Tonight there will be a welcome party for freshmen.

재학생 jae·hak·saeng registered student

졸업생 jo·reop·saeng graduate
재학생과 졸업생은 우리 체육관을 무료로 이용할 수 있습니다. jaehaksaenggwa joreopsaengeun uri cheyukgwaneul muryoro iyonghal su itseumnida. Alumni and current students can use our gym for free.

학생증 hak·saeng·jeung student ID
학생증을 어디서 발급받나요? haksaengjeungeul eodiseo balgeupbannayo? Where can I get a student ID?

선배 seon·bae senior
그는 우리 학교의 3년 선배이다. geuneun uri hakgyoui samnyeon seonbaeida. He was three years my senior in school.

후배 hu·bae junior
내 아내는 내 **대학 후배**야. nae anaeneun nae daehak ubaeya. My wife is my junior in college.

동기 dong·gi person who enters a group at the same time as you

In English, there are no words to really match 선배, 후배, and 동기. Your 선배 is someone who joined an organization like a university or a company earlier than you. A 후배 is the opposite—someone who joined an organization after you did. Your 동기 refers to a person who entered a group at the same time as you.

동창 dong·chang alumnus, alumna
그는 내 **대학 동창**이다. geuneun nae daehak dongchangida. He's an alumnus of the same college I went to.

교사 gyo·sa schoolteacher
그녀는 **교사가 되기** 위해 일을 그만두었다. geunyeoneun gyosaga doegi wihae ireul geumandueotda. She quit her job to become a teacher.

선생 seon·saeng teacher

담임 da·mim homeroom teacher
우리 **담임 선생님**은 아주 엄한 분이세요. uri damim seonsaengnimeun aju eomhan buniseyo. My homeroom teacher is very strict.

교장 gyo·jang principal

교감 gyo·gam vice-principal

(대학)교수 (dae·hak·)gyo·su professor
저는 **대학교수**가 되고 싶어요. jeoneun daehakgyosuga doego sipeoyo. I want to be a professor.

총장 chong·jang chancellor, head of the university

학장 hak·jang dean

강사 gang·sa instructor, lecturer

조교 jo·gyo teaching assistant, research assistant

교실 gyo·sil classroom
우리 **교실**은 3층에 있습니다. uri gyosireun samcheunge itseumnida. My classroom is on the third floor.

교무실 gyo·mu·sil teachers' room

강의실 gang·ui·sil lecture room

양호실 yang·ho·sil school infirmary

캠퍼스 kaem·peo·seu campus

교내 gyo·nae at school, on campus
교내에서는 금연입니다. gyonaeeseoneun geumnyeonimnida. Smoking is not allowed at the school campus.

도서관 do·seo·gwan library
책을 **도서관**에 반납하세요. chaegeul doseogwane bannapaseyo. You should return those books to the library.

매점 mae·jeom cafeteria

강당 gang·dang hall, auditorium
비가 오면 졸업식은 **강당**에서 거행됩니다. biga omyeon joreopsigeun gangdangeseo geohaengdoemnida. In the event of rain, the graduation ceremony will be held in the auditorium.

운동장 un·dong·jang playground
아이들은 **운동장**에서 놀고 있을 거야. aideureun undongjangeseo nolgo isseul geoya. The kids are probably playing on the playground.

교문 gyo·mun school gate

16.2 School Facilities, Stationery

칠판 chil·pan blackboard
누가 수업 후에 **칠판** 지울래? nuga sueop hue chilpan jiullae? Who's going to clean the blackboard after the lesson?

책상 chaek·sang desk
연필이 **책상** 밑으로 떨어졌다. yeonpiri chaeksang miteuro tteoreojyeotda. The pencil fell under the desk.

의자 ui·ja chair
의자가 열 개밖에 없어요. uijaga yeol gaebakke eopseoyo. There are only ten chairs.

분필 bun·pil chalk
분필이 다 떨어졌네. bunpiri da tteoreojyeonne. I'm running out of chalk.

컴퓨터 keom·pyu·teo computer

프린터 peu·rin·teo printer

팩스 paek·seu fax

복사기 bok·sa·gi photocopier

계산기 gye·san·gi calculator

문(방)구 mun(·bang)·gu stationery

학용품 ha·gyong·pum school supplies

공책 = 노트 gong·chaek = no·teu notebook
공책/노트 좀 빌려줄래? gongchaek/noteu jom billyeojullae? Can I borrow your notebook?

필통 pil·tong pencil case

연필 yeon·pil pencil
잠시만. 종이하고 **연필** 가져올게. jamsiman. jongihago yeonpil gajyeoolge. Hold on. I'll get some paper and a pencil.

자루 ja·ru unit for counting pencils
연필 다섯 **자루** yeonpil daseot jaru five pencils

색연필 sae·gyeon·pil colored pencil

샤프 sya·peu mechanical pencil

볼펜 bol·pen ballpoint pen

자 ja ruler

지우개 ji·u·gae eraser, rubber

종이 jong·i paper

장 jang unit for counting paper, tickets, etc.
　종이 두 장 jongi du jang two sheets of paper

가위 ga·wi scissors

풀 pul glue, paste

테이프 te·i·peu tape

봉투 bong·tu envelope, bag

박스 = 상자 bak·seu = sang·ja box

16.3 School and School Life

학교 hak·gyo school
　우리 집은 학교에서 가까워. uri jibeun hakgyo-
　eseo gakkawo. My house is near my school.

국립(학교) gung·nip(·hak·gyo) national
school

사립(학교) sa·rip(·hak·gyo) private school

공립(학교) gong·nip(·hak·gyo) public
school

유치원 yu·chi·won kindergarten

초등학교 cho·deung·hak·gyo elementary
school
　예전에는 초등학교를 국민학교라고 불렀다.
　yejeoneneun chodeunghakgyoreul gungminhak-
　gyorago bulleotda. Elementary school used
　to be called "national school."

중학교 jung·hak·gyo junior high school
　우리 엄마는 중학교 미술 선생님이야. uri
　eommaneun junghakgyo misul seonsaeng-
　nimiya. My mom teaches art at a junior high
　school.

고(등학)교 go(·deung·hak)·gyo high school
　나는 고등학교 때 제2외국어로 일본어를 배
　웠다. naneun godeunghakgyo ttae jeioegu-
　georo ilboneoreul baewotda. I studied Japa-
　nese as a foreign language in high school.

학년 hang·nyeon year, grade
　A: 몇 학년이야? B: 1학년이에요. A: myeot
　tangnyeoniya? B: ilhangnyeonieyo. A: What
　year are you in? B: I'm a freshman.

학기 hak·gi semester
　한 학기 휴학 중이에요. han hakgi hyuhak
　jungieyo. I'm taking a semester off.

과목 gwa·mok subject
　제가 제일 좋아하는 과목은 생물이에요. jega

jeil joahaneun gwamogeun saengmurieyo. My
favorite subject is biology.

국어 gu·geo Korean

영어 yeong·eo English

수학 su·hak mathematics

산수 san·su arithmetic

과학 gwa·hak science

생물 saeng·mul biology

물리 mul·li physics

화학 hwa·hak chemistry

지구과학 ji·gu·gwa·hak earth science

사회 sa·hoe social studies

국사 guk·sa Korean history

역사 yeok·sa history

도덕 do·deok ethics

윤리 yul·li ethics

정치 jeong·chi politics

경제 gyeong·je economics

지리 ji·ri geography

음악 eu·mak music

미술 mi·sul fine arts

체육 che·yuk physical training, physical
education
　체육 시간에 축구를 하다가 다리를 다쳤어요.
　cheyuk sigane chukgureul hadaga darireul
　dachyeosseoyo. I hurt my leg while playing
　soccer in PE class.

한문 han·mun Chinese writing

입학 | ~하다 i·phak | ~·ha·da entrance into a school | to enter a school
저는 일곱 살에 **초등학교에 입학했어요**. jeoneun ilgop sare chodeunghakgyoe iphakaesseoyo. I started elementary school when I was seven.

입학식 i·phak·sik entrance ceremony

재학 | ~하다 jae·hak | ~·ha·da being in school | to be in school
딸아이는 중학교에 **재학** 중입니다. ttaraineun junghakgyoe jaehak jungimnida. My daughter is in middle school.

졸업 | ~하다 jo·reop | ~·ha·da graduation | to graduate
저는 올해 **코스모스 졸업**을 했어요. jeoneun olhae koseumoseu joreobeul haesseoyo. I graduated in August of this year.

나오다 na·o·da to finish
우리 엄마는 **초등학교도** 못 **나왔어요**. uri eommaneun chodeunghakgyodo mon nawasseoyo. My mom didn't even finish elementary school.

졸업식 jo·reop·sik graduation ceremony, commencement ceremony
오늘 딸아이의 **졸업식**이 있어요. oneul ttaraiui joreopsigi isseoyo. Today is my daughter's graduation.

다니다 da·ni·da to go, attend
막내가 **초등학교에 다녀요**. mangnaega chodeunghakgyoe danyeoyo. My youngest one is in elementary school.

등교 | ~하다 deung·gyo | ~·ha·da attending school | to attend school
저는 버스로 **등교해요**. jeoneun beoseuro deunggyohaeyo. I go to school by bus.

출석 | ~하다 chul·seok | ~·ha·da attendance | to attend
출석 부를게. chulseok bureulge. I'll take roll now.

지각 | ~하다 ji·gak | ~·ha·da lateness | to be late
오늘 아침 **학교에 지각했어요**. oneul achim hakgyoe jigakaesseoyo. I was late for school this morning.

조퇴 | ~하다 jo·toe | ~·ha·da early leave | to have an early leave

결석 | ~하다 gyeol·seok | ~·ha·da absence from school | to be absent from school
어릴 때 저는 아파서 **자주 결석했어요**. eoril ttae jeoneun apaseo jaju gyeolseokaesseoyo. When I was little, I was often out sick.

하교 | ~하다 ha·gyo | ~·ha·da coming home from school | to come home from school

학급 = 반 hak·geup = ban class
민수는 우리 **학급에서/반에서** 제일 똑똑한 아이예요. minsuneun uri hakgeubeseo/baneseo jeil ttokttokan aiyeyo. Minsu is the smartest kid in my class.

반장 ban·jang class president
저는 3년 동안 계속해서 **반장**이었습니다. jeoneun samnyeon dongan gyesokaeseo banjangieotseumnida. I was class president for three years in a row.

수업 su·eop class, lecture
한 시간 후에 **수업**이 있어요. han sigan hue sueobi isseoyo. I have class in an hour.

시간표 si·gan·pyo schedule

교시 gyo·si period
1**교시**는 영어야. ilgyosineun nyeongeoya. First period is English.

종 jong bell
마침 쉬는 시간 **종**이 울렸다. machim swineun sigan jongi ullyeotda. Then the bell rang for recess.

배우다 bae·u·da to learn
플루트는 **배우기** 쉬운가요? peulluteuneun baeugi swiungayo? Is the flute easy to learn?

익히다 i·ki·da to master, become proficient
외국어를 **익히는** 데는 시간이 걸린다. oegugeoreul ikineun deneun sigani geollinda. It takes time to learn a foreign language.

가르치다 ← 가르키다 ga·reu·chi·da ← ga·reu·ki·da to teach
저는 학교에서 **음악을 가르칩니다**. jeoneun hakgyoeseo eumageul gareuchimnida. I teach music at school.

지도 | ~하다 ji·do | ~·ha·da guidance, instruction | to teach, instruct
저는 일주일에 두 번 수영 **개인 지도**를 받고 있어요. jeoneun iljuire du beon suyeong gaein jidoreul batgo isseoyo. I take private swimming lessons twice a week.

교과서 gyo·gwa·seo textbook
영어 **교과서** 10쪽을 펴세요. **yeongeo gyogwaseo sipjjogeul pyeoseyo.** Open your English textbook to page 10.

교재 gyo·jae teaching material, textbook

과 gwa lesson, chapter
오늘 몇 **과** 할 차례지? **oneul myeot gwa hal charyeji?** What lesson are we doing today?

진도 jin·do progress
진도가 너무 빨라요. **jindoga neomu ppallayo.** The course is going too fast.

점심시간 jeom·sim·si·gan lunchtime
점심시간은 한 시간이다. **jeomsimsiganeun han siganida.** We have an hour-long lunch break.

도시락 do·si·rak box lunch
저는 **도시락**을 싸 갖고 다녀요. **jeoneun dosirageul ssa gatgo danyeoyo.** I bring my own lunch.

소풍 so·pung picnic, excursion
소풍은 비 때문에 취소되었다. **sopungeun bi ttaemune chwisodoeeotda.** The picnic was called off due to the rain.

방학 bang·hak vacation
방학 숙제가 많이 밀렸어. **banghak sukjega mani millyeosseo.** I have a lot of vacation homework to do.

여름방학 yeo·reum·bang·hak summer vacation

겨울방학 gyeo·ul·bang·hak winter vacation

수학여행 su·hang·nyeo·haeng school trip
내일 학교에서 제주도로 **수학여행**을 가요. **naeil hakgyoeseo jejudoro suhangnyeohaengeul gayo.** We are going on a school trip to Jeju Island tomorrow.

공부 | ~하다 gong·bu | ~·ha·da study | to study
나는 대학에서 경제학을 **공부**하고 싶다. **naneun daehageseo gyeongjehageul gongbuhago sipda.** I want to study economics at college.

학습 | ~하다 hak·seup | ~·ha·da study, learning | to learn, study
그 아이는 **학습** 능력이 뛰어나다. **geu aineun hakseup neungnyeogi ttwieonada.** The boy has outstanding academic aptitude.

예습 | ~하다 ye·seup | ~·ha·da preparation | to prepare (a lesson)
그 다음 장 **예습**해 오세요. **geu daeum jang yeseupae oseyo.** Preview the next chapter.

복습 | ~하다 bok·seup | ~·ha·da review | to review
틀린 문제를 **복습**하는 것은 좋은 방법이다. **teullin munjereul bokseupaneun geoseun joeun bangbeobida.** It's good to review the questions you got wrong.

외우다 oe·u·da to memorize
영어 **단어**를 **외우는** 건 참 지루해요. **yeongeo daneoreul oeuneun geon cham jiruhaeyo.** It is so boring memorizing English vocabulary.

암기 | ~하다 am·gi | ~·ha·da memorization | to memorize
수학 공부는 **공식**을 **암기하는** 것이 아니다. **suhak gongbuneun gongsigeul amgihaneun geosi anida.** The study of mathematics is not about memorizing formulas.

숙제 suk·je homework
숙제 다 했어? **sukje da haesseo?** Did you finish your homework?

준비물 jun·bi·mul preparation material

학원 ha·gwon private educational institute
한국에는 **학원**이 많은 것 같아요. **hangugeneun hagwoni maneun geot gatayo.** There seem to be a lot of private institutes in Korea.

과외 gwa·oe private lesson
한국에서는 많은 학생들이 좋은 대학에 가기 위해 **과외를 받는다.** **hangugeseoneun maneun haksaengdeuri joeun daehage gagi wihae gwaoereul banneunda.** In Korea, many students get private lessons to help them get into good universities.

시험 si·heom exam, test

테스트 te·seu·teu test
테스트 결과는 언제 확인할 수 있나요? **teseuteu gyeolgwaneun eonje hwaginhal su innayo?** When will the test results be available?

퀴즈 kwi·jeu quiz

내다 nae·da to give, write
간단한 **퀴즈**를 **내겠습니다.** **gandanhan kwijeureul naegetseumnida.** I'll give you a simple quiz.

출제 | ~하다 chul·je | ~·ha·da giving an exam | to give (an exam)

여러분이 오늘 배운 것도 **출제 범위**에 포함됩니다. **yeoreobuni oneul baeun geotdo chulje beomwie pohamdoemnida.** The test will cover what you've learned today.

보다 = 치다 bo·da = chi·da to take (an exam)
모든 학생은 학기 말에 **시험을 보게/치게** 됩니다. **modeun haksaengeun hakgi mare siheomeul boge/chige doemnida.** All students will be examined at the end of the term.

중간고사 jung·gan·go·sa midterm exam

기말고사 gi·mal·go·sa final exam

시험지 si·heom·ji test paper
시작 지시가 있을 때까지 **시험지를 엎어 놓으세요.** **sijak jisiga isseul ttaekkaji siheomjireul eopeo noeuseyo.** Leave your test paper face down until told to begin.

문제 mun·je question, problem

풀다 pul·da to solve
어려운 문제는 빼고 다른 것들 먼저 **풀어라.** **eoryeoun munjeneun ppaego dareun geotdeul meonjeo pureora.** Skip the difficult questions and solve the others first.

답 | ~하다 dap | ~·ha·da answer, reply | to answer, reply
다음 **물음**에 답하시오. **daeum mureume dapasio.** Answer the following question.

해답 hae·dap answer, solution
해답은 책 뒷면에 있다. **haedabeun chaek dwinmyeone itda.** The answers are in the back of the book.

정답 jeong·dap correct answer
정답을 알면 버튼을 누르세요. **jeongdabeul almyeon beoteuneul lureuseyo.** If you know the answer, press the button.

맞다 mat·da right, correct
몇 번이 맞아요? **myeot beoni majayo?** What's the correct number?

맞히다 ma·chi·da to guess correctly
열 문제 중 고작 세 개 맞혔어? **yeol munje jung gojak se gae machyeosseo?** Did you get only three questions correct out of ten?

People often confuse 맞히다 with 맞추다. Most of the time they use 맞추다 when they mean to say 맞히다.

틀리다 teul·li·da to be wrong, be incorrect

이번 시험에서 한 개 틀렸어요. **ibeon siheomseo han gae teullyeosseoyo.** I got one problem wrong on this exam.

People often confuse 틀리다 with 다르다. They often say 틀리다 when they should have said 다르다.

맞추다 mat·chu·da to check, compare
우리 서로 **답 맞춰** 보자. **uri seoro dam matchwo boja.** Let's compare our answers.

채점 | ~하다 chae·jeom | ~·ha·da grading, marking | to grade, mark
주말 내내 채점해야 할 시험지가 쌓여 있어요. **jumal laenae chaejeomhaeya hal siheomjiga ssayeo isseoyo.** I've got a pile of tests to grade during the weekend.

성적 seong·jeok grade, mark
정수의 **학교 성적**이 점점 떨어지고 있어요. **jeongsuui hakgyo seongjeogi jeomjeom tteoreojigo isseoyo.** Jeongsu' school grades are going down.

Be careful not to pronounce this as /성쩍/ since this means "sexual."

성적표 seong·jeok·pyo report card, transcript
성적표는 각 가정에 우편으로 보내집니다. **seongjeokpyoneun gak gajeonge upyeoneuro bonaejimnida.** Report cards will be mailed home.

점수 jeom·su score, mark
역사 점수가 안 좋아요. **yeoksa jeomsuga an joayo.** I got a bad score in history.

점 jeom point
몇 점 받았어? **myeot jeom badasseo?** How many points did you get?

만점 man·jeom perfect score
나 **만점 받았어.** **na manjeom badasseo.** I got a perfect score.

등수 deung·su rank

등 deung ranking
이번 시험에서 50명 중 49등을 했어요. **ibeon siheomeseo osimmyeong jung sasipgudeungeul haesseoyo.** I placed 49th out of 50 students in the exam.

입시 ip·si entrance examination
저희는 **대학 입시**에 관한 여러 정보를 제공합

니다. jeohuineun daehak ipsie gwanhan nyeoreo jeongboreul jegonghamnida. We provide various information on college entrance exams.

대입 dae·ip college admission
다음 주에 **대입 시험**이 있습니다. daeum jue daeip siheomi itseumnida. The university entrance exam will be held next week.

진로 jil·lo career
졸업 후 **진로**를 아직 **결정하지** 못했어요. joreop pu jilloreul ajik gyeoljeonghaji motaesseoyo. I haven't decided what to do after I graduate yet.

수험생 su·heom·saeng testee

합격 | ~하다 hap·gyeok | ~·ha·da pass | to pass
그는 **시험**에 **합격**하기 위해 열심히 노력했지만 떨어졌다. geuneun siheome hapgyeokagi wihae yeolsimhi noryeokaetjiman tteoreojyeotda. He strived to pass the exam, but failed.

붙다 but·da to pass
운 좋게 **시험**에 **붙었어요.** un joke siheome buteosseoyo. I was lucky to pass the test.

합격자 hap·gyeok·ja successful candidate

명단 myeong·dan list
제 이름이 **합격자 명단**에 없었어요. je ireumi hapgyeokja myeongdane eopseosseoyo. My name was not on the list of those who passed the test.

불합격 | ~하다 bul·hap·gyeok | ~·ha·da failure | to fail
저는 운전 면허 시험에 총 열두 번 **불합격했어요.** jeoneun unjeon myeonheo siheome chong yeoldu beon bulhapgyeokaesseoyo. I failed the driving test a total of twelve times.

떨어지다 tteo·reo·ji·da to fail
저는 제가 **떨어질** 줄 알았어요. jeoneun jega tteoreojil jul arasseoyo. I knew I would fail the test.

물(을) 먹다 = 미역국(을) 먹다 mul(·eul) meok·da = mi·yeok·guk(·eul) meok·da to fail an exam, mess up
필기 시험에서 **물을/미역국을 먹었어요.** pilgi siheomeseo mureul/miyeokgugeul meogeosseoyo. I failed the written test.

Koreans consider it a taboo to eat seaweed soup on the test day because of the slippery texture of seaweed.

16.4 University and Campus Life

대학 dae·hak college, university

대학교 dae·hak·gyo university
우리 **대학교**는 오랜 역사를 갖고 있다. uri daehakgyoneun oraen nyeoksareul gatgo itda. My university has a long history.

대학원 dae·ha·gwon graduate school
대학원 시험을 준비 중입니다. daehagwon siheomeul junbi jungimnida. I'm preparing for the graduate school exam.

(학)과 (hak·)gwa department, major
이 **과**의 남녀 비율이 어떻게 되죠? i gwaui namnyeo biyuri eotteoke doejyo? What's the ratio of men to women in this department?

전공 | ~하다 jeon·gong | ~·ha·da major | to major in
네 **전공**은 **결정**했니? ne jeongongeun gyeoljeonghaenni? Have you decided on your major?

학위 ha·gwi degree

취득 | ~하다 chwi·deuk | ~·ha·da acquisition | to acquire, obtain
저는 작년에 국문학 박사 **학위를 취득했어요.** jeoneun jangnyeone gungmunhak baksa hagwireul chwideukaesseoyo. I got my doctor's degree in Korean Literature last year.

학사 hak·sa bachelor's degree

석사 seok·sa Master, master

박사 bak·sa doctor's degree

학번 hak·beon student ID number
A: 몇 **학번**이세요? B: 98**학번**입니다. A: myeot takbeoniseyo? B: gupalhakbeonimnida. A: When did you start college? B: In '98.

학번 refers to the student number given to individuals. However, if someone inquires about your 학번, it is highly likely that he or she is asking what year you entered college.

학비 hak·bi school expenses

등록 | ~하다 deung·nok | ~·ha·da registration, enrollment | to register, enroll
등록 마감 기한이 언제예요? deungnok magam gihani eonjeyeyo? When is the deadline for registration?

등록금 deung·nok·geum tuition
납부 | ~하다 nap·bu | ~·ha·da payment | to pay
다음 주 월요일까지 등록금을 납부하셔야 합니다. daeum ju woryoilkkaji deungnokgeumeul lapbuhasyeoya hamnida. You need to pay tuition by next Monday.

장학금 jang·hak·geum scholarship
장학금은 신청했어? janghakgeumeun sincheonghaesseo? Did you apply for a scholarship?

강의 | ~하다 gang·ui | ~·ha·da lecture, class | to lecture
그분 강의는 전혀 지루하지가 않아요. geubun ganguineun jeonhyeo jiruhajiga anayo. His lectures are not boring at all.

수강 | ~하다 su·gang | ~·ha·da attending a course | to attend a course
이번 학기에 어떤 과목을 수강할 거야? ibeon hakgie eotteon gwamogeul suganghal geoya? What classes will you take this semester?

신청 | ~하다 sin·cheong | ~·ha·da application, request | to apply for
이 과목 수강 신청을 취소하려고요. i gwamok sugang sincheongeul chwisoharyeogoyo. I want to drop this course.

신청서 sin·cheong·seo application form

과정 gwa·jeong course (of study)
저는 작년에 석사 과정을 마쳤습니다. jeoneun jangnyeone seoksa gwajeongeul machyeotseumnida. I completed the courses for a master's degree last year.

학점 hak·jeom credit; grade
졸업하려면 130학점을 이수해야 합니다. joreoparyeomyeon baeksamsipakjeomeul isuhaeya hamnida. You must have 130 credits to graduate.
화학에서 A 학점을 받았다. hwahageseo A hakjeomeul badatda. I got an A in chemistry.

이수 | ~하다 i·su | ~·ha·da completion of a course | to complete, finish

보고서 = 리포트 bo·go·seo = ri·po·teu paper, report, essay

과제 gwa·je coursework, assignment

논문 non·mun thesis, dissertation
자네 졸업 논문이 매우 참신하다고 들었네. jane joreop nonmuni maeu chamsinhadago deureonne. I heard your graduate thesis was original.

세미나 se·mi·na seminar
오늘 밤 세미나에 참석하고 싶어요. oneul bam seminae chamseokago sipeoyo. I want to attend tonight's seminar.

동아리 = 서클 dong·a·ri = seo·keul club, society in college
동아리에/서클에 가입했니? dongarie/seokeure gaipaenni? Have you joined any clubs?

스터디 | ~하다 seu·teo·di | ~·ha·da group study | to study in groups

자원봉사 ja·won·bong·sa volunteer work
저는 여름방학이면 자원봉사를 합니다. jeoneun nyeoreumbanghagimyeon jawonbongsareul hamnida. I do volunteer work every summer vacation.

동창회 dong·chang·hoe school reunion
내일 고교 동창회가 있어. naeil gogyo dongchanghoega isseo. I have a high school reunion tomorrow.

학생회 hak·saeng·hoe student government

유학 yu·hak studying overseas
외국 유학을 가기로 결심했어. oeguk nyuhageul gagiro gyeolsimhaesseo. I have decided to study abroad.

어학연수 eo·hang·nyeon·su language study abroad
저는 대학 다닐 때 미국에서 1년간 어학연수를 했습니다. jeoneun daehak danil ttae migugeseo illyeongan eohangnyeonsureul haetseumnida. I studied English in the States for a year when I was in college.

16.5 Studies, Scholars

학문 hang·mun study, learning, science
학문에는 지름길이 없다. **hangmuneneun jireumgiri eopda.** There is no shortcut to learning.

학자 hak·ja scholar
그녀는 세계적으로 유명한 **학자**다. **geunyeoneun segyejeogeuro yumyeonghan hakjada.** She is a scholar with worldwide fame.

인문학 in·mun·hak the humanities

문학 mun·hak literature

역사 | ~적 yeok·sa | ~·jeok history | historic, historical

역사학자 yeok·sa·hak·ja historian

철학 | ~적 cheol·hak | ~·jeok philosophy | philosophical

철학자 cheol·hak·ja philosopher

심리학 sim·ni·hak psychology

심리학자 sim·ni·hak·ja psychologist

언어학 eon·eo·hak linguistics

언어학자 eon·eo·hak·ja linguist

사회과학 sa·hoe·gwa·hak social science

사회학 sa·hoe·hak sociology

사회학자 sa·hoe·hak·ja sociologist

경영학 gyeong·yeong·hak business administration

경제학 gyeong·je·hak economics

경제학자 gyeong·je·hak·ja economist

법학 beo·pak law

정치학 jeong·chi·hak politics

자연과학 ja·yeon·gwa·hak natural science

과학 | ~적 gwa·hak | ~·jeok science | scientific

과학자 gwa·hak·ja scientist

건축학 geon·chu·kak architecture

물리학 mul·li·hak physics

물리학자 mul·li·hak·ja physicist

화학 hwa·hak chemistry

화학자 hwa·hak·ja chemist

수학 su·hak mathematics

수학자 su·hak·ja mathematician

의학 ui·hak medicine

16.6 Academic Activities

학술 | ~적 hak·sul | ~·jeok scholarship | scientific, academic
저희는 사회 과학 분야의 **학술** 도서들을 발행합니다. **jeohuineun sahoe gwahak bunyaui haksul doseodeureul balhaenghamnida.** We publish scholarly books in social sciences.

이론 | ~적 i·ron | ~·jeok theory | theoretical
이것들은 단지 **이론**적으로만 가능하다. **igeotdeureun danji ironjeogeuroman ganeunghada.** These are possible only in theory.

실제 sil·je reality
이론과 **실제**는 종종 다르다. **irongwa siljeneun jongjong dareuda.** Theory and practice are often different.

가설 ga·seol hypothesis
네가 한 말들은 단지 **가설**일 뿐이야. **nega han maldeureun danji gaseoril ppuniya.** What you said is merely a hypothesis.

실험 | ~하다 sil·heom | ~·ha·da experiment, test | to do an experiment
동물 **실험**은 이미 완료되었습니다. **dongmul silheomeun imi wallyodoeeotseumnida.** The animal experiments have already been completed.

실습 | ~하다 sil·seup | ~·ha·da practice | to practice
실습이 꼭 이론보다 중요한 것은 아니다. **silseubi kkok gironboda jungyohan geoseun anida.** Practice is not always more important than theory.

조 jo group, team
다섯 명이서 **조**를 짜세요. daseot myeongiseo joreul jjaseyo. Form groups of five.

기구 gi·gu apparatus, appliance
실험 **기구**는 조심해서 다뤄야 한다. silheom giguneun josimhaeseo darwoya handa. Experimental apparatuses should be handled with care.

기록 | ~하다 gi·rok | ~·ha·da record | to record
나는 실험 중에 있었던 일들을 모두 기록했다. naneun silheom junge isseotdeon ildeureul modu girokaetda. I recorded everything that happened during the test.

설문 | ~하다 seol·mun | ~·ha·da survey | to survey
최근의 **설문 조사** 결과 응답자의 과반수가 새 규정에 반대하는 것으로 나타났다. choegeunui seolmun josa gyeolgwa eungdapjaui gwabansuga sae gyujeonge bandaehaneun geoseuro natanatda. A recent survey showed more than 50 percent of those questioned were against the new regulations.

발견 | ~하다 bal·gyeon | ~·ha·da discovery | to discover
그는 그 기생충을 최초로 발견한 사람이다. geuneun geu gisaengchungeul choechoro balgyeonhan saramida. He was the first to discover that particular parasite.

발명 | ~하다 bal·myeong | ~·ha·da invention | to invent
필요는 발명의 어머니다. piryoneun balmyeongui eomeonida. Necessity is the mother of invention.

· ·

수준 su·jun level, standard
네 기술은 프로 **수준**이다. ne gisureun peuro sujunida. Your technique is of a professional level.

표준 pyo·jun standard, average, norm
아들아이는 그 나이의 **표준** 키예요. adeuraineun geu naiui pyojun kiyeyo. My baby is of average height for his age.

기준 gi·jun standard
이 제품은 **안전 기준**에 맞추어 제작되었습니다. i jepumeun anjeon gijune matchueo jejakdoeeotseumnida. This is designed to meet the safety requirements.

평균 pyeong·gyun average, mean
한국 남성의 **평균 수명**은 약 80세다. hanguk namseongui pyeonggyun sumyeongeun nyak palsipseda. The average life expectancy of Korean men is about eighty years.

기초 | ~적 gi·cho | ~·jeok base, basics | basic, elementary
나는 수학의 **기초**가 **부족하다**. naneun suhagui gichoga bujokada. I have poor basic math skills.

기본 | ~적 gi·bon | ~·jeok basics | basic, fundamental
건강한 생활의 **기본**은 무엇인가요? geonganghan saenghwarui giboneun mueosingayo? What are the basics of a healthy life?
기본적으로 나도 동의해. gibonjeogeuro nado donguihae. Basically, I agree.

근본적 geun·bon·jeok fundamental
인간과 동물 사이에는 **근본적인** 차이가 있다. ingangwa dongmul saieneun geunbonjeogin chaiga itda. There is a fundamental difference between human beings and animals.

초보 | ~적 cho·bo | ~·jeok beginner level | basic, elementary
제가 **초보적인** 실수를 저질렀어요. jega chobojeogin silsureul jeojilleosseoyo. I've made an elementary mistake.

초보(자) cho·bo(·ja) beginner, novice
초보를 위한 수영 강습이 있나요? choboreul wihan suyeong gangseubi innayo? Are there any swimming lessons for beginners?

전문 | ~적 jeon·mun | ~·jeok one's specialty | specialized, technical
그의 설명은 너무 **전문적**이어서 나는 이해할 수 없었다. geuui seolmyeongeun neomu jeonmunjeogieoseo naneun ihaehal su eopseotda. His explanation was too technical for me to understand.

전문가 jeon·mun·ga expert
자전거를 고치는 데 **전문가**여야 할 필요는 없다. jajeongeoreul gochineun de jeonmungayeoya hal piryoneun eopda. You don't have to be an expert to repair a bicycle.

· ·

자료 ja·ryo material, data
아직 **자료**들을 정리해야 해요. ajik jaryodeureul jeongnihaeya haeyo. I still have to arrange the data.

통계 tong·gye statistics
이 **통계** 수치들은 신뢰할 만한가요? i tonggye suchideureun silloehal manhangayo? Are these statistics trustworthy?

지침 ji·chim guidelines
아래의 **지침을** 반드시 **따라야** 합니다. araeui jichimeul bandeusi ttaraya hamnida. You must follow the guidelines below.

법칙 beop·chik law, rule
예외 없는 법칙은 없다. yeoe eomneun beopchigeun eopda. There is no rule that does not have exceptions.

개념 gae·nyeom concept, idea, notion
때로는 정의의 **개념을** 정의하기가 쉽지 않습니다. ttaeroneun jeonguiui gaenyeomeul jeonguihagiga swipji anseumnida. Sometimes it is not easy to define the concept of justice.

관념 gwan·nyeom concept, notion, sense
그는 **위생 관념**이 부족하다. geuneun wisaeng gwannyeomi bujokada. He lacks a sense of hygiene.

사실 sa·sil fact, truth
그것은 **명백한 사실**입니다. geugeoseun myeongbaekan sasirimnida. That is an obvious fact.

진리 jil·li truth
철학자들은 절대 **진리를 추구한다.** cheolhakjadeureun jeoldae jillireul chuguhanda. Philosophers pursue the absolute truth.

지식 ji·sik knowledge
실질적인 경험을 통해 제 **지식을 넓혀** 나가고 싶어요. siljiljeogin gyeongheomeul tonghae je jisigeul leolpyeo nagago sipeoyo. I'm eager to expand my knowledge through practical experience.

정보 jeong·bo information
더 이상의 **정보는** 드릴 수가 없네요. deo isangui jeongboneun deuril suga eomneyo. I can't give you any more information.

상식 sang·sik common sense; common knowledge
당신의 주장은 **상식에 어긋납니다.** dangsinui jujangeun sangsige eogeunnamnida. Your claims go against common sense.

기자가 되려면 **상식이 풍부해야** 합니다. gijaga doeryeomyeon sangsigi pungbuhaeya hamnida. To be a journalist, you should have a great deal of common knowledge.

연구자 = 연구원 yeon·gu·ja = yeon·gu·won researcher

연구소 yeon·gu·so laboratory

결근 경력 경리 경리부 계약직 고용 공고 과장 관리

구조조정 구직 근로 근로자 기획 노동 담당자 도장

동료 마케팅 명함 병가 보너스 본사 부서 부서장 부장

부하직원 비서 비용 비정규직 사무실 사원 사장

사 선전 수당 승진 신입 신제품 아르바이트 업무 연금

연봉 연차 영업 영업팀 예산 외출 원서 월급 은퇴

이력서 이사 인사 인사팀 인원 인재 일 일자리

chapter **17** | **Work and the Workplace**

임원 입사 자기소개서 작성 재무 적성검사 전형 접수 정규직

정년 지각 지원 지위 지점 직급 직원 직위 직장

장인 차장 책임지다 총무부 출근 출장 출퇴근 취업

탈락 퇴근 퇴사 퇴직금 팀 팀원 파견 홍보 홍보부

회의 회의실 회장 휴가 휴직 -부

17.1 Work, Employment, Recruitment

일 | ~하다 il | ~·ha·da work, job | to work
저는 의류 회사에서 일하고 있습니다. **jeoneun uiryu hoesaeseo ilhago itseumnida.** I work for a fashion company.

근로 geul·lo work, labor
근로 시간이 단축되면 **근로 환경**과 근로자들의 삶의 질이 개선될 것입니다. **geullo sigani danchukdoemyeon geullo hwangyeonggwa geullojadeurui salmui jiri gaeseondoel geosimnida.** Reducing working hours will drastically improve the working conditions and the quality of life for workers.

노동 | ~하다 no·dong | ~·ha·da labor, work | to labor, work
아동 노동이 금지되어 있음을 모르는 사람들도 있어요. **adong nodongi geumjidoeeo isseumeul moreuneun saramdeuldo isseoyo.** Some people still don't know child labor is prohibited.

업무 eom·mu work, task, job
민수 씨는 이 **업무**에 꼭 **적합한** 사람입니다. **minsu ssineun i eommue kkok jeokapan saramimnida.** Minsu is definitely the right person for this job.

근무 | ~하다 geun·mu | ~·ha·da work | to work, be at work
나 지금 근무 중이야. **na jigeum geunmu jungiya.** I'm at work right now.

근로자 = 노동자 geul·lo·ja = no·dong·ja worker, laborer
우리는 **외국인 근로자**들의/노동자들의 권익을 보호하기 위해 계속해서 최선을 다할 것입니다. **urineun oegugin geullojadeurui/nodongjadeurui gwonigeul bohohagi wihae gyesokaeseo choeseoneul dahal geosimnida.** We will continue to make utmost efforts to protect the rights and interests of foreign workers.

일자리 il·ja·ri work, job
요즘은 **일자리**를 구하기가 힘들다. **yojeumeun iljarireul guhagiga himdeulda.** It's very hard to find work these days.

고용 | ~하다 go·yong | ~·ha·da employment, engagement | to employ
이 프로그램의 목적은 **장애인 고용**을 촉진하는 것입니다. **i peurogeuraemui mokjeogeun jangaein goyongeul chokjinhaneun geosimnida.** This program is designed to promote the employment of the disabled.

구직 gu·jik job hunting

구직자 gu·jik·ja job seeker
많은 구직자들이 구직 활동을 포기하고 있다. **maneun gujikjadeuri gujik hwaldongeul pogihago itda.** A number of job hunters have given up looking for work.

취직 | ~하다 chwi·jik | ~·ha·da getting a job | to get a job
졸업 후에는 **은행**에 **취직**하고 싶어요. **joreop pueneun eunhaenge chwijikago sipeoyo.** I'd like to work at a bank after graduation.

취업 | ~하다 chwi·eop | ~·ha·da getting a job, employment | to get a job
현재 **취업 준비** 중이에요. **hyeonjae chwieop junbi jungieyo.** I'm looking for a job.

정규직 jeong·gyu·jik permanent position; permanent employee

비정규직 bi·jeong·gyu·jik non-regular position; non-regular worker

계약직 gye·yak·jik contract position; contract worker

임시직 im·si·jik temporary position; temporary worker

아르바이트 = 알바 | ~하다 a·reu·ba·i·teu = al·ba | ~·ha·da part-time job; part-time worker | to work part-time
주말에는 편의점에서 아르바이트를/알바를 합니다. **jumareneun pyeonuijeomeseo areubaiteureul/albareul hamnida.** I work part-time at a convenience store on the weekend.

아르바이트 derives from the German word *Arbeit*.

채용 | ~하다 chae·yong | ~·ha·da recruitment | to recruit
저희 홈페이지에서 **채용 일정**을 확인하세요. **jeohui hompeijieseo chaeyong iljeongeul hwaginhaseyo.** See our website for our recruitment schedule.

공고 | ~하다 gong·go | ~·ha·da announcement, notice | to announce
저희는 지난달에 디자이너 **채용 공고**를 올렸습니다. **jeohuineun jinandare dijaineo chaeyong gonggoreul ollyeotseumnida.** We posted a job opening for a designer last month.

모집 | ~하다 mo·jip | ~·ha·da recruitment | to recruit
신문에 비서 **모집 광고**를 냈어요? sinmune biseo mojip gwanggoreul laesseoyo? Did you put a job advertisement for a secretary in the newspapers?

인원 i·nwon the number of people
올해는 예전보다 더 많은 **인원을 뽑을** 계획입니다. olhaeneun yejeonboda deo maneun inwoneul ppobeul gyehoegimnida. Our company is planning to hire more people than ever this year.

인재 in·jae talented person, talent
우리 회사는 새로운 **인재를 찾고** 있습니다. uri hoesaneun saeroun injaereul chatgo itseumnida. Our company is looking for new talent.

지원 | ~하다 ji·won | ~·ha·da applying | to apply
귀하가 우리가 원하는 요건을 갖추고 있다고 생각되시면 서둘러 인턴직에 지원하십시오. gwihaga uriga wonhaneun nyogeoneul gatchugo itdago saenggakdoesimyeon seodulleo inteonjige jiwonhasipsio. If you feel you possess most of the qualifications we are looking for, go ahead and apply for the internship.

(지)원서 (ji·)won·seo application (form)
원서 접수는 내일이 마감입니다. wonseo jeopsuneun naeiri magamimnida. The application deadline is tomorrow.

이력서 i·ryeok·seo résumé
이력서를 이메일로 보내 주십시오. iryeokseoreul imeillo bonae jusipsio. Please send your résumé by email.

자기소개서 = 자소서 ja·gi·so·gae·seo = ja·so·seo cover letter, résumé

내다 nae·da to submit, hand in
이력서와 **자기소개서를 내기** 전에 다시 한 번 확인하세요. iryeokseowa jagisogaeseoreul laegi jeone dasi han beon hwaginhaseyo. Double check your cover letter and résumé before submitting them.

제출 | ~하다 je·chul | ~·ha·da submission | to submit

전형 jeon·hyeong screening

통과 | ~하다 tong·gwa | ~·ha·da pass | to pass
서류 전형은 통과했어요. seoryu jeonhyeongeun tonggwahaesseoyo. I passed the application phase of the hiring process.

탈락 | ~하다 tal·lak | ~·ha·da being eliminated | to fail, be eliminated
면접에서 또 탈락했어요. myeonjeobeseo tto tallakaesseoyo. I failed the interview again.

접수 | ~하다 jeop·su | ~·ha·da receipt | to accept, receive

적성검사 jeok·seong·geom·sa aptitude test

면접 myeon·jeop interview
면접 볼 때 입을 양복이 필요해요. myeonjeop bol ttae ibeul lyangbogi piryohaeyo. I need a suit for my job interview.

신입 si·nip newcomer
신규 고객을 유치하려고 할 때 하는 것처럼 **신입 사원**을 채용해야 합니다. singyu gogaegeul lyuchiharyeogo hal ttae haneun geotcheoreom sinip sawoneul chaeyonghaeya hamnida. You should recruit new employees the same way you try to attract new customers.

경력 gyeong·nyeok career, work experience
이런 일에 **경력이 있으세요**? ireon ire gyeongnyeogi isseuseyo? Do you have any experience with this kind of work?

17.2 Working Life

입사 | ~하다 ip·sa | ~·ha·da joining a company | to join a company
입사한 지 한 달 되었어요. ipsahan ji han dal doeeosseoyo. It's been a month since I joined this company.

출근 | ~하다 chul·geun | ~·ha·da attendance (at the office) | to go to work
새 직장에는 언제부터 출근하는 거예요? sae jikjangeneun eonjebuteo chulgeunhaneun geoyeyo? When do you start your new job?

퇴근 | ~하다 toe·geun | ~·ha·da leaving the office | to leave the office
저는 보통 여섯 시에 퇴근해요. jeoneun botong yeoseot sie toegeunhaeyo. I usually leave the office at six.

출퇴근 | ~하다 chul·toe·geun | ~·ha·da

commute | to commute
저는 버스로 출퇴근해요. jeoneun beoseuro chultoegeunhaeyo. I commute by bus.

출장 chul·jang business trip
저는 **출장**을 많이 **다녀서** 혼자 있는 때가 많아요. jeoneun chuljangeul mani danyeoseo honja inneun ttaega manayo. Because I travel a lot for my work, I'm often alone.

파견 | ~하다 pa·gyeon | ~·ha·da dispatch | to dispatch, send
1년에 두세 차례 본사에서 기술자들이 파견되어 현지 직원들과 협업합니다. illyeone duse charye bonsaeseo gisuljadeuri pagyeondoeeo hyeonji jigwondeulgwa hyeobeopamnida. Around two to three times a year, technicians are dispatched from the head office to work together with the local staff.

야근 | ~하다 ya·geun | ~·ha·da night overtime | to work overtime at night
일주일에 적어도 이틀은 야근을 합니다. iljuire jeogeodo iteureun nyageuneul hamnida. I work overtime at least two days a week.

지각 | ~하다 ji·gak | ~·ha·da lateness | to be late
오늘 아침 회사에 30분 지각했어요. oneul achim hoesae samsipbun jigakaesseoyo. I was half an hour late for work this morning.

조퇴 | ~하다 jo·toe | ~·ha·da early leave | to have an early leave
임신 중에 조퇴가 불가피한 여러 이유가 있죠. imsin junge jotoega bulgapihan nyeoreo iyuga itjyo. There are many reasons why an early leave from work is unavoidable during pregnancy.

외출 | ~하다 oe·chul | ~·ha·da going out | to go out
김 대리님은 지금 외출 중이세요. gim daerinimeun jigeum oechul jungiseyo. Mr. Kim is out at the moment.

결근 | ~하다 gyeol·geun | ~·ha·da absence (from work) | to be absent from the office
그녀는 잦은 결근으로 회사에서 잘렸다. geunyeoneun jajeun gyeolgeuneuro hoesaeseo jallyeotda. She was fired for frequent absences.

연차(휴가) yeon·cha(·hyu·ga) annual leave
팀장님, 저 내일 연차를 사용할게요. timjangnim, jeo naeil lyeonchareul sayonghalgeyo. Boss, I'll take my annual leave tomorrow.

휴가 hyu·ga leave, vacation

아내는 지금 **출산 휴가** 중이에요. anaeneun jigeum chulsan hyuga jungieyo. My wife is on maternity leave.

병가 byeong·ga sick leave
김효신 씨는 일주일째 **병가** 중이에요. gimhyosin ssineun iljuiljjae byeongga jungieyo. Kim Hyoshin has been off sick for a week.

임금 = 급여 im·geum = geu·byeo wage
매년 물가가 임금/급여 이상으로 올라요. maenyeon mulgaga imgeum/geubyeo isangeuro ollayo. Every year prices rise more than wages.

연봉 yeon·bong annual income
저는 제 연봉에 만족해요. jeoneun je yeonbonge manjokaeyo. I'm satisfied with my income.

월급 wol·geup salary, monthly pay
저는 요즘 제 월급의 대부분을 저축하고 있어요. jeoneun nyojeum je wolgeubui daebubuneul jeochukago isseoyo. I'm saving most of my salary these days.

보너스 = 상여금 bo·neo·seu = sang·yeo·geum bonus
연말에 **보너스가/상여금이** 나옵니다. yeonmare boneoseuga/sangyeogeumi naomnida. Bonuses are given at the end of the year.

수당 su·dang extra pay

연금 yeon·geum pension

퇴직금 toe·jik·geum severance pay

직장 jik·jang workplace, office
직장에서의 성희롱은 해고로 이어질 수 있습니다. jikjangeseoui seonghuirongeun haegoro ieojil su itseumnida. Sexual harassment in the workplace can result in dismissal.

직장인 jik·jang·in office worker
저희 고객들 대부분이 직장인들입니다. jeohui gogaekdeul daebubuni jikjangindeurimnida. Our customers are mostly office workers.

(직장)상사 (jik·jang·)sang·sa one's superior
상사 앞에서 다른 사람들 험담을 하지 마세요. sangsa apeseo dareun saramdeul heomdameul haji maseyo. Don't talk badly about others in front of your boss.

동료 dong·nyo fellow worker, colleague
예진 씨는 단지 회사 동료일 뿐입니다. yejin ssineun danji hoesa dongnyoil ppunimnida. Yejin is just one of my fellow workers.

부하직원 bu·ha·ji·gwon one's subordinate
부하직원이 몇 명인가요? **buhajigwoni myeot myeongingayo?** How many employees are you in charge of?

맡다 mat·da to take care of, take on, assume
이 일은 제가 **맡겠습니다. i ireun jega matgetseumnida.** I'll take care of this job.

담당 | ~하다 dam·dang | ~·ha·da responsibility | to take charge of
그 일은 제 담당이 아닌데요. **geu ireun je damdangi anindeyo.** I am not in charge of it.

담당자 dam·dang·ja the person in charge
담당자가 지금 자리에 없습니다. **damdangjaga jigeum jarie eopseumnida.** The person in charge is away from his desk now.

책임지다 chae·gim·ji·da to take responsibility for
제가 책임지겠습니다. **jega chaegimjigetseumnida.** I'll take responsibility for it.

처리 | ~하다 cheo·ri | ~·ha·da handling, disposal | to handle, dispose of
그 일은 제가 **처리할게요. geu ireun jega cheorihalgeyo.** Let me take care of it.

관리 | ~하다 gwal·li | ~·ha·da administration | to administer, supervise
내 일은 직원들을 **관리하는 것이다. nae ireun jigwondeureul gwallihaneun geosida.** My job is to supervise the staff.

사무실 sa·mu·sil office
앗, 내 열쇠 사무실에 놓아두고 왔어! **at, nae yeolsoe samusire noadugo wasseo!** Oops, I left my keys at the office!

사무소 sa·mu·so office

명함 myeong·ham (business) card
여기, 제 명함입니다. 연락 주세요. **yeogi, je myeonghamimnida. yeollak juseyo.** Here's my business card, so please give me a call.

회의 hoe·ui meeting, conference
회의가 언제 끝날 것 같아요? **hoeuiga eonje kkeunnal geot gatayo?** When do you expect the meeting to finish?

회의실 hoe·ui·sil meeting room
회의실 예약했어요? **hoeuisil yeyakaesseoyo?** Have you reserved a meeting room?

서류 seo·ryu document, paper
아직 그 서류를 갖고 계세요? **ajik geu seo-**

ryureul gatgo gyeseyo? Are you still in possession of your documents?

문서 mun·seo document

작성 | ~하다 jak·seong | ~·ha·da drawing up | to make out, write, draw up
작성한 문서를 닫기 전에 꼭 저장하세요. **jakseonghan munseoreul datgi jeone kkok jeojanghaseyo.** Make sure to save your document before closing it.

도장 do·jang seal, stamp

찍다 jjik·da to stamp
여기에 도장을 찍어 주세요. **yeogie dojangeul jjigeo juseyo.** Please put your seal here.

복사 | ~하다 bok·sa | ~·ha·da duplication | to photocopy, duplicate
이것 좀 복사해 주시겠어요? **igeot jom boksahae jusigesseoyo?** Could you make a copy of this article for me?

비용 bi·yong cost, expense
우리는 **비용을 줄이기** 위해 노력해야 한다. **urineun biyongeul jurigi wihae noryeokaeya handa.** We have got to try to cut down on expenses.

예산 ye·san budget
이번 달은 우리 팀 예산을 초과했어요. **ibeon dareun uri tim yesaneul chogwahaesseoyo.** We are over our team's budget this month.

신제품 sin·je·pum new product
신제품과 관련하여 많은 문제가 발생했다. **sinjepumgwa gwallyeonhayeo maneun munjega balsaenghaetda.** Many problems arose in relation to the new product.

개발 | ~하다 gae·bal | ~·ha·da development | to develop
저희는 최근에 **신제품 개발**에 성공했습니다. **jeohuineun choegeune sinjepum gaebare seonggonghaetseumnida.** We recently succeeded in developing a new product.

기획 | ~하다 gi·hoek | ~·ha·da plan, project | to plan
저는 새로운 **상품을 기획하는** 일을 합니다. **jeoneun saeroun sangpumeul gihoekaneun ireul hamnida.** My job is planning new products.

이직 | ~하다 i·jik | ~·ha·da job change | to change jobs
심각하게 이직을 고민 중이에요. **simgakage ijigeul gomin jungieyo.** I'm seriously considering changing jobs.

휴직 | ~하다 hyu·jik | ~·ha·da leave of absence | to take a leave of absence
저는 건강상의 문제로 현재 **휴직 중**입니다. jeoneun geongangsangui munjero hyeonjae hyujik jungimnida. I am currently on sick leave.

퇴사 | ~하다 toe·sa | ~·ha·da resignation | to resign, leave a company
나영 씨는 지난달에 갑자기 퇴사했어요. nayeong ssineun jinandare gapjagi toesahaesseoyo. Nayeong abruptly left the company last month.

사직 | ~하다 sa·jik | ~·ha·da resignation | to resign

사직서 = 사표 sa·jik·seo = sa·pyo letter of resignation
사직서를/사표를 냈다는 게 사실이에요? sajikseoreul/sapyoreul laetdaneun ge sasirieyo? Is it true that you handed in your letter of resignation?

구조조정 gu·jo·jo·jeong restructuring
회사의 생존을 위해 **대규모 구조조정**이 불가피합니다. hoesaui saengjoneul wihae daegyumo gujojojeongi bulgapihamnida. A large-scale restructuring is inevitable for our company to survive.

해고 | ~하다 hae·go | ~·ha·da dismissal | to dismiss, fire

고용주는 합법적으로 파업 중인 **근로자를 해고**할 수 없다. goyongjuneun hapbeopjeogeuro paeop jungin geullojareul haegohal su eopda. An employer cannot fire employees who are legally on strike.

자르다 ja·reu·da to fire, dismiss

잘리다 jal·li·da to be fired
그는 불성실한 근무 태도로 인해 **회사에서 잘렸다**. geuneun bulseongsilhan geunmu taedoro inhae hoesaeseo jallyeotda. He was fired for his insincere attitude.

은퇴 | ~하다 eun·toe | ~·ha·da retirement | to retire
부모님은 두 분 다 은퇴하셨어요. bumonimeun du bun da euntoehasyeosseoyo. Both of my parents are retired.

퇴직 | ~하다 toe·jik | ~·ha·da retirement | to retire; to resign
퇴직하기까지 얼마나 남으셨어요? toejikagikkaji eolmana nameusyeosseoyo? How much time do you have left before your retirement?

정년 jeong·nyeon retirement age
아버지는 내년이 정년이세요. abeojineun naenyeoni jeongnyeoniseyo. My father will retire next year.

본사 bon·sa head office

지점 = 지사 ji·jeom = ji·sa branch (office)
저는 지점에서/지사에서 본사로 옮겨왔어요. jeoneun jijeomeseo/jisaeseo bonsaro omgyeowasseoyo. I have been transferred from the branch office to the head office.

부서 bu·seo department, division
어느 부서에서 근무하세요? eoneu buseoeseo geunmuhaseyo? Which department do you work in?

-부 = -실 -bu = -sil department

(-)팀 (-)tim team

총무부 = 총무실 = 총무팀 chong·mu·bu = chong·mu·sil = chong·mu·tim general affairs department

총무 chong·mu general affairs; manager

인사팀 = 인사부 in·sa·tim = in·sa·bu personnel department

인사 in·sa personnel matters

영업팀 = 영업부 yeong·eop·tim = yeong·eop·bu sales team, sales department

영업 yeong·eop business, sales

마케팅팀 = 마케팅실 ma·ke·ting·tim = ma·ke·ting·sil marketing team

마케팅 ma·ke·ting marketing

홍보부 = 홍보팀 = 홍보실 hong·bo·bu = hong·bo·tim = hong·bo·sil public relations department

홍보 hong·bo public relations
제가 **홍보 업무**를 담당하고 있습니다. jega hongbo eommureul damdanghago itseumnida. I'm in charge of Public Relations.

광고 gwang·go advertisement

선전 seon·jeon advertisement, commercial

재무팀 jae·mu·tim accounting department

재무 jae·mu financial affairs

경리부 gyeong·ni·bu accounting department

경리 gyeong·ni bookkeeping; bookkeeper

....

직급 jik·geup rank, position
우리 회사에서는 **직급이** 올라가면 연봉도 올라간다. uri hoesaeseoneun jikgeubi ollaga-myeon nyeonbongdo ollaganda. In our company, when someone got promoted, he/she gets a raise.

직위 ji·gwi post, position

지위 ji·wi status, position, rank

회장 hoe·jang chairperson
회장은 다음 달에 물러날 예정이다. hoejang-eun daeum dare mulleonal yejeongida. The chairman is going to retire next month.

부회장 bu·hoe·jang vice chairperson

사장 sa·jang president, CEO
제 꿈은 이 회사의 **사장이** 되는 것입니다. je kkumeun i hoesaui sajangi doeneun geosimni-da. My dream is to be the CEO of this company.

비서 bi·seo secretary, personal assistant

임원 = 간부 i·mwon = gan·bu executive

이사 i·sa director

직원 ji·gwon employee, staff
직원이 몇 명이나 되나요? jigwoni myeon myeongina doenayo? How many employees do you have?

부장 bu·jang general manager

차장 cha·jang deputy general manager

과장 gwa·jang manager

대리 dae·ri assistant manager

사원 sa·won ordinary employee

부서장 bu·seo·jang head of a department

팀장 tim·jang team manager

팀원 ti·mwon team member

승진 | ~하다 seung·jin | ~·ha·da promotion | to be promoted
승진 축하합니다! seungjin chukhahamnida! Congratulations on your promotion!

진급 | ~하다 jin·geup | ~·ha·da promotion | to be promoted, move up
지난달에 대리에서 **과장으로 진급했어요.** ji-nandare daerieseo gwajangeuro jingeupaesseo-yo. I was promoted from assistant manager to manager.

발령 | ~하다 bal·lyeong | ~·ha·da appointment | to appoint
저는 얼마 전에 마케팅팀 팀장으로 **발령을 받았어요.** jeoneun eolma jeone maketingtim tim-jangeuro ballyeongeul badasseoyo. I was made the head of marketing team a while ago.

리다 가위바위보 감상 개봉 게임 경기 경기장 골

또 공격 관광 관광객 관중 구경 구슬 규칙 낚다

사꾼 낚싯대 노래방 농구 놓치다 대회 몇 도전

동물원 두다 등산 따다 라이벌 레슬링 마라톤

표소 모텔 무승부 미끄럼틀 미끼 박 반칙 배구 복권 본선

다 빠뜨리다 사냥 사라지다 산책 상대 천주

수께끼 수집 순위 술래잡기 스케이팅 스트레칭 승부 식물원

chapter **18** | Leisure and Sports

야구 여가 여유 여행 역도 연습 예매하다

계약 예정 올림픽 우승 운동 위 유도 일정

국 자리 조깅 종이비행기 좌석 줄 줄다리기 지니다

다 찍다 챔피언 체력 체육관 출국 출전 취소

카드 카메라 탁구 태권도 팀 판정 패배

팽이치기 해외 해외여행 호텔 화투

18.1 Leisure Time, Hobbies, Games

취미 chwi·mi hobby, interest
특별한 취미가 있으세요? teukbyeolhan chwimiga isseuseyo? Do you have any particular hobbies?

여가 yeo·ga leisure time, spare time
여가 시간에 뭘 하세요? yeoga sigane mwol haseyo? What do you do in your spare time?

여유 yeo·yu extra time
서두를 필요 없어. 아직 여유 있어. seodureul piryo eopseo. ajik yeoyu isseo. We don't have to rush. We still have time.

즐기다 jeul·gi·da to enjoy
저는 드라마를 즐겨 봐요. jeoneun deuramareul jeulgyeo bwayo. I enjoy watching soap operas.

맛(을) 들이다 mat(·eul) deu·ri·da to take an interest in
일단 컴퓨터 게임에 맛을 들이면 그만두기 힘들어요. ildan keompyuteo geime maseul deurimyeon geumandugi himdeureoyo. Once you take an interest in computer games, it's hard to quit.

감상 | ~하다 gam·sang | ~·ha·da appreciation | to appreciate, enjoy
제 취미는 클래식 음악 감상입니다. je chwimineun keullaesik eumak gamsangimnida. My hobby is listening to classical music.

극장 geuk·jang theater
그럼 극장 앞에서 보자, 어때? geureom geukjang apeseo boja, eottae? Then we'll meet in front of the theater, all right?

공연장 gong·yeon·jang performance hall

영화관 yeong·hwa·gwan movie theater
영화관에 자주 가세요? yeonghwagwane jaju gaseyo? Do you often go to the movies?

상영 | ~하다 sang·yeong | ~·ha·da screening, showing | to show, play
마지막 상영이 몇 시죠? majimak sangyeongi myeot sijyo? What time does the last show start?

개봉 | ~하다 gae·bong | ~·ha·da premiere | to release
그 영화는 아직 개봉을 안 했습니다. geu yeonghwaneun ajik gaebongeul an haetseumnida. The movie has not yet been released.

관람 | ~하다 gwal·lam | ~·ha·da seeing, watching | to see, watch
즐거운 관람이 되시기 바랍니다. jeulgeoun gwallami doesigi baramnida. We hope you enjoy the show.

예매하다 ye·mae·ha·da to reserve, book (a ticket)
내가 미리 인터넷으로 예매했어. naega miri inteoneseuro yemaehaesseo. I've already made reservations on the Internet.

표 pyo ticket
표는 끊었어? pyoneun kkeuneosseo? Did you get a ticket?

매표소 mae·pyo·so ticket office
매표소가 어디예요? maepyosoga eodiyeyo? Where can I get a ticket?

창구 chang·gu window, counter

줄 jul line, row
사람들이 창구 앞에 한 줄로 서 있다. saramdeuri changgu ape han jullo seo itda. People are standing in line at the ticket window.

좌석 jwa·seok seat
우리 좌석 번호가 몇 번이야? uri jwaseok beonhoga myeot beoniya? What are our seat numbers?

자리 ja·ri seat
여기 자리 있어요? yeogi jari isseoyo? Is this seat taken?

비다 bi·da empty, vacant, unoccupied
아니요, 여기 자리 비었어요. aniyo, yeogi jari bieosseoyo. No, this seat is empty.

산책 | ~하다 san·chaek | ~·ha·da walk, stroll | to take a walk
밖에 나가서 산책하자. bakke nagaseo sanchaekaja. Let's go out and take a walk.

독서 | ~하다 dok·seo | ~·ha·da reading | to read
독서는 시간을 보내는 좋은 방법이다. dokseoneun siganeul bonaeneun joeun bangbeobida. Reading is a good way to kill time.

노래방 no·rae·bang *noraebang*, karaoke
노래방은 한국에서 인기가 많다. noraebangeun hangugeseo ingiga manta. *Noraebang* is popular in South Korea.

낚시 | ~하다 nak·si | ~·ha·da fishing, angling | to fish
낚시 좋아하세요? **naksi joahaseyo?** Do you like fishing?

낚다 nak·da to catch
고기를 자그마치 열 마리나 **낚았어요**. **gogireul jageumachi yeol marina nakkasseoyo.** I caught as many as ten fish.

그물 geu·mul net
이 강에서 그물로 고기를 잡는 것은 금지되어 있습니다. **i gangeseo geumullo gogireul jamneun geoseun geumjidoeeo itseumnida.** Catching fish with a net in this river is prohibited.

미끼 mi·kki bait
미끼는 뭘 쓰세요? **mikkineun mwol sseuseyo?** What do you use for bait?

낚시꾼 nak·si·kkun angler

낚싯대 nak·sit·dae fishing rod

낚시터 nak·si·teo fishing place

등산 | ~하다 deung·san | ~·ha·da hiking, climbing | to climb
등산 자주 가세요? **deungsan jaju gaseyo?** Do you often go mountain climbing?

등산객 deung·san·gaek mountain hiker

사냥 | ~하다 sa·nyang | ~·ha·da hunting, hunt | to hunt
이 지역에서는 3월부터 10월까지 **사냥이 금지되어** 있다. **i jiyeogeseoneun samwolbuteo siwolkkaji sanyangi geumjidoeeo itda.** Hunting is prohibited from March to October in this area.

덫 deot trap, snare
그들은 여우를 잡을 **덫을 놓았다**. **geudeureun nyeoureul jabeul deocheul loatda.** They set a trap to catch a fox.

사진 sa·jin picture, photo
이 **사진** 정말 잘 **나왔네**. **i sajin jeongmal jal lawanne.** This picture looks great.

사진관 sa·jin·gwan photo studio

촬영 | ~하다 chwa·ryeong | ~·ha·da shooting, filming | to shoot, photograph
사진 **촬영** 금지 **sajin chwallyeong geumji** No Photographs

찍다 jjik·da to take, shoot

저희 **사진** 좀 **찍어** 주시겠어요? **jeohui sajin jom jjigeo jusigesseoyo?** Could you please take a picture of us?

사진을 찍다 **sajineul jjikda** can mean *to take a picture* or *to have one's picture taken*.

카메라 = 사진기 ka·me·ra = sa·jin·gi camera

렌즈 ren·jeu lens

필름 pil·leum film
필름이 몇 장밖에 안 남았어. **pilleumi myeot jangbakke an namasseo.** There are only a few shots left on the roll.

초점 cho·jeom focus
카메라 렌즈 **초점을 맞춰** 봐. **kamera renjeu chojeomeul matchwo bwa.** Adjust the focus of the camera lens.

수집 | ~하다 su·jip | ~·ha·da collection | to collect
제 취미는 **우표 수집**이에요. **je chwimineun upyo sujibieyo.** My hobby is collecting stamps.

모으다 mo·eu·da to gather, collect
언제부터 **동전을 모았어요**? **eonjebuteo dongjeoneul moasseoyo?** How long have you collected coins?

나들이 na·deu·ri trip, outing

교외 gyo·oe suburb, outskirt
이번 연휴에 교외로 가족 나들이를 갈 계획이야. **ibeon nyeonhyue gyooero gajok nadeurireul gal gyehoegiya.** We have plans to go on a family outing in the suburbs this holiday.

동물원 dong·mu·rwon zoo
우리 가족은 오늘 동물원에서 아주 즐거운 시간을 보냈어요. **uri gajogeun oneul dongmurwoneseo aju jeulgeoun siganeul bonaesseoyo.** My family had much fun at the zoo today.

식물원 sing·mu·rwon botanical garden

물놀이 mul·lo·ri playing in water
아이들은 개울에서 물놀이를 하고 있어요. **aideureun gaeureseo mullorireul hago isseoyo.** Children are playing in the stream.

해수욕장 hae·su·yok·jang beach, sunbathing resort
대부분의 **해수욕장들이** 내일 **개장할** 예정입니다. **daebubunui haesuyokjangdeuri naeil gae-**

janghal yejeongimnida. Most beaches will open tomorrow.

....

놀다 nol·da to play
딸아이는 항상 남자 애들하고만 놀아요. **ttaraineun hangsang namja aedeulhagoman norayo.** My daughter always hangs out with boys.

뛰(어)놀다 ttwi(·eo)·nol·da to romp around
아이들이 즐겁게 뛰놀고 있다. **aideuri jeulgeopge ttwinolgo itda.** The kids are romping around.

장난 | ~하다 jang·nan | ~·ha·da fun, joke; prank | to play tricks
화내지 마. 장난이었어. **hwanaeji ma. jangnanieosseo.** Don't get mad. It was all in good fun.

장난 전화 걸지 마라. **jangnan jeonhwa geolji mara.** Don't make prank calls.

놀이터 no·ri·teo playground
아파트 옆에는 큰 놀이터가 있습니다. **apateu yeopeneun keun noriteoga itseumnida.** There's a large playground next to the apartment.

그네 geu·ne swing
아이들이 놀이터에서 그네를 타고 놀고 있어요. **aideuri noriteoeseo geunereul tago nolgo isseoyo.** Children are swinging in the playground.

미끄럼틀 mi·kkeu·reom·teul slide

시소 si·so seesaw
미끄럼틀, 그네, 시소는 대체로 어린 아이들이 이용합니다. **mikkeureomteul, geune, sisoneun daechero eorin aideuri iyonghamnida.** Slides, swings, and seesaws are mostly used by small children.

....

놀이 no·ri play, game
한국의 전통 놀이에는 뭐가 있나요? **hangugui jeontong norieneun mwoga innayo?** What are some traditional games in Korea?

윷놀이 yun·no·ri *yunnori*

Yunnori is a Korean traditional board game using four *yut* sticks as a dice.

제기차기 je·gi·cha·gi *jegichagi*

Jegichagi is a Korean traditional game similar to hacky sack. The person who kicks the *jegi* without letting it fall to the ground wins the game.

팽이치기 paeng·i·chi·gi top-spinning game

줄다리기 jul·da·ri·gi tug-of-war

썰매 sseol·mae sled
썰매 타러 가자. **sseolmae tareo gaja.** Let's go sledding.

종이접기 jong·i·jeop·gi origami

오락 o·rak entertainment, amusement

게임 ge·im (video, computer, etc.) game
우리 아이는 컴퓨터 게임에 푹 빠져 살아요. **uri aineun keompyuteo geime puk ppajyeo sarayo.** My boy is addicted to computer games.

바둑 ba·duk *baduk*, the game of *go*

장기 jang·gi *janggi* (Korean chess)

체스 che·seu chess

두다 du·da to play (*go* or chess)
바둑 한 판 둘까? **baduk han pan dulkka?** How about a game of *go*?

복권 bok·gwon the lottery

당첨 | ~되다 dang·cheom | ~·doe·da prize winning | to win (a prize)
복권에 당첨되면 뭐 할 거야? **bokgwone dangcheomdoemyeon mwo hal geoya?** What would you do if you won the lottery?

카드 ka·deu card, playing card

화투 hwa·tu *hwatu*, flower cards

Hwatu refers to a deck of cards with flower patterns used to play games like Go-Stop.

고스톱 go·seu·top Go-Stop game

Go-Stop is a Korean card game using *hwatu*, a deck of flower cards.

치다 chi·da to play (card)
고스톱은 명절 기간 식구들이 모여 많이들 친다. **goseutobeun myeongjeol gigan sikgudeuri moyeo manideul chinda.** Go-Stop is often played between family members during the holidays.

주사위놀이 ju·sa·wi·no·ri dice

가위바위보 ga·wi·ba·wi·bo rock-paper-scissors

술래잡기 sul·lae·jap·gi tag

숨바꼭질 sum·ba·kkok·jil hide-and-seek

팔씨름 pal·ssi·reum arm wrestling

수수께끼 su·su·kke·kki riddle, puzzle
내가 수수께끼를 낼 테니, 맞혀 봐. **naega su-sukkekkireul lael teni, machyeo bwa.** I'll make a riddle, and you guess the answer, OK?

십자말풀이 sip·ja·mal·pu·ri crossword puzzle

끝말잇기 kkeun·ma·rit·gi *kkeunmaritgi,* word relay

Kkeunmaritgi is a simple popular word game. You are supposed to provide a word beginning with the last syllable of the word given by another.

장난감 jang·nan·gam toy
요즘 애들은 장난감도 얼마나 많은지! **yojeum aedeureun jangnangamdo eolmana maneunji!** Children have so many toys these days!

인형 in·hyeong doll
내 조카는 인형을 좋아해요. **nae jokaneun in-hyeongeul joahaeyo.** My nephew loves dolls.

구슬 gu·seul marble

팽이 paeng·i top

풍선 pung·seon balloon
그 풍선 조금 더 불면 터지겠어. **geu pungseon jogeum deo bulmyeon teojigesseo.** If you blow it any more than that the balloon will burst.

종이비행기 jong·i·bi·haeng·gi paper airplane

연 yeon kite

날리다 nal·li·da to fly
나는 어릴 때 종이비행기를 날리고는 했다. **naneun eoril ttae jongibihaenggireul lalligoneun haetda.** I used to fold and throw paper airplanes when I was little.

띄우다 ttui·u·da to fly, launch
연 띄우러 가자. **yeon ttuiureo gaja.** Let's go fly a kite.

18.2 Traveling

여행 | ~하다 yeo·haeng | ~·ha·da travel, trip | to travel, trip
세계 여행은 언제나 제 꿈이었어요. **segye yeohaengeun eonjena je kkumieosseoyo.** Traveling around the world has always been my dream.

여행사 yeo·haeng·sa travel agency

예정 ye·jeong schedule, plan
원래 어제 떠날 예정이었어요. **wollae eoje tteonal yejeongieosseoyo.** I was scheduled to leave yesterday.

일정 = 스케줄 il·jeong = seu·ke·jul schedule
일정이/스케줄이 너무 빡빡해요. **iljeongi/ seukejuri neomu ppakppakaeyo.** My schedule is too tight.

짜다 jja·da to make out
여행 일정은 짰어? **yeohaeng iljeongeun jja-sseo?** Have you arranged the schedule for the trip?

예약 | ~하다 ye·yak | ~·ha·da reservation | to reserve, book
호텔 예약은 했어? **hotel yeyageun haesseo?** Have you made a hotel reservation?

취소 | ~하다 chwi·so | ~·ha·da cancellation | to cancel
그는 아파서 여행을 취소해야만 했다. **geuneun apaseo yeohaengeul chwisohaeyaman haetda.** He had to cancel his trip due to illness.

놓치다 no·chi·da to miss
비행기를 놓칠 뻔했어요. **bihaenggireul lochil ppeonhaesseoyo.** I almost missed the flight.

짐 jim load, baggage

소지품 so·ji·pum belongings
소지품을 잃어버리지 않도록 주의하십시오. **sojipumeul ireobeoriji antorok juuihasipsio.** Keep an eye on your belongings so that you don't lose them.

싸다 ssa·da to pack
최대한 짐을 가볍게 싸세요. **choedaehan jimeul gabyeopge ssaseyo.** Try to pack as light as possible.

챙기다 chaeng·gi·da to pack, take
약 꼭 챙겨라. **yak kkok chaenggyeora.** Don't forget to take your medicine.

보관 | ~하다 bo·gwan | ~·ha·da storage | to keep, store
귀중품은 금고에 **보관하세요**. gwijungpumeun geumgoe bogwanhaseyo. Keep valuables in the safe.

지니다 ji·ni·da to keep, carry
여권을 늘 지니고 다니세요. yeogwoneul leul jinigo daniseyo. Always carry your passport with you.

휴대 | ~하다 hyu·dae | ~·ha·da carrying | to carry
이 노트북은 **휴대가** 간편합니다. i noteubugeun hyudaega ganpyeonhamnida. This laptop is easy to carry.

빠뜨리다 = 빠트리다 ppa·tteu·ri·da = ppa·teu·ri·da to leave out, miss
단 하나, 돈을 빠뜨렸어/빠트렸어. dan hana, doneul ppatteuryeosseo/ppateuryeosseo. I missed one thing: money.

잃(어버리)다 il(·eo·beo·ri)·da to lose
선글라스를 잃어버렸어요. seongeullaseureul ireobeoryeosseoyo. I've lost my sunglasses.

분실 | ~하다 bun·sil | ~·ha·da loss | to lose, miss
카드를 **분실하거나** 도난 당할 경우 즉시 신고해서 카드를 정지시켜야 합니다. kadeureul bunsilhageona donan danghal gyeongu jeuksi singohaeseo kadeureul jeongjisikyeoya hamnida. If your card gets lost or stolen, please report it immediately so that it can be suspended.

없어지다 eop·seo·ji·da to disappear, be missing
차가 없어졌어요! chaga eopseojyeosseoyo! My car is gone!

사라지다 sa·ra·ji·da to disappear
그 차는 어둠 속으로 사라졌다. geu chaneun eodum sogeuro sarajyeotda. The car disappeared into the dark.

찾다 chat·da to find, look for
가방은 찾았어? gabangeun chajasseo? Have you found your bag?

현지 hyeon·ji local place

가이드 ga·i·deu travel guide
우리는 발리 **현지** 가이드를 고용했다. urineun balli hyeonji gaideureul goyonghaetda. We hired a local guide in Bali.

일행 il·haeng party, company

일행이 있으세요? ilhaengi isseuseyo? Are you in a group?

안내 | ~하다 an·nae | ~·ha·da guidance | to guide, usher

지도 ji·do map
지도를 보면서 안내해 드릴게요. jidoreul bomyeonseo annaehae deurilgeyo. I'll show you on the map.

관광 | ~하다 gwan·gwang | ~·ha·da tour, sightseeing | to go sightseeing
관광하러 왔어요. gwangwanghareo wasseoyo. I'm here for sightseeing.

관광객 gwan·gwang·gaek tourist
매년 **수많은 관광객**들이 경주를 방문한다. maenyeon sumaneun gwangwanggaekdeuri gyeongjureul bangmunhanda. Every year countless tourists visit Gyeongju.

관광지 gwan·gwang·ji tourist attraction
이곳은 한국에서 가장 **인기 있는 관광지** 중 하나입니다. igoseun hangugeseo gajang ingi inneun gwangwangji jung hanaimnida. This place is one of the most popular tourist attractions in Korea.

구경 | ~하다 gu·gyeong | ~·ha·da sightseeing | to see (the sights), look around
어디를 구경하고 싶으세요? eodireul gugyeonghago sipeuseyo? What do you want to see?

기념품 gi·nyeom·pum souvenir
기념품을 살 수 있는 곳이 있나요? ginyeompumeul sal su inneun gosi innayo? Is there a place to buy souvenirs?

바가지(를) 쓰다 ba·ga·ji(·reul) sseu·da to get ripped off
아무래도 나 **바가지 쓴** 것 같아. amuraedo na bagaji sseun geot gata. I think I got ripped off.

바가지(를) 씌우다 ba·ga·ji(·reul) ssui·u·da to overcharge, rip sb off
바가지 씌울 생각 마세요. bagaji ssuiul saenggak maseyo. Don't even think about ripping me off.

숙소 suk·so lodging
숙소는 정했어요? suksoneun jeonghaesseoyo? Have you arranged accommodations?

고급 go·geup high-class
호텔 ho·tel hotel
모텔 mo·tel motel
여관 yeo·gwan inn

펜션 pen·syeon pension

콘도 kon·do membership resort

˙묵다 muk·da to stay, put up
우리는 그날 밤 호텔에서 묵었다. urineun geunal bam hotereseo mugeotda. We stayed at a hotel for the night.

숙박 | ~하다 suk·bak | ~·ha·da lodging | to lodge, stay
이 근처에는 괜찮은 숙박 시설이 없어요. i geuncheoeneun gwaenchaneun sukbak siseori eopseoyo. There are no decent accommodations around here.

˙박 bak night
3박 4일 sambak sail three days and four nights

˙머무르다 = 머물다 meo·mu·reu·da = meo·mul·da to stay, remain
여기에 얼마나 오래 머무르실/머무실 생각이세요? yeogie eolmana orae meomureusil/meomusil saenggagiseyo? How long do you plan to stay here?

˙해외여행 hae·oe·yeo·haeng overseas trip
이번이 제 첫 해외여행입니다. ibeoni je cheot haeoeyeohaengimnida. This is my first overseas trip.

⦂외국 oe·guk foreign country
외국을 여행할 때는 항상 여권을 휴대하고 다녀야 합니다. oegugeul lyeohaenghal ttaeneun hangsang yeogwoneul hyudaehago danyeoya hamnida. You always have to carry your passport when you travel in a foreign country.

˙해외 hae·oe foreign country, overseas country
저는 해외에 나가면 잠을 잘 못 잡니다. jeoneun haeoee nagamyeon jameul jal mot jamnida. I can't sleep well when I visit a foreign country.

˙출국 | ~하다 chul·guk | ~·ha·da departure from a country | to leave a country
다음 주에 출국이에요. daeum jue chulgugieyo. I'm scheduled to leave the country next week.

⦂귀국 | ~하다 gwi·guk | ~·ha·da homecoming | to return to one's country
언제 귀국할 예정입니까? eonje gwigukal yejeongimnikka? When are you planning to return to your home country?

˙입국 | ~하다 ip·guk | ~·ha·da entrance into a country | to enter a country
입국 신고서를 작성해 주세요. ipguk singoseoreul jakseonghae juseyo. Please fill out your disembarkation card.

비자 bi·ja visa
관광 비자로 입국하시는 겁니까? gwangwang bijaro ipgukasineun geomnikka? Are you entering the country on a tourist visa?

˙연장 | ~하다 yeon·jang | ~·ha·da extension | to extend
비자를 6개월 연장하고 싶습니다. bijareul lyukgaewol lyeonjanghago sipseumnida. I would like to extend my visa for another 6 months.

⦂여권 yeo·gwon passport

˙보이다 bo·i·da to show, let sb see
여권 좀 보여 주시겠습니까? yeogwon jom boyeo jusigetseumnikka? May I see your passport?

⦂신고 | ~하다 sin·go | ~·ha·da report, declaration | to report, declare
세관에 신고하실 물건이 있습니까? segwane singohasil mulgeoni itseumnikka? Do you have anything to declare to customs?

18.3 Exercise, Sports

⦂운동 | ~하다 un·dong | ~·ha·da exercise, workout | to exercise
너는 운동을 좀 해야 해. neoneun undongeul jom haeya hae. You ought to get a little exercise.

⦂활동 | ~하다 hwal·dong | ~·ha·da activity | to do, move
다양한 야외 활동을 즐겨보는 건 어때? dayanghan nyaoe hwaldongeul jeulgyeoboneun geon eottae? Why don't you enjoy some outdoor activities?

스트레칭 seu·teu·re·ching stretch

에어로빅 e·eo·ro·bik aerobics
에어로빅을 하기 전에 스트레칭을 하는 걸 잊지 마. eeorobigeul hagi jeone seuteurechingeul haneun geol itji ma. Don't forget to stretch before exercising.

요가 yo·ga yoga

강습 gang·seup lesson, class
저는 일주일에 세 번 **요가 강습**을 받고 있습니다. jeoneun iljuire se beon nyoga gangseubeul batgo itseumnida. I have yoga class three times a week.

달리기 dal·li·gi run, race

조깅 jo·ging jogging

줄넘기 jul·leom·gi jump rope; jumping rope
저는 매일 저녁 공원에서 **줄넘기**를 합니다. jeoneun maeil jeonyeok gongwoneseo julleomgireul hamnida. I jump rope in the park every night.

체력 che·ryeok physical strength, stamina
저는 **체력**이 약해요. jeoneun cheryeogi yakaeyo. I'm not very strong physically.

턱걸이 teok·geo·ri chin-up

팔굽혀펴기 pal·gu·pyeo·pyeo·gi pushup

스포츠 seu·po·cheu sports
저는 **스포츠**를 보는 것도 좋아하고 **하는** 것도 좋아합니다. jeoneun seupocheureul boneun geotdo joahago haneun geotdo joahamnida. I love both watching and playing sports.

대회 dae·hoe competition, championship
그 **대회**에 참가할 거야? geu daehoee chamgahal geoya? Are you going to participate in the competition?

올림픽 ol·lim·pik the Olympics

월드컵 wol·deu·keop World Cup

경기 gyeong·gi game, match
그 축구 **경기**는 무승부로 끝났어. geu chukgu gyeonggineun museungburo kkeunnasseo. The soccer game ended in a tie.

시합 si·hap game, match
우리 **달리기 시합** 할까? uri dalligi sihap halkka? Do you want to race?

게임 ge·im game
이번 한 **게임**에 모든 것을 걸겠어. ibeon han geime modeun geoseul geolgesseo. I'll stake all I've got on this game.

개최하다 gae·choe·ha·da to host, open, hold
2016년 하계 **올림픽**은 브라질 리우데자네이루에서 **개최됩니다**. icheonsimnyungnyeon hagye ollimpigeun beurajil liudejaneirueseo gaechoedoemnida. The 2016 Summer Olympics will be held in Rio de Janeiro, Brazil.

열리다 yeol·li·da to be held, take place
올림픽은 4년마다 **열립니다**. ollimpigeun sanyeonmada yeollimnida. The Olympic Games are held every four years.

프로 peu·ro professional

아마추어 a·ma·chu·eo amateur

훈련 | ~하다 hul·lyeon | ~·ha·da training | to train, exercise
이번에는 **체력 훈련**에 중점을 두었습니다. ibeoneneun cheryeok hullyeone jungjeomeul dueotseumnida. We focused on physical training this time.

컨디션 keon·di·syeon condition
저는 지금 **컨디션**이 **최상**입니다. jeoneun jigeum keondisyeoni choesangimnida. I'm in peak condition.

연습 | ~하다 yeon·seup | ~·ha·da practice | to practice
연습이 몇 시에 끝나? yeonseubi myeot sie kkeunna? What time is the practice over?

참가 | ~하다 cham·ga | ~·ha·da participation | to participate
이 **대회**는 아마추어와 프로 모두 **참가**할 수 있습니다. i daehoeneun amachueowa peuro modu chamgahal su itseumnida. This competition is open to both amateurs and professionals.

출전 | ~하다 chul·jeon | ~·ha·da participation | to participate
그는 부상 때문에 **월드컵 출전**이 불투명하다. geuneun busang ttaemune woldeukeop chuljeoni bultumyeonghada. It's uncertain whether he can participate in the World Cup due to his injuries.

예선 ye·seon the preliminaries, heat
나는 작년에 **예선 탈락**했다. naneun jangnyeone yeseon tallakaetda. Last year I was eliminated in the preliminary round.

본선 bon·seon the finals
우리 팀이 마지막으로 **본선**에 **진출했다**. uri timi majimageuro bonseone jinchulhaetda. Our team was the last to advance to the finals.

결승 gyeol·seung the final

진출 | ~하다 jin·chul | ~·ha·da advance | to advance, enter, go (into)
브라질 축구팀이 또다시 **결승**에 **진출**했어. beurajil chukgutimi ttodasi gyeolseunge jinchulhaesseo. The Brazilian soccer team advanced to the finals again.

승부 seung·bu winning or losing

겨루다 gyeo·ru·da to compete
본선에서 여덟 명의 선수가 **승부를 겨룬다**. bonseoneseo yeodeol myeongui seonsuga seungbureul gyeorunda. Eight players will compete in the finals.

가리다 ga·ri·da to distinguish, determine
승부차기로 **승부를 가리겠습니다**. seungbuchagiro seungbureul garigetseumnida. A penalty shootout will determine the winner.

경쟁 | ~하다 gyeong·jaeng | ~·ha·da competition, rivalry | to compete
한국 팀은 일본 팀과 **경쟁 관계에** 있다. hanguk timeun ilbon timgwa gyeongjaeng gwangye itda. The Korean team is competing against the Japanese team.

그늘에 가리다 geu·neu·re ga·ri·da to be in sb's shadow
저는 이제까지 형의 **그늘에 가려** 부모님께 인정을 못 받았어요. jeoneun ijekkaji hyeongui geuneure garyeo bumonimkke injeongeul mot badasseoyo. I always lived in the shadow of my big brother and never received any recognition from my parents.

챔피언 chaem·pi·eon champion

도전자 do·jeon·ja challenger
챔피언이 도전자를 근소한 차이로 이겼다. chaempieoni dojeonjareul geunsohan chairo igyeotda. The champion barely beat the challenger.

도전 | ~하다 do·jeon | ~·ha·da challenge | to challenge
그의 **도전을 받아들이겠습니다**. geuui dojeoneul badadeurigetseumnida. I accept his challenge.

라이벌 ra·i·beol rival

적수 jeok·su match, rival
너는 내 **적수가 못 돼**. neoneun nae jeoksuga mot dwae. You are no match for me.

상대 sang·dae opponent; match
경기는 상대의 일방적인 승리로 끝났다. gyeonggineun sangdaeui ilbangjeogin seungniro kkeunnatda. The match ended in a lopsided victory for our opponents.

그는 **만만찮은 상대다**. geuneun manmanchaneun sangdaeda. He's quite a match.

상대편 sang·dae·pyeon opponent

승 seung victory
그 투수는 데뷔 이후 **첫 승**을 노리고 있다. geu tusuneun debwi ihu cheot seungeul lorigo itda. The pitcher is chasing his first win since his debut.

승리 | ~하다 seung·ni | ~·ha·da victory | to achieve the victory
경기는 그들의 승리로 끝났다. gyeonggineun geudeurui seungniro kkeunnatda. The game ended in their victory.

이기다 i·gi·da to win, defeat
우리가 70 대 60으로 이겼어. uriga chilsip dae yuksibeuro igyeosseo. We won the game 70 to 60.

우승 | ~하다 u·seung | ~·ha·da victory, title, championship | to win the title
그는 아깝게 **우승을 놓쳤다**. geuneun akkapge useungeul lochyeotda. He narrowly failed to win the championship.

무승부 mu·seung·bu tie, draw
그 게임은 **무승부로 끝났다**. geu geimeun museungburo kkeunnatda. The game ended in a draw.

비기다 bi·gi·da to tie (with)
연장전까지 갔는데, **결국 비겼어요**. yeonjangjeonkkaji ganneunde, gyeolguk bigyeosseoyo. It went into overtime, but the game ended in a tie.

패 | ~하다 pae | ~·ha·da defeat, loss | to be defeated, lose
우리 팀은 현재 1승 1패를 기록하고 있다. uri timeun hyeonjae ilseung ilpaereul girokago itda. Our team record is one win and one loss.

패배 | ~하다 pae·bae | ~·ha·da defeat, loss | to be defeated, lose
그는 **패배를 인정하지 않을** 수 없었다. geuneun paebaereul injeonghaji aneul su eopseotda. He was forced to concede defeat.

지다 ji·da to lose
우리 팀이 2점 **차로 졌다**. uri timi ijeom charo jyeotda. Our team lost by two points.

기록 | ~하다 gi·rok | ~·ha·da record | to record
모든 기록은 깨지기 위해 존재한다. modeun girogeun kkaejigi wihae jonjaehanda. Every record exists to be broken.

순위 su·nwi ranking
한국의 **피파 순위**는 네 계단 상승했다. hangugui pipa sunwineun ne gyedan sang-

seunghaetda. The Korean team climbed up four places in the FIFA rankings.

위 wi unit for counting sb's ranking
제 목표는 이번 대회에서 1위를 차지하는 것입니다. **je mokpyoneun ibeon daehoeeseo irwireul chajihaneun geosimnida.** My goal is to take first place in this competition.

상 sang award, prize
누가 이 **상을 받을지는** 아직 결정되지 않았어요. **nuga i sangeul badeuljineun ajik gyeoljeongdoeji anasseoyo.** It is not decided yet who will get this award.

상금 sang·geum prize money
우승자는 천만 원의 **상금을 받게** 됩니다. **useungjaneun cheonman wonui sanggeumeul batge doemnida.** The winner will receive a cash prize of ten million won.

메달 me·dal medal

따다 tta·da to win, pick, get
제 꿈은 올림픽에서 **메달을 따는** 것입니다. **je kkumeun ollimpigeseo medareul ttaneun geosimnida.** My dream is to win a medal in the Olympics.

금메달 geum·me·dal gold medal

은메달 eun·me·dal silver medal

동메달 dong·me·dal bronze medal
....
경기장 gyeong·gi·jang stadium
경기장 안으로 술을 가지고 들어올 수 없습니다. **gyeonggijang aneuro sureul gajigo deureool su eopseumnida.** You can't bring alcohol into the stadium.

체육관 che·yuk·gwan gym

코트 ko·teu court

팀 tim team
어느 **팀이** 이겼냐? **eoneu timi igyeonnya?** Which team won?

선수 seon·su player, athlete
저 친구처럼 **뛰어난 선수를** 본 적이 없어요. **jeo chingucheoreom ttwieonan seonsureul bon jeogi eopseoyo.** I've never seen such a perfect player before.

감독 gam·dok (head) coach, manager

코치 ko·chi coach
저는 초등학교 **축구 코치를** 하고 있습니다. **jeoneun chodeunghakgyo chukgu kochireul hago itseumnida.** I work as a soccer coach at an elementary school.

심판 sim·pan referee, umpire, judge

판정 | ~하다 pan·jeong | ~·ha·da judgment | to judge, decide
선수들은 심판의 **판정을 존중해야** 한다. **seonsudeureun simpanui panjeongeul jonjunghaeya handa.** Players must respect the referee's call.

규칙 gyu·chik rule, domination
게임의 **규칙을 지켜라.** **geimui gyuchigeul jikyeora.** Follow the rules of the game.

반칙 = 파울 | ~하다 ban·chik = pa·ul | ~·ha·da foul | to foul
그가 골을 넣었지만 심판은 **반칙을/파울을 선언했다.** **geuga goreul neoeotjiman simpaneun banchigeul/paureul seoneonhaetda.** He succeeded in scoring a goal, but the referee called a foul.

관중 gwan·jung spectator
경기장에 만 명이 넘는 **관중이 모였다.** **gyeonggijange man myeongi neomneun gwanjungi moyeotda.** More than 10,000 spectators are present at the stadium.

팬 paen fan
....
육상 yuk·sang track and field, athletics

트랙 teu·raek track

바퀴 ba·kwi turn, lap
트랙 네 **바퀴는** 1마일에 해당한다. **teuraek ne bakwineun ilmaire haedanghanda.** Four laps around a track is equal to a mile.

마라톤 ma·ra·ton marathon
그녀는 이번 마라톤에서 가장 나이 어린 참가자다. **geunyeoneun ibeon maratoneseo gajang nai eorin chamgajada.** She is the youngest participant in this marathon.
....
수영 | ~하다 su·yeong | ~·ha·da swimming | to swim
오후에 수영하러 가자. **ohue suyeonghareo gaja.** Let's go swimming this afternoon.

수영장 su·yeong·jang (swimming) pool

다이빙 | ~하다 da·i·bing | ~·ha·da diving | to dive
....
축구 chuk·gu soccer
너 어제 축구 경기 봤니? **neo eoje chukgu gyeonggi bwanni?** Did you watch the soccer match yesterday?

하키 ha·ki field hockey

농구 nong·gu basketball
키를 보면 그 사람은 하키가 아니라 농구에 어울릴 것 같아. kireul bomyeon geu sarameun hakiga anira nonggue eoullil geot gata. Given his height, he would be better off playing basketball, and not field hockey.

배구 bae·gu volleyball
나는 중학교 때 배구 선수였어. naneun jung-hakgyo ttae baegu seonsuyeosseo. I was a volleyball player in middle school.

야구 ya·gu baseball
류현진은 내가 제일 좋아하는 야구 선수야. ryuhyeonjineun naega jeil joahaneun nyagu seonsuya. Hyunjin Ryu is my favorite baseball player.

볼링 bol·ling bowling

공 gong ball
투수의 공이 너무 빨라서 칠 수가 없어요. tu-suui gongi neomu ppallaseo chil suga eopseoyo. The pitch is too fast to hit.

숏 | ~하다 syut | ~·ha·da shot | to shoot

패스 | ~하다 pae·seu | ~·ha·da pass | to pass
숏 대신 패스를 했었어야지. syut daesin pae-seureul haesseosseoyaji. You should have passed instead of shooting.

골 gol goal
우리가 두 골 차로 지고 있어요. uriga du gol charo jigo isseoyo. We are losing by two goals.

대 dae versus
채널 13번에서 한국 대 일본의 축구 경기를 하고 있다. chaeneol sipsambeoneseo hanguk dae ilbonui chukgu gyeonggireul hago itda. There's a soccer game on Channel 13—Korea versus Japan.

골프 gol·peu golf

테니스 te·ni·seu tennis

탁구 tak·gu table tennis

배드민턴 bae·deu·min·teon badminton

스쿼시 seu·kwo·si squash

치다 chi·da to play (bowling, golf, tennis, table tennis, badminton, squash, billiards, etc.)
테니스 치자. teniseu chija. Let's play tennis.

라켓 ra·ket racket

세트 se·teu set
내가 첫 세트를 6:4로 이겼다. naega cheot se-teureul lyukdaesaro igyeotda. I won the first set six to four.

공격 | ~하다 gong·gyeok | ~·ha·da attack | to attack
공격이 최선의 방어다. gonggyeogi choeseonui bangeoda. A good offense is the best defense.

수비 | ~하다 su·bi | ~·ha·da defense | to defend
저 팀은 공격보다 수비가 강하다. jeo timeun gonggyeokboda subiga ganghada. That team has stronger defense than offense.

씨름 ssi·reum *ssireum*

Ssireum is Korean traditional wrestling. Two people hold each other's belt and the one who flips over or brings the other person down first wins.

태권도 tae·gwon·do taekwondo
어렸을 때 태권도를 배웠어요. eoryeosseul ttae taegwondoreul baewosseoyo. I practiced taekwondo when I was little.

Taekwondo is a Korean traditional martial art which is also recognized worldwide. Both the offensive and the defensive moves are done with the bare hands and feet.

권투 = 복싱 gwon·tu = bok·sing boxing

유도 yu·do judo

검도 geom·do kendo

레슬링 re·seul·ling wrestling

역도 yeok·do weightlifting

체조 che·jo gymnastics

당구 dang·gu billiards

사격 sa·gyeok shooting

양궁 yang·gung archery

스키 seu·ki skiing; skis

스키장 seu·ki·jang ski resort

스케이팅 seu·ke·i·ting skating

타다 ta·da to ski, skate
스키 탈 줄 아니? seuki tal jul ani? Can you ski?

가사 가야금 감독 곡 공연 관객 구성 국악 그리다

그림 글 글쓰기 글씨 내용 노래 대사

도자기 도화지 동요 디자인 뜯다 리듬 마술 만화

멜로디 묘사 물감 미술 미술관 민담 민요 박수 반주

발레 배경 배우 북 비극 비평 색소폰 색칠 서예 설화

성우 소설 소설가 소재 수채화 시 시인 시조 시집

실로폰 쓰다 악기 악보 안무 역 연주 연출 열기

chapter **19** | Arts, Music, Literature

영화 영화제 예술 원고 음반 음악회 인물 일기

작곡가 장면 장편 적다 적히다 전기 조각 조명

조연 주연 주인공 주제 지휘자 창작 첼로

초상화 춤 켜다 코미디 콘서트 판소리 팝송 편

표절 플루트 형식 화가 화음 회화 희곡

19.1 Art, Visual Art

예술 ye·sul art
인생은 짧고 예술은 길다. insaengeun jjalgo yesureun gilda. Art is long, life is short.

예술가 ye·sul·ga artist
박물관에서 일부 예술가들의 조각도 볼 수 있어요. bangmulgwaneseo ilbu yesulgadeurui jogakdo bol su isseoyo. In the museum, you can see some of the artist's sculptures too.

작품 jak·pum work (of art)
작품에 손대지 마시오. jakpume sondaeji masio. Please do not touch the artwork.

장르 jang·neu genre
그 이야기의 장르는 무엇인가요? geu iyagiui jangneuneun mueosingayo? What genre does the story fall into?

형식 hyeong·sik form, formality

내용 nae·yong content, substance
내용뿐 아니라, 형식도 중요해. naeyongppun anira, hyeongsikdo jungyohae. Form is important, as well as substance.

....

만들다 man·deul·da to make, create
그녀는 일생 동안 수많은 **작품을 만들었다**. geunyeoneun ilsaeng dongan sumaneun jakpumeul mandeureotda. She created a large number of artworks during her lifetime.

창작 | ~하다 chang·jak | ~·ha·da creation | to create
그는 20대 초반에 **소설 창작**에 전념하기로 작정했다. geuneun isipdae chobane soseol changjage jeonnyeomhagiro jakjeonghaetda. In his early twenties, he decided to concentrate on writing fiction.

표절 | ~하다 pyo·jeol | ~·ha·da plagiarism | to plagiarize
그 장관은 **표절 시비**에 휘말린 이후 사임했다. geu janggwaneun pyojeol sibie hwimallin ihu saimhaetda. The minister resigned after being caught in a plagiarism scandal.

베끼다 be·kki·da to copy

....

미술 mi·sul (visual) art
저는 **현대 미술**에 관심이 많습니다. jeoneun hyeondae misure gwansimi manseumnida. I'm very much interested in modern visual art.

화가 hwa·ga painter, artist

오늘 저는 어느 **무명 화가**를 소개하려 합니다. oneul jeoneun eoneu mumyeong hwagareul sogaeharyeo hamnida. Today I'm going to introduce an unknown painter.

회화 hoe·hwa picture, painting
초현실주의 **회화**는 어떤 사람에게는 색과 모양을 마구잡이로 섞어 놓은 것처럼 보일 수 있다. chohyeonsiljuui hoehwaneun eotteon saramegeneun saekgwa moyangeul magujabiro seokkeo noeun geotcheoreom boil su itda. A surrealistic painting might look like a collection of random colors and shapes to some people.

그림 geu·rim picture, drawing, painting
이 그림은 얼마인가요? i geurimeun eolmaingayo? How much is this drawing worth?

수채화 su·chae·hwa watercolor

초상화 cho·sang·hwa portrait

스케치 | ~하다 seu·ke·chi | ~·ha·da sketch | to sketch

그리다 geu·ri·da to draw, paint
이거 뭘로 그린 거니? igeo mwollo geurin geoni? What did you paint this with?

색칠 | ~하다 saek·chil | ~·ha·da painting | to paint color

붓 but brush

도화지 do·hwa·ji drawing paper

물감 mul·gam paint

조각 | ~하다 jo·gak | ~·ha·da sculpture | to sculpt
미술은 단지 그리고 조각하고 색칠하는 게 전부는 아니다. misureun danji geurigo jogakago saekchilhaneun ge jeonbuneun anida. Art is not just about drawing, sculpting, or painting.

조각가 jo·gak·ga sculptor

도자기 do·ja·gi ceramics, china

디자인 di·ja·in design
그는 **디자인 전시회**를 준비하고 있다. geuneun dijain jeonsihoereul junbihago itda. He is preparing a design exhibition.

디자이너 di·ja·i·neo designer

만화 man·hwa comic, cartoon

내 어린 조카는 **만화 주인공처럼** 생겼다. nae eorin jokaneun manhwa juingongcheoreom saenggyeotda. My young nephew looks like a cartoon character.

만화가 man·hwa·ga cartoonist

서예 seo·ye calligraphy
이 강좌는 **서예를** 배우고 싶은 사람 누구에게나 열려 있어요. i gangjwaneun seoyereul baeugo sipeun saram nuguegena yeollyeo isseoyo. This class is open to anyone who would like to learn Korean calligraphy.

미술관 = 화랑 mi·sul·gwan = hwa·rang art museum, art gallery

시내에 미술관이/화랑이 있나요? sinaee misulgwani/hwarangi innayo? Is there an art gallery in the city?

전시 | ~하다 jeon·si | ~·ha·da exhibition | to exhibit
이중섭의 유명한 그림 중 다수가 그 미술관에 **전시되어** 있습니다. ijungseobui yumyeonghan geurim jung dasuga geu misulgwane jeonsidoeeo itseumnida. Many of Lee Jungseop's famous paintings are displayed in that gallery.

전시회 jeon·si·hoe exhibition
전시회 입장료가 있습니까? jeonsihoe ipjangnyoga itseumnikka? Is there any admission fee for the exhibition?

19.2 Music, Dance

음악 eu·mak music
음악 많이 들으세요? eumak mani deureuseyo? Do you listen to music a lot?

곡 gok a piece of music; tune, melody
이 **곡은** 제가 가장 좋아하는 곡 중 하나입니다. i gogeun jega gajang joahaneun gok jung hanaimnida. This is one of my favorite pieces of music.

리듬 ri·deum rhythm
그녀는 **리듬** 감각을 타고났다. geunyeoneun lideum gamgageul tagonatda. She has a natural sense of rhythm.

박자 bak·ja beat, time
저는 **박자를** 잘 못 **맞춰요.** jeoneun bakjareul jal mot matchwoyo. I can't get the beat right.

멜로디 = 선율 mel·lo·di = seo·nyul melody, tune
멜로디가/선율이 귀에 익어요. mellodiga/seonyuri gwie igeoyo. This melody sounds familiar to me.

화음 hwa·eum chord, harmony
이 노래는 복잡한 **화음으로** 유명하다. i noraeneun bokjapan hwaeumeuro yumyeonghada. This song is famous for its complex harmonies.

가사 = 노랫말 ga·sa = no·raen·mal lyrics
어린 학생들은 애국가 **가사를/노랫말을** 외워야 한다. eorin haksaengdeureun aegukga gasareul/noraenmareul oewoya handa. School kids should learn the lyrics of the national anthem.

악보 ak·bo music, score
그 곡은 악보 없이 연주해 본 적이 없어요. geu gogeun akbo eopsi yeonjuhae bon jeogi eopseoyo. I've never played it without looking at the score.

음악가 eu·mak·ga musician
제 꿈은 **세계적인 음악가가** 되는 거예요. je kkumeun segyejeogin eumakgaga doeneun geoyeyo. My dream is to become a world-class musician.

가수 ga·su singer
그녀는 **가수가** 되기 위해 서울에 왔다. geunyeoneun gasuga doegi wihae seoure watda. She came to Seoul to be a singer.

연주자 yeon·ju·ja musician, player
그는 작곡가이자 **바이올린 연주자이다.** geuneun jakgokgaija baiollin nyeonjujaida. He is a composer and violinist.

작곡가 jak·gok·ga composer; songwriter
그는 **재능 있는 작곡가로서** 명성을 쌓아 나가고 있다. geuneun jaeneung inneun jakgokgaroseo myeongseongeul ssaa nagago itda. He is building up a reputation as a gifted songwriter.

작사가 jak·sa·ga lyricist

지휘자 ji·hwi·ja conductor

노래 | ~하다 no·rae | ~·ha·da song | to sing
저는 사람들 앞에서 노래하는 걸 좋아하지 않

아요. jeoneun saramdeul apeseo noraehaneun geol joahaji anayo. I don't like singing in front of others.

부르다 bu·reu·da to sing (a song)
그녀는 **노래를** 아주 잘 **부른다.** geunyeoneun noraereul aju jal bureunda. She is very good at singing.

연주 | ~하다 yeon·ju | ~·ha·da musical performance | to play, perform
어머니는 바이올린 연주로 시간을 보내세요. eomeonineun baiollin nyeonjuro siganeul bonaeseyo. My mother plays the violin to pass the time.

반주 | ~하다 ban·ju | ~·ha·da accompaniment | to accompany
그 가수는 아들의 **반주에 맞춰** 노래를 불렀다. geu gasuneun adeurui banjue matchwo noraereul bulleotda. The singer was accompanied on the piano by his son.

작곡 | ~하다 jak·gok | ~·ha·da composition, songwriting | to compose, write music
그 가수는 자신의 모든 노래를 직접 작곡했다. geu gasuneun jasinui modeun noraereul jikjeop jakgokaetda. That singer wrote all of his music himself.

작사 | ~하다 jak·sa | ~·ha·da lyricizing | to write the lyrics
작사할 때 어디에서 영감을 얻으세요? jaksahal ttae eodieseo yeonggameul eodeuseyo? How do you get inspiration for song lyrics?

지휘 | ~하다 ji·hwi | ~·ha·da direction | to conduct, direct
저는 교회 합창단에서 오르간 연주와 **지휘를** 맡고 있어요. jeoneun gyohoe hapchangdaneseo oreugan nyeonjuwa jihwireul matgo isseoyo. I play the organ and direct a church choir.

음반 = 앨범 eum·ban = ael·beom record, album
제가 제일 좋아하는 밴드가 새 **음반을/앨범을 발표했어요.** jega jeil joahaneun baendeuga sae eumbaneul/aelbeomeul balpyohaesseoyo. My favorite band has released a new album.

녹음 | ~하다 no·geum | ~·ha·da recording | to record
이 피아니스트는 베토벤의 소나타를 모두 녹음했다. i pianiseuteuneun betobenui sonatareul modu nogeumhaetda. This pianist has recorded all of Beethoven's sonatas.

연주회 yeon·ju·hoe concert, recital

음악회 eu·mak·oe (classical) concert
음악회 중간에 아이가 울면 공연장 밖으로 즉시 데리고 나가야 합니다. eumakoe junggane aiga ulmyeon gongyeonjang bakkeuro jeuksi derigo nagaya hamnida. Children who are crying during the concert should be taken out of the auditorium immediately.

콘서트 kon·seo·teu concert
오늘밤 콘서트 갈래? oneulbam konseoteu gallae? Would you like to go to a concert tonight?

악기 ak·gi musical instrument
연주할 줄 아는 악기 있어요? yeonjuhal jul aneun akgi isseoyo? Do you play any musical instruments?

북 buk drum

실로폰 sil·lo·pon xylophone

피아노 pi·a·no piano

치다 chi·da to play; to hit
정말 **피아노** 잘 **치시네요.** jeongmal piano jal chisineyo. You play the piano really well.

플루트 peul·lu·teu flute

색소폰 saek·so·pon saxophone

하모니카 ha·mo·ni·ka harmonica

피리 pi·ri pipe

휘파람 hwi·pa·ram whistle

불다 bul·da to blow, play, whistle
그는 유쾌하게 **휘파람을 불며** 해변을 따라 걸었다. geuneun nyukwaehage hwiparameul bulmyeo haebyeoneul ttara georeotda. He walked along the beach whistling merrily.

바이올린 ba·i·ol·lin violin

첼로 chel·lo cello

켜다 kyeo·da to play
바이올린을 잘 **켜려면** 많은 시간과 노력이 필요하다. baiollineul jal kyeoryeomyeon maneun sigangwa noryeogi piryohada. A lot of time and effort are required to play the violin well.

기타 gi·ta guitar
저는 시간이 날 때면 **기타를 치고는** 했어요. jeoneun sigani nal ttaemyeon gitareul chigo-

neun haesseoyo. I used to play the guitar in my free time.

> 치다 **chida,** which means *to hit* or *to beat,* is mostly used for percussion instruments. However, 치다 is also used in 기타를 치다 **gitareul chida** which means *to play the guitar.*

가야금 ga·ya·geum *gayageum*
거문고 geo·mun·go *geomungo*
뜯다 tteut·da to play, pluck, pick
가야금이나 거문고는 손가락으로 뜯어야 합니다. **gayageumina geomungoneun songarageuro tteudeoya hamnida.** You need to play the *gayageum* or *geomungo* with your fingers.

(대중)가요 (dae·jung·)ga·yo popular music
한국의 대중가요가 전 세계에서 인기를 얻고 있다. **hangugui daejunggayoga jeon segyeeseo ingireul eotgo itda.** K-pop is popular all over the world.

팝송 pap·song American pop music
한때 팝송을 즐겨 들었었어요. **hanttae papsongeul jeulgyeo deureosseosseoyo.** I used to listen to American pop music a long time ago.

클래식 keul·lae·sik classical music
클래식은 제 취향이 아니에요. **keullaesigeun je chwihyangi anieyo.** Classical music is not to my taste.

동요 dong·yo children's song

국악 gu·gak Korean traditional music
판소리 pan·so·ri *pansori*

> *Pansori* is a type of Korean traditional folk music.

민요 mi·nyo folk song
재즈 jae·jeu jazz
오페라 o·pe·ra opera

춤 chum dance, dancing
그 가수의 춤 동작은 따라 하기 쉽다. **geu gasuui chum dongjageun ttara hagi swipda.** The singer's dance moves are easy to follow.

추다 chu·da to dance
사람들이 탱고를 추고 있다. **saramdeuri taenggoreul chugo itda.** People are dancing the tango.

안무 an·mu choreography
제가 그 발레 공연의 안무를 담당했습니다. **jega geu balle gongyeonui anmureul damdanghaetseumnida.** I had choreographed the ballet show.

무용 mu·yong artistic dance
저는 현대 무용을 전공했어요. **jeoneun hyeondae muyongeul jeongonghaesseoyo.** I majored in modern dance.

무용가 mu·yong·ga dancer
발레 bal·le ballet
탈춤 tal·chum mask dance

19.3 Literature, Writing

문학 mun·hak literature
문학은 사회를 비추는 거울이다. **munhageun sahoereul bichuneun geourida.** Literature is a mirror of society.

작가 jak·ga writer, author
그 작가는 책을 쓰는 동안에는 외출을 절대 하지 않는다. **geu jakganeun chaegeul sseuneun donganeneun oechureul jeoldae haji anneunda.** The writer never goes out while she is writing a book.

저자 jeo·ja author
그 책의 저자는 누구예요? **geu chaegui jeojaneun nuguyeyo?** What is the name of the author of that book?

시 si poem, poetry
음악은 학생들의 시 감상을 돕는 아주 좋은 매개체예요. **eumageun haksaengdeurui si gamsangeul domneun aju joeun maegaecheyeyo.** Music is a wonderful medium to help students appreciate poetry.

시조 si·jo *sijo*

> *Sijo* is a Korean traditional poetic form which is composed of three lines and a fixed number of syllables.

동시 dong·si children's poem

시집 si·jip collection of poems

시인 si·in poet
윤동주는 가장 **위대한 시인** 중 한 명이다. **yundongjuneun gajang widaehan siin jung han myeongida.** Yun Dongju is one of the greatest poets.

소설 so·seol novel
저는 여가 시간에 주로 **소설을 읽어요**. **jeoneun nyeoga sigane juro soseoreul ilgeoyo.** I usually read novels in my free time.

단편(소설) dan·pyeon(·so·seol) short story

장편(소설) jang·pyeon(·so·seol) novel
저는 세 편의 장편소설과 스무 편의 단편소설을 썼습니다. **jeoneun se pyeonui jangpyeonsoseolgwa seumu pyeonui danpyeonsoseoreul sseotseumnida.** I've written three novels and twenty short stories.

소설가 so·seol·ga novelist

희곡 hui·gok play

극작가 geuk·jak·ga playwright

수필 su·pil essay

일기 il·gi diary
나는 초등학교를 졸업한 이후로 **일기를 써** 본 적이 없다. **naneun chodeunghakgyoreul joreopan ihuro ilgireul sseo bon jeogi eopda.** I haven't kept a diary since I graduated from elementary school.

설화 seol·hwa tale

신화 sin·hwa myth, mythology
단군신화는 우리나라의 건국에 관한 이야기다. **dangunsinhwaneun urinaraui geonguge gwanhan iyagida.** The myth of Dangun tells the story of Korea's foundation.

전설 jeon·seol legend

민담 min·dam folktale

전기 jeon·gi biography

자서전 ja·seo·jeon autobiography

동화 dong·hwa children's story, fairy tale
그의 동화는 아이들뿐 아니라 어른들에게도 인기가 많다. **geuui donghwaneun aideulppun anira eoreundeuregedo ingiga manta.** His children's stories are popular with adults as well as children.

주제 ju·je subject, topic
이 소설의 **주제**가 뭐죠? **i soseorui jujega mwojyo?** What's the theme of this novel?

소재 so·jae material, subject matter
전쟁을 소재로 한 희곡을 쓰고 있어요. **jeonjaengeul sojaero han huigogeul sseugo isseoyo.** I'm writing a play about war.

줄거리 jul·geo·ri summary, outline, synopsis
이 책의 **줄거리**를 쓰시오. **i chaegui julgeorireul sseusio.** Write an outline of this book.

구성 gu·seong plot
매력적인 인물들과 **정교한 구성**이 이 책을 흥미롭게 하는 요소이다. **maeryeokjeogin inmuldeulgwa jeonggyohan guseongi i chaegeul heungmiropge haneun nyosoida.** Attractive characters and an intricate plot are what makes the book so compelling.

(등장)인물 (deung·jang·)in·mul person, character
그녀의 소설은 모든 등장인물들이 저마다의 개성을 갖고 있다. **geunyeoui soseoreun modeun deungjanginmuldeuri jeomadaui gaeseongeul gatgo itda.** All of the characters have their own distinct personalities in her novels.

주인공 ju·in·gong main character, protagonist
많은 경우 추리 소설에서 배경이나 주인공의 직업은 구성에 있어 중요한 요소다. **maneun gyeongu churi soseoreseo baegyeongina juingongui jigeobeun guseonge isseo jungyohan nyosoda.** In many mystery novels, the setting and the main character's job are important elements in the plot.

등장 | ~하다 deung·jang | ~·ha·da appearance | to appear
그의 소설에는 의사가 자주 등장한다. **geuui soseoreneun uisaga jaju deungjanghanda.** Doctors often appear in his novels.

배경 bae·gyeong background, setting

묘사 | ~하다 myo·sa | ~·ha·da description, depiction | to describe, depict
소설의 배경에 대한 **생생한 묘사**가 인상적이었다. **soseorui baegyeonge daehan saengsaenghan myosaga insangjeogieotda.** I was impressed by the vivid depiction of the setting in the novel.

글 geul writing

문법을 이해하면 생각을 글로 명확하게 표현할 수 있다. **munbeobeul ihaehamyeon saeng-gageul geullo myeonghwakage pyohyeonhal su itda.** By understanding grammar, you can express your thoughts clearly in writing.

쓰다 sseu·da to write
저는 그 신문에 글을 쓰고 있어요. **jeoneun geu sinmune geureul sseugo isseoyo.** I'm writing for the newspaper.

쓰이다 sseu·i·da to be written, read
문의 팻말에는 "관계자 외 출입금지"라고 쓰여 있었다. **munui paenmareneun gwangyeja oe churipgeumji rago sseuyeo isseotda.** The sign on the door read "Staff Only."

적다 jeok·da to write, note
여기에 이름과 연락처를 적어 주세요. **yeogie ireumgwa yeollakcheoreul jeogeo juseyo.** Please write down your name and contact information here.

적히다 jeo·ki·da to be written, read
그 종이에는 아무것도 적혀 있지 않았다. **geu jongieneun amugeotdo jeokyeo itji anatda.** There was nothing written on the paper.

글쓰기 geul·sseu·gi (activity of) writing
글쓰기는 말하기와는 많은 점이 다르다. **geulsseugineun malhagiwaneun maneun jeomi dareuda.** Writing is different from speaking in many ways.

번역 | ~하다 beo·nyeok | ~·ha·da translation | to translate
이 단어는 영어로 번역하기가 쉽지 않군요. **i daneoneun nyeongeoro beonyeokagiga swipji ankunnyo.** This word is not easy to translate into English.

글씨 geul·ssi handwriting, letter
죄송해요. 저도 내 글씨가 읽기 힘들다는 거 알아요. **joesonghaeyo. jeodo nae geulssiga ilgi himdeuldaneun geo arayo.** Sorry. I know my handwriting is hard to read.

원고 won·go manuscript
일주일 전에 제 원고의 검토를 의뢰했었습니다. **iljuil jeone je wongoui geomtoreul uiroe-haesseotseumnida.** I requested that you review my manuscript a week ago.

19.4 Movies, Performances

영화 yeong·hwa movie, film
오늘 영화 보러 갈래? **oneul lyeonghwa boreo gallae?** Do you want to go to the movies with me?

공연 | ~하다 gong·yeon | ~·ha·da performance, show | to perform
마지막 공연은 열한 시에 있습니다. **majimak gongyeoneun nyeolhan sie itseumnida.** The last show is at eleven.

연극 yeon·geuk play, theater
그 연극은 5월 1일부터 10월 31일까지 월요일을 제외하고 매일 공연됩니다. **geu yeon-geugeun owol irilbuteo siwol samsibirilkkaji woryoireul jeoehago maeil gongyeondoemnida.** The play is performed daily, except for Mondays, from May 1 until October 31.

오페라 o·pe·ra opera
제가 그 오페라의 주연을 따냈다는 얘기를 들었을 때 저는 정말 믿기지가 않았어요. **jega geu operaui juyeoneul ttanaetdaneun yaegireul deureoseul ttae jeoneun jeongmal mitgijiga anasseoyo.** I couldn't believe it when I was told that I got the leading role in the opera.

뮤지컬 myu·ji·keol musical

마술 ma·sul magic

편 pyeon unit for counting movies, plays, concerts, etc.
영화 한 편 **yeonghwa han pyeon** a movie

연출 | ~하다 yeon·chul | ~·ha·da direction; director | to direct
저는 현재 한 연극의 연출을 담당하고 있습니다. **jeoneun hyeonjae han nyeongeugui yeon-chureul damdanghago itseumnida.** I'm directing a play.

감독 gam·dok director
그는 세계적으로 유명한 한국의 영화 감독이다. **geuneun segyejeogeuro yumyeonghan hangugui yeonghwa gamdogida.** He is a world-famous Korean movie director.

제작 | ~하다 je·jak | ~·ha·da production | to produce
그 소설은 영화로 제작될 예정이다. **geu so-seoreun nyeonghwaro jejakdoel yejeongida.** The novel is going to be made into a movie.

시나리오 = 대본 si·na·ri·o = dae·bon scenario, screenplay
저는 시나리오가/대본이 감독보다 더 중요하

다고 생각해요. jeoneun sinarioga/daeboni gamdokboda deo jungyohadago saenggakaeyo. I believe the script is more important than the director.

각본 = 극본 gak·bon = geuk·bon script

조명 jo·myeong lighting
저는 그 공연의 **조명**을 맡고 있어요. jeoneun geu gongyeonui jomyeongeul matgo isseoyo. I'm in charge of the lighting for the show.

연기자 yeon·gi·ja actor, actress
부모님은 제가 **연기자가 되는** 걸 반대하세요. bumonimeun jega yeongijaga doeneun geol bandaehaseyo. My parents don't want me to become an actor.

배우 bae·u actor, actress
그녀는 배우이자 감독이다. geunyeoneun bae-uija gamdogida. She is an actress and director.

성우 seong·u voice actor, voice actress

(배)역 = 역할 ← 역활 (bae·)yeok = yeo·khal ← yeo·khwal part, role
여러 차례의 오디션을 거쳐 그는 그 **역을/역할을 따냈**다. yeoreo charyeui odisyeoneul geo-chyeo geuneun geu yeogeul/yeokareul ttanaet-da. He won the role after many auditions.

주연 | ~하다 ju·yeon | ~·ha·da lead role, star | to play the lead role
이 영화의 주연은 누구죠? i yeonghwaui juyeo-neun nugujyo? Who's starring in this movie?

조연 jo·yeon supporting role
저는 여러 연극에서 **조연**을 **맡았습니**다. jeoneun nyeoreo yeongeugeseo joyeoneul ma-tatseumnida. I've had supporting roles in many plays.

연기 | ~하다 yeon·gi | ~·ha·da perfor-mance, acting | to perform, act
솔직히 말해, 그녀의 **연기는 형편없었어요**. soljiki malhae, geunyeoui yeongineun hyeong-pyeoneopseosseoyo. Frankly speaking, her acting was poor.

대사 dae·sa lines
무대에서 **대사를 까먹은** 적이 있나요? mu-daeeseo daesareul kkameogeun jeogi innayo? Have you ever forgotten your lines while on stage?

무대 mu·dae stage
내 자리에서 무대가 잘 보여. nae jarieseo mu-daega jal boyeo. I have a good view of the stage from my seat.

자막 ja·mak subtitle, caption
그 뮤지컬은 **영어 자막**과 함께 상연됩니다. geu myujikeoreun nyeongeo jamakgwa hamkke sangyeondoemnida. The musical is per-formed with English subtitles.

장면 jang·myeon scene
영화의 **첫 장면**이 아주 인상적이었어요. yeonghwaui cheot jangmyeoni aju insangjeogieo-sseoyo. The first scene of the movie was so impressive.

관객 gwan·gaek audience

박수 bak·su clap, applause
관객들이 배우들에게 열광적으로 **박수를 보냈다**. gwangaekdeuri baeudeurege yeol-gwangjeogeuro baksureul bonaetda. The audi-ence applauded the actors and actresses with enthusiasm.

관람 | ~하다 gwal·lam | ~·ha·da watch-ing, viewing | to see, watch
이 연극은 **미성년자 관람 불가**예요. i yeon-geugeun miseongnyeonja gwallam bulgayeyo. Underaged people are not allowed to see this play.

열기 yeol·gi excitement, fever
공연장은 **열기로 가득했다**. gongyeonjangeun nyeolgiro gadeukaetda. The concert hall was filled with excitement.

영화제 yeong·hwa·je film festival
부산국제영화제 busangukjeyeonghwaje Bu-san International Film Festival

비극 bi·geuk tragedy
인생은 비극이야. insaengeun bigeugiya. Life is a tragedy.

코미디 = 희극 ← 코메디 ko·mi·di = hui·geuk ← ko·me·di comedy
저는 비극보다 코미디가/희극이 좋아요. jeoneun bigeukboda komidiga/huigeugi joayo. I like comedies more than tragedies.

비평 ≒ 평론 | ~하다 bi·pyeong ≒ pyeong·non | ~·ha·da criticism, review | to criticize, review

평론가 ≒ 비평가 pyeong·non·ga ≒ bi·pyeong·ga critic, reviewer
그 영화는 평론가들에게서/비평가들에게서 높은 평가를 받았다. geu yeonghwaneun pyeong-nongadeuregeseo/bipyeonggadeuregeseo nopeun pyeonggareul badatda. The film received high praise from the critics.

chapter **20** | # Nations and Politics

20.1 **General Terms**

국가 guk·ga nation, country
이 드라마는 특히 **아시아 국가**들 사이에서 인기가 높다. i deuramaneun teuki asia gukgadeul saieseo ingiga nopda. This drama is particularly popular in Asian countries.

나라 na·ra nation, country
어느 나라에 가고 싶어? eoneu narae gago sipeo? Which country do you want to visit?

선진국 seon·jin·guk developed country
선진국은 후진국보다 지구 온난화 문제에 더 많은 책임이 있다. seonjingugeun hujingukboda jigu onnanhwa munjee deo maneun chaegimi itda. Developed countries are more responsible for global warming than underdeveloped countries.

개발도상국 gae·bal·do·sang·guk developing country

후진국 hu·jin·guk underdeveloped country

국내 gung·nae domestic
국내 농산물을 이용합시다. gungnae nongsanmureul iyonghapsida. Let's use domestic farm products.

국제(적) guk·je(·jeok) international
환경에 관한 **국제 회의**가 서울에서 열리고 있다. hwangyeonge gwanhan gukje hoeuiga seoureseo yeolligo itda. An international conference on the environment is taking place in Seoul.

그는 올림픽에서 금메달을 딴 뒤 **국제적 명성**을 얻었다. geuneun ollimpigeseo geummedareul ttan dwi gukjejeok myeongseongeul eodeotda. He gained international recognition, winning a gold medal in the Olympics.

국제화 guk·je·hwa globalization

세계 | ~적 se·gye | ~·jeok world | global, worldwide
중국은 세계에서 가장 큰 나라다. junggugeun segyeeseo gajang keun narada. China is the largest country in the world.

세상 se·sang world
제 꿈은 세상의 모든 나라들을 가 보는 거예요. je kkumeun sesangui modeun naradeureul ga boneun geoyeyo. My dream is to visit all the countries in the world.

우리나라 u·ri·na·ra my country
추석은 우리나라의 제일 큰 명절이에요. chu-

seogeun urinaraui jeil keun myeongjeorieyo. Chuseok is our most important holiday.

각국 gak·guk each country
각국을 대표하는 선수들이 올림픽에 출전한다. gakgugeul daepyohaneun seonsudeuri ollimpige chuljeonhanda. Players representing each country participate in the Olympics.

양국 yang·guk the two countries

국민 gung·min nation, people
대다수 국민들이 정치의 변화를 간절히 바라고 있다. daedasu gungmindeuri jeongchiui byeonhwareul ganjeolhi barago itda. Most people long for political change.

국적 guk·jeok nationality
저는 일본에서 자랐지만 국적은 한국입니다. jeoneun ilboneseo jaratjiman gukjeogeun hangugimnida. I grew up in Japan, but my nationality is Korean.

교포 gyo·po overseas Korean
저는 **재미 교포** 2세입니다. jeoneun jaemi gyopo iseimnida. I'm a second generation Korean-American.

동포 dong·po compatriot

내국인 nae·gu·gin local

외국인 oe·gu·gin foreigner
매년 많은 **외국인 관광객**들이 서울을 방문합니다. maenyeon maneun oegugin gwanggwanggaekdeuri seoureul bangmunhamnida. Every year, many international tourists visit Seoul.

이민 i·min emigration, immigration
제 친구 하나가 작년에 호주로 **이민을 갔어요**. je chingu hanaga jangnyeone hojuro imineul gasseoyo. A friend of mine emigrated to Australia last year.

인구 in·gu population
현재 우리나라의 인구는 5천만이 넘는다. hyeonjae urinaraui inguneun ocheonmani neomneunda. Presently, South Korea's population exceeds 50 million.

민족 min·jok race, people, ethnic group

인종 in·jong race

백인 bae·gin Caucasian, white person

흑인 heu·gin black

동양인 dong·yang·in Asian

서양인 seo·yang·in Westerner
동양인들의 생활 방식은 서양인들과 많이 달라요. dongyangindeurui saenghwal bangsigeun seoyangindeulgwa mani dallayo. The Asian way of life is much different from its Western counterpart.

국기 guk·gi national flag
한국의 국기는 태극기라고 부릅니다. hangugui gukgineun taegeukgirago bureumnida. The national flag of Korea is called the *Taegeuki*.

태극기 tae·geuk·gi *Taegeukgi* (Korean national flag)

국토 guk·to country, territory

영토 yeong·to territory, domain
한국과 일본은 오래 전부터 독도를 둘러싸고 **영토** 분쟁을 벌이고 있다. hangukgwa ilboneun orae jeonbuteo dokdoreul dulleossago yeongto bunjaengeul beorigo itda. Korea and Japan have been engaged in a territorial dispute over Dokdo for a long time.

국경 guk·gyeong border
양국은 **국경이** 접해 있습니다. yanggugeun gukgyeongi jeopae itseumnida. The two countries share a common border.

국가 guk·ga national anthem

애국가 ae·guk·ga the Korean national anthem
애국가는 4절까지 있다. aegukganeun sajeolkkaji itda. The Korean national anthem has four verses.

20.2 Continents, Countries, Peoples

대륙 dae·ryuk continent

동양 dong·yang the East

아시아 a·si·a Asia

동남아(시아) dong·na·ma(·si·a) Southeast Asia

한반도 han·ban·do the Korean Peninsula

서양 seo·yang the West

유럽 yu·reop Europe

아프리카 a·peu·ri·ka Africa

북아메리카 = 북미 bu·ga·me·ri·ka = bung·mi North America

남아메리카 = 남미 na·ma·me·ri·ka = nam·mi South America

오세아니아 o·se·a·ni·a Oceania

남극 nam·geuk the South Pole

북극 buk·geuk the North Pole

한국 han·guk Korea
내년에 다시 한국에 올 거예요. naenyeone dasi hanguge ol geoyeyo. I'll come back to Korea again next year.

한국인 han·gu·gin Korean

대한민국 dae·han·min·guk Korea

남한 nam·han South Korea
일본은 남한 면적의 네 배 정도 된다. ilboneun namhan myeonjeogui ne bae jeongdo doenda. Japan is around four times the size of South Korea.

> 남한 is the term South Koreans call South Korea as opposed to North Korea. In other cases, they will say 한국 **hanguk** or 대한민국 **daehanminguk**.

북한 bu·khan North Korea

> 북한 is the term South Koreans call North Korea. North Koreans, by contrast, call their country 북조선 **bukjoseon** and South Korea 남조선 **namjoseon**.

중국 jung·guk China

중국인 jung·gu·gin Chinese

일본 il·bon Japan
일본 여행은 어땠어? ilbon nyeohaengeun eottaesseo? How was your trip to Japan?

일본인 il·bo·nin Japanese

타이완 = 대만 ta·i·wan = dae·man Taiwan

몽골 mong·gol Mongolia

베트남 be·teu·nam Vietnam

싱가포르 sing·ga·po·reu Singapore
인도네시아 in·do·ne·si·a Indonesia
말레이시아 mal·le·i·si·a Malaysia
타이 = 태국 ta·i = tae·guk Thailand
필리핀 pil·li·pin the Philippines
인도 in·do India
이란 i·ran Iran
이라크 i·ra·keu Iraq
이스라엘 i·seu·ra·el Israel
터키 teo·ki Turkey

러시아 reo·si·a Russia
영국 yeong·guk the United Kingdom
영국인 yeong·gu·gin the British
프랑스 peu·rang·seu France
프랑스인 peu·rang·seu·in French
독일 do·gil Germany
독일인 do·gi·rin German, the German people
스위스 seu·wi·seu Switzerland
네덜란드 ne·deol·lan·deu Netherlands
스페인 seu·pe·in Spain
포르투갈 po·reu·tu·gal Portugal

그리스 geu·ri·seu Greece
노르웨이 no·reu·we·i Norway
덴마크 den·ma·keu Denmark
스웨덴 seu·we·den Sweden
핀란드 pil·lan·deu Finland
폴란드 pol·lan·deu Poland
헝가리 heong·ga·ri Hungary

이집트 i·jip·teu Egypt
케냐 ke·nya Kenya
남아프리카공화국 = 남아공 na·ma·peu·ri·ka·gong·hwa·guk = na·ma·gong the Republic of South Africa

미국 mi·guk the United States of America
미국인 mi·gu·gin American
캐나다 kae·na·da Canada
쿠바 ku·ba Cuba
멕시코 mek·si·ko Mexico
브라질 beu·ra·jil Brazil
아르헨티나 a·reu·hen·ti·na Argentina

오스트레일리아 = 호주 o·seu·teu·re·il·li·a = ho·ju Australia
뉴질랜드 nyu·jil·laen·deu New Zealand

20.3 Politics, Political Systems

정치 jeong·chi politics
종교는 정치와 분리되어야 한다. jonggyoneun jeongchiwa bullidoeeoya handa. Religion has to be separated from politics.

정치인 jeong·chi·in politician
정치인은 많은 후원자를 갖고 있다. jeongchiineun maneun huwonjareul gatgo itda. That politician has many backers.

정치권 jeong·chi·gwon political circles
정치권에서는 그 장관의 사임을 요구하고 있다. jeongchigwoneseoneun geu janggwanui saimeul lyoguhago itda. Political circles call for the minister to resign.

이념 i·nyeom ideology, principle

민주주의의 **근본 이념**은 인간 존중이다. minjujuuiui geunbon inyeomeun ingan jonjungida. Democracy was founded on the basic principle of respect for the individual.

민주주의 min·ju·ju·ui democracy
대한민국은 **민주주의** 국가다. daehanmingugeun minjujuui gukgada. The Republic of Korea is a democracy.

이상 | ~적 i·sang | ~·jeok ideal | ideal, perfect
이곳은 휴가를 보내기에 **이상적인** 곳이다. igoseun hyugareul bonaegie isangjeogin gosida. This is an ideal place for a holiday.

현실 | ~적 hyeon·sil | ~·jeok reality | realistic

현실은 이상과 다릅니다. **hyeonsireun isanggwa dareumnida.** Reality is different from the ideal.

다수 da·su many, majority
다수의 결정이 항상 옳은 것은 아니다. **dasuui gyeoljeongi hangsang oreun geoseun anida.** The majority's decision is not always right.

소수 so·su minority
우리는 소수의 의견을 존중해야 합니다. **urineun sosuui uigyeoneul jonjunghaeya hamnida.** We should respect the opinion of the minority.

대표 | ~하다 dae·pyo | ~·ha·da representative | to represent
양국의 대표들이 그 사안을 논의하기 위해 만났다. **yanggugui daepyodeuri geu saaneul lonuihagi wihae mannatda.** Representatives from the two countries met to discuss the issue.

정책 jeong·chaek policy

외교 oe·gyo diplomacy
야당은 정부의 외교 정책을 비판해 왔다. **yadangeun jeongbuui oegyo jeongchaegeul bipanhae watda.** The opposition has criticized the government's diplomatic policies.

외교관 oe·gyo·gwan diplomat
아버지가 외교관이어서 어릴 때 싱가포르에서 살았어요. **abeojiga oegyogwanieoseo eoril ttae singgaporeueoseo sarasseoyo.** My father is a diplomat, and I lived in Singapore when I was little.

대사 dae·sa ambassador
그는 주미 대사로 임명되었다. **geuneun jumi daesaro immyeongdoeeotda.** He was appointed ambassador to the US.

대사관 dae·sa·gwan embassy
저는 대사관 소속입니다. **jeoneun daesagwan sosogimnida.** I'm affiliated with the embassy.

교류 | ~하다 gyo·ryu | ~·ha·da exchange, interchange | to exchange, interchange
정부는 다른 아시아 나라들과의 문화 교류를 강화하는 데 힘쓰고 있다. **jeongbuneun dareun asia naradeulgwaui munhwa gyoryureul ganghwahaneun de himsseugo itda.** The government is trying to enhance cultural exchanges with other Asian countries.

개방 | ~하다 gae·bang | ~·ha·da opening | to open

도입 | ~하다 do·ip | ~·ha·da introduction

| to introduce, adopt
그는 적극적으로 외국 자본을 도입해야 한다고 주장했다. **geuneun jeokgeukjeogeuro oeguk jaboneul doipaeya handago jujanghaetda.** He insisted that we actively introduce foreign capital.

선거 seon·geo election
저는 이번 선거에 별 관심이 없습니다. **jeoneun ibeon seongeoe byeol gwansimi eopseumnida.** I don't have much interest in this election.

대선 dae·seon presidential election
그는 차기 대선에서 가장 유력한 후보이다. **geuneun chagi daeseoneseo gajang yuryeokan huboida.** He is the strongest candidate in the next presidential election.

총선(거) chong·seon(·geo) general election

지방선거 ji·bang·seon·geo local election

후보(자) hu·bo(·ja) candidate

출마 | ~하다 chul·ma | ~·ha·da candidacy | to run for office
그녀는 이번 선거에 무소속으로 출마했다. **geunyeoneun ibeon seongeoe musosogeuro chulmahaetda.** She ran in this election as an independent candidate.

공약 gong·yak campaign pledge
그 후보는 말도 안 되는 공약을 내걸었다. **geu huboneun maldo an doeneun gongyageul laegeoreotda.** The candidate made empty promises.

선거운동 seon·geo·un·dong campaign
공식 선거운동 기간은 14일이다. **gongsik seongeoundong giganeun sipsairida.** The official campaign period is 14 days.

유세 | ~하다 yu·se | ~·ha·da campaign, electioneering | to campaign
당 대표들은 전국을 돌며 유세를 펼치고 있다. **dang daepyodeureun jeongugeul dolmyeo yusereul pyeolchigo itda.** Leaders from each party are touring the country for their campaigns.

당선 | ~되다 dang·seon | ~·doe·da election | to be elected
그는 작년에 시장으로 당선되었다. **geuneun jangnyeone sijangeuro dangseondoeeotda.** He was elected mayor last year.

선출 | ~하다 seon·chul | ~·ha·da election | to elect

대통령은 5년마다 선출됩니다. **daetongnyeong-eun onyeonmada seonchuldoemnida.** The president is elected every five years.

뽑다 ppop·da to select, elect
도지사로 누구를 뽑을 거야? **dojisaro nugureul ppobeul geoya?** Who are you going to vote for as governor?

뽑히다 ppo·pi·da to be selected, be elected

당선자 dang·seon·ja elected person

지도자 = 리더 ji·do·ja = ri·deo leader
그는 지도자가/리더가 될 자격이 충분하지 않다. **geuneun jidojaga/rideoga doel jagyeogi chungbunhaji anta.** He is not good enough to be a leader.

낙선 | ~하다 nak·seon | ~·ha·da losing an election | to lose an election
그는 이번 총선에서 낙선했다. **geuneun ibeon chongseoneseo nakseonhaetda.** He lost in the general election.

투표 | ~하다 tu·pyo | ~·ha·da vote, ballot | to vote
현 **투표 시간**은 오전 여섯 시에서 오후 여섯 시까지다. **hyeon tupyo siganeun ojeon nyeoseot sieseo ohu yeoseot sikkajida.** The current voting period is from 6 a.m. to 6 p.m.

찍다 jjik·da to vote
저는 이번 선거에서 여당 **후보**를 찍었어요. **jeoneun ibeon seongeoeseo yeodang huboreul jjigeosseoyo.** I voted for the candidate from the ruling party.

기권 | ~하다 gi·gwon | ~·ha·da abstention | to abstain
이번 선거에서 유권자 네 명 중 한 명꼴로 기권한 것으로 드러났다. **ibeon seongeoeseo yugwonja ne myeong jung han myeongkkollo gigwonhan geoseuro deureonatda.** It turned out that around one fourth of the voters abstained from voting.

표 pyo vote, ballot
그는 이번 대선에서 불과 3만 표 차이로 승리했다. **geuneun ibeon daeseoneseo bulgwa sam-man pyo chairo seungnihaetda.** He won the presidential election by only 30,000 votes.

투표소 tu·pyo·so polling place

투표용지 tu·pyo·yong·ji ballot paper

투표함 tu·pyo·ham ballot box

투표권 tu·pyo·gwon the right to vote

한국에서는 만 19세에 **투표권이 부여된다**. **hangugeseoneun man sipgusee tupyogwoni buyeodoenda.** In Korea, people who are 19 or older can vote.

투표율 tu·pyo·yul turnout
이번 선거의 **투표율**은 매우 **낮았다**. **ibeon seongeoui tupyoyureun maeu najatda.** The voter turnout for this election was very low.

유권자 yu·gwon·ja voter
이번 정책은 **중산층 유권자**들에게 환영받을 것으로 예상된다. **ibeon jeongchaegeun jungsancheung yugwonjadeurege hwannyeongbadeul geoseuro yesangdoenda.** These policies are expected to be welcomed by middle-class voters.

개표 | ~하다 gae·pyo | ~·ha·da ballot count | to count the ballots
개표는 여섯 시 정각에 시작합니다. **gaepyoneun nyeoseot si jeonggage sijakamnida.** Vote counting will start at six o'clock.

개표소 gae·pyo·so ballot count place

득표 | ~하다 deuk·pyo | ~·ha·da poll | to poll
그녀는 이번 선거에서 총 투표 수의 51퍼센트를 득표했다. **geunyeoneun ibeon seongeoeseo chong tupyo suui osibilpeoseonteureul deukpyohaetda.** She polled 51% of the vote in the election.

의회 ui·hoe assembly, congress
시 의회는 전체 시 공무원들의 임금을 10퍼센트 인상하기로 결정했다. **si uihoeneun jeonche si gongmuwondeurui imgeumeul sippeoseonteu insanghagiro gyeoljeonghaetda.** The city council has decided to give a 10% raise to all municipal employees.

국회 gu·khoe the National Assembly
국회는 그 예산안을 채택했다. **gukhoeneun geu yesananeul chaetaekaetda.** The National Assembly adopted the budget.

국회의원 gu·khoe·ui·won member of the National Assembly
그는 국회의원으로 당선되었다. **geuneun gukoeuiwoneuro dangseondoeeotda.** He was elected to become a member of the National Assembly.

(정)당 (jeong·)dang (political) party
그들은 새 **정당**을 결성했다. **geudeureun sae jeongdangeul gyeolseonghaetda.** They formed a new political party.

여당 yeo·dang the ruling party

야당 ya·dang the opposition party
이번 지방선거에서 여당이 야당에 승리했다. ibeon jibangseongeoseo yeodangi yadange seungnihaetda. The ruling party defeated the opposition in this local election.

· ·

᠁ (국)왕 (guk·)wang king
세종대왕은 1443년 한글을 만들었다. sejong-daewangeun cheonsabaeksasipsamnyeon han-geureul mandeureotda. Great King Sejong invented the Hangul in 1443.

왕비 wang·bi queen (the wife of the king)

여왕 yeo·wang queen (hereditary ruler)

왕자 wang·ja prince

공주 gong·ju princess

지배 | ~하다 ji·bae | ~·ha·da rule, domination | to rule, dominate

독립 | ~하다 dong·nip | ~·ha·da independence | to become independent
한국은 1945년 일본으로부터 독립했다. hangugeun cheongubaeksasibonyeon ilbo-neurobuteo dongnipaetda. Korea declared independence from Japan in 1945.

20.4 The Government, Executive Branch of Korea

정부 jeong·bu government
노조는 정부의 제안을 거절했다. nojoneun jeongbuui jeaneul geojeolhaetda. The Labor Union rejected the government's proposals.

청와대 cheong·wa·dae *Cheongwadae*, the Korean presidential residence

᠁ 대통령 dae·tong·nyeong president

(국무)총리 (gung·mu·)chong·ni prime minister
대통령은 총리와 대화 중이다. daetongnyeong-eun chongniwa daehwa jungida. The President is in a discussion with the Prime Minister.

장관 jang·gwan government minister

임명 | ~하다 im·myeong | ~·ha·da appointment | to appoint
그는 통일부 장관으로 임명되었다. geuneun tongilbu janggwaneuro immyeongdoeeotda. He was appointed Minister of Unification.

· ·

행정부 haeng·jeong·bu administration, executive branch

기획재정부 gi·hoek·jae·jeong·bu Ministry of Strategy and Finance

미래창조과학부 mi·rae·chang·jo·gwa·hak·bu Ministry of Science, ICT and Future Planning

교육부 gyo·yuk·bu Ministry of Education

외교부 oe·gyo·bu Ministry of Foreign Affairs

통일부 tong·il·bu Ministry of Unification

법무부 beom·mu·bu Ministry of Justice

국방부 guk·bang·bu Ministry of National Defense

안전행정부 an·jeon·haeng·jeong·bu Ministry of Security and Public Administration

문화체육관광부 mun·hwa·che·yuk·gwan·gwang·bu Ministry of Culture, Sports and Tourism

농림축산식품부 nong·nim·chuk·san·sik·pum·bu Ministry of Agriculture, Food and Rural Affairs

산업통상자원부 sa·neop·tong·sang·ja·won·bu Ministry of Trade, Industry and Energy

보건복지부 bo·geon·bok·ji·bu Ministry of Health and Welfare

환경부 hwan·gyeong·bu Ministry of Environment

고용노동부 go·yong·no·dong·bu Ministry of Employment and Labor

여성가족부 yeo·seong·ga·jok·bu Ministry of Gender Equality and Family

국토교통부 guk·to·gyo·tong·bu Ministry of Land, Infrastructure and Transport

해양수산부 hae·yang·su·san·bu Ministry of Oceans and Fisheries

국세청 guk·se·cheong National Tax Service

관세청 gwan·se·cheong Korea Customs Service

조달청 jo·dal·cheong Public Procurement Service

통계청 tong·gye·cheong Statistics Korea

검찰청 geom·chal·cheong Supreme Prosecutors' Office

병무청 byeong·mu·cheong Military Manpower Administration

방위사업청 bang·wi·sa·eop·cheong Defense Acquisition Program Administration

경찰청 gyeong·chal·cheong Korean National Police Agency

소방방재청 so·bang·bang·jae·cheong National Emergency Management Agency

문화재청 mun·hwa·jae·cheong Cultural Heritage Administration

농촌진흥청 nong·chon·jin·heung·cheong Rural Development Administration

산림청 sal·lim·cheong Korea Forest Service

중소기업청 jung·so·gi·eop·cheong Small and Medium Business Administration

특허청 teu·kheo·cheong Korean Intellectual Property Office

기상청 gi·sang·cheong Korea Meteorological Administration

행정중심복합도시건설청 haeng·jeong·jung·sim·bo·khap·do·si·geon·seol·cheong Multifunctional Administrative City Construction Agency

새만금개발청 sae·man·geum·gae·bal·cheong Saemangeum Development Agency

해양경찰청 hae·yang·gyeong·chal·cheong Korea Coast Guard

대통령비서실 dae·tong·nyeong·bi·seo·sil Office of the President

국가안보실 guk·ga·an·bo·sil Office of National Security

대통령경호실 dae·tong·nyeong·gyeong·ho·sil Presidential Security Service

국무조정실 gung·mu·jo·jeong·sil Office for Government Policy Coordination

국무총리비서실 gung·mu·chong·ni·bi·seo·sil Office of the Prime Minister

방송통신위원회 bang·song·tong·sin·wi·won·hoe Korea Communications Commission

공정거래위원회 gong·jeong·geo·rae·wi·won·hoe Korean Fair Trade Commission

금융위원회 geu·myung·wi·won·hoe Financial Services Commission

국민권익위원회 gung·min·gwo·ni·gwi·won·hoe Anti-corruption & Civil Rights Commission

원자력안전위원회 won·ja·ryeo·gan·jeon·wi·won·hoe Nuclear Safety and Security Commission

국가인권위원회 guk·ga·in·gwo·nwi·won·hoe National Human Rights Commission of Korea

법제처 beop·je·cheo Ministry of Government Legislation

국가보훈처 guk·ga·bo·hun·cheo Ministry of Patriots & Veterans Affairs

식품의약품안전처 sik·pu·mui·yak·pu·man·jeon·cheo Ministry of Food and Drug Safety

감사원 gam·sa·won Board of Audit & Inspection

국가정보원 guk·ga·jeong·bo·won National Intelligence Service

20.5 Administrative Districts, Government Offices

시 si city

특별시 teuk·byeol·si special city
서울특별시 seoulteukbyeolsi Seoul Metropolitan City

광역시 gwang·yeok·si megalopolis, metropolitan city
부산광역시 busangwangyeoksi

> South Korea has six metropolitan cities—Busan, Daejeon, Daegu, Incheon, Ulsan, and Gwangju.

도 do *do*, province

> South Korea has six provinces—Gyeonggi, Gangwon, Gyeongsang, Jeolla, Chungcheong, and Jeju.

군 gun *gun*, county

구 gu *gu*, district, borough

읍 eup *eup*, town

면 myeon *myeon*, township

동 dong *dong*, neighborhood

리 ri *li*, village

> 군, 읍, 면, and 리 are used in rural areas, while 구 and 동 are used in urban areas.

관공서 gwan·gong·seo government office

시청 si·cheong city hall

도청 do·cheong provincial government office

군청 gun·cheong *gun* office

구청 gu·cheong *gu* office

읍사무소 eup·sa·mu·so *eup* office

면사무소 myeon·sa·mu·so *myeon* office

동사무소 dong·sa·mu·so *dong* office

시장 si·jang mayor

도지사 do·ji·sa governor

공무원 gong·mu·won public official

가해자 갇히다 감방 강간 강간범 강도 건 검사 검찰

경찰 경찰서 고발 고소 괴롭히다 구하다 깡패

납치 달아나다 대 도둑 도망 도망가다 도주

튀지다 맞다 목격 목격자 몰래 무죄 방지 배심원 벌금

범법 범법자 범죄 범죄자 법률 법원 변호 변호사

변석 보호 불법 빼앗다 살리다 살아나다 살아남다

살인 살인범 석방 선서 성희롱 소송 속다 속이다 수감

chapter **21** | Law and Order

수갑 수사 순찰 슬그머니 슬쩍 신고 안전 용의자 위조

위험 유죄 잡다 잡히다 재소자 재판

전과 전과자 절도 조 조례 죽이다 증거 증언 증인 지구대

쫓다 체포 출소하다 치안 탈출 파출소 판결 폭력 폭행

려나다 피고 피해 해 헌법 현장 혐의 형벌 형사 훔치다

21.1 Law, Crime

법 | ~적 beop | ~·jeok law | legal
저는 대학에서 **법을** 공부하고 있습니다. jeoneun daehageseo beobeul gongbuhago itseumnida. I'm studying law at university.

헌법 heon·beop constitution
표현의 자유는 **대한민국 헌법** 제21조에 의해 보장된다. pyohyeonui jayuneun daehanminguk heonbeop jeisibiljoe uihae bojangdoenda. Freedom of expression is guaranteed by article 21 of the Constitution of the Republic of Korea.

법률 beom·nyul law, act, legislation
저는 법률에 관한 지식이 별로 없어요. jeoneun beomnyure gwanhan jisigi byeollo eopseoyo. I don't have much knowledge of law.

조례 jo·rye ordinance

조 jo article

범죄 beom·joe crime
최근 **길거리 범죄가** 심각한 문제가 되고 있다. choegeun gilgeori beomjoega simgakan munjega doego itda. Recently street crime has been a real problem.

죄 joe crime, misdeed
저는 **죄가** 없어요. jeoneun joega eopseoyo. I'm innocent.

피해 pi·hae damage, harm
다행히 **피해는** 크지 않았다. dahaenghi pihaeneun keuji anatda. Fortunately, the damage was not great.

해 hae harm, damage

불법 = 위법 bul·beop = wi·beop unlawfulness, illegality
한국에서는 대마초를 피우는 것이 불법입니다/위법입니다. hangugeseoneun daemachoreul piuneun geosi bulbeobimnida/wibeobimnida. Smoking marijuana is illegal in Korea.

범법 beom·beop law-breaking
그는 자신이 **범법 행위를** 저질렀음을 시인했다. geuneun jasini beombeop haengwireul jeojilleosseumeul siinhaetda. He admitted that he had committed an illegal act.

범죄자 beom·joe·ja criminal
내가 보기에 그 여자는 보통의 범죄자일 뿐이다. naega bogie geu yeojaneun botongui beomjoejail ppunida. To me, she is nothing more

than a common criminal.

범법자 beom·beop·ja law-breaker
그곳에 갔다는 이유만으로 왜 제가 **범법자 취급을** 받아야 하나요? geugose gatdaneun iyumaneuro wae jega beombeopja chwigeubeul badaya hanayo? Why should I be treated like an offender simply because I went there?

살인 | ~하다 sa·rin | ~·ha·da murder, homicide | to kill, murder
한 30대 남자가 **살인을** 저지르고 달아났다. han samsipdae namjaga sarineul jeojireugo daranatda. A man in his 30s committed homicide and ran away.

죽이다 ju·gi·da to kill
그 죄수는 두 명의 간수를 죽였다. geu joesuneun du myeongui gansureul jugyeotda. The prisoner killed two guards.

살인범 sa·rin·beom murderer, killer
그 **연쇄 살인범은** 사형 선고를 받았다. geu yeonswae sarinbeomeun sahyeong seongoreul badatda. The serial killer was sentenced to death.

폭력 | ~적 pong·nyeok | ~·jeok violence | violent
학교 **폭력이** 매해 늘어나고 있다. hakgyo pongnyeogi maehae neureonago itda. School violence is increasing every year.

폭행 | ~하다 po·khaeng | ~·ha·da assault, attack | to assault, attack
50대 여인이 **경찰을 폭행하여** 기소되었다. osipdae yeoini gyeongchareul pokhaenghayeo gisodoeeotda. A woman in her 50s was charged with assaulting a police officer.

맞다 mat·da to be hit, be struck
저는 얼굴과 **온몸을 맞았습니다.** jeoneun eolgulgwa onmomeul majatseumnida. I was beaten in the face and all over my body.

대 dae blow
나는 얼굴에 주먹을 한 대 맞고 병원에 실려 갔다. naneun eolgure jumeogeul han dae matgo byeongwone sillyeogatda. I was hospitalized after getting hit in the face.

강도 gang·do robbery, mugging; burglar
일주일 전에 길거리에서 **강도를 당했어요.** iljuil jeone gilgeorieseo gangdoreul danghaesseo-

yo. I was robbed on the street a week ago.

그 강도는 마스크를 쓰고 있었다. **geu gang-doneun maseukeureul sseugo isseotda.** The burglar had a mask on.

깡패 ≒ 불량배 kkang·pae ≒ bul·lyang·bae bully, mugger, gangster

위협 | ~하다 wi·hyeop | ~·ha·da threat, menace | to threaten, menace
그는 칼로 우리를 **위협**했다. **geuneun kallo urireul wihyeopaetda.** He threatened us with a knife.

협박 | ~하다 hyeop·bak | ~·ha·da threat, blackmail | to threaten, blackmail
그는 내 비밀을 폭로하겠다며 나를 **협박**했다. **geuneun nae bimireul pongnohagetdamyeo nareul hyeopbakaetda.** He threatened to reveal my secrets.

괴롭히다 goe·ro·pi·da to harass, torment
동네 불량배들이 어린아이들을 **괴롭힌**다. **dongne bullyangbaedeuri eorinaideureul goeropinda.** Bullies in the neighborhood pick on young children.

빼앗다 = 뺏다 ppae·at·da = ppaet·da to take, rob, extort
깡패들이 지역 상인들에게서 돈을 **빼앗았다**/**뺏았다**. **kkangpaedeuri jiyeok sangindeuregeseo doneul ppaeasatda/ppaesatda.** The gangsters extorted money from local businessmen.

빼앗기다 = 뺏기다 ppae·at·gi·da = ppaet·gi·da to be robbed
어제 불량배들한테 돈을 **빼앗겼어**/**뺏겼어**. **eoje bullyangbaedeulhante doneul ppaeatgyeosseo/ppaetgyeosseo.** Some bullies extorted money from me yesterday.

납치 ≒ 유괴 | ~하다 nap·chi ≒ yu·goe | ~·ha·da kidnapping, abduction | to kidnap, abduct
그녀는 한 무리의 괴한들에게 **납치를/유괴를 당했다**. **geunyeoneun han muriui goehandeurege napchireul/yugoereul danghaetda.** She was abducted by a group of gunmen.
유괴된 아이는 무사히 집으로 돌아갔다. **yugoedoen aineun musahi jibeuro doragatda.** The kidnapped child returned home unharmed.

납치범 ≒ 유괴범 nap·chi·beom ≒ yu·goe·beom kidnapper

사기 sa·gi fraud, swindle
그녀는 **사기를 당해** 집을 날렸다. **geunyeoneun sagireul danghae jibeul lallyeotda.** She was swindled out of her home.

속다 sok·da to be deceived, be cheated
그런 뻔한 속임수에 다시는 속지 않을 거야. **geureon ppeonhan sogimsue dasineun sokji aneul geoya.** I'll never fall for such an obvious trick again.

속이다 so·gi·da to deceive, cheat
사람들을 속일 의도는 없었어요. **saramdeureul sogil uidoneun eopseosseoyo.** I had no intention of deceiving others.

위조 | ~하다 wi·jo | ~·ha·da forgery | to forge, fake
일부 강사들은 자신의 **학력을 위조한** 것으로 드러났다. **ilbu gangsadeureun jasinui hangnyeogeul wijohan geoseuro deureonatda.** Some instructors turned out to have faked their academic records.

사기꾼 sa·gi·kkun con man, swindler

강간 = 성폭행 | ~하다 gang·gan = seong·po·khaeng | ~·ha·da rape | to rape
그는 살인, 강도, 강간/성폭행 등 흉악한 범죄를 저질렀다. **geuneun sarin, gangdo, ganggan/seongpokhaeng deung hyungakan beomjoereul jeojilleotda.** He has committed several atrocious crimes: murder, burglary, and rape.

강간범 gang·gan·beom rapist

성추행 | ~하다 seong·chu·haeng | ~·ha·da sexual assault | to sexually assault
그녀는 자신이 기차에서 **성추행을 당했다**고 주장했다. **geunyeoneun jasini gichaeseo seongchuhaengeul danghaetdago jujanghaetda.** She claimed that she had been sexually assaulted on the train.

성희롱 | ~하다 seong·hui·rong | ~·ha·da sexual harassment | to sexually harass
직장 내 **성희롱 예방**을 위해 고용주들은 무엇을 해야 할까요? **jikjang nae seonghuirong yebangeul wihae goyongjudeureun mueoseul haeya halkkayo?** What should employers do to prevent sexual harassment in the workplace?

절도 jeol·do theft, burglary
우리 시의 **차량 절도** 사건이 올해 하반기부터 증가하고 있습니다. **uri siui charyang jeoldo sa-**

geoni olhae habangibuteo jeunggahago itseum-nida. The number of car thefts in our city has been rising since the second half of the year.

훔치다 hum·chi·da to steal
그들은 자기들이 훔치지 않았다고 맹세했다. geudeureun jagideuri humchiji anatdago maengsehaetda. They swore that they didn't steal it.

뒤지다 dwi·ji·da to look through, ransack
왜 내 가방을 뒤지는 거예요? wae nae gabang-eul dwijineun geoyeyo? Why are you going through my bag?

도둑 do·duk thief
그 도둑은 유리창을 통해 침입했다. geu dodu-geun nyurichangeul tonghae chimipaetda. The thief entered through the window.

21.2 Police, the Police Force

경찰 gyeong·chal police, police officer

경찰관 gyeong·chal·gwan police officer

경찰서 gyeong·chal·seo police station

형사 hyeong·sa (police) investigator

파출소 ≒ 지구대 pa·chul·so ≒ ji·gu·dae police substation

치안 chi·an public order
이 지역은 치안이 좋지 않다. i jiyeogeun chiani jochi anta. This area is not safe.

순찰 | ~하다 sun·chal | ~·ha·da patrol | to patrol
저희 경찰들은 3교대로 순찰을 나갑니다. jeo-hui gyeongchaldeureun samgyodaero sun-chareul lagamnida. Our police officers are out on patrol in three shifts.

위험 | ~하다 wi·heom | ~·ha·da danger, risk | dangerous
밤에 밖에 나가면 위험해. bame bakke naga-myeon wiheomhae. It is dangerous to go out at night.

안전 | ~하다 an·jeon | ~·ha·da safety | safe
경찰은 시민의 안전을 책임진다. gyeong-chareun siminui anjeoneul chaegimjinda. The police protect the safety of the people.

방지 ≒ 예방 | ~하다 bang·ji ≒ ye·bang | ~·ha·da prevention | to prevent
사고 방지/예방 대책을 수립해야 한다. sago bangji/yebang daechaegeul suripaeya handa. You should draw up a plan for accident pre-vention.

보호 | ~하다 bo·ho | ~·ha·da protection | to protect, safeguard
우리는 환경을 보호해야 한다. urineun hwangyeongeul bohohaeya handa. We should protect the environment.

구하다 gu·ha·da to rescue, save
그 사람은 나를 구하고 자신은 목숨을 잃었다. geu sarameun nareul guhago jasineun mok-sumeul ireotda. He gave his life to save me.

살리다 sal·li·da to save
의사들은 그녀를 살리려고 모든 노력을 다했다. uisadeureun geunyeoreul salliryeogo modeun noryeogeul dahaetda. Doctors tried every-thing to keep her alive.

살아나다 sa·ra·na·da to revive
나는 운이 좋아 살아났어. naneun uni joa sara-nasseo. I survived by pure luck.

살아남다 sa·ra·nam·da to survive
끝까지 살아남는 사람이 승자야. kkeutkkaji saranamneun sarami seungjaya. People who survive in the end are winners.

사건 sa·geon case, incident
우리 경찰서 내 거의 모든 경찰들이 그 사건에 매달려 있어요. uri gyeongchalseo nae geoui modeun gyeongchaldeuri geu sageone maedal-lyeo isseoyo. Almost all of the police officers in the station are working on the case.

건 geon case, matter
살인 사건 두 건 sarin sageon du geon two murder cases

수사 | ~하다 su·sa | ~·ha·da investiga-tion | to investigate
수사에 진전 사항들이 있나요? susae jinjeon sahangdeuri innayo? Are there any develop-ments in the investigation?

현장 hyeon·jang site, scene
사건 현장을 잘 보존하는 것은 매우 중요하다. sageon hyeonjangeul jal bojonhaneun geo-

seun maeu jungyohada. It is very important to preserve the crime scene.

목격 | ~하다 mok·gyeok | ~·ha·da observation, witnessing | to witness
만약에 사고를 **목격한다면** 어떻게 해야 할까요? mannyage sagoreul mokgyeokandamyeon eotteoke haeya halkkayo? What should I do if I witness an accident?

목격자 mok·gyeok·ja witness, eyewitness
경찰은 **목격자**를 찾고 있다. gyeongchareun mokgyeokjareul chatgo itda. The police are looking for witnesses.

신고 | ~하다 sin·go | ~·ha·da report | to report
경찰에 **신고하려면** 112를 누르세요. gyeongchare singoharyeomyeon illillireul lureuseyo. Call 112 to contact the police.

피해자 pi·hae·ja victim
피해자는 목과 가슴을 찔렸습니다. pihaejaneun mokgwa gaseumeul jjillyeotseumnida. The victim was stabbed in the neck and chest.

가해자 ga·hae·ja attacker
그녀는 **가해자**의 얼굴을 기억해 내지 못했다. geunyeoneun gahaejaui eolgureul gieokae naeji motaetda. She could not recall the attacker's face.

용의자 = 피의자 yong·ui·ja = pi·ui·ja suspect
경찰은 아직 **용의자의/피의자의** 신원을 파악 중에 있다. gyeongchareun ajik nyonguijaui/piuijaui sinwoneul paak junge itda. The police are still verifying the identity of the suspect.

혐의 hyeo·mui suspicion, charge
그녀는 남편을 살해했다는 **혐의를 부인했다.** geunyeoneun nampyeoneul salhaehaetdaneun hyeomuireul buinhaetda. She denied the charge that she had murdered her husband.

범인 beo·min criminal, culprit
범인은 아직 잡히지 않고 있다. beomineun ajik japiji anko itda. The culprit is still at large.

슬그머니 ≒ 슬며시 seul·geu·meo·ni ≒ seul·myeo·si stealthily
그녀는 홀을 **슬그머니/슬며시** 빠져나왔다. geunyeoneun horeul seulgeumeoni/seulmyeosi ppajyeonawatda. She slipped out of the hall.

슬쩍 seul·jjeok stealthily, secretly
몰래 mol·lae secretly

증거 jeung·geo evidence, proof
내가 그 차를 훔쳤다는 **증거라도** 있어요? naega geu chareul humchyeotdaneun jeunggeorado isseoyo? Do you have any proof that I stole the car?

도주 | ~하다 do·ju | ~·ha·da escape, flight | to flee, run away
범인은 현재 **도주** 중이다. beomineun hyeonjae doju jungida. The criminal is now on the run.

도망 do·mang escape, flight

도망가다 = 도망치다 do·mang·ga·da = do·mang·chi·da to escape, run away
경찰이 도착했을 때 도둑들은 이미 **도망가고/도망치고** 없었다. gyeongchari dochakaesseul ttae dodukdeureun imi domanggago/domangchigo eopseotda. By the time the police arrived, the thieves were already gone.

달아나다 da·ra·na·da to escape, run away
경보가 울리자 강도는 놀라 **달아났다.** gyeongboga ullija gangdoneun nolla daranatda. As the alarms sounded, the burglar was frightened and took flight.

꼬리를 감추다 kko·ri·reul gam·chu·da to disappear without a trace
범인들은 **꼬리를 감췄다.** beomindeureun kkorireul gamchwotda. The criminals have all vanished into thin air.

(뒤)쫓다 (dwi·)jjot·da to chase, run after
경찰이 살인범을 **쫓고** 있다. gyeongchari sarinbeomeul jjotgo itda. The police are chasing after the murderer.

쫓기다 jjot·gi·da to be chased, be pursued
그는 경찰에 **쫓기고** 있다. geuneun gyeongchare jjotgigo itda. He is being chased by the police.

(붙)잡다 (but·)jap·da to hold, catch
경찰은 일주일간의 강도 높은 수색 끝에 **용의자를 붙잡았다.** gyeongchareun iljuilganui gangdo nopeun susaek kkeute yonguijareul butjabatda. The police finally caught the suspect after a week of intense searching.

체포 | ~하다 che·po | ~·ha·da arrest, apprehension | to arrest, apprehend
당신을 **체포합니다.** dangsineul chepohamnida. You are under arrest.

구속 | ~하다 gu·sok | ~·ha·da imprisonment, arrest | to imprison, arrest

그는 음주 운전 혐의로 구속되었다. **geuneun eumju unjeon hyeomuiro gusokdoeeotda.** He was arrested on suspicion of driving under the influence of drinks.

수갑 su·gap handcuffs
경찰이 그 여자에게 **수갑을 채웠다. gyeongchari geu yeojaege sugabeul chaewotda.** The police handcuffed the woman.

(붙)잡히다 (but·)ja·pi·da to be arrested, be caught

그녀는 불륜 현장에서 붙잡혔다. **geunyeoneun bullyun hyeonjangeseo butjapyeotda.** She was caught in the act of adultery.

검찰 geom·chal the prosecution
그녀는 검찰 측 증인이다. **geunyeoneun geomchal cheuk jeunginida.** She is a witness for the prosecution.

21.3 Trial, Punishment

법원 beo·bwon court
법원은 그 사건을 기각했다. **beobwoneun geu sageoneul gigakaetda.** The court dismissed the case.

고발 | ~하다 go·bal | ~·ha·da accusation, charge | to accuse, charge
그들은 그녀를 사기죄로 고발했다. **geudeureun geunyeoreul sagijoero gobalhaetda.** They charged her with fraud.

고소 | ~하다 go·so | ~·ha·da accusation, charge | to accuse, charge, sue
나에 대해 계속 나쁜 얘기를 하고 다니면 고소하겠어요. **nae daehae gyesok nappeun yaegireul hago danimyeon gosohagesseoyo.** I'll sue you if you keep saying bad stuff about me.

검사 geom·sa prosecutor, district attorney
검사는 피고에게 10년형을 구형했다. **geomsaneun pigoege simnyeonhyeongeul guhyeonghaetda.** The prosecutor demanded a ten-year prison term for the accused.

기소 | ~하다 gi·so | ~·ha·da prosecution, indictment | to prosecute
그 정치인은 뇌물을 받은 혐의로 기소되었다. **geu jeongchiineun noemureul badeun hyeomuiro gisodoeeotda.** The politician was indicted on suspicion of taking bribes.

재판 jae·pan trial
그 사건은 현재 재판 중이에요. **geu sageoneun hyeonjae jaepan jungieyo.** The case is on trial.

소송 so·song suit, lawsuit
투자자들이 그 회사를 상대로 집단 **소송을 제기했다. tujajadeuri geu hoesareul sangdaero jipdan sosongeul jegihaetda.** Investors brought a class action suit against the company.

원고(인) won·go(·in) plaintiff
원고 측이 재판에서 승리했다. **wongo cheugi jaepaneseo seungnihaetda.** The plaintiff won the case.

피고(인) pi·go(·in) defendant, the accused
판사는 피고가 무죄라고 판결했다. **pansaneun pigoga mujoerago pangyeolhaetda.** The judge determined that the defendant was not guilty.

변호사 byeon·ho·sa lawyer
오늘 오후에 변호사랑 약속이 있어요. **oneul ohue byeonhosarang yaksogi isseoyo.** This afternoon I have an appointment with my lawyer.

변호 | ~하다 byeon·ho | ~·ha·da defense | to defend, plead

배심원 bae·si·mwon juror, jury
한국은 **배심원 제도를** 지난 2008년 도입했다. **hangugeun baesimwon jedoreul jinan icheonpallyeon doipaetda.** South Korea adopted the jury system in 2008.

증인 jeung·in witness
피고의 아내가 **증인으로 소환되었다. pigoui anaega jeungineuro sohwandoeeotda.** The accused's wife was called as a witness.

선서 | ~하다 seon·seo | ~·ha·da oath | to take an oath
진술하기 전에 선서하세요. **jinsulhagi jeone seonseohaseyo.** Please swear an oath before giving your testimony.

증언 | ~하다 jeung·eon | ~·ha·da testimony | to testify, attest, witness

그는 사건 당일 밤 그 여자를 보았다고 증언했다. geuneun sageon dangil bam geu yeojareul boatdago jeungeonhaetda. He testified that he had seen her on the night of the incident.

판사 pan·sa judge

판결 | ~하다 pan·gyeol | ~·ha·da ruling, judgment | to rule, judge

무죄 mu·joe innocence
재심에서 그는 **무죄 판결**을 받고 석방되었다. jaesimeseo geuneun mujoe pangyeoreul batgo seokbangdoeeotda. At his retrial, he was acquitted and released.

유죄 yu·joe guilt

선고 | ~하다 seon·go | ~·ha·da sentence | to sentence
판사는 그에게 **유죄를 선고했다**. pansaneun geuege yujoereul seongohaetda. The judge declared him guilty.

처벌 | ~하다 cheo·beol | ~·ha·da punishment, penalty | to punish, penalize
그 사람들을 처벌하기를 원치 않습니다. geu saramdeureul cheobeolhagireul wonchi anseumnida. I don't want to penalize them.

벌 | ~하다 beol | ~·ha·da punishment | to punish
동수는 같은 반 친구를 주먹으로 때려 **벌을 받았다**. dongsuneun gateun ban chingureul jumeogeuro ttaeryeo beoreul badatda. Dongsu was punished for having punched his classmate.

형벌 hyeong·beol punishment, penalty

벌금 ≒ 과태료 ≒ 범칙금 beol·geum ≒ gwa·tae·ryo ≒ beom·chik·geum fine, penalty
금연 구역에서 담배를 피우면 10만 원의 **벌금**이/과태료가/범칙금이 부과됩니다. geumyeon guyeogeseo dambaereul piumyeon simman wonui beolgeumi/gwataeryoga/beomchikgeumi bugwadoemnida. People who smoke in non-smoking areas will be fined 100,000 won.

감옥 = 교도소 = 형무소 ga·mok = gyo·do·so = hyeong·mu·so prison, jail
그는 신용카드 사기죄로 **감옥에/교도소에/형무소에 갔다**. geuneun sinnyongkadeu sagijoero gamoge/gyodosoe/hyeongmusoe gatda. He went to prison for credit card fraud.

감방 gam·bang prison cell

재소자 = 죄수 jae·so·ja = joe·su prisoner
그 재소자는/죄수는 자신에게 죄가 없다고 주장했다. geu jaesojaneun/joesuneun jasinege joega eopdago jujanghaetda. The prisoner declared that he was innocent.

수감 | ~되다 su·gam | ~·doe·da imprisonment | to be imprisoned, be incarcerated
그는 차를 훔쳐 수감되었다. geuneun chareul humchyeo sugamdoeeotda. He was imprisoned for stealing a car.

갇히다 ga·chi·da to be locked up, be confined
그는 사기죄로 감옥에 갇혀 있다. geuneun sagijoero gamoge gachyeo itda. He is in jail for fraud.

징역 jing·yeok prison labor
그녀는 남자 친구를 살해한 죄로 3년간 **징역**을 살았다. geunyeoneun namja chingureul salhaehan joero samnyeongan jingyeogeul saratda. She served three years in prison for the murder of her boyfriend.

복역 | ~하다 bo·gyeok | ~·ha·da serving one's time | to serve one's time
그는 무죄임이 입증되기 전 5년을 복역했다. geuneun mujoeimi ipjeungdoegi jeon onyeoneul bogyeokaetda. He served five years in prison before he was exonerated.

탈출 | ~하다 tal·chul | ~·ha·da escape | to escape
재소자들이 **탈출을 시도했지만** 성공하지 못했다. jaesojadeuri talchureul sidohaetjiman seonggonghaji motaetda. The prisoners tried to break out of jail but did not succeed.

출소하다 chul·so·ha·da to be released from prison
저는 어제 출소했습니다. jeoneun eoje chulsohaetseumnida. I was released from prison yesterday.

풀려나다 pul·lyeo·na·da to be released, be freed
그는 보석으로 어제 풀려났다. geuneun boseogeuro eoje pullyeonatda. He was freed on bail yesterday.

석방 | ~하다 seok·bang | ~·ha·da release, discharge | to release, discharge

전과 jeon·gwa criminal record
그는 전과 5범이다. **geuneun jeongwa obeomi-da.** He has five previous convictions.

전과자 jeon·gwa·ja ex-convict

보석 bo·seok bail

부 간첩 간부 간첩 경례 계급 공격 공군 국군 국방 군

사 군사력 군인 권총 기지 낙하산 무기 미사일 민간인

민방위 바치다 발사 방어 방패 병사 병역 보안 복무 부대

사관 부하 분단 사격 상관 성 수류탄 신체검사 쏘다 어뢰

군 영장 영창 예비군 육군 임무 입대 자원 작전 잠수함

교 적 전략 전사 전술 전역 전쟁 전쟁터 전투 전투기 지뢰

총 총알 침공 칼 탈영 탱크 터뜨리다 터지다 테러

통일 파괴 포 포로 폭격 폭탄 피난 항복 해군 핵무기

헬리콥터 화살 활 후퇴 훈련소 훈장 희생 경례 계급 공격

chapter **22** | National Defense

공군 국군 국방 군 군사 군사력 군인 권총 기지 낙하산

기 미사일 민간인 민방위 바치다 발사 방어 방패 병사 병역

보안 복무 부대 부사관 부하 분단 사격 상관 성 수류탄

신체검사 쏘다 어뢰 여군 영장 영창 예비군 육군 임무

입대 자원 작전 잠수함 장교 적 전략 전사 전술 전역

전쟁 전쟁터 전투 전투기 지뢰 창 총 총알 침공 칼

영 탱크 터뜨리다 터지다 테러 통일 파괴 포 포로

폭격 폭탄 피난 항복 해군 핵무기 헬리콥터 화살 활

후퇴 훈련소 훈장 희생

22.1 The Military

군(대) gun(·dae) the military, the armed forces
한국 남자들은 모두 **군대에 가야** 한다. hanguk namjadeureun modu gundaee gaya handa. All Korean men must serve in the military.

국군 guk·gun the Korean Armed Forces

국방 guk·bang national defense
정부는 **국방 예산을** 삭감하라는 압력에 직면해 있다. jeongbuneun gukbang yesaneul sakgamharaneun amnyeoge jingmyeonhae itda. The government faces pressure to cut back on defense spending.

군사 gun·sa the military
대통령은 테러리스트에 대해 **군사 행동을** 개시하기로 결정했다. daetongnyeongeun tereoriseuteue daehae gunsa haengdongeul gaesihagiro gyeoljeonghaetda. The President decided to initiate military operations against terrorists.

군사력 gun·sa·ryeok military power
의심의 여지 없이 미국은 **막강한 군사력을** 보유하고 있다. uisimui yeoji eopsi migugeun makganghan gunsaryeogeul boyuhago itda. Undoubtedly the United States possesses great military strength.

보안 bo·an security
....

해군 hae·gun navy

공군 gong·gun air force

육군 yuk·gun the army

예비군 ye·bi·gun reserve forces; reservist

민방위 min·bang·wi civil defense
....

병역 byeong·yeok military service
저는 **병역을 마쳤습니다.** jeoneun byeongyeogeul machyeotseumnida. I've fulfilled my obligation for military service.

신체검사 = 신검 sin·che·geom·sa = sin·geom physical examination, checkup
저는 신체검사에서/신검에서 4급 판정을 받았어요. jeoneun sinchegeomsaeseo/singeomeseo sageup panjeongeul badasseoyo. I received a grade-4 in the military physical examination.

영장 yeong·jang draft notice

나 **영장 나왔어**. na yeongjang nawasseo. I got my draft notice.

입대 | ~하다 ip·dae | ~·ha·da enlistment | to enlist
아들애가 **입대한** 지 3일이 지났어요. adeuraega ipdaehan ji samiri jinasseoyo. Three days have passed since my son joined the army.

자원 | ~하다 ja·won | ~·ha·da volunteering | to volunteer
한 유명 영화배우가 해병에 **자원 입대했다.** han nyumyeong yeonghwabaeuga haebyeonge jawon ipdaehaetda. A movie star volunteered for the marines.

훈련소 hul·lyeon·so training camp
나 3일 후에 **훈련소 들어가.** na samil hue hullyeonso deureoga. I enter boot camp in three days.

부대 bu·dae troops, corps
저는 **보병 부대에** 있었어요. jeoneun bobyeong budaee isseosseoyo. I served in an infantry unit.

군인 gu·nin soldier, military personnel
한국에는 군인이 몇 명이나 있습니까? hangugeneun gunini myeot myeongina itseumnikka? How many soldiers are there in Korea?

병사 ≒ 사병 byeong·sa ≒ sa·byeong solider, enlisted man

간부 gan·bu officer

부사관 bu·sa·gwan noncommissioned officer

장교 jang·gyo commissioned officer

여군 yeo·gun female soldier

계급 gye·geup rank
군대는 **계급 조직**이다. gundaeneun gyegeup jojigida. The military has a hierarchical structure.

상관 sang·gwan one's superior
여러분은 **상관의 명령**에 무조건적으로 복종해야 한다. yeoreobuneun sanggwanui myeongnyeonge mujogeonjeogeuro bokjonghaeya handa. You must obey the orders of your superior unquestioningly.

부하 bu·ha subordinate, one's men

경례 | ~하다 gyeong·nye | ~·ha·da salute | to salute

병사는 간부에게 경례를 해야 한다. **byeong-saneun ganbuege gyeongnyereul haeya handa.** A soldier must salute an officer.

복무 | ~하다 bong·mu | ~·ha·da service | to serve
저는 육군에서 2년 2개월 동안 복무했습니다. **jeoneun nyukguneseo inyeon igaewol dongan bongmuhaetseumnida.** I served two years and two months in the army.

탈영 | ~하다 ta·ryeong | ~·ha·da desertion | to desert

영창 yeong·chang guardhouse, military prison
그는 탈영을 하여 **영창을 갔다. geuneun taryeongeul hayeo yeongchangeul gatda.** He was sent to a military prison for desertion.

전역 = 제대 | ~하다 jeo·nyeok = je·dae | ~·ha·da discharge | to be discharged from military service
저는 육군 병장으로 전역했어요/제대했어요. **jeoneun nyukgun byeongjangeuro jeonyeokaesseoyo/jedaehaesseoyo.** I was discharged from the army as a sergeant.

22.2 War

전쟁 jeon·jaeng war
그 전쟁의 희생자들 대부분 평범한 사람들이었다. **geu jeonjaengui huisaengjadeul daebubun pyeongbeomhan saramdeurieotda.** Most of the victims of the war were ordinary people.

전투 jeon·tu combat, battle
그는 그 전투의 유일한 생존자였다. **geuneun geu jeontuui yuilhan saengjonjayeotda.** He was the only survivor of the battle.

전쟁터 jeon·jaeng·teo battlefield
수도는 전쟁터로 변해 버렸다. **sudoneun jeonjaengteoro byeonhae beoryeotda.** The capital was turned into a battlefield.

테러 te·reo terror, terrorism

적 jeok enemy
남한은 북한을 적으로 규정해 왔다. **namhaneun bukhaneul jeogeuro gyujeonghae watda.** South Korea has declared the North its enemy.

간첩 gan·cheop spy, secret agent
그녀가 **간첩 혐의로 구속되었다. geunyeoga gancheop hyeomuiro gusokdoeeotda.** She was arrested under suspicion of being a spy.

작전 jak·jeon military operation
국방부는 **군사 작전** 중에 다섯 명이 사망했다고 발표했다. **gukbangbuneun gunsa jakjeon junge daseot myeongi samanghaetdago balpyohaetda.** The Ministry of Defense announced that five soldiers were killed during the military operation.

기지 gi·ji base
그 기지에 인접해 있던 마을은 폭격에 의해 아수라장이 되었다. **geu gijie injeopae itdeon maeureun pokgyeoge uihae asurajangi doeeotda.** The village that neighbored the base was ruined by the bombing.

전략 | ~적 jeol·lyak | ~·jeok strategy, tactic | strategic, tactical
그 지역은 위치상 전략적으로 매우 중요하다. **geu jiyeogeun wichisang jeollyakjeogeuro maeu jungyohada.** That area is strategically very important because of its location.

전술 jeon·sul tactics

임무 im·mu duty, mission
국경 방어가 우리에게 주어진 **막중한 임무**입니다. **gukgyeong bangeoga uriege jueojin makjunghan immuimnida.** Defending the borders is an important mission for us.

성 seong castle, fortress
성이 적에게 넘어갔다. **seongi jeogege neomeogatda.** The castle fell to the enemy.

공격 | ~하다 gong·gyeok | ~·ha·da attack, assault | to attack, assault
민간인에 대한 공격은 어떤 경우에라도 정당화될 수 없다. **minganine daehan gonggyeogeun eotteon gyeonguerado jeongdanghwadoel su eopda.** Attacks on civilians can't be justified under any circumstances.

파괴 | ~하다 pa·goe | ~·ha·da destruction | to destroy
전쟁은 도시를 순식간에 파괴해 버렸다. **jeonjaengeun dosireul sunsikgane pagoehae beoryeotda.** The war destroyed the city in a flash.

폭격 | ~하다 pok·gyeok | ~·ha·da bombing | to bomb, bombard

적의 폭격으로 도시는 폐허가 되었다. jeogui pokgyeogeuro dosineun pyeheoga doeeotda. The city was devastated by the enemy's bombing.

침공 = 침략 | ~하다 chim·gong = chim·nyak | ~·ha·da invasion, attack | to invade, attack

방어 | ~하다 bang·eo | ~·ha·da defense | to defend
여러 공격 무기가 개발됨에 따라 **방어** 무기도 다양화된다. yeoreo gonggyeok mugiga gaebaldoeme ttara bangeo mugido dayanghwadoenda. As different offensive weapons are developed, defensive weapons become diverse, too.

후퇴 | ~하다 hu·toe | ~·ha·da retreat | to retreat
그들은 **전략적 후퇴**를 결정했다. geudeureun jeollyakjeok hutoereul gyeoljeonghaetda. They decided to make a strategic retreat.

항복 | ~하다 hang·bok | ~·ha·da surrender, submission | to surrender, yield
항복하느니 차라리 죽음을 택하겠다. hangbokaneuni charari jugeumeul taekagetda. I would rather die than surrender.

전사 | ~하다 jeon·sa | ~·ha·da death in action | to be killed in action
제 남편은 한국전쟁 때 전사했습니다. je nampyeoneun hangukjeonjaeng ttae jeonsahaetseumnida. My husband was killed in the Korean War.

희생 | ~하다 hui·saeng | ~·ha·da sacrifice | to sacrifice
우리는 이 전쟁을 이기기 위해 많은 **희생**을 치렀다. urineun i jeonjaengeul igigi wihae maneun huisaengeul chireotda. We made great sacrifices to win this war.

바치다 ba·chi·da to dedicate, devote
많은 젊은이들이 이 나라를 위해 **목숨을 바쳤다**. maneun jeolmeunideuri i narareul wihae moksumeul bachyeotda. Many young men have given their lives for this country.

훈장 hun·jang medal, badge
그는 한 장교의 목숨을 구해 **훈장**을 받았다. geuneun han janggyoui moksumeul guhae hunjangeul badatda. He was awarded a medal for saving the life of an officer.

포로 po·ro prisoner
전쟁이 끝난 후, 대부분의 포로들은 자기 나라로 돌려보내졌다. jeonjaengi kkeunnan hu, daebubunui porodeureun jagi nararo dollyeobonaejyeotda. After the war, most of the prisoners were returned to their home countries.

민간인 min·ga·nin civilian

피난 | ~하다 pi·nan | ~·ha·da refuge | to take refuge, flee for safety
사람들은 집을 버리고 **피난**을 떠났다. saramdeureun jibeul beorigo pinaneul tteonatda. People fled their homes to take refuge from the war.

분단 | ~되다 bun·dan | ~·doe·da division | to be divided
한국은 세계 유일의 **분단 국가**이다. hangugeun segye yuirui bundan gukgaida. Korea is the only divided country in the world.

통일 | ~하다 tong·il | ~·ha·da unification, unity | to unite
저는 **남북 통일**을 간절히 바라고 있어요. jeoneun nambuk tongireul ganjeolhi barago isseoyo. I long for the unification of South and North Korea.

무기 mu·gi weapon, arms
북한은 여러 다양한 대량 **살상 무기**를 갖고 있는 것으로 알려져 있다. bukhaneun nyeoreo dayanghan daeryang salsang mugireul gatgo inneun geoseuro allyeojyeo itda. North Korea is known to have various weapons of mass destruction.

활 hwal bow

화살 hwa·sal arrow

창 chang spear

방패 bang·pae shield

칼 kal sword

총 chong gun

권총 gwon·chong pistol

총알 chong·al bullet

(대)포 (dae·)po cannon

폭탄 pok·tan bomb, explosive

수류탄 su·ryu·tan hand grenade

지뢰 ji·roe mine, landmine

탱크 = 전차 taeng·keu = jeon·cha tank

어뢰 eo·roe torpedo

잠수함 jam·su·ham submarine

전투기 jeon·tu·gi fighter

헬리콥터 = 헬기 hel·li·kop·teo = hel·gi helicopter

낙하산 na·kha·san parachute
특공대원들이 헬기에서 **낙하산을 타고** 뛰어 내렸다. teukgongdaewondeuri helgieseo na-khasaneul tago ttwieonaeryeotda. The commandos made a parachute jump from the helicopter.

미사일 mi·sa·il missile

핵무기 haeng·mu·gi nuclear weapon

쏘다 sso·da to shoot, fire
총을 쏘지 마세요. chongeul ssoji maseyo. Don't shoot!

발사 | ~하다 bal·sa | ~·ha·da launch, discharge | to launch, shoot

그는 이번 주에 북한이 **미사일을 발사할지도** 모른다고 말했다. geuneun ibeon jue bukhani misaireul balsahaljido moreundago malhaetda. He said North Korea could launch a missile this week.

사격 | ~하다 sa·gyeok | ~·ha·da fire | to shoot, fire
사격 개시! sagyeok gaesi! Fire!

터지다 teo·ji·da to explode
오늘 아침 **폭탄이 터져** 열 명이 넘는 사람이 부상을 입었다. oneul achim poktani teojyeo yeol myeongi neomneun sarami busangeul ibeotda. This morning a bomb exploded and injured more than 10 people.

터뜨리다 teo·tteu·ri·da to explode
수류탄을 터뜨리기 전에 30초를 주겠다! suryutaneul teotteurigi jeone samsipchoreul jugetda! I'll give you 30 seconds before I denote this hand grenade.

가입 가치 가입 가치 갈등 강제 개인 게임 경향 계층 공동체
공중도덕 과정 구성원 권력 권리 권위 규칙 그르다 근원 기관 기구
기성세대 기원 끝나다 나다 나타나다 달라지다 대책
덕 도박 동호회 들다 마약 명예 모임 문제 발생 발전 방해
벌어지다 변하다 변화 불러오다 불평등하다 사회 사회문제 상류층
생겨나다 생기다 서민 세대 속하다 순조롭다 시민 시스템
위 시작 신분 신세대 실업 실업자 악화되다 알코올 야기하다 올바르다
옳다 원인 유래 유발하다 의무 인권 인종차별 일으키다 자극 자살
자유 자율 잔치 잘못 전개 절차 정의 제도 중산층 진보 진실
질서 집단 차례 차별 참여 책임 카페인 캠페인 평등하다 평화
행사 현상 회원 해방 흐름 갈등 강제 개인 게임 경향

chapter **23** | Society

계층 공동체 공중도덕 과정 구성원 권력 권리 권위 규칙 그르다 근원
기관 기구 기성세대 기원 끝나다 나다 나타나다
달라지다 대책 도덕 도박 동호회 들다 마약 명예 모임
문제 발생 발전 방해 벌어지다 변하다 변화 불러오다
불평등하다 사회 사회문제 상류층 생겨나다 생기다 서민 세대
속하다 순조롭다 시민 시스템 시위 시작 신분 신세대 실업 실업자
악화되다 알코올 야기하다 올바르다 옳다 원인 유래 유발하다 의무
인권 인종차별 일으키다 자극 자살 자유 자율 잔치 잘못 전개
절차 정의 제도 중산 진보 진실 질서 집단 차례 차별 참여 책임
카페인 캠페인 평등하다 평화 행사 현상 회원 해방 흐름

23.1 Society

사회 | ~적 sa·hoe | ~·jeok society | social
자본주의 **사회**에서는 소비자가 왕이다. **ja-
bonjuui sahoeeseoneun sobijaga wangida.** In
capitalist societies, the consumer is king.
노인 부양은 큰 **사회적 문제**가 되었다. **noin
buyangeun keun sahoejeok munjega doeeotda.**
Support for senior citizens has become a big
social issue.

가치 ga·chi value
많은 과학자들은 명예에 높은 **가치를 둔다.**
**maneun gwahakjadeureun myeongyee nopeun
gachireul dunda.** Many scientists place a high
value on honor.

자유 ja·yu freedom, liberty
공공 정책에 있어 개인의 **자유**는 우선시되어
야 한다. **gonggong jeongchaege isseo gaeinui
jayuneun useonsidoeeoya handa.** Personal liberty should take priority in public policy.

권리 gwol·li right, claim
대중은 **알 권리**가 있다. **daejungeun al gwolli-
ga itda.** The public has the right to know.

의무 ui·mu obligation, duty, responsibility
우리는 모두 법을 지킬 **의무**가 있다. **urineun
modu beobeul jikil uimuga itda.** We all have responsibility to obey the law.

책임 chae·gim responsibility, blame
자유에는 **책임**이 뒤따른다. **jayueneun chaegimi dwittareunda.** Freedom comes with responsibility.

명예 myeong·ye honor, fame
내 **명예**를 걸고 약속할게. **nae myeongyereul
geolgo yaksokalge.** I promise on my honor.

부 bu wealth, fortune
그녀는 자신의 재능을 이용해 명예와 **부를 추
구하는** 데는 아무 관심이 없었다. **geunyeo-
neun jasinui jaeneungeul iyonghae myeongyewa
bureul chuguhaneun deneun amu gwansimi
eopseotda.** She had no interest in using her
talent to pursue fame or fortune.

권력 gwol·lyeok power, authority

자율 | ~적 ja·yul | ~·jeok autonomy | au-
tonomous
보호 장비의 사용을 직원들의 **자율에 맡겨서
는** 안 됩니다. **boho jangbiui sayongeul ji-
gwondeurui jayure matgyeoseoneun an doemnida.** The use of the protective devices

should not be left to the discretion of the
employees.

강제 | ~적 gang·je | ~·jeok compulsion,
coercion | compulsory
그 계약서에 **강제로 사인하지** 않아도 된다.
**geu gyeyakseoe gangjero sainhaji anado doen-
da.** You are under no obligation to sign the
contract.

인권 in·gwon human rights
강제적인 결혼은 **인권 침해**입니다. **gangjejeo-
gin gyeolhoneun ingwon chimhaeimnida.**
Forced marriage is an abuse of human
rights.

도덕 ≒ 윤리 do·deok ≒ yul·li ethics, mor-
als

옳다 ol·ta right, proper
누가 **옳고** 그른지는 중요하지 않아. **nuga olko
geureunjineun jungyohaji ana.** It doesn't matter who's wrong or right.

바르다 ba·reu·da right, upright
김 교수는 정직하고 **바른** 사람입니다. **gim
gyosuneun jeongjikago bareun saramimnida.**
Professor Kim is an honest and upright
man.

올바르다 ol·ba·reu·da right, proper, upright

그르다 geu·reu·da wrong, false

잘못 | ~하다 jal·mot | ~·ha·da mistake,
fault; by mistake | to make a mistake, do
wrong
다 제 **잘못**입니다. **da je jalmosimnida.** It's all
my fault.
전화 **잘못** 거셨어요. **jeonhwa jalmot geosyeosseoyo.** You called the wrong number.
제가 뭘 **잘못**했죠? **jega mwol jalmotaetjyo?**
What did I do wrong?
컴퓨터가 **잘못**해서 꺼졌다. **keompyuteoga jal-
motaeseo kkeojyeotda.** The computer was
turned off by mistake.

실수 | ~하다 sil·su | ~·ha·da mistake, er-
ror | to make a mistake
제가 말도 안 되는 **실수**를 했어요. **jega maldo
an doeneun silsureul haesseoyo.** I made a hor-
rible mistake.

진실 jin·sil truth, fact
진실은 밝혀지게 되어 있어. jinsireun balkyeo·jige doeeo isseo. The truth will always come out.

거짓 geo·jit lie, untruth
그녀가 한 말은 모두 거짓이었다. geunyeoga han mareun modu geojisieotda. Everything she said was a lie.

정의 jeong·ui justice, righteousness
정의는 우리 편이다. jeonguineun uri pyeonida. Righteousness and justice are on our side.

공중도덕 gong·jung·do·deok public order
관광객들은 **공중도덕**과 사회 도덕을 **지켜야** 한다. gwangwanggaekdeureun gongjung·dodeokgwa sahoe dodeogeul jikyeoya handa. Tourists shall observe public order and respect social morality.

평화 pyeong·hwa peace
비둘기는 **평화를 상징한다**. bidulgineun pyeonghwareul sangjinghanda. The dove symbolizes peace.

질서 jil·seo order
공동 생활에는 질서가 요구된다. gongdong saenghwareneun jilseoga yogudoenda. Communal life requires order.

규칙 ≒ 규정 gyu·chik ≒ gyu·jeong rule, regulation
따님은 학교의 **규칙을/규정을** 존중하지 않아요. ttanimeun hakgyoui gyuchigeul/gyujeong·eul jonjunghaji anayo. Your daughter doesn't respect the school rules.

차례 = 순서 cha·rye = sun·seo order; turn
차례를/순서를 지키세요. charyereul/sunseoreul jikiseyo. Stay in line, please.
오늘은 제가 대접할 차례예요/순서예요. oneureun jega daejeopal charyeyeyo/sunseoyeyo. It's my treat today.

절차 jeol·cha procedure, process
이것은 그저 **형식적인 절차**입니다. igeoseun geujeo hyeongsikjeogin jeolchaimnida. This is just a routine procedure.

지키다 ji·ki·da to keep, obey
모든 학생들은 예외 없이 아래의 **규정을 지켜야** 합니다. modeun haksaengdeureun yeoe eopsi araeui gyujeong·eul jikyeoya hamnida. All of the students must obey the following rules without exception.

제도 je·do system, institution
저는 **사형 제도**가 야만적이라고 생각하지 않아요. jeoneun sahyeong jedoga yamanjeogirago saenggakaji anayo. I don't think capital punishment is barbaric.

시스템 si·seu·tem system
새 시스템은 보다 효율적입니다. sae siseutemeun boda hyoyuljeogimnida. The new system is more efficient.

캠페인 kaem·pe·in campaign, drive
우리는 에너지 절약 **캠페인을 벌이려고** 준비 중입니다. urineun eneoji jeoryak kaempeineul beoriryeogo junbi jungimnida. We are preparing to launch an energy conservation campaign.

....

계층 gye·cheung class, stratum
사회 계층 간의 갈등을 해소하는 일은 매우 중요하다. sahoe gyecheung ganui galdeungeul haesohaneun ireun maeu jungyohada. It is very important to resolve conflicts among social classes.

신분 sin·bun social position, rank
몇몇 나라에서는 아직도 여성의 **사회적 신분**이 낮다. myeonmyeot naraeseoneun ajikdo yeoseongui sahoejeok sinbuni natda. In some countries, women still have a low social status.

권위 gwo·nwi authority
그녀는 언어학 분야에서 **권위 있는 학자**이다. geunyeoneun eoneohak bunyaeseo gwonwi inneun hakjaida. She is an authoritative scholar in linguistics.

평등 | ~하다 pyeong·deung | ~·ha·da equality | equal

불평등 | ~하다 bul·pyeong·deung | ~·ha·da inequality | unfair, unequal

시민 si·min citizen
투표는 **시민의 의무**다. tupyoneun siminui uimuda. Voting is every citizen's obligation.

상류층 sang·nyu·cheung the upper class

중산층 jung·san·cheung the middle class

서민 seo·min ordinary person
서민들의 삶이 더 어려워지고 있다. seomindeurui salmi deo eoryeowojigo itda. The lives of the people are getting worse.

세대 se·dae generation
어떻게 해야 **세대 차이**를 극복할 수 있을까요? eotteoke haeya sedae chaireul geukbokal su isseulkkayo? How can we overcome the generation gap?

신세대 sin·se·dae new generation

기성세대 gi·seong·se·dae older generation

....

개인 gae·in individual
모든 개인은 법 앞에 평등하다. **modeun gaeineun beop ape pyeongdeunghada.** All individuals are equal before the law.

공동 gong·dong association

집단 jip·dan group, body
우리는 사람들이 **집단 생활**에 적응하도록 돕습니다. **urineun saramdeuri jipdan saenghware jeogeunghadorok dopseumnida.** We help people adapt to communal living.

단체 dan·che organization, group
작년에 저희는 열 명의 주부들로 구성된 **단체**를 만들었어요. **jangnyeone jeohuineun nyeol myeongui jubudeullo guseongdoen danchereul mandeureosseoyo.** Last year, we formed a group consisting of ten housewives.

그룹 geu·rup group

조직 | ~하다 jo·jik | ~·ha·da group, organization | to organize
적절한 환경을 구축하면 **조직 문화**를 개선할 수 있습니다. **jeokjeolhan hwangyeongeul guchukamyeon jojik munhwareul gaeseonhal su itseumnida.** You can improve the organizational culture by creating the right environment.

기관 gi·gwan organization, institution
공공 기관들은 경제 성장에서 중요한 역할을 해 왔다. **gonggong gigwandeureun gyeongje seongjangeseo jungyohan nyeokareul hae watda.** Public institutions have played a crucial role in economic growth.

기구 gi·gu organization, institution

모임 mo·im meeting, gathering
우리는 매주 토요일 저녁에 가족 **모임**을 갖습니다. **urineun maeju toyoil jeonyeoge gajok moimeul gatseumnida.** We have a family gathering every Saturday night.

공동체 gong·dong·che community
음악은 **공동체 생활**에서 없어서는 안 될 부분이다. **eumageun gongdongche saenghwareseo eopseoseoneun an doel bubunida.** Music is an integral part of community life.

행사 haeng·sa event, occasion
금요일 **행사**에 **참여**하지 않을 거야. **geumyoil** haengsae chamyeohaji aneul geoya. I'm not going to attend the Friday event.

잔치 jan·chi party, feast
아버지의 **환갑 잔치**에 참석해 주셔서 감사합니다. **abeojiui hwangap janchie chamseokae jusyeoseo gamsahamnida.** Thank you very much for attending my father's sixtieth birthday party.

파티 pa·ti Western style party
파티에 친구들을 데려와도 돼요. **patie chingudeureul deryeowado dwaeyo.** You can bring your friends to the party.

축제 chuk·je festival
그 축제는 전통적으로 유월 마지막 주말 동안 열린다. **geu chukjeneun jeontongjeogeuro yuwol majimak jumal dongan nyeollinda.** The festival is traditionally held on the last weekend of June.

동호회 = 클럽 dong·ho·hoe = keul·leop club, society
최근에 수영 **동호회**에/**클럽**에 가입했어요. **choegeune suyeong donghohoee/keulleobe gaipaesseoyo.** I recently joined a swimming club.

회원 hoe·won member
나는 그 헬스 클럽에 **회원**으로 등록했다. **naneun geu helseu keulleobe hoewoneuro deungnokaetda.** I registered to become a member of the fitness club.

구성원 gu·seong·won member

가입 | ~하다 ga·ip | ~·ha·da entry | to join, enter
그 밴드에 **가입**할지 고민 중이에요. **geu baendeue gaipalji gomin jungieyo.** I'm thinking about joining the band.

들다 deul·da to join, enter
대학에 가면 사진 **동아리**에 **들고** 싶어요. **daehage gamyeon sajin dongarie deulgo sipeoyo.** When I go to college, I want to join the photography club.

참여 | ~하다 cha·myeo | ~·ha·da participation | to participate
저도 이 **모임**에 **참여**하고 싶어요. **jeodo i moime chamyeohago sipeoyo.** I'd love to join this meeting.

소속 | ~되다 so·sok | ~·doe·da one's position | to belong to
어디 **소속**이세요? **eodi sosogiseyo?** Where do you belong?

속하다 so·ka·da to belong to
저는 어느 **팀에도 속해** 있지 않아요. jeoneun eoneu timedo sokae itji anayo. I don't belong to any team.

탈퇴 | ~하다 tal·toe | ~·ha·da withdrawal | to withdraw, drop out

이 사이트에서 **회원 탈퇴**를 하고 싶습니다. i saiteueseo hoewon taltoereul hago sipseumnida. I want to withdraw my membership from this website.

23.2 Social Issues

사회문제 sa·hoe·mun·je social issue

문제(점) mun·je(·jeom) problem
현 정부는 많은 **문제점을** 안고 있다. hyeon jeongbuneun maneun munjejeomeul ango itda. The current government has many problems.

자살 | ~하다 ja·sal | ~·ha·da suicide | to commit suicide
나는 그의 자살에 매우 큰 충격을 받았다. naneun geuui jasare maeu keun chunggyeogeul badatda. I was deeply shocked by his suicide.

실업 si·reop unemployment
청년 실업은 가장 시급한 사회문제 중 하나이다. cheongnyeon sireobeun gajang sigeupan sahoemunje jung hanaida. Youth unemployment is one of the most pressing social issues.

실업자 si·reop·ja unemployed person
1년이 넘도록 **실업자 신세**예요. illyeoni neomdorok sireopja sinseyeyo. I've been unemployed for over one year.

중독 | ~되다 jung·dok | ~·doe·da addiction | to be addicted to
김 과장님은 완전히 **일 중독**이에요. gim gwajangnimeun wanjeonhi il jungdogieyo. Mr. Kim is a complete workaholic.

마약 ma·yak drug
마약 복용이 증가하고 있다. mayak bogyongi jeunggahago itda. Drug use is on the rise.

알코올 ← 알콜 al·ko·ol ← al·kol alcohol
아버지는 **알코올 중독**이셨어요. abeojineun alkool jungdogisyeosseoyo. My father was an alcoholic.

니코틴 ni·ko·tin nicotine

카페인 ka·pe·in caffeine

도박 = 노름 do·bak = no·reum gambling
제 이모는 도박으로/노름으로 전 재산을 날렸어요. je imoneun dobageuro/noreumeuro jeon jaesaneul lallyeosseoyo. My aunt blew all her money on gambling.

게임 ge·im game
온라인 **게임 중독**은 심각한 사회문제다. ollain geim jungdogeun simgakan sahoemunjeda. Online game addiction is a serious issue.

차별 | ~하다 cha·byeol | ~·ha·da discrimination | to discriminate
어떤 종류의 **차별**도 용인될 수 없다. eotteon jongnyuui chabyeoldo yongindoel su eopda. Any kind of discrimination is not tolerated.

성차별 seong·cha·byeol sexual discrimination

인종차별 in·jong·cha·byeol racism

갈등 gal·deung conflict
결혼 생활에 있어 **갈등을 피할** 방법은 없다. gyeolhon saenghware isseo galdeungeul pihal bangbeobeun eopda. There is no way to avoid conflict in your marriage.

시위 ≒ 데모 | ~하다 si·wi ≒ de·mo | ~·ha·da demonstration, protest | to demonstrate, protest
조세 개정에 반대해 금요일에 **평화 시위**가 있었다. jose gaejeonge bandaehae geumyoire pyeonghwa siwiga isseotda. A peaceful demonstration took place against tax reform on Friday.

마찰 ma·chal friction
두 나라 간의 **무역 마찰**이 최고점에 다다랐다. du nara ganui muyeok machari choegojeome dadaratda. Trade friction between the two countries reached its peak.

위기 wi·gi crisis, emergency
이 **위기**를 극복해야 한다. i wigireul geukbokaeya handa. We should overcome this crisis.

대책 dae·chaek countermeasure, measure
최대한 빨리 **대책을 세워야** 한다. choedaehan ppalli daechaegeul sewoya handa. We should set up countermeasures as soon as possible.

해소 | ~하다 hae·so | ~·ha·da solution, settlement | to solve, resolve
지역 **갈등을 해소하기** 위해서는 선거 제도의 개선이 필요하다. jiyeok galdeungeul haesohagi wihaeseoneun seongeo jedoui gaeseoni piryohada. We need to reform the electoral system to remove regionalism.

해결 | ~하다 hae·gyeol | ~·ha·da settlement, solution | to settle

이 요구는 두 달 이내에 해결될 겁니다. i yoguneun du dal inaee haegyeoldoel geomnida. This claim will be settled within two months.

발등의 불을 끄다 bal·deung·ui bu·reul kkeu·da to deal with an urgent matter
저는 지금 **발등의 불을 끄느라** 정신이 없어요. jeoneun jigeum baldeungui bureul kkeuneura jeongsini eopseoyo. I'm busy taking care of what's on my plate.

23.3 Social Phenomena

현상 hyeon·sang phenomenon

원인 wo·nin cause
인스턴트 식품은 비만의 **주요 원인** 중 하나다. inseuteonteu sikpumeun bimanui juyo wonin jung hanada. Junk food is one of the main causes of obesity.

근원 geu·nwon root, source
스트레스는 모든 **병의 근원**이다. seuteureseuneun modeun byeongui geunwonida. Stress is the cause of all illnesses.

자극 | ~하다 ja·geuk | ~·ha·da stimulation, stimulus | to stimulate, provoke
그의 강의는 학생들의 지적 **호기심을 자극했**다. geuui ganguineun haksaengdeurui jijeok hogisimeul jageukaetda. His lecture encouraged the students' intellectual curiosity.

(불러)일으키다 (bul·leo·)i·reu·ki·da to cause, arouse
그 보고서는 엄청난 대중의 **관심을 불러일으켰**다. geu bogoseoneun eomcheongnan daejungui gwansimeul bulleoireukyeotda. The report aroused a great deal of public interest.

유발하다 yu·bal·ha·da to cause, arouse
스트레스는 온갖 건강 **문제를 유발할** 수 있다. seuteureseuneun ongat geongang munjereul lyubalhal su itda. Stress can cause all kinds of health problems.

야기하다 ya·gi·ha·da to cause, arouse
한순간의 부주의가 치명적인 **사고를 야기할** 수도 있습니다. hansunganui bujuuiga chimyeongjeogin sagoreul lyagihal sudo itseumnida. A moment's carelessness can cause a fatal accident.

초래하다 cho·rae·ha·da to cause, bring about
과도한 운동은 나쁜 **결과를 초래할** 수 있다. gwadohan undongeun nappeun gyeolgwareul choraehal su itda. Excessive exercise can have a negative effect.

가져오다 ga·jyeo·o·da to cause, bring about
인터넷은 우리의 일상 생활에 거대한 **변화를 가져왔**다. inteoneseun uriui ilsang saenghware geodaehan byeonhwareul gajyeowatda. The Internet has brought about huge changes to our daily lives.

불러오다 bul·leo·o·da to cause, bring about
긍정적인 생각이 긍정적인 **변화를 불러올** 수 있습니다. geungjeongjeogin saenggagi geungjeongjeogin byeonhwareul bulleool su itseumnida. Positive thoughts bring about positive changes.

끼치다 = 미치다 kki·chi·da = mi·chi·da to affect, have influence

벌어지다 beo·reo·ji·da to happen, take place
길에서 **싸움이 벌어졌**다. gireseo ssaumi beoreojyeotda. A fight broke out on the street.

발생 | ~하다 bal·saeng | ~·ha·da occurrence | to occur
오늘 오후 세 시경, **지진이 발생했**다. oneul ohu se sigyeong, jijini balsaenghaetda. An earthquake took place around three o'clock in the afternoon.

(일어)나다 (i·reo·)na·da to happen
어떻게 **사고가 났**어요? eotteoke sagoga nasseoyo? How did the accident happen?

나타나다 na·ta·na·da to appear
어머니가 어젯밤 꿈에 **나타났**다. eomeoniga eojetbam kkume natanatda. My mother appeared in my dream last night.

출현 | ~하다 chul·hyeon | ~·ha·da emergence, appearance | to emerge, appear
뉴스에서 그러는데, 상어가 해안에 출현했대. nyuseueseo geureoneunde, sangeoga haeane chulhyeonhaetdae. The news said a shark was sighted near the coast.

생기다 saeng·gi·da to happen, occur
문제는 생기기 마련이야. munjeneun saenggi·gi maryeoniya. Problems are expected to arise.

생겨나다 saeng·gyeo·na·da to originate
그 질병은 아프리카에서 생겨났어요. geu jil·byeongeun apeurikaeseo saenggyeonasseoyo. That disease originated in Africa.

비롯되다 bi·rot·doe·da to begin, derive
말다툼은 실없는 농담에서 비롯됐다. malda·tumeunn sireomneun nongdameseo birotdwaet·da. The argument started with a silly joke.

유래 | ~하다 yu·rae | ~·ha·da origin, beginning | to originate, derive
많은 영어 단어가 고대 그리스어에서 유래했다. maneun nyeongeo daneoga godae geuri·seueoeoseo yuraehaetda. Many English words originated from ancient Greek.

시작 | ~하다 si·jak | ~·ha·da beginning, start | to begin
앉아주세요, 곧 시작합니다. anjajuseyo, got sijakamnida. Sit down, please. We'll start soon.

기원 gi·won origin, beginning
이 책은 생명의 기원을 다루고 있다. i chae·geun saengmyeongui giwoneul darugo itda. This book is about the origins of life.

진행 | ~하다 jin·haeng | ~·ha·da progress, progression | to progress; to emcee
프로젝트는 순조롭게 진행되고 있다. peuro·jekteuneun sunjoropge jinhaengdoego itda. The project is progressing smoothly.

전개 | ~하다 jeon·gae | ~·ha·da development | to develop
우리는 기다리면서 상황의 전개를 지켜보기로 결정했다. urineun gidarimyeonseo sang·hwangui jeongaereul jikyeobogiro gyeoljeong·haetda. We decided to wait and see how the situation developed.

흐름 heu·reum flow, stream

경향 gyeong·hyang tendency, trend
그래프는 어떤 경향을 나타내고 있는가? geu-raepeuneun eotteon gyeonghyangeul latanaego inneunga? What trend does the graph show?

과정 gwa·jeong process

단계 dan·gye stage, phase, step
사업은 계획 단계에 있습니다. saeobeun gye·hoek dangyee itseumnida. My business is in the planning stages.

순조롭다 sun·jo·rop·da smooth

IDM 감(을) 잡다 gam(·eul) jap·da to get the picture
이제야 감을 좀 잡겠어요. ijeya gameul jom japgesseoyo. Now I get the picture.

방해 | ~하다 bang·hae | ~·ha·da disturbance, interruption | to disturb
제가 방해가 됐나요? jega banghaega dwaen·nayo? Am I bothering you?

훼방 hwe·bang disturbance, interruption

IDM 고춧가루(를) 뿌리다 go·chut·ga·ru (·reul) ppu·ri·da to spoil, ruin
넌 꼭 분위기 좋을 때 고춧가루를 뿌리는구나. neon kkok bunwigi joeul ttae gochutgarureul ppurineunguna. You always spoil the mood.

IDM 물(을) 흐리다 mul(·eul) heu·ri·da to exert a bad influence on others
괜히 물 흐리지 말고 딴 데 가라. gwaenhi mul heuriji malgo ttan de gara. Don't spoil the mood! Go somewhere else.

IDM 발목(을) 잡다 bal·mok(·eul) jap·da to drag sth down
정치가 기업의 발목을 잡아서는 안 됩니다. jeongchiga gieobui balmogeul jabaseoneun an doemnida. Politics should not drag businesses down.

변화 | ~하다 byeon·hwa | ~·ha·da change | to change (to)
이 지역에서는 날씨의 갑작스런 변화가 아주 빈번합니다. i jiyeogeseoneun nalssiui gapjak·seureon byeonhwaga aju binbeonhamnida. In this area, sudden changes in the weather are quite frequent.

바뀌다 ba·kkwi·da to change (to)
신호가 녹색으로 바뀌었어. sinhoga noksae·geuro bakkwieosseo. The lights changed to green.

변하다 byeon·ha·da to change, vary
너 많이 변했구나. neo mani byeonhaetguna. You've changed a lot.

달라지다 dal·la·ji·da to alter, become different
세상이 지난 십 년 동안 아주 많이 달라졌다. sesangi jinan sim nyeon dongan aju mani dallajyeotda. The world has changed a lot in the last ten years.

되다 doe·da to become
얼음이 녹아서 물이 되었다. eoreumi nogaseo muri doeeotda. The ice has melted into water.

발달 | ~하다 bal·dal | ~·ha·da development, growth | to develop, grow
과학이 발달할수록 윤리 교육이 더 필요하다. gwahagi baldalhalsurok nyulli gyoyugi deo piryohada. We need more training in ethics as science develops.

발전 | ~하다 bal·jeon | ~·ha·da development, growth | to develop
우리는 이 프로그램이 경제 발전을 촉진시킬 것이라고 기대하고 있습니다. urineun i peurogeuraemi gyeongje baljeoneul chokjinsikil geosirago gidaehago itseumnida. We expect that this program will expedite economic development.

진보 | ~하다 jin·bo | ~·ha·da progress, advance | to make progress
산업혁명은 급격한 기술의 진보를 가져왔다. saneopyeongmyeongeun geupgyeokan gisurui jinboreul gajyeowatda. The Industrial Revolution resulted in a rapid advancement in technology.

향상 | ~시키다 hyang·sang | ~·si·ki·da improvement | to improve
어떻게 해야 한국어 실력을 향상시킬 수 있을까요? eotteoke haeya hangugeo sillyeogeul hyangsangsikil su isseulkkayo? How can I improve my Korean?

악화되다 a·khwa·doe·da to become worse
그의 발언으로 상황이 악화되었다. geuui bareoneuro sanghwangi akhwadoeeotda. His remarks have worsened the situation.

끝나다 kkeun·na·da to end, come to an end
내일이면 방학이 끝나요. naeirimyeon banghagi kkeunnayo. School vacation ends tomorrow.

개종 관습 교황 교회 기도 기독교 기적

대중문화 목사 무슬림 문화 문화재 미신

믿다 믿음 박물관 보존 부처 불교

사원 설교 성경 성당 세례 수녀 스님

식 신 신도 신부 신앙 십자가 악마 영혼 예배

예수 유령 유물 유적 유적지 육체 이슬람교

장 전통 전통문화 절 절 정신 제사

조상 종교 주 중 지내다 지옥 창조

천국 천사 천주교 치르다 탑 풍습 하나님

하느님 효녀 효도 효자 힌두교

24.1 Culture

문화 | ~적 mun·hwa | ~·jeok culture | cultural
여기에 처음 왔을 때 나는 이곳 문화에 익숙하지 않았다. yeogie cheoeum wasseul ttae naneun igot munhwae iksukaji anatda. I was not familiar with the culture the first time I came here.

대중문화 dae·jung·mun·hwa popular culture
그는 한국 **대중문화의 상징**이다. geuneun hanguk daejungmunhwaui sangjingida. He is an icon of Korean pop culture.

전통문화 jeon·tong·mun·hwa traditional culture
모든 나라가 저마다의 전통문화를 갖고 있다. modeun naraga jeomadaui jeontongmunhwareul gatgo itda. Every country has its own traditional culture.

전통 | ~적 jeon·tong | ~·jeok tradition | traditional
우리 대학은 백 년의 전통을 자랑한다. uri daehageun baeng nyeonui jeontongeul jaranghanda. Our university boasts a tradition that goes back 100 years.

풍습 pung·seup custom
우리는 새해에 떡국을 먹는 풍습이 있습니다. urineun saehaee tteokgugeul meongneun pungseubi itseumnida. We have a custom of eating rice cake soup on New Year's Day.

관습 gwan·seup custom, convention
외국에서는 새로운 관습에 적응할 필요가 있다. oegugeseoneun saeroun gwanseube jeogeunghal piryoga itda. In a foreign country, you need to adapt yourself to new customs.

(의)식 (ui·)sik ceremony, ritual
결혼은 인생에서 가장 중요한 의식 중 하나예요. gyeolhoneun insaengeseo gajang jungyohan uisik jung hanayeyo. A wedding is one of the most important ceremonies.

치르다 chi·reu·da to hold, carry out
덕분에 **초상**을 무사히 **치렀습니다**. deokbune chosangeul musahi chireotseumnida. Thanks to you the funeral went well.

지내다 ji·nae·da to hold, carry out
장례를 지내야 한다는 법이 있지는 않다. 장례는 단지 보편적인 작별 의식이다. jangnyereul jinaeya handaneun beobi itjineun anta. jangnyeneun danji bopyeonjeogin jakbyeol uisigida. There is no legal requirement to have a funeral; it's just a common practice as a way of saying goodbye.

박물관 bang·mul·gwan museum
박물관은 연중 무휴입니다. bangmulgwaneun nyeonjung muhuimnida. The museum is open all the year round.

유물 yu·mul relic, artifact
문화 유물들은 잘 보존되어야 한다. munhwa yumuldeureun jal bojondoeeoya handa. Cultural relics must be carefully preserved.

유적 yu·jeok remains, ruins

유적지 yu·jeok·ji historical site
경주에는 유적지가 많아요. gyeongjueneun nyujeokjiga manayo. There are lots of historical sites in Gyeongju.

문화재 mun·hwa·jae cultural assets
문화재를 훼손할 수 있으므로 실내에서 장난을 금합니다. munhwajaereul hwesonhal su iseumuro sillaeeseo jangnaneul geumhamnida. No horseplay allowed in this room. You might damage some cultural assets.

보존 | ~하다 bo·jon | ~·ha·da preservation | to preserve
그 오래된 집은 잘 보존되어 있다. geu oraedoen jibeun jal bojondoeeo itda. The old house is well preserved.

탑 tap tower, pagoda
다보탑은 신라 시대의 유명한 석탑이다. dabotabeun silla sidaeui yumyeonghan seoktabida. Dabotap is a famous stone pagoda from the Silla Dynasty.

조상 jo·sang ancestor
속담에는 **조상들의 지혜**가 담겨 있다. sokdameneun josangdeurui jihyega damgyeo itda. Proverbs contain the wisdom of our ancestors.

제사 je·sa ancestral rites, memorial service
저희 집은 일 년에 한 번 **제사를 지내요**. jeohui jibeun il lyeone han beon jesareul jinaeyo. We hold ancestral rites once a year.

효도 | ~하다 hyo·do | ~·ha·da filial duty | to be a good son or daughter
부모님께 효도해라. bumonimkke hyodohaera.

Be good to your parents.

• **효자** hyo·ja good son

효녀 hyo·nyeo good daughter

24.2 Religion

: **종교** jong·gyo religion
한국에서는 헌법에 의해 **종교의 자유**가 보장 된다. hangugeseoneun heonbeobe uihae jong-gyoui jayuga bojangdoenda. Freedom of religion is guaranteed by the Korean Constitution.

신앙 si·nang faith, religious belief
신앙 생활은 믿음의 실천을 동반해야 한다. sinang saenghwareun mideumui silcheoneul dongbanhaeya handa. Living a life of faith should involve putting our faith into practice.

: **믿음 ≒ 신앙심** mi·deum ≒ si·nang·sim belief, faith
그분은 **믿음이/신앙심이** 아주 깊어요. geubuneun mideumi/sinangsimi aju gipeoyo. He's very religious.

미신 mi·sin superstition
나는 그것들이 미신이라고 생각해. naneun geugeotdeuri misinirago saenggakae. I think they are superstitions.

• **신** sin god, God
저는 신을 믿지 않습니다. jeoneun sineul mitji anseumnida. I don't believe in God.

• **하느님** ha·neu·nim God

유령 ≒ 귀신 yu·ryeong ≒ gwi·sin ghost, spirit
저는 유령을/귀신을 본 적이 있어요. jeoneun nyuryeongeul/gwisineul bon jeogi isseoyo. I have seen a ghost before.

: **믿다** mit·da to believe in, have faith in
나는 귀신을 안 믿어. naneun gwisineul an mideo. I don't believe in ghosts.

개종 | ~하다 gae·jong | ~·ha·da conversion | to convert
최근에 기독교에서 불교로 개종하기로 마음 먹었어요. choegeune gidokgyoeseo bulgyoro gaejonghagiro maeummeogeosseoyo. I have recently decided to convert from Christianity to Buddhism.

신도 = 신자 sin·do = sin·ja believer

• **영혼** yeong·hon soul, spirit

저는 그의 영혼이 지금 제가 있는 이 방에 있다 고 믿습니다. jeoneun geuui yeonghoni jigeum jega inneun i bange itdago mitseumnida. I think his spirit is right here in the room with me.

: **정신** jeong·sin mind, spirit
내가 정신이 나갔었나 봐. naega jeongsini nagasseonna bwa. I must have been out of my mind.

• **육체** yuk·che body

: **불교** bul·gyo Buddhism
불교에서 손을 모으는 것이 뭘 의미하나요? bulgyoeseo soneul moeuneun geosi mwol uimi-hanayo? In Buddhism, what does it mean to hold one's hands together?

: **부처 = 석가(모니)** bu·cheo = seok·ga (·mo·ni) Buddha

: **절 = 사찰** jeol = sa·chal Buddhist temple
한국에는 절이/사찰이 아주 많아요. hanugeneun jeori/sachari aju manayo. There are a lot of temples in Korea.

중 jung Buddhist monk

: **스님** seu·nim Buddhist monk
한국에서 가장 존경 받는 스님 중 한 명인 법정 스님이 2010년에 세상을 떠났다. hangugeseo gajang jongyeong banneun seunim jung han myeongin beopjeong seunimi icheon-simnyeone sesangeul tteonatda. Beopjeong, one of the most respected Buddhist monks in Korea, passed away in 2010.

• **기독교 = 크리스트교** gi·dok·gyo = keu·ri·seu·teu·gyo Christianity
저는 작년에 기독교로/크리스트교로 개종했 어요. jeoneun jangnyeone gidokgyoro/keuri-seuteugyoro gaejonghaesseoyo. I converted to Christianity last year.

: **교회** gyo·hoe church
아내와 저는 매주 일요일 아침에 **교회에 갑니 다**. anaewa jeoneun maeju iryoil achime gyo-hoee gamnida. My wife and I go to church every Sunday morning.

: **목사** mok·sa minister, pastor

설교 | ~하다 seol·gyo | ~·ha·da sermon, preach | to preach, give a sermon
목사님의 설교는 너무 길고 지루해서 나는 말씀 중에 계속해서 졸았다. moksanimui seolgyoneun neomu gilgo jiruhaeseo naneun malsseum junge gyesokaeseo joratda. The minister's sermon was so long and boring that I kept dozing off.

예배 ye·bae worship, service
저는 수요일과 일요일에 예배에 참석합니다. jeoneun suyoilgwa iryoire yebaee chamseokamnida. I attend church services on Wednesdays and Sundays.

천주교 = 가톨릭(교) ← 카톨릭 cheon·ju·gyo = ga·tol·lik(·gyo) ← ka·tol·lik Catholic, Catholicism
저는 천주교를/가톨릭을 믿습니다. jeoneun cheonjugyoreul/gatolligeul mitseumnida. I am a practitioner of Catholicism.

성당 seong·dang Catholic church, cathedral
그 성당은 우리나라에서 가장 오래된 성당이다. geu seongdangeun urinaraeseo gajang oraedoen seongdangida. It is the oldest Catholic church in Korea.

신부 sin·bu priest

수녀 su·nyeo nun, sister

교황 gyo·hwang Pope

성경 seong·gyeong the Bible
그녀는 기독교 신자가 아닌 사람에게 자신의 믿음을 설명할 때 곧잘 성경을 인용한다. geunyeoneun gidokgyo sinjaga anin saramege jasinui mideumeul seolmyeonghal ttae gotjal seonggyeongeul inyonghanda. She often quotes the Bible to non-Christians to explain why she believes something.

장 jang chapter

절 jeol verse
창세기 1장 1절 changsegi iljang iljeol Genesis Chapter 1, Verse 1

하나님 ha·na·nim Christian God

주 ju the Lord

예수 (그리스도) ye·su (geu·ri·seu·do) Jesus (Christ)
우리 주 예수 그리스도의 이름으로 기도 드립니다, 아멘. uri ju yesu geuriseudoui ireumeuro gido deurimnida, amen. We pray in the name of Jesus Christ our Lord. Amen.

창조 | ~하다 chang·jo | ~·ha·da creation | to create
기독교에서는 하나님이 세상을 창조했다고 믿는다. gidokgyoeseoneun hananimi sesangeul changjohaetdago minneunda. Christians believe that God made the world.

기적 gi·jeok miracle
의사 말로는 할머니가 3주 만에 깨어나신 건 기적이래요. uisa malloneun halmeoniga samju mane kkaeeonasin geon gijeogiraeyo. The doctor said it was a miracle my grandmother came around after three weeks.

기도 | ~하다 gi·do | ~·ha·da pray | to pray
널 위해 기도할게. neol wihae gidohalge. I'll pray for you.

세례 se·rye baptism
저는 아기일 때 세례를 받았어요. jeoneun agiil ttae seryereul badasseoyo. I was baptized as a baby.

천국 = 천당 cheon·guk = cheon·dang Paradise, Heaven
천국에/천당에 가고 싶으면 신을 믿으세요. cheonguge/cheondange gago sipeumyeon sineul mideuseyo. Believe in God if you want to go to Heaven.

지옥 ji·ok hell

천사 cheon·sa angel

악마 ang·ma Satan, the Devil

십자가 sip·ja·ga cross

힌두교 hin·du·gyo Hinduism
힌두교에서 소는 신성한 동물로 여겨진다. hindugyoeseo soneun sinseonghan dongmullo yeogyeojinda. Cows are considered sacred in Hinduism.

이슬람교 = 회교 i·seul·lam·gyo = hoe·gyo Islam

무슬림 = 회교도 mu·seul·lim = hoe·gyo·do Muslim
아프가니스탄 인구의 약 99퍼센트가 무슬림이다/회교도이다. apeuganiseutan inguui yak gusipgupeosenteuga museullimida/hoegyodoida. About 99% of the Afghan population is Muslim.

사원 sa·won temple; mosque
이슬람 사원에 들어가기 전에는 신을 벗어야 합니다. iseullam sawone deureogagi jeoneneun sineul beoseoya hamnida. You need to take off your shoes before entering the mosque.

가동 갈다 거두다 건축 건축가 곡물 곡식 공구 공사

공장 과수원 광업 괭이 구제역 귀농 금 금광 기사 낙농

낫 논 농가 농민 농사 농산물 농약 농업 농장

농촌 다이아몬드 도색 드라이버 드릴 망치 매다 매매 먹이

목록 목장 목재 밭농사 벌집 베다 벼 벼농사 뿌리다

사다리 사육 산업 삽 상업 석탄 설계 설비 소매 수확

chapter 25 | Industries

시장 아스팔트 알루미늄 양계 양봉 양식 양식장

양잠 어민 어촌 업종 외양간 용접 우리 원료 유통 은

작물 작업 장비 장사 쟁기 전구 제조 제조업 제조업체

조류독감 조립 짓다 짓다 철 철 추수 축사 축산

물 칠 콩 탄광 통 품목 해산물 허수아비 헐다 흉년

25.1 Farming

산업 sa·neop industry
관광은 남극에서 급성장하고 있는 산업이다. gwangwangeun namgeugeseo geupseongjanghago inneun saneobida. Tourism is a fast-growing industry in the Antarctica.

업종 eop·jong type of business

농업 nong·eop agriculture, farming (industry)
이 지역 주민들 중 대부분은 **농업에 종사하고** 있다. i jiyeok jumindeul jung daebubuneun nongeobe jongsahago itda. Most of the inhabitants in this region are occupied with agriculture.

농촌 nong·chon farm village
저는 작은 농촌 마을에서 태어났습니다. jeoneun jageun nongchon maeureseo taeeonatseumnida. I was born in a small farming community.

농가 nong·ga farmhouse, farm family
폭설로 이 지역 농가들이 큰 피해를 입었다. pokseollo i jiyeok nonggadeuri keun pihaereul ibeotda. The heavy snow caused great damage to the farms in this area.

농민 nong·min farmer, peasant

농부 nong·bu farmer, peasant

. . . .

벼농사 = 논농사 = 쌀농사 byeo·nong·sa = non·nong·sa = ssal·long·sa rice farming

밭농사 ban·nong·sa dry-field farming

. . . .

과수원 gwa·su·won orchard
어머니는 과수원에서 사과를 따고 계세요. eomeonineun gwasuwoneseo sagwareul ttago gyeseyo. My mother is picking apples in the orchard.

비닐하우스 bi·nil·ha·u·seu vinyl greenhouse

농장 nong·jang farm
저희 가족은 주말이면 부모님 농장에서 일합니다. jeohui gajogeun jumarimyeon bumonim nongjangeseo ilhamnida. My family works on my parents' farm on weekends.

농(경)지 nong(·gyeong)·ji farmland
많은 **농경지가** 침수되었다. maneun nonggyeongjiga chimsudoeeotda. Much farmland was flooded.

논 non rice paddy
예전에 이 지역은 논이었다. yejeone i jiyeogeun nonieotda. All of this area used to be rice paddies.

밭 bat dry field
아버지는 하루 종일 밭에서 일하세요. abeojineun haru jongil bateseo ilhaseyo. My father works in the field all day long.

농사 nong·sa farming

짓다 jit·da to farm
그 땅은 **농사를 짓기**에 부적합하다. geu ttangeun nongsareul jitgie bujeokapada. The land is not suitable for farming.

경작 | ~하다 gyeong·jak | ~·ha·da cultivation | to cultivate, farm
다음 주에 농민들에게 옥수수 **경작하는** 법을 교육할 예정입니다. daeum jue nongmindeurege oksusu gyeongjakaneun beobeul gyoyukal yejeongimnida. We're going to teach farmers how to grow corn next week.

갈다 gal·da to plow
농부가 밭을 갈고 있다. nongbuga bateul galgo itda. The farmer is plowing his fields.

매다 mae·da to weed
온종일 부모님을 도와 논을 **맸어요**. onjongil bumonimeul dowa noneul maesseoyo. I helped my parents weed the rice paddy all day long.

비료 bi·ryo fertilizer
이 비료에는 식물의 생장에 필요한 모든 영양소가 들어 있습니다. i biryoeneun singmurui saengjange piryohan modeun nyeongyangsoga deureo itseumnida. This fertilizer has all the nutrients essential for a plant to grow.

농약 nong·yak agricultural pesticides

거름 geo·reum manure

뿌리다 ppu·ri·da to sow, spread
저희는 정기적으로 작물들에 **농약을 뿌립니다**. jeohuineun jeonggijeogeuro jangmuldeure nongyageul ppurimnida. We regularly spray crops with pesticide.

허수아비 heo·su·a·bi scarecrow
까마귀는 **허수아비**를 전혀 무서워하지 않았다. kkamagwineun heosuabireul jeonhyeo museowohaji anatda. The crows weren't scared of the scarecrows at all.

관개 | ~하다 gwan·gae | ~·ha·da irrigation | to irrigate
농민들은 **관개 시설** 덕분에 가까스로 가뭄을 이겨낼 수 있었다. nongmindeureun gwangae siseol deokbune gakkaseuro gamumeul igyeonael su isseotda. Farmers managed to withstand the drought due to the irrigation system.

대다 dae·da to supply
이 호수의 물이 마을 주변의 땅에 **물을 대는**데 사용됩니다. i hosuui muri maeul jubyeonui ttange mureul daeneun de sayongdoemnida. The water from this lake is used to irrigate the land around the village.

베다 be·da to cut
지금이 **벼를 베기**에 가장 좋은 시기야. jigeumi byeoreul begie gajang joeun sigiya. Now is the best time to harvest rice.

수확 | ~하다 su·hwak | ~·ha·da harvest | to harvest
가을은 **수확의** 계절이다. gaeureun suhwagui gyejeorida. Fall is the harvest season.

거두다 geo·du·da to collect, gather, harvest
추수 | ~하다 chu·su | ~·ha·da harvest | to harvest
추수하기 참 좋은 날씨야. chusuhagi cham joeun nalssiya. The weather is perfect for harvesting.

풍년 pung·nyeon bumper year
흉년 hyung·nyeon bad year
귀농 | ~하다 gwi·nong | ~·ha·da turning to farming | to turn to farming

그는 은퇴 후 **귀농했다**. geuneun euntoe hu gwinonghaetda. He became a farmer after retirement.

농기구 nong·gi·gu farming tool
낫 nat sickle, scythe
삽 sap shovel
(곡)괭이 (gok·)gwaeng·i pickax
쟁기 jaeng·gi plow
호미 ho·mi hoe
농기계 nong·gi·gye farm machine
경운기 gyeong·un·gi cultivator
트랙터 teu·raek·teo tractor

농산물 nong·san·mul farm produce
농가들이 **잉여 농산물**을 놓고 고심하고 있다. nonggadeuri ingyeo nongsanmureul loko gosimhago itda. Farming households are grappling with surplus produce.

(농)작물 (nong·)jang·mul crop, produce
태풍으로 **농작물**이 큰 피해를 입었다. taepungeuro nongjangmuri keun pihaereul ibeotda. The typhoon did great damage to the crops.

곡식 gok·sik grain
그 창고는 습기가 많아서 **곡식을/곡물을** 장기간 **보관하기는** 어렵다. geu changgoneun seupgiga manaseo goksigeul/gongmureul janggigan bogwanhagineun eoryeopda. The warehouse was too humid to store grain for a long time.

곡물 gong·mul grain
벼 byeo rice
콩 kong bean
보리 bo·ri barley

25.2 Livestock, Fishing, Mining

축산 chuk·san stockbreeding
축산물 시장 개방으로 국내 **축산 농가**들이 어려움을 겪고 있다. chuksanmul sijang gaebangeuro gungnae chuksan nonggadeuri eoryeoumeul gyeokgo itda. Domestic farmers are suffering due to the opening of the livestock market.

낙농 nang·nong dairying
우유는 대표적인 **낙농 제품**이다. uyuneun daepyojeogin nangnong jepumida. Milk is a typical dairy product.

목장 mok·jang farm, ranch
부모님은 **목장**을 운영하세요. bumonimeun

mokjangeul unyeonghaseyo. My parents run a ranch.

외양간 oe·yang·gan barn, stable

양계 yang·gye poultry farming
이 마을은 양계가 활발합니다. i maeureun nyanggyega hwalbalhamnida. Poultry farming thrives in this village.

양계장 yang·gye·jang poultry farm
저희 양계장에는 약 5만 마리의 닭이 있어요. jeohui yanggyejangeneun nyak oman mariui dalgi isseoyo. I have about 50,000 chickens in my chicken farm.

양돈 yang·don hog raising
양돈 사업은 앞으로 전망이 밝습니다. yangdon saeobeun apeuro jeonmangi bakseumnida. Hog raising has a promising future.

우리 u·ri pen, cage
이런, 우리 문이 열려 있어! ireon, uri muni yeollyeo isseo! Oops, the door to the pen is open!

축사 chuk·sa cattle shed
간밤에 돼지 축사에서 화재가 있었다. ganbame dwaeji chuksaeseo hwajaega isseotda. There was a fire in the pigpen last night.

양봉 yang·bong beekeeping
이 마을은 양봉으로 유명하다. i maeureun nyangbongeuro yumyeonghada. This village is famous for beekeeping.

벌집 beol·jip (bee)hive

벌꿀 beol·kkul honeybee

채취 | ~하다 chae·chwi | ~·ha·da collection | to gather, collect
벌집에서 벌꿀을 채취하는 것은 때로는 위험하다. beoljibeseo beolkkureul chaechwihaneun geoseun ttaeroneun wiheomhada. It is sometimes dangerous to gather honey from a beehive.

양잠 yang·jam silkworm farming

누에 nu·e silkworm

사육 | ~하다 sa·yuk | ~·ha·da breeding, raising | to breed, raise
저희 농장에서는 돼지나 닭, 그 밖에도 여러 동물들을 사육하고/기르고/키우고 있습니다. jeohui nongjangeseoneun dwaejina dak, geu bakkedo yeoreo dongmuldeureul sayukago/gireugo/kiugo itseumnida. We raise pigs, chickens, and other animals on the farm.

기르다 ≒ 키우다 gi·reu·da ≒ ki·u·da to breed, keep

사료 sa·ryo feed
저희는 소에게 특수 사료를 먹입니다. jeohui- neun soege teuksu saryoreul meogimnida. We give the cattle special feed.

먹이 meo·gi food, feed

모이 mo·i food, feed (of birds or chickens)

먹이다 meo·gi·da to feed
저는 아침마다 닭에게 모이를 먹입니다. jeoneun achimmada dalgege moireul meogimnida. I feed the chickens every morning.

축산물 chuk·san·mul livestock products

광우병 gwang·u·byeong BSE

구제역 gu·je·yeok foot-and-mouth disease
구제역은 전국으로 빠르게 확산되었다. gujeyeogeun jeongugeuro ppareuge hwaksandoeeotda. Foot-and-mouth disease has spread quickly nationwide.

조류독감 jo·ryu·dok·gam avian influenza

....

수산업 su·sa·neop fishing industry
그 나라의 수산업이 위기에 빠졌다. geu naraui susaneobi wigie ppajyeotda. The country's fishing industry is in crisis.

어업 eo·eop fishing industry

양식 | ~하다 yang·sik | ~·ha·da culture, farming | to raise, farm (marine products)
굴 양식은 단순히 굴을 채취하는 것과는 완전히 다르다. gul lyangsigeun dansunhi gureul chaechwihaneun geotgwaneun wanjeonhi dareuda. Oyster farming is totally different from just harvesting oysters from their beds.

양식장 yang·sik·jang fish farm
기름 유출로 인해 지역 내 거의 모든 물고기 양식장들이 파괴되었다. gireum nyuchullo inhae jiyeok nae geoui modeun mulgogi yangsikjangdeuri pagoedoeeotda. The oil spill has destroyed almost all of the fish farms in the region.

어촌 eo·chon fishing village

어민 = 어부 eo·min = eo·bu fisherman
어민들은/어부들은 생계를 바다에 의존한다. eomindeureun/eobudeureun saenggyereul badae uijonhanda. Fishermen depend on the seas for their livelihood.

수산물 su·san·mul marine products
한국은 방사능 오염에 대한 우려로 일본 **수산물의 수입**을 금지했다. hangugeun bangsaneung oyeome daehan uryeoro ilbon susanmurui suibeul geumjihaetda. South Korea banned imports of seafood from Japan over fears of radioactive contamination.

해산물 hae·san·mul seafood

광(산)업 gwang(·san)·eop mining (industry)

광산 gwang·san mine
그 **광산**은 오래전에 **폐쇄되었다**. geu gwangsaneun oraejeone pyeswaedoeeotda. The mine was shut down long ago.

금광 geum·gwang gold mine

탄광 tan·gwang coal mine

광부 gwang·bu miner
남편은 **탄광의 광부**입니다. nampyeoneun tangwangui gwangbuimnida. My husband is a coal miner.

광물 gwang·mul mineral

석탄 seok·tan coal

구리 gu·ri copper

납 nap lead

철 cheol iron

금 geum gold
그는 **금**을 캐며 평생을 보냈다. geuneun geumeul kaemyeo pyeongsaengeul bonaetda. He spent his whole life mining for gold.

은 eun silver

다이아몬드 da·i·a·mon·deu diamond

25.3 Manufacturing, Construction, Commerce

공업 gong·eop manufacturing industry

제조업 je·jo·eop manufacturing industry
이 나라의 경제는 대체로 제조업에 기반을 두고 있다. i naraui gyeongjeneun daechero jejoeobe gibaneul dugo itda. The economy of this country is largely based on manufacturing.

제조업체 = 제조사 je·jo·eop·che = je·jo·sa manufacturer
제조업체의/제조사의 지시를 따르라. jejoeopcheui/jejosaui jisireul ttarara. Follow the manufacturer's instructions.

작업자 ja·geop·ja worker
우리는 **작업자의 안전**을 최우선으로 생각합니다. urineun jageopjaui anjeoneul choeuseoneuro saenggakamnida. We believe the safety of workers is our first priority.

기사 ≒ 기술자 gi·sa ≒ gi·sul·ja technician, engineer
기사에게/기술자에게 기계를 점검해 보라고 하겠습니다. gisaege/gisuljaege gigyereul jeomgeomhae borago hagetseumnida. I'll have a technician check the machine.

공장 gong·jang factory, plant

설비 seol·bi facilities, equipment
그 공장은 최신 **설비**를 갖추고 있다. geu gongjangeun choesin seolbireul gatchugo itda. The factory has up-to-date facilities.

기술 gi·sul skill, technique, technology
한국의 휴대폰 **기술**은 고도로 발달했다. hangugui hyudaepon gisureun godoro baldalhaetda. Korea's cell phone technology is highly advanced.

작업 | ~하다 ja·geop | ~·ha·da work, job | to work
저희는 **작업 환경**을 개선하기 위해 최선을 다하고 있습니다. jeohuineun jageop hwangyeongeul gaeseonhagi wihae choeseoneul dahago itseumnida. We are doing our best to improve the work environment.

기계 gi·gye machine
이 **기계 고장** 난 것 같아. i gigye gojang nan geot gata. This machine seems to be broken.

가동 | ~하다 ga·dong | ~·ha·da operation | to operate
에어컨이 24시간 가동되고 있다. eeokeoni isipsasigan gadongdoego itda. The air conditioners are operating twenty four hours a day.

제품 ≒ 상품 je·pum ≒ sang·pum product, goods

물품 mul·pum article, goods

품목 pum·mok item

목록 = 리스트 mong·nok = ri·seu·teu list, inventory

모델 mo·del model
이 제품은 여러 면에서 이전 모델과 다릅니다. i jepumeun nyeoreo myeoneseo ijeon model-gwa dareumnida. This product is different from the earlier model in many ways.

(품)질 (pum·)jil quality
이 상품은 품질과 내구성 면에서 최고입니다. i sangpumeun pumjilgwa naeguseong myeoneseo choegoimnida. This product is the best in quality and durability.

제조 | ~하다 je·jo | ~·ha·da production | to produce, make
김 대리가 **제조 공정**에 관해 설명해 드리겠습니다. gim daeriga jejo gongjeonge gwanhae seolmyeonghae deurigetseumnida. Mr. Kim will explain the manufacturing process.

부품 bu·pum part, component

조립 | ~하다 jo·rip | ~·ha·da assembly | to assemble

원료 wol·lyo raw material
나무는 종이의 원료가 된다. namuneun jongiui wollyoga doenda. Trees provide the raw material for paper.

건설 | ~하다 geon·seol | ~·ha·da construction, building | to construct, build
그 **댐의 건설**에 5년 이상이 걸렸다. geu daemui geonseore onyeon isangi geollyeotda. The construction of the dam took more than five years.

건축 | ~하다 geon·chuk | ~·ha·da construction, building | to construct, build
건축 비용이 제 예상보다 너무 많이 나왔어요. geonchuk biyongi je yesangboda neomu mani nawasseoyo. The cost of the building construction came out to be far more expensive than I expected.

건설사 = 시공사 geon·seol·sa = si·gong·sa builder, construction company
그 회사가 아파트 **건설사로/시공사로** 선정되었다. geu hoesaga apateu geonseolsaro/sigongsaro seonjeongdoeeotda. The company was designated the builder for the apartment complex.

건축가 geon·chuk·ga architect
저는 **건축가가 되기** 위한 공부를 하고 있습니다. jeoneun geonchukgaga doegi wihan gongbureul hago itseumnida. I'm studying to be an architect.

공사 gong·sa construction work
공사로 인해 불편을 드려 대단히 죄송합니다. gongsaro inhae bulpyeoneul deuryeo daedanhi joesonghamnida. We're very sorry for the inconvenience caused by the construction work.

짓다 jit·da to build, construct
제가 살 **집을 짓고** 싶어요. jega sal jibeul jitgo sipeoyo. I want to build my own house.

헐다 heol·da to pull down, tear down
벽을 헐어서 침실을 넓히고 싶어요. byeogeul heoreoseo chimsireul leolpigo sipeoyo. I'd like to tear down the wall to enlarge my bedroom.

설계 | ~하다 seol·gye | ~·ha·da design | to design, lay out
이 건물은 친환경적으로 설계되었다. i geonmureun chinhwangyeongjeogeuro seolgyedoeeotda. This building was designed to be eco-friendly.

설계도 seol·gye·do blueprint
내일 고객과 함께 **설계도를 검토해** 봐야 합니다. naeil gogaekgwa hamkke seolgyedoreul geomtohae bwaya hamnida. I need to go over the blueprints with the customer tomorrow.

용접 | ~하다 yong·jeop | ~·ha·da welding | to weld

도색 | ~하다 do·saek | ~·ha·da painting | to paint
선박은 현재 도색 중입니다. seonbageun hyeonjae dosaek jungimnida. The ship is now being painted.

칠 | ~하다 chil | ~·ha·da painting | to paint
벽을 흰색으로 다시 칠하고 싶어요. byeogeul huinsaegeuro dasi chilhago sipeoyo. I feel like painting the wall white again.

자재 ja·jae material
이 **건축 자재**는 화재에 강해요. i geonchuk jajaeneun hwajaee ganghaeyo. This building material is fire-resistant.

목재 mok·jae lumber
방 안의 모든 가구는 목재로 만들어졌어요. bang anui modeun gaguneun mokjaero mandeureojyeosseoyo. All the furniture in the room was made of wood.

통 tong container, barrel
이 통은 저것보다 네 배 더 많은 물을 담을 수

있다. i tongeun jeogeotboda ne bae deo ma-neun mureul dameul su itda. This barrel can hold four times as much water as that one.

벽돌 byeok·dol brick
작업자들이 **벽돌을** 쌓고 있다. jageopjadeuri byeokdoreul ssako itda. Workers are laying some bricks.

시멘트 si·men·teu cement
집을 지으려면 시멘트, 콘크리트, 모래 등이 필요하다. jibeul jieuryeomyeon simenteu, konkeuriteu, morae deungi piryohada. To build a house you need cement, concrete, sand, and so forth.

알루미늄 al·lu·mi·nyum aluminum

철 = 쇠 cheol = soe iron

플라스틱 peul·la·seu·tik plastic

유리 yu·ri glass

페인트 pe·in·teu paint
아직 **페인트** 냄새가 나요. ajik peinteu naem-saega nayo. I can still smell the paint.

아스팔트 a·seu·pal·teu asphalt
이 길에 **아스팔트를** 깐다는 게 누구 생각이었는지 궁금해요. i gire aseupalteureul kkanda-neun ge nugu saenggagieonneunji gung-geumhaeyo. I wonder whose idea it was to pave this street with asphalt.

전구 jeon·gu bulb
전구 갈아야겠어. jeongu garayagesseo. The bulb needs to be changed.

스위치 seu·wi·chi switch
스위치를 눌러라. seuwichireul lulleora. Switch it on.

공구 = 연장 gong·gu = yeon·jang tool
공구를/연장을 사용할 때 장갑을 꼭 껴라. gonggureul/yeonjangeul sayonghal ttae jang-gabeul kkok kkyeora. Don't forget to wear gloves when using the hand tools.

도구 do·gu tool, kit
이 작업에는 도구가 몇 개 필요하다. i jageo-beneun doguga myeot gae piryohada. I need a couple of tools for this job.

드라이버 deu·ra·i·beo screwdriver

나사 na·sa screw
드라이버로 **나사를** 풀어라. deuraibeoro na-sareul pureora. Loosen the screw with a screwdriver.

드릴 deu·ril drill
벽에 구멍을 뚫어야 하니 드릴을 가져올게요. byeoge gumeongeul ttureoya hani deurireul ga-jyeoolgeyo. I need to make a hole in the wall, so I'll bring a drill.

망치 mang·chi hammer

못 mot nail
망치로 벽에 **못** 좀 **박아** 줄래? mangchiro byeoge mot jom baga jullae? Could you ham-mer the nail into the wall?

톱 top saw
그는 판자를 톱으로 잘랐다. geuneun pan-jareul tobeuro jallatda. He sawed the board.

장비 jang·bi equipment, gear

사다리 sa·da·ri ladder
남자가 사다리 위에서 작업 중이다. namjaga sadari wieseo jageop jungida. A man is work-ing on the ladder.

굴착기 gul·chak·gi excavator

상업 sang·eop commerce, business
공원 주변에 **상업** 시설들이 들어설 겁니다. gongwon jubyeone sangeop siseoldeuri deureo-seol geomnida. The park will be surrounded by commercial facilities.

상인 sang·in merchant, dealer
대형 마트 때문에 소규모 **상인들이** 어려움을 겪고 있다. daehyeong mateu ttaemune sogyu-mo sangindeuri eoryeoumeul gyeokgo itda. Small merchants are having a hard time due to the big supermarkets.

장사 | ~하다 jang·sa | ~·ha·da business, commerce | to sell, deal in
장사는 잘 되세요? jangsaneun jal doeseyo? How's business?

영업 | ~하다 yeong·eop | ~·ha·da busi-ness, sales | to do business
토요일은 오후 다섯 시까지 영업합니다. to-yoireun ohu daseot sikkaji yeongeopamnida. We're open until 5 pm on Saturdays.

매매 | ~하다 mae·mae | ~·ha·da dealing | to trade
다음 주에 **매매** 계약을 체결할 예정입니다. daeum jue maemae gyeyageul chegyeolhal yejeongimnida. We'll sign the sales contract next week.

거래 | ~하다 geo·rae | ~·ha·da deal | to deal, trade

온라인 거래 전에 다음 약관을 잘 읽어 주십시오. **ollain georae jeone daeum nyakgwaneul jal ilgeo jusipsio.** Please read the following terms and conditions carefully before making transactions online.

계약 | ~하다 gye·yak | ~·ha·da contract | to contract
이 계약은 10년간 유효하다. **i gyeyageun simnyeongan nyuhyohada.** This contract is good for ten years.

계약서 gye·yak·seo contract
먼저 계약서를 좀 살펴보겠습니다. **meonjeo gyeyakseoreul jom salpyeobogetseumnida.** Let me take a look at the contract first.

시장 si·jang market
우리의 올해 과제는 새로운 시장을 개척하는 것입니다. **uriui olhae gwajeneun saeroun sijangeul gaecheokaneun geosimnida.** Our mission this year is to penetrate a new market.

유통 | ~되다 yu·tong | ~·doe·da distribution, circulation | to be distributed
이것들의 유통 가격은 얼마인가요? **igeotdeurui yutong gagyeogeun eolmaingayo?** What's the current market price for these?

거래처 geo·rae·cheo account, customer
방금 거래처에서 팩스를 받았어요. **banggeum georaecheoeseo paekseureul badasseoyo.** I just received a fax from our client.

도매 do·mae wholesale

소매 so·mae retail, retailing

가계 거액 가계 거액 건강보험 경기 경영 경제
경제적 계좌 계좌번호 공과금 공급 공황 관세 기업 나르다
납입 낭비 담보 대기업 대출 대출금 돈 망하다 매출 먹고살다
물가 밑천 배당 벌다 법인 보장 보험료 보험사 부가가치세
부자 부잣집 분배 불경기 사업 사업가 사회주의 상장하다
상환 생계 생산 생산자 세관 소득 소비세 소비자 손해 수입
수입품 수출 신다 안 액수 엔 연체하다 외제 외화 용돈
운반 운송 유산 융자 은행 이득 이윤 이율 인출 인플레이션
입금 자금 자원 잔돈 재산 산세 적자 절약 주가 주식
중소기업 지급 지출 지폐 직접세 창구 채무 청구 통장
통화 투자 투자자 현금지급기 혜택 화물 화폐 환전 흑자 건강보험

chapter 26 | The Economy

경기 경영 경제 경제적 계좌 계좌번호 공과금 공급 공황
관세 기업 나르다 납입 낭비 담보 대기업 대출 대출금
돈 망하다 매출 먹고살다 물가 밑천 배당 벌다 법인 보장
보험료 보험사 부가가치세 부자 부잣집 분배 불경기 사업 사업가
사회주의 상장하다 상환 생계 생산 생산자 세관 소득 소비세
소비자 손해 수입 수입품 수출 신다 안정 액수 엔
연체하다 외제 외화 용돈 운반 운송 유산 융자 은행
이득 이윤 이율 인출 인플레이션 입금 자금 자원 잔돈 재산 재산세
적자 절약 주가 주식 중소기업 지급 지출 지폐 직접세
창구 채무 청구 통장 통화 투자 투자자 현금지급기 혜택
화물 화폐 환전 흑자

26.1 The Economy, Trade

경제 gyeong·je the economy
세계 경제는 저성장 국면에 있습니다. segye gyeongjeneun jeoseongjang gungmyeone itseumnida. The world economy has been in a phase of decelerated growth.

자본주의 ja·bon·ju·ui capitalism

사회주의 sa·hoe·ju·ui socialism
북한은 아직도 **사회주의** 체제를 유지하고 있다. bukhaneun ajikdo sahoejuui chejereul lyujihago itda. North Korea still maintains the socialist system.

공산주의 gong·san·ju·ui communism

수요 su·yo demand
2013년에는 작은 아파트에 대한 **수요가 급증**할 것으로 예상된다. icheonsipsamnyeoneneun jageun apateue daehan suyoga geupjeunghal geoseuro yesangdoenda. We expect to see a sharp rise in demand for small apartments in 2013.

공급 | ~하다 gong·geup | ~·ha·da supply | to supply
수천 가정에 **전력 공급**이 중단되었다. sucheon gajeonge jeollyeok gonggeubi jungdandoeeotda. The electrical supply has been cut off for thousands of households.

생산 | ~하다 saeng·san | ~·ha·da production | to produce, manufacture
이 공장은 하루에 3만 개가 넘는 **제품을 생산**한다. i gongjangeun harue samman gaega neomneun jepumeul saengsanhanda. This factory produces more than 30,000 products a day.

국민총생산 gung·min·chong·saeng·san GNP (Gross National Product)

국내총생산 gung·nae·chong·saeng·san GDP (Gross Domestic Product)

생산자 saeng·san·ja producer, manufacturer

소비 | ~하다 so·bi | ~·ha·da consumption | to consume, spend
우리의 목표는 **에너지 소비**를 10% 줄이는 것입니다. uriui mokpyoneun eneoji sobireul sippeosenteu jurineun geosimnida. Our goal is to achieve a ten percent reduction in energy consumption.

소비자 so·bi·ja consumer
소비자 불만에 잘 대응하는 것은 매우 중요합니다. sobija bulmane jal daeeunghaneun geoseun maeu jungyohamnida. Handling customer complaints well is very important.

소득 ≒ 수입 so·deuk ≒ su·ip income, profit
소득 신고 했어? sodeuk singo haesseo? Have you declared your income?
저는 수입의/소득의 절반을 저축합니다. jeoneun suibui/sodeugui jeolbaneul jeochukamnida. I save half of my earnings.

국민소득 gung·min·so·deuk national income
2012년 우리나라의 1인당 국민소득은 미화 2만 달러가 넘었다. icheonsibinyeon urinaraui irindang gungminsodeugeun mihwa iman dalleoga neomeotda. In 2012, South Korea's per capita income surpassed 20,000 USD.

분배 | ~하다 bun·bae | ~·ha·da distribution | to distribute
부의 **균등한 분배**란 누구도 기아로 죽지 않는 것을 의미합니다. buui gyundeunghan bunbaeran nugudo giaro jukji anneun geoseul uimihamnida. Equal distribution of wealth means no one should die of hunger.

지출 ji·chul expense
저는 수입보다 지출이 많아요. jeoneun suipboda jichuri manayo. My expenses always exceed my income.

물가 mul·ga price
서울은 세계에서 가장 **물가가 비싼** 도시 중 하나예요. seoureun segyeeseo gajang mulgaga bissan dosi jung hanayeyo. Seoul is one of the most expensive cities in the world.

경기 gyeong·gi economy
경기가 작년보다 더 안 **좋아요**. gyeonggiga jangnyeonboda deo an joayo. The economy is worse than last year.

안정 | ~되다 an·jeong | ~·doe·da stability | to be stabilized
이 계획은 **물가 안정**에 초점을 맞추고 있다. i gyehoegeun mulga anjeonge chojeomeul matchugo itda. This plan focuses on price stabilization.

불경기 = 불황 bul·gyeong·gi = bul·

hwang recession, slump
불경기가/불황이 계속되면서 사람들의 구매가 줄고 있다. **bulgyeonggiga/bulhwangi gyesokdoemyeonseo saramdeurui gumaega julgo itda.** As the recession continues, people are buying less.

호경기 = 호황 ho·gyeong·gi = ho·hwang economic boom
제주도의 관광 산업이 호경기를/호황을 누리고 있다. **jejudoui gwangwang saneobi hogyeonggireul/hohwangeul lurigo itda.** The tourism industry on Jeju Island is booming.

인플레이션 in·peul·le·i·syeon inflation

(경제)공황 (gyeong·je·)gong·hwang economic crisis, depression

....

가계 ga·gye household budget
가계 지출을 줄이는 제 비결을 알려드리려고 해요. **gagye jichureul jurineun je bigyeoreul allyeodeuriryeogo haeyo.** I'd like to share my tips for saving on household expenses.

생계 saeng·gye living, livelihood
이 월급으로는 생계를 유지하기가 힘들어요. **i wolgeubeuroneun saenggyereul lyujihagiga himdeureoyo.** It's hard to make a living on this salary.

먹고살다 meok·go·sal·da to earn a living
먹고살기가 더 힘들어진 느낌이에요. **meokgosalgiga deo himdeureojin neukkimieyo.** I find it harder to make ends meet.

뼈(가) 빠지게 일하다 ppyeo(·ga) ppa·ji·ge il·ha·da to work one's fingers to the bone
아버지는 우리 가족을 위해 **뼈가 빠지게** 일하셨어요. **abeojineun uri gajogeul wihae ppyeoga ppajige ilhasyeosseoyo.** My father worked his fingers to the bone supporting my family.

벌다 beol·da to make (money)
당신이 **돈** 벌면 내가 아이 볼게. **dangsini don beolmyeon naega ai bolge.** I'll take care of the children if you make the money.

절약 | ~하다 jeo·ryak | ~·ha·da saving, conservation | to save, conserve
저는 늘 전기를 절약하려고 노력합니다. **jeoneun neul jeongireul jeollyakaryeogo noryeokamnida.** I always try to save electricity.

아끼다 a·kki·da to save, conserve
물을 아껴 씁시다. **mureul akkyeo sseupsida.** Let's not waste water.

경제적 gyeong·je·jeok economical
어느 쪽이 더 경제적이야? **eoneu jjogi deo gyeongjejeogiya?** Which one is more economical?

낭비 | ~하다 nang·bi | ~·ha·da waste, dissipation | to waste
그건 시간 낭비일 뿐이야. **geugeon sigan nangbiil ppuniya.** It's only a waste of time.

용돈 yong·don allowance
용돈 좀 제발 올려주세요. **yongdon jom jebal ollyeojuseyo.** Can I get a raise on my allowance, please?

재산 jae·san property, wealth
나는 부모님으로부터 많은 재산을 물려받았다. **naneun bumonimeurobuteo maneun jaesaneul mullyeobadatda.** I inherited a huge property from my parents.

부자 bu·ja rich person
부자라고 반드시 행복한 것은 아니다. **bujarago bandeusi haengbokan geoseun anida.** The rich are not necessarily happy.

부잣집 bu·jat·jip rich family
아내는 부잣집 외동딸이에요. **anaeneun bujatjip oedongttarieyo.** My wife is the only daughter of a wealthy family.

유산 yu·san legacy, bequest

....

무역 mu·yeok trade, commerce
저는 해외 무역 일을 하고 있어서 외국에 자주 나갑니다. **jeoneun haeoe muyeok ireul hago isseoseo oeguge jaju nagamnida.** I'm engaged in foreign trade and often go abroad.

세관 se·gwan customs
세관을 통과할 때 문제가 있었나요? **segwaneul tonggwahal ttae munjega isseonnayo?** Did you have any trouble getting through customs?

관세 gwan·se duty, tariff
정부는 수입 위스키에 대한 관세를 낮추기로 결정했다. **jeongbuneun suip wiseukie daehan gwansereul latchugiro gyeoljeonghaetda.** The government has decided to lower customs duties on imported whisky.

화물 hwa·mul freight, cargo

운송 | ~하다 un·song | ~·ha·da transportation, shipping | to transport, carry
이 배는 무거운 화물을 운송할 수 있게 설계되어 있다. **i baeneun mugeoun hwamureul unsonghal su itge seolgyedoeeo itda.** This boat is

designed for transporting heavy loads.

운반 | ~하다 un·ban | ~·ha·da transportation | to transport
상품들은 기차로 운반됩니다. sangpumdeureun gicharo unbandoemnida. The goods are transported by train.

나르다 na·reu·da to carry, transport

싣다 sit·da to load
트럭에 짐을 다 실었어? teureoge jimeul da sireosseo? Have you finished loading the truck?

송장 song·jang invoice
첨부된 송장 사본을 확인 바랍니다. cheombudoen songjang saboneul hwagin baramnida. Please find the attached copy of your invoice.

수출 | ~하다 su·chul | ~·ha·da exportation, export | to export
저희 제품은 전 세계 30개국 이상으로 수출되고 있습니다. jeohui jepumeun jeon segye samsipgaeguk isangeuro suchuldoego itseumnida. Our products are being exported to more than 30 countries around the world.

수출품 su·chul·pum export
한국의 **주요 수출품**에는 전자제품, 기계, 자동차, 철강, 조선 등이 있다. hangugui juyo suchulpumeneun jeonjajepum, gigye, jadongcha, cheolgang, joseon deungi itda. South Korea's main exports include electronic products, machinery, automobiles, steel, and ships.

수입 | ~하다 su·ip | ~·ha·da importation, import | to import
이 판매대에 놓인 모든 상품들이 중국에서 수입된 것입니다. i panmaedaee noin modeun sangpumdeuri junggugeseo suipdoen geosimnida. All of the items you see on this counter were imported from China.

수입품 su·ip·pum imports
값싼 수입품이 국내 산업을 위협하고 있다. gapssan suippumi gungnae saneobeul wihyeopago itda. Cheap imports are threatening domestic industry.

국산 guk·san domestic, domestically produced

외제 oe·je foreign, imported
이 시계 국산이야, 외제야? i sigye guksaniya, oejeya? Is this watch a domestic brand or a foreign brand?

자원 ja·won resources
우리나라는 **자원**이 부족합니다. urinaraneun jawoni bujokamnida. My country is poor in resources.

26.2 Money, Finance

돈 don money
지금 당장은 **돈**이 없어요. jigeum dangjangeun doni eopseoyo. I have no money right now.

통화 tong·hwa currency
유럽 국가들 중 다수가 유로를 **통화 단위**로 사용한다. yureop gukgadeul jung dasuga yuroreul tonghwa danwiro sayonghanda. Many of the countries in Europe use the Euro as their currency.

화폐 hwa·pye money, currency
한국의 **화폐 단위**는 '원'입니다. hangugui hwapye danwineun wonimnida. The monetary unit of Korea is the won.

지폐 ji·pye bill, note
만 원짜리 지폐를 잔돈으로 바꿀 수 있을까요? man wonjjari jipyereul jandoneuro bakkul su isseulkkayo? Do you have change for a ten thousand won bill?

동전 dong·jeon coin, change
A: 동전 있어? B: 아니, 지폐뿐이야. A: dongjeon isseo? B: ani, jipyeppuniya. A: Do you have any coins? B: No, only bills.

잔돈 jan·don small change
잔돈 없으세요? jandon eopseuseyo? Do you have smaller bills?

액수 aek·su sum (of money)
간단한 비법 몇 개를 따라 하면 **상당한 액수**의 돈을 아낄 수 있습니다. gandanhan bibeop myeot gaereul ttara hamyeon sangdanghan aeksuui doneul akkil su itseumnida. You can save a good amount of money by following a few simple tips.

금액 geu·maek sum of money
모두 합해서 금액이 얼마입니까? modu hapaeseo geumaegi eolmaimnikka? How much is it all together?

거액 geo·aek fortune, large sum of money
침몰한 배를 구조하는 비용은 거액에 달한다. chimmolhan baereul gujohaneun biyongeun geoaege dalhanda. The cost for salvaging a sunken ship amounts to a huge sum.

원 won won (the monetary unit of Korea)

외화 oe·hwa foreign currency
수출은 우리나라의 주 **외화 획득원**이다. su-chureun urinaraui ju oehwa hoekdeugwonida. Exports are Korea's biggest foreign currency earner.

달러 dal·leo dollar
1달러는 1000원 가량 됩니다. ildalleoneun cheonwon garyang doemnida. One dollar is equivalent to around a thousand won.

엔 en yen

금융 geu·myung finance
여러분은 **금융 기관**들로부터 우편물을 대거 받으실 겁니다. yeoreobuneun geumyung gi-gwandeullobuteo upyeonmureul daegeo badeusil geomnida. You may receive a multitude of mailings from financial institutions.

주식 ju·sik stock, share
주식 거래에는 늘 위험이 따른다. jusik geo-raeeneun neul wiheomi ttareunda. There is always a risk in trading stocks.

증권 jeung·gwon securities, stock
전문가들은 **증권 시장** 붕괴에 대비해야 한다고 조언한다. jeonmungadeureun jeunggwon sijang bunggoee daebihaeya handago joeon-handa. Experts warn people to prepare for a stock market crash.

주주 ju·ju stockholder
모든 직원들이 주주는 아니지만 모든 주주는 직원입니다. modeun jigwondeuri jujuneun ani-jiman modeun jujuneun jigwonimnida. Not all employees are shareholders but all share-holders are employees.

주가 ju·ga stock price
지난달에 **주가가** 급격히 **하락했다**. jinandare jugaga geupgyeoki harakaetda. There was a severe downswing in stock prices last month.

투자 | ~하다 tu·ja | ~·ha·da investment | to invest
저는 **주식 투자**로 많은 돈을 벌었습니다. jeoneun jusik tujaro maneun doneul beoreot-seumnida. I made a lot of money by investing in stocks.

투자자 tu·ja·ja investor
주식에 대한 투자자들의 관심이 높아지고 있다. jusige daehan tujajadeurui gwansimi nopa-jigo itda. Investors are becoming more interested in stocks.

배당 | ~하다 bae·dang | ~·ha·da distri-bution, allocation | to distribute, allocate, pay a dividend
우리는 연말에 주주들에게 배당을 합니다. urineun nyeonmare jujudeurege baedangeul hamnida. We pay dividends to shareholders at the end of the year.

상장하다 sang·jang·ha·da to list a com-pany on the stock market
저희 회사는 2년 전에 주식 시장에 상장되었어요. jeohui hoesaneun inyeon jeone jusik si-jange sangjangdoeeosseoyo. Our company was listed on the stock market two years ago.

증권사 jeung·gwon·sa stock trading firm

채권 chae·gwon bond
이 채권들은 3년 후에 만기가 된다. i chae-gwondeureun samnyeon hue mangiga doenda. These bonds reach maturity in three years.

보험 bo·heom insurance
어떤 **보험**을 드셨어요? eotteon boheomeul deusyeosseoyo? What kind of insurance do you have?

건강보험 geon·gang·bo·heom health in-surance

보장 | ~하다 bo·jang | ~·ha·da coverage | to cover
그 보험은 어떤 것들을 보장해 주나요? geu boheomeun eotteon geotdeureul bojanghae ju-nayo? What is covered by the insurance?

보험사 bo·heom·sa insurance company

보험료 bo·heom·nyo premium
보험료가 50퍼센트 **인상되었어요**. boheom-nyoga osippeosenteu insangdoeeosseoyo. In-surance premiums have increased by 50 percent.

납입 = 납부 | ~하다 na·bip = nap·bu | ~·ha·da payment | to pay
매달 **보험료를 납입하는/납부하는** 것이 한 번에 큰돈을 내는 것보다 낫다. maedal boheom-nyoreul labipaneun/napbuhaneun geosi han beone keundoneul laeneun geotboda natda. Paying a monthly fee for insurance is better than paying a lot of money at once.

보험금 bo·heom·geum insurance

청구 | ~하다 cheong·gu | ~·ha·da claim, charge | to demand, claim
보험 약관에 따라 **보험금을 청구하려고** 할 때 다음 순서를 따르세요. **boheom nyakgwane ttara boheomgeumeul cheongguharyeogo hal ttae daeum sunseoreul ttareuseyo.** If you need to make an insurance claim, follow these steps.

지급 | ~하다 ji·geup | ~·ha·da payment | to pay, give, provide
보험사는 **보험금 지급을** 거부했다. **boheomsaneun boheomgeum jigeubeul geobuhaetda.** The insurance company refused to pay.

펀드 peon·deu fund

경매 gyeong·mae auction

····················

은행 eun·haeng bank
은행 문을 몇 시에 닫나요? **eunhaeng muneul myeot sie dannayo?** What time does the bank close?

창구 chang·gu counter
2번 창구에서 공과금을 납부하실 수 있습니다. **ibeon changgueseo gonggwageumeul lapbuhasil su itseumnida.** You can pay your utility bills at Counter 2.

계좌 gye·jwa account
저희 은행에 **계좌를** 갖고 계신가요? **jeohui eunhaenge gyejwareul gatgo gyesingayo?** Do you have an account with our bank?

계좌번호 gye·jwa·beon·ho account number
계좌번호가 어떻게 되세요? **gyejwabeonhoga eotteoke doeseyo?** What is your account number, please?

통장 tong·jang bankbook
통장 정리를 하고 싶어요. **tongjang jeongnireul hago sipeoyo.** I want to update my bankbook.

저축 ≒ 저금 | ~하다 jeo·chuk ≒ jeo·geum | ~·ha·da saving; savings, deposit | to save, deposit
저축/저금 많이 하세요? **jeochuk/jeogeum mani haseyo?** Do you save a lot of money?

예금 | ~하다 ye·geum | ~·ha·da saving; savings, deposit | to save, deposit
얼마나 예금하시겠습니까? **eolmana yegeumhasigetseumnikka?** How much would you like to deposit?

대출 | ~하다 dae·chul | ~·ha·da loan | to loan
대출을 좀 **받고** 싶은데요. **daechureul jom batgo sipeundeyo.** I want to take out a loan.

융자 | ~하다 yung·ja | ~·ha·da financing, loan | to loan
이 집은 **은행 융자**를 받아 산 거예요. **i jibeun eunhaeng yungjareul bada san geoyeyo.** We bought this house with a bank loan.

빌리다 bil·li·da to borrow, take out a loan

담보 dam·bo security, collateral
집을 담보로 돈을 빌렸어요. **jibeul damboro doneul billyeosseoyo.** I borrowed money using my house as collateral.

보증 bo·jeung surety
대출을 위해서는 **보증을** 서실 분이 필요합니다. **daechureul wihaeseoneun bojeungeul seosil buni piryohamnida.** A person who will stand surety for the loan is required.

대출금 dae·chul·geum loan

채무 chae·mu debt, liabilities, payables
이 프로그램은 과도한 **채무 부담**을 경감하기 위해 만들어졌습니다. **i peurogeuraemeun gwadohan chaemu budameul gyeonggamhagi wihae mandeureojyeotseumnida.** This program is designed to relieve excessive debt burdens.

대금 dae·geum payment

빚 bit debt, liabilities

지다 ji·da to owe
그 사람한테 **빚을** 얼마나 **진** 거야? **geu saramhante bijeul eolmana jin geoya?** How much do you owe him?

갚다 gap·da to repay
대출금은 다 **갚았어? daechulgeumeun da gapasseo?** Did you pay back your loan?

상환 | ~하다 sang·hwan | ~·ha·da repayment | to pay back, repay
대출금은 이번 달 말까지 **상환해야** 합니다. **daechulgeumeun ibeon dal malkkaji sanghwanhaeya hamnida.** The loan is due by the end of the month.

연체하다 yeon·che·ha·da to fall behind
귀하의 신용카드 **대금이 연체**되었습니다. **gwihaui sinnyongkadeu daegeumi yeonchedoeeotseumnida.** You've fallen behind on your credit card payments.

원금 won·geum principal

이자 i·ja interest
갚아야 할 **원금과 이자**를 모두 합하면 3억에 달한다. gapaya hal wongeumgwa ijareul modu hapamyeon sameoge dalhanda. Total principal and interest to be repaid amount to 300 million won.

이(자)율 = 금리 i(·ja)·yul = geum·ni interest rate
현재 **은행 예금 이율**은/금리는 5퍼센트도 채 안 된다. hyeonjae eunhaeng yegeum iyureun/geumnineun opeosenteudo chae an doenda. The current interest rate of bank deposits is less than 5 percent.

현금(자동)지급기 = 현금인출기 hyeon·geum(·ja·dong)·ji·geup·gi = hyeon·geu·min·chul·gi ATM
가까운 **현금지급기가/현금인출기**가 어디에 있나요? gakkaun hyeongeumjigeupgiga/hyeongeuminchulgiga eodie innayo? Where is the nearest ATM?

인출 | ~하다 in·chul | ~·ha·da withdrawal | to withdraw
귀하는 하루에 5백만 원까지 인출하실 수 있습니다. gwihaneun harue obaengman wonkkaji inchulhasil su itseumnida. You can withdraw a maximum of five million won a day.

이체 | ~하다 i·che | ~·ha·da transfer | to transfer
그 돈을 제 계좌로 이체해 주실 수 있습니까? geu doneul je gyejwaro ichehae jusil su itseumnikka? Can you transfer the money to my savings account?

입금 | ~하다 ip·geum | ~·ha·da deposit | to deposit
돈은 일주일 후에 귀하의 **계좌에 입금**될 것입니다. doneun iljuil hue gwihaui gyejwae ipgeum-

doel geosimnida. The money will be deposited into your bank account in a week.

환율 hwa·nyul exchange rate
환율이 급격히 **떨어졌다**. hwanyuri geupgyeo-ki tteoreojyeotda. The exchange rate has fallen sharply.

환전 | ~하다 hwan·jeon | ~·ha·da exchange | to exchange, change
원화를 달러로 환전하고 싶은데요. won-hwareul dalleoro hwanjeonhago sipeundeyo. I need to change won into dollars.

금고 geum·go safe, strongbox

세금 se·geum tax
어째서 세금은 항상 오르기만 하는 겁니까? eojjaeseo segeumeun hangsang oreugiman haneun geomnikka? How come taxes go up all the time?

간접세 gan·jeop·se indirect tax

직접세 jik·jeop·se direct tax

국세 guk·se national tax

지방세 ji·bang·se local tax

부가가치세 bu·ga·ga·chi·se value-added tax

소득세 so·deuk·se income tax

소비세 so·bi·se sales tax

재산세 jae·san·se property tax

주민세 ju·min·se residence tax

공과금 gong·gwa·geum utility bill
저는 **공과금**을 자동 이체로 납부합니다. jeoneun gonggwageumeul jadong ichero napbu-hamnida. I pay my utility bills via automatic withdrawal.

26.3 Business

사업 sa·eop business, enterprise
내 **개인 사업**을 시작할까 생각 중이야. nae gaein saeobeul sijakalkka saenggak jungiya. I'm thinking of starting my own business.

사업가 sa·eop·ga entrepreneur
제 아버지는 **타고난 사업가**세요. je abeoji-neun tagonan saeopgaseyo. My father is a born businessman.

매출 mae·chul sales
이번 분기 **매출**이 두 배로 **상승했어요**. ibeon bungi maechuri du baero sangseunghaesseoyo. Sales figures this quarter have doubled.

이익 i·ik profit, gain
어떤 기업도 **이익**을 창출하지 않고 오래 살아 남을 수 없다. eotteon gieopdo iigeul chang-chulhaji anko orae saranameul su eopda. No company survives long without profits.

이윤 i·yun profit, gain
올해는 우리 회사 역사상 최고의 **이윤을 올린**
해였습니다. olhaeneun uri hoesa yeoksasang
choegoui iyuneul ollin haeyeotseumnida. We
had the most profitable year in the history
of our company.

수익 su·ik profit, gain
우리 회사의 **수익이** 작년에 비해 크게 **떨어졌**
다. uri hoesaui suigi jangnyeone bihae keuge
tteoreojyeotda. Our company's earnings have
dropped significantly compared to the previous year.

이득 i·deuk profit, benefit
양쪽에 모두 **이득이 있습니다.** yangjjoge
modu ideugi itseumnida. There are benefits
for both parties.

혜택 hye·taek benefit
회원이 되면 어떤 **혜택이 있나요?** hoewoni
doemyeon eotteon hyetaegi innayo? What are
the benefits of becoming a member?

흑자 heuk·ja surplus
작년에 한국은 사상 최고의 무역 **흑자를 기록**
했다. jangnyeone hangugeun sasang choegoui
muyeok eukjareul girokaetda. Last year, Korea
recorded its largest trade surplus ever.

손실 son·sil loss
그 회사는 화재로 큰 금전적 **손실을 입었다.**
geu hoesaneun hwajaero keun geumjeonjeok
sonsireul ibeotda. The company has lost a lot
of money due to the fire.

손해 son·hae damage, loss
그들은 큰 **손해를 입고** 회사를 매각했다. geudeureun keun sonhaereul ipgo hoesareul mae-
gakaetda. They sold the business at a big
loss.

적자 jeok·ja deficit, loss
지금으로서는 **적자를 메울** 방법이 없다. ji-
geumeuroseoneun jeokjareul meul bangbeobi
eopda. There is no way to make up for the
deficit at the moment.

밑천 mit·cheon seed money, seed capital
이 사업은 상대적으로 적은 밑천으로 시작할
수 있어요. i saeobeun sangdaejeogeuro jeogeun
mitcheoneuro sijakal su isseoyo. You can start
this business with relatively little money.

자금 ja·geum funds, money
회사의 **자금 사정이** 악화되고 있습니다. hoe-
saui jageum sajeongi akhwadoego itseumnida.
The company's financial situation is deteriorating.

자본 ja·bon capital
외국 자본이 엄청난 속도로 국내로 유입되고
있다. oeguk jaboni eomcheongnan sokdoro
gungnaero yuipdoego itda. Foreign capital is
flowing into the country at an enormous
pace.

망하다 mang·ha·da to go bankrupt, go
broke
지난 한 달간 얼마나 많은 **회사들이 망했는지**
아세요? jinan han dalgan eolmana maneun hoe-
sadeuri manghaenneunji aseyo? Do you know
how many companies have gone bankrupt
during the last month?

회사 hoe·sa company
저는 작은 **회사를** 운영하고 있습니다. jeo-
neun jageun hoesareul unyeonghago itseumnida. I run a small business.

기업 gi·eop business, enterprise, company
우리는 **외국 기업과의** 기술 협력을 추진하고
있습니다. urineun oeguk gieopgwaui gisul
hyeomnyeogeul chujinhago itseumnida. We are
seeking a technological partnership with a
foreign company.

법인 beo·bin corporation, corporate body
중국에 **해외 법인을** 설립하고자 한다면 고려
해야 할 사항이 몇 가지 있습니다. jungguge
haeoe beobineul seollipagoja handamyeon
goryeohaeya hal sahangi myeot gaji itseumnida. If you would like to establish a foreign
corporation in China, there are a few things
to consider.

대기업 dae·gi·eop major company; con-
glomerate
저희는 **대기업과** 거래하고 있습니다. jeohuineun daegieopgwa georaehago itseumnida.
We are making a deal with a major company.

중소기업 jung·so·gi·eop small and medi-
um-sized businesses
정부는 **중소기업 지원을** 약속했다. jeongbuneun jungsogieop jiwoneul lyaksokaetda.
The government promised to help small
businesses.

세우다 se·u·da to establish, found
내년에 인도에 **공장을 세울** 예정입니다. nae-
nyeone indoe gongjangeul seul yejeongimnida.
We're planning to establish a factory in India next year.

설립 | ~하다 seol·lip | ~·ha·da establishment, foundation | to establish, found, set up

우리는 1990년에 **회사를 설립한** 이래 많은 외국인들을 지원해 왔습니다. urineun cheongubaekgusimnyeone hoesareul seollipan irae maneun oegugindeureul jiwonhae watseumnida. We have supported many foreigners since we set up our firm in 1990.

경영 | ~하다 gyeong·yeong | ~·ha·da management | to manage

올해에는 **경영 환경**에 중대한 변화가 있었습니다. olhaeeneun gyeongyeong hwangyeonge jungdaehan byeonhwaga isseotseumnida. There was a significant change in the business environment this year.

운영 | ~하다 u·nyeong | ~·ha·da management | to manage, run, operate

저희는 직원들을 위해 탁아 **프로그램을 운영하고** 있습니다. jeohuineun jigwondeureul wihae taga peurogeuraemeul unyeonghago itseumnida. We run a daycare program for the employees' children.

검색 광고 검색 광고 그래픽카드 기사 기자 깔다 끄다
다 내려받다 내보내다 녹화방송 뉴스 다큐멘터리 데스크톱
드라마 매스컴 메모 바꾸다 바이러스 발행 방송 방영되다
백과사전 백업 복사 본문 부 부수 부치다 불러오다 붙여넣다 블로그
빠른우편 사이트 사전 삭제 생방송 서핑 소식 쇼 수화기
스마트폰 스타 스튜디오 스팸 시청률 시청자 신문사 싣다
아이디 업그레이드 업데이트 업로드 엽서 영상 예능 오류 온라인
올리다 우체국 우표 위성방송 유선전화 음성 인쇄 입력
잡지 잡지사 재방송 저장하다 전화기 제목 즐겨찾기 지우다
동 쪽 채팅 청취 출연자 취재 커서 컴퓨터 켜다 클릭 키보드
탤런트 통 통신 팬 페이지 프로그램 프린터 피디 하드
핸드폰 형성 확장자 회견 그래픽카드 기사 기자 깔다

chapter **27** | Communications

끄다 끝다 내려받다 내보내다 녹화방송 뉴스 다큐멘터리 달다
데스크톱 드라마 매스컴 메모 바꾸다 바이러스 발행 방송
방영되다 방청 백과사전 백업 복사 본문 부 부수 부치다 불러오다
붙여넣다 블로그 빠른우편 사이트 사전 삭제 생방송 서핑 소식
수화기 스마트폰 스타 스튜디오 스팸 시청률 시청자 신문사 싣다
아이디 업그레이드 업데이트 업로드 엽서 영상 예능 오류 온라인
올리다 우체국 우표 위성방송 유선전화 음성 인쇄 입력
잡지 잡지사 재방송 저장하다 전화기 제목 즐겨찾기 지우다
진동 쪽 채팅 청취 출연자 취재 커서 컴퓨터 켜다
클릭 키보드 탤런트 통 통신 팬 페이지 프로그램 프린터
피디 하드 핸드폰 형성 확장자 회견

27.1 Postal Service, Telecommunications

통신 tong·sin communication
악천후로 두 섬 간의 **통신이** 끊겼다. akcheon-huro du seom ganui tongsini kkeunkyeotda. Bad weather interrupted telephone communications between the two islands.

(의사)소통 (ui·sa·)so·tong communication
우리는 의사소통에 문제가 없습니다. urineun uisasotonge munjega eopseumnida. We have no communication problem.

전달 | ~하다 jeon·dal | ~·ha·da delivery | to deliver, pass on
영어로 **의사를 전달하지** 못해 답답했어요. yeongeoro uisareul jeondalhaji motae dapdapaesseoyo. I felt frustrated because I could not express myself properly in English.

전하다 jeon·ha·da to tell, convey
그 사람한테 제가 전화했었다고 전해 주세요. geu saramhante jega jeonhwahaesseotdago jeonhae juseyo. Could you let him know that I called?

소식 so·sik news, word
몇 가지 **좋은 소식이** 있어요. myeot gaji joeun sosigi isseoyo. I have some good news for you.

·······································

우편 u·pyeon mail

빠른우편 ppa·reu·nu·pyeon express mail

보통우편 bo·tong·u·pyeon regular mail
빠른우편과 보통우편 중에 어느 것으로 보내시겠어요? ppareunupyeongwa botongupyeon junge eoneu geoseuro bonaesigesseoyo? Do you want to send this by express or regular mail?

편지 pyeon·ji letter
이 편지를 우체통에 넣어야 하거든요. i pyeonjireul uchetonge neoeoya hageodeunnyo. I have to put this letter in the mailbox.

엽서 yeop·seo postcard

소포 so·po parcel
저는 여기에 **소포 찾으러** 왔는데요. jeoneun nyeogie sopo chajeureo wanneundeyo. I'm here to pick up a parcel.

우체국 u·che·guk post office
우체국은 어느 쪽이에요? uchegugeun eoneu jjogieyo? Which way is to the post office?

우체통 u·che·tong mailbox

우편번호 u·pyeon·beon·ho postal code, zip code
주소와 **우편번호를** 입력하세요. jusowa upyeonbeonhoreul imnyeokaseyo. Type in your address and zip code.

우표 u·pyo stamp

붙이다 bu·chi·da to stick, attach, glue
봉투에 **우표 붙였어?** bongtue upyo buchyeosseo? Did you put a stamp on the envelope?

부치다 bu·chi·da to send, mail
어제 집으로 **소포를 부쳤어요.** eoje jibeuro soporeul buchyeosseoyo. I sent a package home yesterday.

보내다 bo·nae·da to send, mail
매주 **엽서 보낼게.** maeju yeopseo bonaelge. I'll send you a postcard every week.

답장 | ~하다 dap·jang | ~·ha·da reply, answer | to reply, answer
우리는 그들의 **답장을 기다리고** 있어요. urineun geudeurui dapjangeul gidarigo isseoyo. We are waiting for their reply.

연락 | ~하다 yeol·lak | ~·ha·da contact | to contact
저는 예전 직장 동료들과 아직도 연락하고 지내요. jeoneun yejeon jikjang dongnyodeulgwa ajikdo yeollakago jinaeyo. I'm still in contact with my former colleagues.

·······································

전화 | ~하다 jeon·hwa | ~·ha·da telephone | to call

통 tong unit for counting phone calls
전화 한 통 써도 될까요? jeonhwa han tong sseodo doelkkayo? Can I use your phone?

전화번호 jeon·hwa·beon·ho phone number
전화번호 알려주시면 내일 제가 전화할게요. jeonhwabeonho allyeojusimyeon naeil jega jeonhwahalgeyo. Give me your phone number and I will call you tomorrow.

연락처 yeol·lak·cheo contact number
연락처를 남겨 주세요. yeollakcheoreul lamgyeo juseyo. Please leave your contact number here.

번 beon number

몇 번으로 거셨어요? myeot beoneuro geosyeosseoyo? What number did you call?

전화기 jeon·hwa·gi telephone set

수화기 su·hwa·gi telephone receiver

집전화 jip·jeon·hwa home phone
점점 더 많은 사람들이 집전화 대신 무선전화를 사용한다. jeomjeom deo maneun saramdeuri jipjeonhwa daesin museonjeonhwareul sayonghanda. More and more people use their cell phones instead of their home phones.

유선전화 yu·seon·jeon·hwa corded telephone

무선전화 mu·seon·jeon·hwa cordless phone

핸드폰 = 휴대폰 = 휴대전화 haen·deu·pon = hyu·dae·pon = hyu·dae·jeon·hwa cell phone
운전 중 핸드폰/휴대폰/휴대전화 사용은 법으로 금지되어 있습니다. unjeon jung haendeupon/hyudaepon/hyudaejeonhwa sayongeun beobeuro geumjidoeeo itseumnida. Using a cell phone while driving is prohibited by law.

스마트폰 seu·ma·teu·pon smartphone
스마트폰으로 다양한 일을 할 수 있어요. seumateuponeuro dayanghan ireul hal su isseoyo. You can do various things with a smartphone.

공중전화 gong·jung·jeon·hwa pay phone, public phone
요즘은 공중전화를 보기가 힘들어. yojeumeun gongjungjeonhwareul bogiga himdeureo. These days, it is hard to find a pay phone.

전화벨 jeon·hwa·bel ring

벨소리 bel·so·ri ringtone
이거 네 벨소리 아냐? igeo ne belsori anya? Isn't your telephone ringing?

진동 jin·dong vibration
지하철에서는 핸드폰을 진동으로 하세요. jihacheoreseoneun haendeuponeul jindongeuro haseyo. Put your cell phone on vibration mode.

메시지 me·si·ji message

메모 | ~하다 me·mo | ~·ha·da note, message | to make a note
메모를 남기시겠어요? memoreul lamgisigesseoyo? Would you like to leave a message?

문자 (메시지) mun·ja (me·si·ji) text message
내 문자 받았어? nae munja badasseo? Did you get my text message?

음성 (메시지) eum·seong (me·si·ji) voice message

통화 | ~하다 tong·hwa | ~·ha·da telephone conversation | to speak over the phone
그 사람 지금 통화 중이야. geu saram jigeum tonghwa jungiya. He's on the phone now.

걸다 geol·da to call, phone
제가 전화를 잘못 걸었나 봐요. jega jeonhwareul jalmot georeonna bwayo. I think I have the wrong number.

울리다 ul·li·da to sound, ring
전화벨이 시끄럽게 울렸다. jeonhwaberi sikkeureopge ullyeotda. The phone rang loudly.

여보세요 yeo·bo·se·yo hello
여보세요. yeoboseyo. Hello.

바꾸다 ba·kku·da to change, switch
은지 좀 바꿔 주시겠어요? eunji jom bakkwo jusigesseoyo? Can I talk to Eunji?

부재중 bu·jae·jung one's absence
저는 지금 부재중이니 메시지를 남겨 주세요. jeoneun jigeum bujaejungini mesijireul lamgyeo juseyo. I'm out now. Please leave a message.

부재중전화 bu·jae·jung·jeon·hwa missed call
부재중전화가 세 통 와 있네. bujaejungjeonhwaga se tong wa inne. There are three missed calls.

끊다 kkeun·ta to hang up
전화 끊고 다시 걸게요. jeonhwa kkeunko dasi geolgeyo. I'll hang up and dial again.

끊기다 kkeun·ki·da to be disconnected, be cut off
전화가 끊겼어요. jeonhwaga kkeunkyeosseoyo. I was disconnected.

27.2 The Press, Broadcasts

언론 eol·lon the press
언론은 여론의 형성에 큰 역할을 한다. eol-loneun nyeoronui hyeongseonge keun nyeokareul handa. The media plays a major role in forming people's opinions.

미디어 = 매체 mi·di·eo = mae·che media

매스컴 mae·seu·keom the mass media
매스컴에서 계속해서 그 사건을 다루고 있다. maeseukeomeseo gyesokaeseo geu sageoneul darugo itda. The media has been covering the story for days.

> 매스컴 is from the English word *mass communication*. However, it actually refers to the mass media.

대중 dae·jung the public
대중은 전혀 현명하지 않다. daejungeun jeonhyeo hyeonmyeonghaji anta. The public is not smart at all.

여론 yeo·ron public opinion
정치인들은 여론에 민감하다. jeongchiindeureun nyeorone mingamhada. Politicians are sensitive to public opinion.

형성 | ~하다 hyeong·seong | ~·ha·da formation | to form

방송 | ~하다 bang·song | ~·ha·da broadcasting, broadcast | to broadcast, air
그 경기 언제 방송해요? geu gyeonggi eonje bangsonghaeyo? When will the game be broadcast?

생방송 saeng·bang·song live broadcast

녹화방송 no·khwa·bang·song filmed TV broadcast
A: 저 게임 생방송이에요? B: 아뇨, 녹화방송이요. A: jeo geim saengbangsongieyo? B: anyo, nokhwabangsongiyo. A: Is that game a live broadcast? B: No, it is recorded.

중계방송 jung·gye·bang·song relay broadcasting

공개방송 gong·gae·bang·song public broadcasting

위성방송 wi·seong·bang·song satellite broadcasting

유선방송 = 케이블(방송) yu·seon·bang·song = ke·i·beul(·bang·song) cable

재방송 | ~되다 jae·bang·song | ~·doe·da rerun | to rerun
대부분의 채널이 재방송을 내보내고 있다. daebubunui chaeneori jaebangsongeul laebonaego itda. Most of the channels are broadcasting reruns.

방송국 bang·song·guk broadcasting station

스튜디오 seu·tyu·di·o studio

방송사 bang·song·sa broadcasting company

광고 gwang·go advertisement, commercial
너무 잦은 중간 광고는 정말 짜증 나. neomu jajeun junggan gwanggoneun jeongmal jjajeung na. Having too many commercial interruptions is really annoying.

텔레비전 = 티브이 tel·le·bi·jeon = ti·beu·i television

영상 yeong·sang picture, image

화면 hwa·myeon screen
왜 티브이 화면이 이렇게 어둡지? wae tibeui hwamyeoni ireoke eodupji? Why is the TV screen so dark?

채널 chae·neol channel
7번 채널에서는 무슨 프로그램 해? chilbeon chaeneoreseoneun museun peurogeuraem hae? What program is on channel seven?

켜다 kyeo·da to turn on
저는 집에 오면 버릇처럼 텔레비전을 켭니다. jeoneun jibe omyeon beoreutcheoreom tellebijeoneul kyeomnida. I come home and turn on the TV out of habit.

끄다 kkeu·da to switch off
아직 티브이 끄지 마. ajik tibeui kkeuji ma. Don't switch the TV off yet.

돌리다 dol·li·da to change, convert
채널 좀 그만 돌려. chaeneol jom geuman dollyeo. Stop changing the channels.

시청 | ~하다 si·cheong | ~·ha·da watching | to watch
그녀는 아이의 TV 시청을 일주일 동안 금지했다. geunyeoneun aiui tibeui sicheongeul iljuil

dongan geumjihaetda. She banned her kid from watching TV for a week.

시청자 si·cheong·ja viewer
시청자들에게 새 앨범에 대해 말씀해 주시겠어요? **sicheongjadeurege sae aelbeome daehae malsseumhae jusigesseoyo?** Could you tell our viewers about your new album?

시청률 si·cheong·nyul (viewer) ratings
지난 한 달 사이에 **시청률이** 약간 **떨어졌다**. jinan han dal saie sicheongnyuri yakgan tteoreojyeotda. Ratings have slightly fallen over the past month.

출연 | ~하다 chu·ryeon | ~·ha·da appearance | to appear
그는 **텔레비전에** 한 번 **출연한** 다음 갑자기 유명해졌다. geuneun tellebijeone han beon churyeonhan daeum gapjagi yumyeonghaejyeotda. He became famous overnight after appearing on television.

출연자 chu·ryeon·ja program guest

드라마 = 연속극 deu·ra·ma = yeon·sok·geuk soap opera

탤런트 tael·leon·teu TV actor, TV actress

방영되다 bang·yeong·doe·da to be broadcast
그 **드라마는** 매주 토요일 저녁에 **방영된다**. geu deuramaneun maeju toyoil jeonyeoge bangyeongdoenda. The drama is aired every Saturday night.

예능 ye·neung entertainment

프로(그램) peu·ro(·geu·raem) program, show
아버지는 **텔레비전 프로라고는** 뉴스밖에 안 보세요. abeojineun tellebijeon peurorogoneun nyuseubakke an boseyo. My father watches nothing but the news on TV.

쇼 syo show
주부들을 위한 **퀴즈 쇼가** 몇 개 있습니다. jubudeureul wihan kwijeu syoga myeot gae itseumnida. There are a few quiz programs for housewives.

진행 | ~하다 jin·haeng | ~·ha·da hosting (a show) | to host a show
저는 **라디오 진행을** 할 때 마음이 편해서 라디오가 좋아요. jeoneun ladio jinhaengeul hal ttae maeumi pyeonhaeseo radioga joayo. I like hosting a radio program because it makes

me feel comfortable.

진행자 jin·haeng·ja MC, host

사회자 sa·hoe·ja chairperson, MC
사회자는 청중에게 간단히 인사를 한 후 초대 손님들을 소개했다. sahoejaneun cheongjungege gandanhi insareul han hu chodae sonnimdeureul sogaehaetda. The host briefly greeted the audience and introduced the guests.

방청 | ~하다 bang·cheong | ~·ha·da attending | to attend

방청객 bang·cheong·gaek audience, spectator

연예인 yeo·nye·in entertainer
딸아이 방 벽은 온통 연예인 사진이야. ttarai bang byeogeun ontong yeonyein sajiniya. My daughter's room is plastered with pictures of celebrities.

스타 seu·ta star
많은 십대들이 **스타들을** 동경한다. maneun sipdaedeuri seutadeureul donggyeonghanda. Many teenagers admire celebrities.

팬 paen fan

뉴스 nyu·seu news
오늘 아침에 정호가 **뉴스에** 나왔어. oneul achime jeonghoga nyuseue nawasseo. Jeongho was on the news this morning.

피디 pi·di producer

기자 gi·ja reporter, journalist
기자들은 유명한 사람들을 따라다닌다. gijadeureun nyumyeonghan saramdeureul ttaradaninda. The reporters follow famous people around.

아나운서 a·na·un·seo announcer, anchor
저는 티브이 **방송국의 아나운서입니다**. jeoneun tibeui bangsonggugui anaunseoimnida. I'm an anchor for a TV station.

보도 | ~하다 bo·do | ~·ha·da report, coverage | to report
당국은 그 보도를 완강하게 부인하고 있다. danggugeun geu bodoreul wanganghage buinhago itda. The authorities are vehemently denying the report.

인터뷰 | ~하다 in·teo·byu | ~·ha·da interview | to interview, give an interview
오늘 오후에 기자와 인터뷰하기로 되어 있어요. oneul ohue gijawa inteobyuhagiro doeeo

isseoyo. I'll give an interview to a reporter this afternoon.

회견 hoe·gyeon interview, press conference

그 탤런트는 **기자 회견**을 소집했다. **geu taelleonteuneun gija hoegyeoneul sojipaetda.** The TV actor held a press conference.

취재 | ~하다 chwi·jae | ~·ha·da collecting news material | to cover

많은 기자들이 그 **사건을 취재하기** 위해 경쟁을 벌였다. **maneun gijadeuri geu sageoneul chwijaehagi wihae gyeongjaengeul beoryeotda.** Many reporters competed to cover the case.

다큐멘터리 da·kyu·men·teo·ri documentary

라디오 ra·di·o radio

이 **라디오 채널**은 주로 팝송을 틀어 준다. **i radio chaeneoreun juro papsongeul teureo junda.** This radio channel plays mostly pop music.

청취 | ~하다 cheong·chwi | ~·ha·da listening | to listen

청취해 주셔서 감사드립니다. **cheongchwihae jusyeoseo gamsadeurimnida.** Thanks for tuning in.

청취자 cheong·chwi·ja listener

우리 프로의 주된 청취자는 20대 여성입니다. **uri peuroui judoen cheongchwijaneun isipdae yeoseongimnida.** The listeners of our program are mainly women in their twenties.

비디오 bi·di·o video, VCR

녹화 | ~하다 no·khwa | ~·ha·da recording | to record, videotape

그녀는 자신이 출연한 방송을 모두 녹화했다. **geunyeoneun jasini churyeonhan bangsongeul modu nokhwahaetda.** She has videotaped every TV program she has appeared on.

27.3 The Print Media

신문 sin·mun newspaper

어떤 **신문 봐? eotteon sinmun bwa?** Which newspaper do you read?

잡지 jap·ji magazine, journal

발행 | ~하다 bal·haeng | ~·ha·da publication | to publish, issue

저희 **잡지는** 매달 초에 **발행됩니다. jeohui japjineun maedal choe balhaengdoemnida.** Our magazine is published at the beginning of every month.

구독 | ~하다 gu·dok | ~·ha·da subscription | to subscribe

정기 **구독하고** 있는 신문이 있나요? **jeonggi gudokago inneun sinmuni innayo?** Do you subscribe to any newspapers?

잡지사 jap·ji·sa magazine publisher

저는 한 패션 **잡지사의 기자**입니다. **jeoneun han paesyeon japjisaui gijaimnida.** I'm a journalist for a fashion magazine.

신문사 sin·mun·sa newspaper (company)

저는 **신문사 편집부**에서 일하고 있습니다. **jeoneun sinmunsa pyeonjipbueseo ilhago itseumnida.** I work for a newspaper in the editorial department.

부수 bu·su circulation, number of copies

부 bu copy

그 신문은 하루 판매 부수가 백만 부가 넘는다. **geu sinmuneun haru panmae busuga baengman buga neomneunda.** The newspaper has a daily circulation of more than one million.

싣다 sit·da to carry, run, put in

우리는 신문에 신제품 **광고를 싣기로** 결정했다. **urineun sinmune sinjepum gwanggoreul sitgiro gyeoljonghaetda.** We decided to put an ad in the newspapers to promote our new product.

기사 gi·sa article

이 기사는 아무런 가치가 없다. **i gisaneun amureon gachiga eopda.** This article is of no value.

사설 sa·seol editorial

오늘 신문 사설 읽었어? **oneul sinmun saseol ilgeosseo?** Did you read the editorial in today's paper?

책 chaek book, volume

죄송하지만 이 책은 절판되었습니다. **joesonghajiman i chaegeun jeolpandoeeotseumnida.** I'm sorry but this book is out of print.

서적 seo·jeok books

저희는 중고 서적을 사고 팝니다. **jeohuineun**

junggo seojeogeul sago pamnida. We buy and sell used books.

도서 do·seo book
아동 도서 시장은 빠르게 성장하고 있다. adong doseo sijangeun ppareuge seongjanghago itda. The market for children's books is growing fast.

권 gwon unit for counting books
그 책은 여태까지 전 세계에서 천만 권 이상 팔렸다. geu chaegeun nyeotaekkaji jeon segyeeseo cheonman gwon isang pallyeotda. That book has sold over 10 million copies so far worldwide.

제목 je·mok title
그 시 제목을 잊어버렸어. geu si jemogeul ijeoboryeosseo. I've forgotten the title of the poem.

목차 mok·cha table of contents
책을 구입하기 전에 목차를 꼭 확인해라. chaegeul guipagi jeone mokchareul kkok waginhaera. Make sure to check the table of contents before purchasing a book.

머리말 = 서문 meo·ri·mal = seo·mun preface, foreword

본문 bon·mun the body

부록 bu·rok supplement, appendix

색인 sae·gin index

페이지 pe·i·ji page
오른쪽 페이지를 보세요. oreunjjok peijireul boseyo. Look at the right-hand page.

쪽 jjok page
그 보고서는 100쪽이 넘는다. geu bogoseoneun baekjjogi neomneunda. The report is over 100 pages long.

독자 dok·ja reader
이 책의 독자는 대부분 십대들입니다. i chaegui dokjaneun daebubun sipdaedeurimnida. Most of the readers of this book are teenagers.

서점 = 책방 seo·jeom = chaek·bang bookstore
서점에/책방에 가면 그 책 좀 사다 줘. seojeome/chaekbange gamyeon geu chaek jom sada jwo. If you go to the bookstore, get me the book.

사전 sa·jeon dictionary
나한테 적당한 사전 좀 추천해 줄래? nahante jeokdanghan sajeon jom chucheonhae jullae? Can you recommend a good dictionary to me?

백과사전 baek·gwa·sa·jeon encyclopedia

출판 | ~하다 chul·pan | ~·ha·da publication | to publish
저의 새 책이 내년에 출판됩니다. jeoui sae chaegi naenyeone chulpandoemnida. My new book will be out next year.

출판사 chul·pan·sa publisher
저는 출판사에서 일해요. jeoneun chulpansaeseo ilhaeyo. I work at a publishing company.

편집 | ~하다 pyeon·jip | ~·ha·da edit, editing | to edit
편집이 아직 끝나지 않았어요. pyeonjibi ajik kkeunnaji anasseoyo. The editing has not been completed yet.

인쇄 | ~하다 in·swae | ~·ha·da printing | to print
인쇄가 선명하지 않아요. inswaega seonmyeonghaji anayo. The print is not clear.

찍다 jjik·da to print, publish, issue
초판을 보통 몇 부 찍나요? chopaneul botong myeot bu jjingnayo? How many copies do you usually print for a first edition?

인쇄소 in·swae·so printing house

27.4 Computers, the Internet

컴퓨터 keom·pyu·teo computer
이 컴퓨터 잠시 좀 써도 되나요? i keompyuteo jamsi jom sseodo doenayo? Can I use this computer for a moment?

피시 pi·si personal computer

태블릿피시 tae·beul·lit·pi·si tablet PC

노트북 no·teu·buk laptop

데스크톱 de·seu·keu·top desktop
저는 데스크톱보다 노트북을 더 좋아합니다.

jeoneun deseukeutopboda noteubugeul deo jo-ahamnida. I prefer a laptop to a desktop.

....

• **하드웨어** ha·deu·we·eo hardware

그래픽카드 geu·rae·pik·ka·deu graphics card

사운드카드 sa·un·deu·ka·deu sound card

모뎀 mo·dem modem

램 raem RAM

중앙처리장치 jung·ang·cheo·ri·jang·chi CPU

메인보드 me·in·bo·deu mainboard

하드(디스크) ha·deu(·di·seu·keu) hard disk drive

: **모니터** mo·ni·teo monitor
모니터는 1년간 품질 보증이 됩니다. moni-teoneun illyeongan pumjil bojeungi doemnida. The monitor comes with a one-year warranty.

커서 keo·seo cursor

마우스 ma·u·seu mouse
마우스가 안 돼요. mauseuga an dwaeyo. The mouse isn't working.

키보드 = 자판 ki·bo·deu = ja·pan key-board
키보드에서/자판에서 F1 키를 눌러 주세요. kibodeueseo/japaneseo epeuwon kireul lulleo juseyo. Press the F1 key on your keyboard.

....

• **프린터(기)** peu·rin·teo(·gi) printer

....

• **소프트웨어** so·peu·teu·we·eo software

: **프로그램** peu·ro·geu·raem program

• **깔다** kkal·da to install, set up
프린터 드라이버는 깔았어요? peurinteo deuraibeoneun kkarasseoyo? Have you in-stalled the printer driver?

• **설치 | ~하다** seol·chi | ~·ha·da installa-tion | to install
설치 중에는 컴퓨터를 끄지 마시오. seolchi jungeneun keompyuteoreul kkeuji masio. Do not turn off the computer during the instal-lation process.

• **바이러스** ba·i·reo·seu virus
아무래도 내 컴퓨터가 바이러스에 걸린 것 같아. amuraedo nae keompyuteoga baireoseue geollin geot gata. I think my computer has a virus.

파일 pa·il file

아이콘 a·i·kon icon

클릭 | ~하다 keul·lik | ~·ha·da click | to click
아이콘을 클릭하면 프로그램이 실행됩니다. aikoneul keullikamyeon peurogeuraemi sil-haengdoemnida. If you click on the icon, the program will run.

폴더 pol·deo folder

파일명 pa·il·myeong filename

확장자 hwak·jang·ja extension

: **열다** yeol·da to open
파일을 열지 못했습니다. paireul lyeolji mo-taetseumnida. We could not open the file.

불러오다 bul·leo·o·da to import

• **내보내다** nae·bo·nae·da to export
내 컴퓨터의 즐겨찾기를 다른 컴퓨터로 내보내려면 어떻게 해야 하죠? nae keompyuteoui jeulgyeochatgireul dareun keompyuteoro nae-bonaeryeomyeon eotteoke haeya hajyo? How do I export my bookmarks to another computer?

저장 | ~하다 jeo·jang | ~·ha·da storage | to save

: **닫다** dat·da to close
파일을 닫기 전에 저장해라. paireul datgi jeone jeojanghaera. Save the file before clos-ing it.

백업 | ~하다 bae·geop | ~·ha·da backup | to back up
마지막으로 파일을 백업한 게 언제였죠? ma-jimageuro paireul baegeopan ge eonjeyeotjyo? When was the last time you backed up your files?

: **날아가다** na·ra·ga·da to be gone
정전이 되는 바람에 파일들이 모두 날아갔다. jeongjeoni doeneun barame paildeuri modu naragatda. I lost all the files because of the blackout.

내려받다 nae·ryeo·bat·da to download
내 컴퓨터는 영화 한 편을 내려받는 데 5분도 안 걸린다. nae keompyuteoneun nyeonghwa han pyeoneul laeryeobanneun de obundo an geollinda. My computer takes less than 10 minutes to download a movie.

다운(로드) | 다운로드하다 da·un (·no·deu) | da·un·no·deu·ha·da download | to download

업로드 | ~하다 eom·no·deu l ~·ha·da up-loading | to upload
당신의 **사진을 업로드하고** 당신의 관심사를 다른 사람과 공유할 수 있습니다. dangsinui sajineul eomnodeuhago dangsinui gwansimsareul dareun saramgwa gongyuhal su itseumnida. You can upload your photos and share your interests with others.

올리다 ol·li·da to upload, post

복사 | ~하다 bok·sa l ~·ha·da copy | to copy

붙여넣다 bu·chyeo·neo·ta to paste
이것은 복사해서 붙여넣는 간단한 작업입니다. igeoseun boksahaeseo buchyeoneonneun gandanhan jageobimnida. This is a simple copy and paste job.

삭제 | ~하다 sak·je l ~·ha·da deletion | to delete
실수로 중요한 **파일을 삭제해** 버렸어요. silsuro jungyohan paireul sakjehae beoryeosseoyo. I deleted an important file by mistake.

지우다 ji·u·da to delete

실행 | ~하다 sil·haeng l ~·ha·da execution | to run, execute
파일을 실행하는 중에 오류가 발생했습니다. paireul silhaenghaneun junge oryuga balsaenghaetseumnida. An error occurred while trying to execute the file.

오류 o·ryu error

다운되다 da·un·doe·da to crash
갑자기 **컴퓨터가 다운됐어.** gapjagi keompyuteoga daundwaesseo. Suddenly, the computer crashed.

부팅 | ~하다 bu·ting l ~·ha·da booting | to boot
컴퓨터를 다시 **부팅해** 봐. keompyuteoreul dasi butinghae bwa. Reboot the computer.

업그레이드 | ~하다 eop·geu·re·i·deu l ~·ha·da upgrade | to upgrade
네 **컴퓨터 업그레이드해야겠어.** ne keompyuteo eopgeureideuhaeyagesseo. You need to upgrade your computer.

업데이트 | ~하다 eop·de·i·teu l ~·ha·da update | to update
아이콘을 누르면 **업데이트가** 시작됩니다. aikoneul lureumyeon eopdeiteuga sijakdoemnida. Press the icon and the update will start.

인터넷 in·teo·net the Internet

얼마나 자주 **인터넷에 접속하십니까?** eolmana jaju inteonese jeopsokasimnikka? How often do you go online?

온라인 ol·la·in online
온라인으로 표를 예매하면 10% 할인이 됩니다. ollaineuro pyoreul ryemaehamyeon sippeosenteu harini doemnida. You will get a 10% discount if you reserve tickets online.

(웹)사이트 (wep·)sa·i·teu website

홈페이지 hom·pe·i·ji homepage; website
mp3 파일을 홈페이지에서 다운로드 받으시기 바랍니다. empisseuri paireul hompeijieseo daunnodeu badeusigi baramnida. Please download the mp3 files from our homepage.

블로그 beul·lo·geu blog

게시판 ← 계시판 ge·si·pan ← gye·si·pan noticeboard, bulletin board
게시판에 글 좀 올려. gesipane geul jom ollyeo. Post something on the bulletin board.

접속 | ~하다 jeop·sok l ~·ha·da access | to access
투숙객들은 호텔 내 모든 장소에서 **인터넷에 접속할** 수 있습니다. tusukgaekdeureun hotel lae modeun jangsoeseo inteonese jeopsokal su itseumnida. Guests can access the Internet everywhere in the hotel.

로그인 | ~하다 ro·geu·in l ~·ha·da login | to log in
로그인이 안 돼요. rogeuini an dwaeyo. I'm having trouble logging in.

아이디 a·i·di ID

비밀번호 bi·mil·beon·ho password, PIN

입력 | ~하다 im·nyeok l ~·ha·da entry | to enter, input
아이디와 **비밀번호를** 정확히 **입력하시오.** aidiwa bimilbeonhoreul jeonghwaki imnyeokasio. Enter your ID and password correctly.

로그아웃 | ~하다 ro·geu·a·ut l ~·ha·da logout | to log out
창을 닫기 전에 로그아웃을 꼭 해라. changeul datgi jeone rogeuauseul kkok haera. Make sure to log out before closing the window.

네티즌 ne·ti·jeun netizen

검색 | ~하다 geom·saek l ~·ha·da search | to search, browse
검색 문구가 너무 길어요. geomsaek munguga neomu gireoyo. Your search query is too long.

서핑 | ~하다 seo·ping | ~·ha·da surfing | to surf, browse

인터넷 서핑 중이에요. inteonet seoping jung-ieyo. I'm surfing the Internet.

댓글 = 덧글 = 답글 daet·geul = deot·geul = dap·geul comment

달다 dal·da to post, put, make

제 블로그에 **댓글을 달아** 주셔서 감사합니다. je beullogeue daetgeureul dara jusyeoseo gamsahamnida. Thanks for leaving comments on my blog.

(이)메일 (i·)me·il e-mail

제 **메일** 주소를 알려 드릴게요. je meil jusoreul allyeo deurilgeyo. I'll give you my e-mail address.

스팸(메일) seu·paem(·me·il) spam, junk mail

이 프로그램은 **스팸메일을 차단해** 줍니다. i peurogeuraemeun seupaemmeireul chadanhae jumnida. This program blocks junk mail.

답메일 dam·me·il reply

아직 **답메일을 못 받았어요.** ajik dammeireul mot badasseoyo. I haven't gotten a reply to my e-mail.

채팅 | ~하다 chae·ting | ~·ha·da online chat | to do online chat

저는 아내를 채팅으로 알게 됐어요. jeoneun anaereul chaetingeuro alge dwaesseoyo. I met my wife in a chat room.

와이파이 wa·i·pa·i Wi-Fi

이곳은 무료 **와이파이 구역**입니다. igoseun muryo waipai guyeogimnida. This is a free Wi-Fi zone.

조회 | ~하다 jo·hoe | ~·ha·da inquiry | to inquire

제 **블로그 조회** 수는 하루 500회 정도 됩니다. je beullogeu johoe suneun haru obaekoe jeongdo doemnida. My blog has about 500 hits a day.

방문자 bang·mun·ja visitor

한 달에 평균적으로 **사이트 방문자** 수가 몇 명이나 됩니까? han dare pyeonggyunjeogeuro saiteu bangmunja suga myeot myeongina doemnikka? How many visitors does your website get each month on average?

즐겨찾기 jeul·gyeo·chat·gi bookmark, favorite

현재 페이지를 **즐겨찾기** 목록에 추가하고 싶으면 "추가" 버튼을 누르세요. hyeonjae peijireul jeulgyeochatgi mongnoge chugahago sipeumyeon chuga beoteuneul lureuseyo. Click the "add" button to add the current web page to your Favorites list.

아타다 갓길 객실 거리 거스름돈 검색대 경유하다 경차

고속버스 고장 고치다 교체 교통 교통카드 국내선 국도

국제선 기어 기장 기차 길 깜빡이 끊다 노선 대

합실 도로 뒷문 딱지 뜨다 뜨다 면허 면허증 무사하다

다 배 버스 번호판 벌금 부딪히다 붐비다 브레이크

행 비행기 뺑소니 사거리 선장 손잡이 수동 수리 승객

용차 시외버스 신호 신호등 안장 어기다 엔진 역

chapter **28** Traffic, Modes of Transportation

차 와이퍼 왕복v 요금 운전 운전사 운전자 턴 육교

이륙 인도 잃다v자동 자동차 정류장 조수석

주차장 중고차 중형차 지름길 지하도 차량 차선 철도

인 출입문 칸 큰길 타다 택시 트럭 트렁크 편도

표지판 피하다 항공 헤매다 헬멧 혼잡하다 활주로 휴게소

28.1 Cars

차 cha car
차를 정비소에 가져가세요. chareul jeongbi-soe gajyeogaseyo. Take your car to the repair shop.

차량 cha·ryang car, vehicle
현재 **차량** 흐름은 원활합니다. hyeonjae char-yang heureumeun wonhwalhamnida. Current-ly, the traffic is flowing smoothly.

대 dae   unit for counting vehicles, ma-chines, instruments, etc.
차 한 대 cha han dae a car

자동차 ja·dong·cha car, automobile
자동차에 또 문제가 있어요? jadongchae tto munjega isseoyo? Are you having problems with your car again?

승용차 seung·yong·cha passenger car

자가용 ja·ga·yong (one's own) car
저는 자가용으로 출퇴근을 합니다. jeoneun jagayongeuro chultoegeuneul hamnida. I go to and from work using my own car.

트럭 teu·reok truck
큰 트럭이 길을 막고 있다. keun teureogi gireul makgo itda. The road is blocked by a large truck.

구급차 gu·geup·cha ambulance
구급차를 불러 주세요. gugeupchareul bulleo juseyo. Please call an ambulance.

소방차 so·bang·cha fire engine
열 대가 넘는 소방차가 화재 현장에 도착했다. yeol daega neomneun sobangchaga hwajae hyeonjange dochakaetda. More than ten fire trucks arrived at the fire scene.

중고차 jung·go·cha used car

신차 sin·cha new car
저는 신차보다 중고차를 선호합니다. jeoneun sinchaboda junggochareul seonhohamnida. I prefer a used car to a new one.

경차 gyeong·cha light vehicle

소형차 so·hyeong·cha small car, compact car

중형차 jung·hyeong·cha mid-size car

대형차 dae·hyeong·cha large car

백미러 baeng·mi·reo rearview mirror
후진하기 전에 **백미러를** 확인해라. hujinhagi jeone baengmireoreul hwaginhaera. Check the rearview mirror before backing up.

사이드미러 sa·i·deu·mi·reo side-view mirror

번호판 beon·ho·pan license plate

와이퍼 wa·i·peo wiper

트렁크 teu·reong·keu trunk
여분 타이어는 트렁크 안에 있어요. yeobun taieoneun teureongkeu ane isseoyo. The spare tire is in the trunk.

깜빡이 = 방향 지시등 kkam·ppa·gi = bang·hyang ji·si·deung turn signal, blinker
깜빡이도/방향 지시등도 안 켜고 당신이 차선을 바꿨잖아요. kkamppagido/banghyang jisi-deungdo an kyeogo dangsini chaseoneul ba-kkwotjanayo. You changed lanes without us-ing the turn signal.

비상등 bi·sang·deung hazard light

바퀴 ba·kwi wheel

타이어 ta·i·eo tire
제 차 **타이어가** 펑크 났어요. je cha taieoga peongkeu nasseoyo. My car has a flat tire.

액셀 aek·sel accelerator

브레이크 beu·re·i·keu brake
브레이크가 말을 듣지 않았어요. beureikeuga mareul deutji anasseoyo. My brakes didn't work.

클러치 keul·leo·chi clutch

운전대 = 핸들 un·jeon·dae = haen·deul steering wheel
운전대를/핸들을 편안하게 **잡으세요.** unjeon-daereul/haendeureul pyeonanhage jabeuseyo. Ease your grip on the steering wheel.

안전벨트 = 안전띠 = 좌석벨트 an·jeon·bel·teu = an·jeon·tti = jwa·seok·bel·teu seat belt
안전벨트를/안전띠를/좌석벨트를 매 주세요. anjeonbelteureul/anjeonttireul/jwaseokbel-teureul mae juseyo. Please fasten your seat belt.

경적 = 클랙슨 gyeong·jeok = keul·laek·seun horn
이 구역에서 **경적을/클랙슨을** 울리는 것은 금지되어 있습니다. **i guyeogeseo gyeongjeogeul/keullaekseuneul ullineun geoseun geumjidoeeo itseumnida.** It is prohibited to honk your horn in this area.

운전석 un·jeon·seok driver's seat
그녀가 **운전석**에 **타** 시동을 걸었다. **geunyeoga unjeonseoge ta sidongeul georeotda.** She got into the driver's seat and started the engine.

조수석 jo·su·seok passenger seat

기어 gi·eo gear
기어를 후진에 놓아. **gieoreul hujine noa.** Shift the car into reverse gear.

자동 (변속기) ja·dong (byeon·sok·gi) automatic transmission

수동 (변속기) su·dong (byeon·sok·gi) manual transmission
이 차 자동이에요, 수동이에요? **i cha jadongieyo, sudongieyo?** Does this car have an automatic or a manual transmission?

• 엔진 en·jin engine
사고의 원인은 **엔진** 고장이었다. **sagoui wonineun enjin gojangieotda.** The cause of the accident was engine failure.

연비 yeon·bi gas mileage
이 모델은 **연비**가 좋습니다. **i modereun nyeonbiga josseumnida.** This model has good gas mileage.

오토바이 o·to·ba·i motorcycle, motorbike
저는 오토바이로 출퇴근을 합니다. **jeoneun otobairo chultoegeuneul hamnida.** I commute to work on a motorbike.

: 자전거 ja·jeon·geo bicycle
밖에서 **자전거** 타도 돼요? **bakkeseo jajeongeo tado dwaeyo?** Can I ride my bicycle outside?

페달 pe·dal pedal, treadle
페달을 힘껏 **밟아라**. **pedareul himkkeot balbara.** Pedal hard.

헬멧 hel·met helmet
자전거 탈 때 **헬멧** 쓰는 거 잊지 마. **jajeongeo tal ttae helmet sseuneun geo itji ma.** Don't forget to wear a helmet when you're riding a bicycle.

안장 an·jang saddle
자전거 **안장**을 조정해 봐. **jajeongeo anjangeul jojeonghae bwa.** Adjust the seat on the bike.

체인 che·in chain
자전거 **체인**에 기름칠을 해야겠어. **jajeongeo cheine gireumchireul haeyagesseo.** You need to lube the bicycle chain.

28.2 Roads, Driving, Accidents

: 길 gil street, way, path, road
이 길을 따라 가세요. **i gireul ttara gaseyo.** Go this way.

: 도로 do·ro road
교통 체증을 피하려면 이 **도로**를 **이용해라**. **gyotong chejeungeul piharyeomyeon i dororeul iyonghaera.** Use this road to avoid traffic.

• 인도 = 보도 in·do = bo·do sidewalk
오늘 오후 차가 인도로/보도로 뛰어들어 지나가던 사람 한 명이 다쳤습니다. **oneul ohu chaga indoro/bodoro ttwieodeureo jinagadeon saram han myeongi dachyeotseumnida.** This afternoon a car drove onto the sidewalk and a passerby was injured.

차도 cha·do road

고속도로 go·sok·do·ro expressway
경부고속도로를 타셔야 해요. **gyeongbugosokdororeul tasyeoya haeyo.** You will have to take the Gyeongbu Expressway.

국도 guk·do highway, route

: 골목(길) gol·mok(·gil) alley
그 골목은 아주 좁았다. **geu golmogeun aju jobatda.** The alley was very narrow.

: 큰길 keun·gil main street

• 지름길 ji·reum·gil shortcut
제가 지름길을 알아요. **jega jireumgireul arayo.** I know a shortcut.

: (길)거리 (gil·)geo·ri street, road
길거리에 사람이 많아요. **gilgeorie sarami manayo.** There are many people in the street.

사거리 = 네거리 sa·geo·ri = ne·geo·ri

crossroads, four-way stop
다음 사거리에서/네거리에서 우회전하세요. daeum sageorieseo/negeorieseo uhoejeonhaseyo. Turn right at the next crossroads.

교차로 gyo·cha·ro crossroads, intersection

횡단보도 ≒ 건널목 hoeng·dan·bo·do ≒ geon·neol·mok crosswalk
저 횡단보도에서/건널목에서 내려 주시겠어요? jeo hoengdanbodoeseo/geonneolmogeseo naeryeo jusigesseoyo? Will you drop me off at that crosswalk?

신호등 sin·ho·deung traffic light
이 횡단보도는 신호등이 없어서 위험합니다. i hoengdanbodoneun sinhodeungi eopseoseo wiheomhamnida. This crossing is dangerous because there is no traffic light.

표지판 pyo·ji·pan sign, notice
도로 표지판이 헷갈려요. doro pyojipani hetgallyeoyo. The road signs are confusing.

차선 cha·seon (traffic) lane

육교 yuk·gyo overpass

지하도 ji·ha·do underpass
시청 오른쪽에 지하도가 있어요. sicheong oreunjjoge jihadoga isseoyo. There is an underpass to the right of City Hall.

보행자 bo·haeng·ja pedestrian
골목에서는 차가 보행자에게 양보해야 한다. golmogeseoneun chaga bohaengjaege yangbohaeya handa. Cars should give way to pedestrians in alleys.

갓길 gat·gil shoulder
다음 10킬로미터 내 갓길 없음. daeum sipkillomiteo nae gatgil eopseum. No shoulder for the next 10 kilometers.

터널 teo·neol tunnel

휴게소 hyu·ge·so rest area
다음 휴게소에서 잠깐 쉬었다 가자. daeum hyugesoeseo jamkkan swieotda gaja. Let's stop at the next rest area.

잃(어버리)다 il(·eo·beo·ri)·da to lose, stray
길을 잃어버리신 것 같군요. gireul ireobeorisin geot gatgunnyo. You seem to be lost.

헤매다 he·mae·da to wander, roam
길을 잃어서 몇 시간을 헤맸어요. gireul ireo-

seo myeot siganeul hemaesseoyo. I got lost and I wandered for hours.

찾다 chat·da to find, look for
너희 집 찾느라 애 먹었어. neohui jip channeura ae meogeosseo. I had a hard time finding your house.

교통 gyo·tong traffic
이 시간에는 늘 교통이 혼잡합니다. i siganeneun neul gyotongi honjapamnida. The road traffic is always heavy at this time.

밀리다 mil·li·da to be congested
사고가 나서 차가 많이 밀려 있어요. sagoga naseo chaga mani millyeo isseoyo. The traffic is congested due to an accident.

막히다 ma·ki·da to be stuck, be blocked
차가 막혀 늦었어요. chaga makyeo neujeosseoyo. I was late because of a traffic jam.

혼잡하다 hon·ja·pa·da congested, jammed
저는 혼잡한 도로를 운전하는 것에 익숙하지가 않아요. jeoneun honjapan dororeul unjeonhaneun geose iksukajiga anayo. I'm not familiar with driving on busy streets.

붐비다 bum·bi·da to be crowded
강남은 언제나 붐벼요. gangnameun eonjena bumbyeoyo. Gangnam is always crowded.

운전 | ~하다 un·jeon | ~·ha·da driving | to drive
여기서 운전하시면 안 됩니다. yeogiseo unjeonhasimyeon an doemnida. You can't drive through here.

운전자 un·jeon·ja driver
운전자가 누구였어요? unjeonjaga nuguyeosseoyo? Who drove this car?

몰다 mol·da to steer, drive (a car)
저는 열아홉 살 때부터 트럭을 몰아 왔어요. jeoneun nyeorahop sal ttaebuteo teureogeul mora wasseoyo. I have been driving trucks since I was 19.

끼어들다 kki·eo·deul·da to cut in

양보 | ~하다 yang·bo | ~·ha·da yield | to yield
다른 차가 끼어들 때는 그냥 양보해라. dareun chaga kkieodeul ttaeneun geunyang yangbohaera. Give way when another car cuts in front of you.

추월 | ~하다 chu·wol | ~·ha·da passing | to pass

나는 **버스를 추월하기** 위해 가속 페달을 밟았다. naneun **beoseureul chuwolhagi** wihae gasok pedareul balbatda. I stepped on the accelerator to overtake the bus.

앞지르다 ap·ji·reu·da to pass
터널 내에서는 **앞지르기**가 금지되어 있습니다. teoneol laeeseoneun **apjireugi**ga geumjidoeeo itseumnida. In the tunnel, no passing is allowed.

유턴 | ~하다 yu·teon | ~·ha·da U-turn | to make a U-turn
저기서 **유턴**해. jeogiseo **yuteon**hae. Make a U-turn over there.

정차 | ~하다 jeong·cha | ~·ha·da stop | to stop
정차 금지 jeongcha geumji No Standing

주차 | ~하다 ju·cha | ~·ha·da parking | to park
도시 한복판에서 **주차**하는 것은 거의 불가능합니다. dosi hanbokpaneseo **jucha**haneun geoseun geoui bulganeunghamnida. It's almost impossible to park in the town center.

주차장 ju·cha·jang parking lot
고객 전용 **주차장** gogaek jeonyong **juchajang** Customer Parking Only

신호 sin·ho signal, sign

어기다 eo·gi·da to break, violate
그는 **신호를 어기지** 않았다고 주장했다. geuneun **sinhoreul eogiji** anatdago jujanghaetda. He insisted that he didn't disobey the signal.

위반 | ~하다 wi·ban | ~·ha·da violation | to violate

속도 sok·do speed

시속 si·sok speed per hour
이 도로에서 **제한 속도**는 시속 80킬로미터입니다. i doroeseo **jehan sokdo**neun sisok palsipkillomiteoimnida. The speed limit on this road is 80 kph.

제한 | ~하다 je·han | ~·ha·da limit | to limit
한국의 고속도로에서는 **속도 제한**이 있습니다. hangugui gosokdoroeseoneun **sokdo jehan**i itseumnida. On Korean highways, there is a speed limit.

음주운전 eum·ju·un·jeon DUI
그녀는 **음주운전**으로 면허가 취소되었다. geunyeoneun **eumjuunjeon**euro myeonheoga chwisodoeeotda. She had her license revoked for drunk driving.

딱지 ttak·ji ticket

떼다 tte·da to give a ticket, get a ticket
신호 위반으로 **딱지**를 **뗐어요**. sinho wibaneuro **ttakji**reul **ttesseoyo**. I got a ticket for running a red light.

벌금 ≒ 과태료 ≒ 범칙금 beol·geum ≒ gwa·tae·ryo ≒ beom·chik·geum fine, penalty
범칙금은 현금으로 내야 합니다. **beomchikgeum**eun hyeongeumeuro naeya hamnida. Fines must be paid in cash.

사고 sa·go accident
그 음주 운전자는 결국 **사고**를 냈다. geu eumju unjeonjaneun gyeolguk **sago**reul laetda. The drunk finally got into a car accident.

교통사고 gyo·tong·sa·go traffic accident
오는 길에 **교통사고**가 있었어. oneun gire **gyotongsago**ga isseoseo. There was a traffic accident on the way.

뺑소니 ppaeng·so·ni hit-and-run
남편은 **뺑소니** 사고로 목숨을 잃었어요. nampyeoneun **ppaengsoni** sagoro moksumeul ireosseoyo. My husband died in a hit-and-run accident.

충돌 | ~하다 chung·dol | ~·ha·da collision, crash | to collide, crash
오늘 아침 제 차가 버스랑 **충돌했어요**. oneul achim je chaga beoseurang **chungdol**haesseoyo. My car crashed into a bus this morning.

부딪히다 bu·di·chi·da to be bumped
유조선이 암초에 **부딪혀** 최소 천만 갤런의 기름을 바다에 쏟아냈다. yujoseoni amchoe **budichyeo** choeso cheonman gaelleonui gireumeul badae ssodanaetda. An oil tanker hit a reef and spilled at least 10 million gallons of oil into the ocean.

당하다 dang·ha·da to go through, suffer
A: 무슨 일이에요? B: 며칠 전에 **교통사고**를 **당했어요**. A: museun irieyo? B: myeochil jeone **gyotongsago**reul **dang**haesseoyo. A: What happened? B: I had a car accident a couple of days ago.

피하다 pi·ha·da to avoid, escape
우리는 **교통 체증**을 **피하**려고 일찍 출발했다. urineun **gyotong chejeung**eul **piha**ryeogo iljjik

chulbalhaetda. We left early to avoid the traffic.

무사하다 mu·sa·ha·da safe, intact
무사해서 다행이야. musahaeseo dahaengiya.
I'm happy you're okay.

면허 myeon·heo license (permission)

면허증 myeon·heo·jeung license (document)
면허증을 보여 주세요. myeonheojeungeul boyeo juseyo. Show me your license.

운전면허 un·jeon·myeon·heo driver's license
나는 아직 운전면허가 없어요. naneun ajik gunjeonmyeonheoga eopseoyo. I don't have a driver's license yet.

고장 go·jang trouble, breakdown
차가 아주 혼잡한 도로 한복판에서 **고장이 났다**. chaga aju honjapan doro hanbokpaneseo gojangi natda. My car broke down in the middle of a very busy road.

수리 | ~하다 su·ri | ~·ha·da repair | to repair, fix
제 차는 **수리를** 맡겼어요. je chaneun surireul matgyeosseoyo. I had my car sent to an auto repair shop.

고치다 go·chi·da to repair, fix
뭐든 고칠 수 있다고 했잖아요. mwodeun

gochil su itdago haetjanayo. You said you can fix anything.

손(을) 보다 son(·eul) bo·da to repair, touch up
A: 다 됐어? B: 아니. 아직 **손을** 좀 더 **봐야** 해. A: da dwaesseo? B: ani. ajik soneul jom deo bwaya hae. A: Are you done? B: Not yet. It needs a little more touch-up.

정비 | ~하다 jeong·bi | ~·ha·da maintenance, service | to maintain, service
마지막으로 **차량 정비**를 받으신 게 언제죠? majimageuro charyang jeongbireul badeusin ge eonjejyo? When was the last time you had your car checked?

정비소 jeong·bi·so repair shop, garage
제 차는 엔진에 문제가 있어서 정비소에 있어요. je chaneun enjine munjega isseoseo jeongbisoe isseoyo. My car is at the auto repair shop now because of engine problems.

갈다 gal·da to change, replace
타이어 갈 줄 알아? taieo gal jul ara? Do you know how to change a tire?

교체 | ~하다 gyo·che | ~·ha·da change, replacement | to change, replace
고장 난 **부품** 하나만 **교체하시면** 됩니다. gojang nan bupum hanaman gyochehasimyeon doemnida. All you need to do is have the broken one replaced.

28.3 Public Transportation

대중교통 dae·jung·gyo·tong public transportation
대중교통을 이용하는 게 어때요? daejunggyotongeul iyonghaneun ge eottaeyo? How do you like using public transportation?

표 = 티켓 pyo = ti·ket ticket
표를/티켓을 보여주시겠어요? pyoreul/tikeseul boyeojusigesseoyo? Can I see your ticket?

끊다 kkeun·ta to buy
표부터 끊어야겠어. pyobuteo kkeuneoyagesseo. I need to get the ticket first.

편도 pyeon·do one way

왕복 wang·bok round-trip
편도입니까, 왕복입니까? pyeondoimnikka,

wangbogimnikka? Do you want a one-way or round-trip ticket?

운전(기)사 un·jeon(·gi)·sa driver, chauffeur

승객 seung·gaek passenger

승강장 seung·gang·jang (taxi) stand; platform
택시 승강장이 어디에 있어요? taeksi seunggangjangi eodie isseoyo? Where's the taxi stand?
지하철 승강장에서 열차가 들어오기를 기다리고 있었어요. jihacheol seunggangjangeseo yeolchaga deureoogireul gidarigo isseoyo. I was waiting on the subway platform for the train to arrive.

정류장 = 정거장 jeong·nyu·jang = jeong·geo·jang stop
이 근처에 **버스 정류장**이/**정거장**이 있습니까? i geuncheoe beoseu jeongnyujangi/jeonggeojangi itseumnikka? Is there a bus stop near here?

터미널 teo·mi·neol terminal
제주행 비행기는 5번 터미널에서 출발합니다. jejuhaeng bihaenggineun obeon teomineoreseo chulbalhamnida. Flights for Jeju depart from Terminal 5.

요금 yo·geum fee, fare
요금이 얼마인가요? yogeumi eolmaingayo? How much is the fare?

운임 u·nim fare
65세 이상은 **지하철 운임**이 무료다. yuksibose isangeun jihacheol unimi muryoda. People aged 65 or older can use the subway for free.

태우다 tae·u·da to take, give a ride
버스가 정거장에서 **승객들**을 **태웠다**. beoseuga jeonggeojangeseo seunggaekdeureul taewotda. The bus picked up passengers at the bus stop.

타다 ta·da to ride, get on, take
134번 **버스**를 **타세요**. baeksamsipsabeon beoseureul taseyo. Take bus number 134.

내리다 nae·ri·da to get off
뒷문으로 내리세요. dwinmuneuro naeriseyo. Get off at the rear door.

운행 | ~하다 un·haeng | ~·ha·da operation | to run
오늘 아침 폭설로 **열차 운행**이 한 시간 동안 중단되었다. oneul achim pokseollo yeolcha unhaengi han sigan dongan jungdandoeeotda. This morning train service was interrupted for an hour due to heavy snowfall.

운항 | ~하다 un·hang | ~·ha·da sailing; flight | to sail; to fly
1월부터 4월까지 여객선은 주말에만 운항합니다. irwolbuteo sawolkkaji yeogaekseoneun jumareman unhanghamnida. From January to April, the ferry is in service during the weekends.

버스 beo·seu bus

마을버스 ma·eul·beo·seu town shuttle bus

시내버스 si·nae·beo·seu city bus

시외버스 si·oe·beo·seu intercity bus

고속버스 go·sok·beo·seu express bus

교통카드 gyo·tong·ka·deu transportation card

단말기 dan·mal·gi card reader
교통카드를 **단말기**에 대세요. gyotongkadeureul danmalgie daeseyo. Swipe the transportation card over the card reader.

앞문 am·mun front door

뒷문 dwin·mun rear door

손잡이 son·ja·bi grip, strap
손잡이를 꽉 잡으세요. sonjabireul kkwak jabeuseyo. Hold onto the rail.

택시 taek·si taxi

거스름돈 = 잔돈 geo·seu·reum·don = jan·don change
거스름돈은/**잔돈**은 가지세요. geoseureumdoneun/jandoneun gajiseyo. Keep the change.

기차 gi·cha train
이거 부산행 기차 맞아요? igeo busanhaeng gicha majayo? Is this the right train for Busan?

열차 yeol·cha train, subway
다음 열차는 몇 시에 있어요? daeum nyeolchaneun myeot sie isseoyo? When does the next train leave?

철도 cheol·do train track, railroad; train
그 **철도**는 아직 건설 중입니다. geu cheoldoneun ajik geonseol jungimnida. The railroad is still under construction.
저는 **철도 여행**을 좋아합니다. jeoneun cheoldo yeohaengeul joahamnida. I like traveling by train.

철로 cheol·lo train track, railroad

역 yeok station

기차역 gi·cha·yeok train station

대합실 dae·hap·sil waiting room

칸 kan car
식당 칸은 어디예요? sikdang kaneun eodiyeyo? Where's the dining car?

지하철 = 전철 ji·ha·cheol = jeon·cheol subway

제 고향에는 아직 지하철이/전철이 없어요. je gohyangeneun ajik jihacheori/jeoncheori eopseoyo. In my hometown, there's no subway yet.

지하철역 = 전철역 ji·ha·cheol·lyeok = jeon·cheol·lyeok subway station
여기서 지하철역이/전철역이 얼마나 멀어요? yeogiseo jihacheollyeogi/jeoncheollyeogi eolmana meoreoyo? How far is the subway station from here?

노선 no·seon route, line
서울의 **지하철 노선**은 상당히 복잡하다. seourui jihacheol loseoneun sangdanghi bokjapada. The subway lines in Seoul are quite complicated.

호선 ho·seon line
A: 몇 호선을 타야 하죠? B: 1호선을 타세요. A: myeot toseoneul taya hajyo? B: ilhoseoneul taseyo. A: Which line should I take? B: Take line number one.

개찰구 gae·chal·gu turnstile

입구 ip·gu entrance
지하철 **입구**는 어디에 있어요? jihacheol ipguneun eodie isseoyo? Where is the entrance to the subway?

출구 chul·gu exit; way out
3번 **출구로 나가세요**. sambeon chulguro nagaseyo. Go out Exit 3.

출입문 chu·rim·mun door, gate
열차가 **출입문 고장**으로 한 시간 가량 지연되었다. yeolchaga churimmun gojangeuro han sigan garyang jiyeondoeeotda. The train was delayed for about an hour due to a door malfunction.

갈아타다 ga·ra·ta·da to change (cars), to transfer (to)
시청으로 가려면 어디에서 **지하철을 갈아타야** 합니까? sicheongeuro garyeomyeon eodieseo jihacheoreul garataya hamnikka? Where should I transfer to get to City Hall?

환승 | ~하다 hwan·seung | ~·ha·da transfer | to transfer (to)

비행기 bi·haeng·gi airplane
비행기는 5분 후에 이륙할 예정입니다. bihaenggineun obun hue iryukal yejeongimnida. The plane will take off in 5 minutes.

항공 hang·gong aviation, flight

항공사 hang·gong·sa airline

국내선 gung·nae·seon domestic flight

국제선 guk·je·seon international flight

기장 gi·jang captain

승무원 seung·mu·won flight attendant

객실 gaek·sil cabin
승객들과 승무원들은 객실에 있다. seunggaekdeulgwa seungmuwondeureun gaeksire itda. The passengers and the crew are in the cabin.

기내 gi·nae cabin
기내에서는 흡연이 금지되어 있습니다. ginaeeseoneun heubyeoni geumjidoeeo itseumnida. Smoking is prohibited inside the aircraft.

통로 tong·no aisle

창가 chang·ga window
창가하고 통로 쪽 중에 어느 쪽으로 드릴까요? changgahago tongno jjok junge eoneu jjogeuro deurilkkayo? Would you prefer a window or an aisle seat?

공항 gong·hang airport
공항에 세 시까지 오셔야 합니다. gonghange se sikkaji osyeoya hamnida. You need to arrive at the airport by three.

검색대 geom·saek·dae security check
승객들이 **검색대를 통과하고** 있다. seunggaekdeuri geomsaekdaereul tonggwahago itda. Passengers are going through security check.

활주로 hwal·ju·ro runway

뜨다 tteu·da to take off
기술적인 문제가 있어서 **비행기가 뜰** 수 없대요. gisuljeogin munjega isseoseo bihaenggiga tteul su eopdaeyo. I was told that the plane can't take off due to a technical hitch.

이륙 | ~하다 i·ryuk | ~·ha·da take-off | to take off
우리 비행기는 10분 후에 이륙합니다. uri bihaenggineun sipbun hue iryukamnida. The flight will take off in ten minutes.

착륙 | ~하다 chang·nyuk | ~·ha·da landing | to land
저희 비행기가 정시에 착륙하고 있습니다. jeohui bihaenggiga jeongsie changnyukago itseumnida. We're landing at the airport on time.

비행 | ~하다 bi·haeng | ~·ha·da flight | to fly

비행 시간이 얼마나 되나요? bihaeng sigani eolmana doenayo? What's the flight time?

경유하다 ≒ 거치다 gyeong·yu·ha·da ≒ geo·chi·da to pass via

이 비행기는 도쿄를 경유해서/거쳐서 인천으로 갑니다. i bihaenggineun dokyoreul gyeongyuhaeseo/geochyeoseo incheoneuro gamnida. This flight is heading for Incheon by way of Tokyo.

....

배 bae boat, ship

척 cheok unit for counting ships

배 한 척 bae han cheok one ship

항구 hang·gu port, harbor

배가 항구로 들어왔다. baega hangguro deureowatda. The ship steamed into the harbor.

부두 bu·du wharf, dock

등대 deung·dae lighthouse

선원 seo·nwon crewman, sailor

선장 seon·jang captain of a ship

뜨다 tteu·da to float; to leave

배는 어떻게 떠 있을 수 있을까? baeneun eotteoke tteo isseul su isseulkka? How is it that a boat floats?

오늘은 날씨 때문에 **배가** 안 **뜹니다**. oneureun nalssi ttaemune baega an tteumnida. There's no ship because of the bad weather.

가라앉다 ga·ra·an·da to sink, go under

작은 구멍이 큰 배를 가라앉게 하는 법이다. jageun gumeongi keun baereul garaange haneun beobida. A small leak can sink a great ship.

정박 | ~하다 jeong·bak | ~·ha·da anchoring | to anchor, berth

배가 부두에 정박 중이다. baega budue jeongbak jungida. The ship is anchored at the dock.

강가 강물 개다 건조하다 걷히다 공기 공중 관측 구름

굴 궤도 금성 기상 기압 기온 낙엽 난리 내리다 눈사태

늪 달 달빛 대기 덥다 도 땅 땅바닥 땅속 맑다

맺히다 모래 무더위 무덥다 무지개 물결 밀물 바람

바위 반달 별 불다 비 비바람 빗물 빗방울 빗줄기

빛 사막 산 산꼭대기 산성비 산소 산속 서늘하다 섬

흙질오염 숲 쌩쌩 썰물 쓰나미 언덕 얼다 얼음 연못 열대기후

chapter **29** The Universe
and Nature

영상 오존층 온실효과 온천 우물 우주 우주선 위성 일기예보

자연현상 저기압 절벽 중력 지구 지다 천둥 초승달 태풍

파도 폭발 폭포 한대기후 해 해안 해왕성 행성 오수 홍수

화성 화창하다 환경 황사 흐르다 흐리다 흙

29.1 The Universe, Earth

우주 u·ju space, the universe
우주의 기원을 이해하는 것은 인류의 오랜 소망 중 하나다. ujuui giwoneul ihaehaneun geoseun illyuui oraen somang jung hanada. Understanding the origins of the universe is one of the oldest dreams of mankind.

우주선 u·ju·seon spacecraft

로켓 ro·ket rocket
로켓이 성공적으로 과학 위성을 궤도에 진입시켰다. rokesi seonggongjeogeuro gwahak wiseongeul gwedoe jinipsikyeotda. The rocket successfully put a scientific satellite into orbit.

위성 wi·seong satellite, moon
지구에는 위성이 단 하나 있는데 그것이 바로 달이다. jiguneun wiseongi dan hana inneunde geugeosi baro darida. The Earth has a single satellite—the Moon.

인공위성 in·gong·wi·seong satellite

궤도 gwe·do orbit
인공위성이 궤도를 벗어났다. ingongwiseongi gwedoreul beoseonatda. The satellite has left its orbit.

....

행성 haeng·seong planet

수성 su·seong Mercury

금성 geum·seong Venus

화성 hwa·seong Mars

목성 mok·seong Jupiter

토성 to·seong Saturn

천왕성 cheo·nwang·seong Uranus

해왕성 hae·wang·seong Neptune

....

지구 ji·gu Earth
지구가 둥글다는 것은 상식이 되었다. jiguga dunggeuldaneun geoseun sangsigi doeeotda. It became common knowledge that the Earth is round.

중력 jung·nyeok gravity
중력의 법칙은 우주에서도 적용된다. jungnyeogui beopchigeun ujueseodo jeogyongdoenda. The laws of gravity apply even in space.

태양 tae·yang the Sun
지구는 태양의 주위를 돈다. jiguneun taeyangui juwireul donda. The Earth revolves around the Sun.

해 hae the Sun

별 byeol star
지금은 날이 흐려서 별이 보이지 않는다. jigeumeun nari heuryeoseo byeori boiji anneunda. I can't see the stars because the sky is cloudy.

달 dal the Moon
달이 구름 사이로 나타났다. dari gureum sairo natanatda. The Moon appeared through the clouds.

초승달 ← 초생달 cho·seung·dal ← cho·saeng·dal new moon

반달 ban·dal half moon

보름달 bo·reum·dal full moon

....

뜨다 tteu·da to float, rise
해는 동쪽에서 뜬다. haeneun dongjjogeseo tteunda. The Sun rises in the east.

솟다 sot·da to soar, rise
구름 사이로 해가 솟았다. gureum sairo haega sosatda. The Sun rose through the clouds.

지다 ji·da to set
여름에는 해가 늦게 진다. yeoreumeneun haega neutge jinda. The Sun sets late in summer.

29.2 Natural Phenomena, Environmental Issues

자연 ja·yeon nature
인간은 자연과 조화를 이루며 살아야 한다. inganeun jayeongwa johwareul irumyeo saraya handa. Men should live in harmony with nature.

자연현상 ja·yeon·hyeon·sang natural phenomenon

빛 bit light
빛은 소리보다 훨씬 빨리 이동한다. bicheun

soriboda hwolssin ppalli idonghanda. Light travels much faster than sound.

햇빛 haet·bit sunlight, sunshine
햇빛에 눈이 부셨다. **haetbiche nuni busyeot-da.** The sunlight dazzled my eyes.

햇볕 haet·byeot sunlight, sunshine
쨍쨍 jjaeng·jjaeng blazingly, brightly
햇볕이 **쨍쨍** 내리쬐고 있다. **haetbyeochi jjaengjjaeng naerijjoego itda.** The Sun is shining bright.

햇살 haet·sal sunshine, Sun
햇살이 따가우니까 자외선 차단제 꼭 발라라. **haetsari ttagaunikka jaoeseon chadanje kkok ballara.** The Sun is very hot. Don't forget to put on sunscreen.

달빛 dal·bit moonlight

그림자 geu·rim·ja shadow
지구의 그림자가 달을 가렸다. **jiguui geurim-jaga dareul garyeotda.** Earth's shadow blotted out the Moon.

그늘 geu·neul shade
그 정원은 오후가 되면 **그늘이 진다.** **geu jeongwoneun ohuga doemyeon geuneuri jinda.** The garden is shaded in the afternoon.

구름 gu·reum cloud
끼다 kki·da to hang, cloud
산에 **구름이 끼기** 시작했다. **sane gureumi kkigi sijakaetda.** It started to become cloudy over the mountain.

안개 an·gae fog, mist
안개가 꼈을 때는 천천히 운전해라. **angaega kkyeosseul ttaeneun cheoncheonhi unjeon-haera.** Drive slowly in foggy conditions.

자욱하다 ja·u·ka·da dense, thick
오늘 아침은 **안개가 자욱하다.** **oneul achi-meun angaega jaukada.** It is misty this morning.

비 bi rain
오늘 저녁 **비가** 올 확률이 60퍼센트입니다. **oneul jeonyeok biga ol hwangnyuri yuksip-peoseonteuimnida.** There's a 60 percent chance of rain tonight.

가랑비 ga·rang·bi drizzle
소나기 = 소낙비 so·na·gi = so·nak·bi shower

오늘 오후 한때 소나기가 예상됩니다. **oneul ohu hanttae sonagiga yesangdoemnida.** We expect a brief shower in the afternoon.

빗물 bin·mul rainwater
빗방울 bit·bang·ul raindrop
빗방울이 점점 굵어진다. **bitbanguri jeomjeom gulgeojinda.** The raindrops are getting bigger.

빗줄기 bit·jul·gi rain streak
비바람 bi·ba·ram rainstorm
장마 jang·ma rainy season
우리나라는 여름에 장마가 있습니다. **urinara-neun nyeoreume jangmaga itseumnida.** In Korea, the rainy season is part of the summer.

무지개 mu·ji·gae rainbow
비 온 뒤에 **무지개가 떴다.** **bi on dwie mujigae-ga tteotda.** There was a rainbow after the rain.

이슬 i·seul dew
맺히다 mae·chi·da to form
나뭇잎에 **이슬이 맺혔다.** **namunnipe iseuri maechyeotda.** The dew gathered on the leaves.

천둥 cheon·dung thunder
번개 = 벼락 beon·gae = byeo·rak lightning
번쩍 beon·jjeok with a flash
치다 chi·da to strike, flash
어젯밤 **번개가** 번쩍 **쳤다.** **eojetbam beonga-ga beonjjeok chyeotda.** Lightning flashed in the sky last night.

눈 nun snow
하루 종일 **눈이 오네.** **haru jongil luni one.** It's been snowing all day.

내리다 nae·ri·da to fall
어제 **눈 내리는** 거 봤어? **eoje nun naerineun geo bwasseo?** Did you see the snow fall yesterday?

그치다 geu·chi·da to stop, cease
빨리 **눈이 그쳤으면** 좋겠어요. **ppalli nuni geuchyeosseumyeon jokeseoyo.** I wish it would stop snowing soon.

쌓이다 ssa·i·da to pile up, be stacked up
밤새 **눈이 많이 쌓였다.** **bamsae nuni mani ssayeotda.** The snow piled up throughout the night.

얼음 ← **어름** eo·reum ice

얼다 eol·da to be frozen, freeze
호수에 **얼음**이 **얼었다**. hosue eoreumi eoreotda. The lake has frozen up.

녹다 nok·da to melt, thaw
얼음이 **녹고** 있어요. eoreumi nokgo isseoyo. The ice is melting.

바람 ba·ram wind

쌩쌩 ssaeng·ssaeng hard, strongly

불다 bul·da to blow
바람이 **쌩쌩 불고** 있어요. barami ssaengssaeng bulgo isseoyo. The wind is howling.

파도 pa·do wave
배가 파도에 심하게 좌우로 흔들렸다. baega padoe simhage jwauro heundeullyeotda. The boat rocked from side to side in the waves.

물결 mul·gyeol wave

밀물 mil·mul rising tide

썰물 sseol·mul ebb

화산 hwa·san volcano

폭발 | ~하다 pok·bal | ~·ha·da explosion, eruption | to explode, erupt
화산이 **폭발해서** 수많은 사람들이 사망했다. hwasani pokbalhaeseo sumaneun saramdeuri samanghaetda. A volcano erupted and killed numerous people.

자연재해 ja·yeon·jae·hae natural disaster

태풍 tae·pung typhoon
태풍이 진로를 서쪽으로 바꾸었다. taepungi jilloreul seojjogeuro bakkueotda. The typhoon has turned its course westward.

홍수 hong·su flood
이번 홍수로 모든 것을 잃었습니다. ibeon hongsuro modeun geoseul ireotseumnida. I lost everything in the flood.

가뭄 ga·mum drought
강들이 가뭄으로 바싹 말랐다. gangdeuri gamumeuro bassak mallatda. The rivers all dried up due to the drought.

폭설 pok·seol heavy snow
오늘 오전 강원도에 **폭설이** 내렸습니다. oneul ojeon gangwondoe pokseori naeryeotseumnida. There was a very heavy snowfall in Gangwon Province this morning.

눈사태 nun·sa·tae avalanche

지진 ji·jin earthquake
어젯밤 광주에서 강력한 **지진이 발생했다**. eojetbam gwangjueseo gangnyeokan jijini balsaenghaetda. There was a huge earthquake in Gwangju last night.

해일 hae·il tidal wave

쓰나미 sseu·na·mi tsunami
쓰나미는 광범위한 피해를 가져왔다. sseunamineun gwangbeomwihan pihaereul gajyeowatda. The tsunami brought widespread damage.

황사 hwang·sa yellow dust
한국에서는 봄에 부는 황사가 심각한 문제입니다. hangugeseoneun bome buneun hwangsaga simgakan munjeimnida. In Korea, yellow dust is a serious problem in spring.

난리 nal·li panic, mess
지진으로 전국이 **난리가 났다**. jijineuro jeongugi nalliga natda. An earthquake caused panic all over the country.

환경 hwan·gyeong environment

자연환경 ja·yeon·hwan·gyeong natural environment
우리는 **자연환경을 보호해야** 한다. urineun jayeonhwangyeongeul bohohaeya handa. We should try to protect our environment.

환경문제 hwan·gyeong·mun·je environmental problem
저는 환경문제에 깊은 관심을 갖고 있습니다. jeoneun hwangyeongmunjee gipeun gwansimeul gatgo itseumnida. I care deeply about environmental issues.

오염 | ~시키다 o·yeom | ~·si·ki·da pollution, contamination | to pollute

환경오염 hwan·gyeong·o·yeom environmental pollution, environmental contamination

대기오염 dae·gi·o·yeom air pollution
전문가들은 **대기오염의 위험성**에 대해 오랫동안 경고해 왔다. jeonmungadeureun daegioyeomui wiheomseonge daehae oraetdongan gyeonggohae watda. Experts have been warning about the dangers of air pollution for a long time.

수질오염 su·ji·ro·yeom water pollution
산업 하수는 **수질오염**을 유발한다. saneop hasuneun sujiroyeomeul lyubalhanda. Indus-

trial sewage causes water pollution.

토양오염 to·yang·o·yeom soil pollution

공해 gong·hae (environmental) pollution
공해를 막을 더 많은 대책이 필요합니다. gonghaereul mageul deo maneun daechaegi piryohamnida. We need more action to stop pollution.

매연 mae·yeon exhaust

소음 so·eum noise
우리 집은 길가에 있어서 특히 밤에 **소음**이 심하다. uri jibeun gilgae isseoseo teuki bame soeumi simhada. My house is right by the road, so it's very noisy, particularly at night.

스모그 seu·mo·geu smog
자동차 매연은 **스모그**의 주요 원인 중 하나다. jadongcha maeyeoneun seumogeuui juyo wonin jung hanada. Vehicle exhaust fumes are one of the major causes of smog.

산성비 san·seong·bi acid rain

산성비가 내릴 때 비를 맞지 않도록 조심해라. sanseongbiga naeril ttae bireul matji antorok josimhaera. Be careful not to get wet when acid rain falls.

열대야 yeol·dae·ya tropical night, hot night
열대야는 지구온난화와 밀접한 관련이 있다. yeoldaeyaneun jiguonnanhwawa miljeopan gwallyeoni itda. Tropical nights are closely associated with global warming.

지구온난화 ji·gu·on·nan·hwa global warming

오존층 o·jon·cheung the ozone layer
오존층 파괴는 지구온난화의 원인이 되고 있다. ojoncheung pagoeneun jiguonnanhwaui wonini doego itda. Ozone destruction is contributing to global warming.

온실효과 on·sil·hyo·gwa the greenhouse effect

29.3 The Air, Mountains, Land, Bodies of Water

하늘 ha·neul sky
하늘이 잔뜩 찌푸려 있어요. haneuri jantteuk jjipuryeo isseoyo. The sky is clouded over.

공중 gong·jung the air
몇몇 사람들은 자신이 **공중에** 뜰 수 있다고 주장한다. myeonmyeot saramdeureun jasini gongjunge tteul su itdago jujanghanda. Some people insist that they can float in the air.

공기 gong·gi air
신선한 **공기**를 마시니 기분이 좋아져요. sinseonhan gonggireul masini gibuni joajyeoyo. Breathing some fresh air has made me feel better.

대기 dae·gi the atmosphere, the air
높은 산에서는 **대기**가 맑고 깨끗하다. nopeun saneseoneun daegiga malgo kkaekkeutada. In the high mountains the air is fresh and pure.

산소 san·so oxygen
높은 지대에는 **산소**가 **희박해요**. nopeun jidaeneun sansoga huibakaeyo. There is sparse oxygen at high altitudes.

산 san mountain
어제 **산**을 내려오다 발을 삐었어요. eoje

saneul laeryeooda bareul ppieosseoyo. I sprained my ankle while coming down the mountain yesterday.

풍경 pung·gyeong landscape, scene
사람들이 멈춰 서서 **풍경**을 **감상했다**. saramdeuri meomchwo seoseo punggyeongeul gamsanghaetda. People stopped to admire the scenery.

경치 gyeong·chi scenery, scene
지리산은 **경치**가 아주 **아름다워요**. jirisaneun gyeongchiga aju areumdawoyo. Mount Jiri has marvelous scenery.

정상 jeong·sang top, summit
마침내 우리는 산 **정상**에 올랐다. machimnae urineun san jeongsange ollatda. Finally we reached the top of the mountain.

산꼭대기 san·kkok·dae·gi mountaintop
산꼭대기에서 보는 경치는 정말 아름다웠다. sankkokdaegieseo boneun gyeongchineun jeongmal areumdawotda. The view from the top of the mountain was really beautiful.

(산)봉우리 (san·)bong·u·ri mountaintop

계곡 = 골짜기 gye·gok = gol·jja·gi valley
새 한 마리가 계곡/골짜기 위를 날고 있었다.

sae han mariga gyegok/goljjagi wireul lalgo isseotda. A bird was flying above the valley.

산길 san·gil mountain path

산속 san·sok in the mountains
산속에서 길을 잃는 것은 매우 위험하다. **sansogeseo gireul illeun geoseun maeu wiheomhada.** It is very dangerous to get lost in the mountains.

절벽 jeol·byeok cliff
그 호텔은 절벽 끝에 위치해 있다. **geu hotereun jeolbyeok kkeute wichihae itda.** The hotel is located on a cliff.

언덕 eon·deok hill, slope
이 언덕에는 대나무 숲이 있어요. **i eondeogeneun daenamu supi isseoyo.** This hill has bamboo forests.

고개 go·gae hill, mountain pass

숲 sup forest
사람들이 숲에서 야영을 하고 있다. **saramdeuri supeseo yayeongeul hago itda.** People are camping in the forest.

(동)굴 (dong·)gul cave
실종자는 동굴에서 사망한 채로 발견되었다. **siljongjaneun donggureseo samanghan chaero balgyeondoeeotda.** The missing person was found dead in the cave.

단풍 dan·pung fall foliage
설악산은 아름다운 **가을 단풍**으로 유명하다. **seoraksaneun areumdaun gaeul danpungeuro yumyeonghada.** Mt. Seorak is famous for its beautiful autumn foliage.

낙엽 na·gyeop fallen leaves, autumn leaves
벌써 **낙엽이** 지기 시작했다. **beolsseo nagyeobi jigi sijakaetda.** The autumn leaves have already started to fall.

땅 ttang earth, land, ground
이 **땅은** 아주 **비옥하다**. **i ttangeun aju biokada.** This land is very fertile.

땅바닥 ttang·ba·dak (bare) ground

땅속 ttang·sok underground

들(판) deul(·pan) field
소들이 들판에서 풀을 뜯고 있다. **sodeuri deulpaneseo pureul tteutgo itda.** The cows are grazing in the fields.

평야 pyeong·ya plains

흙 heuk earth, soil, dirt

지렁이는 축축한 흙에서 산다. **jireongineun chukchukan heulgeseo sanda.** Earthworms live in the moist soil.

돌 dol stone
그 집은 돌로 지어졌다. **geu jibeun dollo jieojyeotda.** The house was built of stone.

돌멩이 dol·meng·i stone

자갈 ja·gal gravel, pebble

바위 ba·wi rock
바위가 너무 **무거워서** 움직일 수가 없어. **bawiga neomu mugeowoseo umjigil suga eopseo.** The rock is too heavy to move.

모래 mo·rae sand
신발에 모래가 들어갔어. **sinbare moraega deureogasseo.** I have sand in my shoe.

사막 sa·mak desert
호주의 내륙은 하나의 거대한 **사막 지역**이다. **hojuui naeryugeun hanaui geodaehan samak jiyeogida.** The interior of Australia is one big desert region.

바다 ba·da sea, ocean
언덕에서 바다가 내려다보여요. **eondeogeseo badaga naeryeodaboyeoyo.** The hill commands a fine view of the sea.

바닷가 = 해변 ba·dat·ga = hae·byeon beach, coast
이번 휴가에 바닷가에/해변에 갈 거야. **ibeon hyugae badatgae/haebyeone gal geoya.** I will go to the beach during my vacation.

해안 hae·an coast, seashore

바닷물 ba·dan·mul seawater
바닷물 색깔 좀 봐! **badanmul saekkkal jom bwa!** Look at the color of the sea!

강 gang river
한강은 한국에서 가장 큰 강이다. **hangangeun hangugeseo gajang keun gangida.** The Han River is the biggest river in Korea.

강가 = 강변 gang·ga = gang·byeon riverside
아침마다 강가를/강변을 따라 걷습니다. **achimmada ganggareul/gangbyeoneul ttara geotseumnida.** I walk along the river every morning.

강물 gang·mul river
그녀가 강물에 뛰어들었다. **geunyeoga gangmure ttwieodeureotda.** She jumped into the river.

호수 ho·su lake
보트를 타고 **호수를** 건너고 싶어요. boteureul tago hosureul geonneogo sipeoyo. I would like to go across the lake in a sailboat.

하천 ha·cheon river, stream

개울 gae·ul brook, stream

시내 si·nae stream, brook

폭포 pok·po waterfall

연못 yeon·mot pond
이 연못의 물을 마시지 마시오. i yeonmosui mureul masiji masio. Do not drink water from the pond.

우물 u·mul well
오랜 가뭄으로 **우물이 말라** 버렸다. oraen gamumeuro umuri malla beoryeotda. The wells have dried up due to the long drought.

샘 saem spring

온천 on·cheon hot spring

늪 neup marsh, swamp
그 늪에는 온갖 곤충들이 산다. geu neupeneun ongat gonchungdeuri sanda. The marsh is swarming with a variety of insects.

섬 seom island
그 섬은 아름다운 해변으로 유명하다. geu seomeun areumdaun haebyeoneuro yumyeonghada. The island is famous for its beautiful beaches.

물속 mul·sok underwater
개구리는 물속과 땅 위 양쪽에서 살 수 있다. gaegurineun mulsokgwa ttang wi yangjjogeseo sal su itda. Frogs can live both in water and on land.

흐르다 heu·reu·da to flow, run
한강은 도심을 가로질러 흐른다. hangangeun dosimeul garojilleo heureunda. The Han River flows through the heart of the city.

29.4 The Climate, Weather

날씨 nal·ssi weather
오늘 날씨 어때요? oneul lalssi eottaeyo? How's the weather today?

맑다 mak·da clear, sunny
하루 종일 맑겠습니다. haru jongil malgetseumnida. It looks like it will be clear all day.

화창하다 hwa·chang·ha·da clear, sunny
남부 캘리포니아는 일 년 내내 화창합니다. nambu kaelliponianeun il lyeon naenae hwachanghamnida. It's sunny in southern California all year round.

온화하다 on·hwa·ha·da mild, temperate

흐리다 heu·ri·da cloudy
흐린 날씨가 이어지겠습니다. heurin nalssiga ieojigetseumnida. The cloudy weather will continue.

개다 gae·da to become clear
일기예보에서 오후에는 **날씨가 갠대**. ilgiyeboeseo ohueneun nalssiga gaendae. The weather forecast said it would become clear in the afternoon.

걷히다 geo·chi·da to lift, clear up
구름이 걷히기 시작했어요. gureumi geochigi sijakaesseoyo. The clouds have begun to clear.

따뜻하다 tta·tteu·ta·da warm
올해 겨울은 이상하게 따뜻하다. olhae gyeoureun isanghage ttatteutada. It's unusually warm this winter.

덥다 deop·da hot
여기는 일 년 내내 더워. yeogineun il lyeon naenae deowo. It's hot all year round here.

더위 deo·wi the heat
더위를 많이 타세요? deowireul mani taseyo? Are you very sensitive to the heat?

무덥다 mu·deop·da stifling, sweltering
한낮에는 무더웠는데 지금은 시원해. hannajeneun mudeowonneunde jigeumeun siwonhae. It was stifling at midday, but now it is cool.

무더위 mu·deo·wi heat wave

찌다 jji·da to steam, get steaming hot
날이 찌는 듯이 덥다. nari jjineun deusi deopda. It is steaming hot.

춥다 chup·da cold
밖은 아직도 추워. bakkeun ajikdo chuwo. It's still cold outside.

추위 chu·wi the cold

추위 때문에 몸이 안 움직여요. **chuwi ttae-mune momi an umjigyeoyo.** I can't move my body because of the cold.

° **서늘하다 seo·neul·ha·da** cool
여름이라도 저녁에는 서늘하다. **yeoreumirado jeonyeogeneun seoneulhada.** It gets cold at night, even during the summer.

쌀쌀하다 ssal·ssal·ha·da chilly
어젯밤에 비가 많이 와서 오늘 아침은 쌀쌀하네. **eojetbame biga mani waseo oneul achimeun ssalssalhane.** It rained a lot last night, so it's chilly this morning.

° **습기 seup·gi** moisture, humidity
이곳은 **습기**가 **많아요**. **igoseun seupgiga manayo.** This place is humid.

습하다 seu·pa·da damp, humid
지금은 장마철이어서 **습한 날씨**가 이어져요. **jigeumeun jangmacheorieoseo seupan nalssiga ieojyeoyo.** It's rainy season, so the humid days will continue.

° **건조하다 geon·jo·ha·da** dry, arid
날씨가 너무 **건조해서** 자주 감기에 걸려. **nalssiga neomu geonjohaeseo jaju gamgie geollyeo.** I catch a cold very often because the weather is too dry.

일기예보 il·gi·ye·bo weather forecast

기상 gi·sang weather conditions
오늘 경기는 **기상 악화**로 취소되었습니다. **oneul gyeonggineun gisang akhwaro chwisodoeeotseumnida.** Today's game has been canceled due to deteriorating weather conditions.

관측 | ~하다 gwan·cheuk | ~·ha·da observation | to observe
이번 일식은 약 5분간 관측되었다. **ibeon ilsigeun nyak obungan gwancheukdoeeotda.** The solar eclipse was observed for about five minutes.

° **기온 gi·on** (atmospheric) temperature
아침저녁으로 **기온 변화**가 심합니다. **achimjeonyeogeuro gion byeonhwaga simhamnida.**

The temperature fluctuates considerably from night to day.

° **도 do** degree
기온이 어제보다 15도 떨어졌어요. **gioni eojeboda sibodo tteoreojyeosseoyo.** The temperature has dropped 15 degrees since yesterday.

° **최고 choe·go** the highest
° **최저 choe·jeo** the lowest
° **영상 yeong·sang** over zero
낮 최고 기온은 영상 2도로 예상됩니다. **nat choego gioneun nyeongsang idoro yesangdoemnida.** During the daytime high temperatures will be two degrees above zero.

° **영하 yeong·ha** below zero
밤에는 기온이 영하로 떨어지겠습니다. **bameneun gioni yeongharo tteoreojigetseumnida.** The temperature will drop below zero at night.

습도 seup·do humidity
오늘은 습도가 30%입니다. **oneureun seupdoga samsippeosenteuimnida.** There is 30 percent humidity today.

° **강수량 gang·su·ryang** precipitation
기압 gi·ap atmospheric pressure
고기압 go·gi·ap high pressure
저기압 jeo·gi·ap low pressure

° **기후 gi·hu** climate
열대기후 yeol·dae·gi·hu tropical climate
건조기후 geon·jo·gi·hu dry climate
온대기후 on·dae·gi·hu temperate climate
한국은 온대기후에 속합니다. **hangugeun ondaegihue sokamnida.** Korea has a temperate climate.

냉대기후 naeng·dae·gi·hu subarctic climate
한대기후 han·dae·gi·hu polar climate

가꾸다 가로수 가시 가지 갈대 갈매기 강아지 개나리

미 게 고래 곰 국화 그루 기린 기생충 길들이다 까악까악 까치

껍질 꼬끼오 꼬리 꽃 꽃씨 꽃잎 꿀꿀 나방 나비 나팔꽃

날다 늑대 달걀 닭 대나무 독 독수리 돌고래 돼지

둥지 매 매미 맴맴 멍멍 멸종 모기 무리 미생물 민들레

이러스 박쥐 박테리아 뱀 벌 벚꽃 부리 비둘기 뿌리 뿔

새 새끼 생명 소 소나무 송이 심다 싹 씨 알

chapter 30 | Plants and Animals

야옹 양 어미 여우 열리다 열매 염소 오리 은행나무

인삼 잎 잔디 잠자리 잡아먹다 조개 줄기 지느러미

진달래 짐승 짖다 쪼다 참새 카네이션 코끼리 코스모스

트다 파리 풀 피다 호랑이 화분 히힝

30.1 Plants, Cultivation

식물 sing·mul plant
식물의 성장에는 햇빛이 반드시 필요하다. singmurui seongjangeneun haetbichi bandeusi piryohada. Sunlight is essential for plant growth.

뿌리 ppu·ri root

줄기 jul·gi stem, stalk

가지 ga·ji branch, sprig

나뭇가지 na·mut·ga·ji tree branch

잎 ip leaf
대부분의 나무는 가을에 잎이 떨어진다. daebubunui namuneun gaeure ipi tteoreojinda. Most trees lose their leaves in autumn.

나뭇잎 na·mun·nip leaf, foliage

꽃잎 kkon·nip petal

가시 ga·si thorn, prickle

껍질 kkeop·jil bark

꽃 kkot flower
나비가 꽃에 앉아 있다. nabiga kkoche anja itda. A butterfly is sitting on the flower.

송이 song·i unit for counting flowers
장미 한 송이 jangmi han songi a rose

개나리 gae·na·ri forsythia

진달래 jin·dal·lae azalea

벚꽃 beot·kkot cherry blossoms

민들레 min·deul·le dandelion

튤립 tyul·lip tulip

나팔꽃 na·pal·kkot morning glory

장미 jang·mi rose

해바라기 hae·ba·ra·gi sunflower

카네이션 ka·ne·i·syeon carnation

무궁화 mu·gung·hwa the rose of Sharon

국화 gu·khwa chrysanthemum

코스모스 ko·seu·mo·seu cosmos

나무 na·mu tree
이 나무는 백 년이 넘었다고 알려져 있다. i namuneun baeng nyeoni neomeotdago allyeojyeo itda. This tree is known to be more than one hundred years old.

그루 geu·ru unit for counting trees
소나무 한 그루 sonamu han geuru a pine tree

소나무 so·na·mu pine tree

은행나무 eun·haeng·na·mu ginkgo

가로수 ga·ro·su trees along the street

풀 pul grass

갈대 gal·dae reed

잔디 jan·di grass, lawn

대나무 dae·na·mu bamboo

인삼 in·sam ginseng
인삼은 이 지방의 특산물이다. insameun i jibangui teuksanmurida. Ginseng is a specialty of this region.

씨(앗) ssi(·at) seed
며칠 있으면 씨앗에서 싹이 틀 거야. myeochil isseumyeon ssiaseseo ssagi teul geoya. The seeds will sprout in a few days.

꽃씨 kkot·ssi flower seeds

싹 ssak sprout, shoot

트다 teu·da to bud, sprout
나무에 벌써 싹이 텄다/돋았다/났다. namue beolsseo ssagi teotda/dodatda/natda. The tree is in bud already.

돋다 dot·da to bud, sprout

나다 na·da to bud, sprout

활짝 hwal·jjak in full bloom

피다 pi·da to bloom, blossom
나무에 꽃이 활짝 피었다. namue kkochi hwaljjak pieotda. The tree is in full bloom.

열매 yeol·mae fruit, nut

맺다 maet·da to bear
식물이 열매를 맺기 시작하면 많은 물을 필요로 한다. singmuri yeolmaereul maetgi sijakamyeon maneun mureul piryoro handa. As plants start to bear fruit, they need a lot of water.

열리다 yeol·li·da to be born

이 나무는 **열매가** 많이 **열린다**. i namuneun nyeolmaega mani yeollinda. This tree bears a lot of fruit.

시들다 si·deul·da to wilt, wither
화분에 심은 꽃이 시들었다. hwabune simeun kkochi sideureotda. My potted flower wilted.

지다 ji·da to fall
이달 말이면 **벚꽃이** 질 거야. idal marimyeon beotkkochi jil geoya. By the end of the month, the cherry blossoms will be gone.

화분 hwa·bun flowerpot
나 없는 동안 화분에 물 좀 줄래? na eomneun dongan hwabune mul jom jullae? Can you water the plant while I'm gone?

심다 sim·da to plant
이번 주말에는 산에 가서 **나무를 심을** 생각입니다. ibeon jumareneun sane gaseo namureul simeul saenggagimnida. I'm going to the mountains to plant some trees this weekend.

가꾸다 ga·kku·da to grow, raise, tend
어머니는 뜰에서 **채소를 가꾸세요**. eomeonineun tteureseo chaesoreul gakkuseyo. My mother grows vegetables in the backyard.

30.2 Animals, Keeping Animals

생물 saeng·mul life, organism

생명 saeng·myeong life
화성에는 **생명의 흔적이** 없었다. hwaseongeneun saengmyeongui heunjeogi eopseotda. There was no sign of life on Mars.

동물 dong·mul animal

짐승 jim·seung animal, beast

마리 ma·ri unit for counting animals
새 두 마리 sae du mari two birds

암컷 am·keot female

수컷 su·keot male
암컷이야, 수컷이야? amkeosiya, sukeosiya? Is it a she or he?

무리 = 떼 mu·ri = tte group, crowd, herd
꿀벌은 **무리를/떼를** 지어 산다. kkulbeoreun murireul/tteureul jieo sanda. Honeybees live in communities.

새끼 sae·kki baby, young
어젯밤에 우리 집 고양이가 **새끼를 낳았어요**. eojetbame uri jip goyangiga saekkireul laasseoyo. Last night our cat gave birth to a kitten.

어미 eo·mi mother (animal)
어미 새가 새끼들에게 먹이를 주고 있다. eomi saega saekkideurege meogireul jugo itda. A mother bird is feeding her young.

꼬리 kko·ri tail
그가 고양이의 꼬리를 잡아당기자 고양이가 그를 물었다. geuga goyangiui kkorireul jabadanggija goyangiga geureul mureotda. The cat bit him because he pulled her tail.

애완동물 ae·wan·dong·mul pet

반려동물 bal·lyeo·dong·mul animal companion

기르다 ≒ 키우다 gi·reu·da ≒ ki·u·da to raise, rear, grow
저희 집에서는 개와 닭을 기릅니다/키웁니다. jeohui jibeseoneun gaewa dalgeul gireumnida/kiumnida. We keep dogs and poultry.
엄마, 거북이 키우고/기르고 싶어요. eomma, geobugi kiugo/gireugo sipeoyo. Mom, I'd like to raise a tortoise.

개 gae dog
개는 냄새를 잘 맡는다. gaeneun naemsaereul jal manneunda. Dogs have good noses.

강아지 gang·a·ji puppy

멍멍 meong·meong sound of dogs

짖다 jit·da to bark
우리 집 개는 낯선 사람을 봐도 짖지를 않아. uri jip gaeneun natseon sarameul bwado jitjireul ana. Our dog never barks at strangers.

고양이 go·yang·i cat
우리 집 고양이는 쥐 잡는 데 관심이 없어요. uri jip goyangineun jwi jamneun de gwansimi eopseoyo. My cat is not interested in catching mice.

야옹 ya·ong sound of cats

가축 ga·chuk stock, livestock

길들이다 gil·deu·ri·da to train, domesticate

소 so cow, cattle

송아지 song·a·ji calf

음메 eum·me sound of cows or goats

말 mal horse
말 타 본 적 있어? mal ta bon jeok isseo? Have you ever ridden a horse?

히힝 hi·hing sound of horses

돼지 dwae·ji pig

꿀꿀 kkul·kkul sound of pigs

닭 dak chicken, hen, rooster

꼬끼오 kko·kki·o sound of roosters

병아리 byeong·a·ri chick

삐악삐악 ppi·ak·ppi·ak sound of chicks

알 al egg

달걀 = 계란 dal·gyal = gye·ran hen's egg
우리 집 닭은 달걀을/계란을 하루에 한 개씩 낳는다. uri jip dalgeun dalgyareul/gyeraneul harue han gaessik nanneunda. Each of our hens lays one egg a day.

토끼 to·kki rabbit

양 yang sheep

염소 yeom·so goat

오리 o·ri duck

거위 geo·wi goose

꽥꽥 kkwaek·kkwaek sound of ducks or geese

사자 sa·ja lion
사자는 동물의 왕이다. sajaneun dongmurui wangida. The lion is the king of the animals.

호랑이 ho·rang·i tiger
호랑이는 아시아에 살아요. horangineun asi-ae sarayo. Tigers live in Asia.

어흥 eo·heung sound of tigers

곰 gom bear
사람들은 곰이 느리다고 생각하지만 실제로는 그렇지 않다. saramdeureun gomi neurida-go saenggakajiman siljeroneun geureochi anta. People think bears are slow but actually they are not.

늑대 neuk·dae wolf

여우 yeo·u fox

공룡 gong·nyong dinosaur

멸종 | ~하다 myeol·jong | ~·ha·da extinction | to die out
공룡의 멸종에 대해 많은 가설들이 있다. gongnyongui myeoljonge daehae maneun ga-seoldeuri itda. There are many assumptions about the extinction of dinosaurs.

잡아먹다 ja·ba·meok·da to prey on, feed on
어제 고양이가 쥐를 잡아먹는 것을 보았다. eoje goyangiga jwireul jabameongneun geo-seul boatda. Yesterday I saw a cat catch a mouse.

고래 go·rae whale

고릴라 go·ril·la gorilla

원숭이 won·sung·i monkey

기린 gi·rin giraffe

사슴 sa·seum deer

코끼리 ko·kki·ri elephant
코끼리는 보통 떼를 지어 산다. kokkirineun botong ttereul jieo sanda. Elephants usually live in herds.

코뿔소 ko·ppul·so rhinoceros

뿔 ppul horn

쥐 jwi rat, mouse
이웃집 다락에 쥐가 있어요. iutjip darage jwiga isseoyo. Our neighbors have mice in their attic.

거북(이) geo·buk(·i) turtle, tortoise

악어 a·geo crocodile, alligator

뱀 baem snake

개구리 gae·gu·ri frog

개굴개굴 gae·gul·gae·gul sound of frogs

올챙이 ol·chaeng·i tadpole

새 sae bird
일찍 일어나는 새가 벌레를 잡는다. iljjik ireo-naneun saega beollereul jamneunda. The early bird catches the worm.

날개 nal·gae wing

깃털 git·teol feather, plumage

부리 bu·ri beak, bill

쪼다 jjo·da to peck
닭들이 **모이를 쪼고** 있다. dakdeuri moireul jjogo itda. The chickens are pecking at their feed.

훨훨 hwol·hwol lightly

날다 nal·da to fly
나비 한 마리가 하늘을 **훨훨 날고** 있다. nabi han mariga haneureul hwolhwol lalgo itda. A butterfly is flying freely in the sky.

둥지 dung·ji nest
뻐꾸기는 다른 새의 둥지에 알을 낳는다. ppeokkugineun dareun saeui dungjie areul lanneunda. The cuckoo lays its eggs in other birds' nests.

제비 je·bi swallow
조상들은 제비가 낮게 날면 비가 온다는 것을 알았다. josangdeureun jebiga natge nalmyeon biga ondaneun geoseul aratda. Our ancestors knew that it was about to rain when swallows flew low to the ground.

까치 kka·chi magpie
한국 사람들은 까치가 울면 반가운 손님이 온다고 생각한다. hanguk saramdeureun kkachiga ulmyeon bangaun sonnimi ondago saenggakanda. Korean people think a welcome guest may be visiting them when they see a magpie cawing.

까마귀 kka·ma·gwi crow

까악까악 kka·ak·kka·ak sound of crows

독수리 dok·su·ri eagle

매 mae hawk, falcon

비둘기 bi·dul·gi dove, pigeon

구구 gu·gu sound of doves

참새 cham·sae sparrow

짹짹 jjaek·jjaek sound of sparrows

지저귀다 ji·jeo·gwi·da to sing, chirp

갈매기 gal·mae·gi seagull

기러기 gi·reo·gi wild goose

박쥐 bak·jwi bat

펭귄 peng·gwin penguin

물고기 mul·go·gi fish
안전을 위해 떼를 지어 사는 물고기들이 많다. anjeoneul wihae ttereul jieo saneun mulgogideuri manta. Many kinds of fish live in schools for protection.

상어 sang·eo shark

돌고래 dol·go·rae dolphin

금붕어 geum·bung·eo goldfish

지느러미 ji·neu·reo·mi fin

비늘 bi·neul scales

아가미 a·ga·mi gill

게 ge crab

조개 jo·gae clam

껍질 kkeop·jil shell

곤충 gon·chung bug, insect
저는 곤충을 별로 좋아하지 않아요. jeoneun gonchungeul byeollo joahaji anayo. I don't like bugs very much.

벌레 beol·le bug, insect

잠자리 jam·ja·ri dragonfly

벌 beol bee
손가락이 **벌에 쏘였어요**. songaragi beore ssoyeosseoyo. I was stung on my finger by a bee.

꿀벌 kkul·beol honeybee

나비 na·bi butterfly

나방 na·bang moth

매미 mae·mi cicada

맴맴 maem·maem sound of cicadas

모기 mo·gi mosquito

파리 pa·ri fly

개미 gae·mi ant
개미가 설탕 주변에 모여 있다. gaemiga seoltang jubyeone moyeo itda. Ants are swarming around the sugar.

거미 geo·mi spider

독 dok poison

지렁이 ji·reong·i earthworm

달팽이 dal·paeng·i snail

미생물 mi·saeng·mul microorganism

(세)균 (se·)gyun germ

상처 부위에 **균이** 들어가지 않게 해라.
sangcheo buwie gyuni deureogaji anke haera.
Make sure to keep the wound from getting
infected.

박테리아 bak·te·ri·a bacterium

바이러스 ba·i·reo·seu virus

그 바이러스는 신체 접촉을 통해 전염된다.
**geu baireoseuneun sinche jeopchogeul tonghae
jeonyeomdoenda.** The virus is transmitted
through physical contact.

곰팡이 gom·pang·i mold

음식에 **곰팡이가** 피었어. **eumsige gompangi-
ga pieosseo.** The food is green with mold.

기생충 gi·saeng·chung parasite

갓 결말 곡우 곧장 그때 그전 그제 근대 금세 기원전

기원후 김 끝 낮 느리다 닷새 당시 당장 동시 동지

되다 뒤 때로 뜸하다 막상 만 매번 매일 먼저

명절 방금 백로 벌써 분 비로소 사월 새해 소만

한 수년 시 시각 시간 시기 시점 식목일 아흐레 양력

어린이날 어버이날 어제 오늘날 오후 이때

이르다 이어 이월 이제 이후 일 일요일

chapter **31** | Time and
Time Concepts

입춘 자꾸 잘 장래 장차 잦다 절기 정각 정기적 주

줄곧 중세 지금 직후 짧다 차츰 채 채 처음

천천히 초 초기 초여름 초저녁 최초 추석 춘분

칠월 토요일 팔월 한글날 한낮 한로 한순간

한여름 후년 훗날 흐르다 흔하다

31.1 Days of the Week and Dates

날 nal day
졸업할 날이 얼마 안 남았다. joreopal lari eolma an namatda. The date of my graduation is not far off.

일 il day
5일 정도 걸립니다. oil jeongdo geollimnida. It takes about five days.

하루 ha·ru a day

이틀 i·teul two days

사흘 sa·heul three days

나흘 na·heul four days

닷새 dat·sae five days

엿새 yeot·sae six days

이레 i·re seven days

여드레 yeo·deu·re eight days

아흐레 a·heu·re nine days

열흘 yeol·heul ten days

보름 bo·reum fifteen days

며칠 ← 몇일 myeo·chil a few days
A: 그 사람 언제 떠났는지 아세요? B: 글쎄요, **며칠 전**인 것 같은데요. A: geu saram eonje tteonanneunji aseyo? B: geulsseyo, myeochil jeonin geot gateundeyo. A: Do you know when he left here? B: Well, I think a few days ago.

주 ju week
다음 주에 봐요. daeum jue bwayo. See you next week.

주(일) ju(·il) week
이사 온 지 2주가 지났어요. isa on ji ijuga jinasseoyo. It's been two weeks since I moved in.

지난주 ji·nan·ju last week
A: 오늘은 좀 어때요? B: 지난주보다는 훨씬 좋아. A: oneureun jom eottaeyo? B: jinanjubodaneun hwolssin joa. A: How are you today? B: Much better than last week.

매주 mae·ju every week

요일 yo·il day of the week
무슨 요일에 가고 싶어? museun nyoire gago sipeo? What day of the week would you like to go?

일주일 il·ju·il a week, one week
A: 왜 그렇게 바쁘세요? B: 일주일 동안 쉬었거든요. A: wae geureoke bappeuseyo? B: iljuil dongan swieotgeodeunnyo. A: Why are you so busy? B: I took a week's vacation.

월요일 wo·ryo·il Monday

화요일 hwa·yo·il Tuesday

수요일 su·yo·il Wednesday

목요일 mo·gyo·il Thursday

금요일 geu·myo·il Friday

토요일 to·yo·il Saturday

일요일 i·ryo·il Sunday
우리는 금요일 오후에 떠나 일요일 저녁에 돌아올 수 있을 거라 생각했어요. urineun geumyoil ohue tteona iryoil jeonyeoge doraol su isseul geora saenggakaeseoyo. We thought we could leave Friday afternoon and come back Sunday evening.

평일 pyeong·il weekday
오늘은 평일이라서, 주말만큼 바쁘지는 않아요. oneureun pyeongiriraseo, jumalmankeum bappeujineun anayo. Today's a weekday, so it's not as busy as the weekends.

주말 ju·mal weekend
주말 어떻게 보냈어? jumal eotteoke bonaesseo? How did you spend the weekend?

휴일 hyu·il holiday
휴일을 어떻게 보낼 거야? hyuireul eotteoke bonael geoya? How are you going to spend the holidays?

공휴일 gong·hyu·il national holiday
3월 1일은 한국에서 공휴일이다. samwol irireun hangugeseo gonghyuirida. March 1 is a national holiday in Korea.

날짜 ← 날자 nal·jja ← nal·ja date
결혼 **날짜**를 아직 결정하지 못했어요. gyeolhon naljjareul ajik gyeoljeonghaji motaesseoyo. I haven't decided on a date for the wedding yet.

언제 eon·je when
언제 왔어? eonje wasseo? When did you get here?

며칠 ← 몇일 myeo·chil date

오늘이 며칠이죠? **oneuri myeochirijyo?** What is the date?

: **년 nyeon** year
2014년 월드컵은 브라질에서 열렸다. **icheonsipsanyeon woldeukeobeun beurajireseo yeolleotda.** The 2014 World Cup was held in Brazil.

: **월 wol** month
오늘은 2014년 12월 30일이에요. **oneureun icheonsipsanyeon sibiwol samsibirieyo.** Today is December 30, 2014.

> Dates in Korean are written in the year, month, and day format.

: **일 il** day
A: 생일이 몇 월 며칠이세요? B: 9월 28일이에요. **A: saengiri myeot wol myeochiriseyo? B: guwol isipparirieyo.** A: When is your birthday? B: September 28.

31.2 Months

: **달 dal** month
이번 달 전기 요금이 너무 많이 나왔어요. **ibeon dal jeongi yogeumi neomu mani nawasseoyo.** The electricity bill is too high this month.
여기서 일한 지 벌써 석 달이 넘었어요. **yeogiseo ilhan ji beolsseo seok dari neomeosseoyo.** I've been working here for more than three months.

: **개월 gae·wol** month
A: 아기가 몇 살이에요? B: 11개월 됐어요. **A: agiga myeot sarieyo? B: sibilgaewol dwaesseoyo.** A: How old is your baby? B: She is 11 months old.

· **이달 i·dal** this month
이달 말에 겨울 휴가를 갈 거야. **idal mare gyeoul hyugareul gal geoya.** At the end of this month I will leave for winter vacation.

: **지난달 ji·nan·dal** last month
여동생이 지난달에 아이를 낳았어요. **yeodongsaengi jinandare aireul laasseoyo.** My younger sister gave birth last month.

· **내달 nae·dal** next month
새 학기가 내달에 시작된다. **sae hakgiga naedare sijakdoenda.** The new semester starts next month.

· **매달 mae·dal** every month
월급은 매달 25일입니다. **wolgeubeun maedal isiboirimnida.** My salary is paid on the 25th of the month.

· **초순 cho·sun** the first ten days of a month

일월 초순에 파리로 갈 거야. **irwol chosune pariro gal geoya.** I'm going to go to Paris in early January.

· **중순 jung·sun** the middle ten days of a month

· **하순 ha·sun** the last ten days of a month

: **일월 i·rwol** January
: **이월 i·wol** February
: **삼월 sa·mwol** March
: **사월 sa·wol** April
: **오월 o·wol** May
: **유월 yu·wol** June
올해 유월은 쌀쌀하네. **olhae yuworeun ssalssalhane.** It's chilly this June.

> For easy pronunciation, the original spelling of 육월 has been changed to 유월. The same also applies to 시월 **siwol**, which means *October*.

: **칠월 chi·rwol** July
: **팔월 pa·rwol** August
: **구월 gu·wol** September
: **시월 si·wol** October
: **십일월 si·bi·rwol** November
: **십이월 si·bi·wol** December

31.3 Year, Seasons, Periods

해 hae year
해가 바뀌었습니다. **haega bakkwieotseumnida.** The new year has begun.

년 nyeon year
우리는 3년 전에 처음 만났다. **urineun samnyeon jeone cheoeum mannatda.** We first met three years ago.

올해 = 금년 ol·hae = geum·nyeon this year
올해에는/금년에는 담배를 끊기로 결심했어요. **olhaeeneun/geumnyeoneneun dambaereul kkeunkiro gyeolsimhaesseoyo.** I've decided to quit smoking this year.

지난해 = 작년 ji·nan·hae = jang·nyeon last year
지난해에/작년에 일을 그만뒀어. **jinanhaee/jangnyeone ireul geumandwosseo.** I quit my job last year.

지지난해 = 재작년 ji·ji·nan·hae = jae·jang·nyeon the year before last
나는 지지난해에/재작년에 이혼했다. **naneun jijinanhaee/jaejangnyeone ihonhaetda.** I got divorced two years ago.

내년 nae·nyeon next year
나 내년에 결혼할 거야. **na naenyeone gyeolhonhal geoya.** I'm going to get married next year.

후년 hu·nyeon the year after next

내후년 nae·hu·nyeon three years from now

새해 sae·hae new year, the New Year
새해 복 많이 받으세요. **saehae bong mani badeuseyo.** Happy New Year!

그해 geu·hae that year

주년 ju·nyeon anniversary (for counting how many years have passed after a certain time)
결혼 10주년 **gyeolhon sipjunyeon** tenth wedding anniversary

매년 = 해마다 mae·nyeon = hae·ma·da every year
저는 매년/해마다 새로운 악기를 배웁니다. **jeoneun maenyeon/haemada saeroun akgireul baeumnida.** Every year I learn a new musical instrument.

수년 su·nyeon several years
우리는 수년 동안 편지를 교환해 왔다. **urineun sunyeon dongan pyeonjireul gyohwanhae watda.** We've been exchanging letters for years.

년대 nyeon·dae (certain times of) age, era
1990년대에는 많은 역사적 사건들이 있었다. **cheongubaekgusimnyeondaeeneun maneun nyeoksajeok sageondeuri isseotda.** There were many historic events in the 1990s.

년도 nyeon·do year
몇 년도에 졸업했니? **myeon nyeondoe joreopaenni?** What year did you graduate?

연초 yeon·cho the beginning of the year

연말 yeon·mal the end of the year
연말에는 술자리가 많습니다. **yeonmareneun suljariga manseumnida.** There are lots of drinking parties at the end of the year.

상반기 sang·ban·gi the first half of the year

하반기 ha·ban·gi the second half of the year

계절 gye·jeol season
어떤 계절을 제일 좋아하세요? **eotteon gyejeoreul jeil joahaseyo?** What season do you like best?

철 cheol season, time

사계절 sa·gye·jeol four seasons
1년은 사계절로 이루어져 있다. **illyeoneun sagyejeollo irueojyeo itda.** There are four seasons in a year.

봄 bom spring
오늘은 꼭 날씨가 봄 같아. **oneureun kkok nalssiga bom gata.** Today's weather is like spring.

여름 yeo·reum summer
올해 여름은 참을 수 없이 더워. **olhae yeoreumeun chameul su eopsi deowo.** This summer is unbearably hot.

한여름 han·nyeo·reum midsummer

초여름 cho·yeo·reum early summer

가을 ga·eul fall, autumn
가을에는 잎들이 붉은 색으로 변한다. **gaeure-**

neun ipdeuri bulgeun saegeuro byeonhanda. In the autumn the leaves turn red.

* **늦가을** neut·ga·eul late fall

: **겨울** gyeo·ul winter
작년 겨울에는 기온이 영하 10도까지 떨어졌었죠. jangnyeon gyeoureneun gioni yeongha sipdokkaji tteoreojyeosseotjyo. Last winter the temperature was as low as minus 10 degrees.

* **한겨울** han·gyeo·ul midwinter

: **때** ttae time, the time, the moment
아무 때나 괜찮아. amu ttaena gwaenchana. Any time will do.

* **세월** se·wol time
세월 참 빠르네! sewol cham ppareune! How time flies!

: **시절** si·jeol days, years
나는 한국에서 보낸 시절을 잊지 못할 거야. naneun hangugeseo bonaen sijeoreul itji motal geoya. I'll never forget the days I spent in Korea.

* **시기** si·gi time, period
청소년기는 아주 **중요한 시기**야. cheongso-nyeongineun aju jungyohan sigiya. Adolescence is a very important period in life.

* **시점** si·jeom time

현 시점의 주 관심사는 자원을 확보하는 데 있습니다. hyeon sijeomui ju gwansimsaneun jawoneul hwakbohaneun de itseumnida. The main concern at the moment is securing resources.

: **기간** gi·gan period (of time), term
나는 **계약 기간**을 채울 수 없었다. naneun gyeyak giganeul chaeul su eopseotda. I couldn't fulfill the contract period.

: **시대** si·dae period, epoch, era
불국사는 통일신라 시대에 세워졌다. bulguk-saneun tongilsilla sidaee sewojyeotda. Bulguksa was built during the United Silla era.

: **세기** se·gi century
산업혁명은 19세기에 시작했다. saneopyeong-myeongeun sipgusegie sijakaetda. The Industrial Revolution began in the nineteenth century.

* **기원전** gi·won·jeon B.C., B.C.E.

기원후 = 서기 gi·won·hu = seo·gi A.D., C.E.

고대 go·dae ancient times

중세 jung·se the Middle Ages

: **근대** geun·dae modern times

: **현대** hyeon·dae today, modern times

31.4 The Time, Time of Day

: **시간** si·gan time, hour
어제 두 시간밖에 못 잤어요. eoje du sigan-bakke mot jasseoyo. I slept for only two hours last night.

* **시각** si·gak (a certain point of) time, hour
현지 시각은 새벽 두 시입니다. hyeonji siga-geun saebyeok du siimnida. The local time is 2 a.m.

정각 jeong·gak the exact time
기차는 아홉 시 정각에 출발합니다. gichaneun ahop si jeonggage chulbalhamnida. The train leaves at 9 o'clock sharp.

: **몇** myeot what (time)

: **시** si time, hour, o'clock

: **분** bun minute
A: 몇 시야? B: 세 시 사십 분. A: myeot siya?

B: se si sasip bun. A: What time is it? B: It's 3:40.

: **초** cho second
1분은 60초다. ilbuneun nyuksipchoda. One minute is made up of sixty seconds.

> Pure Korean numerals—한 han, 두 du, 세 se, 네 ne, ...—are used before 시 si, while Sino-Korean numerals—일 il, 이 i, 삼 sam, 사 sa, ...—are used before 분 bun and 초 cho.

: **빠르다** ppa·reu·da early, fast
서울은 발리보다 한 시간 빨라요. seoureun balliboda han sigan ppallayo. Seoul is one hour ahead of Bali.

: **느리다** neu·ri·da slow
제 시계는 5분 느려요. je sigyeneun obun neu-ryeoyo. My watch is five minutes slow.

걸리다 geol·li·da to take (time)
여기서 걸어서 얼마나 걸리나요? yeogiseo georeoseo eolmana geollinayo? How long does it take to get there from here on foot?

들다 deul·da to take (time, cost, etc.)
프린터를 고치려면 **시간이** 얼마나 **들까요?** peurinteoreul gochiryeomyeon sigani eolmana deulkkayo? How much time is needed to repair the printer?

들이다 deu·ri·da to spend
이것을 조립하는 데 많은 **시간과 노력을 들였어요.** igeoseul joripaneun de maneun sigangwa noryeogeul deullyeosseoyo. It took a lot of time and effort to put this together.

오늘 o·neul today

어제 eo·je yesterday
오늘은 어제보다 더 춥네요. oneureun eojeboda deo chumneyo. It's colder today than yesterday.

그제 = 그저께 geu·je = geu·jeo·kke the day before yesterday
이모가 그제/그저께 돌아가셨어요. imoga geuje/geujeokke doragasyeosseoyo. My aunt went back the day before yesterday.

내일 nae·il tomorrow

모레 mo·re the day after tomorrow
내일 출발 비행기 티켓을 모레로 바꾸고 싶은데요. naeil chulbal bihaenggi tikeseul morero bakkugo sipeundeyo. I'd like to change my flight for tomorrow to the day after tomorrow.

새벽 sae·byeok dawn, daybreak
새벽에 잠이 깼어요. saebyeoge jami kkaesseoyo. I woke up at dawn.

아침 a·chim morning
오늘 아침은 꽤 쌀쌀하네. oneul achimeun kkwae ssalssalhane. It's quite chilly this morning.

오전 o·jeon morning, a.m.
오전 열 시에 보자. ojeon nyeol sie boja. Let's meet up at 10 a.m.

정오 jeong·o noon
점심시간은 정오부터 오후 한 시까지입니다. jeomsimsiganeun jeongobuteo ohu han sikkajiimnida. Lunch time is from noon to 1 p.m.

점심때 jeom·sim·ttae lunchtime

낮 nat day, daytime
낮에는 사무실에 없을 겁니다. najeneun samusire eopseul geomnida. I won't be in the office during the day.

한낮 han·nat midday
한낮에는 너무 더워 밖에 나가고 싶지 않아. hannajeneun neomu deowo bakke nagago sipji ana. I don't want to go outside because it's too hot at midday.

오후 o·hu afternoon; p.m.
이따 오후에 오세요. itta ohue oseyo. Come by this afternoon.

저녁(때) jeo·nyeok(·ttae) evening
오늘 저녁에 시간 있어요? oneul jeonyeoge siga nisseoyo? Do you have time this evening?

초저녁 cho·jeo·nyeok early evening
할머니는 초저녁에 주무세요. halmeonineun chojeonyeoge jumuseyo. My grandmother goes to bed early in the evening.

밤 bam night
밤이 되자 다시 눈이 오기 시작했다. bami doeja dasi nuni ogi sijakaetda. It began to snow again at night.

야간 ya·gan night
오늘은 **야간** 근무가 있어요. oneureun nyagan geunmuga isseoyo. I'm on the night shift today.

(한)밤중 (han·)bam·jung the middle of the night
그녀는 밤중에 일한다. geunyeoneun bamjunge ilhanda. She works in the middle of the night.

자정 ja·jeong midnight
자정이 지나면 기본 요금이 오릅니다. jajeongi jinamyeon gibon nyogeumi oreumnida. After midnight the basic charge goes up.

밤낮 bam·nat night and day

31.5 The Present, Past, Future

현재 hyeon·jae the present
현재로서는 바빠서 나갈 수가 없어. hyeonjaeroseoneun bappaseo nagal suga eopseo. I am busy now and can't go out.

최근 = 근래 choe·geun = geul·lae recent days, lately
최근에/근래에 뮤지컬 본 적 있니? choegeune/geullaee myujikeol bon jeok inni? Have you seen any musicals lately?

요즈음 = 요즘 = 요사이 = 요새 yo·jeu·eum = yo·jeum = yo·sa·i = yo·sae these days, recently
요즈음/요즘/요사이/요새 입맛이 없어요. yojeueum/yojeum/yosai/yosae immasi eopseoyo. I have no appetite these days.

평소 = 평상시 pyeong·so = pyeong·sang·si usual day
평소보다/평상시보다 더 바쁜 하루였다. pyeongsoboda/pyeongsangsiboda deo bappeun haruyeotda. It was a busier day than usual.

오늘날 o·neul·lal today, present
오늘날 여성의 사회적 역할은 과거에 비해 훨씬 중요해지고 있다. oneullal lyeoseongui sahoejeok nyeokareun gwageoe bihae hwolssin jungyohaejigo itda. The role of women in society is becoming much more important compared to the past.

이날 i·nal this day, today

이때 i·ttae now, this day
저는 이날 이때까지 다른 사람에게 피해를 준 적이 없습니다. jeoneun inal ittaekkaji dareun saramege pihaereul jun jeogi eopseumnida. To this very day, I've never done anyone else any harm.

올 ol of this year
올 시월에 전세 계약이 끝납니다. ol siwore jeonse gyeyagi kkeunnamnida. The lease expires in October of this year.

현 hyeon current, present
현 상태로는 전혀 만족스럽지 않습니다. hyeon sangtaeroneun jeonhyeo manjokseureopji anseumnida. As it stands, this is not satisfactory at all.

방금 bang·geum just now

막 mak just
그는 방금 막 집에 왔다. geuneun banggeum mak jibe watda. He has just come home.

갓 gat just
대학을 갓 졸업했습니다. daehageul gat joreopaetseumnida. I have just graduated from college.

지금 ji·geum now
지금 어디 계세요? jigeum eodi gyeseyo? Where are you now?

이제 = 인제 i·je = in·je now, from now on
이제/인제 그만 갈게요. ije/inje geuman galgeyo. I have to leave now.

즉시 jeuk·si immediately, instantly
즉시 집으로 가라! jeuksi jibeuro gara! I want you to go home immediately!

당장 dang·jang right now, at once; for the time being
나가! 여기서 당장 나가라고! naga! yeogiseo dangjang nagarago! Out! Get out of here right now!

(곧)바로 (got·)ba·ro right away, immediately
내가 곧바로 다시 전화할게. naega gotbaro dasi jeonhwahalge. I'll call you right back.

얼른 eol·leun at once, quickly
얼른 대답해. eolleun daedapae. Answer me quickly.

곧장 got·jang right away, straight
회사 끝나고 곧장 왔어요. hoesa kkeunnago gotjang wasseoyo. I came straight from the office.

과거 gwa·geo the past
과거 이 지역에는 공장이 없었어요. gwageo i jiyeogeneun gongjangi eopseosseoyo. In the past, there were no plants in this area.

옛날 yen·nal the old days, the past
모든 게 옛날이 좋았어요. modeun ge yennari joasseoyo. Things were better in the old days.

지난날 ji·nan·nal the past, the old days
지난날이 그립습니다. jinannari geuripseumnida. I miss the old days.

(예)전 (ye·)jeon the old days
예전에 어디선가 그 커플을 본 적이 있다. yejeone eodiseonga geu keopeureul bon jeogi

itda. I've seen that couple somewhere before.

° **그전** geu·jeon the old days
저는 그전의 제가 아닙니다. jeoneun geu-jeonui jega animnida. I'm not what I used to be.

° **옛** yet old
오늘 옛 친구와 길에서 마주쳤다. oneul yet chinguwa gireseo majuchyeotda. I bumped into an old friend of mine on the street today.

° **당시** dang·si (at) that time

° **그때** geu·ttae (at) that time
그때 당시 저는 고작 세 살이었어요. geuttae dangsi jeoneun gojak se sarieosseoyo. At that time, I was only three.

당일 dang·il that day
당일에 신분증을 지참하셔야 합니다. dangire sinbunjeungeul jichamhasyeoya hamnida. You are required to bring your ID with you on that day.

: **그날** geu·nal that day

: **이튿날** i·teun·nal next day, the following day

° **한때** han·ttae at one time, once
한때는 나도 날씬했었다. hanttaeneun nado nalssinhaesseotda. At one time, I was slim.

: **언젠가** eon·jen·ga sometime, before
언젠가 우리 만난 적이 있던가요? eonjenga uri mannan jeogi itdeongayo? Have we met before?

° **일찍이 ← 일찌기** il·jji·gi before, in the past
그렇게 똑똑한 사람은 일찍이 본 적이 없어요. geureoke ttokttokan sarameun iljjigi bon jeogi eopseoyo. I have never seen such a smart person.

° **아까** a·kka a while ago
아까 뭐라고 하셨어요? akka mworago hasyeosseoyo? What did you say a while ago?

: **미래** mi·rae the future
이 회사의 미래는 매우 밝다고 생각합니다. i hoesaui miraeneun maeu bakdago saenggakamnida. I think the future of this company is very promising.

: **앞** ap the future
시험이 한 달 앞으로 다가왔어요. siheomi han

dal apeuro dagawasseoyo. The examination is a month away.

° **앞날** am·nal the future
앞날이 불확실하다. amnari bulhwaksilhada. The future looks uncertain.

: **장래** jang·nae the future
부모님은 저의 장래에 큰 기대를 걸고 계세요. bumonimeun jeoui jangnaee keun gidaereul geolgo gyeseyo. My parents have great expectations for my future.

° **훗날** hun·nal the future
우리는 훗날 다시 만날 것을 약속했다. urineun hunnal dasi mannal geoseul lyaksokaetda. We promised to meet again in the future.

° **장차** jang·cha in the future
장차 어떤 사람이 되고 싶니? jangcha eotteon sarami doego simni? What do you want to be in the future?

° **이내** i·nae soon, shortly, right away
이내 도착할 거야. inae dochakal geoya. I'll be there soon.

° **금세 ← 금새** geum·se ← geum·sae soon, shortly
주말에는 시간이 금세 지나간다. jumareneun sigani geumse jinaganda. Time passes quickly on the weekend.

: **금방** geum·bang soon
저녁 금방 차릴게. jeonyeok geumbang charilge. I'll get dinner ready shortly.

: **곧** got soon, shortly, right away
곧 돌아올게. got doraolge. I'll be right back.

: **이따(가)** i·tta(·ga) later
이따 전화할게. itta jeonhwahalge. I'll call you later.

: **나중에** na·jung·e later
나중에 보자. najunge boja. See you later.

° **차차** cha·cha later
그 문제에 대해서는 차차 의논해 보자. geu munjee daehaeseoneun chacha uinonhae boja. Let's discuss that issue later.

: **언제** eon·je sometime, someday
언제 한번 들러. eonje hanbeon deulleo. Drop by sometime.

: **언젠가** eon·jen·ga sometime, someday
언젠가는 꼭 그곳에 가고 싶어요. eonjenganeun kkok geugose gago sipeoyo. I want to go there someday.

31.6 Time Concepts

처음 cheo·eum beginning, start

첫 cheot first
언제 첫 키스를 했는지 잘 기억이 안 나요. eonje cheot kiseureul haenneunji jal gieogi an nayo. I can't remember exactly when I had my first kiss.

초 cho beginning
4월 초는 아직 춥습니다. sawol choneun ajik chupseumnida. It's still cold in early April.

애초 ae·cho beginning, start

최초 choe·cho the first
에디슨이 최초의 전구를 만든 게 언제인지 아니? ediseuni choechoui jeongureul mandeun ge eonjeinji ani? Do you know when Edison made the first electric light bulb?

초기 cho·gi the early days, early stage

원래 = 본래 wol·lae = bol·lae originally, by nature
저는 원래/본래 왼손잡이였어요. jeoneun wollae/bollae oensonjabiyeosseoyo. I was originally left-handed.

중간 jung·gan the middle
영화 중간에 잠이 들었어요. yeonghwa junggane jami deureosseoyo. I fell asleep in the middle of the movie.

중 jung the middle
지금 회의 중이라서 전화를 받을 수가 없습니다. jigeum hoeui jungiraseo jeonhwareul badeul suga eopseumnida. I'm not available because I'm in a conference now.

도중 do·jung the middle
나는 집에 오는 도중에 서점에 들렀다. naneun jibe oneun dojunge seojeome deulleotda. I stopped by a bookstore on the way home.

한창 han·chang the peak
파티가 한창이다. patiga hanchangida. The party is in full swing.

끝 kkeut end, finish, close
내 말 끝까지 좀 들어 봐. nae mal kkeutkkaji jom deureo bwa. Please hear me out.

마지막 ma·ji·mak the last
이번이 너의 마지막 기회야. ibeoni neoui majimak gihoeya. This is your last chance.

말 mal end, close
이달 말까지 이 쿠폰을 사용하셔야 합니다. idal malkkaji i kuponeul sayonghasyeoya hamnida. You need to use this coupon by the end of the month.

결말 gyeol·mal end, finish, close
그 영화의 결말은 실망스러웠다. geu yeonghwaui gyeolmareun silmangseureowotda. The ending of the film was disappointing.

최후 choe·hu the last, the end
이것을 최후의 수단으로 남겨두세요. igeoseul choehuui sudaneuro namgyeoduseyo. Use this as the last resort.

최종 choe·jong the final
최종 점수는 11 대 8이었어. choejong jeomsuneun sibil dae parieosseo. The final score was 11-8.

말기 mal·gi end, late stage
아버지는 폐암 말기 선고를 받으셨다. abeojineun pyeam malgi seongoreul badeusyeotda. My father was diagnosed with late-stage lung cancer.

궁극적 = 최종적 gung·geuk·jeok = choe·jong·jeok ultimate, eventual
행복이 제 궁극적인/최종적인 목표입니다. haengbogi je gunggeukjeogin/choejongjeogin mokpyoimnida. Happiness is my ultimate goal.

비로소 ← 비로서 bi·ro·so ← bi·ro·seo at last, not ... until
그가 죽은 후에야 비로소 내가 그 사람을 얼마나 사랑했는지 알았습니다. geuga jugeun hueya biroso naega geu sarameul eolmana saranghaenneunji aratseumnida. It was not until his death that I realized how much I loved him.

드디어 ≒ 마침내 ≒ 이윽고 deu·di·eo ≒ ma·chim·nae ≒ i·euk·go finally, at last
드디어/마침내/이윽고 우리가 떠날 날이 왔다. deudieo/machimnae/ieukgo uriga tteonal lari watda. Finally the day came for us to leave.

결국 gyeol·guk finally, after all
옆집 사는 부부 결국 이혼했어요. yeopjip saneun bubu gyeolguk ihonhaesseoyo. The married couple next door finally got divorced.

끝내 kkeun·nae to the end, in the end
그는 끝내 나타나지 않았다. geuneun kkeunnae natanaji anatda. In the end, he didn't appear.

막상 mak·sang ultimately, actually
보기에는 간단해 보였지만 막상 해 보니 그렇지 않았다. bogieneun gandanhae boyeotjiman maksang hae boni geureochi anatda. It looked simple, but in reality it was not.

- -

전 jeon before; previous
어두워지기 전에 집에 가자. eoduwojigi jeone jibe gaja. Let's go home before it gets dark.
이 사람은 제 전 남편입니다. i sarameun je jeon nampyeonimnida. This is my ex-husband.

직전 jik·jeon just before
저는 항상 시험 직전에 공부해요. jeoneun hangsang siheom jikjeone gongbuhaeyo. I always study just before an exam.

전날 jeon·nal the day before
결혼식 전날 밤에 잠을 거의 못 잤어요. gyeolhonsik jeonnal bame jameul geoui mot jasseoyo. I hardly slept the night before the wedding.

저번 = 지난번 jeo·beon = ji·nan·beon the last time, the other day
저번/지난번 시간에 선생님이 출석 불렀어? jeobeon/jinanbeon sigane seonsaengnimi chulseok bulleosseo? Did the teacher call the roll last time?

전기 jeon·gi the former period

먼저 meon·jeo first, in advance
먼저 가세요. meonjeo gaseyo. Go first.

우선 u·seon first, above all
우선 엄마한테 물어봐야 해요. useon eommahante mureobwaya haeyo. I have to ask mom first.

일단 il·dan first
일단 밥부터 먹자. ildan bapbuteo meokja. Let's eat first.

앞서 ap·seo before, ahead of
선수들은 경기에 앞서 저마다 몸을 풀었다. seonsudeureun gyeonggie apseo jeomada momeul pureotda. Every player loosened up prior to the match.

미리 mi·ri beforehand, in advance
미리 알려 주세요. miri allyeo juseyo. Let me know beforehand.

벌써 beol·sseo already
벌써 가려고? beolsseo garyeogo? Are you leaving already?

이미 i·mi already
이미 7시가 넘었다. imi ilgopsiga neomeotda. It is past seven o'clock already.

진작 jin·jak beforehand, in advance
왜 진작 말 안 했어? wae jinjak mal an haesseo? Why didn't you say that beforehand?

미처 mi·cheo in advance
그건 미처 생각하지 못했어요. geugeon micheo saenggakaji motaesseoyo. I didn't think of that.

- -

이번 i·beon this time
이번 수학 시험은 지난번보다 더 어려웠어. ibeon suhak siheomeun jinanbeonboda deo eoryeowosseo. This math test was more difficult than the last one.

아직 a·jik still
아직 자? ajik ja? Are you still sleeping?

여전히 yeo·jeon·hi still, as ever
여전히 통화 중인데요. yeojeonhi tonghwa jungindeyo. The line's still busy.

여태(껏) yeo·tae(·kkeot) still, so far
여태 이 문제로 끙끙대고 있어? yeotae i munjero kkeungkkeungdaego isseo? Are you still struggling with this problem?

채 chae still, so far
경찰은 5분이 채 안 되어 현장에 도착했다. gyeongchareun obuni chae an doeeo hyeonjange dochakaetda. The police arrived at the scene within less than five minutes.

동시 dong·si same time
그들은 나와 동시에 떠났다. geudeureun nawa dongsie tteonatda. They left at the same time I did.

차 cha the moment
잠이 막 들려던 차에 전화가 왔다. jami mak deullyeodeon chae jeonhwaga watda. My phone rang when I was just about to fall asleep.

김 gim chance, opportunity
일어나는 김에 가져올게요. ireonaneun gime gajyeoolgeyo. I'll get it for you since I'm about to get up anyway.

채 chae just as it is
어젯밤에는 너무 피곤해서 옷을 입은 채로 잠

이 들었다. **eojetbameneun neomu pigonhaeseo oseul ibeun chaero jami deureotda.** Yesterday I was so tired that I fell asleep with my clothes on.

....

후 hu after
나는 고등학교를 졸업한 후 바로 군대에 갔다. **naneun godeunghakgyoreul joreopan hu baro gundaee gatda.** I went straight into the service after I graduated from high school.

직후 ji·khu right after
나는 사고 직후에 의식을 잃었다. **naneun sago jikhue uisigeul ireotda.** I passed out immediately after the accident.

이후 i·hu after
그날 이후, 그녀는 다시 보이지 않았다. **geunal ihu, geunyeoneun dasi boiji anatda.** After that day, she was never seen again.

뒤 dwi after, since

다음 da·eum next
이 프로그램은 다음 시간에 계속됩니다. **i peurogeuraemeun daeum sigane gyesokdoemnida.** This program will be continued next time.

다음번 da·eum·beon next time
다음번에는 어머니와 같이 와야겠어. **daeum-beoneneun eomeoniwa gachi wayagesseo.** I think I should come with my mother next time.

후기 hu·gi the latter period

(곧)이어(서) (got·)i·eo(·seo) and then
곧이어 애국가 제창이 있겠습니다. **godieo aegukga jechangi itgetseumnida.** Now, we will sing the national anthem.

....

항상 ≒ 언제나 ≒ 늘 hang·sang ≒ eon·je·na ≒ neul always
저는 평일에는 항상/언제나/늘 바빠요. **jeoneun pyeongireneun hangsang/eonjena/neul bappayo.** I'm always busy on weekdays.

언제든(지) eon·je·deun(·ji) anytime
궁금한 게 있으면 언제든 전화해. **gunggeumhan ge isseumyeon eonjedeun jeonhwahae.** Feel free to call if you have any questions.

매번 = 번번이 mae·beon = beon·beo·ni all the time
내가 그를 보러 갔을 때마다 매번/번번이 그는 잠을 자고 있었다. **naega geureul boreo gasseul ttaemada maebeon/beonbeoni geuneun**

jameul jago isseotda. Every time I went to see him, he was sleeping.

매일 mae·il every day
매일 일기를 써라. **maeil ilgireul sseora.** Keep a diary every day.

맨날 = 만날 maen·nal = man·nal every day
누나는 맨날/만날 책만 읽어. **nunaneun maennal/mannal chaegman ilgeo.** My sister is always reading books.

앉으나 서나 an·jeu·na seo·na always
그 사람은 앉으나 서나 일 생각만 해요. **geu sarameun anjeuna seona il saenggangman haeyo.** He thinks about work 24/7.

대개 ≒ 보통 dae·gae ≒ bo·tong usually, generally
저는 대개/보통 점심을 걸러요. **jeoneun daegae/botong jeomsimeul geolleoyo.** I usually skip lunch.
쓰레기는 대개/보통 밤에 걷어간다. **sseuregineun daegae/botong bame geodeoganda.** Garbage is usually collected at night.

주로 ju·ro mostly, mainly
손님은 주로 외국인이에요. **sonnimeun juro oeuginieyo.** The customers are mostly foreigners.

으레 eu·re usually, always

대체로 dae·che·ro generally, overall
대체로 재미있었어. **daechero jaemiisseosseo.** Overall, it was fun.

일반적 il·ban·jeok generally
일반적으로 여자가 남자보다 오래 산다. **ilbanjeogeuro yeojaga namjaboda orae sanda.** In general, women live longer than men.

(곧)잘 (got·)jal often
저는 학생들로부터 그런 질문을 곧잘 받아요. **jeoneun haksaengdeullobuteo geureon jilmuneul gotjal badayo.** I often get such questions from my students.

자주 ja·ju often, frequently
그는 자주 식사를 거른다. **geuneun jaju siksareul georeunda.** He often skips meals.

잦다 jat·da frequent
민주는 학교에 지각이 너무 잦아요. **minjuneun hakgyo jigagi neomu jajayo.** Minju is late for school too often.

빈번하다 bin·beon·ha·da frequent
이곳은 추락 사고가 빈번하게 발생합니다. igoseun churak sagoga binbeonhage balsaenghamnida. This is where accidental falls happen frequently.

수시로 su·si·ro frequently, often
저는 수시로 부모님께 전화를 드립니다. jeoneun susiro bumonimkke jeonhwareul deurimnida. I often call my parents.

사흘이 멀다 하고 sa·heu·ri meol·da ha·go very often
신랑은 사흘이 멀다 하고 술을 마셔요. sillangeun saheuri meolda hago sureul masyeoyo. My husband drinks very often.

자꾸(만) ja·kku(·man) repeatedly, often
전화가 자꾸 끊어져요. jeonhwaga jakku kkeuneojyeoyo. My phone line keeps getting disconnected.

일쑤 il·ssu common thing
그때는 끼니를 거르기가 일쑤였다. geuttaeneun kkinireul georeugiga ilssuyeotda. Skipping meals was common at that time.

흔하다 | 흔히 heun·ha·da | heun·hi common | commonly, often
전립선암은 아주 흔한 암이다. jeollipseonameun aju heunhan amida. Prostate cancer is a very common type of cancer.

규칙적 gyu·chik·jeok regular
제 건강의 비결은 규칙적으로 먹고 자는 겁니다. je geongangui bigyeoreun gyuchikjeogeuro meokgo janeun geomnida. The secret of my health is to eat and sleep regularly.

정기적 jeong·gi·jeok regular, periodic
정기적으로 복용하는 약이 있나요? jeonggijeogeuro bogyonghaneun nyagi innayo? Are you taking any medications regularly?

가끔 = 이따금 ga·kkeum = i·tta·geum sometimes, occasionally
사람은 모두 가끔/이따금 실수를 한다. saramnun modu gakkeum/ittageum silsureul handa. We all make mistakes sometimes.

종종 = 왕왕 ≒ 간혹 jong·jong = wang·wang ≒ gan·hok sometimes, occasionally
정확한 번역이 불가능할 때가 종종/왕왕/간혹 있다. jeonghwakan beonyeogi bulganeunghal ttaega jongjong/wangwang/ganhok itda. An accurate translation is sometimes impossible.

어쩌다(가) eo·jjeo·da(·ga) sometimes, occasionally
술은 어쩌다 한 번씩 마셔요. sureun eojjeoda han beonssik masyeoyo. I drink once in a while.

때(때)로 ttae(·ttae)·ro sometimes, occasionally
때로는 거짓말을 하지 않을 수 없다. ttaeroneun geojinmareul haji aneul su eopda. Lies are unavoidable from time to time.

뜸하다 tteum·ha·da infrequent
요즘 걔한테서 소식이 뜸해. yojeum gyaehanteseo sosigi tteumhae. I haven't heard much from him these days.

드물다 deu·mul·da rare, uncommon
그 사람이 화를 내는 건 드문 일이다. geu sarami hwareul laeneun geon deumun irida. It is unusual for him to get angry.

갑작스럽다 gap·jak·seu·reop·da sudden, abrupt
우리는 갑작스럽게 여행을 취소해야 했다. urineun gapjakseureopge yeohaengeul chwisohaeya haetda. We suddenly had to cancel our trip.

갑자기 gap·ja·gi suddenly, abruptly
갑자기 문이 열리고 한 남자가 들어왔다. gapjagi muni yeolligo han namjaga deureowatda. Suddenly the door opened and a man came in.

문득 mun·deuk suddenly
문득 그 여자 생각이 났다. mundeuk geu yeoja saenggagi natda. Suddenly, I thought of her.

별안간 ≒ 느닷없이 ≒ 돌연 byeo·ran·gan ≒ neu·da·deop·si ≒ do·ryeon suddenly, abruptly

어느덧 = 어느새 eo·neu·deot = eo·neu·sae without one's knowing, already
그 꼬마가 어느덧/어느새 커서 어른이 되었구나. geu kkomaga eoneudeot/eoneusae keoseo eoreuni doeeotguna. The little kid has already grown up.

급격하다 | 급격히 geup·gyeo·ka·da | geup·gyeo·ki rapid, sharp | rapidly, sharply

점차 = 점점 jeom·cha = jeom·jeom gradually, by degrees
점차/점점 좋아지고 있습니다. jeomcha/jeomjeom joajigo itseumnida. I am gradually getting better.

차츰 cha·cheum gradually, little by little

조금씩 jo·geum·ssik little by little
사람들이 조금씩 모이고 있어. saramdeuri jo·geumssik moigo isseo. People are gathering little by little.

갈수록 gal·su·rok as time goes by
갈수록 흰머리가 늘어요. galsurok huinmeoriga neureoyo. I'm getting more gray hair as days go by.

서서히 seo·seo·hi gradually, slowly

동안 dong·an during, for
겨울방학 동안 졸업 논문 준비를 할 생각입니다. gyeoulbanghak dongan joreop nonmun junbireul hal saenggagimnida. I'm going to work on my graduation thesis during winter vacation.

사이 sa·i during, for
새벽 한 시에서 두 시 사이였을 거예요. saebyeok han sieseo du si saiyeosseul geoyeyo. It must be between one and two o'clock in the morning.

-간 -gan during, for
3일간 묵을 겁니다. samilgan mugeul geomnida. I'll stay for three nights.

순간 | ~적 sun·gan | ~·jeok moment | momentary
확실해? 마지막 순간에 마음 바꾸면 안 돼! hwaksilhae? majimak sungane maeum bakkumyeon an dwae! Are you sure? Don't change your mind at the last minute.

한순간 han·sun·gan moment
한순간의 부주의가 사고를 불러올 수 있다. hansunganui bujuuiga sagoreul bulleool su itda. A moment of carelessness can cause an accident.

일시적 il·si·jeok temporary, momentary
이 치료의 효과는 일시적입니다. i chiryoui hyogwaneun ilsijeogimnida. The effect of this treatment is temporary.

순식간 sun·sik·gan brief instant
순식간에 일어난 일이야. sunsikgane ireonan iriya. It all happened in a flash.

눈 깜짝할 사이 nun kkam·jja·kal sa·i in the blink of an eye
모든 게 눈 깜짝할 사이에 일어났어요. modeun ge nun kkamjjakal saie ireonasseoyo. It all happened so fast!

언뜻 = 얼핏 eon·tteut = eol·pit in an instant

언뜻/얼핏 봐도 그녀가 깊은 잠에 빠졌다는 것을 알 수 있었다. eontteut/eolpit bwado geunyeoga gipeun jame ppajyeotdaneun geoseul al su isseotda. One glance was enough to know that she is in deep sleep.

잠시 = 잠깐 jam·si = jam·kkan (for) a moment
잠시/잠깐 얘기 좀 할래? jamsi/jamkkan yaegi jom hallae? Can I talk to you for a moment?

당분간 dang·bun·gan for the time being, for a while
당분간 술은 피하셔야 합니다. dangbungan sureun pihasyeoya hamnida. You should avoid drinking for a while.

얼마간 eol·ma·gan some time, a while
얼마간 여기 머물 예정입니다. eolmagan nyeogi meomul yejeongimnida. I'll stay here for a while.

한동안 han·dong·an for a while
한동안 영화 보러 가지 못했어요. handongan nyeonghwa boreo gaji motaesseoyo. I haven't been to the movies for a long time.

한참 han·cham for a while
걔 본 지 한참 됐어요. gyae bon ji hancham dwaesseoyo. It's been a while since I saw him.

오래(도록) o·rae(·do·rok) for a long time
오래 기다리시게 해서 죄송합니다. orae gidarisige haeseo joesonghamnida. I am so sorry for having kept you waiting for so long.

오랫동안 ← 오랜동안 o·raet·dong·an ← o·raen·dong·an long, for a long time
우리는 오랫동안 알고 지내왔습니다. urineun oraetdongan algo jinaewatseumnida. We've known each other for a long time.

(온·)종일 (on·)jong·il all day (long), the whole day
너 어디 있었어? 온종일 너 찾아다녔잖아. neo eodi isseoseo? onjongil leo chajadanyeotjana. Where have you been? I've been looking for you all day.

한나절 han·na·jeol half a day
아마도 수리하는 데 한나절 걸릴 거예요. amado surihaneun de hannajeol geollil geoyeyo. Probably it'll take half a day to repair it.

반나절 ban·na·jeol a quarter of a day

영원하다 | 영원히 yeong·won·ha·da | yeong·won·hi permanent, everlasting | forever

영원한 것은 없다. yeongwonhan geoseun eop-da. Nothing lasts forever.

빠르다 ppa·reu·da fast, quick, rapid
빠르면 빠를수록 좋죠. ppareumyeon ppareulsurok jochyo. The sooner, the better.

신속하다 sin·so·ka·da quick, prompt
신속한 답변 부탁합니다. sinsokan dapbyeon butakamnida. I would appreciate your prompt reply.

빨리 ppal·li quickly, fast
아이들은 참 빨리 큰다. aideureun cham ppalli keunda. Children grow up so fast.

재빨리 jae·ppal·li quickly, fast
그는 재빨리 쪽지를 주머니에 넣었다. geuneun jaeppalli jjokjireul jumeonie neoeotda. He quickly pocketed the note.

느리다 neu·ri·da slow
컴퓨터가 갑자기 느려졌어요. keompyuteoga gapjagi neuryeojyeosseoyo. My computer suddenly became slow.

천천히 cheon·cheon·hi slowly
천천히 먹어라. cheoncheonhi meogeora. Take your time with the food.

안 = (이)내 an = (i·)nae within
한 시간 안으로/내로 돌아와. han sigan aneuro/naero dorawa. Come back within an hour.

넘다 neom·da to pass, exceed
벌써 다섯 시가 넘었어. beolsseo daseot siga neomeoseo. It's already past five o'clock.

넘기다 neom·gi·da to pass, exceed
다행히 위험한 고비는 넘겼습니다. dahaenghi wiheomhan gobineun neomgyeotseumnida. Fortunately, he has passed the critical stage.

지나다 ji·na·da to pass, go by
이 요구르트는 유통기한이 지났는데. i yogureuteuneun nyutonggihani jinanneunde. This yogurt is past its expiration date.

흐르다 heu·reu·da to pass, go by, elapse
흐르는 시간을 멈출 수는 없어. heureuneun siganeul meomchul suneun eopseo. You can't stop the flow of time.

가다 ga·da to pass, go by
시간이 가면 잊혀질 거야. sigani gamyeon ichyeojil geoya. You'll forget it as time goes by.

보내다 bo·nae·da to spend, pass
크리스마스는 보통 가족과 함께 보냅니다. keuriseumaseuneun botong gajokgwa hamkke bonaemnida. I usually spend Christmas with my family.

쏜살같다 sson·sal·gat·da swift
시간이 참 쏜살같군요. sigani cham ssonsalgatgunnyo. How time flies!

더디다 deo·di·da slow, tardy
오늘따라 시간이 더디게 가는 것 같아요. oneulttara sigani deodige ganeun geot gatayo. Time is passing so slowly today.

길다 gil·da long, lengthy
하루가 너무 길었어. haruga neomu gireosseo. I had a very long day.

짧다 jjal·da short
일주일은 발리를 충분히 즐기기에는 너무 짧았다. iljuireun ballireul chungbunhi jeulgigieneun neomu jjalbatda. One week was too short to enjoy Bali fully.

이르다 i·reu·da early
이렇게 이른 시각에 무슨 일이세요? ireoke ireun sigage museun iriseyo? What are you doing here so early?

일찍 il·jjik early
아침 일찍 집을 나섰어요. achim iljjik jibeul naseosseoyo. I left home early in the morning.

늦다 neut·da (to be) late
서둘러. 우리 늦겠다. seodulleo. uri neutgetda. Hurry up. We are going to be late.

뒤늦다 dwi·neut·da belated

이래 i·rae since, after
지난주 시위가 시작된 이래 서른 명이 넘는 사람이 사망했습니다. jinanju siwiga sijakdoen irae seoreun myeongi neomneun sarami samanghaetseumnida. Over thirty people have died thus far in the demonstrations that began last week.

지 ji since
졸업한 지 3년이 지났어요. joreopan ji samnyeoni jinasseoyo. Three years have passed since I graduated.

적 jeok time, experience
수원에 가 본 적 있으세요? suwone ga bon jeok gisseuseyo? Have you ever been to Suwon?

만 man after, since, time
이게 얼마 만이니? ige eolma manini? How long has it been?

되다 doe·da to become, reach

엄마가 돌아가신 지 벌써 1년이 되었어요. **eommaga doragasin ji beolsseo illyeoni doeeosseoyo.** It has been a year already since mom died.

오래되다 o·rae·doe·da old, long
이발소에 간 지 오래됐어요. **ibalsoe gan ji oraedwaesseoyo.** It's been a long time since I went to the barber.

오래되다 is always used in the past tense.

오랜만 ← 오랫만 o·raen·man long time (since we met before)
오랜만이네요. **oraenmanineyo.** Long time no see.

모처럼 mo·cheo·reom after a long time
모처럼 좋은 소식이군요. **mocheoreom joeun sosigigunnyo.** It's good news for a change.

그동안 = 그간 = 그사이 = 그새 geu·dong·an = geu·gan = geu·sa·i = geu·sae so far

그동안/그간/그사이/그새 어떻게 지냈어요? **geudongan/geugan/geusai/geusae eotteoke jinaesseoyo?** How have you been?

지금껏 ji·geum·kkeot so far
지금껏 어디에 있었어? **jigeumkkeot eodie isseosseo?** Where have you been all this time?

밤새 bam·sae all night long
밤새 잘 잤어? **bamsae jal jasseo?** Did you sleep well last night?

내내 nae·nae throughout, all the time
제가 거기 있는 내내 눈이 왔어요. **jega geogi inneun naenae nuni wasseoyo.** It snowed the whole time I was there.

줄곧 jul·got continuously, all the time
나는 줄곧 네 생각뿐이었어. **naneun julgot ne saenggakppunieosseo.** I was thinking about you all the time.

31.7 Calendar, Special Days

달력 dal·lyeok calendar

양력 yang·nyeok solar calendar

음력 eum·nyeok lunar calendar
오늘이 음력으로 며칠이지? **oneuri eumnyeogeuro myeochiriji?** What day is it on the lunar calendar?

명절 myeong·jeol holiday

연휴 yeon·hyu holiday; long weekend
연휴 동안 많은 가게들이 문을 열지 않는다. **yeonhyu dongan maneun gagedeuri muneul lyeolji anneunda.** Many stores will be closed during the holidays.

설(날) seol(·lal) Lunar New Year's Day
설날에 한국인들은 떡국을 먹는다. **seollare hangugindeureun tteokgugeul meongneunda.** On the Lunar New Year's Day, Koreans eat rice cake soup.

추석 chu·seok Chuseok, Korean Thanksgiving Day (August 15 on the lunar calendar)
추석 때 거의 모든 한국 사람들이 고향을 방문한다. **chuseok ttae geoui modeun hanguk saramdeuri gohyangeul bangmunhanda.** During Chuseok, almost everyone in Korea visits his or her hometown.

국경일 guk·gyeong·il national holiday

삼일절 sa·mil·jeol Independence Movement Day (March 1)

제헌절 je·heon·jeol Constitution Day (July 7)

광복절 gwang·bok·jeol Liberation Day (August 15)

개천절 gae·cheon·jeol National Foundation Day (October 3)

한글날 han·geul·lal Hangul Proclamation Day (October 9)

기념일 gi·nyeo·mil anniversary

식목일 sing·mo·gil Arbor Day (April 5)

노동절 no·dong·jeol May Day (May 1)

어린이날 eo·ri·ni·nal Children's Day (May 5)

어버이날 eo·beo·i·nal Parents' Day (May 8)

스승의날 seu·seung·ui·nal Teachers' Day (May 15)

석가탄신일 seok·ga·tan·si·nil Buddha's Birthday (April 8 on the lunar calendar)

현충일 hyeon·chung·il Memorial Day (June 6)

국군의날 guk·gun·ui·nal Armed Forces Day (October 1)

크리스마스 keu·ri·seu·ma·seu Christmas

절기 jeol·gi solar term

According to Korean thinking, each year has 24 solar terms. These are points on the calendar that correspond to some natural phenomena.

입춘 ip·chun Start of Spring (February 4)

우수 u·su Rain Water (February 19)

경칩 gyeong·chip Awakening of Insects (March 6)

춘분 chun·bun the Vernal Equinox (March 21)

청명 cheong·myeong Clear and Bright (April 5)

곡우 go·gu Grain Rain (April 20)

입하 i·pha Start of Summer (May 6)

소만 so·man Grain Filling Out (May 21)

망종 mang·jong Grain in the Ear (June 6)

하지 ha·ji the Summer Solstice (June 21)

소서 so·seo Moderate Heat (July 7)

대서 dae·seo Great Heat (July 23)

입추 ip·chu the Start of Autumn (August 8)

처서 cheo·seo End of Heat (August 23)

백로 baeng·no White Dew (September 8)

추분 chu·bun the Autumnal Equinox (September 23)

한로 hal·lo Cold Dew (October 8)

상강 sang·gang Descent of Frost (October 23)

입동 ip·dong the Start of Winter (November 7)

소설 so·seol Light Snow (November 22)

대설 dae·seol Heavy Snow (December 7)

동지 dong·ji the Winter Solstice (December 22)

소한 so·han Moderate Cold (January 6)

대한 dae·han Severe Cold (January 20)

가리키다 가운데 가장자리 거기 겓너펀 겉

경계 곁 곳 구석 군데 그곳 그리 그쪽

근처 꼭대기 나란히 나침반 남쪽 내부

너머 데 동쪽 뒤 뒤쪽 마주 맞은편

모서리 밑 바깥쪽 바다 밖 반대편 방향 부근

북쪽 서쪽 속 아래 안 안쪽 앞 앞뒤

앞쪽 양쪽 여기 여기저기 옆

chapter **32** | Locations and Directions

옆쪽 오른쪽 외부 왼쪽 위 위아래 위치

이곳 이리 이리저리 이쪽 인근 장소

저곳 저기 지리 저쪽 정면 주변 중간

중심 중앙 지점 쪽 한가운데 한쪽 향하다

32.1 Locations, Places

위치 | ~하다 wi·chi | ~·ha·da position, location | to be located
집은 괜찮은데 위치가 맘에 안 들어요. jibeun gwaenchaneunde wichiga mame an deureoyo. The house itself is good, but I don't like the location.
저희 집은 언덕 꼭대기에 위치해 있어요. jeohui jibeun eondeok kkokdaegie wichihae isseoyo. My house is located on top of a hill.

앞 ap the front
죽기를 두려워하지 않는다면 앞으로 나오시오. jukgireul duryeowohaji anneundamyeon apeuro naosio. Come to the front if you're not afraid to die.

정면 jeong·myeon front
정면에 보이는 건물이 학생회관이다. jeongmyeone boineun geonmuri haksaenghoegwanida. The building in front is the Student Union Building.

뒤 dwi back, the rear
내 뒤에 서 있어라. nae dwie seo isseora. Stand behind me.

앞뒤 ap·dwi the front and the rear
배가 앞뒤로 흔들리고 있었다. baega apdwiro heundeulligo isseotda. The boat was rocking back and forth.

위 wi top, above
위로 올라와. wiro ollawa. Come up here.

꼭대기 kkok·dae·gi top, summit
책장 꼭대기에 팔이 안 닿아. chaekjang kkokdaegie pari an daa. I can't reach the top bookshelf.

아래 a·rae the lower part
나무 아래에서 좀 쉬자. namu araeeseo jom swija. Let's get some rest under the tree.

밑 mit the lower part
노트가 침대 밑에 있어. noteuga chimdae mite isseo. The notebook is under the bed.

바닥 ba·dak floor, ground, the bottom
바닥이 왜 이리 지저분해? badagi wae iri jijeobunhae? Why is the floor so dirty?

위아래 wi·a·rae top and the lower part
내 생각에는 위아래가 뒤바뀐 것 같아. nae saenggageneun wiaraega dwibakkwin geot gata. I think it's upside down.

옆 yeop side
옆으로 비켜 주세요. yeopeuro bikyeo juseyo. Please step aside.

곁 gyeot sb's side
네가 곁에 있어서 다행이야. nega gyeote isseoseo dahaengiya. I am happy you are with me.

안 an the inside
주사위를 상자 안에 넣어라. jusawireul sangja ane neoeora. Put the dice in the box.

속 sok the inside, interior
서랍 속의 너비는 약 20센티쯤 됩니다. seorap sogui neobineun nyak gisipsentijjeum doemnida. The width of the inside of a drawer is about 20 cm.

내부 nae·bu the inside, interior
건물 내부는 2007년에 수리되었다. geonmul laebuneun icheonchillyeone suridoeeotda. The interior of the building was repaired in 2007.

밖 = 바깥 bak = ba·kkat the outside
선 밖으로/바깥으로 나가면 반칙이야. seon bakkeuro/bakkateuro nagamyeon banchigiya. Crossing the line is a foul.

겉 geot the outside, exterior, surface
스테이크가 겉만 익었어요. seuteikeuga geonman igeosseoyo. The steak was cooked only on the outside.

외부 oe·bu the outside
외부에서는 열쇠가 없으면 문을 못 열어요. oebueseoneun nyeolsoega eopseumyeon muneul mon nyeoreoyo. You cannot open the door from the outside without a key.

중간 jung·gan the middle, medium
중간에서 만납시다. junggganeseo mannapsida. I'll meet you in the middle.

중심 jung·sim center, the middle
제 집은 서울 중심에 있습니다. je jibeun seoul jungsime itseumnida. My house is located in the center of Seoul.

중앙 jung·ang the middle
방의 중앙에 의자를 놓으세요. bangui jungange uijareul loeuseyo. Put the chair in the middle of the room.

가운데 ga·un·de center, the middle

강이 시 가운데를 흐르고 있습니다. **gangi si gaundereul heureugo itseumnida.** The river runs through the city.

한가운데 han·ga·un·de the very middle

구석 = 모퉁이 = 코너 gu·seok = mo·tung·i = ko·neo corner
왜 너는 늘 구석에/모퉁이에/코너에 앉니? **wae neoneun neul guseoge/motungie/koneoe anni?** Why are you always sitting in the corner?

가장자리 ga·jang·ja·ri edge, border

모서리 mo·seo·ri corner, edge
식탁 모서리에 앉지 마. **siktak moseorie anji ma.** Don't sit at the corner of the table.

경계 gyeong·gye boundary, border
한강은 서울의 북쪽과 남쪽을 가르는 경계 역할을 한다. **hangangeun seourui bukjjokgwa namjjogeul gareuneun gyeonggye yeokareul handa.** The Han River acts as a boundary between northern and southern Seoul.

인근 in·geun vicinity
주차는 인근 공영 주차장에서 가능합니다. **juchaneun ingeun gongyeong juchajangeseo ganeunghamnida.** Parking is available in a nearby public parking lot.

근처 geun·cheo neighborhood, vicinity
실례지만, 이 근처 식당 좀 가르쳐 주실래요? **sillyejiman, i geuncheo sikdang jom gareuchyeo jusillaeyo?** Excuse me, can you give me the name of a restaurant in this neighborhood?

부근 bu·geun neighborhood, vicinity
오늘 아침 학교 부근에서 큰 사고가 났다. **oneul achim hakgyo bugeuneseo keun sagoga natda.** There was a major accident near the school this morning.

주변 = 주위 ju·byeon = ju·wi surroundings
주변에/주위에 사람이 많으니까 긴장돼. **jubyeone/juwie sarami maneunikka ginjangdwae.**

I'm nervous because there are many people around.

장소 jang·so place
시간이랑 장소는 정했어? **siganirang jangsoneun jeonghaesseo?** Have you decided on the time and place?

지점 ji·jeom point, spot, place
그들이 발견된 **정확한 지점**이 어디입니까? **geudeuri balgyeondoen jeonghwakan jijeomi eodiimnikka?** Where is the exact spot they were discovered?

곳 got place, location, lot
여기가 내가 **태어난 곳**이야. **yeogiga naega taeeonan gosiya.** This is the place where I was born.

군데 gun·de place
몇 해 전에 커피숍이 몇 군데 생겼어요. **myeot hae jeone keopisyobi myeot gunde saenggyeosseoyo.** Coffee shops started opening in a few places several years ago.

여기 yeo·gi here

거기 geo·gi there

저기 jeo·gi there

이곳 i·got here, this place

그곳 geu·got there, that place

저곳 jeo·got there, that place

데 de place, part
다친 데 없어요? **dachin de eopseoyo?** Are you all right?

여기저기 = 이곳저곳 yeo·gi·jeo·gi = i·got·jeo·got here and there
주말이면 여기저기/이곳저곳 돌아다녀요. **jumarimyeon nyeogijeogi/igotjeogot doradanyeoyo.** I go here and there on the weekends.

이리저리 i·ri·jeo·ri here and there

32.2 Directions

방향 bang·hyang direction
우리가 옳은 방향으로 가고 있는 거야? **uriga oreun banghyangeuro gago inneun geoya?** Are you sure we're driving in the right direction?

쪽 ≒ 편 jjok ≒ pyeon direction, side
어느 쪽이 남쪽이야? **eoneu jjogi namjjogiya?** Which direction is South?

이쪽 ≒ 이편 i·jjok ≒ i·pyeon this way

이리 i·ri here, this way
이리 와. **iri wa.** Come here.

그쪽 ≒ 그편 geu·jjok ≒ geu·pyeon that way

그리 geu·ri that way

저쪽 ≒ **저편** jeo·jjok ≒ jeo·pyeon that way

저리 jeo·ri that way
저리 가! **jeori ga!** Go away!

동쪽 dong·jjok east

서쪽 seo·jjok west

남쪽 nam·jjok south

북쪽 buk·jjok north

나침반 na·chim·ban compass

가리키다 ga·ri·ki·da to point, indicate
나침반이 **남쪽을 가리키고** 있다. **nachimbani namjjogeul garikigo itda.** The compass is pointing south.

앞쪽 ap·jjok the front

뒤쪽 = **뒤편** dwi·jjok = dwi·pyeon back, the rear

옆쪽 yeop·jjok side

왼쪽 = **왼편** oen·jjok = oen·pyeon the left

오른쪽 = **오른편** o·reun·jjok = o·reun·pyeon the right

한쪽 han·jjok one side

양쪽 yang·jjok both sides, both directions, both parties
양쪽 다리가 부었어요. **yangjjok dariga bueosseoyo.** Both of my legs are swollen.

안쪽 an·jjok the inside

바깥쪽 ba·kkat·jjok the outside

맞은편 ma·jeun·pyeon opposite side
우리 학교는 은행 맞은편에 있어. **uri hakgyoneun eunhaeng majeunpyeone isseo.** Our school is on the opposite side of the bank.

반대편 = **반대쪽** ban·dae·pyeon = ban·dae·jjok opposite side
도서관은 입구의 반대편에/반대쪽에 있습니다. **doseogwaneun ipguui bandaepyeone/bandaejjoge itseumnida.** The library is located on the opposite side of the entrance.

건너편 geon·neo·pyeon opposite side, the other side
그 건물은 길 건너편에 있어요. **geu geonmureun gil geonneopyeone isseoyo.** The building is on the other side of the street.

너머 neo·meo beyond
산 너머로 해가 졌다. **san neomeoro haega jyeotda.** The sun has set beyond the mountains.

나란히 na·ran·hi side by side
우리는 한참을 나란히 걸었다. **urineun hanchameul laranhi georeotda.** We walked side by side for a long time.

마주 ma·ju face to face
그들은 한마디 말도 없이 마주 보고 앉았다. **geudeureun hanmadi maldo eopsi maju bogo anjatda.** They sat face to face without saying a word.

향하다 hyang·ha·da to face
그녀는 우리를 향해 손을 흔들었다. **geunyeoneun urireul hyanghae soneul heundeureotda.** She waved at us.

까이. 가까이 각 간격 갈색 꾸로 거품 검은색 공간 구 구부러
지다 구성 구조 굵기 굵다 규모 기능 기울이다 기체 납작하다 낮다
낮추다 넓다 넓이 노란색 노랗다 높다 대각선 데시리터 도형
동그랗다 둔각 둘레 똑바로 똑바르다 뚜렷하다 멀다 멀리 면
무겁다 미터 밀리 바래다 반듯하다 반짝거리다 밝다 방울
벌어지다 범위 보라색 볼록하다 부피 비치다 빨간색 삼각형 색
생기다 선명하다 성분 성질 센티 속성 액체 얕다 어둡다
연두색 연하다 열다 예각 오므라들다 요소 원 원기둥 원뿔 일반 자리
작다 재다 점 제곱미터 좁히다 직선 진하다 축소 측량 측정 직직하다
커다랗다 크다 톤 투명하다 특징 평행 하늘색 하얀색
하얗다 형태 화려하다 휘다 흑백 희미하다 각 간격 갈색 거꾸로
거품 검은색 공간 구 구부러지다 구성 구조 굵기 굵다 규모 기능

chapter **33** | Describing Objects

기울이다 기체 납작하다 낮다 낮추다 넓다 넓이 노란색
노랗다 높다 대각선 데시리터 도형 동그랗다 둔각 둘레 똑바로
똑바르다 뚜렷하다 멀다 멀리 면 무겁다 미터 밀리 바래다
반듯하다 반짝거리다 밝다 방울 벌어지다 범위 보라색 볼록하다
부피 비치다 빨간색 삼각형 색 생기다 선명하다 성분
성질 센티 속성 액체 얕다 어둡다 연두색 연하다 다 예각 오므라들다
요소 원 원기둥 원뿔 일반 자리 작다 재다 점 제곱미터
좁히다 직선 진하다 축소 측량 측정 직직하다 커다랗다 크다
톤 투명하다 특징 평행 하늘색 하얀색 하얗다 형태
화려하다 휘다 흑백 희미하다

33.1 Physical States, Properties

물질 mul·jil matter, substance
얼음과 물은 같은 물질이다. eoreumgwa mureun gateun muljirida. Ice and water are the same substance.

물체 mul·che object
물체는 중력 때문에 지면으로 떨어지게 돼 있다. mulcheneun jungnyeok ttaemune jimyeoneuro tteoreojige dwae itda. Things fall to the ground because of gravity.

사물 sa·mul thing, object
어린아이들은 사물에 대한 호기심이 많다. eorinaideureun samure daehan hogisimi manta. Children are curious and inquisitive about things.

상태 sang·tae condition, state
액체 상태의 물 1킬로는 1리터의 부피를 차지한다. aekche sangtaeui mul ilkilloneun illiteoui bupireul chajihanda. One kilo of liquid water takes up the space of one liter.

기체 gi·che gas

고체 go·che solid

덩어리 deong·eo·ri lump, mass

가루 ga·ru powder

액체 aek·che liquid

방울 bang·ul drop

거품 geo·pum lather, bubble, foam
많은 아이들이 거품을 가지고 노는 것을 좋아한다. maneun aideuri geopumeul gajigo noneun geoseul joahanda. Many kids like to play with bubbles.

성질 seong·jil nature, quality, properties
이 비누는 살균 성질이 있습니다. i binuneun salgyun seongjiri itseumnida. This soap has antiseptic properties.

특성 teuk·seong characteristic, nature, quality
선인장은 혹독한 환경에 잘 적응하는 특성이 있다. seoninjangeun hokdokan hwangyeonge jal jeogeunghaneun teukseongi itda. Cacti are characterized by their adaptation to harsh environments.

특징 teuk·jing distinctive characteristic, feature
상자는 별다른 특징이 없었다. sangjaneun byeoldareun teukjingi eopseotda. The box had

nothing distinctive about it.

본질 | ~적 bon·jil | ~·jeok essence, essentials | essential
그 두 방법은 본질적으로 동일하다. geu du bangbeobeun bonjiljeogeuro dongilhada. The two methods are basically the same.

속성 sok·seong attribute, properties
권력을 동경하는 것은 인간의 속성 중 일부다. gwollyeogeul donggyeonghaneun geoseun inganui sokseong jung ilbuda. It is part of human nature to yearn for power.

일반 il·ban general
그 TV프로그램은 **일반 상식**을 시험하기 위해 만들어졌다. geu tibeuipeurogeuraemeun ilban sangsigeul siheomhagi wihae mandeureojyeotda. The TV program is designed to test general knowledge.

특수 teuk·su special
저는 군대에서 **특수 훈련**을 받았어요. jeoneun gundaeeseo teuksu hullyeoneul badasseoyo. I received special training in the army.

특수성 teuk·su·seong special characteristics
이 문제에 있어 남북 관계의 **특수성을 고려해야** 합니다. i munjee isseo nambuk gwangyeui teuksuseongeul goryeohaeya hamnida. We should consider the special nature of inter-Korean relations.

구조 gu·jo structure
문장 구조가 좀 이상해. munjang gujoga jom isanghae. The structure of this sentence is a little bit strange.

구성 | ~하다 gu·seong | ~·ha·da composition | to compose, form
물은 수소와 산소로 구성된다. mureun susowa sansoro guseongdoenda. Water is composed of hydrogen and oxygen.

성분 seong·bun ingredient, component
바닷물의 주 **성분**은 소금이다. badanmurui ju seongbuneun sogeumida. The main component of seawater is salt.

요소 yo·so element, factor

기능 gi·neung function
이 텔레비전에는 어떤 기능이 있어요? i tellebijeoneneun eotteon gineungi isseoyo? What functions does this TV have?

33.2 Shapes, Figures

모양 mo·yang shape
A: 책상은 어떤 모양이에요? B: 동그래요. **A: chaeksangeun eotteon moyangieyo? B: donggeuraeyo.** A: What shape is the desk? B: It's round.

형태 hyeong·tae shape, form
얼음, 눈, 수증기는 물의 다른 형태들이다. **eoreum, nun, sujeunggineun murui dareun hyeongtaedeurida.** Ice, snow, and steam are different forms of water.

둥글다 dung·geul·da round
지구는 둥글다. **jiguneun dunggeulda.** The earth is round.

동그랗다 dong·geu·ra·ta round
각 조각을 동그랗게 만드세요. **gak jogageul donggeurake mandeuseyo.** Mold each piece into a ball.

타원형 = 계란형 ta·won·hyeong = gye·ran·hyeong oval
왜 럭비공은 타원형이죠/계란형이죠? **wae reokbigongeun tawonhyeongijyo/gyeranhyeongijyo?** Why does a rugby ball have an oval shape?

네모나다 ne·mo·na·da square
나는 케이크를 네모나게 잘라 접시에 담았다. **naneun keikeureul lemonage jalla jeopsie damatda.** I cubed the cake and put it into a dish.

똑바로 ttok·ba·ro straight
똑바로 서라! **ttokbaro seora!** Stand up straight!

거꾸로 ← 꺼꾸로 geo·kku·ro ← kkeo·kku·ro upside down, inside out, backward
저는 모자를 거꾸로 씁니다. **jeoneun mojareul geokkuro sseumnida.** I like to wear my cap backwards.

똑바르다 ttok·ba·reu·da straight
그림을 보면 하얀 기둥이 완전히 똑바르지 않다는 걸 보실 수 있습니다. **geurimeul bomyeon hayan gidungi wanjeonhi ttokbareuji antaneun geol bosil su itseumnida.** If you look at the picture, you can see the white post isn't quite straight.

곧다 got·da straight
등을 곧게 펴라. **deungeul gotge pyeora.** Keep your back straight.

반듯하다 ban·deu·ta·da straight
선생님은 우리에게 책상 줄을 반듯하게 맞추도록 시켰다. **seonsaengnimeun uriege chaeksang jureul bandeutage matchudorok sikyeotda.** The teacher made us line up the desks in straight rows.

기울다 gi·ul·da to incline, tilt
지구의 자전축은 중심에서 23.5도 기울어 있다. **jiguui jajeonchugeun jungsimeseo isipsamjeomodo giureo itda.** The earth's axis is tilted 23.5 degrees off center.

기울이다 gi·u·ri·da to lean
몸을 살짝 앞으로 기울여 보세요. **momeul saljjak apeuro giullyeo boseyo.** Lean forward slightly.

구부러지다 gu·bu·reo·ji·da to bend, curve
도로는 오른쪽으로 완만하게 구부러져 나무로 된 다리로 이어진다. **doroneun oreunjjogeuro wanmanhage gubureojyeo namuro doen dariro ieojinda.** The road bends in a slight curve to the right that leads to a wooden bridge.

굽다 gup·da to bend, curve
할머니는 나이 때문에 **허리가 굽으셨다.** **halmeonineun nai ttaemune heoriga gubeusyeotda.** My grandmother is hunched over because of her age.

휘다 hwi·da to bend, curve
제 아들은 **어깨가** 구부정하게 **휘었어요.** **je adeureun eokkaega gubujeonghage hwieosseoyo.** My son's shoulders are bent in a slight curve.

비뚤다 bi·ttul·da crooked, atilt
왜 모자를 **비뚤게 쓰니? wae mojareul bittulge sseuni?** Why do you wear your cap at an angle?

비스듬하다 bi·seu·deum·ha·da askew, oblique
액자가 벽에 비스듬하게 걸려 있다. **aekjaga byeoge biseudeumhage geollyeo itda.** The frame is hung askew on the wall.

납작하다 nap·ja·ka·da flat
반죽을 납작하게 누르세요. **banjugeul lapjakage nureuseyo.** Flatten the dough into a disk.

볼록하다 bol·lo·ka·da bulging, protruding

그의 호주머니는 돈으로 볼록했다. **geuui ho-jumeonineun doneuro bollokaetda.** His pocket bulged with cash.

오목하다 o·mo·ka·da dented, concave
사람들은 멀리 있는 사람을 부를 때 흔히 손을 오목하게 만들어 입가에 댑니다. **saram-deureun meolli inneun sarameul bureul ttae heunhi soneul omokage mandeureo ipgae daemnida.** People often cup their hands around their mouth to call someone far away.

도형 do·hyeong figure
점 jeom dot, point
선 seon line
직선 jik·seon straight line
곡선 gok·seon curve
포물선 po·mul·seon arc, parabola
대각선 dae·gak·seon diagonal
수직 su·jik verticality
두 선은 수직으로 교차한다. **du seoneun suji-geuro gyochahanda.** The two lines cross at right angles.
수직선 su·jik·seon vertical line
주어진 선의 주어진 지점에 **수직선을 그으시오. jueojin seonui jueojin jijeome sujikseoneul geueusio.** Draw a line perpendicular to a given line from a given point.

수평 su·pyeong horizontality
평행 | ~하다 pyeong·haeng | ~·ha·da parallel | to parallel
선 AB와 A'B'는 평행이다. **seon eibiwa eipeuraimbipeuraimeun pyeonghaengida.** Lines AB and A'B' are parallel.
면 myeon face, side
주사위는 면이 여섯 개다. **jusawineun myeoni yeoseot gaeda.** A die has six sides.
삼각형 ≒ 세모 sam·ga·kyeong ≒ se·mo triangle
사각형 ≒ 네모 sa·ga·kyeong ≒ ne·mo quadrangle
원 ≒ 동그라미 won ≒ dong·geu·ra·mi circle
주어진 **원의 넓이**를 구하시오. **jueojin wonui neolbireul guhasio.** Figure out the area of the given circle.
타원 ta·won oval, ellipse
구 gu sphere
원기둥 won·gi·dung cylinder
원뿔 won·ppul cone
각뿔 gak·ppul pyramid
정육면체 jeong·yung·myeon·che cube

33.3 Colors and Brightness

색(깔) ≒ 빛깔 saek(·kkal) ≒ bit·kkal color
그 아이는 하늘을 **어두운 색**으로 칠했다. **geu aineun haneureul eoduun saegeuro chilhaetda.** The child painted the sky in a dark color.
컬러 keol·leo color
제가 어렸을 때는 동네에 **컬러 텔레비젼**이 있는 집이 하나도 없었어요. **jega eoryeosseul ttaeneun dongnee keolleo tellebijeoni inneun jibi hanado eopseosseoyo.** When I was young, there was no household with a color TV set in my neighborhood.
흑백 heuk·baek black and white
그 영화는 의도적으로 흑백으로 촬영되었다. **geu yeonghwaneun uidojeogeuro heukbae-geuro chwaryeongdoeeotda.** The movie was intentionally shot in black and white.

검다 = 까맣다 geom·da = kka·ma·ta black
검은색 = 검정(색) = 까망 = 까만색 = 흑색 geo·meun·saek = geom·jeong(·saek) = kka·mang = kka·man·saek = heuk·saek black
갈색 gal·saek brown
회색 hoe·saek gray
파랗다 pa·ra·ta blue
푸르다 pu·reu·da blue, azure, green
파란색 = 파랑 = 푸른색 = 청색 pa·ran·saek = pa·rang = pu·reun·saek = cheong·saek blue

하늘색 ha·neul·saek sky-blue

초록색 ≒ 녹색 cho·rok·saek ≒ nok·saek green

연두색 yeon·du·saek yellowish green

보라색 bo·ra·saek violet, purple

빨갛다 ≒ 붉다 ppal·ga·ta ≒ buk·da red

빨간색 = 빨강 = 적색 ppal·gan·saek = ppal·gang = jeok·saek red

분홍(색) bun·hong(·saek) pink

노랗다 no·ra·ta yellow

노란색 = 노랑 no·ran·saek = no·rang yellow

하얗다 = 희다 ha·ya·ta = hui·da white

하얀색 = 흰색 = 하양 = 백색 ha·yan·saek = huin·saek = ha·yang = baek·saek white

··

선명하다 seon·myeong·ha·da clear, distinct, vivid
색이 참 **선명하**군요. saegi cham seonmyeonghagunnyo. The color is very clear.

뚜렷하다 = 또렷하다 ttu·ryeo·ta·da = tto·ryeo·ta·da clear, distinct
한국은 사계절이 **뚜렷합니다/또렷합니다.** hangugeun sagyejeori tturyeotamnida/ttoryeotamnida. Korea has four distinct seasons.

흐리다 = 흐릿하다 heu·ri·da = heu·ri·ta·da dim, faint
인쇄가 너무 **흐려서/흐릿해서** 읽을 수가 없어요. inswaega neomu heuryeoseo/heuritaeseo ilgeul suga eopseoyo. The print is too faint to read.

희미하다 hui·mi·ha·da dim, faint
그녀는 **희미한 불빛** 아래서 잠이 들었다. geunyeoneun huimihan bulbit araeseo jami deureotda. She fell asleep in the dim light.

투명하다 tu·myeong·ha·da transparent
잠자리의 날개는 거의 투명하다. jamjariui nalgaeneun geoui tumyeonghada. The wings of dragonflies are almost transparent.

화려하다 hwa·ryeo·ha·da fancy, colorful
저는 화려한 것을 별로 좋아하지 않아요. jeoneun hwaryeohan geoseul byeollo joahaji anayo. I don't like fancy things very much.

은은하다 eu·neun·ha·da soft, subdued, subtle

나는 그들에게 벽을 **은은한 색**으로 칠해 달라고 부탁했다. naneun geudeurege byeogeul euneunhan saeguro chilhae dallago butakaetda. I asked them to paint the walls in subtle colors.

진하다 jin·ha·da dark, deep, thick
저는 아내가 **화장을 진하게 하는** 것을 좋아하지 않습니다. jeoneun anaega hwajangeul jinhage haneun geoseul joahaji ansseumnida. I don't like my wife wearing too much makeup.

짙다 jit·da deep, dark
그 립스틱은 색깔이 너무 **짙어** 보여. geu ripseutigeun saekkkari neomu jiteo boyeo. The lipstick looks too dark.

연하다 yeon·ha·da light, soft, weak
그는 목에 **연한** 갈색 목도리를 두르고 있었다. geuneun moge yeonhan galsaek mokdorireul dureugo isseotda. He had a light brown scarf round his neck.

옅다 = 엷다 yeot·da = yeol·da light, pale
저는 **화장을 옅게/엷게 하는** 걸 좋아해요. jeoneun hwajangeul lyeotge/yeolge haneun geol joahaeyo. I like to wear light makeup.

화사하다 hwa·sa·ha·da colorful, beautiful
새 집의 **화사한 컬러** 덕분에 기분이 좋아져요. sae jibui hwasahan keolleo deokbune gibuni joajyeoyo. The cheerful colors of my new home help to keep my spirit up.

칙칙하다 chik·chi·ka·da dark, dull
칙칙한 색깔은 사람을 피곤하고 우울하게 할 수 있습니다. chikchikan saekkkareun sarameul pigonhago uulhage hal su itseumnida. Somber colors can make you feel fatigued and depressed.

··

밝다 bak·da bright, light
오늘 밤은 **달이** 정말 **밝아요**. oneul bameun dari jeongmal balgayo. The moon is so bright tonight.

환하다 hwan·ha·da bright, light
밤에는 **환한 색** 옷을 입는 게 안전합니다. bameneun hwanhan saek oseul imneun ge anjeonhamnida. It's safer to wear bright-colored clothes at night.

빛나다 bin·na·da to shine, sparkle
구름 한 점 없는 하늘에서 해가 **밝게 빛나고** 있었다. gureum han jeom eomneun haneureseo haega balge binnago isseotda. The sun was shining brightly in the cloudless sky.

반짝거리다 = 반짝이다 ban·jjak·geo·ri·da = ban·jja·gi·da to glitter, sparkle
머리 위로 무수한 **별들이 반짝거리고/반짝이고** 있다. meori wiro musuhan byeoldeuri banjjakgeorigo/banjjagigo itda. Myriads of stars were twinkling overhead.

어둡다 eo·dup·da dark, gloomy
이제 밖은 어두워요. ije bakkeun eoduwoyo. It is dark outside now.

어둠 eo·dum darkness

캄캄하다 kam·kam·ha·da very dark
일곱 시밖에 안 되었는데 밖이 벌써 캄캄하네요. ilgop sibakke an doeeonneunde bakki beolsseo kamkamhaneyo. It's only seven, but it's already dark outside.

바래다 ba·rae·da to fade
티셔츠가 **빛이 바랬어요**. tisyeocheuga bichi baraesseoyo. The T-shirt has faded.

비추다 bi·chu·da to shine, light
그는 자신의 모습을 거울에 비춰 보았다. geuneun jasinui moseubeul geoure bichwo boatda. He looked at himself in the mirror.

비치다 bi·chi·da to shine, light
나무 사이로 햇빛이 비췄다. namu sairo haetbichi bichyeotda. The sun shone through the trees.

33.4 Area, Dimensions

공간 gong·gan space, room
기증품이 계속 들어오면서 우리는 **저장 공간**이 부족하다는 사실을 깨달았어요. gijeungpumi gyesok deureoomyeonseo urineun jeojang gonggani bujokadaneun sasireul kkaedarasseoyo. As donations continue to come in, we found ourselves short of storage space.

자리 ja·ri space, room
침대를 하나 더 놓을 자리는 없어. chimdaereul hana deo noeul jarineun eopseo. There's no room for another bed.

간격 gan·gyeok interval, space, gap
앞 차하고 안전 **간격을 유지하세요**. ap chahago anjeon gangyeogeul lyujihaseyo. You should keep a safe distance from the car ahead.

사이 sa·i gap, space
소파하고 침대 사이는 봤어? sopahago chimdae saineun bwasseo? Did you look between the sofa and the bed?

틈 teum crack, gap, space
갈라진 벽 **틈 사이로** 희미한 빛이 들어왔다. gallajin byeok teum sairo huimihan bichi deureowatda. A glimmer of light shone through a crack on the wall.

금 geum crack

생기다 saeng·gi·da to be formed
충격으로 벽에 **금이 생겼어요**. chunggyeogeuro byeoge geumi saenggyeosseoyo. The wall cracked from the impact.

갈라지다 gal·la·ji·da to split, crack
지진으로 **지붕이 갈라졌다**. jijineuro jibungi gallajyeotda. The roof cracked during the earthquake.

벌어지다 beo·reo·ji·da to widen

오므라들다 o·meu·ra·deul·da to close up
꽃잎은 기온이 높을 때 벌어지고 기온이 낮을 때 오므라든다. kkonnipeun gioni nopeul ttae beoreojigo gioni najeul ttae omeuradeunda. The flower petals open when the temperature is high and close when the temperature is low.

길이 gi·ri length
길이가 얼마나 됩니까? giriga eolmana doemnikka? How long is it?

둘레 dul·le circumference

가로 ga·ro width

세로 se·ro length
이 상자는 가로 30, 세로 50, 높이 20센티다. i sangjaneun garo samsip, sero osip, nopi isipsentida. This box is 30 centimeters wide, 50 centimeters long, and 20 centimeters high.

길다 gil·da long, lengthy
이 바지는 나한테는 너무 길어. i bajineun nahanteneun neomu gireo. The pants are too long for me.

늘이다 neu·ri·da to stretch, lengthen
고무줄을 늘이면 열을 발산한다. gomujureul leurimyeon nyeoreul balsanhanda. Stretching a rubber band will cause it to release heat.

짧다 jjal·da short
그 **치마**는 너한테 너무 **짧아**. **geu chimaneun neohante neomu jjalba.** The skirt is too short for you.

넓이 = 면적 neol·bi = myeon·jeok area, extent
이 가게는 넓이가/면적이 얼마나 됩니까? **i gageneun neolbiga/myeonjeogi eolmana doemnikka?** How big is this store?

범위 beo·mwi scope, range
이 바지는 내 **예산 범위** 밖이다. **i bajineun nae yesan beomwi bakkida.** These pants are way over budget.

폭 = 너비 pok = neo·bi width, breadth
이 복도는 **폭이/너비가** 너무 **좁다**. **i bokdoneun pogi/neobiga neomu jopda.** This hallway is too narrow.

넓다 neol·da large, extensive, big
그들은 **넓은** 집을 사고 싶어 한다. **geudeureun neolbeun jibeul sago sipeo handa.** They wish to buy a big house.

넓히다 neol·pi·da to widen, extend
저는 내년에 **집을 넓힐** 계획이 있습니다. **jeoneun naenyeone jibeul leolpil gyehoegi itseumnida.** I plan to expand my house next year.

확장 | ~하다 hwak·jang | ~·ha·da extension, enlargement | to extend, enlarge
도로를 2차로에서 4차로로 **확장하는** 공사가 곧 시작된다. **dororeul icharoeseo sacharoro hwakjanghaneun gongsaga got sijakdoenda.** The project to widen the road from two lanes to six lanes will begin soon.

좁다 jop·da narrow, small
길이 너무 **좁아**. **giri neomu joba.** The road is too narrow.

좁히다 jo·pi·da to narrow
범위를 좀 **좁혀** 봅시다. **beomwireul jom jopyeo bopsida.** Let's narrow it down.

높이 no·pi height; high
이 건물은 높이가 얼마나 되나요? **i geonmureun nopiga eolmana doenayo?** How tall is this building?
동의한다면 손을 **높이 들어** 주세요. **donguihandamyeon soneul lopi deureo juseyo.** Please raise your hand high if you agree.

높다 nop·da high, tall
이 가게는 **천장이 높아서** 마음에 들어요. **i gageneun cheonjangi nopaseo maeume deureoyo.** I like this shop because of its high ceiling.

높이다 ← 높히다 no·pi·da to make sth high, increase
담장을 높인다고 문제가 해결되지는 않을 것이다. **damjangeul lopindago munjega haegyeoldoejineun aneul geosida.** Heightening the fence won't solve the problem.

낮다 nat·da low
책상이 너무 **낮아요**. **chaeksangi neomu najayo.** The desk is too low for me.

낮추다 nat·chu·da to lower, reduce
몸을 낮추고 앞쪽 발에 체중을 실어라. **momeul latchugo apjjok bare chejungeul sireora.** Lower your body with your weight on the front foot.

크기 keu·gi size, bulk
중간 크기의 양파를 길게 자르세요. **junggan keuguiui yangpareul gilge jareuseyo.** Cut a medium onion into strips.

대형 dae·hyeong large size
간밤에 **대형 화재**가 발생했다. **ganbame daehyeong hwajaega balsaenghaetda.** Last night there was a big fire.

소형 so·hyeong small size
저는 **소형 아파트**에서 혼자 살고 있습니다. **jeoneun sohyeong apateueseo honja salgo itseumnida.** I live alone in a small apartment.

규모 gyu·mo scale, size
이 근처에는 **규모가** 큰 병원이 없습니다. **i geuncheoeneun gyumoga keun byeongwoni eopseumnida.** There are no large hospitals near here.

대규모 dae·gyu·mo large scale
대규모 시위가 내일 예정되어 있다. **daegyumo siwiga naeil yejeongdoeeo itda.** A large demonstration is planned tomorrow.

소규모 so·gyu·mo small scale
이곳은 **소규모 사업**을 하기에 최적의 장소이다. **igoseun sogyumo saeobeul hagie choejeogui jangsoida.** This is a best place for small businesses.

부피 bu·pi volume, bulk
이 **상자의 부피**를 계산하세요. **i sangjaui bupireul gyesanhaseyo.** Calculate the volume of this box.

크다 keu·da big, large

이 냉장고는 우리 집에서 쓰기에는 너무 커. **i naengjanggoneun uri jibeseo sseugieneun neomu keo.** This refrigerator is too big for my house.

커다랗다 keo·da·ra·ta big, large
그는 **커다란 상자**를 안고 내 쪽으로 걸어왔다. **geuneun keodaran sangjareul ango nae jjogeuro georeowatda.** He walked toward me, hugging a big box.

거대하다 geo·dae·ha·da huge, great
그 **거대한 바위**는 꿈쩍도 하지 않았다. **geu geodaehan bawineun kkumjjeokdo haji anatda.** The huge rock won't budge an inch.

작다 jak·da small, little
글자가 너무 **작아서** 못 알아보겠어요. **geuljaga neomu jagaseo mo darabogesseoyo.** The letters are too small to make out.

조그마하다 = 조그맣다 jo·geu·ma·ha·da = jo·geu·ma·ta small, little, tiny

확대 | ~하다 hwak·dae | ~·ha·da expansion, enlargement | to extend, enlarge, magnify
이 서류를 **확대 복사해** 주시겠어요? **i seoryureul hwakdae boksahae jusigesseoyo?** Can you make an enlarged copy of this document?

축소 | ~하다 chuk·so | ~·ha·da reduction, cut | to reduce, cut
우리 회사는 아직도 **규모를 축소해야** 합니다. **uri hoesaneun ajikdo gyumoreul chuksohaeya hamnida.** Our company should downsize some more.

무게 mu·ge weight
짐의 **무게를 재** 봐야 합니다. **jimui mugereul jae bwaya hamnida.** I have to weigh the baggage.

나가다 na·ga·da to weigh
이 노트북은 무게가 얼마나 **나가나요**? **i noteubugeun mugega eolmana naganayo?** How much does this laptop weigh?

무겁다 mu·geop·da heavy
그렇게 **무거운 가방**은 못 들어요. **geureoke mugeoun gabangeun mot deureoyo.** I can't lift such a heavy suitcase.

가볍다 ga·byeop·da light
이 **상자는 가볍습니다. i sangjaneun gabyeopseumnida.** This box is light.

깊이 gi·pi depth; deeply, deep

이 지점은 깊이가 2미터 정도 됩니다. **i jijeomeun gipiga imiteo jeongdo doemnida.** It's two meters deep at this point.
좀 더 **깊이 파라. jom deo gipi para.** Dig deeper.

깊숙이 gip·su·gi deep
나는 그 사진을 서랍 **깊숙이 넣었다. naneun geu sajineul seorap gipsugi neoeotda.** I put the picture deep into a drawer.

깊다 gip·da deep
이 **개울은 아이들이 놀기에는 너무 깊다. i gaeureun aideuri nolgieneun neomu gipda.** This stream is too deep for children to play in.

얕다 yat·da shallow
남은 음식을 **얕은 용기에 넣어 두세요. nameun eumsigeul lyateun nyonggie neoeo duseyo.** Place the leftovers in shallow containers.

거리 geo·ri distance
하이힐을 신고 **먼 거리**는 걸을 수가 없어요. **haihireul singo meon georineun georeul suga eopseoyo.** I can't walk long distances in high heels.

멀다 meol·da far, distant
저희 집은 여기에서 꽤 **멀어요. jeohui jibeun nyeogieseo kkwae meoreoyo.** My house is quite far from here.

멀리 meol·li far, far away
부모님은 도시에서 **멀리** 떨어진 시골에 사세요. **bumonimeun dosieseo meolli tteoreojin sigore saseyo.** My parents live in the countryside far from the city.

가깝다 ga·kkap·da close, near
슈퍼가 우리 집에서 **가까운 곳**에 있어. **syupeoga uri jibeseo gakkaun gose isseo.** There is a supermarket near my house.

가까이 ga·kka·i close, near
가까이 와 봐. **gakkai wa bwa.** Come closer.

엎어지면 코 닿을 곳 eo·peo·ji·myeon ko da·eul got within a stone's throw
저는 학교에서 **엎어지면 코 닿을 곳**에 살아요. **jeoneun hakgyoeseo eopeojimyeon ko daeul gose sarayo.** I live within a stone's throw of school.

두께 du·kke thickness
책의 **두께가 얇군요. chaegui dukkega yalgunnyo.** The book is thin.

두껍다 du·kkeop·da thick, dense
두꺼운 안개가 그 지역을 뒤덮었다. **dukkeoun**

angaega geu jiyeogeul dwideopeotda. A thick mist covered the region.

얇다 yal·da thin, flimsy
왜 겨울에 **얇은 옷**을 입고 있냐? **wae gyeoure yalbeun oseul ipgo innya?** Why are you wearing flimsy clothes in winter?

굵기 gul·gi thickness
굵기가 적어도 10밀리는 되는 나무가 필요합니다. **gukgiga jeogeodo simmillineun doeneun namuga piryohamnida.** I need wood at least 10 mm thick.

굵다 guk·da thick, big
더 **굵은 밧줄**을 가져와라. **deo gulgeun batjureul gajyeowara.** Bring me a thicker rope.

가늘다 ga·neul·da thin, slender
내 **머리카락**은 가는 편이다. **nae meorikarageun ganeun pyeonida.** My hair is rather silky.

각(도) gak(·do) angle
사각형의 네 각은 모두 직각이다. **sagakyeongui ne gageun modu jikgagida.** The four angles of a square are all right angles.

직각 jik·gak right angle

예각 ye·gak acute angle

둔각 dun·gak obtuse angle

온도 on·do temperature
방 안 **온도**가 너무 **낮다. bang an ondoga neomu natda.** The temperature in the room is too low.

33.5 Measuring, Units of Measurement

재다 jae·da to take, measure, weigh
혈압을 **재겠습니다. hyeorabeul jaegetseumnida.** Let me take your blood pressure.

측정 | ~하다 cheuk·jeong | ~·ha·da measurement | to measure
천문학자들은 항성 간의 **거리를** 어떻게 **측정하죠? cheonmunhakjadeureun hangseong ganui georireul eotteoke cheukjeonghajyo?** How do astronomers measure the distance to stars?

측량 | ~하다 cheung·nyang | ~·ha·da measurement | to measure, survey
토지를 **측량하려면** 전문 장비와 훈련이 필요하다. **tojireul cheungnyangharyeomyeon jeonmun jangbiwa hullyeoni piryohada.** You need specialized equipment and training to survey land.

달다 dal·da to weigh

저울 jeo·ul scale, balance
이 소포 저울에 좀 달아 봐. **i sopo jeoure jom dara bwa.** Weigh this package on the scales.

단위 da·nwi unit, measure
우리나라는 **측정 단위**로 미터법을 사용합니다. **urinaraneun cheukjeong danwiro miteobeobeul sayonghamnida.** Korea uses the metric system.

미터 mi·teo meter

밀리(미터) mil·li(·mi·teo) millimeter

센티(미터) sen·ti(·mi·teo) centimeter

킬로(미터) kil·lo(·mi·teo) kilometer

제곱미터 je·gom·mi·teo square meter

평 pyeong *pyeong*

A *pyeong* is Korean traditional measurement of an area which is equal to 3.3 m².

리터 ri·teo liter

데시리터 de·si·ri·teo deciliter

밀리(리터) mil·li(·ri·teo) milliliter

시시 si·si cc

세제곱미터 se·je·gom·mi·teo cubic meter

그램 geu·raem gram

킬로(그램) kil·lo(·geu·raem) kilogram

톤 ton ton

도 do degree

분 bun minute

가득 가득 갖가지 개수 거의 곱하기 공구 구구단 나누다
남기다 넉넉하다 넷 늘리다 늘어나다 다 다섯째
다양성 다양하다 대부분 더하기 더하다 둘 등 많이
모든 모조리 몽땅 배 백만 부분 부족 분량 분수 분자 비다
배다 사 사십 삼 상당수 상당하다 석 세다 셋 소수
소수 수 수만 수많은 수십 수천 숫자 십오 십육 십이 십일 십팔
억 여러 여럿 여섯 열네 열다섯 열두 열둘 열세 열아홉 열일곱
열한 영 예순 오 오십 온갖 유형 이십 일 일부 일체
자연수 잔뜩 저마다 전 전부 정수 종류 줄이다 증가 차
다 천만 첫째 총 칠 텅 팔십 풍족하다 하나 합하다 횟수
갖가지 개수 거의 곱하기 공구 구구단 나누다 남기다

chapter **34** | **Numbers and Quantities**

넉넉하다 넷 늘리다 늘어나다 다 다섯째 다양성
다양하다 대부분 더하기 더하다 둘 등 많이 모든
모조리 몽땅 배 백만 부분 부족 분량 분수 분자 비다
배다 사 사십 삼 상당수 상당하다 석 세다 셋 소수
소수 수 수만 수많은 수십 수천 숫자 십오 십육 십이 십일
팔 억 여러 여럿 여섯 열네 열다섯 열두 열둘 열세 열아홉 열일곱
열한 영 예순 오 오십 온갖 유형 이십 일 일부
일체 자연수 잔뜩 저마다 전 전부 정수 종류 줄이다
증가 차 차다 천만 첫째 총 칠 텅 팔십 풍족하다
하나 합하다 횟수

34.1 Numbers and Counting Words

개수 gae·su the number
개수를 확인해 보세요. **gaesureul hwaginhae boseyo.** Check the number.

번호 beon·ho number
번호를 부를 때까지 로비에서 기다려 주십시오. **beonhoreul bureul ttaekkaji robieseo gidaryeo jusipsio.** Please wait in the lobby until we call out your number.

횟수 hoet·su number (of times)

번 beon time, occasion
저는 하루에 두 번 샤워를 해요. **jeoneun harue du beon syaworeul haeyo.** I take a shower twice a day.

회 hoe time, occasion
모임은 연 4회 열립니다. **moimeun nyeon sa-hoe yeollimnida.** The meeting is to be held four times a year.

세다 se·da to count
1에서 10까지 세어 봐. **ireseo sipkkaji seeo bwa.** Count from one to ten.

·····································

하나 ha·na one

한 han one (modifier form)

둘 dul two

두 du two (modifier form)

셋 set three

세 se three (modifier form)

석 seok three (modifier form)
석 달 **seok dal** three months

> 석 or 넉 is mostly used only for months.

넷 net four

네 ne four (modifier form)

넉 neok four (modifier form)
종이 넉 장 **jongi neok jang** four sheets of paper

다섯 da·seot five

여섯 yeo·seot six

일곱 il·gop seven

여덟 yeo·deol eight

아홉 a·hop nine

열 yeol ten

열하나 yeol·ha·na eleven

열한 yeol·han eleven (modifier form)

열둘 yeol·dul twelve

열두 yeol·du twelve (modifier form)

열셋 yeol·set thirteen

열세 yeol·se thirteen (modifier form)

열넷 yeol·let fourteen

열네 yeol·le fourteen (modifier form)

열다섯 yeol·da·seot fifteen

열여섯 yeol·lyeo·seot sixteen

열일곱 yeo·ril·gop seventeen

열여덟 yeol·lyeo·deol eighteen

열아홉 yeo·ra·hop nineteen

스물 seu·mul twenty

스무 seu·mu twenty (modifier form)

서른 seo·reun thirty

마흔 ma·heun forty

쉰 swin fifty

예순 ye·sun sixty

일흔 il·heun seventy

여든 yeo·deun eighty

아흔 a·heun ninety

·····································

영 yeong zero

공 gong zero
제 전화번호는 010-1234-5678입니다. **je jeonhwabeonhoneun gongilgongillisamsaoryuk-chilparimnida.** My number is 010-1234-5678.

> 공 is often preferred over 영 when reading a number digit by digit.

일 il one

이 i two

삼 sam three

사 sa four

오 o five

육 yuk six

칠 chil seven

팔 pal eight

구 gu nine

십 sip ten

십일 si·bil eleven

십이 si·bi twelve

십삼 sip·sam thirteen

십사 sip·sa fourteen

십오 si·bo fifteen

십육 sim·nyuk sixteen

십칠 sip·chil seventeen

십팔 sip·pal eighteen

십구 sip·gu nineteen

이십 i·sip twenty

삼십 sam·sip thirty

사십 sa·sip forty

오십 o·sip fifty

육십 yuk·sip sixty

칠십 chil·sip seventy

팔십 pal·sip eighty

구십 gu·sip ninety

백 baek one hundred

천 cheon one thousand

만 man ten thousand

십만 sim·man one hundred thousand

백만 baeng·man one million

천만 cheon·man ten million

억 eok one hundred million

첫째 cheot·jjae first

둘째 dul·jjae second

셋째 set·jjae third

넷째 net·jjae fourth

다섯째 da·seot·jjae fifth

번째 beon·jjae unit for counting the order
첫 번째, 두 번째, 세 번째, 네 번째, 다섯 번째 **cheot beonjjae, du beonjjae, se beonjjae, ne beonjjae, daseot beonjjae** first, second, third, fourth, fifth

수십 su·sip dozens

수백 su·baek hundreds

수천 su·cheon thousands

수만 su·man tens of thousands

34.2 Mathematics

수 su number

숫자 sut·ja number, digit, figure
나이는 숫자에 불과하다. **naineun sutjae bul-gwahada.** Age is nothing but a number.

자리 ja·ri digit, figure
이 수의 십의 자리 숫자는 일의 자리 숫자의 세 배이다. 각 숫자의 합은 8이다. 이 수는? **i suui sibui jari sutjaneun irui jari sutjaui se baeida. gak sutjaui habeun palsibida. i suneun?** The tens digit of this number is three times the ones digit. The sum of the digits in the number is 8. What is the number?

실수 sil·su real number

정수 jeong·su integer, whole number

자연수 ja·yeon·su natural number

소수 so·su prime number

분수 bun·su fraction

분모 bun·mo denominator

분자 bun·ja numerator

-분 -bun part, portion
4분의1 **sabunui il** one fourth

소수 so·su decimal

더하다 deo·ha·da to add

더하기 deo·ha·gi addition
1 더하기 3은 4. il deohagi sameun sa. One plus three equals four.

합하다 ≒ 합치다 ha·pa·da ≒ hap·chi·da to add up, total
1에서 100까지의 자연수를 모두 합하시오. ireseo baekkkajiui jayeonsureul modu hapasio. Add all the natural numbers from 1 to 100.

덧셈 deot·sem addition

빼다 ppae·da to subtract, take out
5에서 2를 빼면 3이 남는다. oeseo ireul ppaemyeon sami namneunda. If you take two from five, you get three.

빼기 ppae·gi subtraction

뺄셈 ppael·sem subtraction

차 cha difference, margin
한 점 차로 이겼어요. han jeom charo igyeosseoyo. We won the game by one point.

곱하다 go·pa·da multiply

곱하기 go·pa·gi multiplication
4 곱하기 2는 8. sa gopagi ineun pal. Four times two is eight.

곱셈 gop·sem multiplication

구구단 gu·gu·dan multiplication table, times table

구구단 외울 수 있어? gugudan oeul su isseo? Can you memorize the times table?

제곱 je·gop square
5의 제곱은 25다. oui jegobeun isiboda. Five squared is twenty five.

배 bae times, -fold
하루 사이에 값이 두 배로 올랐어요. haru saie gapsi du baero ollasseoyo. The price went up twice in one day.

나누다 na·nu·da to divide, split
13을 5로 나누면 몫은 2, 나머지는 3이다. sipsameul oro nanumyeon mokseun i, nameojineun samida. If you divide thirteen by five, the quotient is two and the remainder is three.

나눗셈 na·nut·sem to be divided

몫 mok quotient

나머지 na·meo·ji remainder

비율 bi·yul ratio, proportion
우리 회사의 **남녀 비율**은 대략 2 대 1이다. uri hoesaui namnyeo biyureun daeryak i dae irida. The ratio of women to men in my office is about 2:1.

퍼센트 = 프로 peo·sen·teu = peu·ro percent

프로 derives from the Dutch word *procent*.

34.3 Concepts of Quantity

양 yang quantity, amount
사람들은 매일 **엄청난 양**의 기름을 소비한다. saramdeureun maeil eomcheongnan nyangui gireumeul sobihanda. We consume a huge quantity of oil every day.

분량 bul·lyang amount, quantity
그 질문은 답변이 책 한 권 분량은 나올 겁니다. geu jilmuneun dapbyeoni chaek han gwon bullyangeun naol geomnida. That's a question to which the answer could fill a book.

대량 dae·ryang great quantities
대량 구매를 하시면 할인을 해 드립니다. daeryang gumaereul hasimyeon harineul hae deurimnida. We offer you a discount on volume purchases.

많다 man·ta many, much

저는 이곳에 친구가 많아요. jeoneun igose chinguga manayo. I have many friends here.

많이 ma·ni a lot
많이 드세요. mani deuseyo. Help yourself.

수많은 su·ma·neun a lot of, numerous
매일 수많은 사람들이 교통사고로 사망한다. maeil sumaneun saramdeuri gyotongsagoro samanghanda. Every day numerous people die in car accidents.

수없이 su·eop·si innumerably
내가 수없이 경고했잖아! naega sueopsi gyeonggohaetjana! I've warned you a million times!

무수히 mu·su·hi innumerably
기업의 가치를 평가하는 **무수히 많은** 방법이 있다. gieobui gachireul pyeonggahaneun mu-

suhi maneun bangbeobi itda. There are a myriad ways of valuing a company.

상당하다 sang·dang·ha·da considerable, sizeable
그를 찾는 데 **상당한 시간**이 소모되었다. geureul channeun de sangdanghan sigani somodoeeotda. A considerable amount of time was spent finding him.

풍부하다 pung·bu·ha·da rich, plentiful
한국은 **천연자원이 풍부하지** 않습니다. hangugeun cheonyeonjawoni pungbuhaji anseumnida. Korea is not rich in natural resources.

풍족하다 pung·jo·ka·da rich, affluent
다행히 먹을 것은 풍족하게 있어요. dahaenghi meogeul geoseun pungjokage isseoyo. We are lucky that we have plenty of food to eat.

충분하다 | 충분히 chung·bun·ha·da | chung·bun·hi enough | enough, fully
이 정도면 충분해. i jeongdomyeon chungbunhae. This is enough.

넉넉하다 neong·neo·ka·da enough, sufficient
돈은 넉넉하게 있어요. doneun neongneokage isseoyo. I have enough money.

잔뜩 jan·tteuk fully
저녁을 **잔뜩 먹었더니** 잠이 와. jeonyeogeul jantteuk meogeotdeoni jami wa. I feel sleepy because I had a big dinner.

적다 jeok·da few, little, small
그 영화는 **적은 예산**으로 만들어졌다. geu yeonghwaneun jeogeun yesaneuro mandeureojyeotda. The film was made on a small budget.

부족 | ~하다 bu·jok | ~·ha·da shortage, lack | short, insufficient
많은 사람들이 식량 **공급 부족**으로 고통 받고 있다. maneun saramdeuri singnyang gonggeup bujogeuro gotong batgo itda. Many are suffering from a shortage of food.

모자라다 mo·ja·ra·da to be short, be insufficient
시간이 모자라. sigani mojara. I don't have enough time.

증가 | ~하다 jeung·ga | ~·ha·da increase | to increase
최근 몇 년 사이에 **수입이** 3퍼센트 **증가했어요**. choegeun myeon nyeon saie suibi sampeosenteu jeunggahaesseoyo. In recent years, imports have increased by three percent.

늘다 neul·da to increase, rise
전 세계적으로 **수명이 늘고** 있다. jeon segyejeogeuro sumyeongi neulgo itda. The human life expectancy is rising around the globe.

늘어나다 neu·reo·na·da to grow, increase
정부 발표에 따르면 사망자 수가 30명으로 늘어났다. jeongbu balpyoe ttareumyeon samangja suga samsimmyeongeuro neureonatda. According to a government announcement, the death toll has risen to 30.

급증하다 geup·jeung·ha·da to increase rapidly

늘리다 neul·li·da to increase, expand, extend
우리의 올해 목표는 수출량을 늘리는 것입니다. uriui olhae mokpyoneun suchullyangeul leullineun geosimnida. Our goal of this year is to increase exports.

감소 | ~하다 gam·so | ~·ha·da decrease, decline | to decrease
농촌 **인구는** 꾸준히 **감소해** 왔다. nongchon inguneun kkujunhi gamsohae watda. Population in the countryside has steadily declined.

줄다 jul·da to decrease
이번 달 매출이 3퍼센트 **줄었어요**. ibeon dal maechuri sampeosenteu jureosseoyo. This month's sales figures dropped by 3%.

줄어들다 ju·reo·deul·da to decrease, shrink
남성 흡연자의 수가 **줄어들고** 있어요. namseong heubyeonjaui suga jureodeulgo isseoyo. The number of male smokers is decreasing.

줄이다 ju·ri·da to decrease
음식물 **섭취를** 아주 많이 **줄여야** 합니다. eumsingmul seopchwireul aju mani juryeoya hamnida. You need to cut down on your food intake significantly.

가득(히) | 가득하다 ga·deuk(·i) | ga·deu·ka·da fully | full, crammed
가득 넣어 주세요. gadeuk neoeo juseyo. Fill it up, please.
상자 안에는 잡동사니들이 가득했다. sangja aneneun japdongsanideuri gadeukaetda. The box was full of odds and ends.

차다 cha·da to be full, be occupied
자리가 꽉 찼는데요. jariga kkwak channeundeyo. The seats are all occupied.

텅 teong completely

비다 bi·da to be empty, be vacant
누군가의 발자국 소리가 텅 **빈 방**을 울렸다.
nugungaui baljaguk soriga teong bin bangeul
ullyeotda. Footsteps echoed in the empty
room.

남다 nam·da to remain, be left
시험까지 일주일 남았다. siheomkkaji iljuil
lamatda. I have one week left before the
exam.

남기다 nam·gi·da to leave
남기지 말고 다 먹어. namgiji malgo da meogeo. Don't leave anything on your plate.

종류 jong·nyu kind, sort, type
나는 모든 면 종류를 싫어한다. naneun modeun
myeon jongnyureul sireohanda. I dislike all
kinds of noodles.

가지 ga·ji kind, sort
스크린샷을 찍는 두 가지 방법이 있어요. seu-
keurinsyaseul jjingneun du gaji bangbeobi
isseoyo. There are two ways to take screen-
shots.

유형 yu·hyeong type, class, pattern
인간의 성격은 몇 가지 유형으로 분류될 수
없다. inganui seonggyeogeun myeot gaji
yuhyeongeuro bullyudoel su eopda. Human
characters cannot be categorized into a few
types.

여러 yeo·reo many, several
여러 나라를 가 보고 싶어요. yeoreo narareul
ga bogo sipeoyo. I'd like to visit many countries.

여럿 yeo·reot many
이건 단지 여럿 가운데 하나예요. igeon danji
yeoreot gaunde hanayeyo. This is just one out
of many.

온갖 on·gat all, every kind of
주말이면 온갖 사람들이 그곳에 모인다. ju-
marimyeon ongat saramdeuri geugose moinda.
All kinds of people gather there on weekends.

갖가지 gat·ga·ji various, several kinds of
그는 왜 자신이 전화를 받지 못했는지 **갖가지
핑계**를 댔다. geuneun wae jasini jeonhwareul
batji motaenneunji gatgaji pinggyereul daetda.
He made various excuses as to why he
couldn't answer the phone.

각종 gak·jong various
병원에는 **각종 질병**으로 고통받는 많은 사람

들이 있다. byeongwoneneun gakjong jilbyeong-
euro gotongbanneun maneun saramdeuri itda.
There are many people suffering from various diseases in the hospital.

다양하다 da·yang·ha·da various
우리는 학생들에게 **다양한 서비스**를 제공합
니다. urineun haksaengdeurege dayanghan
seobiseureul jegonghamnida. We offer various services for students.

다양성 da·yang·seong diversity

등(等) deung(·deung) etc.
여러분은 이곳에서 장미, 백합, 튤립 등 다양
한 종류의 꽃들을 보실 수 있습니다. yeoreo-
buneun igoseseo jangmi, baekhap, tyullip deung
dayanghan jongnyuui kkotdeureul bosil su itseumnida. You can see several kinds of flowers—roses, lilies, tulips, etc., here.

모두 mo·du all
여러분 모두 이것에 동의하세요? yeoreobun
modu igeose donguihaseyo? Do you all agree
with this?

전부 jeon·bu all
이 시간이 전부 함께 모일 수 있는 좋은 기회
야. i sigani jeonbu hamkke moil su inneun joeun
gihoeya. This time is a good chance to get
everyone together.

몽땅 mong·ttang all
몽땅 다 먹은 거야? mongttang da meogeun
geoya? Did you eat it all?

모조리 mo·jo·ri all, completely
가방 속에 있는 것들을 모조리 꺼내 보세요.
gabang soge inneun geotdeureul mojori kkeo-
nae boseyo. I want you to completely empty
your bag.

죄다 joe·da all, entirely
알고 있는 것들을 죄다 말해. algo inneun geotdeureul joeda malhae. Tell me everything you
know.

다 da all; almost
모두 다 왔을 때 파티는 거의 다 끝나 있었다.
modu da wasseul ttae patineun geoui da kkeunna isseotda. The party was almost over when
everyone arrived.

하나부터 열까지 ha·na·bu·teo yeol·kka·ji
from A to Z
하나부터 열까지 다 다시 설명을 해야 했다.
hanabuteo yeolkkaji da dasi seolmyeongeul
haeya haetda. I had to explain again from A
to Z.

한꺼번에 han·kkeo·beo·ne all at once, all together
한꺼번에 먹기에는 너무 많아. **hankkeobeone meokgieneun neomu mana.** There is too much food to eat all at once.

일체 il·che all, everything
제가 **경비 일체**를 부담하겠습니다. **jega gyeong-bi ilchereul budamhagetseumnida.** I'll bear all the costs.

온통 on·tong all, entirely
머릿속이 온통 담배 생각뿐이에요. **meoritsogi ontong dambae saenggakppunieyo.** All I think about is smoking.

전 jeon all, entire
이것들이 내 **전 재산**이에요. **igeotdeuri nae jeon jaesanieyo.** This is all my property.

총 chong total
참가 인원은 총 열 명입니다. **chamga inwo-neun chong yeol myeongimnida.** The total number of participants is ten.

온 on all, entire
나는 **온 힘**을 다해 벽을 밀었다. **naneun on himeul dahae byeogeul mireotda.** I pushed against the wall with all my strength.

모든 mo·deun all, every
시간이 모든 것을 해결해 줄 거야. **sigani mo-deun geoseul haegyeolhae jul geoya.** Time will solve everything.

거의 geo·ui almost, nearly
올해에는 거의 눈이 내리지 않았다. **olhaeeneun geoui nuni naeriji anatda.** This year there was hardly any snow.

전체 | ~적 jeon·che | ~·jeok the whole | overall
전쟁 중에 그 지역 전체가 파괴되었다. **jeon-jaeng junge geu jiyeok jeonchega pagoedoeeot-da.** The whole district was destroyed during the war.

일부 il·bu part, portion
운동은 제 생활의 일부예요. **undongeun je saenghwarui ilbuyeyo.** Exercise is a part of my life.

부분 | ~적 bu·bun | ~·jeok part | partial
그 영화에서 가장 좋은 부분이 뭐였어? **geu yeonghwaeseo gajang joeun bubuni mwoyeo-sseo?** What was your favorite part of that movie?

대부분 dae·bu·bun most
그 기사의 대부분은 거짓이야. **geu gisaui dae-bubuneun geojisiya.** Most of the article is false.

대다수 dae·da·su majority
주민들 대다수가 높은 만족감을 표시했다. **ju-mindeul daedasuga nopeun manjokgameul pyo-sihaetda.** The majority of the residents expressed high levels of satisfaction.

상당수 sang·dang·su considerable number
상당수 학생들이 그 행사에 참여했다. **sang-dangsu haksaengdeuli geu haengsae chamyeo-haetda.** A considerable number of students joined the event.

(절)반 (jeol·)ban half
시작이 반이다. **sijagi banida.** Well begun is half done.

각(각) gak(·gak) each, every
나머지 세 강의는 각각 한 시간씩이야. **nameo-ji se ganguineun gakgak han siganssigiya.** The other three classes are one hour each.

저마다 jeo·ma·da each, respectively
사람들은 저마다 꿈이 있다. **saramdeureun jeomada kkumi itda.** Each person has his or her own dream.

가량 가장 가치 간단하다 간신히 강력하다 겨우 고유

공통점 과연 관계없이 굉장하다 귀하다 균형 그냥

그런대로 기타 나쁘다 내외 다소 단 단순하다 닮다

대단하다 더욱 도저히 되게 두드러지다 마찬가지

명확하다 몹시 무렵 바람직하다 반대 별다르다 분명하다

불편 불필요하다 불확실하다 빼놓다 뿐 상관 설사 수월하다

쉽다 신규 실컷 심하다 썰렁하다 쓸모 아늑하다 아주

chapter **35** | **General Concepts**

약간 어려움 어찌나 엄청 엄청나다 엉터리 여간 여전하다

오직 오히려 완전히 외 유난히 유리하다 의외로

이롭다 이상 일정하다 잇다 적어도 적합하다 전혀 전후

정도 정말 정상 제법 조화 좀처럼 좋다 중대하다

중요하다 차이점 참 최대한 통 특별히 픽 편

편리하다 포근하다 필요 필요성 하도 한층 혹시 -경

35.1 Degree

가장 ga·jang most, best
가장 최근에 본 영화가 뭐야? **gajang choegeune bon nyeonghwaga mwoya?** What's the most recent film you saw?

제일 je·il (the) first, (the) most
건강이 제일이야. **geongangi jeiriya.** Health is most important.

맨 maen the very, the most
맨 처음 뭘 할까? **maen cheoeum mwol halkka?** What shall we do first?

(지)극히 (ji·)geu·ki extremely
개가 아이를 무는 일은 **극히 드뭅니다. gaega aireul muneun ireun geuki deumumnida.** It is very rare for a dog to bite a kid.

최대 choe·dae maximum, the biggest
2학년은 최대 15학점까지 수강할 수 있습니다. **ihangnyeoneun choedae sibohakjeomkkaji suganghal su itseumnida.** The maximum number of credits allowed for sophomores is 15.

최고 choe·go (the) best
걷기는 **최고의 운동**이다. **geotgineun choegoui undongida.** Walking is the best exercise.

완전히 wan·jeon·hi perfectly, completely
어젯밤에 너 완전히 취했었어. **eojetbame neo wanjeonhi chwihaesseoseo.** You were totally wasted last night.

싹 ssak completely, entirely
싹 버리고 새 것을 사세요. **ssak beorigo sae geoseul saseyo.** Throw them away and buy new ones.

무척 = 매우 mu·cheok = mae·u very, extremely
신입 사원 여러분들에 대한 사장님의 기대가 무척/매우 크십니다. **sinip sawon nyeoreobundeure daehan sajangnimui gidaega mucheok/maeu keusimnida.** Our CEO has high expectations of you, new recruits.

몹시 mop·si very, really, extremely
이런 날씨에 밖에 나가는 것은 몹시 위험하다. **ireon nalssie bakke naganeun geoseun mopsi wiheomhada.** It is very dangerous to go out in this weather.

되게 doe·ge very, extremely
딸아이는 요즘 외모에 되게 신경을 써요. **tta-**

raineun nyojeum oemoe doege singyeongeul sseoyo. My daughter is particular about her appearance these days.

아주 a·ju very, extremely
아내는 처형하고 아주 달라요. **anaeneun cheohyeonghago aju dallayo.** My wife is quite different from her sister.

너무(나) neo·mu(·na) too
이 생선은 가시가 너무 많아. **i saengseoneun gasiga neomu mana.** This fish has too many bones in it.

네가 너무나 보고 싶었어. **nega neomuna bogo sipeosseo.** I missed you so much.

> 너무 is often used to mean *very*, but this usage is regarded as technically incorrect.

엄청나다 eom·cheong·na·da huge, great
이 상자들의 **무게가 엄청나요. i sangjadeurui mugega eomcheongnayo.** These boxes are quite heavy.

엄청 eom·cheong very, extremely
요즘 회사에서 스트레스를 엄청 받아요. **yojeum hoesaeseo seuteureseureul eomcheong badayo.** I'm under a lot of stress at the office these days.

대단하다 | 대단히 dae·dan·ha·da | dae·dan·hi great, important, serious | very, really, extremely
그는 고집이 대단하다. **geuneun gojibi daedanhada.** He is very stubborn.

대단히 감사합니다. **daedanhi gamsahamnida.** Thank you very much.

굉장하다 | 굉장히 goeng·jang·ha·da | goeng·jang·hi wonderful, great | very, extremely
경치가 굉장하군요. **gyeongchiga goengjanghagunnyo.** The view is breathtaking.

회의가 굉장히 지루했어요. **hoeuiga goengjanghi jiruhaesseoyo.** The meeting was extremely boring.

어찌나 eo·jji·na very, so
그 사람이 코를 **어찌나** 심하게 고는지 잠을 잘 수가 없었어. **geu sarami koreul eojjina simhage goneunji jameul jal suga eopseosseo.** I couldn't sleep because he was snoring so much.

얼마나 eol·ma·na how
시험에 통과하면 얼마나 좋을까! **siheome tonggwahamyeon eolmana joeulkka!** How great it would be to pass the test!

무려 mu·ryeo as much as
무려 천 명이나 모였어요. **muryeo cheon myeongina moyeosseoyo.** As many as a thousand people gathered.

하도 ha·do very, much
일이 하도 많아서 점심도 못 먹었어요. **iri hado manaseo jeomsimdo mon meogeosseoyo.** I couldn't have lunch because I have so much work to do.

워낙 wo·nak so, very, remarkably
요즘 워낙 바빠서 연락 못 했어. **yojeum wonak bappaseo yeollak mo taesseo.** I have been so busy recently that I didn't have time to call you.

정말(로) = 진짜(로) jeong·mal(·ro) = jin·jja(·ro) really
오늘 저녁은 정말/진짜 환상적이었어요. **oneul jeonyeogeun jeongmal/jinjja hwansangjeogieosseoyo.** Today's dinner was really fantastic.

참(으로) cham(·eu·ro) truly, really
세월 참 빠르네. **sewol cham ppareune.** Time flies.

그야말로 geu·ya·mal·lo really, simply, truly
불꽃놀이는 그야말로 대단했다. **bulkkonnori-neun geuyamallo daedanhaetda.** The fireworks were really spectacular.

실로 sil·lo really, truly
실로 충격적이다. **sillo chunggyeokjeogida.** It is really shocking.

실컷 sil·keot as much as one likes
실컷 드세요. **silkeot deuseyo.** Eat as much as you like.

마음껏 ma·eum·kkeot as much as one likes
들어오셔서 마음껏 둘러보세요. **deureo-osyeoseo maeumkkeot dulleoboseyo.** You are welcome to come in and take a look around.

힘껏 him·kkeot with all one's strength
힘껏 밀어 봐. **himkkeot mireo bwa.** Push harder.

그만 geu·man to that extent
그만 좀 떠들어. **geuman jom tteodeureo.** Stop talking.

제법 je·beop pretty, fairly
저 아이는 나이에 비해 제법 어른스러워. **jeo aineun naie bihae jebeop eoreunseureowo.** The child is fairly mature for his age.

꽤 kkwae quite, fairly
시간이 꽤 늦었네. **sigani kkwae neujeonne.** It's getting quite late.

퍽 peok quite, fairly

상당히 sang·dang·hi considerably, quite
결과는 상당히 놀라웠어요. **gyeolgwaneun sangdanghi nollawosseoyo.** The result was something of a surprise.

약간 yak·gan a little, a bit
약간 비싼데요. **yakgan bissandeyo.** It's a little expensive.

조금 = 좀 jo·geum = jom a little, a bit
조금/좀 이따 전화해라. **jogeum/jom itta jeonhwahaera.** Call again a little later.

살짝 sal·jjak slightly
고개를 오른쪽으로 살짝 돌려 보세요. **gogaereul oreunjjogeuro saljjak dollyeo boseyo.** Please turn your head slightly to the right.

다소 da·so somewhat, a little
교장 선생님의 말씀은 다소 지루했다. **gyojang seonsaengnimui malsseumeun daso jiruhaetda.** The principal's speech was a little boring.

그런대로 geu·reon·dae·ro somehow
그런대로 괜찮아. **geureondaero gwaenchana.** Not bad.

편 pyeon side, rather
아내는 말이 없는 편이에요. **anaeneun mari eomneun pyeonieyo.** My wife is the quiet type.

겨우 = 고작 gyeo·u = go·jak barely, only
지금 우리에게 남은 돈은 겨우/고작 5000원 뿐이야. **jigeum uriege nameun doneun gyeou/gojak ocheonwonppuniya.** All we have is mere 5000 won.

단지 = 다만 dan·ji = da·man only, just, simply
배는 별로 안 고픈데, 단지/다만 너무 졸려요. **baeneun byeollo an gopeunde, danji/daman neomu jollyeoyo.** I'm not so hungry. I'm just really sleepy.

그냥 = 그저 geu·nyang = geu·jeo just
우리는 그냥/그저 친구 사이예요. urineun geu·nyang/geujeo chingu saiyeyo. We are just friends.

단 dan just, only
이번에는 단 한 번의 실수도 용납되지 않아. ibeoneneun dan han beonui silsudo yongnapdoeji ana. Not even a single mistake is allowed this time.

뿐 ppun just, only
그건 시간 낭비일 뿐이야. geugeon sigan nangbiil ppuniya. It's just a waste of time.

오직 = 오로지 o·jik = o·ro·ji only, solely, exclusively
오직/오로지 한 가지 방법만이 남았어. ojik/oroji han gaji bangbeommani namasseo. There's only one way left.

불과 | ~하다 bul·gwa | ~·ha·da only, just | to be only
이것은 시작에 불과해. igeoseun sijage bulgwahae. This is just the start.

간신히 = 가까스로 gan·sin·hi = ga·kka·seu·ro barely, narrowly
그는 경기 시작 세 시간 만에 간신히/가까스로 시합에서 승리했다. geuneun gyeonggi sijak se sigan mane gansinhi/gakkaseuro sihabeseo seungnihaetda. He won the game by a narrow margin after three hours on the court.

그리 = 그다지 = 별로 = 썩 geu·ri = geu·da·ji = byeol·lo = sseok (not) very much
나는 소주를 그리/그다지/별로/썩 좋아하지 않아. naneun sojureul geuri/geudaji/byeollo/sseok joahaji ana. I don't like soju very much.

전혀 = 전연 jeon·hyeo = jeo·nyeon (not) at all
A: 그거 재미있었어? B: 아뇨, 전혀/전연 재미 없었어요. A: geugeo jaemiisseosseo? B: anyo, jeonhyeo/jeonyeon jaemieopseosseoyo. A: Did you enjoy it? B: No, it was not fun at all.

도무지 do·mu·ji (not) at all
이게 무슨 말인지 도무지 모르겠어요. ige museun marinji domuji moreugesseoyo. I have no idea what this means.

(도)통 (do·)tong (not) at all
요즘 그 사람을 통 못 봤어요. yojeum geu sarameul tong mot bwasseoyo. I haven't seen much of him recently.

영 yeong totally; at all
너는 엄마랑은 영 딴판이구나. neoneun eommarangeun nyeong ttanpaniguna. You are totally different from your mother.
요즘 영 기운이 없어요. yojeum yeong giuni eopseoyo. I'm feeling really low these days.

결코 = 절대로 gyeol·ko = jeol·dae·ro never
저는 결코/절대로 그런 말을 한 적이 없어요. jeoneun gyeolko/jeoldaero geureon mareul han jeogi eopseoyo. I have never said such a thing.

목에 칼이 들어와도 mo·ge ka·ri deu·reo·wa·do come what may
목에 칼이 들어와도 비밀을 지킬게. moge kari deureowado bimireul jikilge. I'll keep the secret come what may.

도저히 do·jeo·hi never
도저히 못 참겠어. dojeohi mot chamgesseo. It is more than I can bear.

여간 yeo·gan ordinarily
그 사람하고 대화를 한다는 건 **여간** 힘든 일이 **아냐.** geu saramhago daehwareul handaneun geon nyeogan himdeun iri anya. It is never easy talking to him.

좀처럼 ← 좀체로 jom·cheo·reom ← jom·che·ro easily
아버지는 좀처럼 화를 내지 않으세요. abeojineun jomcheoreom hwareul laeji aneuseyo. My father rarely gets angry.

약 yak about, approximately
1인치는 약 2.54센티미터입니다. irinchineun nyak ijeomosasentimiteoimnida. One inch is approximately 2.54 centimeters.

대략 dae·ryak approximately, roughly
대략 얼마예요? daeryak geolmayeyo? How much is it approximately?

대충 = 대강 dae·chung = dae·gang approximately, roughly
대충/대강 훑어봤어요. daechung/daegang hulteobwasseoyo. I've run my eyes over it.

내외 = 안팎 nae·oe = an·pak approximately, roughly
용의자는 쉰 살 내외의/안팎의 남자입니다. yonguijaneun swin sal laeoeui/anpakkui namjaimnida. The suspect is a man of about fifty.

전후 jeon·hu around, about
어머니는 실제로는 일흔이지만 예순 전후로

보입니다. eomeonineun siljeroneun ilheuniji-man yesun jeonhuro boimnida. My mother is seventy but she looks like she's around sixty.

정도 jeong·do around, about; degree
집에서 회사까지는 버스로 반 시간 정도 걸립니다. jibeseo hoesakkajineun beoseuro ban sigan jeongdo geollimnida. It takes about half an hour by bus to get from my house to my office.

그 정도면 충분해. geu jeongdomyeon chung-bunhae. That is enough.

-쯤 -jjeum around, about
아마 한 시간쯤 걸릴 거예요. ama han sigan-jjeum geollil geoyeyo. Maybe it will take an hour or so.

가량 ga·ryang around, about

-경 -gyeong around, about
두 시경에 점심을 먹었어요. du sigyeonge jeomsimeul meogeosseoyo. I had lunch at around two o'clock.

무렵 mu·ryeop around
어제는 자정 무렵에 집에 들어갔어요. eoje-neun jajeong muryeobe jibe deureogasseoyo. I came back home around midnight yester-day.

더 deo more
딸아이는 저보다 키가 더 커요. ttaraineun jeo-boda kiga deo keoyo. My daughter is taller than I am.

덜 deol less
오늘은 어제보다 덜 더운 것 같아요. oneureun eojeboda deol deoun geot gatayo. I think today is not as hot as yesterday.

더욱(더) deo·uk(·deo) much more, increasingly
밤이 되자 그녀의 상태가 더욱 나빠졌다. bami doeja geunyeoui sangtaega deouk nappa-jyeotda. That night her condition got worse.

한층 = 한결 han·cheung = han·gyeol much more
날씨가 한층/한결 시원해졌어요. nalssiga hancheung/hangyeol siwonhaejyeosseoyo. It became much cooler.

비교적 bi·gyo·jeok relatively, comparatively
이번 겨울은 비교적 따뜻하다. ibeon gyeou-reun bigyojeok ttatteutada. It's comparatively warm this winter.

훨씬 hwol·ssin much, far
말을 안 하는 게 말을 잘하는 것보다 훨씬 더 어려워요. mareul an haneun ge mareul jalha-neun geotboda hwolssin deo eoryeowoyo. It is much more difficult not to speak than it is to speak well.

이상 i·sang and above
B 이상의 학점은 만족스러운 점수로 생각된다. B isangui hakjeomeun manjokseureoun jeomsuro saenggakdoenda. A "B" or above is the desired grade.

이하 i·ha and under
그녀의 점수는 반 평균 이하였다. geunyeoui jeomsuneun ban pyeonggyun ihayeotda. Her score was below the class average.

> If you say "A 이상/이하," you include A itself, while 미만 does not. For example, 18 이하 means "18 or under" as opposed to 18 미만 which means "17 or under" (excluding 18).

미만 mi·man under
18세 미만 출입 금지 sippalse miman churip geumji No admittance to anyone under 18.

낫다 nat·da better, superior
올해 수확이 작년보다 낫다. olhae suhwagi jangnyeonboda natda. This year's harvest is better than last year's.

못하다 mo·ta·da inferior
이곳 서비스가 예전보다 못하다. igot seobi-seuga yejeonboda motada. The service here is not as good as it used to be.

못지않다 mot·ji·an·ta as ... as
오늘도 어제 못지않게 더워요. oneuldo eoje motjianke deowoyo. It is just as hot as yester-day.

만큼 man·keum as ... as
저는 단지 일한 만큼 받고 싶을 뿐이에요. jeoneun danji ilhan mankeum batgo sipeul ppu-nieyo. I just want to get paid for the work done.

달리 dal·li unlike
자기 형하고는 달리, 진수는 수줍음이 많다. jagi hyeonghagoneun dalli, jinsuneun suju-beumi manta. Jinsu is shy, unlike his brother.

그나마 geu·na·ma at least, still
죽지 않은 게 그나마 다행이야. jukji aneun ge geunama dahaengiya. At least, it's fortunate that he is not dead.

최소(한) choe·so(·han) at least

이 건물을 다시 짓는 데는 최소한 2년이 걸릴 거야. i geonmureul dasi jinneun deneun choesohan inyeoni geollil geoya. The reconstruction of this building will take at least two years.

적어도 jeo·geo·do at least

최대한 choe·dae·han to the maximum
최대한 협조하겠습니다. choedaehan hyeopjohagetseumnida. I'll give you my full cooperation.

차라리 cha·ra·ri rather
거기 가느니 차라리 집에서 잠이나 자겠다. geogi ganeuni charari jibeseo jamina jagetda. I would rather sleep at home than go there.

특별히 teuk·byeol·hi particularly, especially
특별히 찾으시는 브랜드가 있으세요? teukbyeolhi chajeusineun beuraendeuga isseuseyo? Do you have any particular brand in mind?

특히 teu·ki particularly, especially
특히 이 부분을 주의해서 보세요. teuki i bubuneul juuihaeseo boseyo. Pay particular attention to this.

유난히 = 유달리 yu·nan·hi = yu·dal·li particularly, especially
올 겨울은 유난히/유달리 춥네요. ol gyeoureun nyunanhi/yudalli chumneyo. It's exceptionally cold this winter.

35.2 Certainty, Supposition

확실하다 | 확실히 hwak·sil·ha·da | hwak·sil·hi sure, certain | surely, certainly
확실해요? hwaksilhaeyo? Are you sure?
A: 그럼 누구 잘못이야? B: 몰라, 확실히 내 잘못은 아냐. A: geureom nugu jalmosiya? B: molla, hwaksilhi nae jalmoseun anya. A: Whose fault is it then? B: I don't know, but it's certainly not mine.

틀림없다 | 틀림없이 teul·li·meop·da | teul·li·meop·si sure, certain | certainly, surely
그 이야기는 틀림없이 거짓이다. geu iyagineun teullimeopsi geojisida. The story is certainly a lie.

분명하다 | 분명히 bun·myeong·ha·da | bun·myeong·hi clear, distinct | clearly, obviously
나는 매사 분명한 것을 좋아한다. naneun maesa bunmyeonghan geoseul joahanda. I like it when things are clear.
좀 더 분명히 말해 봐. jom deo bunmyeonghi malhae bwa. Speak more clearly.

명백하다 myeong·bae·ka·da obvious, certain
언어가 시간에 따라 변화한다는 것은 **명백한 사실**이다. eoneoga sigane ttara byeonhwahandaneun geoseun myeongbaekan sasirida. It is an obvious fact that a language changes over time.

명확하다 myeong·hwa·ka·da clear, obvious

명확한 증거가 있나요? myeonghwakan jeunggeoga innayo? Do you have any definite evidence?

정확하다 | 정확히 jeong·hwa·ka·da | jeong·hwa·ki accurate, correct | exactly
수업이 정확히 8시에 시작합니다. sueobi jeonghwaki yeodeolsie sijakamnida. Class begins exactly at 8 o'clock.

마련 ma·ryeon bound, certain
사람은 죽게 마련이다. sarameun jukge maryeonida. Humans will die eventually.

반드시 ≒ 꼭 ban·deu·si ≒ kkok surely, certainly
저는 반드시/꼭 살아남겠습니다. jeoneun bandeusi/kkok saranamgetseumnida. I'll surely survive.
문 꼭 잠가라. mun kkok jamgara. Make sure to lock the door.

무조건 mu·jo·geon unconditionally, at any cost
이번 시합은 무조건 이겨야 한다. iben sihabeun mujogeon igyeoya handa. We must win this game at any cost.

불확실하다 bul·hwak·sil·ha·da uncertain, unclear
그가 나를 도와줄지는 불확실하다. geuga nareul dowajuljineun bulhwaksilhada. It is uncertain whether he will help me out or not.

아마(도) a·ma(·do) probably, perhaps
아마 그럴 거야. ama geureol geoya. Probably.

듯(이) | 듯하다 deut(·i) | deu·ta·da as if, like | look like, seem

그 사람은 죽은 듯이 자고 있었다. **geu sara-meun jugeun deusi jago isseotda.** He was sleeping like a log.

일기예보가 아무래도 틀린 듯하다. **ilgiyeboga amuraedo teullin deutada.** The weather forecast seems to be wrong.

같다 gat·da feel like, look like

그 사람 나쁜 사람 같아요. **geu saram nappeun saram gatayo.** He seems like a bad guy.

비가 쏟아질 것 같아요. **biga ssodajil geot gatayo.** It looks like it's going to pour.

터 teo must, would

배고플 텐데, 밥 먹으러 가자. **baegopeul tende, bam meogeureo gaja.** You must be hungry. Let's go get some food.

> When 터 is combined with 이다, 터이 is usually shortened to 테.

어쩌면 eo·jjeo·myeon maybe, perhaps

어쩌면 진짜일지도 몰라. **eojjeomyeon jinjjailjido molla.** That might be true.

아무래도 a·mu·rae·do how hard I think

아무래도 우리가 질 것 같아. **amuraedo uriga jil geot gata.** I think we will lose.

혹시 hok·si by any chance, in case

혹시 모르니까 우산 가져가라. **hoksi moreunikka usan gajyeogara.** Take an umbrella just in case.

왠지 = 어쩐지 ← 웬지 waen·ji = eo·jjeon·ji ← wen·ji somehow

왠지/어쩐지 기분이 이상해. **waenji/eojjeonji gibuni isanghae.** I feel strange somehow.

설마 seol·ma not likely

설마 마음이 변한 건 아니겠죠? **seolma maeumi byeonhan geon anigetjyo?** Don't tell me you have changed your mind.

과연 gwa·yeon indeed, really

그 여자 말이 과연 사실일까요? **geu yeoja mari gwayeon sasirilkkayo?** Are her words true?

오히려 = 도리어 o·hi·ryeo = do·ri·eo on the contrary

오히려/도리어 제가 고마워요. **ohiryeo/dorieo jega gomawoyo.** I should be thanking you.

의외로 ui·oe·ro unexpectedly

그녀는 의외로 날씬했다. **geunyeoneun uioero nalssinhaetda.** She was unexpectedly slim.

뜻밖에 tteut·ba·kke unexpectedly

뜻밖에도 그 자리에는 그가 와 있었다. **tteut-bakkedo geu jarieneun geuga wa isseotda.** He was there unexpectedly.

....

가령 ga·ryeong if, supposing

가령 우리가 이겼다고 하자. **garyeong uriga igyeotdago haja.** Let's say, we won.

예컨대 ← 예컨데 ye·keon·dae ← ye·keon·de for example, supposing

인스턴트 식품, 예컨대 햄버거나 핫도그를 그만 먹어야 합니다. **inseuteonteu sikpum, ye-keondae haembeogeona hatdogeureul geuman meogeoya hamnida.** Stop eating junk food such as burgers and hot dogs.

만약 = 만일 ma·nyak = ma·nil just in case, if

만약을/만일을 대비해서, 매달 돈을 저축해라. **manyageul/manireul daebihaeseo, maedal doneul jeochukaera.** Just in case, save some money every month.

만약/만일 안 맞으면 교환할 수 있나요? **ma-nyak/manil an majeumyeon gyohwanhal su innayo?** Can I return it if it doesn't fit?

설사 = 설령 seol·sa = seol·lyeong even if, even though

설사/설령 알고 있어도 말하지 않겠어. **seol-sa/seollyeong algo isseodo malhaji ankesseo.** I would not tell you even if I knew.

비록 bi·rok though, although

비록 짧은 시간이었지만 그곳에서 만든 추억은 영원할 거예요. **birok jjalbeun siganieot-jiman geugoseseo mandeun chueogeun nyeong-wonhal geoyeyo.** Even though it was a short time, the memories I made there will last a lifetime.

아무리 a·mu·ri no matter how

사람은 자신이 좋아하는 일을 하면 **아무리** 힘들어도 늘 즐거운 법이다. **sarameun jasini joa-haneun ireul hamyeon amuri himdeureodo neul jeulgeoun beobida.** When you are doing something you like, it is always fun no matter how hard the work is.

35.3 Relations

관계 gwan·gye relationship
이 일은 저와 아무 **관계가** 없어요. i ireun jeowa amu gwangyega eopseoyo. This has nothing to do with me.

관련 ≒ **연관** | ~**되다** gwal·lyeon ≒ yeon·gwan | ~·doe·da relation, connection | to be related (to), be connected to
많은 사람들이 이 사고에 관련되어/연관되어 있다. maneun saramdeuri i sagoe gwal-lyeondoeeo/yeongwandoeeo itda. Many people are connected to this accident.

상관 | ~**하다** sang·gwan | ~·ha·da relation, connection | to care
네가 **상관할** 문제가 아니야. nega sanggwan-hal munjega aniya. It's none of your business.

관계없이 ≒ **상관없이** gwan·gye·eop·si ≒ sang·gwa·neop·si irrespectively, regardless of
나이에 **관계없이/상관없이** 누구나 참여할 수 있습니다. naie gwangyeeopsi/sanggwaneopsi nuguna chamyeohal su itseumnida. Everyone can participate regardless of age.

연결 | ~**하다** yeon·gyeol | ~·ha·da connection | to connect
잘못된 부서로 연결되었어요. jalmotdoen buseoro yeongyeoldoeeosseoyo. I've been connected to the wrong department.

잇다 it·da to connect, join
두 점을 자와 연필을 이용해 이으시오. du jeomeul jawa yeonpireul iyonghae ieusio. Connect the two dots with your ruler and pencil.

합치다 hap·chi·da to combine
그 두 회사는 합치기로 결정했다. geu du hoe-saneun hapchigiro gyeoljeonghaetda. The two companies decided to merge.

통합 | ~**하다** tong·hap | ~·ha·da combination, integration | to combine, integrate

교대 | ~**하다** gyo·dae | ~·ha·da rotation | to rotate
우리 집은 아이들이 교대로 설거지를 합니다. uri jibeun aideuri gyodaero seolgeojireul ham-nida. My kids take turns doing the dishes.

대신 | ~**하다** dae·sin | ~·ha·da instead (of) | to replace, substitute
당신을 대신할 사람은 많아요. dangsineul daesinhal sarameun manayo. There are many people that can replace you.

(똑)같다 ≒ **동일하다** (ttok·)gat·da ≒ dong·il·ha·da same, identical
저는 누나랑 키가 같아요. jeoneun nunarang kiga gatayo. I'm as tall as my sister.

비슷하다 ≒ **유사하다** bi·seu·ta·da ≒ yu·sa·ha·da similar, alike, like
네 옷 내 거랑 비슷한데/유사한데. ne ot nae georang biseutande/yusahande. Your clothes are similar to mine.
이 두 곡은 되게 유사해. i du gogeun doege yu-sahae. These two songs are very alike.

공통점 gong·tong·jeom common feature
형과 저는 **공통점이** 전혀 없어요. hyeonggwa jeoneun gongtongjeomi jeonhyeo eopseoyo. My older brother and I have nothing in common.

닮다 dam·da to resemble, look like
부모님 중에 누구를 더 닮았어요? bumonim junge nugureul deo dalmasseoyo? Who do you resemble more, your father or your mother?

Note that the past tense 닮았다 **dalmatda** is used to describe two people or things which ARE similar to each other.

여전하다 yeo·jeon·ha·da still the same
부지런한 건 여전하구나. bujireonhan geon nyeojeonhaguna. You are as diligent as ever.

일정하다 il·jeong·ha·da uniform, fixed

해당하다 hae·dang·ha·da to be relevant, be applicable
해당되는 단어에 밑줄을 그어라. haedangdoe-neun daneoe mitjureul geueora. Underline applicable words.

마치 ma·chi like, as if
마치 새 것 같아요. machi sae geot gatayo. It looks like new.

다름없다 da·reu·meop·da as good as, same
이 펜은 새 거나 다름없어. i peneun sae geona dareumeopseo. This pen is as good as new.

마찬가지 ma·chan·ga·ji the same

역시 yeok·si also, too, as well

나도 **역시 마찬가지야**. nado yeoksi machanga-jiya. Same here.

일치 │ ~하다 il·chi │ ~·ha·da agreement, concordance │ to agree, match
암호가 **일치하지** 않습니다. amhoga ilchihaji anseumnida. The password doesn't match.

조화 jo·hwa harmony
그 집은 자연환경과 **조화를 이룬다**. geu jibe-un jayeonhwangyeonggwa johwareul irunda. The house is in harmony with the environment.

균형 gyun·hyeong balance, equilibrium
보존과 개발 사이에 **균형을 맞추는** 일은 쉽지 않다. bojongwa gaebal saie gyunhyeongeul matchuneun ireun swipji anta. It's not easy to keep a balance between conservation and development.

포함 │ ~하다 po·ham │ ~·ha·da inclusion │ to include, contain
이 가격은 **세금을 포함하지** 않습니다. i gagyeo-geun segeumeul pohamhaji anseumnida. This price does not include the tax.

제외 │ ~하다 je·oe │ ~·ha·da exclusion │ to exclude, leave out
우리 가게는 현충일만 **제외하고** 365일 문을 엽니다. uri gageneun hyeonchungilman jeoe-hago sambaengnyuksiboil muneul lyeomnida. Our store is open every day except Memorial Day.

빼놓다 ppae·no·ta to leave out, miss

딴 = 다른 ttan = da·reun another, other
미안, 잠시 **딴/다른 생각**을 하고 있었어. mian, jamsi ttan/dareun saenggageul hago isseoseo. Sorry. I was thinking about something else.
저는 **딴/다른 사람**들과는 달라요. jeoneun ttan/dareun saramdeulgwaneun dallayo. I'm different from other people.

별도 byeol·do exception
부가세는 **별도**입니다. bugaseneun byeoldoimnida. Surcharges are excluded.

예외 ye·oe exception

이 규정에 누구도 **예외가 될 수 없습니다**. i gyujeonge nugudo yeoega doel su eopseumnida. There is no exception to this rule.

(이)외 (i·)oe except (for), but (for)
그는 자신 **외에는** 아무도 믿지 않는다. geune-un jasin oeeneun amudo mitji anneunda. He doesn't believe anyone except himself.

말고 mal·go except
너 **말고** 그렇게 말하는 사람은 아무도 없다. neo malgo geureoke malhaneun sarameun amu-do eopda. No one else says that except you.

기타 gi·ta the others

다르다 da·reu·da different
서울은 몇 가지 점에서 **다른** 아시아 도시들과 다르다. seoureun myeot gaji jeomeseo dareun asia dosideulgwa dareuda. Seoul is different from other Asian cities in some respects.

차(이) cha(·i) difference, gap
그 둘 사이에는 **뚜렷한 차이**가 있다. geu dul saieneun tturyeotan chaiga itda. There is a distinct difference between the two.

하늘과 땅 차이 ha·neul·gwa ttang cha·i a world of difference
1등과 2등은 **하늘과 땅 차이**예요. ildeunggwa ideungeun haneulgwa ttang chaiyeyo. There's a world of difference between first place and second.

차이점 cha·i·jeom difference, different point

비하다 bi·ha·da to compare
나이에 **비해** 어려 보이시네요. naie bihae eo-ryeo boisineyo. You look young for your age.

반하다 ban·ha·da to be opposed to
저는 키가 큰 **데 반해**, 아버지는 키가 작으세요. jeoneun kiga keun de banhae, abeojineun kiga jageuseyo. I am tall, while my father is short.

반대 ban·dae the opposite

정반대 jeong·ban·dae the exact opposite
제 쌍둥이 형은 저랑 **정반대**예요. je ssang-dungi hyeongeun jeorang jeongbandaeyeyo. My twin brother is the complete opposite of me.

35.4 General States

있다 it·da to be, stay, exist
지갑은 침대 옆 탁자 위에 있어요. jigabeun chimdae yeop takja wie isseoyo. The wallet is on the table next to the bed.

계시다 gye·si·da honorific of 있다 itda
엄마 집에 계셔? eomma jibe gyesyeo? Is your mom at home?

없다 eop·da not exist, not have
날개가 없는 새가 있어요? nalgaega eomneun saega isseoyo? Is there a bird that doesn't have wings?

없이 eop·si without
사람은 물 없이는 살 수 없다. sarameun mul eopsineun sal su eopda. We can't survive without water.

존재 | ~하다 jon·jae | ~·ha·da existence | to exist
달에 생명체가 존재할까? dare saengmyeong-chega jonjaehalkka? Does life exist on the Moon?

쉽다 swip·da easy, simple
한글은 배우기 쉬워요. hangeureun baeugi swiwoyo. Hangul is easy to learn.

수월하다 su·wol·ha·da easy

식은 죽 먹기 = 땅 짚고 헤엄 치기 = 누워서 떡 먹기 si·geun jung meok·gi = ttang jip·go he·eom chi·gi = nu·wo·seo tteong meok·gi a piece of cake
이번 수학 시험은 식은 죽 먹기/땅 짚고 헤엄 치기/누워서 떡 먹기였어. ibeon suhak siheomeun sigeun jung meokgi/ttang jipgo heeomchigi/nuwoseo tteong meokgiyeosseo. This math exam was as easy as pie.

만만하다 man·man·ha·da easy to deal with
아기를 돌보는 일은 결코 만만한 일이 아니에요. agireul dolboneun ireun gyeolko manman-han iri anieyo. It's no easy task taking care of a baby.

어렵다 eo·ryeop·da difficult, hard
생물 시험이 아주 어려웠어요. saengmul si-heomi aju eoryeowosseoyo. The biology exam was very difficult.

어려움 eo·ryeo·um difficulty, trouble
수면을 취하는 데 **어려움을 겪은** 적이 있나 요? sumyeoneul chwihaneun de eoryeoumeul gyeokkeun jeogi innayo? Have you ever experienced any trouble getting to sleep?

하늘의 별 따기 ha·neu·rui byeol tta·gi one in a million chance
요즘은 집 구하기가 **하늘의 별 따기**야. yo-jeumeun jip guhagiga haneurui byeol ttagiya. These days it's almost impossible to find a good house.

힘들다 him·deul·da hard, difficult
코로 숨을 쉬기가 힘들어요. koro sumeul swi-giga himdeureoyo. It is hard for me to breathe through my nose.

단순하다 | 단순히 dan·sun·ha·da | dan·sun·hi simple, naive | simply
단순한 게 좋은 거예요. dansunhan ge joeun geoyeyo. To be simple is to be good.

그건 단순히 이기고 지는 문제가 아니야. geugeon dansunhi igigo jineun munjega aniya. It's not simply a question of winning or losing.

간단하다 | 간단히 gan·dan·ha·da | gan·dan·hi simple, easy, brief | simply, briefly
이 카메라는 사용이 간단합니다. i kameraneun sayongi gandanhamnida. This camera is quite easy to use.

간단히 말해 시험을 망쳤어요. gandanhi mal-hae siheomeul mangchyeosseoyo. In short, I screwed up the exam.

복잡하다 bok·ja·pa·da complicated, complex
알고 보니 그 문제는 예상한 것보다 더 복잡 했다. algo boni geu munjeneun yesanghan geotboda deo bokjapaetda. The problem has turned out to be more complicated than expected.

자세하다 ≒ 상세하다 | 자세히 ≒ 상세히 ja·se·ha·da ≒ sang·se·ha·da | ja·se·hi ≒ sang·se·hi detailed | in detail
자세한/상세한 얘기는 이따 하죠. jasehan/sangsehan yaegineun itta hajyo. We can go into details later.

더 자세히 설명할까요? deo jasehi seol-myeonghalkkayo? Do you want me to elaborate?

구체적 gu·che·jeok detailed, specific

좀 더 구체적으로 말씀해 주세요. **jom deo gu-chejeogeuro malsseumhae juseyo.** Please be more specific.

간편하다 gan·pyeon·ha·da simple and convenient
이 배낭은 휴대가 간편해요. **i baenangeun hyudaega ganpyeonhaeyo.** This backpack is convenient to carry around.

편리하다 pyeol·li·ha·da convenient
대중교통으로 오시는 게 더 편리하실 거예요. **daejunggyotongeuro osineun ge deo pyeollihasil geoyeyo.** It would be more convenient to come here using public transportation.

불편 | ~하다 bul·pyeon | ~·ha·da inconvenience | inconvenient
불편하시게 해서 죄송합니다. **bulpyeonhasige haeseo joesonghamnida.** I'm sorry for the inconvenience.

번거롭다 beon·geo·rop·da inconvenient, cumbersome

좋다 jo·ta good, fine
이보다 더 좋을 수는 없다. **iboda deo joeul suneun eopda.** This is as good as it gets.

완벽 | ~하다 wan·byeok | ~·ha·da perfection | perfect
완벽한 사람은 없어. **wanbyeokan sarameun eopseo.** Nobody is perfect.

완전 | ~하다 wan·jeon | ~·ha·da completeness | complete, perfect
이건 완전한 문장이 아냐. **igeon wanjeonhan munjangi anya.** This is not a complete sentence.

바람직하다 ba·ram·ji·ka·da desirable
경제가 빨리 성장한다는 것이 항상 바람직한 것은 아니다. **gyeongjega ppalli seongjanghandaneun geosi hangsang baramjikan geoseun anida.** It's not always desirable for the economy to grow rapidly.

나쁘다 na·ppeu·da bad, poor
저는 기억력이 나빠요. **jeoneun gieongnyeogi nappayo.** I have a bad memory.

불완전하다 bu·rwan·jeon·ha·da incomplete, imperfect

엉터리 eong·teo·ri nonsense, sham

약점 yak·jeom weakness, weak point
왜 내 약점을 건드리는 거예요? **wae nae yakjeomeul geondeurineun geoyeyo?** Why are

you picking on my weak points?

흠 heum fault, flaw

강하다 gang·ha·da strong, powerful
그는 책임감이 강하다. **geuneun chaegimgami ganghada.** He has a strong sense of responsibility.

강력하다 | 강력히 gang·nyeo·ka·da | gang·nyeo·ki strong, powerful | strongly
2010년 아이티에서 강력한 지진이 발생했다. **icheonsimnyeon aitieseo gangnyeokan jijini balsaenghaetda.** In 2010, there was a devastating earthquake in Haiti.

세다 se·da strong, powerful
딸아이가 고집이 엄청 세요. **ttaraiga gojibi eomcheong seyo.** My daughter is so stubborn.

굳다 gut·da strong, firm
나는 다시 돌아오지 않겠다고 굳게 결심했다. **naneun dasi doraoji anketdago gutge gyeolsimhaetda.** I've made up my mind not to come back.

약하다 ya·ka·da weak, feeble
저는 추위에 약해요. **jeoneun chuwie yakaeyo.** I'm weak to the cold.

필요 | ~하다 pi·ryo | ~·ha·da need, necessity | necessary
걱정할 필요 없어. **geokjeonghal piryo eopseo.** There is no need to worry.

필요성 pi·ryo·seong need, necessity

필수 | ~적 pil·su | ~·jeok must | essential
규칙적인 운동은 건강에 필수적이다. **gyuchikjeogin undongeun geongange pilsujeogida.** Regular exercise is essential for good health.

불필요하다 bul·pi·ryo·ha·da unnecessary, useless

중요하다 jung·yo·ha·da important
중요한 부분에 밑줄을 그어라. **jungyohan bubune mitjureul geueora.** Underline the important sections.

중요성 jung·yo·seong importance

주요 ≒ 주 ju·yo ≒ ju main, major
외국인이 많기 때문에, 언어 장벽이 주요 문제다. **oegugini manki ttaemune, eoneo jangbyeogi juyo munjeda.** Because there are so many foreigners, the language barrier is the main problem.

귀(중)하다 gwi·(·jung)·ha·da　precious, valuable
귀중한 정보를 제공해 주셔서 감사합니다. gwijunghan jeongboreul jegonghae jusyeoseo gamsahamnida. Thank you for providing valuable information.

중대하다 jung·dae·ha·da important, serious
이것은 중대한 실수예요. igeoseun jungdaehan silsuyeyo. This is a serious mistake.

사소하다 sa·so·ha·da trivial, minor

....

소용 so·yong use, good
쓸모 ≒ 쓸데 sseul·mo ≒ sseul·de use
그의 발명품은 전혀 쓸모가/쓸데가 없다. geuui balmyeongpumeun jeonhyeo sseulmoga/sseuldega eopda. His inventions are totally useless.

가치 ga·chi value, worth
이 책은 읽을 가치가 없어. i chaegeun ilgeul gachiga eopseo. This book is not worth reading.

이롭다 i·rop·da beneficial, advantageous
어떤 기생충은 인간에게 이로울 수 있다. eotteon gisaengchungeun inganege iroul su itda. Certain parasites can be very beneficial to humans.

유리하다 yu·ri·ha·da favorable
현재 상황은 우리에게 유리하다. hyeonjae sanghwangeun uriege yurihada. The current situation is favorable for us.

소용없다 so·yong·eop·da no use
모르는 체해도 소용없다. moreuneun chehaedo soyongeopda. It's no use pretending like you don't know.

입만 아프다 im·man a·peu·da to waste one's breath
말해 봤자 입만 아파. malhae bwatja imman apa. What's the use talking about it? I'll just be wasting my breath.

쓸데없다 | 쓸데없이 sseul·de·eop·da | sseul·de·eop·si unnecessary, useless | to no purpose
쓸데없는 말 좀 하지 마. sseuldeeomneun mal jom haji ma. Don't speak nonsense.

해롭다 hae·rop·da harmful, bad
말할 필요도 없이, 술은 건강에 해롭다. malhal piryodo eopsi, sureun geongange haeropda. Needless to say, drinking alcohol is harmful to your health.

불리하다 bul·li·ha·da unfavorable

새롭다 sae·rop·da new, fresh
당신 디자인에는 새로운 게 없어요. dangsin dijaineneun saeroun ge eopseoyo. There is nothing new in your design.

새 sae new
저는 새 요리법을 개발하는 것을 좋아해요. jeoneun sae yoribeobeul gaebalhaneun geoseul joahaeyo. I love creating new recipes.

신규 sin·gyu new
제 일은 신규 고객을 확보하는 것입니다. je ireun singyu gogaegeul hwakbohaneun geosimnida. My job is to solicit new customers.

새로 sae·ro newly
새로 산 거야? saero san geoya? Is this new?

오랜 o·raen long, old
한국은 오랜 역사를 갖고 있습니다. hangugeun oraen nyeoksareul gatgo itseumnida. Korea has a long history.

낡다 nak·da old, worn out
이사를 하면서 낡은 옷들을 모두 버렸어요. isareul hamyeonseo nalgeun otdeureul modu beoryeosseoyo. When I moved out, I threw away all my shabby clothes.

헌 heon old, worn out, used
헌 돈을 새 돈으로 교환해 주실 수 있나요? heon doneul sae doneuro gyohwanhae jusil su innayo? Could you please exchange the old notes for new ones?

....

적당하다 | 적당히 jeok·dang·ha·da | jeok·dang·hi moderate, suitable | moderately, suitably
평상시에 사용하기에 적당해 보이네요. pyeongsangsie sayonghagie jeokdanghae boineyo. It looks suitable for everyday use.

알맞다 al·mat·da appropriate, proper, suitable
빈 칸에 알맞은 말을 쓰시오. bin kane almajeun mareul sseusio. Fill in the blanks with the appropriate words.

적절하다 jeok·jeol·ha·da right, proper, appropriate
그 예는 적절하지 않아요. geu yeneun jeokjeolhaji anayo. The example is not appropriate.

적합하다 jeo·kha·pa·da right, proper, suitable, fit
그는 이 일에 적합하지 않아. geuneun i ire

jeokhapaji ana. He is not fit for this job.

지나치다 ji·na·chi·da excessive, immoderate
장난이 지나치시네요. jangnani jinachisineyo. Your pranks have gone too far.

심하다 sim·ha·da heavy, severe
치통이 너무 심해. chitongi neomu simhae. I have a terrible toothache.

정상 | ~적 jeong·sang | ~·jeok normality | normal
체온은 정상입니다. cheoneun jeongsangimnida. Your temperature is normal.

이상하다 i·sang·ha·da strange, odd
우리가 만난 적이 없다니 이상하군요. uriga mannan jeogi eopdani isanghagunnyo. I find it strange that we've never met before.

독특하다 = 특이하다 dok·teu·ka·da = teu·gi·ha·da peculiar, distinctive, unique
그 물은 독특한/특이한 냄새가 있다. geu mureun dokteukan/teugihan naemsaega itda. There's a peculiar smell to the water.

고유 | ~하다 go·yu | ~·ha·da essence, nature | unique, characteristic
우리는 모두 자신만의 고유한 재능을 갖고 있다. urineun modu jasinmanui goyuhan jaeneungeul gatgo itda. We all have talents of our own.

특별하다 teuk·byeol·ha·da special
그의 시에는 특별한 무엇인가가 있다. geuui sieneun teukbyeolhan mueosingaga itda. There is something special about his poems.

별다르다 byeol·da·reu·da particular, special
이번 주말에 별다른 계획 없어요. ibeon jumare byeoldareun gyehoek eopseoyo. I don't have any special plans this weekend.

색다르다 saek·da·reu·da unusual, unconventional
그것은 색다른 경험이었어요. geugeoseun saekdareun gyeongheomieosseoyo. It was a novel experience.

두드러지다 du·deu·reo·ji·da remarkable, noticeable
지난 12개월 동안 그 회사는 두드러진 성장을 보였다. jinan sibigaewol dongan geu hoesaneun dudeureojin seongjangeul boyeotda. The company has shown exceptional growth over the past 12 months.

분위기 bu·nwi·gi atmosphere, mood
여기 분위기가 마음에 들어요. yeogi bunwigiga maeume deureoyo. I like the atmosphere here.

아늑하다 a·neu·ka·da cozy

포근하다 po·geun·ha·da cozy, snug
침대가 참 포근하네요. chimdaega cham pogeunhaneyo. I feel cozy in bed.

익숙하다 ik·su·ka·da familiar
저는 기차로 출퇴근하는 데 익숙합니다. jeoneun gicharo chultoegeunhaneun de iksukamnida. I'm used to commuting by train.

엄숙하다 eom·su·ka·da solemn, sober

심각하다 sim·ga·ka·da serious, grave
왜 그렇게 표정이 심각해? wae geureoke pyojeongi simgakae? Why do you look so serious?

썰렁하다 sseol·leong·ha·da awkward

평화롭다 pyeong·hwa·rop·da peaceful
우리는 평화로운 날들을 보냈다. urineun pyeonghwaroun naldeureul bonaetda. We spent some very peaceful days.

자유롭다 ja·yu·rop·da free, liberal
우리 회사는 분위기가 자유로운 편이에요. uri hoesaneun bunwigiga jayuroun pyeonieyo. Our company has a relatively relaxed atmosphere.

가다 가지다 같이 것 -겠- 계시다 그 그

것 그대 그래도 그래야 그러므로 그런 그런데

그리고 께서 당신 대로 도 드리다 든 또는 랑

로 로서 마다 말다 매- 못 밖에 보다 보다 뿐

실 생- 실은 싶다 아/야 아니다 아무 아무것

아무튼 아울러 -았-/-었/였 -애- 어찌하다 에 에게

에서 외- 요 -우- 우리 의 -이- 이/가

chapter **36** | Structural
Words

이러하다 이렇게 있다 자기 저 저대로

러하다 저런 저렇게 저희 제 주다 쫌 최- -추-

치우다 하지만 한테 혹은 -하- -받다

-는데/ㄴ데/은데 -이 -냐 -자 -더니 -려

면 -히 -을래/ㄹ래 -음/ㅁ -든지 -거든 -기

-아/어/여 -도록 -십시오 -니까 -다랗다 -려면

-습디까/ㅂ니까 -아야/어야/여야 -아/어/여

36.1 Particles

(이)다 (i·)da to be
이 책은 한국어 교과서이다. **i chaegeun hangugeo gyogwaseoida.** This is a Korean language textbook.

요 yo politeness particle
어렵지 않을걸요. **eoryeopji aneulgeoryo.** That shouldn't be hard.

이/가 i/ga subject particle, complement particle
커서 선생님이 되고 싶어요. **keoseo seonsaengnimi doego sipeoyo.** I want to be a teacher when I grow up.
네가 한 말은 사실이 아냐. **nega han mareun sasiri anya.** What you said is not true.
내가 그랬어. **naega geuraesseo.** I did it.

> Nouns/pronouns ending in a consonant take –이, and nouns/pronouns ending in a vowel take –가. When pronouns like 나 na (I), 너 neo (you), 저 jeo (honorific of 나 na), 누구 nugu (who) combine with –가, they change respectively to 내 nae, 네 ne, 제 je, and 누 nu.

께서 kke·seo subject particle (honorific)

을/를 eul/reul object particle
아버지께서 운전을 가르쳐 주셨어요. **abeojikkeseo unjeoneul gareuchyeo jusyeosseoyo.** My father taught me how to drive.
요즘 중국어 공부를 하고 있어요. **yojeum junggugeo gongbureul hago isseoyo.** I'm studying Chinese these days.

의 ui of
그 사람의 전화번호가 뭐죠? **geu saramui jeonhwabeonhoga mwojyo?** What's his phone number?

> To make it easier to say, the particle 의 is often pronounced as 에 e.

에게 e·ge to (sb)
그 돈을 친구에게 주었어요. **geu doneul chinguege jueosseoyo.** I gave my friend the money.

한테 han·te to (sb)
제가 누구한테 말하면 돼요? **jega nuguhante malhamyeon dwaeyo?** Who should I talk to?

께 kke honorific of 에게 ege
선생님께 말씀드려 봐. **seonsaengnimkke malsseumdeuryeo bwa.** Talk to your teacher.

에 e at, in, to, from
어제 미술관 옆 동물원에 갔어요. **eoje misulgwan nyeop dongmurwone gasseoyo.** I went to the zoo next to the art museum yesterday.
저는 보통 아침 7시에 일어나요. **jeoneun botong achim ilgopsie ireonayo.** I usually wake up at seven.

에서 e·seo at, in, to, from
어디에서 오셨어요? **eodieseo osyeosseoyo?** Where are you from?
어제 지하철에서 담임 선생님을 우연히 만났어요. **eoje jihacheoreseo damim seonsaengnimeul uyeonhi mannasseoyo.** I ran into my homeroom teacher on the subway.

(으)로 (eu·)ro by, with; to (somewhere)
밖으로 나가! **bakkeuro naga!** Get out!
여기까지 자전거로 왔어요. **yeogikkaji jajeongeoro wasseoyo.** I came here by bicycle.

(으)로서 (eu·)ro·seo as
저는 영업 사원으로서 10년의 경험을 갖고 있습니다. **jeoneun nyeongeop sawoneuroseo simnyeonui gyeongheomeul gatgo itseumnida.** I have ten years of experience as a salesperson.
그는 남자 친구로서는 완벽하지만, 남편으로서는 아니다. **geuneun namja chinguroseoneun wanbyeokajiman, nampyeoneuroseoneun anida.** He is perfect as a boyfriend, but not as a husband.

(으)로써 (eu·)ro·sseo with, by means of, using
사람은 먹음으로써 살 수 있다. **sarameun meogeumeurosseo sal su itda.** Humans have to eat to stay alive.

아/야 a/ya vocative particle
소영아! **soyeonga!** Soyoung!

와/과 wa/gwa and, with
나와 녀석은 둘도 없는 친구다. **nawa nyeoseogeun duldo eomneun chinguda.** He and I are best friends.
친구들과 내일 려행 가기로 했어요. **chingudeulgwa naeil lyeohaeng gagiro haesseoyo.** I decided to take a trip with my friends.

하고 ha·go with, and
저는 동생하고 사이가 좋아요. **jeoneun dongsaenghago saiga joayo.** I'm on good terms with my younger brother.

(이)랑 (i·)rang with, and
내일 나랑 영화 보러 갈래? **naeil larang yeonghwa boreo gallae?** Do you want to go to the movies with me tomorrow?

은/는 eun/neun particle of contrast or sentence topic
저는 먹는 것은 좋아하지만 요리는 좋아하지 않아요. **jeoneun meongneun geoseun joahajiman nyorineun joahaji anayo.** I love to eat but I don't like cooking.

그 여자는 젊었을 때는 미인이었어요. **geu yeojaneun jeolmeosseul ttaeneun miinieosseoyo.** She was beautiful when she was young.

도 do also, too
나도 밖에서 놀고 싶어요. **nado bakkeseo nolgo sipeoyo.** I want to play outside, too.

만 man only
왜 엄마는 형만 사랑해? 저도 엄마 아들이라고요. **wae eommaneun hyeongman saranghae? jeodo eomma adeuriragoyo.** Why do you only love my brother? I'm your son, too.

뿐 ppun only, merely, just
우리 둘뿐이야. **uri dulppuniya.** Just the two of us.

든(지) deun(·ji) any
노력하면 누구든지 성공할 수 있다. **noryeokamyeon nugudeunji seonggonghal su itda.** Anyone can succeed if he or she tries.

마다 ma·da every, each
저는 일요일 아침마다 산에 갑니다. **jeoneun iryoil achimmada sane gamnida.** I go to the mountains on Sunday mornings.

밖에 ba·kke not more than, only
저는 그것밖에 몰라요. **jeoneun geugeotbakke mollayo.** I know nothing other than that.

부터 bu·teo from, since

까지 kka·ji to, until, by
저는 9시부터 6시까지 일합니다. **jeoneun ahopsibuteo yeoseotsikkaji ilhamnida.** I work from nine to six.

처럼 cheo·reom like, as
평소처럼 그 사람은 활기가 넘쳤다. **pyeongsocheoreom geu sarameun hwalgiga neomchyeotda.** As usual, he was full of energy.

같이 ga·chi like, as
저와 남편은 매일같이 싸웠어요. **jeowa nampyeoneun maeilgachi ssawosseoyo.** My husband and I quarreled almost every day.

만큼 man·keum like, as
누나는 저만큼 만화를 좋아해요. **nunaneun jeomankeum manhwareul joahaeyo.** My sister likes comics as much as I do.

대로 dae·ro like, as
약속대로 네가 저녁 해. **yaksokdaero nega jeonyeok hae.** Make dinner as you promised.

보다 bo·da than
저는 커피보다 차를 좋아해요. **jeoneun keopiboda chareul joahaeyo.** I prefer tea to coffee.

(이)나 (i·)na or; as much as
대회는 보통 1월 말이나 2월 초에 열립니다. **daehoeneun botong irwol marina iwol choe yeollimnida.** The competition is held mostly in late January or early February.

나 30분이나 기다렸어. **na samsipbunina gidaryeosseo.** I've been waiting for as long as thirty minutes.

커피나 차 중에 뭘 마실래? **keopina cha junge mwol masillae?** Do you want coffee or tea?

36.2 Auxiliary Verbs/Adjectives, Negative Expressions

가다 ga·da to go, continue
날이 건조해서 농작물이 죽어 가요. **nari geonjohaeseo nongjangmuri jugeo gayo.** The weather is dry and the crops are dying.

오다 o·da to come, continue
그는 30년간 한 회사에서 일해 왔다. **geuneun samsimnyeongan han hoesaeseo ilhae watda.** He has worked for one company for thirty years.

있다 it·da to be doing; to be in a state, remain
음악을 듣고 있어요. **eumageul deutgo isseoyo.** I am listening to the music.

저는 아침이 될 때까지 깨어 있었어요. **jeoneun achimi doel ttaekkaji kkaeeo isseosseoyo.** I stayed awake until the morning.

계시다 gye·si·da honorific of 있다 **itda**

:**내다** nae·da to see sth through, get sth done
마침내 제가 **해 냈어요**. machimnae jega hae naesseoyo. Finally, I did it.

:**나다** na·da after
숙제하고 **나서** 놀아라. sukjehago naseo norara. You can play after finishing your homework.

:**버리다** beo·ri·da to do completely
돈을 다 **써 버렸어요**. doneul da sseo beoryeosseoyo. I used up the money.

:**먹다** meok·da to do sth negative
아차! 통장 가져온다는 걸 **잊어 먹었네**. acha! tongjang gajyeoondaneun geol ijeo meogeonne. Oh dear! I forgot to bring my bankbook.

:**말다** mal·da to end up doing
회사가 결국 망하고 **말았다**. hoesaga gyeolguk manghago maratda. The company ended up going bankrupt.

:**치우다** chi·u·da to do thoroughly
그는 밥을 세 그릇이나 **먹어 치웠다**. geuneun babeul se geureusina meogeo chiwotda. He ate three bowls of rice.

:**주다** ju·da to do as a favor
제발 도**와 줘**. jebal dowa jwo. Please help me.

:**드리다** deu·ri·da humble word of 주다 juda
아버지 도**와 드려라**. abeoji dowa deuryeora. Help your father.

:**보다** bo·da to try
제가 **해 볼게요**. jega hae bolgeyo. Let me try it.

:**놓다 = 두다** no·ta = du·da to keep
창문을 열어 **놓아라/두어라**. changmuneul lyeoreo noara/dueora. Leave the window open.

:**가지다 = 갖다** ga·ji·da = gat·da to do sth and with it
지금처럼 놀**아 가지고는/갖고는** 이 시험에 합격할 수 없어. jigeumcheoreom nora gajigoneun/gatgoneun i siheome hapgyeokal su eopseo. You won't pass this exam if you keep playing like this.

> –아/어 가지고 **-a/eo gajigo** has the same meaning as the connective ending –아서/어서 **-aseo/eoseo**.

:**싶다** sip·da to want to do
밥 먹고 **싶어요**. bam meokgo sipeoyo. I want to eat rice.

:**만하다** man·ha·da worth
이 책은 읽을 **만하다**. i chaegeun ilgeul manhada. This book is worth reading.

:**뻔하다** ppeon·ha·da almost
약속 시간에 늦을 **뻔했어요**. yaksok sigane neujeul ppeonhaesseoyo. I was almost late for the appointment.

···

:**못** mot (can)not
요즘에 잠을 잘 **못** 자. yojeume jameul jal mot ja. I can't sleep well these days.

:**못하다** mo·ta·da cannot
저는 한국말을 하**지 못해요**. jeoneun hangungmareul haji motaeyo. I can't speak Korean.

:**없다** eop·da cannot
정말? 믿을 **수 없어**! jeongmal? mideul su eopseo! Really? I can't believe it!

:**않다** an·ta (do) not
좋지도 **않지만** 나쁘지도 **않아**. jochido anchiman nappeujido ana. Not good, but not bad.

:**안** an (be) not, (do) not
A: 추워? B: 아니, **안** 추워. A: chuwo? B: ani, an chuwo. A: Do you feel cold? B: No, I'm okay.

:**아니다** a·ni·da (be) not
그건 네가 걱정할 일이 **아니다**. geugeon nega geokjeonghal iri anida. It is nothing you should be concerned about.

:**말다** mal·da stop, (do) not
걱정하**지 말고** 좀 쉬어. geokjeonghaji malgo jom swieo. Stop worrying and take a break.

36.3 Personal Pronouns

나 na I
아들 녀석은 나보다 키가 커. adeul lyeoseo-geun naboda kiga keo. My son is taller than me.

내 nae I; my
파티에 온 사람들은 모두 내가 모르는 사람들이었다. patie on saramdeureun modu naega moreuneun saramdeurieotda. Everyone at the party was a stranger to me.
이 모자가 내 마음에 들어. i mojaga nae maeume deureo. I like this hat.

저 jeo humble word of 나 na
저를 아세요? jeoreul aseyo? Do I know you?

제 je I; my
이건 제가 주문한 게 아니에요. igeon jega jumunhan ge anieyo. This is not what I ordered.
제 방이 지금 엉망이에요. je bangi jigeum eongmangieyo. My room is a total wreck now.

우리 u·ri we; our
우리는 작년에 여기에서 처음 만났어요. urineun jangnyeone yeogieseo cheoeum mannasseoyo. We met here for the first time a year ago.

저희 jeo·hui humble word of 우리 uri
문제가 생기면 저희한테 알려 주세요. munjega saenggimyeon jeohuihante allyeo juseyo. Let us know if you have any problems.

너 neo you
너는 정말 용감하구나. neoneun jeongmal lyonggamhaguna. You are so brave.

네 ne you; your
이건 네가 상관할 문제가 아니야. igeon nega sanggwanhal munjega aniya. This is none of your business.
그건 네 잘못이 아니었다. geugeon ne jalmosi anieotda. It was not your fault.

당신 dang·sin you
여보, 당신을 영원히 사랑할 거야. yeobo, dangsineul lyeongwonhi saranghal geoya. Honey, I will love you forever.

그대 geu·dae you
자네 ja·ne you
자네는 직업이 뭔가? janeneun jigeobi mwonga? What do you do for a living?

너희 neo·hui you; your
너희 둘이 사귀는 줄 몰랐어. neohui duri sagwineun jul mollasseo. I didn't know you two were together.

여러분 yeo·reo·bun all of you, everyone (honorific of 너희 neohui)
여러분 잠시만 주목해 주십시오. yeoreobun jamsiman jumokae jusipsio. Attention please, everyone.

그 geu he
그녀 geu·nyeo she
그녀는 그보다 키가 더 크다. geunyeoneun geuboda kiga deo keuda. She is taller than him.

그분 geu·bun he, she (honorific of 그 사람 geu saram)

이분 i·bun this person (honorific of 이 사람 i saram)

얘 yae this (shortened form of 이 아이 i ai)

걔 gyae he, she (shortened form of 그 아이 geu ai)
걔가 전에 말한 걔예요. yaega jeone malhan gyaeyeyo. This is the one I told you about before.

쟤 jyae that (shortened form of 저 아이 jeo ai)

자기 ja·gi oneself
쟤는 항상 자기 얘기만 한다. jyaeneun hangsang jagi yaegiman handa. She always only talks about herself.

자신 ja·sin oneself
너 자신을 알라. neo jasineul alla. Know yourself.

아무 a·mu anyone, anybody, no one
아무도 오지 않았다. amudo oji anatda. No one came.

36.4 Demonstratives

이 i this
이 근처 사세요? **i geuncheo saseyo?** Do you live around here?

그 geu the, that
나는 그 사람 마음에 안 들어. **naneun geu saram maeume an deureo.** I don't like that guy.

저 jeo that
저기 저 그림 좀 봐. **jeogi jeo geurim jom bwa.** Look at that picture over there.

> 이 **i** and 그 **geu** are used to refer to something close to the speaker and the listener, respectively; 저 **jeo** is used for something far from both the speaker and the listener. This rule applies to the following word pairs: 이것/그것/저것 **igeot/geugeot/jeogeot**, 이런/그런/저런 **ireon/geureon/jeoreon**, and 여기/거기/저기 **yeogi/geogi/jeogi**.

것 = 거 geot = geo thing, fact
이 책 네 것이야/거야? **i chaek ne geosiya/geoya?** Is this your book?

이것 = 이거 i·geot = i·geo this
이것/이거 좀 봐. **igeot/igeo jom bwa.** Look at this.

그것 = 그거 geu·geot = geu·geo it, that

저것 = 저거 jeo·geot = jeo·geo that

이것저것 = 이거저거 i·geot·jeo·geot = i·geo·jeo·geo this and that
이것저것/이거저거 샀어요. **igeotjeogeot/igeojeogeo sasseoyo.** I bought this and that.

아무것 a·mu·geot anything
오늘 아무것도 안 먹었어. **oneul amugeotdo an meogeosseo.** I didn't eat anything today.

이런 i·reon such, this

그런 geu·reon such, that
저는 그런 사람이 아닙니다. **jeoneun geureon sarami animnida.** I'm not that kind of person.

저런 jeo·reon that, such

어떤 eo·tteon some, certain; any
어떤 사람들은 컴퓨터가 우리 생활을 보다 편리하게 만들었다고 말한다. **eotteon saramdeureun keompyuteoga uri saenghwareul boda pyeollihage mandeureotdago malhanda.** Some people say that computers have made life more convenient.

어떤 일이 있어도 거기 갈 거야. **eotteon iri isseodo geogi gal geoya.** No matter what happens, I'll be there.

어느 eo·neu some, certain; any
어느 비 내리는 아침, 그가 내 사무실에 찾아왔다. **eoneu bi naerineun achim, geuga nae samusire chajawatda.** One rainy morning, he stopped by my office.
어느 때고 와. **eoneu ttaego wa.** You are welcome anytime.

아무 a·mu any
아무 때나 좋아요. **amu ttaena joayo.** Any time will do.

이러하다 = 이렇다 i·reo·ha·da = i·reo·ta like this
내 생각은 이래. **nae saenggageun irae.** Here's what I think.

그러하다 = 그렇다 geu·reo·ha·da = geu·reo·ta like that
A: 배고파. B: 나도 그래. **A: baegopa. B: nado geurae.** A: I'm hungry. B: So am I.

저러하다 = 저렇다 jeo·reo·ha·da = jeo·reo·ta like that

아무렇다 a·mu·reo·ta concerned, meaningful
저는 아무렇지도 않아요. **jeoneun amureochido anayo.** I'm fine.

어찌하다 = 어쩌다 eo·jji·ha·da = eo·jjeo·da to do sth
그럼 나더러 어쩌라고? **geureom nadeoreo eojjeorago?** What do you want me to do, then?

이렇게 = 이리 i·reo·ke = i·ri this, like this
왜 이렇게/이리 늦었어? **wae ireoke/iri neujeosseo?** Why are you so late?

그렇게 = 그리 geu·reo·ke = geu·ri that, like that

저렇게 = 저리 jeo·reo·ke = jeo·ri that, like that
바깥이 왜 저렇게/저리 시끄러워? **bakkachi wae jeoreoke/jeori sikkeureowo?** What is all that racket outside?

이대로 i·dae·ro as it is, like this

그대로 geu·dae·ro as it is, like that

저대로 jeo·dae·ro as it is, like that

36.5 Conjunctive Adverbs

그리고 geu·ri·go and
뭐 좀 먹어. 그리고 좀 쉬어. **mwo jom meogeo. geurigo jom swieo.** Eat something. And get some rest.

그래서 geu·rae·seo so, therefore
그 애를 사랑해. 그래서 그 가족과도 잘 지내려고 노력하고 있어. **geu aereul saranghae. geuraeseo geu gajokgwado jal jinaeryeogo noryeokago isseo.** I love her, so I try to get along with her family, too.

그러니까 geu·reo·ni·kka so
그 사람 안 올 거야. 그러니까 기다리지 마. **geu saram a nol geoya. geureonikka gidariji ma.** He won't come, so don't wait for him.

따라서 tta·ra·seo so, therefore, accordingly
이 서명은 제 것이 아닙니다. 따라서 이 계약은 무효입니다. **i seomyeongeun je geonni animnida. ttaraseo i gyeyageun muhyoimnida.** This is not my signature, so this contract is void.

그러므로 geu·reo·meu·ro so, therefore, accordingly
나는 그 사람을 만난 적도 없습니다. 그러므로 이 기사는 말도 안 됩니다. **naneun geu sarameul mannan jeokdo eopseumnida. geureomeuro i gisaneun maldo an doemnida.** I've never seen him. Therefore, this article is complete nonsense.

그리하여 geu·ri·ha·yeo so, therefore

그러면 geu·reo·myeon and, then, if you do so
네가 먼저 가. 그러면 내가 따라갈게. **nega meonjeo ga. geureomyeon naega ttaragalge.** You go first, and then I'll follow you.

그래야 geu·rae·ya and, so
말을 해. 그래야 네 생각을 알지. **mareul hae. geuraeya ne saenggageul alji.** Talk to me so I can know what you're thinking.

그런데 = 근데 geu·reon·de = geun·de well, by the way; however
그런데/근데 점심은 뭐 먹을까? **geureonde/geunde jeomsimeun mwo meogeulkka?** By the way, what do you want for lunch?

그러나 geu·reo·na but, however

저는 술을 좋아합니다. 그러나 자주 마시지는 않습니다. **jeoneun sureul joahamnida. geureona jaju masijineun anseumnida.** I enjoy drinking, though I don't drink often.

하지만 ha·ji·man but, however
그 애는 좋아. 하지만 그 언니가 맘에 안 들어. **geu aeneun joa. hajiman geu eonniga mame an deureo.** I like her, but I do not like her sister.

그렇지만 geu·reo·chi·man but, however

그래도 geu·rae·do but, nevertheless, still
사실 지금 좀 피곤해. 그래도 나도 갈래. **sasil jigeum jom pigonhae. geuraedo nado gallae.** Actually I'm a little tired, but I'll go with you.

아무튼 = 하여튼 = 어쨌든 = 좌우간 ← 아뭏든 a·mu·teun = ha·yeo·teun = eo·jjaet·deun = jwa·u·gan anyway
아무튼/하여튼/어쨌든/좌우간 모두 무사해서 다행이야. **amuteun/hayeoteun/eojjaetdeun/jwaugan modu musahaeseo dahaengiya.** Anyway, I'm happy to see everybody is safe.

한편 han·pyeon meanwhile

반면 ban·myeon while, on the other hand
저는 바다를 좋아하는 반면 아내는 산을 더 좋아해요. **jeoneun badareul joahaneun banmyeon anaeneun saneul deo joahaeyo.** I like the sea, while my wife prefers the mountains.

내지 nae·ji to, or
보험회사가 보험료를 1 내지 5퍼센트 인상했어. **boheomhoesaga boheomnyoreul il laeji opeosenteu insanghaesseo.** The insurance company raised the premium by 1 to 5 percent.

및 mit and, as well as
식사 및 음료는 무료입니다. **siksa mit eumnyoneun muryoimnida.** Food and beverages are free.

또는 tto·neun or

혹은 ho·geun or

게다가 = 더구나 = 더욱이 ← 더우기 ge·da·ga = deo·gu·na = deo·u·gi besides, moreover
이 차 마음에 들어요. 게다가/더구나/더욱이 가격도 괜찮아요. **i cha maeume deureoyo. gedaga/deoguna/deougi gagyeokdo gwaencha-**

nayo. I like this car. Besides, the price is reasonable.

솔직히 거기 가고 싶지 않아. 더구나 시간도 너무 늦었어. **soljiki geogi gago sipji ana. deoguna sigando neomu neujeosseo.** Frankly, I don't want to go there. Besides, it's too late.

°아울러 a·ul·leo in addition

ᛁ또(한) tto(·han) also, too

ᛁ왜냐하면 wae·nya·ha·myeon because

나는 그녀를 사랑하는데 왜냐하면 그녀가 아주 귀엽기 때문이다. **naneun geunyeoreul saranghaneunde waenyahamyeon geunyeoga aju gwiyeopgi ttaemunida.** I love her because she is so cute.

왜냐하면 is usually followed by 때문 **ttaemun** or −(으)니까 **-(eu)nikka.**

°즉 jeuk in other words, that is

미성년자, 즉 19세 미만인 자에게 담배를 파는 것은 불법이다. **miseongnyeonja, jeuk sipguse mimanin jaege dambaereul paneun geoseun bulbeobida.** It is illegal to sell cigarettes to minors, i.e. people under the age of 19.

ᛁ사실 sa·sil actually, in fact

사실 내 생각은 달라. **sasil lae saenggageun dalla.** Actually I don't agree.

°실은 si·reun actually, in fact

실은 나도 잘 모르겠어. **sireun nado jal moreugesseo.** Actually I don't know, either.

°사실상 sa·sil·sang actually, in fact

이 두 노래는 사실상 같다. **i du noraeneun sasilsang gatda.** These two songs are, in fact, identical.

36.6 Endings

ᛁ-는다/ㄴ다 -neun·da/n·da declarative ending of verbs

나는 점심시간을 이용해 신문을 읽는다. **naneun jeomsimsiganeul iyonghae sinmuneul ingneunda.** I use my lunchtime to read the newspaper.

제주도에는 눈이 잘 안 온다. **jejudoeneun nuni jal an onda.** It rarely snows on Jeju Island.

ᛁ-다 -da present ending of adjectives; basic ending of verbs/adjectives

요즘 TV에는 광고가 너무 많다. **yojeum tibeuieneun gwanggoga neomu manta.** There are too many commercials on TV these days.

산에 오르다 **sane oreuda** climb a mountain

ᛁ-습니다/ㅂ니다 -seum·ni·da/m·ni·da declarative ending

오후에는 약속이 있습니다. **ohueneun nyaksogi itseumnida.** I have an appointment in the afternoon.

저는 담배 없이는 하루도 못 삽니다. **jeoneun dambae eopsineun harudo mot samnida.** I can't live a day without cigarettes.

ᛁ-았-/었/였 -at-/eot/yeot past

알았어요. **arasseoyo.** Okay.

우리는 아무 말 없이 한참을 걸었다. **urineun amu mal eopsi hanchameul georeotda.** We walked for a while without a word.

ᛁ-겠- -get- intention or will; supposition

꼭 암을 이겨내겠어요. **kkok ameul igyeonaegesseoyo.** I will overcome cancer.

오늘 밤 많은 비가 오겠습니다. **oneul bam maneun biga ogetseumnida.** There may be heavy rain tonight.

ᛁ-아/어/여 -a/eo/yeo declarative ending; interrogative ending; imperative ending

네 말이 맞아. **ne mari maja.** You're right.

뭐가 그리 우스워? **mwoga geuri useuwo?** What's so funny?

얼른 말해. **eolleun malhae.** Spit it out.

ᛁ-야 -ya declarative ending; interrogative ending

그 사람은 참 좋은 사람이야. **geu sarameun cham joeun saramiya.** He's a very nice person.

두 사람 친구 아니야? **du saram chingu aniya?** Aren't you two buddies?

ᛁ-에요 -e·yo declarative ending; interrogative ending

그 사람은 참 좋은 사람이에요. **geu sarameun cham joeun saramieyo.** He's a very good person.

두 사람 친구 아니에요? **du saram chingu anieyo?** Aren't you two buddies?

에요 combines with the stem of 이다 ida and 아니다 anida to form 이에요 ieyo and 아니에요 anieyo, respectively. 이에요 can be shortened to 예요 yeyo.

-지 -ji declarative ending; interrogative ending; imperative ending
두고 봐야 알지. dugo bwaya alji. We'll have to wait and see.
누가 안 왔지? nuga an watji? Who's not here today?
잠깐 산책하러 나가지요. jamkkan sanchaekareo nagajiyo. Let's go out for a quick walk.

-네 -ne exclamatory ending
집이 참 예쁘네요. jibi cham yeppeuneyo. Your house looks lovely.

-(으)세요 -(eu·)se·yo declarative ending; interrogative ending; imperative ending
아버지는 저한테 바라는 게 많으세요. abeojineun jeohante baraneun ge maneuseyo. My father has high expectations for me.
여기는 웬일이세요? yeogineun weniriseyo? What brings you here?
먼저 가세요. 곧 따라갈게요. meonjeo gaseyo. got ttaragalgeyo. Go ahead first. I'll be right with you.

-거든 -geo·deun declarative ending
아마 철수는 그걸 들 수 있을 거예요. 걔가 저보다 힘이 세거든요. ama cheolsuneun geugeol deul su isseul geoyeyo. gyaega jeoboda himi segeodeunnyo. Maybe Cheolsu can lift it. He is stronger than me.

-을게/ㄹ게 -eul·ge/l·ge (I, we) promise
며칠 내로 꼭 갚을게. myeochil laero kkok gapeulge. I promise to pay you back in a few days.
제가 알아서 할게요. jega araseo halgeyo. I'll take care of it.

-을래/ㄹ래 -eul·lae/l·lae will do, want to do
오늘 밤은 그냥 집에 있을래요. oneul bameun geunyang jibe isseullaeyo. I'll just stay home tonight.
나는 차라리 집에서 숙제나 할래. naneun charari jibeseo sukjena hallae. I'd rather stay home and do my homework.

-냐 -nya interrogative ending
얘가 네 동생이냐? yaega ne dongsaenginya? Is this your younger sibling?

-나 -na interrogative ending
이 지폐를 잔돈으로 좀 바꿔 주실 수 있나요? i jipyereul jandoneuro jom bakkwo jusil su innayo? Can you break this bill for me?

-니 -ni interrogative ending
밥 먹다 말고 어디 가니? bam meokda malgo eodi gani? Where are you going in the middle of dinner?

-습니까/ㅂ니까 -seum·ni·kka/m·ni·kka interrogative ending
이곳에서 오래 사셨습니까? igoseseo orae sasyeotseumnikka? Have you lived here for a long time?
여기는 처음이십니까? yeogineun cheoeumisimnikka? Is this your first time here?

-을까/ㄹ까 -eul·kka/l·kka interrogative ending
누구한테 물어보면 제일 좋을까요? nuguhante mureobomyeon jeil joeulkkayo? Who do you think is the best person to ask?
오늘 한잔할까? oneul hanjanhalkka? How about a drink tonight?

-아라/어라/여라 -a·ra/eo·ra/yeo·ra imperative ending
내 손 잡아라. nae son jabara. Hold my hand.
천천히 먹어라. cheoncheonhi meogeora. Take your time with the food.
필요한 게 있으면 말해라. piryohan ge isseumyeon malhaera. Tell me if you need anything.

-(으)십시오 -(eu·)sip·si·o imperative ending
원하는 곳에 앉으십시오. wonhaneun gose anjeusipsio. You can sit wherever you want.
잠시 여기서 기다려 주십시오. jamsi yeogiseo gidaryeo jusipsio. Wait here for a moment, please.

-자 -ja propositive ending
나가서 뭐 좀 먹자. nagaseo mwo jom meokja. Let's go out and eat something.

-읍시다/ㅂ시다 -eup·si·da/p·si·da propositive ending
구석 자리에 앉읍시다. guseok jarie anjeupsida. Let's take the corner seats.
그만 끝내고 집에 갑시다. geuman kkeunnaego jibe gapsida. Let's call it a day and go home.

-는 -neun present modifier
한국어를 배우는 사람이 늘고 있다. **hangugeo-reul baeuneun sarami neulgo itda.** The number of people who are learning Korean is increasing.

-은/ㄴ -eun/n past modifier
그 책 다 읽은 후에 빌려 줄래? **geu chaek da ilgeun hue billyeo jullae?** Can I borrow that book after you are done reading it?

-을/ㄹ -eul/l future modifier
비자를 받을 필요가 없어요. **bijareul badeul piryoga eopseoyo.** You don't have to get a visa.

-음/ㅁ -eum/m nominal ending, ...ing
출구 없음 **chulgu eopseum** No Exit
그 사람이 범인임이 분명해. **geu sarami beo-minimi bunmyeonghae.** I'm sure he is the criminal.

-기 -gi nominal ending, ...ing
요즘은 책을 보기도 귀찮아요. **yojeumeun chaegeul bogido gwichanayo.** I don't feel like reading books these days.

-고 -go and
아내는 서울에 있고, 저는 직장 때문에 제주도에 있습니다. **anaeneun seoure itgo, jeoneun jikjang ttaemune jejudoe itseumnida.** My wife lives in Seoul, but I live on Jeju Island because of my work.

-거나 -geo·na or
주말에는 보통 영화를 보거나 책을 읽어요. **jumareneun botong yeonghwareul bogeona chaegeul ilgeoyo.** On weekends, I usually watch movies or read books.

-든지 -deun·ji whether ... or
하든지 말든지 이제 상관 안 할래. **hadeunji maldeunji ije sanggwan an hallae.** I don't care whether you do it or not anymore.

-아도/어도/여도 -a·do/eo·do/yeo·do (even) if, though
이제 집에 가도 돼요? **ije jibe gado dwaeyo?** Can I go home now?
내일 비가 내려도 소풍을 가나요? **naeil biga naeryeodo sopungeul ganayo?** Is the picnic still on even if it rains tomorrow?
부탁 하나 해도 될까요? **butak hana haedo doelkkayo?** May I ask a favor of you?

-지만 -ji·man but, yet
바지는 잘 맞지만 셔츠는 너무 껴요. **bajineun**

jal matjiman syeocheuneun neomu kkyeoyo. The pants fit fine, but the shirt is too tight.

-는데/ㄴ데/은데 -neun·de/n·de/eun·de and, but, so
비가 많이 오는데, 꼭 나가야 해요? **biga mani oneunde, kkok nagaya haeyo?** It's pouring. Do you still have to go?
여기는 추운데 그곳 날씨는 어때요? **yeogineun chuunde geugot nalssineun eottaeyo?** It's cold here. How is the weather there?
품질은 좋은데 약간 비싸네요. **pumjireun jo-eunde yakgan bissaneyo.** The quality is good, but it's a little expensive.

-(으)면서 -(eu·)myeon·seo while, at the same time
우리 걸으면서 얘기 좀 하자. **uri georeu-myeonseo yaegi jom haja.** Let's talk as we walk.
거울 보면서 연습하고 있어요. **geoul bo-myeonseo yeonseupago isseoyo.** I'm practicing in front of the mirror.

-아/어/여 -a/eo/yeo ending linking prime verbs/adjectives and auxiliary ones
눈을 감아 봐. **nuneul gama bwa.** Close your eyes.
찬성하시면 손을 들어 주세요. **chanseong-hasimyeon soneul deureo juseyo.** Raise your hands if you're in favor.
들어와서 커피 한 잔 해. **deureowaseo keopi han jan hae.** Come in for a cup of coffee.

-더라도 -deo·ra·do (even) if, though
무슨 일이 있더라도 나는 네 편이야. **museun iri itdeorado naneun ne pyeoniya.** Whatever happens, I'm on your side.

-(으)러 -(eu·)reo for the purpose of
점심 먹으러 식당에 가다가 소영이를 만났어요. **jeomsim meogeureo sikdange gadaga soyeongireul mannasseoyo.** On the way to the cafeteria to eat lunch, I met Soyoung.
누구 만나러 오셨어요? **nugu mannareo osyeo-sseoyo?** Who have you come to meet?

-(으)려고 -(eu·)ryeo·go for the purpose of
좀 적게 먹으려고 노력 중이야. **jom jeokge meogeuryeogo noryeok jungiya.** I'm trying to eat less.
제 집을 마련하려고 저축을 하고 있습니다. **je jibeul maryeonharyeogo jeochugeul hago itseumnida.** I have saved up to buy a house.

-도록 -do·rok so that, until
아버지가 편히 주무시도록 조용히 해라.
abeojiga pyeonhi jumusidorok joyonghi haera.
Your dad is sleeping so be quiet.

-을수록/ㄹ수록 -eul·su·rok/l·su·rok the
more ... the more
이 노래는 들을수록 좋아. **i noraeneun
deureulsurok joa.** The more I hear this song,
the more I like it.
생각할수록 더 화가 나. **saenggakalsurok deo
hwaga na.** The more I think about it, the an-
grier I become.

-(으)면 -(eu·)myeon if, provided, when
돈이 있으면 좀 빌려 줄래? **doni isseumyeon
jom billyeo jullae?** If you have any money, can
you lend me some?
서두르면 기차를 탈 수 있을 거야. **seo-
dureumyeon gichareul tal su isseul geoya.** If
you hurry, you'll catch the train.

-거든 -geo·deun if
시간이 있거든 놀러 와라. **sigani itgeodeun
nolleo wara.** If you have time, come on over.

-아야/어야/여야 -a·ya/eo·ya/yeo·ya only
when
미국에 가려면 영어를 배워야 한다. **miguge
garyeomyeon nyeongeoreul baewoya handa.** If
you want to go to America, you should learn
English.
사람은 먹어야 산다. **sarameun meogeoya sanda.** Humans have to eat to live.
건강해야 일도 할 수 있죠. **geonganghaeya
ildo hal su itjyo.** You can work when you are
healthy.

-(으)려면 -(eu·)ryeo·myeon if you want
to do, in order to
좋은 자리를 잡으려면 서둘러야 해. **joeun jarireul jabeuryeomyeon seodulleoya hae.** We
must hurry if we want to get good seats.
성공을 하려면 남들보다 더 노력해야 해.
**seonggongeul haryeomyeon namdeulboda deo
noryeokaeya hae.** If you want to succeed, you
should work harder than others.

-듯(이) -deu(·si) as if, like
땀이 비 오듯이 쏟아져요. **ttami bi odeusi
ssodajyeoyo.** I'm sweating buckets.

-(으)니까 -(eu·)ni·kka since, and so
늦었으니까 택시를 탑시다. **neujeosseunikka
taeksireul tapsida.** We are late, so let's take a
taxi.
밖이 추우니까 옷을 따뜻하게 입어라. **bakki
chuunikka oseul ttatteutage ibeora.** It's cold
outside, so make sure to dress warm.

-게 -ge adverbial ending
행복하게 살아라. **haengbokage sarara.** Live
happily.

-지 -ji connective ending followed by negative expressions
춥지 않아? **chupji ana?** Aren't you cold?

-더니 -deo·ni since, as
너무 많이 먹었더니 배가 터질 것 같아요.
**neomu mani meogeotdeoni baega teojil geot ga-
tayo.** I ate too much and now I feel like my
stomach is about to burst.

36.7 Prefixes and Suffixes

매- mae- each, every
매년 **maenyeon** every year
매달 **maedal** every month

외- oe- only, single
외아들 **oeadeul** only son

총- chong- all, whole
총액 **chongaek** total amount

최- choe- the most
최우수 **choeusu** the best
최소 **choeso** the smallest

한- han- the peak, the extreme

한밤중 **hanbamjung** middle of the night
한여름 **hannyeoreum** midsummer

생- saeng- raw, natural, unripe
생맥주 **saengmaekju** draft beer
생쌀 **saengssal** uncooked rice

-간 -gan among, between
형제간 **hyeongjegan** between brothers
며칠간 **myeochilgan** for a few days

-기 -gi nominal suffix
굵기 **gukgi** thickness
달리기 **dalligi** running

-ㅁ -m nominal suffix
꿈 **kkum** dream
잠 **jam** sleep

-하다 -ha·da verbal or adjectival suffix
공부하다 **gongbuhada** study
건강하다 **geonganghada** healthy

-되다 -doe·da become, be, get
시작되다 **sijakdoeda** begin
해결되다 **haegyeoldoeda** get solved

-받다 -bat·da become, be, get
버림받다 **beorimbatda** be abandoned
사랑받다 **sarangbatda** be loved

-시키다 -si·ki·da make, have, let
진정시키다 **jinjeongsikida** calm, pacify
오염시키다 **oyeomsikida** contaminate, pollute

-드리다 -deu·ri·da do, give
말씀드리다 **malsseumdeurida** tell, say, speak

-거리다 = -대다 -geo·ri·da = -dae·da do repeatedly
두근거리다/두근대다 **dugeungeorida/dugeundaeda** pound
중얼거리다/중얼대다 **jungeolgeorida/jungeoldaeda** mumble

-이- -i- make, have, let; become, be, get
보이다 **boida** show
쌓이다 **ssaida** be piled

-히- -hi- make, have, let; become, be, get
괴롭히다 **goeropida** harass, bully
닫히다 **dachida** be closed

-리- -ri- make, have, let
울리다 **ullida** make sb cry
팔리다 **pallida** be sold

-기- -gi- make, have, let
웃기다 **utgida** make sb laugh
쫓기다 **jjotgida** be chased

-우- -u- make, have, let
깨우다 **kkaeuda** wake sb up
비우다 **biuda** empty

-구- -gu- make, have, let
달구다 **dalguda** heat

-추- -chu- make, have, let
맞추다 **matchuda** set, adjust
낮추다 **natchuda** lower

-애- -ae- make, have, let
없애다 **eopsaeda** remove

-다랗다 -da·ra·ta rather
커다랗다 **keodarata** rather large

-답다 -dap·da like
남자답게 굴어라. **namjadapge gureora.** Be a man.

-스럽다 -seu·reop·da like
사랑스럽다 **sarangseureopda** lovely

-지다 -ji·da have, like
멋지다 **meotjida** nice

-이 -i adverbial suffix
많이 **mani** much

-히 -hi adverbial suffix
조용히 **joyonghi** quietly

Romanized Index

English Index

The Hangul Index is downloadable from **www.tuttlepublishing.com**